RECENT CATHOLIC PHILOSOPHY
THE TWENTIETH CENTURY

RECENT CATHOLIC PHILOSOPHY
THE TWENTIETH CENTURY

by

ALAN VINCELETTE

MARQUETTE
UNIVERSITY
PRESS

MARQUETTE STUDIES IN PHILOSOPHY
NO. 71
ANDREW TALLON, SERIES EDITOR

LIBRARY OF CONGRESS CATALOGING-IN-PUBLICATION DATA

Vincelette, Alan Roy.
Recent Catholic philosophy : the Twentieth Century / by Alan Vincelette.
    p. cm. — (Marquette studies in philosophy ; no. 71)
Includes bibliographical references and index.
ISBN-13: 978-0-87462-803-6 (pbk. : alk. paper)
ISBN-10: 0-87462-803-2 (pbk. : alk. paper)
1. Christianity—Philosophy—History—20th century. 2. Catholic Church and philosophy—History—20th century. I. Title.
BR100.V56 2011190.9'04--dc22

                                              2011008997

© 2011 Marquette University Press
Milwaukee, Wisconsin 53201-3141
All rights reserved.
www.marquette.edu/mupress/

Reprinted 2015

∞The paper used in this publication meets the minimum requirements of the
American National Standard for Information Sciences—
Permanence of Paper for Printed Library Materials, ANSI Z39.48-1992.

Association of American
University Presses

MARQUETTE UNIVERSITY PRESS
MILWAUKEE

The Association of Jesuit University Presses

TABLE OF CONTENTS

INTRODUCTION

This work continues the discussion of recent Catholic philosophy begun in *Recent Catholic Philosophy: The Nineteenth Century* (Milwaukee: Marquette University Press, 2009), treating Catholic philosophy through the end of the twentieth-century.[1] There have been approximately 3000 Catholic philosophers who made significant contributions to philosophy in the twentieth-century [including around 70 bishops, two popes—Leo XIII (1810-1903) and John Paul II (1920-2005), and over 130 converts]. Hence a survey of twentieth-century Catholic philosophy cannot be anything but selective.

I have hence chosen those who I think are the 21 most important and representative of the twentieth-century Catholic philosophers in seven major movements [with the percentage in each movement given in brackets]: Phenomenology [6%], Neo-Thomism [52%], Transcendental Thomism [8%], Personalism [4%], Existentialism [11%], Analytic Philosophy [7%], and Postmodernism [4%]—two other common movements in the twentieth-century are Augustinianism [4%] and Idealism, typically Hegelianism [1%]). Interestingly, Thomism—which makes up a combined 60% of twentieth-century Catholic philosophers—is particularly rare in the Continental philosophers born between 1930 and 1960 (except for Spain), even as it has maintained a popularity in America and Britain (and in Continental philosophers born after 1960). I discuss two philosophers in some depth and include a shorter account of one additional figure for each movement (with a focus as before on Western European and North American thought, and also on epistemology, ethics, metaphysics, and the philosophy of religion).[2]

I

PHENOMENOLOGY

1900-2000 in Austria, Belgium, Germany, France, Liechtenstein,
Netherlands, Poland, & the United States

With the rise of National Socialism (1933-1945) under Adolph Hitler in Germany, the lives of two notable German Catholic phenomenologists, namely Edith Stein and Dietrich von Hildebrand, were imperiled—and indeed in the former case tragically put to an end. A third celebrated thinker, Martin Heidegger, however, had already abandoned his Catholic roots and was now a member of the Nazi Party. Meanwhile, the Jesuit Alfred Delp, who had written a book critical of Heidegger called *Tragic Existence* [*Tragische Existenz*] (1935), sadly and ironically suffered his own tragic existence and was put to death by the Nazis in 1945 on account of his efforts on behalf of the resistance group Kreisau Circle. Such was Catholic intellectual life in Austria and Germany during the Nazi Era.

Initially the German Catholic bishops (who had earlier often been critical of National Socialism) agreed to a Concordat with the Nazi Party in 1933. This Concordat allowed for the continued functioning of the Catholic hierarchy, private Catholic schools, seminaries, charitable organizations, and Catholic Theological Faculties at the universities (though open advocacy for Catholicism was considered unprofessional in the German university system of the day), state funding of the Church, the publication of pastoral letters and Catholic journals, and expanded religious education in the public schools. In turn the Catholic Church agreed to forbid priests from making overt political criticisms of National Socialism, to disband the Catholic German Center Party, and to merge the Catholic Youth Organizations with the National Socialist Youth Organizations (the Hitler Youth and the

Company of German Girls). It was an uneasy compromise at best as the Catholic Church was vociferously opposed to the Nazi support of the euthanasia of those considered mentally and physically unfit, and to its encouragement of abortion for Jews, Gypsies, and Slavs (though not for Aryans); and many Catholic bishops and faithful were deeply troubled by its anti-Semitic platform.

The German Catholics were right to be worried. For though the National Socialists initially paid lip-service to religion (such as in Hitler's Reichstag Address of March 23, 1933), their true feelings began to surface. So it is that in 1933 many German Catholic newspapers were shuttered. National Socialist anti-Catholicism (the so-called Kirchenkampf) especially surfaced after 1935 when from 1935-1941 the Nazis worked to de-Catholicize education and society by removing crucifixes from public schools; by paganizing Christian festivals by replacing the name Christmas (with its overt reference to Christ) with that of Yuletide and introducing elements of sun and fertility celebrations and changing other Church festivals into commemorative days for Woden and Thor; by reducing the attendance at private Catholic schools through having parents "choose" to send their children to Catholic or National Socialist schools in front of Nazi SA witnesses who implicitly or explicitly threatened parents with loss of employment if they made the wrong choice (hence Catholic schools in Munich saw their attendance shrink from 84% to 65% of the city from 1934-1935); by replacing religious sisters with laity in public schools from 1936-1937 (so for instance Bavaria saw 600 out of 1600 nuns be replaced with laity in 1936); and if that was not enough by the outright conversion of around 13,000 Catholic schools in Hildensheim, Bavaria, and the Rhineland from 1937-1939 into National Socialist community schools (with Christian prayers being replaced by National Socialist prayers by 1941). In response to harsher church criticism, the National Socialists went after the Catholic priests as well with trials of priests for financial corruption (1935) [for the "illegal" use of foreign currency in missionary work] and moral corruption such as having birthed children (1936-1937) [some of the priests reported they had received urgent calls to administer the last rites and when they arrived to do so would find themselves being photographed with a planted prostitute by Nazi agents], and in 1939 priests were forbidden to teach or administer in secondary schools.

The Nazi Kirchenkampf reached its peak from 1938-1941 when the Austrian Concordat of 1933 was abolished (1938) which reestablished civil marriages and confiscated the Austrian Endowment Fund for Religion (reestablished in 1950); when the German Association of Catholic Academicians (1938), the Austrian Catholic Popular Union (1938), and several Catholic charitable and youth organizations were closed (1938); when in 1938 cities such as Baden offered state employment for any nuns who would renounce their vocation; when some German bishops (such as Faulhaber, Innitzer, Sproll, and von Preysing) were subject to Nazi violence or expulsion in 1938; when in 1938-1939 the Catholic Theological Faculties of the Universities of Gießen, Graz, Innsbruck (Jesuit), Munich and Salzburg and the Jesuit Colleges of Sankt Blasien and Feldkirch were all closed [and an additional fifteen Catholic philosophers lost their posts elsewhere in Germany (in some cases through the actions of Heidegger)]; when over 200 monasteries and convents, including the Benedictine Abbeys of Melk, Michelsberg, Scheyern, and St. Matthias, and the Seminary of Trier, were confiscated for military purposes in Germany and Austria (in the 1938-1941 Aktion Klosterturm); when the Polish intellectuals were murdered after the invasion of Poland (1939); when the Catholic Journals Gral (1939), Hochland (1941), and Stimmen der Zeit (1941) were forced to shut down (the Nazi SS journal Das Schwarze Korps, however, with its fervent attacks on the Catholic church continued to operate); when the Catholic Kindergartens were shuttered in 1941; and when the Catholic scholarly group Görres-Gesellschaft (1941) was dissolved. Indeed in 1943 the Nazis contemplated kidnapping Pope Pius XII but eventually decided against it.

With the threat National Socialism posed to the Catholic Church and the German people becoming ever clearer, the German Catholic hierarchy increasingly spoke out against it (even if they didn't always speak out as forcefully and explicitly as they might have). Hence, the Austrian Bishops wrote a pastoral letter in 1933 very critical of National Socialism for its racism, violence, and nationalism. For their part, the German Bishops issued pastoral letters in 1935, 1936, 1938, 1941, 1942, and 1943 which contained criticisms of National Socialism (especially in regard to its Aktion T4 Euthanasia Program of 1939-1941—in which over 70,000 people were killed including a cousin of Pope Benedict XVI with Down Syndrome—persecution of Catholics, and occasionally in regard to its racism), as did the Dutch

Bishops in 1942 (as we will see this ultimately was one factor that led to the death of Edith Stein and others in reprisal). Especially prominent Nazi critics were the German bishops Adolf Bertram (1859-1945), Michael von Faulhaber (1869-1942), who had been a long-time member of the Catholic League against Anti-Semitism *Amici Israël* (1925-1928), Johannes Baptista Sproll (1870-1949) [who was expelled from his diocese by the Nazis in 1938], Ludwig Maria Hugo (1871-1935), Clemens August Graf von Galen (1878-1946), and Konrad von Preysing (1880-1950) [who was expelled from his diocese by the Nazis in 1938]. Additionaly, Pope Pius XI issued the German encyclical *Mit Brennender Sorge* (1937) and Pius XII his *Summi Pontificatus* (1939) [though Pius XII has received criticism for his alleged overall "silence" in such matters]. Unfortunately, due in part to the premature death of Pius XI, a more strongly worded encyclical, *Humani Generis Unitas* (1938), was never released (though elements of it were incorporated into the *Summi Pontificatus*).

Many Catholic faithful also took up the fight against National Socialism, including two members of the White Rose Group, namely, the students Willi Graf (1918-1943) and Cristoph Probst (1919-1943) at the University of Munich, who produced anti-Nazi leaflets from 1941-1942 and paid for it with their lives; Rupert Mayer, S.J. (1876-1945) [who was imprisoned in a concentration camp]; Theodor Haecker (1879-1945) [a convert and supporter of the White Rose group and someone whom Heidegger spoke out against]; Dietrich von Hildebrand (1889-1977) [who was threatened with imprisonment as we shall see]; Heinrich Rommen (1897-1967) [who was briefly arrested]; Ignatius Eschmann, O.P. (1898-1968) [who was imprisoned in a concentration camp]; Eberhard Welty, O.P. (1902-1965) of the Cologne Circle; Gustav Siewerth (1903-1963) [whom Heidegger spoke out against]; Canon Josef Teusch (1902-1976) who wrote *Studien zum Mythos des XX. Jahrhunderts* (1934) in response to the work of Alfred Rosenberg; Max Müller (1906-1994) [another supporter of the White Rose group and one whom Heidegger spoke out against]; the aforementioned Alfred Delp, S.J. (1907-1945) of the Kreisau Circle, Alois Grimm, S.J. (1886-1944), and Josef Mayr-Nusser (1910-1945) [all of whom were executed by the Nazis]. Another National Socialist martyr was Edith Stein as we have seen.[3]

On March 23, 1938 Edith Stein wrote to a fellow religious sister and phenomenologist, Adelgundis Jaegerschmid, O.S.B., in regard to the looming death of their "Master" Edmund Husserl: "I am not at all worried about my dear Master. It has always been far from me to think that God's mercy allows itself to be circumscribed by the visible church's boundaries. God is truth. All who seek truth seek God, whether this is clear to them or not" (*Self-Portrait in Letters*, Letter 259, p. 272). This quote would apply equally well to the life of Edith Stein who spent her life seeking the truth about reality and came to find that truth in both phenomenology and Catholicism.

Phenomenology is a philosophical method which consists in focusing one's attention on and describing the phenomena, or immediate experiences, present to one's consciousness. Hence, its founder, Edmund Husserl (1859-1938) sometimes called it a "descriptive psychology," i.e. a descriptive science of phenomena (LI, I, Introduction, 6, pp. 261-263). In such a phenomenology we engage in a description of the immanent content of consciousness (ID, I, 2:19, pp. 74-76), for as Husserl describes his "principle of principles": "every originary presentative intuition is a legitimizing source of cognition ... everything originarily ... offered to us in intuition is to be accepted simply as what it is presented as being, but also only within the limits in which it is presented there" (ID, I, 2:24, p. 83; cf. CM, III, 24, pp. 57-58).[4]

Phenomenology then in Husserl's famous turn of phrase represents a "return to the things themselves" [*die Sachen selbst zurückgehen*] (LI, I, Introduction, 2, p. 252). In this way, says Husserl, we can free our mind of any presuppositions and attend merely to what is given to it (LI, II, Introduction, 7, pp. 263-266; V, Introduction, 2, p. 537; ID, III, 7:63, pp. 171-173).

Furthermore, by describing the immediate data given (*es gibt*) to one's mental experience one can extract what is essential to a given appearance or phenomenon (i.e. what is the necessary ideal condition of an object, the essence [*eidos*; *Wesen*]). This, for Husserl, constitutes the first reduction, the eidetic reduction (LI, I, Introduction, 6, p. 262; II, 3:14, pp. 365-368; V, 2:21, pp. 590-593; ID, I, 1, pp. 46-57). Consequently Husserl explains that phenomenology is a "pure description ... [a] contemplation of pure essences on a basis of exemplary individual intuitions of experiences" (LI, I, Introduction, 6, p. 261) and so "phenomenology must bring to pure expression, must describe in terms of their essential concepts and their governing formulae of essence, the essences which directly make themselves known in intuition" (LI, I, Introduction, 2, p. 249). We can enter into such an eidetic reduction either a) by focusing on what is common to all appearances of a given type (i.e. by examining several examples of the same phenomenon); or b) by engaging in a free imaginative variation in which we one-by-one imaginatively remove the features of an object until we find those features which are invariably necessary for the object to be what it is (i.e. features that can't be removed without the object losing its identity) (LI, II, 1:1, p. 340; ID, III, 7:70, pp. 181-184; CM, IV, 34, pp. 69-72; EJ, Part Three, II, 87, pp. 340-348). While Husserl himself primarily engaged in a phenomenology of perception, and other phenomenologists went on to give descriptions of memory and time, Catholic phenomenologists tended to describe the a priori experiences of freedom, values, and God. Indeed, apart from Thomism, phenomenology may be the most popular philosophy among recent Catholic philosophers.

Edith Stein [Steinová] (1891-1942) was born in Breslau [Wrocław], Silesia, Poland in 1891 (then part of Germany). Regrettably, Stein's father died of heat stroke before she had reached the age of two leaving her mother and siblings to raise her (Edith was the youngest of eleven siblings, four of whom died as children). Her parents were observant Jews, although by age thirteen Edith Stein (through the reading of Spinoza) had lost her faith in prayer and by age nineteen in a personal God and described herself as a non-believer (see Life in a Jewish Family, pp. 60, 70, 138, 148, 193, 260, 316).

In 1911-1913 Stein studied psychology with William Stern and philosophy with Richard Höningswald and Eugen Kühnermann at the Friedrich Wilhelm University in Breslau [women only recently having been allowed to attend German Universities in 1908]. There she also joined the Pedagogical Society for Women's Right to Vote and was something of a feminist. Philosophy became her first love and so Stein went on to pursue phenomenological studies with "the Master" Edmund Husserl at the University of Göttingen in 1913 (besides the important influence of Husserl, Stein was also influenced by Roman Ingarden, Adolf Reinach, Hans Lipps, and Wilhelm Dilthey). Her studies were briefly interrupted by the First World War when in 1915 Stein volunteered as a nurse's aid in the Red Cross. Stein then followed Husserl to the University of Freiberg in 1916 where she received her doctorate (she was the second German women, after her friend Hedwig Conrad-Martius, to get a doctorate). Stein was delighted when Husserl requested that she become his first Freiburg assistant (she had to study Gabelsberger shorthand in order to be able to edit his books *Ideas Pertaining to a Pure Phenomenology* [ID] (books II and III) and *On the Phenomenology of the Consciousness of Inner Time*). Stein, however, quit as Husserl's assistant after two years and returned to Wroclaw in 1918 due to her frustration with the ever-increasing and ever-changing manuscripts being produced and then cast-aside by Husserl.

Many of the phenomenologists had recently converted to some form of Christianity (for instance Edmund Husserl, Adolf Reinach, Theodor Conrad and his wife Hedwig Conrad-Martius to Lutheranism, and Max Scheler and Dietrich von Hildebrand to Catholicism). Hence Stein developed a newfound appreciation for religious world-views and on occasion attended Lutheran services with her colleagues. Eventually Stein herself was inspired to convert to Catholicism (particularly on account of the great strength the widow of Adolf Reinach found in Lutheranism after her husband's death on the WWI front and by her discovery of the writings of Teresa of Avila in 1921 while on vacation with Hedwig Conrad-Martius). So it is that in 1922 Edith Stein was baptized a Catholic at St. Martin's Church in Bergzabern.

Stein sought a teaching position in one of the German Universities; unfortunately her being female and of Jewish descent precluded this (and her applications were rejected at the Universities of Göttingen and Kiel in 1919 and the Universities of Breslau and Freiburg in 1931 [where though she had the initial support of Martin Honecker and Martin Heidegger, it seems Honecker and Heidegger (who was turning to National Socialism) developed a dislike of her combination of phenomenology and Thomism (cf. *Never Forget*, pp. 199-201)]). Still Stein was able to teach Greek, Latin, and German languages as well as history at St. Magdalene's Dominican School [Mädchen-Lyzeum] for girls in Speyer, Germany from 1923-1931. Stein additionally became a spokesperson for the Catholic Women's Movement throughout Germany in 1928-1932 (giving talks in such places as Bendorf, Ludwigshafen, Augsburg, Münster, Heidelberg, Zurich, Salzburg, Vienna, and Zurich) and she also attended the Juvisy Thomistic Society conference in 1931 where she befriended Jacques Maritain and his wife. Finally, in 1932 Stein was able to secure a favorable teaching position at the German Institute for Scientific Pedagogy (Deutsches Institut für wissenschaftliche Pädagogik; the Marianum) in Münster (she also joined the International Phenomenological Society in 1940).

Stein's academic career was short-lived, however, as in 1933 she was forced to resign due to Nazi anti-Jewish laws [as an interesting aside Stein (after a failed attempt at a meeting) wrote Pope Pius X a letter in 1933 in which she described the great injustices perpetrated on Jews by the National Socialists and urged him to not remain silent but speak out against the Nazi movement and its anti-Jewish laws].

With her hopes for an academic career dashed (Stein had additionally turned down a teaching position in Argentina as it would take her too far away from her mother), Edith Stein decided to go through with her plans of becoming a Carmelite nun ["What did not lie in my plan lay in God's plan" (FEB, III, 12, p. 113)]. Hence she entered the Lindenthal Carmel of Cologne in 1933 taking the name Sister Teresa Benedicta a Cruce [of the Cross]. The growth of National Socialism, however, continued to threaten her life goals and indeed her life itself. Thus it proved impossible for Edith Stein to publish her books in Germany given her Jewish ancestry (and the passage of the Nuremberg Laws of 1935). Stein was even forced to flee Germany for the Carmel of Echt in the Netherlands following the Kristallnacht pogrom in 1938 wherein Jewish synagogues, homes, and businesses were destroyed. This new location, however, was no safer than the previous one when the Nazi's invaded the Netherlands in 1940. Hence Stein and her sister (who had also become a Carmelite nun) had to wear the Yellow Star of David to identify themselves as Jews and had to report regularly to the Gestapo there. Stein and her sister attempted to once again flee to safer territories, this time to the Le Pâquier Carmel in Switzerland, but the arrangements for Stein's sister were held up and Stein refused to leave her behind. Then in 1942 the Dutch bishops published a pastoral letter condemning the anti-Semitic Nazi measures which denied the right of Jewish-descended Catholic children to attend Catholic schools as well as the ongoing Jewish deportations including the deportation of several hundred Catholic priests, religious, and laity of Jewish descent. In reprisal the Nazi's earmarked all the Jewish converts to Catholicism for imprisonment. Thus Stein and her sister were arrested by Nazi SS agents and taken to camps in Amersfoort and Westerbork, Netherlands and then on to Birkenau, Auschwitz where both were executed in the gas chamber (Edith Stein's purported last words to her sister as she left the convent were "Come, let us go for our people") [attributed to a lay co-worker witness at the convent]. Edith Stein accordingly saw her last earthly day in Birkenau, Auschwitz in 1942.

Edith Stein was beatified in 1987 and canonized in 1998 (a matter of some consternation to several Jews). And in 1999 Stein was declared co-patroness of Europe and the year before she had been singled out as a great example of a Catholic philosopher in Pope John Paul II's encyclical *Fides et Ratio* (1998).[5] There are additionally schools named after Stein in Darmstadt, Germany and Hengelo, Netherlands and an Edith Stein Guild was founded in 1955 in New York. Lastly, in Germany, a dormitory in the University of Tübingen, a street in Bad Bergzabern, and a statue in the Walhalla Temple of Regensburg all bear her name.

As mentioned above, the encyclical *Fides et Ratio* (1998) of Pope John Paul II proclaimed that Stein is to be counted among those great Christian philosophers who displayed the "same fruitful relationship between philosophy and the word of God" (section 74). Stein did so in her phenomenological works *Psychical Causality* [*Psychische Kausalität*] [PC] (written in 1919; published in 1922) and *Individual and Community* [*Individuum und Gemeinschaft*] [IC] (written in 1919; published in 1922).[6] These works attempt to develop a phenomenology of the human person, especially a phenomenology of joy (lifepower) and freewill.

Stein, in her early phenomenological description of the human being, held that the human contains four realms: 1) physical; 2) sensate [soul; sentient; psychic; *psychische*]; 3) mental [spiritual; *geistige*]; and 4) personal [core; *Kern*] (IC, II, 1, p. 200; II, 3, pp. 226-229, 237-238; Conclusion, p. 298; FEB, III, 3, p. 72; IV, 5, pp. 272-275; VII, 3, pp. 363-364, 367, 376-377; VII, 5, pp. 391-392; VII, 7-9, pp. 422-423, 425, 433-435, 462-463; VIII, 2-3, pp. 501-502, 506, 519; n. 39 on p. 590; SHP, I, pp. 52-53; III, pp. 61-65; IV-V, pp. 70-71, 74-78, 84; VI, pp. 112-118; VII, pp. 129-130, 133-137; WIH?, I, pp. 15-22; PA, V, 2, pp. 86-88; V, 8, p. 117, 126-153; VI, 2, pp. 158-182; VI, 23, pp. 236-281; Conclusion, p. 283; SIP, I, pp. 41; II, pp. 135-143, 156-161).

The physical realm of the human being consists of the outer physical body (*Körper*). This is our material body which is given in outer perception (perceived) and which is subject to the causal laws of nature and hence physiological processes. This realm, while private to each individual, allows the human being to be sunk deep into and interface with the physical world (FEB, VII, 3, pp. 365-367; VII, 7, p. 422; OPE, III, p. 41 [44]).

The sensate (psychical) realm on the other hand consists of the living body (Leib) wherein the physical body is animated by a soul [Seele]. That is to say, here the human exists as an inner living body, a body which is internally sensed (experienced) and which has various attendant sensations (pain, hot, cold, sounds, sights, etc.) and feelings (joy, weariness, etc.) (FEB, VII, 3, pp. 365-367, 369; VII, 7, p. 422; OPE, III, pp. 41-42 [44-45]; 45 [49]; 47-49 [52-53]; 56 [63]; "WKG," II, 4, p. 99 and n. 49 on p. 142; WP, pp. 142-148, 172-185). The sensate realm is also subject to the causality of nature yet is both private and interpersonal. For at one level (that of sheer sensuality) one's sensations are private to oneself and so intrapersonal, such as with sensations of pain, a shimmering before the eyes, a ringing in the ear, an itch (IC, I, 2, p. 145, 154, 166; Conclusion, p. 295). Yet at another level the sensate realm is interpersonal as when, for example, other humans can come to grasp my inner feelings through empathy and indeed be affected by them (IC, II, 3, pp. 230, 232; II, 4, p. 271; Conclusion, p. 295).

The third human realm is that of the mental. This refers to the mind which is capable of acts of intellection and meaning (combination, comparison, comprehension, facility in grasping, inference, perspicacity, shrewdness, etc.) and which allows for rational motivations (IC, I, 2, pp. 152, 154; II, 3, p. 225; Conclusion, pp. 295-296). This realm of meaning is sharable between humans, and so two humans can share the ideas (object constitution) of a dog, a triangle, or courage (IC, I, 2, pp. 146-147, 150, 152-154, 157; Conclusion, p. 295).

Finally, the core of the human being consists of the person or spirit [Geist]. Within this personal core the human possesses a unique and incommunicable 'I' or ego (it has its own life and subsists for itself) whereby it has self-awareness, a self immediately given in consciousness [though not necessarily a deep self-knowledge] (FEB, II, 6, pp. 48, 54; VI, 4, p. 343; VII, 1-2, 3, 5, pp. 356, 361-362, 375, 411; VII, 9, pp. 428-431; SHP, II, pp. 53-54; VI, pp. 105-115). This ego is also the bearer of experiences; it is continually present as the carrier of experiential contents (OPE, II, p. 5 [3]; III, p. 40 [44]; FEB, II, 6, pp. 48, 54; III, 4, p. 76; VI, 4, p. 344; VII, 2, p. 362; n. 25 on p. 555; IC, II, 3, p. 230). The ego or 'I' can accordingly be called "the subject of experience living in experience" (OPE, II, 29 [32]; cf. OPE, p. 5 [3]; 29 [32]; III,

38-39 [41-42]; IV, p. 98 [110]; PC, Introduction, p. 8; I, 1-2, pp. 9, 13; IC, I, 1, pp. 133, 135, 140; Conclusion, p. 309).

This personal core also includes free will and so "denotes an incorporeal, rational, and freely active essence or nature" (FEB, VII, 7, p. 422).[7] The personal core is lastly what allows for humans to be open to the world of value and to religious and mystical experiences (PC, I, 4, p. 17; IC, I, 2, pp. 158-160, I, 3, p. 195; II, 3-4, pp. 226-229, 263-264, 275, 278, 294; Conclusion, pp. 309, 313-314; FEB, V, 17, pp. 316-317; VI, 4, p. 343; VI, 2, p. 363; VII, 3, pp. 373, 376-377; VII, 4, p. 380; VII, 5, pp. 394-396; VII, 5, p. 400; VII, 9, pp. 429, 441-442, 444-445; n. 91 on p. 604; VIII, 3, p. 504; OPE, II, pp. 7, 31 [6, 35]; IV, pp. 97, 101, 108, 110-111, 113, 116 [108, 113, 121, 123-124, 128, 130]; "WKG," II, 4, pp. 104-105, and Appendix, p. 122; PA, V, 8, pp. 139-151; SIP, I, p. 115; II, pp. 144; WP, pp. 46-48). For the core contains a moral conscience wherein humans experience the value-ladenness of objects (their being 'good-if-so' and not 'just-so'), making the human a "value-tropic being" and permeable to values (which can then be shared with other humans) (PC, III, 1, p. 43; V, 3, p. 86; IC, I, 2, pp. 164, 166; II, 3, pp. 226-227, 231, 234-238; II, 4, p. 253; OPE, IV, p. 108 [121]; FEB, VII, 3, p. 373; ICS, II, 4, pp. 155-156).

Stein, in particular, focuses her phenomenological analysis of the soul on the sensate realm and describes the various life feelings (*Lebensgefühl*) which constitute "the experiencing of a status of living," or the recognition of the "changing conditionalities of life" (PC, II, 1, p. 24; II, 2, p. 27)]. These life feelings include such things as admiration, alertness, confidence, fear, gloominess, gratitude, hate, hope, irritability, joy (vigor), love, nervousness, relief, serenity, trust, vengeance, and weariness (exhaustion, fatigue, tiredness) (PC, I, 4, pp. 14-16, 19; II, 1, p. 22; II, 2, p. 27; II, 3, pp. 34-36; V, 3, pp. 81, 86; IC, I, 2-3, pp. 163-164, 173; II, 2, pp. 201, 217-218; OPE, III, pp. 49-50, 68 [53-55, 77]; IV, pp. 99, 100-101 [111-113]; FEB, VII, 3, pp. 365-366; SHP, VI, pp. 104-105; VII, pp. 137-162).

These life feelings [general feelings], moreover, affect our experience of and receptivity to sense impressions. This is especially so for the continuum of life feeling (life-status) stretching from weariness to vigor. The more vigor I have, the more the intensity of an experience (its aliveness, clarity, and salience) increases, and the more weariness I have, the more the intensity of experience decreases: "The more refreshed I feel myself to be, the more 'alertly' my 'mental eye' looks around, the more intense is the orientation toward the objects, and the livelier the apprehension" (PC, V, 1, p. 74; cf. PC, II, 2, p. 30; II, 3, pp. 35-36). Stein appeals here to the metaphor of the life feelings bathing and coloring our experiences—with one's cheerfulness or vigor giving them warmth and color, but one's gloominess or sluggishness giving them coldness and hollowness [for if one is weary then colors are colorless and tones are hollow] (PC, I, 4, pp. 14-15, 19-20; II, 1-3, pp. 25-27, 29, 32; V, 1-2, pp. 74-75; V, 3, p. 81; IC, I, 3, pp. 189-190; II, 1, p. 198; II, 2, pp. 217-218; OPE, III, pp. 48-49, 68 [53-54, 77]; IV, p. 100 [112]; cf. n. 126 on p. 129). As Stein puts it: "The feeling either impels the rest of the flowing current forward more rapidly or paralyzes it, and colors it either 'brighter' or 'gloomier'" (PC, V, 2, p. 75).

With this in mind Stein arrives at the fecund idea of lifepower [Lebenskraft] which we can define (though unfortunately Stein never gives it an explicit definition) as a current of vital energy whose presence causes vigor and whose absence causes weariness of life. Stated otherwise, lifepower is a continuum of increments of weariness and vigor (joy) wherein "the changing conditionalities of life signify an increase or decrease of lifepower, and different life feelings correspond to that as 'manifestations'" (PC, II, 1, p. 24; see PC, I, 4, pp. 19, 22; II, 2-3, pp. 27, 30, 32-33, 36; V, 2, p. 78). Thus lifepower goes through various influxes and outflows which increases or reduces its level or supply of energy (PC, II, 1, p. 22, n. 34 on p. 23; II, 1, p. 24; IV, 2, p. 67-68; V, 5, p. 93; IC, I, 2, p. 173; II, 1-2, pp. 197-198, 201; II, 3, pp. 232, 235; Conclusion, p. 304).

The first thing that reduces our level of lifepower is experiencing itself. For according to Stein all experience depends on lifepower in a certain sense and would not enter into sensation (i.e. into our awareness) without it (PC, II, 2, pp. 29-30): "Lifepower ... serves to maintain the current of sensate living" (PC, II, 3, p. 37). Hence each sensate occurrence or experience costs us a certain expenditure of lifepower, causing our level of vigor to diminish and turn to weariness (PC, I, 3, pp. 4, 20; II, 1-3, pp. 25, 27-32, 32; II, 3, p. 37; IV, 2, p. 66-67; V, 1-2, pp. 74-75; V, 5, p. 92; IC, I, 3, p. 190; II, 2, pp. 202-203; II, 3-4, pp. 236, 249; Conclusion, p. 304; FEB, VII, 9, p. 435). Thus while a high level of lifepower (vigor) increases the intensity of our experiences (there is a conversion of lifepower into active experiencing), it is also the case that this active experiencing utilizes lifepower (experiencing drains our lifepower). Ultimately then experiencing sensations can lead to a tiredness wherein the current of energy slackens and shuts itself off from future experiences (PC, I, 4, p. 20).

Secondly, hard physical labor [indeed bodily fatigue or illness in general] as well as intense mental activity also decrease our level of lifepower (PC, IV, 2, 4, pp. 67-68, 74; V, 5, p. 92). In this way physical events can have an effect on the mental life and vice versa. Thus if I am fatigued I may not be able to engage in arduous mental activities such as mathematics (a tired person has a hard time doing calculus) or philosophy or reading, or appreciate a book, film, or someone's love or worth (PC, II, 3, pp. 36-37; V, 3, pp. 81, 83-84; Conclusion, p. 115). Indeed, according to Stein, the very act of willing reduces our lifepower (PC, V, 4-5, pp. 87, 89, 92): "And it can be that the resolve, coming to life from a free impulse but feeding on the lifepower, completely consumes the lifepower" (PC, V, 4, p. 89).

Finally, for Stein feelings of anxiety, distrust, fright, grief, hatred, sluggishness, or sorrow drain our lifepower and steal our vigor and vitality rather than replenishing them; they hobble our impulse to activity (PC, V, 2-3, pp. 79-80, 84; IC, II, 2, pp. 212, 217). Hence my sorrow can prevent me from sharing in a friend's joyful news (OPE, II, p. 15 [15]; 18 [18]; III, p. 49 [54]; FEB, II, 5, p. 47). Or to take a similar example if I am weary then the joy that would normally come from hearing a favorable report may be diminished (PC, V, 2, p. 75). Nor can we appreciate values when weary. "I recognize the value of an artwork, but I'm not able to get excited about it; I recognize the meanness of a sentiment, but I can't rouse myself to indignation over it; I recognize the unique worth of a human being, but I don't love him" (PC, V, 3, p. 84). It is even the case that the presence of these feelings in other humans can affect me. For example, the anxiety, grief, or weariness of other humans with low lifepower can rub off on me (be a form of contagion) and reduce my own lifepower (IC, I, 1, p. 136; I, 2, pp. 158, 164, 189; II, 2, pp. 211-212, 217; II, 4, pp. 251, 253, 267, 288-291, n. 237 on pp. 288-289; PC, V, 5, p. 107; OPE, II, p. 23 [24]; III, pp. 71-72 [81]).

Fortunately, though sensation, intense physical or mental labor, and negative emotions reduce our lifepower, there are other factors by which we can maintain and even increase lifepower. One basic way in which we can replenish our lifepower is by resting. As Stein remarks "But rest doesn't mean just a halt of expenditure of lifepower, but simultaneously a supplementation, a replenishment of available lifepower, which is manifested in a fading of the tiredness and in a decisive transition to a new vigor and a positive urge toward activity corresponding to it" (PC, IV, 2, pp. 67-68). We could even say, says Stein, that there are feedback loops operating here within the human being. When lifepower is at a low level, humans develop a feeling of fatigue and a desire for rest. And when humans rest they replenish their lifepower (PC, IV, 2, pp. 67-68): "If the reservoir of power is filled, then it converts itself into activity impulses in which its surplus is used up. If it's near to exhaustion, so that a failure of the functions of the mechanism is imminent, then it sounds out 'impulses of need' whose fulfillment brings it an influx of new power" (PC, IV, 2, p. 68).

Secondly, ideas (especially ones that are motivational or have a positive meaning), moral values, and the beauty of art or nature can build up one's lifepower (PC, III, 1, pp. 42; V, 2-3, pp. 78-79, 82, 83; Conclusion, pp. 115-116; IC, I, 2, pp. 173-175, 187-188; II, 2, pp. 212-213, 217, 219; Conclusion, p. 309). Suppose I hear a favorable report, for example; this good news can bring me joy and put me in a happy mood for the rest of the day (PC, V, 2, pp. 75; FEB, II, 5, p. 47; III, 4, p. 74; n. 26 on p. 555). Here "The joy is not merely joy at the report, but at the same time it fills 'me' up, it impinges upon the status of my life feeling. The joy is a new current, as it were, that gushes into the lifestream from elsewhere, 'churns it up,' influences its subsequent flow, and colors it in a determinate manner" (PC, V, 2, p. 75). So too reading a pleasant work of literature or historical work with particularly heroic figures (or we could use the contemporary example of watching an inspiring film) can result in an increase in lifepower and a feeling of vigor in our lives (PC, V, 2, pp. 77-78; IC, I, 2, p. 175; II, 2, pp. 213, 216; OPE, II, p. 32 [35]). Stein describes such an occurrence as follows: "Suppose that in a state of fatigue in which I feel 'lifeless' or inwardly numb, I reach for a book, for a literary work that I love, and suppose that delight over its beauty takes hold of me ... as the content begins to course through me, fills me more and more, and finally inundates me entirely, the fatigue goes away and I feel myself to be as though 'newborn,' refreshed and lively and full of incentive for new life activity" (PC, V, 2, pp. 76-77). The process is similar with other forms of art wherein observing them can increase our vigor and zest and additionally motivate us to act: "The beauty of a figure that I behold ignites in me the enthusiasm that spurs me to artistic creation. The hero of an epic poem fills me with admiration, and out of that admiration the urge wells up to emulate him" (IC, II, 2, p. 216).

Thirdly, encounters with the life feelings of other persons (and resting in God), or merely a resolve of my own will (i.e. willpower), can also increase my own lifepower (PC, V, 3-5, pp. 84-86, 88-91, 97; Conclusion, pp. 115-116; IC, II, 2-4, pp. 203-205, 206-208, 213, 216, 234-235, 266; Conclusion, p. 3Q9). Here again there is a kind of contagiousness of life feelings wherein the joy and vigor (or alternatively sadness or weariness) of another person can rub off on me (unconsciously or consciously), as with a Mardi Gras celebration (PC, V, 2, p. 76; V, 5, pp. 106-107; IC, I, 2-3, pp. 174-176, 184-185, 187-190, n. 86-87 on pp. 187-189, 192; II, 2, pp. 217-218; II, 4, pp. 251, 253, 267, 288-291, n. 237 on p. 288-289; see also OPE, II, p. 23 [24]; III, pp. 71-72 [81]). So when I want to stop worrying I can seek out a happy companion, and their life feelings of gratitude, love, and trust can generate lifepower for myself (OPE, II, pp. 11, 13, 14, 23-24 [10, 13, 24-25]; FEB, VII, 9, pp. 435-436; IC, II, 2, pp. 203-206, 208-209, 211-212, 215). Stein discusses this ability of other persons (through their presence, ideas, values, and feelings) to enhance my lifepower and give me vigor and joy in life in some notable passages:

> The love which I meet with strengthens and invigorates me and grants me the power for unexpected achievements (IC, II, 2, p. 212).
> ... in the communications of one person with another. The love with which I embrace a human being may be sufficient to fill him with new lifepower if his own breaks down. Indeed, the mere contact with human beings of more intense aliveness may exert an enlivening effect upon those who are jaded or exhausted, who have no activeness as a presupposition on their side (PC, V, 3, p. 85).
> Suppose, for example, a new instructor gives an 'invigorating jolt' to a sluggish and sleepy class, not through the intellectual contents he introduces to it, but rather through the contagious vigor that emanates from him (IC, II, 2, p. 206).
> There is a state of resting in God, of complete relaxation of all mental activity, in which you make no plans at all, reach no decision, much less take action, but rather leave everything that's future to the divine will, 'consigning yourself entirely to fate.' This state might have befallen me after an experience that exceeded my power, and that has completely consumed my mental lifepower and deprived me of all activeness. Compared to the cessation of activeness from the lack of lifepower, resting in God is something completely new and unique. The former was dead silence. Now its place is taken by the feeling of being safe, of being ex-

empted from all anxiety and responsibility and duty to act. And as I surrender myself to this feeling, new life begins to fill me up, little by little, and impels me – without any voluntary exertion – toward new activation. This reviving infusion appears as an emanation of a functionality and a power which is not my emanation and which becomes operative within me without my asking for it (PC, V, 3, pp. 84-85).

Now an important feature of Stein's notion of lifepower is that the influence of feelings, moral values, beauty, ideas (even a vivid image of one's family) coming from our environment or other people can increase our lifepower in ways that go beyond the physical and sensate realm and their laws (PC, V, 3, 5, pp. 81, 85-86, 97; Conclusion, p. 115). For as a person, with our four levels of reality, we are open to influxes coming from the realms beyond the sensory and sensate realms (i.e. from the mental and personal realms), and the impulse power flowing in from these realms can replenish our lifepower (PC, V, 3, pp. 81-82, 84; Conclusion, p. 115; IC, Introduction, p. 129; II, 2, pp. 208-210). As Stein writes in regard to a resolve of my own free will:

> In any event, it seems as though wherever the requisite objective foundations are available but any lifepower emanating from them is lacking, the resolve of the will itself can produce itself in the same way it generates other free acts. This marvelous capability of generating 'impulse powers' out of itself obviously indicates a power source lying beyond the mechanism of the individual personality, which flows into the willing ego and in which the willing ego is anchored (PC, V, 4, p. 89; cf. PC, V, 4, p. 90; V, 5, pp. 96-98; Conclusion, p. 116; IC, I, 3, pp. 191, 194; II, 3, p. 233; SHP, VII, pp. 157-162).
>
> Fatigue, and therefore the shortage of impulse power that's manifested in fatigue, can be made to disappear when its place is taken by the power arising from the will (PC, V, 4, p. 91).

In point of fact this ability of lifepower to be revivified is a phenomenon that violates the law of the conservation of energy (it goes beyond the law of physics) and so is a non-natural phenomenon (PC, II, 2, p. 27; Appendix I, pp. 117-118; IC, I, 3, pp. 187-188 including n. 3; II, 2-3, pp. 203-206, 208-211). Stein writes:

> The love which I meet with strengthens and invigorates me and grants me the power for unexpected achievements. ... He who loves me doesn't lose power proportionately with how he enlivens me. ... On the contrary, love operates within the one who loves as an invigorating force that might even develop more power within him than experiencing it costs

him. ... Thus, love and the positive attitudes in general don't feed upon themselves; rather, they are a font from which I can nourish others without impoverishing myself. This font is inexhaustible in itself; the only reason why it fails from time to time, or entirely, is because my power is so taken up with the other mental occupations that it doesn't cover the experiencing of such life-contributing contents. Thus, in subjectivity we already have sources of life which elude all measure and all calculation, which benefit the causal mechanism as propellant powers, but are not subject to any control themselves (IC, II, 2, p. 212).

Lifepower then (mental and spiritual/personal lifepower at least) can give out energy without itself being decreased (other persons can fill me up with energy without any diminution of their own lifepower). This suggests then that humans are not purely physical beings but spiritual as well (and that humans transcend the laws of physics) as such a non-abating source of energy does not occur with physical energy.[8]

Another Catholic phenomenologist on the run from the Nazi party was **Dietrich Richard Alfred von Hildebrand (1889-1977)**.[9] Dietrich von Hildebrand was born in 1889 in Florence, Italy at the former Minim monastery of San Francesco which his father had purchased (it had been secularized by Napoleon). His father was the famous German sculptor Adolf von Hildebrand (known for such works as the Hubertus, Vater-Rhein, and Wittelsbacher fountains in Munich and a statue of Bismark in Bremen and as the author of the aesthetical work *Das Problem der Form*, 2 vols. [1893-1897]). Dietrich von Hildebrand grew up in both Florence, Italy and Munich, Germany where he was home-schooled by various tutors such as Walter Rietzler, Ludwig Curtius, and Alois Fischer (Curtius and Fischer were fallen Catholics and his parents were non-practicing Protestants; indeed his father embraced a moral relativism and pantheism), and von Hildebrand learned to speak English, French, German, and Italian and to read Greek and Latin. He studied philosophy at the University of Munich from 1906 to 1909, with Theodor Lipps, Alexander Pfänder, Alois Fischer, and Moritz Geiger, where he also joined the Academic Association for Psychology. Even more influential was his friendship with Max Scheler who was responsible for von Hildebrand eventually converting to Catholicism in 1914. He then left for Göttingen where he studied with Husserl and became a disciple of phenomenology (he was also influenced by Clemens Baeumker, Friedrich Wilhelm Foerster, and Adolf Reinach) and joined the Göttingen Philosophical Association. The year 1912 was very significant to Von Hildebrand as that was the year he received his doctorate in philosophy and also married his first wife, Margarete (Gretchen) Denck (von Hildebrand had consummated their relationship and gotten his girlfriend pregnant after his parents refused to grant him the necessary legal permission—needless to say they relented; their son's name was Franz von Hildebrand).

During the First World War, von Hildebrand worked as a doctor's assistant for the Red Cross (c. 1915). He then began his academic career at the University of Munich in 1918 as a lecturer (Privatdozent), becoming a professor of philosophy there in 1924 (unfortunately Husserl did not support him for a position at the University of Freiburg in 1921). Von Hildebrand first came to the attention of the National Socialists in 1921 when he gave a political speech in Paris at the invitation of Marc Sangnier of Le Sillon fame (he returned to Paris in 1934 to lecture at the Catholic Institute of Paris where he met Jacques Maritain). Shortly thereafter an article appeared in Germany criticizing his views which led to a university inquest which came to naught. Not one to rest on his laurels, from 1924-1930 von Hildebrand started ed a philosophical discussion group (which included such participants as Erich Przywara, Martin Grabmann, Fernand van Steenbergen, and the aforementioned Cardinal Konrad von Preysing) and also became a member of the Association of Catholic Academicians. In 1933 he gave another talk at a pacifist congress in Munich and this time it was directly disrupted by Nazi agents.

Hence von Hildebrand was forced to flee Germany in 1933 for Florence when the Nazi party came to power. He then made his way to Vienna, Austria. In Austria von Hildebrand further angered the National Socialists by founding the journal *Der christliche Ständestaat* for which reason his books were censored in Germany, he was declared an enemy of the Nazi's, and he was given a death sentence by them *in abstentia*. Von Hildebrand took up a position at the University of Vienna in 1935 in spite of the fact that, apart from the anti-Nazi logical positivist Moritz Schlick, most of the faculty were opposed to his nomination and even held a demonstration to prevent it. Austria itself, however, fell under the sway of the Nazis in 1938, and so von Hildebrand fled to France and joined the Catholic Institute of Toulouse. Yet

France was not safe for long and after the fall of France to Germany in 1940, he fled first to Portugal (with the assistance of a Dominican army officer, a Fr. Duployer [possibly Pie Duployé, O.P. who founded the French Liturgical Movement in 1943 as we will soon see], and the famous French politician Edmond Michelet), and then to the United States (through a Rockefeller Foundation Scholarship Maritain had helped to set up) where he taught at Fordham University in New York from 1942 until his retirement in 1960 (he had turned down a position at the New School for Social Research). As his first wife had died in 1957, just before his retirement (in 1959) von Hildebrand married a former student of his Alice Jourdain (1923-) (she went on to become a well-known philosopher and speaker herself). He founded the Roman Forum for the defense of Catholic doctrine and culture in 1968 and died in 1977 in New Rochelle, New York. There is a Dietrich von Hildebrand Institute (1968) and a Dietrich von Hildebrand Legacy Project (2004), and von Hildebrand has been praised by Pius XII (who called him the Doctor of the Church of the Twentieth-Century), Benedict XVI, and the Austrian Cardinal Christoph Schönborn. It is also said that over 100 people converted to Catholicism due to his influence.

Von Hildebrand's key work is his *Christian Ethics* [CE] (1953).[10] He is quite upfront in stating that this book is an attack on moral relativism and represents a defense of "the inalterable character of the moral law, the absolute nature of moral values" (CE, Preface, p. vi; cf. CE, Preface, p. v).

In this moral investigation the method of phenomenology is especially valuable in that it forces us to suspend all the theories we may happen to hold with regard to a philosophical sphere and instead let "the evident, as well as anything which is really given, ... have undisputed precedence over any hypothesis, explanation, or interpretation" (CE, Prolegomena, p. 16). In this manner we are able to reject any construction or explanation which fails to do justice to the data presented in our experience, and indeed avoid any thesis which is not imposed on us by the data (CE, Prolegomena, pp. 1, 4, 8-9, 13-18).

One of the things that phenomenology lets us recognize by removing all preconceptions is the incorrectness of a radical empiricism which holds that only the senses provide us with knowledge. For in addition to the empirical data which derives from reflection upon our sense-experience (giving us a knowledge of real existence; a posteriori knowledge) there is also the data which derives from reflection on more mental experiences comprising what von Hildebrand calls such-being [*Die Sachverhalt*] (giving us knowledge of ideal existence; a priori knowledge wherein we find strict necessity, incomparable intelligibility, and absolute certainty). Such-being in particular comprises the necessary essences we discover in the realms of logic (i.e. the principle of contradiction, efficient cause, final cause, syllogisms, etc.), mathematics, value, beauty, self-consciousness, and freedom (CE, Prolegomena, pp. 9, 13-14; Part One, I, 2, pp. 31-33; II, 8, p. 102; Part Two, I, 17, n. 37 on pp. 229-230; WIP, IV, pp. 63-74, 77, 83, 86-92, 98, 108, 120-131, 136; V, 159-165; IMA, II, 1, 3, pp. 69-74, 88-112). Von Hildebrand explains:

> ... the possibility of a priori knowledge, that is, absolutely certain knowledge of essentially necessary states of facts, is grounded in the type of such-beings of certain objects. It is grounded in an object's constitutive unity which has been intuitively revealed to our mind.... A priori knowledge bears upon states of facts which possess two characteristics. First, they are necessarily grounded in a necessary such-being unity; second, they can be understood by us with absolute certainty, either through the intuitive givenness of the necessary such-being unity, or through a deductive inference from a directly understood necessary state of facts. The possibility of a priori knowledge, therefore, is provided by objects having a necessary essence which can be intuitively seized. Hence, it follows that the circumference of a priori knowledge is much larger than it is often thought to be. A priori knowledge is not only possible, it is also the only possible and suitable knowledge, not simply in the fields of mathematics and logic but also in metaphysics, especially the ontology of the person, in ethics, aesthetics, and many other areas of human knowledge (WIP, IV, pp. 127-129).

Thus phenomenology shows us that knowledge arises from a reflection upon experience broadly understood. To claim that only that which can be physically sensed is real, as Hume and the positivists do, is to impose an arbitrary theory on experience (CE, Prolegomena, p. 10).

Von Hildebrand, as we have seen, found his philosophical calling in engaging in a phenomenological description of moral experience: "we must ... come back to the most explicit and unrestricted experience of moral data, and confront every result of our exploration with the full flavor of the experienced data themselves. The task of ethics is to attain to a full philosophical *prise de conscience* [awareness; literally 'taking into awareness'] of moral data (i.e. a philosophical awareness implying an explicit and fully conscious grasping of these data) and to arrive thereby at a precise notion of their specific nature, of their full significance, and of the presuppositions of man's conduct required for the possession of moral goodness" (CE, Prolegomena, p. 2; cf. CE, Prolegomena, pp. 1, 11; cf. WIP, I, pp. 15-25; "PV," p. 5; MOR, I, 1, p. 47). Von Hildebrand's particular genius, in fact, was to engage in a defense of absolute moral values through the phenomenological analysis of moral importance [*Bedeutsamkeit*; the *bonum* or good]. He does so by distinguishing between three kinds of importance: the important-in-itself (value), the objective good for a person, and the subjectively satisfying.

With the important-in-itself [*Das in sich Bedeutsame*], or what is more commonly called a value [*Das Wert*], we grasp that something has this value independent of our interest, need, pleasure, or satisfaction. We recognize that it is better in itself that something occurs, that this something ought to be [*Gesolltsein*], as it is noble, sublime, or heroic. This occurs, for instance, when we observe moral acts (such as charity, forgiveness, humility, gratitude, justice, or purity), the beauty of art, music, or nature (such as with sunsets and stars), or the majesty of truth (CE, Prolegomena, p. 1; Part One, I, 3, pp. 34-35, 43, 48; II, 7, p. 90; II, 8, pp. 95, 101-102, 104; Part Two, III, 28, p. 379; IV, 31, p. 412; WIP; IV, p. 122; FMA, I, pp. 1-3, 5; V, 61; TMC, V, pp. 66-69; X, p. 130; MOR, I, 1, pp. 40-59; NL, II, pp. 51-54; VII, pp. 146-154, 164-167, 174; "ROG," p. 975). As von Hildebrand describes:

> Whether we praise a human as just, or as reliable; whether we want to persuade someone that science is important; whether in reading a poem, we find it beautiful; whether we praise a symphony as powerful and sublime; whether we rejoice about the blossoming trees in spring; whether we are moved by the generosity of another person; whether we strive for freedom; whether our conscience forbids us to profit by injuring another—there is always presupposed the notion of something important-in-itself. ... In all indignation at something mean and debased; in every exclamation that one philosopher ranks higher than another, that one painter is a greater genius than another, we always presuppose the datum of value (CE, Part One, I, 6, p. 75).

The objective good for a person [*objektiver Güter für eine Person*], on the other hand and as the name suggests, consists of things which are objective goods for someone, things which are conducive to someone's true interest (CE, Part One, I, 3, pp. 50-51, 54; II, 7, pp. 80-81, 84; II, 8, p. 105; Part Two, III, 29, p. 395; MOR, I, 3, pp. 91-97, 117-128; "MPV," pp. 75-77; NL, VII, pp. 154-155). Objective goods for a person include such things as 1) moral values (conversion, forgiveness of evil, or gratitude for a benefactor); 2) goods of high value such as art, beauty, friendship, liturgical praise of God, love, philosophy, truth, and our ultimate eternal communion with God; 3) elementary goods which are necessities such as clothing, food, freedom, health, money, order, peace, shelter, and other things useful for a minimal degree of life; 4) agreeable things such as a comfortable bed and gourmet foods [which the noblest people, such as saints, do not seek] (CE, Part One, I, 4, pp. 67, 69; II, 7, p. 90; Part Two, III, 29, pp. 393-394, 398-403). Von Hildebrand contrasts values (the important-in-itself) and goods for a person as follows: "In hearing of the conversion of a sinner, we rejoice in a twofold direction. We rejoice first over the intrinsic goodness of the conversion, its importance-in-itself or its value, which glorifies God; and secondly, we rejoice for the man, because he did what is in the direction of his true good, because of the priceless gift he received in his conversion" (CE, Part One, I, 3, p. 58).

Lastly, the subjectively satisfying [*subjektiv Befriedigende*] is something which is important to a human only in that it gives pleasure or is agreeable. The subjectively satisfying accordingly denotes such things as a complement, a cool breeze or swim on a hot day, eating a meal or drinking water or wine, a game of bridge, resting in a chair or bed when tired, or a warm bath (CE, Part One, I, 3, pp. 34-35, 38-40; II, 7, p. 80; Part Two, II, 23, p. 302; IV, 33, p. 427; MOR, I, 8, pp. 135-148).

Von Hildebrand is especially attentive to contrasting the important-in-itself (value) with the subjectively satisfying. He does so by noting four distinguishing marks. First, while intrinsically important things do provide joy and satisfaction, their value is independent of the happiness they provide (independent even of our knowledge of them). For we discern that the happiness which a value imparts to us is based on an awareness of its intrinsic importance (CE, Part One, I, 3, pp. 36, 38-39; Part Two, II, 25, p. 317; IV, 32, pp. 415, 425). He goes on to proclaim:

> The delight and emotion which we experience in witnessing a noble moral action or in gazing at the beauty of a star-studded sky essentially

presupposes the consciousness that the importance of the object is in no way dependent on the delight it may bestow on us. Indeed, this bliss arises from our confrontation with an object having an intrinsic importance; an object standing majestically before us, autonomous in its sublimity and nobility. Our bliss implies in fact that here is an object which depends in no way on our reaction to it, an object whose importance we cannot alter, which we can neither increase nor diminish: for it draws its importance not from its relation to us, but from its own rank; it stands before us, a message, as it were, from on high, elevating us beyond ourselves. ... our engagement with a value elevates us, liberates us from self-centeredness, reposes us in a transcendent order which is independent of us, of our moods, of our dispositions. This blissful experience presupposes a participation in the intrinsically important; it implies a harmony which is given forth by the intrinsically good, the essentially noble alone; and it displays to us a rightness which is 'consubstantial' (congenial) with the intrinsic beauty and splendor of the value. In this priceless contact with the intrinsically and autonomously important, the important in itself, it is the object which shelters and embraces our spirit (CE, Part One, I, 3, pp. 36-37).

So although it is a trait of a value (even necessary to it and its "essential mark") that it bestows delight, the resulting delight is something secondary to the value itself, it is an epiphenomenon which flows from the value and is not its root (CE, Part One, I, 3, pp. 35-37; II, 7, p. 90; Part Two, I, 18, pp. 258, 278; II, 23, p. 309; IV, 33, pp. 428-429; "MPV," pp. 70-75, 77-80): "Authentic happiness, on the contrary, by its very nature cannot be the end of our actions, but it is definitely a gift bestowed on us when we abandon ourselves to a good endowed with a genuine value" (CE, Part Two, II, 23, p. 309). Happiness therefore is best considered as a gift, a return, a superabundance, a surplus that comes to us when we seek the good for itself (CE, Part Two, II, 23, pp. 303, 305, 309; III, 29, pp. 398-399; NTB, I, pp. 24-27; "HC," pp. 453-454). Or as von Hildebrand comments "no one would ever say I have heard love is such a blissful experience; therefore I want to fall in love in order to experience the bliss of love" ("HC," p. 454; cf. NL, V, pp. 101-122; VI, p. 139; X, pp. 221-234). What it is important to take home from this then is that a value is not good merely because it provides joy or because it is beneficial (or similarly a vice bad because it provides unhappiness or punishment) but on account of itself (CE, Part One, I, 3, pp. 56-57, 60).

Secondly every value calls for a human to transcend its own self-centeredness, it calls for a value-response (*Wertantwort*). So a decisive mark of a value response "is its character of self-abandonment. ... we break open our self-centeredness and conform to the important-in-itself. Our interest in the object is completely based on and completely nourished by the intrinsic goodness, beauty and preciousness of the object, and the mysterious rhythm of its intrinsic importance. The value response is, therefore, essentially a conforming of ourselves to the logos of the value" (CE, Part Two, I, 17, pp. 214-215; cf. Part Two, I, 17, p. 218; cf. IMA, III, 2, pp. 74-87; MOR, I, 1, pp. 36-46, 64-73; LP, VI, pp. 50, 53; TIC, XVIII, pp. 481-485, 495-498; NL, I, pp. 15-19, 28-35; II, pp. 52-54; III, pp. 77-79; IV, pp. 118-122; XII, pp. 300-307; Conclusion, pp. 373-374; "PV," pp. 6-8; "MPV," pp. 60-65). To embrace a value then is to engage in an act of self-donation or self-abandonment, to reverently submit to something greater than ourselves and respect it as good and precious in its own right, as worthy of being loved (CE, Part Two, I, 17, pp. 215-216, 218-222, 225, 228; I, 19, n. 2 on p. 258; FMA, I, pp. 304, 10-11; III, pp. 35-36, 43-46; V, pp. 71-72). In short the "general will to be good of the morally conscious man is a pure value response free of any egocentric taint" (CE, Part Two, I, 19, p. 274), "the pure gift of oneself to the value for its own sake, without the commingling of anything egocentric" (LP, VI, p. 50).

The subjectively satisfying, quite to the reverse, reposes us in ourselves, in our self-centeredness. For the subjectively satisfying occurs when we relate an object to ourselves; at its core it is based on a search for self-centered satisfaction, i.e. egoism (CE, Part One, I, 3, p. 39; I, 6, p. 75; Part Two, I, 17, p. 215). This is why in the end, by imprisoning us in ourselves, a life based solely on the pursuit of the subjectively satisfying wears itself out and leaves us with boredom and emptiness (CE, Part One, I, 3, pp. 36-37; I, 6, p. 76).

Thirdly, a value with its call addresses our free spiritual center; it acts unobtrusively and respects our conscience (CE, Part One, I, 3, p. 38). That is to say, when we enter into a meaningful concerting with a value and its intrinsic importance we light upon a "luminous harmony, inner freedom and serenity, the victorious superiority of love —which is the secret of eager and ready service—openness to the life of other men, warmth, ardor, meekness, and mildness, all-embracing breadth, awakedness, and the capacity to grasp values" (FMA, V, p. 70; cf. CE, Part Two, I, 17, pp. 217). The subjectively satisfying, by way of contrast, wants us to yield to instinct; it is a temptation that tries to silence our conscience, and acts in an obtrusive manner (CE, Part One, I, 3, p. 38).

Fourthly every good imposes on us the obligation to give it an adequate response; it is not left to us to determine how we should respond to it (we have no choice in the matter of doing good or avoiding evil). The subjectively satisfying, on the other hand, does not demand a response from us; how we respond to it is up to us (whether to eat a delectable dish or not is a real choice) (CE, Part One, I, 3, pp. 38-39).

With these contrasts of the important-in-itself (value) and the subjectively satisfying in mind, we can say that in the end morality comes down to a fundamental choice of values over and above the subjectively satisfying, and in two ways (CE, Part One, I, 3, pp. 43-44, 49, 61; II, 7, p. 83; Part Two, II, 23, pp. 304, 306; II, 24, pp. 320, 323-324, 327, 336-337; III, 28, p. 379). First, to truly be moral, one must be good for the sake of goodness. That is to say one must consciously will to be good out of an awareness of the moral significance of one's act and the call to engage in it, and in this way acquire a "concerting" with values (CE, Part Two, I, 18, p. 258; II, 23, p. 303; III, 28, pp. 348, 377-378; III, 29, p. 396; IV, 31, p. 410; "MPV," pp. 80-83).

Being moral furthermore requires us to develop what von Hildebrand calls a "superactual will," a will which is always ready to conform to the good (even in the absence of the object). So "every eternal truth and every authentic value ... which has been revealed to us should form a durable measure for our life" (CE, Part Two, IV, 32, p. 425; cf. CE, Part Two, I, 17, pp. 242-243; I, 18, pp. 257; I, 19, pp. 266-269, 276-277; II, 25, pp. 321-322, 325-326, 331; II, 27, pp. 358, 366, 376-378; IV, 32, pp. 416-419; IV, 32, p. 425, 428-429; TIC, IX, pp. 231-232; NL, II, pp. 43-48). Von Hildebrand spells out these two requirements of moral behavior thusly: "... a value response acquires the character of a fully valid moral response only when it implies the awareness of the moral significance of a morally relevant good, the response to this moral significance, and the superactual will to be good. Now we have to add a new indispensable requirement: the cooperation of our free spiritual center" (CE, Part Two, II, 25, p. 323).

Not surprisingly von Hildebrand was a great defender of moral realism. He sharply rejects a reductionist account of values wherein beauty is nothing but a contraction of the viscera, love nothing but a sublimated sexual instinct, and justice nothing but a bitter grievance of the weak and mediocre. This is to abdicate the philosophical method for that of natural science and reduce the spiritual realm to that of impersonal causes (CE, Prolegomena, p. 5, pp. 16-17; Part One, I, 2, p. 29; "PV," pp. 8-10). Hence Von Hildebrand remarks: "If anything calls for a psychoanalytic investigation, it is the artificial and desperate effort to deny the most obvious data and to make of them innumerably different things—anything in fact except what they distinctly reveal themselves to be" (CE, Part One, II, 9, p. 128).

Firstly, values, such as love and justice (as well as other phenomena such as space and time; truth; numbers; knowledge; will; and joy) are real as they have an intrinsic necessity (consistency) and intelligibility. They are entities of ultimate meaningfulness (intelligible essences) that are grasped in an original intuition (consequently they are ultimate data; non-deducibles; a *principium* [principle, i.e. source] not a *principiatum* [principled, i.e. effect]) (CE, Prolegomena, pp. 6-7; Part One, I, 1, pp. 26-27; I, 2, pp. 29-32; I, 3, pp. 37-38; II, 7, pp. 89-90, 95; II, 8, p. 104; II, 9, pp. 113, 115, 118, 120, 127; Part Two, I, 15, p. 187; NL, I, p. 29). Secondly, in moral experience we grasp an essential link between an object and its value (such as grasping the beloved as precious, as important-in-itself). Phenomenologically values appeal to us as something good in themselves and not just as what will appease an urge or desire [again it is only because it is a value that it can appease us as it does] (CE, Part One, I, 8, pp. 98-99; II, 7, pp. 87-89; II, 8, pp. 96-97, 103; Part Two, I, 17, n. 23 on pp. 215-216, 220, 231; MKMV, I, 2, pp. 130-141). Hence values cannot be reduced to a mere appearance or aspect of something which is in reality different from our mental experience (they are not mere psychical happenings in our soul or physical events in our brain). Values are rather undeniably real; they are realities as objective and independent of our consciousness as are movements of objects in the material world, it is just that they belong to the spiritual sphere (CE, Part One, I, 6, p. 76; II, 9, pp. 115, 117, 120-121, 124): "the intrinsic movement of value with its splendor and oughtness ... is in truth the heart and soul of being" (CE, I, 6, p. 78; cf. CE, Part One, I, 5, p. 72-74; II, 7, p. 89; II, 8, p. 102). Von Hildebrand spells this out by arguing:

> In contemplating charity, we grasp at once that it is necessarily good; we do not just bluntly state it, but we understand that it is so and must always be so. ... [In] acts of charity or justice ... the value discloses itself as a property of these acts ... the moral goodness of justice, the beauty of a

star-covered sky, the value of a human person, or his dignity as an *imago Dei* [image of God] are in the fullest sense properties of these being (CE, Part One, II, 7, p. 88; cf. Part Two, III, 29, p. 408).

In saying beautiful or good, we mean an importance-in-itself, something which not only is but ought to be. And if we examine what is given to us in the face of a morally good action, or of the dignity of a person, or of the beauty of nature, we immediately grasp that the datum confirms what we mean by those predications; that what we mean in saying good, beautiful, noble, or sublime is not something to which no reality corresponds, but on the contrary something which has the character of an importance-in-itself, which is univocally manifested in reality, and which reveals itself in the data of our experience (CE, Part One, II, 8, p. 104; cf. NTB, VI, pp.159-160, 167-170).

A careful analysis of moral values moreover shows us that God exists (hence von Hildebrand accepts a moral argument for God). It is true that someone does not need to believe in a supernatural Revelation or even in God's existence to grasp most moral values. People can be honest or dishonest, loyal or disloyal, selfish or unselfish on a purely natural level (here Socrates comes to mind as exemplifying the natural law, as do various non-Christians and atheists) (CE, Part One, II, 7, p. 93; III, 12, p. 154; III, 13, pp. 157-158; Part Two, V, 36, pp. 453-456, and n. 2 on pp. 453-454; TMC, XI, p. 155; "PV," pp. 10-12). Yet ultimately we cannot understand the nature of moral values, of the mysterious important-in-itself, if we look upon the moral sphere as merely human or natural (CE, Part One, II, 14, p. 179). In other words, moral values ultimately presuppose the infinite goodness and beauty of God as their source (CE, Part One, I, 6, p. 78; III, 11, pp. 134, 144; III, 12, pp. 150, 152; III, 14, pp. 161-162; Conclusion, p. 456; NTB, VI, pp. 168-171, 174-175; TIC, V, pp. 96-98; TMC, XI, p. 156; "MPV," pp. 59-60). Thus in the end "all natural goodness—the attitude of Socrates who not only taught but lived the truth that it is better for man to suffer injustice than to commit it, the sacrifice of Alcestis [by Euripides], the piety and the moral strength of Antigone [by Sophocles], the faithfulness of Pylades—all in their touching beauty and depth are reflections of the infinite goodness of God" (CE, Part Two, III, 14, p. 178; cf. MOR, I, 18, pp. 198-199).

In the first place qualitative values such as the beauty of a glorious sunset, the purity of Joseph in refusing to yield to the wife of Potiphat (Genesis 39:1-23), or an act of deep contrition, lead us to God as they all imply a message from above. Such values imply a promise that all

the splendor and intrinsic light shining forth from them is a triumphant metaphysical reality, that a final word occurs in the order of
actual being, that their ultimate intelligibility lies in a final cause which
is Absolute Being and Goodness (CE, Part One, II, 8, p. 105; III, 13,
pp. 159-160; III, 14, p. 162; Part Two, I, 16, p. 194; V, 36, pp. 455-
456). One could even say that moral values are God's "most intimate
reflection and message in the natural realm" (CE, Part One, III, 14, p.
165; cf. LP, V, pp. 42-43) for they contain "the implicit message that
moral goodness is for us an objective good, transcending the boundaries of our earthly existence" (CE, Part Two, III, 14, p. 176). Moral
values then indicate that humans are called to partake in a dialogue
with God; they represent God's chosen form of communication to us
humans (CE, Part One, III, 11, p. 134 and n. 8 on p. 138; III, 14, p.
162; Part Two, I, 17, p. 217, 221-222; III, 29, p. 393; IV, 31, p. 413;
V, 36, n. 5 on p. 456, pp. 456-457; JD, II, pp. 16-17). Von Hildebrand
expounds his position at length stating:

> But even though such values can be grasped without referring to God,
> objectively God is definitely presupposed by them. We have here a situ-
> ation analogous to the relation between the existence of God and the
> existence of contingent things. We do not need to know God in order to
> grasp the existence and nature of contingent beings, but in the ontologi-
> cal order the existence of a contingent being necessarily presupposes the
> existence of God. So here too the ontological value can be grasped with-
> out referring to God, but objectively it presupposes God... We do not
> claim that this ascent has the same character of a strict demonstration of
> God's existence as the argument based on the contingency of all created
> beings. But it cannot be denied that it is at least a starting point toward
> God, an indication, a hinting at God. ...
>
> Though this character of a message from above reaches still a new
> and higher level in moral values, beauty also throws into relief this more
> intimate reflection of God proper to qualitative values. ... the beauty of
> visible and audible things, the beauty of nature, of fine arts and music;
> ... this beauty is not simply the efflorescence of corporeal beings or of
> the sequence of sounds in which it manifests itself, but ... it definitely
> surpasses in its quality the ontological rank of these beings. We cannot
> expound this deep problem here. But it should be stressed that there is
> a special message of God, a specific reflection of God's infinite beauty,
> contained in a glorious landscape, such as the one seen from the Par-
> thenon in Athens or from the Giannicolo in Rome; in the sublimity of
> a church such as San Marco in Venice, and in the transfigured music of
> Beethoven's Ninth Symphony or in one of his last quartets. This beauty

speaks of a world above; it is a ray of the Father of all Lights; it elevates our spirit and fills our heart with a longing for this higher world (CE, Part One, III, 14, pp. 162-164; cf. "Beauty and the Christian," pp. 100-111; and "Zum Problem der Schönheit des Sichtbaren und Hörnbaren," pp. 180-191).

In the second place, moral values reveal the divine transcendent or an Absolute Goodness in that the moral actions to which we are called (or the immoral ones to which we are not) themselves call for a reward (or a punishment), both earthly and non-earthly. Values thus imply a mysteriously intimate connection with what awaits us in another life (CE, Part One, III, 14, p. 176). So to be endowed with moral values "is decisive for man's eternal fate, for they hint at eternity and the fact that man's existence is not exhausted by his earthly life" (CE, Part Two, III, 14, p. 176; cf. JD, I, pp. 7-8; II, pp. 16-17; III, pp. 20-21).

Indeed moral obligation implies not just the existence of a God that is Absolute Goodness, but also a personal God; for only a personal God could impose absolute obligations, obligations with weightiness and splendidness (as well as create human persons of great value). Von Hildebrand explains: "But as soon as one philosophically contemplates and analyzes the message embodied in moral values, in their unique gravity, in the categorical character of the obligation which can be grasped by us, we discover that only the existence of a personal God who is the Infinite Goodness can fulfill the message of moral values or can ultimately justify the validity of this obligation. ... moral values only possess the ultimate reality which justifies the gravity of the moral order, of its majestic obligation, if they are ultimately rooted and embodied in the Absolute Person of God" (CE, Part Two, V, 36, p. 456; MOR, Introduction, pp. 21-27; I, 1, pp. 59-68; I, 9, pp. 145-148; II, 32, pp. 360-364).

Yet while reason can establish the existence and objectivity of values (a natural ethics) and hint at the existence of God we require faith with its grace to perfect our natural knowledge and practice of ethics, and our natural knowledge and worship of God (CE, Preface, p. vii; Prolegomena, p. 19; Part Two, I, 18, p. 250; XX, pp. 182-187; WIP; VII, pp. 236-238; NTB, II, pp. 82-90; NL, XI, pp. 235-273).

Firstly with grace we can more fully rid ourselves of the stain of the Fall (namely, the pride revealed in the Scriptures and the concupiscence philosophically found in our hearts) (CE, Part Two, III, 29, p. 397; IV, 31, p. 412; IV, 32, n. 2 on p. 412, pp. 414-415, 429; IV, 34, pp. 431-440; IV, 35, pp. 441-450; V, 36, n. 2 on pp. 453-454; n. 3 on p. 454, p. 463; FMA, I, pp. 6-8; GI, II, pp. 15-22; III, pp. 84-95; III, p. 107; TIC, VII, pp. 149-151).

Secondly with grace we can transform the natural virtues displayed by Socrates and others (such as faithfulness, fortitude, justice, prudence (wisdom), reliability, reverence, temperance, and veracity) and give them an entirely new meaning in the light of eternity. This is seen above all in moral actions of such saints as Paul, Francis of Assisi, Catherine of Siena, Ignatius of Loyola, Rose of Lima, and John Bosco where the natural virtues take on a new depth, inner freedom, seriousness, realism, and splendor (CE, Part One, III, 14, p. 166; III, 14, pp. 177-179; Part Two, I, 19, pp. 265, 277, 276, 29; II, 27, n. 18 on pp. 353-354, 356-357; II, 28, pp. 391-392; V, 36, n. 2 on pp. 453-454, and p. 454; n. 9 on p. 458; V, 36, pp. 459-460, 463; GI, VIII, pp. 117-119; XI, pp. 178-179, 182-183, 187; TMC, X, pp. 147-154; XI, pp. 158-170; SH, II, 2, pp. 173-182; NL, XI, pp. 235-274). For example, in the saint, temperance becomes love keeping itself entire and incorrupt for God; fortitude becomes love bearing all for God; justice becomes love serving God only; and prudence becomes love making the right distinction between what helps it and what hinders it in order to approach God (CE, Part Two, V, 36, pp. 459-460).

Thirdly, by grace we can acquire the full spectrum of the virtues by taking on new supernatural ones. The saint, for instance, displays an ever-present readiness to be changed, elevation above oneself, freedom, genuine contrition, humility, meekness, mercifulness, patience, peacefulness, simplicity, a standing in the light of full truth, and an unlimited and irresistible charity.[11] He or she is zealous yet gentle and kind, courageous yet modest and meek (CE, Part Two, V, 36, pp. 458, 461; "MPV," pp. 65-66). For example, St. Teresa of Ávila displayed the humbleness and meekness to throw away all honors and to accept all humiliations (even to the point of claiming to be a great sinner), something which is a scandal and foolishness to a natural morality (CE, Part Two, V, 36, pp. 460-461; TIC, VII, pp. 157-163, 178-180, 184-188; XIV, pp. 397-398, 402-409, 412-421). Again St. Stephen's prayer for his murderers, and St. Francis of Assisi's embrace of a leper show that active charity and mercy are at the very core of the saint's being (rather than the natural virtues or mere abstention from evil) (CE, Part Two, V, 36, pp. 461-462; GI, XI, pp. 184-188; TIC, XV, pp. 423-427, 435-440). Thus while the pagan has a value-responding center, the Christian has a "reverent, humble, loving center" (CE, Part Two, IV, 31, pp. 412; IV, 32, p. 422; V, 6, p. 463). This is because in a supernatural condition the love of an Absolute Person who is Infinite Goodness pervades every act of the will (every virtue) and is the first and last word of the human being (CE, Part Two, V, 36, pp. 458, 462). So by grace we become new creatures in Christ (we are transformed in Christ) and are able to possess a more perfect *similitudo Dei* [likeness to God] as with the saints.

Fourthly and lastly, revelation tells us that God is Love (indeed charity, goodness, justice, mercy, and veracity itself) and not just the One Who Is (CE, Part One, III, 12, p. 151; III, 13, p. 160; III, 14, p. 179; Part Two, II, 27, p. 361). Let us now turn to a phenomenologist from Mexico.

The Catholic phenomenologist **Enrique Dussel (1934-)**[12] has become well-known for incorporating the phenomenological views of Emmanuel Levinas (1906-1995) into a Catholic philosophy of liberation. Dussel was born in La Paz, Mendoza, Argentina in 1934. Dussel lived through the rule of Juan Peron (1946-1955) who suppressed religious teachings in the schools, removed crucifixes from the government offices, legalized divorce, imprisoned priests, and in general was oppressive of the Argentinian Catholic Church. Dussel completed a bachelor's degree in philosophy at the Universidad Nacional de Cuyo (1957), a doctorate in philosophy at the University of Madrid (1959), a Master's in Theology at the Catholic Institute of Paris (1965), and a doctorate in history at the Sorbonne (1967). Beginning in the same year as the famous Medellin Bishops Conference of Latin American which gave impetus to liberation theology, Dussel taught at the Universidad Nacional de Cuyo in Argentina from 1968-1975, but was expelled during the Isabel Perón (1974-1976) presidency due to his Marxist sympathies (just before the Argentinian Dirty War that led to so much violence, wherein a bishop and several priests lost their lives, and for which the Catholic hierarchy apologized in 1996 for not speaking out enough against the governmental persecutions). Dussel then moved to Mexico City where he has taught at the Universidad Autónoma Metropolitana-Iztapalapa (1975-) and the Universidad Nacional Autónoma de México [UNAM] (1976-). He is married and has two children.

Dussel's main works are his *Philosophy of Liberation* [*Filosofía de la Liberación*] [PL] and his *Theology of Liberation and Ethics* [*Teología de la liberación y ética*] [TLE], both published in 1975.[13]

Dussel's philosophy of liberation, inspired by Levinas as mentioned above, is based on a phenomenological analysis of the encounter with another person, with "the other" [*el otro*] (PL, II, 1, pp. 16-17; TLE, V, pp. 120-141). The other represents the human being who has been excluded from society, oppressed and forgotten, humans who form the "underside of history." Classical examples include the poor, orphans, and widows, but "the other" can represent anyone debarred in any way whatsoever (PL, II, 1, pp. 3-5; EL, I, 3-4, pp. 16-22; I, 6, pp. 26-30; TELAL, v. IV, IX, 61, pp. 40-43). As Dussel notes: "The other encompasses the peripheral colonial world, the sacrificed Indian, the enslaved black, the oppressed women, the subjugated child, the alienated popular culture" (IA, Appendix II, p. 137).

The other has been maltreated and rejected on account of the operation of what Dussel calls the totality (*la totalidad*). The totality is the dominant socio-political or cultural system which envelops humans and excludes those who don't accord with it, the other. It does so by imposing its own (false) ideology and value-system on the world, one wherein the periphery does not exist (PL, II, 1, p. 6; II, 2, pp. 21-28; II, 4, pp. 43-44; TLE, I, pp. 4-17, 17-21; II, pp. 29-31; EL, II, 1, pp. 44-45; TELAL, v. I, III, 13-14, pp. 97-108; v. III, Appendix, 54-56, pp. 199-211; EC, Appendix, p. 238). To redress the injustices done to the other, we accordingly need to liberate the other from the oppressive system (establishment), i.e. from the totality. Such a liberation is a "movement on behalf of the one who stands beyond the horizon of the world" (PL, II, 6, p. 62).

We liberate the other in the first place simply by grasping the other (in his or her exteriority or transcendence) as independent of the system (of the totality). And this in turn happens through our seeing the face (*el cara; el rostro*) of the other and listening to the other's voice.[14] Merely encountering the face of the other allows for an acknowledgement that the other escapes from the system and a visualization of a new freedom and future for the other [the other is seen as *poder-ser* (able-to-be something else)] Additionally by having a face-to-face (*cara-a-cara*) encounter with the other (with for instance a hungry face) we come to recognize the other's ultimate incomprehensibility and inability to be mastered, and to affirm the priority of the other over us and our responsibility to help him or her (PL, II, 1, pp. 18-20; II, 4, pp. 40, 43-44; II, 6, pp. 60-62; Appendix, p. 192; TELAL, vol. I, I, 4-6, pp. 47-64, III, 16, pp. 118-128; vol. II, IV, 22, pp. 34-41; V, 27-28, pp. 74-89; V, 30-31, pp. 97-127; VI, 36, pp. 156-174).

After our face-to-face encounter with the other we can liberate the other in the second place by directly acting to free the other from the repression of the subjugators and their ideology and system (PL, II, 4, pp. 39-42, 47-48; II, 6, pp. 56-65; V, 9, pp. 170-180; TEL, II, pp. 33-36, 38-41; VI, pp. 165-167; TELAL, vol. II, IV, 20-22, pp. 13-41; IV, 24, pp. 52-59; VI, 36, 156-174; vol. III, VIII, 53, pp. 183-198; v. IV, IX, 66, pp. 109-123; EC, Appendix, pp. 240-242; HTL, I, pp. 4-5). Hence Dussel remarks: "When I do something for the Other as other, that is the praxis of liberation" (TLE, II, p. 38).

In this vein, Dussel recasts the traditional virtues (both the cardinal virtues of wisdom, justice, courage, and temperance, and the theological virtues of faith, hope, and love) in light of his philosophy of liberation. With regard to the cardinal virtues, to have wisdom (prudence) is to listen to the voice of the other (to know how to tactically orchestrate service toward it). To have justice is to give to all people what is due to them and to help create a more just order. To have courage (fortitude) is to commit oneself to liberating the other even to the point of death. And to have temperance is to have no fear of losing one's comfort or possessions in this struggle for liberation.

With regard to the theological virtues, to have faith is to accept (believe) the word of the other out of a concrete praxis of commitment. To have hope is to desire that those who have appealed to oneself and told one of their hunger (or suffering) are liberated. And finally to have charity is to love the other as other [el amor al Otro como otro], to enagage in a commitment, surrender, and self-donation to the other without regard for any reciprocity, recompense, gratitude, or gratification (PL, II, 4, pp. 46-47; TLE, II, pp. 46-48; VI, pp. 153-157, 159-162, 167-173; EC, I, 1, pp. 9-10; Appendix, pp. 238-239).

These virtues of liberation have the added blessing of allowing us to imitate and come to know and love God, the Infinite and Absolute Other [el Otro absolutamente absoluto], who died on the cross for our own liberation, our liberation from sin (HTL, I, pp. 2, 4-5; EC, I, 1, pp. 13-14; TELAL, vol. V, X, 69, pp. 49-59).[15]

2

NEO-THOMISM

1900-1970 at its Peak (Continuing on into 2000) in Australia, Austria, Belgium, Canada, England, France, Germany, Ireland, Italy the Netherlands, Poland, Portugal, Scotland, Spain, Switzerland & the United States

In 1903 a French atheistic couple attending the Sorbonne, a couple who had put their faith in science as the savior of society, became increasingly troubled by the inability of science to give a meaning to life (and to show how truth was possible and how there can be a distinction between good and evil). They accordingly forged a suicide pact in the Jardin des Plantes: unless they discovered a solution to life's dilemmas within a few years they would commit suicide together. Fortunately they lighted upon the thought of the Jewish philosopher Henri Bergson who was then teaching at the nearby Collège de France (and who was later desirous of entering the Catholic Church though his premature death prevented it) and the Catholic novelist Léon Bloy. Through these fortuitous meetings the couple found the meaning of life they had been so desperately seeking in Catholicism and married and converted to that faith. The wife went on to become a noted poet and the husband one of the greatest Thomists of the twentieth-century – his name was Jacques Maritain.

Thomism came to be revived in Catholic philosophical circles when in 1879 Pope Leo XIII wrote the encyclical *Aeterni Patris* which strongly encouraged all Catholic philosophers and theologians to turn to the thought of Thomas Aquinas as a model. Indeed in 1914 the Congregation of Sacred Studies published their famous Twenty-Four Thomistic Theses as the centerpiece of Catholic seminary education. The year 1914 also saw the beginning of the First World War which was to end the French Anti-Catholicism of the Third Republic (1870-1914).

For the philosophy of positivism, which limited reality to what could be uncovered by science (and so denied the existence of a divine supersensible being), had made great inroads into the French mentality and its educational and governmental institutions in the nineteenth-century. Consequently the stated goal of the positivist Minister of Education Jules Ferry (with the support of his liberal Protestant and Deistic administrators Ferdinand Buisson, Félix Pécaut, and Jules Steeg) was to reconstitute society "without God and king."

So it is that in 1879 the French senate passed legislation that excluded the clergy from the administration of hospitals, charities, military or hospital chaplainships, and the Council of the University (additionally Catholic Universities had to operate under the lesser title of Instituts Catholiques and could no longer confer degrees); in 1880 Bastille Day was made the national holiday (in honor of the French Revolution), work was allowed on Sundays, parliamentary sessions no longer began with prayers, and the Jesuits were outlawed; and in 1884 divorce was legalized. Finally in 1882 and 1886 education was secularized, made obligatory and free (l'obligation, la gratuité, la laicité) and given exclusively in the French language. As a result of these laws priests and nuns were forbidden to teach in the state schools (5000 of whom had to be expelled by force after they refused to comply), religion itself could no longer be taught in these state schools, textbooks had to remove the words God, Providence, and Creator, newly-opened schools were not allowed to put up crucifixes or other religious symbols, and the state religious fund was eliminated.

This Anti-Catholicism received new impetus on account of the prominent Catholic support (especially the Assumptionists and their vehicle La Croix) for the army during the unfortunate Dreyfus Affair (1894-1899) in which the Jewish army officer Alfred Dreyfus had been accused of selling military secrets to the Germans and imprisoned in 1894 (Dreyfus was cleared of charges in 1906 and in 1995 the French Army admitted framing him). Accordingly the Assumptionists were dissolved in 1900, and 1901 saw the passage of the René Waldeck-Rousseau law whereby religious congregations of men and women, in order to operate, had to be authorized by the state (which was not overly-inclined to grant authorization). Subsequently around 16,000 "unauthorized" religious congregations with their nearly 14,000 associated schools were dissolved (including such major orders as the Benedictines, Carmelites, Dominicans, Oratorians, and Salesians), leaving only around 3200 authorized congregations (including the Brothers of the Christian Schools, Lazarists, and Sulpicians). Nor did it surprise anyone when the properties of these unauthorized religious congregations were appropriated by the state and sold off (in 1903-1903). In the years that followed (1903-1904) soldiers were forbidden from frequenting Catholic social clubs, crucifixes were removed from the courts of law, and the French government severed diplomatic relations with the Vatican. Then in 1904 Émile Combes (a former seminarian) had the Falloux Law repealed and religious priests lost even the option of teaching at private schools and so the remaining 3000 schools operated by authorized congregations were closed (it should be noted that though initially most of the members of unauthorized religious congregations fled France many of them returned and their existence, including that of the Jesuits, was tacitly permitted in France). Combes also undertook an inventory of Church property forecasting his future malicious intentions, and sent teachers into the French villages to try and secularize the populace there.

Secularization reached its peak in 1905 when a law formally separated Church and State in France. Henceforth the Concordat of 1801 was revoked and Catholicism was no longer recognized as the religion of the majority of the French people; the state no longer paid the salaries of Catholic priests (the state pay had originally been invoked to compensate the Church for the property taken from it during the French Revolution); church buildings were overseen by Catholic lay associations (Associations Culturelles) instead of the clergy; bishop houses, presbyteries, and seminaries were charged rent after a limited rent-free period (two to five years) and then in 1908 seized altogether; the Catholic theological faculties of Aix, Bordeaux, Lyons, Paris, and Rouen were shuttered; crucifixes were now removed from all of the state schools; religious symbols were not allowed in any public spaces (including cemeteries); the mass to start the term at naval academy was eliminated; and a battleship was named the Ernest Renan in honor of the French deist.

This was the world into which the French Thomist **Étienne Gilson (1884-1978)** was born in 1884 in Paris. After attending the seminary of Notre-Dame-des-Champs from 1895-1902 where he studied philosophy under the priest Lucien Paulet (1876-1915), a priest who gave up his life in the first world war, Gilson decided against the priesthood for himself and studied philosophy at the Sorbonne from 1905-1907 [under the Catholic Victor Delbos (1862-1916), and also Lucien Levy-Bruhl (1857-1939), Émile Durkheim (1858-1917), and Léon Brunschvicg (1869-1944)] to prepare for a teaching career (he also sat in on the lectures of Henri Bergson at the nearby Collège de France). Gilson received his agrégation in 1907, married Thérèse Ravisé in 1908, and taught at lycées in Bourge-en-Bresse (1907-1908), Rochefort-sur-Mer (1908-1910), Tour (1910-1911), Saint-Quentin (1911-1912), and Angers (1912-1913). At the first of these institutions, he was accused of teaching religious propaganda in his medieval philosophy class but he quelled these worries after he offered to teach modern philosophy instead. Gilson went on to attain his doctorate in philosophy from the Sorbonne in 1913 with a work on Descartes and the Scholastic tradition, research which introduced him to the thought of his beloved Aquinas. When the First World War broke out Gilson served as an officer in the army from 1914 to 1916 when he was captured at Verdun and became a prisoner of war until cessation of hostilities in 1918 (he received the Croix de Guerre in 1918 for his war-time efforts). With the termination of the Great War and his incarceration, Gilson returned to academia as a professor of philosophy at the University of Strasbourg from 1919 to 1921. He then made a triumphant return to the Sorbonne where he held the chair of medieval philosophy from 1921-1932 and demonstrated the continuing importance of medieval thought. Gilson eventually achieved great prominence in France and secured a position at the Collège de France from 1932-1951. In 1951, however, with his wife being deceased for two years, Gilson decided to journey overseas and assumed the directorship of the Institute of Medieval Studies at the University of Toronto until 1968 (an Institute which he had helped to found in 1929).[16] Besides his academic work, Gilson was a French delegate to the San Francisco Conference which helped found the United Nations in 1945. He died in 1978.[17]

Gilson's gave the Gifford Lectures in 1931-1932 at the University of Aberdeen, was elected a member of the French Academy in 1947 (and was also made a Conseil de la Republique in 1946 and received the German Order of Merit), gave the Aquinas Lecture at Marquette University in 1947 and 1951, and received the Aquinas Medal from the American Catholic Philosophical Association in 1952. Gilson also received honorary doctorates from the Universities of Aberdeen,

Freiburg, Harvard, Milan, Montreal, Oxford, Pennsylvania, and the Sapienza. His lasting influence is also apparent in the Etienne Gilson Series of Books (1979-) and Lectures (1980-) at the Pontifical Institute of Medieval Studies at the University of Toronto and a Chaire Etienne Gilson at the Catholic Institute of Paris (1995-).

The key works of Gilson are his *The Spirit of Medieval Philosophy* [*L'esprit de la philosophie médiévale*] [SMP], 2 vols. (1932; 1944) [reproducing the Gifford Lectures from 1931-1932]; *Methodical Realism* [*Le réalisme methódique*] [MR] (1936); and *God and Philosophy* [GP] (1941) [Mahlon Powell Lectures at the University of Indiana in 1939-1940].[18]

Gilson, along with Maritain, was a great proponent of Neo-Thomism in the Twentieth Century (see *Fides et Ratio*, 1998, n. 74). Both of these thinkers focused on the existential aspects of Thomist metaphysics, and so their worldview is often called existential Thomism. Subsequently, both of them also came to teach in North America and influenced many of the teachers of Thomism in the United States at the Catholic University of America, Notre Dame University, Fordham University, Marquette University, and St. Louis University.

One particular area of Gilson's influence was in epistemology. Gilson is quite critical of the idealistic approach to knowledge advocated by Descartes, Kant, Berkeley, Wolff, and his teacher Léon Brunschvicg (1869-1944), as well as by those "Cartesio-Thomists" coming under their influence, and the later Transcendental Thomists such as the Oratorian Gaston Rabeau (1877-1945) and Joseph Maréchal, S.J. (1878-1944).[19]

These idealistically-inclined thinkers argue that philosophical reflection ought to proceed from thought to things, hence the first task of a "critical idealism" (or a "critical realism") is to prove that knowledge of the external world is possible (MR, I, pp. 17-22, 29; II, pp. 38-42, 79; IV, pp. 110, 115, 123; TR, Preface, p. 25; I, pp. 44-51; I, n. 28 on p. 47, p. 52, n. 32 on p. 52; II, pp. 55-61; n. 5 on p. 61; V, pp. 158, 162; VI, pp. 152-154; n. 2 on pp. 152-153; n. 5-8 on pp. 165-167; VII, pp. 190, 192; VIII, pp. 195, 209-214). For instance the Cartesio-Thomist Mercier, in his mediate criteriological realism, begins by reflecting on the inner impression of passivity in regard to our sensation, and then by a principle of causality goes on to posit the external reality of the objects of sensation (MR, II, pp. 39-43, 45-47, 55; TR, I, n. 2 on pp. 29-30). And another Cartesio-Thomist Noël develops an epistemology that shows the logic of the transition from an object as a "reality apprehended" to an object as an "apprehended reality" (MR, II, pp. 68-69, 75; TR, I, n. 30-31 on pp. 49-50; II, pp. 60-61).

In opposition, Gilson defends a "methodical realism" (or a "philosophical realism") in which one immediately grasps both the reality and the nature of an object: "what St. Thomas says and psychological experience confirms is that what is first given us is the existence of things" (MR, II, p. 76; cf. MR, I, pp. 24, 30; II, pp. 37, 77-79; V, pp. 129, 132; TR, I, p. 52; VI, p. 169; ST, IV, pp. 86-88; SMP, XII, pp. 229-247; ECP, X, pp. 238-240). For according to Gilson sensation carries with itself an irresistible sentience that what it presents is something really existing outside of the mind. In other words sensible objects are given to us in thought as not dependent upon thought. So the testimony of sensible experience yields an evident certitude of the reality of the external world (MR, II, p. 50-51; II, n. 11 on p. 59; II, pp. 63-64; II, n. 17 on p. 65; II, pp. 77-79; IV, p. 126; V, p. 133; TR, II, p. 62). Realism then starts "with knowledge, that is, with an act of the intellect which consists essentially in grasping an object. ... [with] the lived and experienced unity of an intellect with an apprehended reality" (MR, V, pp. 128-129; cf. MR, II, p. 46).

This being the case, there is no need to make the existence of the world a postulate that one must prove or demonstrate (or translate into a certitude of the intellect) as the Cartesian idealists do (MR, I, pp. 31-32; II, pp. 66-67; TR, Preface, n. 1 on p. 23; I, pp. 27, 30-31, 40; I, n. 32 on p. 51; II, pp. 74-75, 83; VII, pp. 180-181, 183-185; VIII, pp. 212-214; PCB, I-III, pp. 15-122). For "while the idealist thinks, the realist knows" (MR, V, p. 128). Indeed it is only after the subject first grasps an existence which is not its own, that it can secondarily grasp that it knows this and has self-awareness (MR, II, pp. 73-76; IV, p. 121; V, p. 134; TR, V, p. 140; VIII, p. 205): "The awakening of intelligence coincides with the apprehension of things" (MR, V, p. 132). So rather than the subject finding its object through an analysis of knowledge, it discovers its knowledge and itself in the analysis of the object (MR, II, p. 77). In Gilson's trenchant words then "The first step on the realist path is to recognize that one has always been a realist; the second is to recognize that, however, hard one tries to think differently, one will never manage to; the third is to realize that those who claim to think differently, think as realists as soon as they forget to act the part" (MR, V, p. 127).

Moreover, if one tries to critically proceed from thought to the world one will find it impossible to avoid being imprisoned in one's own mind, in a subjectivism (MR, I, pp. 18-23, 27-30, 33, 36; II, pp. 71, 73; II, n. 27 on p. 77; IV, pp. 115, 118; V, pp. 127-128; TR, II, pp. 81-84; V, p. 142). Thus critical realism ends up as self-contradictory as a square-circle: "You must either begin as a realist with being, in which case you will have a knowledge of being, or begin as a critical idealist with knowledge, in which case you will never come in contact with being" (TR, VI, p. 149; cf. MR, I, p. 28; TR, II, p. 84).

A realist must therefore replace the Cartesian and Idealistic mottos *cogito, ergo sum* [I think, therefore I am], *a nosse ad esse valet consequentia* [it is valid to infer being from knowing], and *percipi* [being perceived] with *sum, ergo cogito* [I am, therefore I think], *ab esse ad nosse valet consequentia* [it is valid to infer knowing from being], and *esse* [being] (MR, I, pp. 18-23, 27-30, 33, 36; II, pp. 71, 73; II, n. 27 on p. 77; IV, pp. 115, 118; V, pp. 127-128; TR, II, pp. 81-84; V, p. 142).

Following Aquinas, Gilson also rejects fideism along with its views that reason cannot show that God exists and that Greek philosophy tends to corrupt the faith, witnessed by the fact that God chose twelve simple men not twelve professors of philosophy to help proselytize the world (and that children can be saved without a need to grasp rationally demonstrable conclusions) (SMP, II, pp. 30-31; CRPH, I, pp. 2-5; GR, X, pp. 180-181).

Certainly it is true, says Gilson, that salvation comes through faith and not through metaphysics, and so children (and other humans) can be saved without being philosophers (ICP, Preface, pp. 9, 11-12). Yet natural reason represents an image of the divine in us and is not to be rejected but embraced. Indeed utilization of the intellect in science and philosophy, and in constructing the geometrical architecture of churches, are all ways of serving God. Furthermore, we find that dialectic and philosophy (such as the development of proofs of God and the soul's immortality) were widely practiced by the early Christian Apologists, grew continuously in the Middle Ages, and that their general use was never censored by the Church (if anything the reverse is true with about twenty popes being philosophers, including Peter of Spain who possibly wrote the key medieval textbook of logic, and about two-hundred bishops). Thus by the Middle Ages philosophy was a standard preparation for budding theologians (CRPH, I, pp. 4-6; II, pp. 35-37; V, pp. 105, 115; GR, X, pp. 174-176).

The fideists are also correct in asserting that the God of faith infinitely transcends the God of the philosophers. This is not to say though that we need accept with Pascal and the fideists that the God of the philosophers is different from the God of Abraham, Isaac, and Jacob. For the God whose existence we rationally know is the very same God of whom we believe by faith what we cannot rationally know. Or to put it conversely, even if Prime Mover is not Yahweh, Yahweh is the Prime Mover. So the philosopher who knows God in part can also prays to God in His entirety (ICP, Preface, pp. 9, 11-12; CRPH, II, pp. 71-72; III, p. 77; ICP, Preface, pp. 9-12; I, p. 9; ECP, II, pp. 25-28; III, pp. 52-54).

Gilson does not hesitate then to grant the viability of natural theology (MR, II, p. 72; II, n. 27 on p. 77; TR, V, pp. 146-147; ECP, III, pp. 48-49, 51, 57). Gilson in particular grants credence to Aquinas's five ways for God, of which he prefers the third and fifth ways. The first way begins with the observed motion of things. Now motion occurs when being in potency is affected by being in act (for nothing can be brought from potency to act except by something in act). And since there cannot be an infinite series of things which are both mover and moved (in which case there would be lacking being in act), there must be a prime mover, God (ECP, III, pp. 58-68). The second way is based on the observation of efficient causes or one thing causing another in the world. Now here we have to reject the view that causality is merely a relation of attending, that for A to be a cause of B means that B is always accompanied by A (i.e. the Humean view of causation). For causality involves not just an attendance of two events but an ontological primacy of one causing the other. Indeed B attends A for the very reason that A is the cause of B. This being so, there must be a first efficient cause, as there cannot be an infinite series of things that are caused (ECP, III, pp. 68-72, 84).

Gilson's favored third way commences with the fact that it is possible for things to be or not to be (i.e. things are contingent and might not have existed). Now a universe in which all things were merely possible would never occur, for at one time nothing would have occurred and from this nothing, nothing could have come about. Thus there must be a necessary being, God, a being whose very act is to be, to account for what things have of being. Or put more technically, as all that exists on earth has an essence distinct from its existence (and so its existence is limited by its essence), it receives its participated existence from a being in which essence and existence are identical (the infinite act of existence of God) (ECP, III, p. 74; IV, p. 93; GP, II, pp. 52-53; SMP, IV, pp. 72-80; ICP, II, pp. 18-23; IX, pp. 101-104; BSP, V, pp. 178-181; "OBHM," pp. 236-249). As Gilson says "The only possible explanation for the presence of such finite and contingent beings is that they have been freely given existence by 'Him who is,' and not as parcels of his own existence, which, because it is absolute and total, is also unique, but as finite and partial imitations of what He himself eternally is in his own right" (GP, II, p. 53).

Gilson's other favorite argument for God is the fifth way—which he interprets as an argument to the effect that a great number of events of the world exhibit a regularity and so cannot be the result of chance. For the vast order in the universe, even if there is disorder, requires a cause, and the cause of this order is found above the universe in God, in a mind that orders the world (ECP, III, pp. 78-80; SMP, IV, pp. 78-80).

We know then by reason that there exists a divine being who is the Prime Mover, Prime Cause, and Ultimate End. Yet Gilson is at times downright agnostic when it comes to philosophy being able to disclose the full nature of God. He, in fact, has no qualms saying that we do not really know God's essence at all, or that we only really know what God is not (ECP, III, pp. 86-87; IV, p. 108; X, pp. 233-235; ST, III, pp. 77-83). For while the proofs give us a knowledge of God's existence, they fail to give us any concept of God's essence: they tell us that God is [*an est* (whether He is)] but not what He is [*quid est*] (GP, II, pp. 63-67; see Aquinas, *Summa Theologiae*, I, q. 3 a. 3 and I q. 3 a. 4 ad 2).

It is true that we can predicate such creaturely perfections of God as being (the most proper name of God), truth, goodness, justice, and Father (i.e. the transcendentals); for God is the cause of things and their perfections, and the cause of these perfections rightly bears their names (ICP, IV, p. 35; ECP, VI, pp. 137-140, 159-160; cf. Aquinas, *Summa Contra Gentiles*, I, 38, 2; *Summa Theologiae* I, q. 5 a. 2; ad 1). Yet the world is but a feeble analogue of God and every concept gleaned from creation breaks down in some way when applied to God who in His overflowingness and perfection eludes our grasp (SMP, III, pp. 54-56). So in the end all we can really say is that God is the cause of these worldly perfections and we are left ignorant of how exactly to represent the divine perfections in themselves. So, for instance, though we can say God is our Father, we remain ignorant of just how

God is a Father. Indeed there are a multitude of names which could with equal justification be applied to God (ICP, III, p. 38; IV, p. 40; n. 5 on pp. 40-41; ECP, III, pp. 86-87; IV, pp. 108-110; VI, p. 144; n. 15 on p. 309; see Aquinas, *Disputed Questions in Power*, VII, 2, ad 1; *On Truth*, II, 11; *Summa Contra Gentiles*, I, 12, 7; *De Potentia* q. 1 a. 2 ad 1 and q. 7 a. 1 ad 1; *Summa Theologiae* I q. 3 a. 4 ad 2; I. q. 12 a. 12 ad 1; I q. 13 a. 10 ad 5).[20] Natural theology for Gilson then "offers for our love an unknown God whose infinite and inexpressible grandeur, defying knowledge, can only be embraced by love" (ICP, IV, p. 39).

Gilson is perhaps most famous and controversial on account of his notion of "Christian philosophy." Gilson asserts, following the tradition of Justin Martyr, Lactantius, Augustine, Anselm, Albert the Great, Aquinas, and the encyclical *Aeterni Patris* of 1879 (or so he claims),[21] that not only does revelation correct the work of philosophers, not only does it supply mysteries of the faith ever beyond the reach of reason (i.e. the notions of the Trinity and the Incarnation), but that it also supplies philosophy itself with new content. That is to say, "Christian philosophy" defines the view that revelation can and has supplied truths to philosophy which, while capable of being justified in the light of reason alone, hitherto philosophy had not yet discovered on its own [and indeed which it was incapable of discovering on its own, as we will see] (GP, II, pp. 38, 43-44; SMP, I, pp. 11-12; II, pp. 31-32; XVII, p. 362; XX, p. 409; GR, XI, p. 181; ECP, Foreword, p. 5; II, p. 37; PT, V, pp. 97-101; CRPH, II, pp. 36-39; III, pp. 55-57, 75-77). To quote Gilson here:

A philosophy open to the supernatural would certainly be compatible with Christianity, but it would not necessarily be a Christian philosophy [contra Blondel]. If it is to deserve that name the supernatural must descend as a constitutive element not, of course, into its texture which would be a contradiction, but into the work of its constitution. Thus I call Christian, every philosophy which, although keeping the two orders formally distinct, nevertheless considers the Christian revelation as an indispensable auxiliary of reason. ... It is but one of the species of the genus philosophy and includes in its extension all those philosophical systems which were in fact what they were only because a Christian religion existed and because they were ready to submit to its influence (SMP, II, p. 37).

A true philosophy, taken absolutely in itself, owes all its truth to its rationality and to nothing other than its rationality; ... But the constitution
of this true philosophy could not in fact be achieved without the aid of
revelation, acting as an indispensable moral support to reason ... in spite
of the purely rational texture of their [Christian] systems, we can still
today discern the mark of the influence of their faith on the conduct of
their thought (SMP, II, pp. 40-41).

In light of the above quotes Gilson makes it clear that Christian
philosophy is the work of natural reason as such, i.e. it is constructed
in the light of the intellect and its principles rather than in the light
of faith. Hence it is truly a philosophy. Yet he argues that human nature is a fallen one and so there are truths of the philosophical domain which historically reason only discovered through the assistance
of revelation. Indeed Gilson seems to suggest that reason could not
have discovered certain philosophical claims unless aided by divine
revelation—as with his phrase quoted above "revelation, acting as an
indispensable moral support to reason." Or with his suggestion: "... it is
incorrect to call these notions essentially religious, they are essentially
rational and belong therefore of full right to philosophy. True, the
Greeks never clearly conceived them, but they might well have done
so on the basis of their own principles, or at least by purely rationally
perfecting their own principles. ... I would by no means deny that as a
matter of right the Greeks could well have conceived [these things]; I
simply state it as a fact that they lacked the strength to do so" (SMP,
XVII, pp. 361-362). Thus in Gilson's conception of Christian philosophy, revelation does not substitute itself for natural reason. Rather
revelation allows reason to better perform its natural operations by
showing reason uses of itself that it could not have anticipated (ICP, I,
pp. 21-26; III, pp. 80-81; IV, p. 101; V, pp. 110-113; ECP, II, pp. 39-
40; III, p. 55; SMP, I, p. 12; XX, p. 409; PT, VI, pp. 101-105; IX, pp.
191-198; X, p. 214; XI, pp. 228-229). And so whether it be a natural
morality, a natural theology, or a natural metaphysics, "... the content
of Christian philosophy is that body of rational truths, discovered,
explored or simply safeguarded, thanks to the help that reason receives
from revelation" (SMP, II, p. 35).

Consequently—contra René Descartes and Sorbonne rationalists
such as Étienne Vacherot (1809-1897) [who lost his position in 1851
due to his critique of Christianity], Émile Bréhier (1876-1952), and
Léon Brunschvicg (1869-1944)[22]—philosophy is no less a philosophy

when it is Christian and philosophizes in the light of revelation. Indeed Gilson goes so far as to assert that to be a real philosopher one must first be a theologian. For theology helps the intellect see truths towards which it ought to steer its course and which it should demonstrate (CRPH, III, p. 79; IV, p. 87; SMP, II, p. 36; n. 13 on p. 429; XX, pp. 405-406). This being the case, one should not strive for a "separate philosophy," i.e. for a philosophy separated from theology in the sphere of its exercise, and philosophize as if one were not a Christian (CRPH, III, pp. 68-70; IV, pp. 84-85, 89, 92-95; SMP, I, p. 12; II, p. 34; ECP, II, pp. 33-35, 37-38; GR, IX, pp. 165-166; XX, pp. 333-336; PT, VI, pp. 97-101). So, just as Christianity has had a great influence in the arts, it must also descend into the sciences and philosophy (CRPH, V, pp. 114, 118-120, 123; ICP, II, p. 21; III, pp. 27-28; V, pp. 45-50; VI, p. 66).

Gilson expent a great deal of historical research spelling out exactly where revelation provided new content to philosophy, content philosophy previously was not aware of but which once discovered it could set out to rationally justify. First and perhaps most importantly, in the Scriptures, God reveals Himself as 'I am who am' (Ex 3:13-15), i.e. as a somebody, a He, and not an It (GP, II, pp. 39-41, 51-52; ECP, V, pp. 124-133; ICP, I, pp. 5-9, 13; III, pp. 24-32; ST, III, pp. 73-77; BSP, I, pp. 31-31; GR, XV, pp. 230-235; PCB, VII-VIII, pp. 169-253). And this statement has become epoch making in the history of philosophy. First, with this claim, God reveals Himself to be not just a prime mover but a personal being. As Gilson argues:

> The Greeks had never gone further than the natural theology of Plato and of Aristotle, not on account of intellectual weakness on their part, but, on the contrary, because both Plato and Aristotle had pushed their investigations almost as far as human reason alone can take us. By posting, as the supreme cause of all that which is, somebody who is, and of whom the very best that can be said is that 'He is,' Christian revelation was establishing existence as the deepest layer of reality as well as the supreme attribute of that divinity (GP, II, pp. 43-44; cf. GP, II, pp. 41-42).

Second, God here reveals Himself to be a pure act of existing: 'I am' (GP, II, pp. 51-52). And this served as the clue that allowed Christians to grasp the metaphysical import of their religious belief (GP, II, pp. 39, 41, 43).[23] For God is not just a being [ens], but, beyond this, being itself [esse]. Or, more metaphysically speaking, God is a pure act of being (the fullness of existence), without any limiting essence (a being in which essence and existence are identical), and so God is infinite, self-sufficient, and necessary [*ipsum esse per se subsistens*; self-subsisting being] (ICP, III, pp. 28-30; IV, pp. 34-35; SMP, III, pp. 51-55; ECP, IV, pp. 113-124). Gilson states: "the supreme principle is a God whose true name is 'He who is.' A pure Act of existing, taken as such and without any limitation, necessarily is all that which it is possible to be" (GP, II, p. 51; cf. GP, II, pp. 41-42, 63-67; SMP, III, p. 51; IV, p. 71; ECP, IV, pp. 113-119; BSP, V, pp. 180-185).

Third, this Bible passage, and others like it, inspired Christians to come up with the metaphysical distinction between essence and existence in finite beings. For with the Greeks everything immaterial was pure act, but for Christians there existed immaterial angels who were not pure act but who possessed a potency in terms of their own existence. For Christians then all save God might not have existed, i.e. there is a contingency of existence in all finite beings. And on this basis Christians were able to recognize that all finite beings have an existence separate from their essence and depend upon a creative (and conservative) act of a self-subsistent being (SMP, IV, pp. 68-71; XX, p. 410; GR, VIII, pp. 146-147; ECP, V, pp. 131-132).[24] Thus, says Gilson, there is a profound difference between the Christian and pagan mental universes:

> On the one side we have a god defined by a perfection in the order of quality; Plato's Good; or by a perfection in one of the orders of being: Aristotle's Thought; on the other side stands the Christian God Who is first in the order of being. ... On the Greek side stands a god who is doubtless the cause of all being, including its intelligibility, efficiency and finality—all, save existence itself; on the Christian side a God Who causes the very existence of being. On the Greek side we have a universe eternally informed or eternally moved; on the Christian side a universe which begins to be by a creation. On the Greek side stands a universe contingent in the order of intelligibility or in the order of becoming; on the Christian side a universe contingent in the order of existence. On the Greek side, there is the immanent finality of an order interior to beings; on the Christian side the transcendent finality of a Providence who creates the very being of order along with that of the things ordered (SMP, IV, p. 81).

Other truths of Christian philosophy, truths that were only known historically because philosophers were inspired by revelation [besides the previous claims that there exists a unique God (monotheism) who is personal, a God of pure being who freely creates the world, that all finite beings are contingent, and that there exist non-material individual substances or angels (and so individuation is not solely due to matter)] include the philosophical claims that: there is a divine creation from nothing (rather than the Greek idea of God creating through rearranging eternal matter), humans have free will or the power to freely choose to act or not, humans exist as a substantial composite of soul and body, God is a God of love not just of justice, a transcendent God is our true end, God can and does call humans to eternal blessedness (a beatific vision of Himself), God implants a moral law in our consciences that yields moral obligations, morality does not just deal with virtues or external acts but also with interior intentions and ultimate ends, sin can occur whereby we offend God (as opposed to merely harming ourselves) since we act in disaccord with the divine will, sin and vice occur not just out of ignorance but can be a deliberate refusal of the divine order, evil is due to a divine desire to create corruptible and free beings (versus due to matter or chance), and only divine grace can heal our corrupt nature (ST, II, p. 53; SMP, VI, pp. 116-121; VIII, pp. 148-156; XI, pp. 199-206; XV, pp. 304-314; XVI, pp. 324-342; XVII, pp. 345-347, 353-358, 361-363). According to Gilson then there are the numerous ways in which philosophy only progressed after it had come into contact with Christian Revelation.

Let us now turn our attention to the previously mentioned Thomist who found Catholicism and did not end his life (literally) as a positivist, Jacques Maritain (1882-1973), whose goal was to apply Thomism to contemporary philosophical, scientific, and societal issues.

Maritain was born in 1882 in Paris. He was raised in a liberal Protestant environment (his grandfather Jules Favre was a senator in the anti-clerical Third Republic government though he became a liberal Protestant toward the end of his life) and studied at the Lycée Henri IV and then philosophy and science at the Sorbonne from 1900-1906 (with the Catholic Victor Delbos as well as with Émile Durkheim, Lucien Lévy-Bruhl, and Félix Le Dantec). The Sorbonne, besides introducing Maritain to the sciences and influencing him to become a positivist and atheist, also introduced him to the Russian Jew and atheist, Raïssa Oumansov, who was to become his future wife. Yet marriage was not in their initial plans, since, as we noted above, they both began to question the extent to which a positivist life, one that held that all the answers to life are to be found in science, was worth living, and they together forged the suicide pact that unless they found more to life they would commit suicide together within a short time. Fortunately, taking the advice of their friend Charles Péguy (the poet and future Catholic convert himself), they took a course with Henri Bergson at the Collège de France and came under his influence. Bergson's critique of the narrow positivistic views at the Sorbonne appealed to them and gave them a philosophy by which they could live and so they married in 1904.

Besides Bergson, the Maritain's fell under the influence of the Catholic novelist Léon Bloy and so in 1906 converted to Catholicism (Maritain was also initially involved with the conservative Action Française political movement but after Rome condemned it in 1926 he began to favor a more liberal political position). That same year, Jacques Maritain went to the University of Heidelberg in Germany where he studied biology for two years with the vitalist Hans Driesch and philosophy with Wilhelm Windelband. Returning to France, Jacques Maritain met another individual who would change the direction of his life, his spiritual director, Fr. Humbert Clérissac, O.P. For it was Clérissac who suggested Maritain read the writings of Aquinas in 1910, and shortly thereafter Maritain became a dedicated Thomist (he hence formed his famous Thomistic circle in 1919). Maritain unfortunately had to give up the pursuit of an academic career in the state universities of France due to their blatant anti-Catholicism (he worked on a *Lexique Orthographique* and a *Dictionnaire de la vie practique* for the Hatchette publishing company for a while), but he did find a position in 1912 at the Catholic Collège Stanislas in Paris, and in 1914 moved to the Catholic Institute of Paris where he taught until 1940 (with a stint at the minor seminary of Versailles in 1916-1917). The Maritain's were also prominent supporters of the arts (Raïssa herself was a poet as noted above) and they held many meetings in Versailles and Meudon with famous French figures (such as the painters Marc Chagall, André Girard, Georges Rouault, Christine van der Meer, and Gino Severini; and the authors Georges Bernanos, Léon Bloy, Jean Cocteau, Henri Ghéon, Julien Green, Charles Péguy, Ernest Psichari, and Pierre van der Meer; in addition Maritain was friends with the politicians Saul Alinsky, Avshalom Feinberg, and the atheist Sydney Hook; and the composer Arthur Lourié wrote a song for Maritain, "De Ordinatione Angelorum").

In 1940, in the heart of World War II, Maritain and his wife left France and came to live in Canada and the United States [he had written the manifesto "Pour le bien commune" (For the Common Good)] in 1934 with Maurice de Gandillace—a manifesto also signed by Étienne Gilson, Gabriel Marcel, Étienne Borne, Jean Lacroix, Emmanuel Mounier, Yves Simon and around fifty others—and had spoken out against Anti-Semitism in 1937-1938 and so was not safe living under the new Vichy Regime]. Maritain thus taught consecutively at the Institute of Medieval Studies in Toronto, Columbia University (where he also helped to found the École Libre de Hautes Études with Jean Wahl and Gustave Cohen and served as its president until 1944), the University of Notre Dame, and the University of Chicago. At the end of World War II, Maritain returned to France to become the French Ambassador to the Vatican (1945-1948), president of the French delegation to UNESCO in 1947, and co-founder [with Jacques Madaule] of the Grand Prix catholique de littérature (1945-). The year 1948, however, saw his return to North America and in 1948 he settled in as a professor at Princeton University where he resided until 1960 at the Institute for Advanced Studies (along with Albert Einstein) and where he had to weather the attacks of the chaplain Hugh Halton, O.P., who from 1955-1957 considered Maritain too liberal and unorthodox and who denied him permission to address the Aquinas Foundation at Princeton. Upon the death of Maritain's wife in 1960 he went back to France, declined a position at the Collège de France, and instead lived with the religious community Little Brothers of Jesus in Toulouse (an order of which he himself became a member in 1970).[25] Maritain died in 1973 in Toulouse, France and is buried in a cemetery in Kolbsheim with his wife.[26]

Maritain achieved great recognition during his life and became a member of the Academia Brasileira de Lettres in 1936, was granted the Leo XIII Award from the Sheil School of Social Studies in Chicago in 1948, received the very first Aquinas Medal from the American Catholic Association in 1951 (and an honorary degree from Manhattan College that same year and one from Boston College in 1958), received the Campion Award from the Catholic Book Club in 1955, as well as the Grand Prize for Literature from the French Academy in 1961 and the Edith Stein Guild Award that same year. He has also inspired many groups such as the Jacques Maritain Center at Notre Dame (1957-); the Cercle d'Études Jacques et Raïssa Maritain in Kolbsheim (1962-); the Fondation Jacques et Raïssa Maritain at the Séminaire de Sainte-Thérèse, Quebec (1964); the Institut International Jacques Maritain (1974-) in Rome, Trieste, and Treviso with its journal *Notes et documents* [*Notas y documentos*] (1975-); the American Maritain Association (1976-); the *Cahiers Jacques Maritain* (1980-); the journal *Études maritainiennes* [*Maritain Studies*] (1984-); and the *Bulletin Jacques et Raissa Maritain* (1993-1996).

Among his voluminous philosophical writings, the following can be singled out as Maritain's key works: *Distinguishing in Order to Unite, or The Degrees of Knowledge* [*Distinguer pour unir, ou les degrees du savoir*] [DK] (1932) and *Approaches to God* [*Approches de Dieu*] [AG] (1953).[27]

Maritain held that Thomism was a perennial philosophy and so valid at all times and places; otherwise the work of a philosopher would be mistaken for that of a tailor wherein fashions change frequently (DK, I, pp. 1, 18; II, p. 54). So in a fine Maritainian turn of phrase, "Truth cannot be subjected to a chronological test" (PM, I, p. 11; cf. ECHP, IV, p. 45). Still Maritain wanted a "living Thomism" and not an "archaeological Thomism"—a Thomism that could be applied to and take into account contemporary thought. In fact, according to Maritain, Thomism is an essentially progressive and assimilative doctrine, and so while it remains the same in terms of its basic truths, it can grow in its understanding of them (DK, Preface, pp. xii-xiv; Foreword, p. xviii; EE, Introduction, p. 11-12; PM, I, pp. 9-10, 19-21). Maritain explains:

> Thomism is not a museum piece. ... It is relevant to every epoch. It answers modern problems, both theoretical and practical. .. We must defend the traditional wisdom and the continuity of the *Philosophia Perennis* [Perennial Philosophy] against the prejudices of modern individualism, insofar as it values, seeks, and delights in novelty for its own sake, and is interested in a system of thought only insofar as it is a creation, the creation of a novel conception of the world. But equally we must show that this wisdom is eternally young and always inventive, and involves a fundamental need, inherent in its very being, to grow and renew itself (PM, pp. 9-10).[28]

Martain's particular excellence lies in his differentiation and description of the various kinds (degrees) of knowledge, and so the avoidance of a monolithic account of knowing (DK, Preface, p. ix). Firstly, he recognizes that there are both natural (i.e. science and philosophy) and supernatural forms of knowledge (i.e. faith or mysticism). Secondly, within the domain of natural knowledge he admits both discursive and intuitive varieties. Lastly, for Maritain there are three types of discursive knowledge: perinoetic, dianoetic, and ananoetic. Let us examine each of these kinds of knowing in turn.

Discursive knowledge is a form of natural knowledge that arises from a step-by-step reasoning process. Maritain's discussion of discursive knowledge is centered around a notion of three degrees of abstraction (which he ultimately borrows from the Renaissance Thomist Cajetan).

The first degree of abstraction occurs when reason abstracts universal forms from the observed matter of concrete singulars. In so doing all of the accidental properties of material beings are abstracted away (such as color) and what one is left with is changing being—or what Maritain calls corporeal, sensible and mobile being [ens mobile]—and its accompanying properties (DK, II, pp. 37-38; IV, p. 146; V, pp. 222-223; UA, XIV, pp. 337-349; PM, IV, pp. 79-85). This is the kind of reasoning that is utilized in the natural sciences and the philosophy of nature and allows for a "scientific" knowledge of the necessary, abstract, and ideal constancies found in the contingent, concrete, flowing world of things (DK, II, pp. 26, 29-30; n. 7 on p. 27; n. 11 on p. 30).

Now in the natural sciences—or what Maritain calls the empiriological sciences—the first degree of abstraction allows us to uncover the scientific necessities found in changing beings: we can grasp the abstract natures and necessary relations or laws at play in the universe of individuals and events. Still while in the empiriological sciences we can grasp the necessities of objects, strictly speaking we do not come to know the essences of objects themselves but only the signs of their essences (that is to say here we do not know the essences of things in themselves but only in their manifestation as external properties). Maritain accordingly calls the knowledge found in the natural sciences perinoetic knowledge (from the Greek preposition peri [around or about]) as it is a knowledge of an object through its sign substitutes, a peripheral or circumferential knowledge of an object where our intellect bears on an essence without being able to discern the essence itself.

That is not to say that this type of knowledge should be depreciated. For even though the essence itself (and so the ultimate explanation, cause, and reason for being) of things is inaccessible, we can still develop an extensive body of knowledge about the specificities of the corporeal world (based on the intelligible necessities of things insofar as they are manifested by signs). For example, we can determine the common accidents of things such as the boiling point, density, and atomic weight of various chemicals, and learn that heat expands metals, and that ruminants have cloven hooves (DK, II, pp. 35-36, 58-59; IV, pp. 145-147, 189-190; V, pp. 215, 218-220). Furthermore, since in this perinoetic knowledge of science we proceed from the visible to the visible in order to determine the laws of phenomena (by linking up one concrete observable with another so as to yield observed regularities which are in turn linked up with mathematical formulas), we must refer back to observations to verify our scientific hypotheses (DK, II, pp. 51, 56-61).

There is, however, at the level of the first degree of abstraction, another form of knowledge wherein we do acquire a knowledge of the essences themselves of sensible changing beings. This occurs in the philosophy of nature, wherein we can grasp the essential and constitutive notes of changing reality, the essences of things, through the proper accidents of objects. Such a philosophy of nature accordingly gives us what Maritain labels dianoetic knowledge (from the Greek preposition dia [through]). In so doing it generates principles of explanation, ultimate causes, and reasons for being of things and reveals the object-essences immanent in the sensible. Even here, however, lacking the intuition of angels and God, we do not immediately grasp the essences of things, but attain them through the signs (common accidents) which manifest them. So ultimately this is still an indirect form of knowledge, albeit one which allows us to grasp the intelligible constitution or essence itself of objects (DK, II, pp. 25, 35-38, 40-41, 44, 50, 58-59, 71; n. 28 on p. 40; V, pp. 215-217, 220; n. 1 on pp. 215-218; VIII, p. 330-331; PM, II, pp. 28, 34; EE, I, p. 21; PN, III, pp. 73-156; IP, II, 3, pp. 106-110; SW, II, pp. 34-69; PG, Appendix, pp. 270-273). Such a philosophy of nature grasps such universal notes of things as corporeal substance and accidents, actuality and potentiality, matter and form, number, motion, causality, space, and time [and also life and soul (the animal as sensible and the human as risible)] (DK, IV, pp. 186-189; V, pp. 219, 231; PM, II, pp. 25-28; IV, pp. 67-68, 75-

76). With the philosophy of nature then we proceed from the visible to the invisible, to what is outside the order of sensible apprehension or imaginative representation as it is a pure object of the understanding (an intelligible essence). This is because the philosophy of nature begins with metaphysical facts (and so must initially justify itself by referencing experience) but it seeks to find essences and the necessities they imply by deduction (DK, II, pp. 51, 56-61).

In the second degree of abstraction, the mind abstracts out all aspects of change and motion (all matter and sensible qualities as it were), and focuses on being as discrete and quantified, i.e. quantitative being (and as such it no longer deals with existent being). This second degree of abstraction is what allows for the development of logic and mathematics (the study of quantity and number). This is also a form of dianoetic knowledge (though now at the second level of abstraction and moreover we here know the essences of things directly) and it allows us to grasp such essences as the geometric properties of a table, or the fact that the diagonal of a square is incommensurable with its side (DK, II, pp. 25, 38, 44, 50; PM, II, p. 29). So whereas the perinoetic knowledge (under the first degree of abstraction) of the natural sciences is a knowledge of things by signs and not in their essences, and the dianoetic knowledge (again under the first degree of abstraction) of the philosophy of nature is an explanatory knowledge of things in their essences but by proper accidents, the dianoetic knowledge (under the second degree of abstraction) of mathematics and logic is an explanatory knowledge of things by their essences.

Finally we have the third degree of abstraction wherein we go beyond both mobile and quantitative being and consider things in their very being as such, being qua being, being in all its fullness, purity, and intelligibility. Here we engage in a metaphysics proper and study the abstract nature of being (both possible and actual being, material and immaterial being) with its various properties (essence or what is and existence or the actuality of whatever is; and the transcendentals of goodness and beauty) [ontology], its principles [the first principles of logic], as well as the existence and nature of God [natural theology]. Such a metaphysics is like the philosophy of nature in that it bears on what exists (unlike mathematics) and begins with experience, albeit at a more general level in both cases, but it does not have to verify its conclusions through a reference back to empirical experience (unlike the sciences) but instead gains them through deduction (DK, II, p. 39;

PM, II, p. 29, 31-35; ECHP, II, p. 12; EE, I, pp. 34-44). Maritain summarizes the path taken by the three degrees of abstraction as follows:

From the flux of singular and contingent things, such as they are given to the apprehension of the sense, a first glance of the intellectual eye causes the world of corporeal substances and their properties to burst forth. A second glance of the eye causes quite another universe to burst forth, the ideal world of the extended number. A third glance of the eye causes a still wholly different, universe to burst forth, the world of being as being and all the transcendental perfections common to spirits and bodies, wherein we can attain purely spiritual realities and the principle of all reality, as in a mirror (DK, II, p. 40 [75-76]).

Now in the metaphysics achieved through the third degree of abstraction, from reflection on being as being we can develop a body of metaphysical and logical knowledge. In the first place we find that being implies the logical first principles of identity (being is being), sufficient reason (everything which is possesses a sufficient reason for its being), causality (every contingent thing, wherein essence is distinct from existence or wherein both act and potency occur, has a cause lying outside of itself, i.e. in a necessary being or God), and finality (all beings act for an end) (DK, III, pp. 80-82; V, pp. 228-229, V, n. 24 on p. 237; PM, III, pp. 60-61; IV, pp. 67-68; V, pp. 90-106; VI, pp. 107-126; VII, pp. 125-132, 141-142; AG, II, p. 21).

And these principles form the philosophical basis of our proofs for God, or a natural theology which reasons to God as an invisible cause of the world on the basis of the vestiges of God here below (i.e. it is *a posteriori*) (AG, I, pp. 13, 12; II, pp. 18-22; III, pp. 67-68, 70-72; OUP, III, pp. 56-60; ECHP, III, p. 20; PG, VI, pp. 141-146). Moreover, as a Thomist Maritain grants pride of place to the five ways of Aquinas.

The first way is based on the fact that our world is a world of becoming or change (motion), and change involves a passing from being in potency to being in act. Now only something already in act can effect such a change; everything which moves is thus moved by another. Moreover, if the agent that effects a change itself moves from potency to act we must posit another agent that moves it, and so on, until we find a First Agent exempt from all becoming (AG, II, pp. 23-33).

The second way notes that there are efficient causes at work in the world and that they are linked in a series. Now as it is impossible to go on from cause to cause to infinity, we must reach a First Cause lacking a cause without which all those other causes would never have been (Maritain notes that this First Cause is not necessarily a cause in time, but only an intelligible conditions for things) (AG, II, pp. 33-40).

The third way commences from the fact that things in the world are contingent (their non-occurrence is not an impossibility). For plants, animals, stars, and atoms are all perishable and can cease to be (for they are subject to the universal rhythm of destruction and production, i.e. change). Now if everything were purely contingent, nothing would now exist, for that which is not necessary cannot have always been. Thus there must be a Necessary Being, a being which is necessary through itself [per se] (in its essence), that causes other things to be [again things occur by reason of themselves or by reason of something else, and we have to posit a being which is the total reason for its own being in order to explain contingent things] (AG, I, pp. 3-10; II, pp. 43-49; DK, VI, p. 297; RR, VII, pp. 86-90). Thus, says Maritain, it is enough to grant ontological reality to a bit of moss or the smallest ant to grasp the Hand that made them (DK, III, p. 117; PM, VII, pp. 125-132, 139-142).

The fourth way, a more Augustinian approach, holds that there are degrees of value or perfection in things (i.e. things differ in their degree of being, truth (knowledge), life, beauty, and goodness (love)). Now there must exist a maximum of these values and one that possesses these perfections through its own essence (for these are transcendental modes of being that exist by participation and surpass every genus and category versus mere qualities such as hot, red, or solid). Thus there is a being which is pure being, beauty, and goodness (AG, II, pp. 50-57).

The fifth way follows upon the observation that objects in the world are arranged in reoccurrences of constant periodicity, that is to say, in a system of regular relations and stably defined orientations. Now such constancies and stable orientations, even if they have developed out of a simple initial state, require an explanatory reason (raison d'être). For regular relations and stable orientations show that things have root tendencies, tendencies to something, ends. And ends are always the object of the intention of an intellect, an intellect on which things depend, a first cause which is intellection itself. Nor can one say here that the order of the world is due to chance, similar to how a book could arise from the random throwing of letters. For an effect is only due to chance if there is another datum apart from chance, a mutual encounter of independent lines of causation, i.e. letters and hands that casts the letters. Thus the chance events of a die that can fall on any side, or a lottery that can produce a number, are themselves based on ordered sequences of events, and similarly the statistics of nature presuppose causal laws that operate in certain given fields. Thus the very fact that there is an order in the world shows it has a divine origination (AG, II, pp. 57-67; DK, II, p. 28; PM, VII, pp. 133-139).[29] Maritain summarizes the proofs thusly:

The first way proceeds from Motion or Change. There is no fact more obvious here below than the fact of change, through which a thing becomes what it was not. But one thing cannot give to itself what it does not have, at least in potency, and potency cannot pass to actuation by itself alone. Everywhere where there is motion or change (even if it is self-motion as in living beings), there is something else which is causing the change. Now if the cause in question is itself subject to change, then it in moved or activated by another agent. But it is impossible to regress from agent to agent without end; if there were not a First Agent, the reason for the action of all others would never be posited in existence. So it is necessary to stop at a Prime Cause, itself uncaused, absolutely exempt from any change for it is absolutely perfect.

In the same manner the second way, which proceeds from Efficient Causes at work in the world, and the third way, which proceeds from Contingency and Necessity in things, lead to a Prime Cause without which all other causes would neither be nor act, and which exists with absolute necessity, in the infinite transcendence of the very *esse* [being] subsisting by itself.

The fourth way proceeds from the Degrees which are in things. It is a fact that there are degrees of value or perfection in things. But on the one hand wherever there are degrees it is necessary that there exist, somewhere, a supreme degree; and on the other hand one thing is good and another is better, but there can always be another still better, so that there is no supreme degree in the possible degrees of goodness or beauty, or finally being, of which things are capable. Goodness, beauty, being are not in their fullness in any one of the things we touch and see. The supreme degree of goodness of beauty, of being, exists elsewhere in a Prime Being which causes all that there is of goodness, beauty and being in things, a First Cause which does not have goodness, beauty and being, but is self-subsisting Being, Goodness and Beauty.

The fifth way proceeds from the intrinsic Order and purposeful Governance of the world. The very fact that in the material universe things are engaged in a system of stable relations, and that a certain order among them exists and endures, shows that they do not result from chance. A purpose is at work in that republic of natures which is the world. But such purpose cannot proceed from the things which compose the world of matter, and which are devoid of understanding. This purpose or intention must exist in an intellect on which things depend in their very essence and natural activities. Thus in the last analysis it is necessary to recognize the existence of a transcendent Intelligence, the existing of which is its very intellection, and which is the Cause of all beings (OUP, III, pp. 61-62).

In terms of God's nature, Maritain is less skeptical than Gilson about philosophy's ability to know it. He does grant that metaphysical approaches to God are ultimately unworthy of God as they are irreparably defective and lack a due proportion to the object known. For God is not a thing like other things, but greater and higher, and indeed their creator. Thus there is always the danger that metaphysics will try to submit God to human grapplings, manipulate God, define or take possession of Him. Moreover, metaphysical approaches reveal more what God is not rather than what God is, for God's perfections exist in a manner surpassing our earthly way of conceiving them (DK, I, pp. 14-15; V, pp. 244-245; UA, XII, pp. 252-264).

Still this doesn't mean we don't know what predicates should be attributed to the divine. For even if we cannot grasp God's essence formally while on earth (i.e. as a reason of being or explanation), we can conceive the divine perfections contained in that essence from our knowledge of created participations of God on earth. In this way we grasp that the being, unity, goodness, and beauty of the world (the transcendentals) reflect God's nature [as do life, knowledge, and love] (DK, II, p. 60; III, p. 139; V, pp. 224-228, 234; VI, pp. 264, 269; Appendix, pp. 442-445; AG, II, pp. 20, 52; AS, V, pp. 19-27; PM, IV, pp. 67-70). Maritain thus calls natural theology a form of ananoetic knowledge (from the Greek preposition *ana* [up]) as from the analogical properties of creation we can move upward to discover the nature of God (DK, V, pp. 231-232; VI, p. 267; PM, IV, pp. 67-70; IP, VIII, pp. 180-181).

In such a manner metaphysics tells us that God is an uncreated being, a being who exists from Himself [*a se*—rather than being self-caused, *causa sui*, as with Descartes] (AG, I, pp. 14-15; IP, II, 8, p. 180; UA, V, pp. 69-84). God indeed is Pure Act, a being in whom essence and existence are identical (AG, II, pp. 69-70; DK, V, pp. 245-248; PM, I, p. 13; V, p. 98; VI, pp. 112-115). As uncreated and pure being, God also has no composition and is immutable (DK, V, p. 249).

Besides possessing the transcendental of pure being, God also possesses the transcendentals of goodness (including mercy and justice) and beauty (DK, V, pp. 241-242; n. 32 on p. 242). God finally is a person with an individuality, unity, integrity, and subsistence (an individual substantial nature), as well as one with an intellect and will, and an incommunicable possession of itself (DK, V, p. 245-248; n. 38 on p. 246; VI, p. 272; PM, IV, p. 75; V, p. 95). In Maritain's own words, "God exists by His essence and His essence is His very act of knowing ... God is in virtue of Himself, because He is intellection, He exists because He knows Himself and His truth, because He is the infinite fullness of intelligibility in pure act thinking Itself, because His existence, His nature, is the eternally subsistent act of understanding. Moreover, in knowing He wills Himself, loves Himself, and this also is His existence, an existence of love" (PM, V, pp. 99, 251-259).

So through analogical or ananoetic reasoning we can at least have a diminutive knowledge of God's essence, a knowledge of the perfections of God in a limited, uncircumscriptive, and imperfect manner. The divine essence is attained but without delivering itself fully and its mystery remains intact and unpenetrated (in this way metaphysics places reason in an attitude of adoration and intellectual admiration with respect to God) (DK, I, pp. 14-15; V, pp. 228, 239-245, 251-259; Appendix, pp. 446-453; UA, XII, pp. 252-264; AG, I, p. 13; IP, II, 8, p. 141; cf. Aquinas, *Summa Theologiae*, I q. 13 a. 3 ad 2; I a. 13 a. 12 ad 1; *Summa Contra Gentiles*, I, 30; III, 49; *De Trinitate*, q. 1 a. 2 ad 1; *De Potentia*, VII, 5 d 14; *Commentary on the Divine Names*, VII, l. 4).

So far we have examined the various discursive forms of knowledge found in the natural sciences (the perinoetic first degree of abstraction), the philosophy of nature (the dianoetic first degree of abstraction), mathematics (the dianoetic second degree of abstraction), and metaphysics and natural theology (the ananoetic third degree of abstraction). Let us now look at the intuitive forms of knowledge, or what Maritain calls knowledge through connaturality.

Knowledge through connaturality is a non-discursive knowledge gained by immediate intuition. Hence it occurs "through inclination or through connaturality, not through conceptual knowledge and by way of reasoning" (RR, III, p. 26; cf. DK, III, n. 91 on p. 116; IV, p. 145; V, n. 47 on p. 253; RR, I, pp. 16-18; III, pp. 22-29; RT, X, pp. 255-264; NLW, I, pp. 15-20). Connatural knowledge is thus a knowledge founded upon the affective inclinations, dispositions, or congenialities of our being (NLW, I, pp. 15-16, 20-21; II, pp. 33-34; III, p. 45; DK, Appendix, pp. 477-480).

There is a natural connatural knowledge of poetry, morality, and the self, and a supernatural connatural knowledge of God in mysticism.

In connatural poetic knowledge we are immediately emotionally moved by something, we are sympathetic with the beauty of an object of art, literature, music, or nature (DK, VI, p. 299; VI, n. 88 on pp. 299-300). Maritain also suggests that humans can have an implicit germ of an intuition of themselves, at least of their existence if not their essence (DK, III, n. 46 on p. 95; III, p. 99; III, n. 116 on p. 131; IV, pp. 188-189) [and one might add here our eidetic intuition of being and its accompanying logical first principles]. Finally humans know the basic precepts of the natural law in an indemonstrable manner through inclination. This is because humans are connatured with the good in their very being (especially through habitually good behavior wherein humans become attuned to the good and morally sensitive to value) (DK, VI, p. 277, 298-299; IP, II, 8, p. 187; EE, II, pp. 59-69; cf. Aquinas, I-II q. 26 a. 1 I-II q. 94 a. 2-3 and I-II q. 93 a. 6; II-II q. 45 a. 2—"one who has the habit of chastity judges rightly [ad ipsa recte judicat] of these things through a kind of connaturality" [per quandam connaturalitatem]). The natural law consequently is based on the fact that certain ends are in tune with our essential constitution. From the natural law we can also derive the rights to existence, to be treated as a person and not a thing, to pursue moral perfection, to pursue eternal life along a path of conscience, to freedom of association, employment, expression, and religion, to marry and have a family, and to employment and social security, private ownership, and suffrage (NLW, II, pp. 27-31; III, pp. 58-59; IV, pp. 75-78, 97-98; "Natural Law and Moral Law," pp. 62-70).[30]

Besides these natural forms of connaturality, there is also the supernatural connatural knowledge of the mystic. Certainly says Maritain, there can be a natural contemplation or spirituality of God (a homesickness for God, a natural sympathy for God). Yet in order to have a mysticism proper, an intuitive awareness of God wherein the self is ineffably touched by divinity, one needs supernatural charity. For only the supernatural can elevate our faculties to God and render possible an experience of God's inner depths, a felt contact with God (DK, I, pp. 11-13; V, p. 255; VI, pp. 263, 270, 276-279, 282-290, 295, 298, 300, 306, n. 42 on pp. 278-279, n. 1 on p. 263, n. 66 on p. 288; VI, p.

278-279; RT, X, pp. 263-266; AG, IV, p. 88; UA, IX, pp. 164-183). Of course it must be recognized that this mystical experience of God is not absolutely immediate as with the supernatural beatific vision which sees God by and in His essence, i.e. as He is in Himself [*sicut in se est*]. Rather it is an obscure and apophatic knowledge of affective experience wherein concepts sleep and God is hidden in darkness (DK, I, p. 6; VI, pp. 265, 271, 280-281; VIII, pp. 329, 343; RT, X, pp. 283-289; AG, IV, p. 88).

Lastly there is the non-connatural supernatural knowledge of God found in earthly faith. Faith in God lets us comprehend what God, the First Truth, reveals of Himself in the Scriptures. Faith then is a knowledge illuminated by grace wherein we know God as He knows Himself, or at least insofar as He can communicate His being to worldly humans (and we entrust ourselves to God in a personal relation). Yet though faith reaches God in His inwardness and proper life, still it does so at a distance and obscurely and remains a mediate knowledge, one making use of means proportionate to the natural human mode of knowing such as concepts, metaphors, and parabolic analogies with created things overflowing with meaning. Thus by faith we do not know the divine essence in and by itself, even if we do know God in virtue of His essence as revealed to us. In some ways faith is even less perfect than mysticism, at least in its manner of knowing (as God is felt more deeply by the mystic) if not in the object known. Nor must we forget that the supernatural beatific vision of the next life is superior to both mysticism and faith as it represents a direct knowledge of God through His essence (DK, Preface, p. x; V, pp. 255-258; VI, pp. 265-268, 276, 289, 305; n. 50 on p. 257; n. 53 on p. 258; n. 11 on p. 266; n. 91 on pp. 302-304; VIII, pp. 344-346; AG, V, pp. 110-114; n. 1 on p. 111; n. 3 on p. 113; ECHP, IV, pp. 34, 39; Appendix, p. 91; RR, XVI, pp. 205-215; UA, XII, pp. 246-251; PM, I, pp. 17-18).[31]

Let us close our discussion of Maritain with this fine quote: "On all sides—even among the new humanists or the partisans of dialectical materialism (as formerly among the followers of Maurice Barrès [*les barrésiens*])—the cry is head: spirit, spirituality! But what spirit are you invoking? If it is not the Holy Spirit, one might as well invoke the spirit of wood or the spirit of wine" (DK, I, p. 17 [32-33]).

One of the better known Thomists of recent times was **Karol Wojtyła (1920-2005)**, who developed a phenomenological and

Thomistic philosophy of ethics and the person before he became Pope John Paul II. Karol Wojtyła was born in 1920 in Wadowice, Poland and sadly his mother died when he was just eight years old. In 1938 he began higher studies at Jagiellonian University, Cracow where he studied language (he eventually learned to speak twelve languages) and theater (he acted and wrote several plays). In 1938, however, the Nazis invaded Poland, closed down Jagiellonian University, and forced many of its professors into concentration camps where several would perish. Wojtyła joined the Polish resistance and wrote the aforementioned plays to try and preserve Polish culture which the Nazis wanted to now Germanize. Wojtyła also continued his studies at a secret underground continuation of Jagiellonian University in Cracow. In 1942 Wojtyła decided to study for the priesthood at an underground seminary in Cracow and he was ordained in 1946, having avoided the seizure of Polish Youth during Black Sunday 1944 by hiding in the Archbishop's House. In 1945 the Germans fled Cracow to avoid the advancing Soviet troops and Wojtyła assisted the Polish Jews left behind.

Karol Wojtła then went to Rome where he completed a doctorate in theology at the Angelicum in 1948, writing on St. John of the Cross. From 1951 to 1954 he completed his habilitation (a second doctorate required for teaching) at Jagiellonian University on the moral philosophy of Max Scheler. He then joined the theological faculty of Jagiellonian University in 1949 and had just begun teaching when the Soviet Communists, who were now in control of Cracow, closed it down (indeed the Communists prevented him from receiving his second doctorate until 1957). Wojtła accordingly joined the Catholic University of Lublin where he taught ethics for over twenty years. During this time Wojtyła wrote for the local Catholic newspaper *Tygodnik Powszechny* and he also wrote poems and plays under the pseudonyms of Andrzej Jawień and Stanisław Andrzej Gruda

Destined for a career in the Church hierarchy, in 1958 he became auxiliary bishop of Cracow, in 1964 the Archbishop of Cracow, and in 1967 he was elevated to a Cardinal. From 1962-1965 he was active at the Second Vatican Council where he helped draft the documents *Dignitatis Humanae* and *Gaudium et Spes* (he also helped draft the papal encyclical *Humanae Vitae* in 1967). As is well-known in 1978 Karol Wojtyła became Pope John Paul II (almost dying in 1981 during an assassination attempt which may have been orchestrated by the

Soviet Government). As Pope he drafted 12 encyclicals and helped to establish World Youth Day in 1984, in 1992 and 1996 he wrote letters arguing that Galileo's theory of the cosmos and the theory of evolution were compatible with Catholicism, and in 1999 he helped institute the Joint Declaration on the Doctrine of Justification with the Lutheran and Methodist confessions and restructure the Pontifical Academy of St. Thomas Aquinas (1879-) in Rome. He died in 2005.[32]

Karol Wojtyła received the Aquinas Medal from the American Catholic Philosophical Association in 1979 and the United States Presidential Medal of Freedom in 2004 (he was also nominated for a Nobel Peace Prize that year for his role in the Fall of Communism in Poland). He was beatified in 2011. There is a Pontifical John Paul II Institute for Studies on Marriage and the Family at the Lateran University in Rome and at the Catholic University of America in Washington (1981-); a John Paul II Institute at the Catholic University of Lublin in Poland (1982-) [now rechristened the John Paul II Catholic University of Lublin]; a Pope John Paul II Bioethics Center (1991-) with its Pope John Paul II Lecture Series in Bioethics (1991-) at Holy Apostle's College in Cromwell, Connecticut; a John Paul II Cultural Center in Washington (2001-); a John Paul II Institute in Melbourne (2001-) [with other branches around the world in Vallina, Changanacherry, Cotonou, Gaming, Guadalajara, Mexico City, Salvador de Bahia, and Valencia]; and a John Paul II Center in Milwaukee (2006-). We can also mention the John Paul II Railway Station in Rome, John Paul II Airports in Cracow and the Azores, a John Paul II Square in Sofia, Bulgaria, a Place Jean Paul II in Paris, a John Paul II Drive in Chicago, a Pope John Paul II Park in Boston, and a John Paul II Peninsula (Ioannes Paulus II Peninsula) on Livingston Island in the Antarctic.

The key works of Karol Wojtyła are his *Love and Responsibility* [*Milosc i odpowiedzialnosc*] [LR] (1960) and his *The Acting Person* [*Osoba i czyn; Person and Act*] [AP] (1969; 1979).[33] In these works Wojtyła combines the philosophy of being of Aristotle and Aquinas with the modern phenomenology of consciousness of Descartes, Husserl, and Scheler.

Wojtyła asserts that the human being is a *suppositum* [supposit], i.e. a self-subsistent reality or substance (its objective side), with a self-consciousness or self-reflection (its subjective side) (PEC, XV, pp. 209-217; XVI, pp. 221-223). Thus as a human I have experiences of external objects and of myself. It is the latter inner experience of my own existence (I am), however, which is first, closest, and most immediate. Indeed my inner experience (subjectification) accompanies all my outer experiences of other things (objectification), keeps them present to myself, and so allows for what Wojtyła calls a mirroring (AP, Introduction, pp, 3-4, 9, 19, 22; I, pp. 31-34, 36, 40-41, 45, 58-59; V, p. 191; VI, pp. 230-231). Accompanying self-consciousness (self-reflection), the experience of the I, is self-knowledge (self-reflexion) wherein I am both subject (experiencer) and object (what is known) and where I am aware of my acts as my own (AP, I, pp. 33, 38, 40-44, 48-51, 59; II, p. 85). So as Wojtyła explains "Every human being is given in a total or simple experience as an autonomous, individual real being, as existing and acting. But every human is also given to himself as the concrete ego, and this is achieved by means of both self-consciousness and self-knowledge. ... not only am I conscious of my ego (on the ground of self-knowledge, but owing to my consciousness in its reflexive function I also experience my ego" (AP, I, p. 46).

Another important characteristic of the person is the fact that the person has possession of itself, indeed, it is its own sole and exclusive possession (AP, III, p. 105, 131, 147). Besides my self-reflection, self-knowledge, and self-possession, I also experience myself as enacting my being, as engaging in action (AP, Preface, pp. vii-viii, xiv; Introduction, pp. 9-12, 15, 19-20; I, pp. 26-29, 42-43, 46, 59; II, pp. 60, 96; IV, p. 186; n. 2 on p. 301; n. 12 on p. 303; Appendix, pp. 317, 320-323, 356; PEC, X, pp. 165-168 XI, pp. 177-180; XVI, pp. 223-225, 232-236; XVI, n. 6 on p. 260): "action serves as a particular moment of apprehending—that is, of experiencing—the person" (AP, Introduction, p. 10).

Moreover, in experiencing myself as acting I also grasp my self-determination (efficacy), that I am the one who determines myself and so am an agent. Here I recognize that besides the things that happen in me—the passive structures of my consciousness—I also experience my acting as a doing of which I am the agent—the active structures of my consciousness (AP, Introduction, p. 20; I, pp. 48, 53, 56-58; II, pp. 61-62, 65-71, 75, 78-84, 87, 100-101; III, pp. 108, 112-113, 116-122, 127; IV, pp. 182-184; V, p. 196-199; LR, II, p. 47; PEC, I, pp. 7-16; VI, pp. 97-99; X, p. 172). Or in Thomistic terms, besides being subject to an *actus humanae* [an act of the human], or a happening, I can engage in an *actus humanus* [human act] or *actus voluntarius* [voluntary act], a conscious, deliberate, and purposeful action. So I possess a free will, an ability to voluntarily will an act (which is best character-ized as an autodeterminism versus an indeterminism or independence of all factors) (AP, I, pp. 26-27, 31, 38; II, pp. 68-69; III, pp. 120-126; PEC, X, pp. 169-171; XV, pp. 209-216; XVI, pp. 225-228). Through this free will therefore I manifest the characteristics of self-reliance, self-governance, and self-responsibility wherein I exercise a power over myself that no one else can (AP, I, pp. 48-49, 67; II, pp. 98-100; III, pp. 106-110; PEC, XVI, pp. 231-232). Wojtyła explains:

> This structure differentiates the person from a merely natural being, for the elements of self-determination, of freedom, and of the consciousness of it, are wholly alien to nature as is also the transcendence in action formed by the person by his freedom and his conscious efficacy. It is that efficacy which is derived from freedom as the essential factor in the dynamic reality of the person and revealed by the experience of 'the hu-man acts.' The experience of being the agent, of being the actor, makes of acting the action of a person that distinguishes it from the other, numer-ous manifestations of the human dynamism, in which the moment of a conscious efficacy of the personal ego is lacking. The dynamic specificity of that action, the specificity molded by conscious efficacy and freedom, is brought into even greater prominence in contrast with that which only happens in man as the subject. ... For we call transcendence the aspect that consists in one's governance and possession of oneself and these are connected with self-determination, that is, with will (AP, V, pp. 189-190).

Now due to the fact that the human person has its own self-con-sciousness and power of self-determination, it is incommunicable (in-effable in its inner life), non-transferable (it cannot be made someone else's property), and intrinsically valuable. For each person is an au-tonomous self-centered being, with its own inner reality, is its own master and capable of making its own decisions, and is unique and irreproducible (AP, I, p. 45; III, pp. 106-108, 136; LR, Introduction, pp. 12-13, 17; I, pp. 22-24; II, pp. 46, 84, 96, 121-126; IV, pp. 245-249; n. 1 on p. 289; n. 21 on pp. 295-296; EV, 2, 34, 39-40, 54-55, 72).

This then gives rise to what Wojtyła, following Kant and Scheler, calls the personalistic norm. That is to say, we cannot treat other peo-ple as a means for our own use or enjoyment, i.e. as a means to an end, but instead we must treat people as ends in themselves (LR, I, pp. 25-29, 33-34, 41-42; II, pp. 87-88, 121-126; n. 3 on p. 289; n. 13 on pp.

292-293). Wojtyła explicates the personalistic norm in the following manner: "The norm, in its negative aspect, states that the person is the kind of good which does not admit of use and cannot be treated as an object of use and as such the means to an end. In its positive form the personalistic norm confirms this: the person is a good towards which the only proper and adequate attitude is love" (LR, I, p. 41; cf. LR, I, pp. 27-28; n. 61 on p. 307). A person therefore cannot be made an object of consumption or instrument of use but must be loved for his or her own sake.

Ideally this love of another person encompasses eight aspects: 1) attraction (*amor complacentiae*)—wherein others posses a charm, fascination, and beauty and are seen as a value or a good; 2) desire (*amor concupiscentiae*)—wherein we need another person and long for them as a good for ourselves; 3) goodwill (*amor benevolentiae*)—wherein we are concerned for the beloved's own good; 4) reciprocity—wherein love involves a union of two persons who have committed to each other and possess a community of feeling; 5) sympathy—wherein we have emotional warmth for another and feel close to them; 6) friendship (*amor amicitiae*)—wherein we engage our whole being for the sake of the other and the self of another becomes in some sense one's own; 7) comradeship—wherein there are common goals, shared concerns, and joint labors; and finally 8) bethrothed love—which is a giving of oneself to another, a surrendering and transfer of one's incommunicable I to another person (LR, I, pp. 21-24; II, pp. 96, 101-118; II, pp. 74-100, 125-128, 131-139; IV, pp. 255-258; n. 11 on p. 292; n. 32 on p. 298; n. 37 on p. 300; n. 55 on p. 305; PEC, XIV, pp. 199-202; XVI, pp. 240-252; XX, pp. 313-322; XXI, pp. 329-335; VS, 87-89; CA, 41; FR, 32, 93; EV, 76). This bethrothed love (which can occur between spouses, mother and child, doctor and patient, teacher and pupil, pastor and flock, or public figures and public) is the ultimate pinnacle of love: "The fullest, the most uncompromising form of love consists precisely in self-giving, in making one's inalienable and nontransferable I someone else's property" (LR, II, p. 97). With such a love we can love others in full awareness of both their virtues and faults (LR, II, p. 135).

Karol Wojtyła, as Pope John Paul II, more fully expresses his moral views in the encyclical *The Splendor of Truth* [*Veritatis Splendor*] [VS] (1993). In this encyclical John Paul II defends a natural law-based ethics and so argues that God has established a natural moral law in which humans participate through their reason (VS, 12, 32, 35-36, 40, 42, 44-47, 51, 53, 84; EV, 70; FR, 69-72, 87, 95-96; PEC, XII, pp. 181-185). Here human reason can grasp what is good and evil and so what is in accord with human nature. Importantly, John Paul II makes it clear that what is "natural" for humans should not be taken to refer to either one's irrational human nature or biological human nature (a physicalist or naturalist interpretation of the natural law), but to one's proper nature as ordered by and to God (VS, 44, 46-47, 50; AP, III, p. 147; IV, pp. 156, 160-166; VI, pp. 232-234, 248-253; LR, I, p. 38; II, pp. 57, 67; III, p. 77; n. 22 on p. 296; n. 46 on p. 303; n. 52 on p. 304; n. 54 on p. 305; PEC, I, pp. 5, 14-21; IV, pp. 67-70; V, pp. 88-93; VI, pp. 96-97; VIII, pp. 107-125; IX, pp. 130-136; XVI, p. 234; FR, 24-25). He writes: the natural law "refers to man's proper and primordial nature, the 'nature of the human person,' which is *the person himself in the unity of soul and body*, in the unity of his spiritual and biological inclinations and of all the other specific characteristics necessary for the pursuit of his end. ... Only in reference to the human person in his 'unified totality,' that is, as 'a soul which expresses itself in a body and a body informed by an immortal spirit' can the specifically human meaning of the body be grasped. Indeed, natural inclinations take on moral relevance only insofar as they refer to the human person and his authentic fulfillment, a fulfillment which for that matter can take place always and only in human nature" (VS, 50; cf. VS, 42, 46-47, 79; AP, V, pp. 215-219; LR, II, pp. 57, 67; n. 22 on p. 296).

Now the natural law commands that "the person must do good and avoid evil, be concerned for the transmission and preservation of life, refine and develop the riches of the material world, cultivate social life, seek truth, practice good and contemplate beauty" (VS, 51; cf. VS, 72). It also shows that keeping the law is a matter of having a pure attitude of love for others, a proper intention, and not just behaving in certain ways.

In light of his support for natural law theory, Pope John Paul II sharply rejects the utilitarianism ("consequentialism," or "teleologism") found in Bentham and Mill (as well as in Henry Sidgwick, Jonathan Bennett, Richard Hare, Richard Brandt, John Smart, Jonathan Glover, Peter Unger, James Rachels, and Peter Singer), as well as the similar Catholic system of proportionalism[34] (VS, 47, 56, 74-75, 84, 90). For both of these systems of ethics argue that there are few or no moral absolutes, moral norms that are never to be violated. Utilitarianism does so on the basis of claiming that what ultimately determines whether an action is good or bad is its consequences. Hence one may have to sacrifice the good of a few people for an overall good (at least in a form of act-utilitarianism such as that advocated by Bentham). Proportionalism similarly asserts that the moral law gives us "practical absolutes" which are "virtually exceptionless" (especially the commands to love God and neighbor) but which may occasionally be violated in order to create the highest proportion of good over evil. Proportionalists thus at times defend the morality of contraception, sterilization, or the taking of an innocent life such as in abortion, wherein one sacrifices a so-called "pre-moral good" (health, life, material goods) for a greater end. As the proportionalist Richard McCormick writes: "Common to all so-called proportionalists ... is the insistence that causing certain disvalues (nonmoral, premoral evils such as sterilization, deception in speech, wounding and violence) in our conduct does not by that very fact make the action morally wrong, as certain traditional formulations supposed. The action becomes morally wrong when, all things considered, there is not a proportionate reason in the act justifying the disvalue. Thus, just as not every killing is murder, not every falsehood is a lie, so not every artificial intervention preventing or promoting conception in marriage is necessarily an unchaste act" ("Veritatis Splendor in Focus: Killing the Patient," *Tablet* (October 30, 1993), pp. 1410-1411).

Yet John Paul II, in opposition, argues that besides intention and consequences, the morality of an act depends on its object (species) and whether it is ordered to God (VS, 78, 82). The mere weighing of goods and evils forseeable as consequences of an action is thus not an adequate method for determining whether a concrete behavior is 'according to its species,' or 'in itself,' morally licit or illicit. For circumstances or intentions can never transform an act intrinsically evil by virtue of its object into a good act (VS, 77; cf. VS, 95-97; EV, 62). Indeed John Paul II authoritatively reaffirms: "Each of us knows how important is the teaching which represents the central theme of this Encyclical and which is being re-stated with the authority of Peter, namely, the reaffirmation of the universality and immutability of the moral commandments, particularly those which prohibit always and without exception intrinsically evil acts" (VS, 115).

As a result, there are intrinsically evil acts which are never to be done, "even in the most dire of circumstance, and the refusal to betray those commandments, even for the sake of one's saving one's own life. For such acts are intrinsically evil according to their species or object" (VS, 20-21, 46, 50-52, 74-75, 78-83, 90-91, 95-97; EV, 53-57, 76-77; LR, I, pp. 36-37, 40; cf. Rom 3:8).[35] So as John Paul II remarks "The *negative precepts* of the natural law are universally valid. They oblige each and every individual, always and in every circumstance. It is a matter of prohibitions which forbid a given action *semper et pro semper* [always and forever], without exception, because the choice of this kind of behavior is in no case compatible with the goodness of the will of the acting person, with his vocation to life with God and to communion with his neighbor" (VS, 52). Or at greater length:

> The morality of the human act depends primarily and fundamentally on the 'object' rationally chosen by the deliberate will, as is borne out by the insightful analysis, still valid today, made by Saint Thomas. ... Reason attests that there are objects of the human act which are by their nature 'incapable of being ordered' to God, because they radically contradict the good of the person made in his image. These are the acts which, in the Church's moral tradition, have been termed 'intrinsically evil [*intrinsece malum*]: they are such always and *per se*, in other words, on account of their very object, and quite apart from the ulterior intentions of the one acting and the circumstances. ... The Second Vatican Council itself, in discussing the respect due to the human person, gives a number of examples of such acts: 'Whatever is hostile to life itself, such as any kind of homicide, genocide, abortion, euthanasia and voluntary suicide; whatever violates the integrity of the human person, such as mutilation, physical and mental torture and attempts to coerce the spirit; whatever is offensive to human dignity, such as subhuman living conditions, arbitrary imprisonment, deportation, slavery, prostitution and trafficking in women and children; degrading conditions of work which treat labourers as mere instruments of profit, and not as free responsible persons: all these and the like are a disgrace, and so long as they infect human civilization they contaminate those who inflict them more than those who suffer injustice, and they are a negation of the honor due to the Creator' (VS, 80; cf. VS, 78-81; *Gaudium et Spes*, 27).

Besides the prohibition against intrinsically evil acts, the natural law also reveals certain positive values that are good in all times and places: "It is right and just, always and for everyone, to serve God, to render Him the worship which is His due and to honor one's parents as they deserve" (VS, 52); and "to do good and avoid evil, be concerned for the transmission and preservation of life, refine and develop the riches of the material world, cultivate social life, seek truth, practice good, and contemplate beauty" (VS, 51; cf. VS, 32).

Pope John II's other philosophical encyclical is his *Fides et Ratio* [FR] (1998), which, as the title would imply, affirms that we know God through both faith and reason: "Faith and reason are like two wings on which the human spirit rises to the contemplation of truth; and God has placed in the human heart a desire to know the truth—in a word, to know himself—so that, by knowing and loving God, men and women may also come to the fullness of truth about themselves" (FR, Opening Address; cf. FR, 20, 48, 56, 104). For "Although faith, a gift from God, is not based on reason, it can certainly not dispense with it. At the same time, it becomes apparent that reason needs to be reinforced by faith, in order to discover horizons it cannot reach on its own" (FR, 67; cf. FR, 42, 73). Thus for John Paul II, faith and reason are both necessary and complementary for a Catholic (FR, 9, 34, 48-49, 73, 80-83, 100, 105-108): "philosophical wisdom, which is based upon the capacity of the intellect, for all its natural limitations, to explore reality, and theological wisdom, which is based upon Revelation and which explores the contents of faith, entering the very mystery of God" (FR, 44; cf. FR, 41).

Philosophy can be quite useful to theology in explicating a perennial philosophy with regard to the first principles of thought, the nature of knowledge, the notion of a person as a free and intelligent subject, personal communication and relations between God and human and in the Trinity, Christ as God and human, language and the meaning of texts (hermeneutics), God's creative activity in the world (natural theology), the meaning of life, the limits of science, a metaphysical understanding of being, the moral law, virtues, and goodness, conscience, freedom, and personal responsibility, human nature and society, the notion of truth, and in leading us to revelation through seeking the ultimate explanation that puts an end to all questioning (FR, 4-5, 8, 19, 22, 36, 55, 60-61, 66-68, 83-84, 96-99; cf. Wis 13:5; Rom 1:19-21, 2:14-15; Acts 14:16-17). Here we have a situation of not just *credo ut intelligam* [I believe that I might understand] but also *intellego ut credam* [I understand that I might believe] following Blondel and Lonergan) (FR, 27, 33, 75, 80-81). As John Paul II puts it consequently, "Theology in fact has always needed and still needs philosophy's contribution. As a work of critical reason in the light of faith, theology presupposes and requires in all its research a reason formed and edu-

cated to concept and argument. Moreover, theology needs philosophy as a partner in dialogue in order to confirm the intelligibility and
universal truth of its claims. It was not by accident that the Fathers
of the Church and the Medieval theologians adopted non-Christian
philosophies" (FR, 77).

Revelation in turn gives us a knowledge he objects of faith that surpasses human reason (such as of the Incarnation, part of the seminal
divine plan of love beginning with creation) (FR, 6-9, 12-15, 21, 23,
64-65, 97, 106): "Based upon God's testimony and enjoying the supernatural assistance of grace, faith is of an order other than philosophical knowledge, which depends upon sense perception and experience
and which advances by the light of the intellect alone" (FR, 9). And
faith, while it does not abolish the autonomy of reason, can help in
sharpening our inner eye, whereby we can follow the path to truth
more quickly and unhindered (FR, 16, 75).

John Paul II indeed gives credence to Gilson's (or perhaps Maritain's, depending on whether we take the subjunctive as indicating
'would' or 'might') notion of Christian Philosophy as philosophical
speculation conceived in dynamic union with faith. Here faith goes
beyond seeking to not contradict reason and yields developments in
philosophical thinking which might [would] not have happened [qui
numquam contigissent] without the direct or indirect contribution of
the Christian faith. That is to say, here revelation proposes truths
which philosophy might [would] never have discovered [nunquam tamen easdem repperisset], though not inaccessible to reason (FR, 74-76,
79-80, 101, 108) [such as with the problem of evil, the nature of God
as free, personal, and creative, the meaning of life, why there is something rather than nothing, personal sin, human dignity, equality, and
freedom, the person as a spiritual being, history as event, original sin
and a supernatural vocation].[36]

3

TRANSCENDENTAL THOMISM

1910-1970 at its Peak (Continuing on into 2000) in Austria, Belgium, Canada, France, Germany, Netherlands, & the United States

In 1914, as World War I commenced, the young Jesuit Pierre Rousselot, a philosopher and theologian who had recently published influential works on epistemology, love, and faith, decided to join the French Army. Rousselot might have gone on become one of the most prominent theologians of the twentieth-century, but alas we will never know, as one year later he died at the young age of 36 as a Sergeant in the trenches at Les Éparges. For since Rousselot spoke German, he was asked to negotiate with the opposing German forces who had surrounded the French troops entrenched on the hill of Éparges. Rousselot said 'I obey' and on his way across the trenches he was hit with two bullets in the chest and died.[37] The Germans eventually won the battle and as Rousselot was being carried off the battlefield by his fellow French prisoners he uttered the words 'My friends I am going to die, it is useless to go any further ... I shall give you my blessing.' His body was abandoned and lost track of and so likely lies in one of the tombs marked 'unknown French soldier—died for France' [*soldat français inconnu—mort pour la France*] in the cemetery of Les Eparges.

This sacrifice of Rousselot and that of other priests was instrumental in changing the fortunes of the French Church at the beginning of the twentieth-century. For the French populace, faced with a common enemy and seeing the willingness to serve and die for the country on the part of the clergy,[38] could no longer view the Catholics with the same suspicion. Thus it was that in 1914 a Union sacrée truce occurred between the various French factions, the largely unenforced French governmental measures against religious congregations were suspended, some of their property returned, and their schools allowed to unofficially reopen, in 1919 the Concordat was restored in Alsace-

Lorraine (which had been returned to France at the end of World War I), and in 1921 Briand-Ceretti Agreement diplomatic relations were reestablished between the French government and the Vatican and power to nominate French bishoprics restored to Rome. What is more, the state Astier Law of 1919 (as well as the later Marie and Barangé Laws of 1951 and the Debré law of 1959) helped subsidize the cost of education at Catholic schools.

Rousselot, incidentally, was the founder of Transcendental Thomism, a philosophy that has its foundation in the thought of Thomas Aquinas but incorporates ideas from such modern philosophers as Kant, Fichte, Schelling, Blondel, Bergson, and Heidegger. A consequence of this latter influence is that instead of centering philosophy on an investigation of objective being and its metaphysical properties, Transcendental Thomism seeks a subjective or epistemological point of departure. As its name suggests, it focuses on the transcendental conditions of knowledge, that is to say, what must occur in any act of knowing for it to even be possible.

Moreover, in this regard, the central conclusion of Transcendental Thomism is that the dynamism of a knowing subject toward Infinite and Absolute Being (i.e. God) is just such an a priori condition of knowledge. That is to say, God is in some way always present as a horizon and necessarily co-affirmed with every act of human knowledge. There are two distinct schools of thought, however, in regard to just how this occurs. According to some proponents of Transcendental Thomism, an a priori *desire* for knowledge of the Absolute Being of God is the transcendental condition of all acts of knowledge [Rousselot; Lonergan]: others argue that what allows for knowledge is that to some degree humans have an a priori *apprehension* of God as Absolute Being (by the light of the agent intellect) [Maréchal, Rahner]. The world is intelligible then for Transcendental Thomists because we either seek or actually ascend to God (Perfectly Intelligible Being) in every act of knowing.

Not surprisingly, the Transcendental Thomists stress an a priori or anthropomorphic approach to natural theology, rather than the a posteriori or cosmocentric approach of traditional Thomism. In their unique proof of God's existence (although echoing earlier thinkers such as Malebranche—who argued for a vision of all things in God— and Ontologists such as Rosmini), Transcendental Thomists assert that God is not known (primarily) by reasoning from the effects observed in the world to God as their cause. Rather God is known as the Infinite Reality that lies in the background of our judgments (as the term of our striving or as an implicit horizon, depending upon the school of thought), making it possible for us humans to grasp limited and finite beings. Or as Joseph Donceel puts it, Transcendental Thomism "reaches God not as the cause of the universe, but as the whereunto of the basic thrust of our intellect and will" ("God in Transcendental Thomism," *Logos* 1 (1980), p. 53). This truth furthermore allows Transcendental Thomists to affirm, following Blondel, that supernatural grace is always present to the natural world, and so all humans, even atheists, have a basic desire for or implicit awareness of God.[39]

The French Jesuit **Pierre Rousselot (1878-1915)** was born in 1878 in Nantes, France. He attended the Sorbonne around 1891-1895 and subsequently joined the Jesuits in 1895 in Canterbury, England, as the Jesuits previously had been expelled from France due to laws of 1880 and 1901.[40] After studies at the Jesuit Scholasticate in Canterbury and the Sorbonne (c. 1904-1908 under the Catholics Émile Boutroux and Victor Delbos), Rousselot received a doctorate in philosophy from the Sorbonne in 1908, the same year in which he was ordained. Rousselot unfortunately had only just begun his teaching career at the Catholic Institute of Paris from 1909-1914 (where as a Jesuit in France, his presence was tolerated though officially illegal—explaining perhaps why he sometimes wrote under a pseudonym), when World War I commenced. And as we saw, on that tragic day of April 25, 1915, as an obedient Sergeant in the trenches at Les Éparges (he had previously served in the military in 1899 in Nantes as well), Rousselot followed the orders of his commander ('I obey'), and made his way over to talk to the opposing German leaders, whereupon he was mortally wounded by gunfire.[41]

The main works of Pierre Rousselot were his book *The Intellectualism of Saint Thomas* [*L'intelletualisme de Saint Thomas*] [ISTH] (1908; 1924; 1936), and his essay "The Eyes of Faith" ["EF"] (1910; 1913).[42] Both works impacted the oeuvre of many of the giants of twentieth century Catholicism such as Henri Bouillard, Henri de Lubac, Avery Dulles, Karl Rahner, and Hans Urs von Balthasar.

Whereas in wartime Rousselot fought against the German incursion into France, in peacetime he directed his efforts towards combating what he felt were the pernicious philosophical influences of Romanticism and Traditionalism (as well as a Theological Rationalism or Modernism). These views held that only or primarily revelation (Traditionalism) or feeling (Romanticism), and not reason, gives humans a knowledge of God. Hence both of these movements were oftentimes couched in terms of an anti-intellectualism (one diametrically opposed to Scholasticism) which claimed that reason was detrimental to religious belief, and this for two main reasons.

In the first place Traditionalism and Romanticism held that the practitioners of a rational philosophy (Aquinas included) engage in an idolatry of abstraction wherein the intellect "deforms and mutilates being." For by classifying objects into categories, a stated goal of reason, one abstracts away the living and individual reality of each thing and reduces it to a shadow or fragment of its former self (for instance in naming a flower a narcissus one loses touch with its individual color and perfume) (ISTH, Introduction, pp. 2-6 [v]). Abstraction is thus "the arbitrary creation of a number of artificial unities substituted, by decree of spirit, for the inexpressible unity of the given" (ISTH, Introduction, p. 3 [vi]). Besides ignoring the individuality and complexity of reality, abstraction also ignores the vital movement or change found in the world: it postulates permanence where there is flux and freezes what flows. Abstraction then creates rigid and static entities that do not correspond to the diffuse and flowing nature of reality. Or in the words of Rousselot, abstraction constructs "an empire of stiff, rigid entities [roides (sic for raides) entités figées], a kind of intellectual chinashop [Chine] ... pale and abstract notions, their life has vanished—these are deformed cadavers" (ISTH, Introduction, pp. 3, 5-6 [vii, ix]; ELK, V, pp. 148-149; VII, pp. 225, 228, 232).

In the second place, rationalists are said to enter into a rashness of affirmation (excessive dogmatism; intemperate assertion) by making presumptuous, absolute, and exclusive assertions. For reason finds itself impelled to create a definite system of stable propositions which completely explain reality (indeed reason often tries to explain reality solely in terms of itself). Yet this is to ignore history, psychology, and the supernatural, and to improperly seek to express all things in a definitive and unrevisable manner. Such a rashness of affirmation is especially problematic when one attempts to treat God in purely rational terms and in dogmatic formulae. For in that case an idea is substituted for a spiritual person (i.e. the divine is spatialized and depersonalized), and vital development in religious knowledge is ignored in an attempt to express the divine through unchanging dogmas (ISTH, Introduction, pp. 2-6, 10; Concl., p. 180).

Now against this twofold critique of the "destructive" activity of reason, Rousselot wants to show how reason is the highest faculty of the human being (as opposed to faith or sentiment), and yet that reason can still claim to know God and do so without destroying the religious life (ISTH, Conclusion, p. 179; ELK, VII, p. 246). Or as he puts it "By intellectualism I understand a doctrine that places all value, all intensity of life, and the very essence of the good, identical with being, in the act of intelligence" (ISTH, Introduction, p. 1 [iii]; cf. ISTH, Introduction, pp. 2, 11; I, p. 39; II, 1, p. 56; II, 6, pp. 140, 143, 158-160-161; III, p. 162; cf. *Summa Contra Gentiles*, I, 102, 6). For with Aquinas "Intelligence ... is everything that is most perfect in life" (*Commentary on Metaphysics*, XII, 5; ISTH, I, p. 13).

Rousselot begins his counter-attack by arguing that for Thomas there is no opposition between idea and spiritual person. For as Aquinas sees it, pure spirits are subsisting intelligibles or ideas (ISTH, Introduction, p. 7; I, pp. 14-15, 18, 27; Conclusion, p. 179-181; ELK, I, pp. 54, 59; VII, p. 231). This is at bottom because nothing can exist without being intelligible, without being an object of divine intellection: "to be able to be is first of all to be able to be thought by God" (ISTH, II, 1, p. 56 [62]). Furthermore, to be immaterial is to be an intellect for Aquinas, that is to say, the less one is material, the more one is an intelligence. All pure spirits, therefore, are intelligent beings with ideas, and the very being of God, who has no matter and indeed is pure act, is identical with intelligence. God then is Absolute Life and Living Spirit as well as Infinite Reason and Subsisting Truth—God is a person who is the source of all thoughts, doctrines, and ideas—and no opposition can be found between these two sides of God (ISTH, II, 3, pp. 92-94, n. 2 on p. 92; Conclusion, p. 182; ELK, I, n. 8 on p.59).

Secondly, Rousselot argues that the true role of intelligence is not to fabricate concepts or string propositions together, but instead to capture beings. Intelligence in itself, therefore, rather than being a faculty of abstraction, is a taking faculty [*faculté prenante*], a faculty of interpenetration (intussusception), a faculty of acquiring and seizing reality (ISTH, I, p. 25; II, 1, p. 50, 55; ELK, II, pp. 101, 110; IV, p. 140; VII, p. 237). Rousselot consequently insists that "To know [*Connaître*] is principally and primarily to seize and embrace within yourself an other who is capable of seizing and embracing you: it is to live by the life of another living being" (ISTH, Introduction, p. 7 [xi]). With this in mind, "intelligence must not be defined as the faculty of discerning, of linking up, of ordering, of deducing, of assigning the causes or the reasons of beings. ... but of directly grasping their in-itself [en-soi], of assimilating to itself the interiority of things, which naturally is supposed to be diaphanous and translucent to the spirit" (ISTH, I, p. 26 [20]). Truth then is less an adequation of a thing to the spirit, as in Aquinas' classical definition [adequatio rei et intellectus], than a conformity, assimilation and union of the spirit with a thing (ISTH, I, p. 26): "But in immaterial things ... a thing is not only what it is, but in some fashion it is other beings as well" (Aquinas, Commentary on the Analytics, II, 5; cf. ISTH, I, p. 13).

This being the case, why is it that so many philosopher's have condemned reason and have failed to see that reason's highest purpose is not to abstract but to grasp and know being? The primary reason for this, says Rousselot, is because they have failed to see that there are two forms intelligence takes in humans, and instead identify intelligence with its lower form which they subsequently critique.

Intelligence in its higher form is found in the intellect [intellectio]. The intellect is characterized by a primacy of contemplation and acquires knowledge through an immanent and immediate intuition of a given reality. Hence the intellect gives us knowledge by "perfect vision, ... possession through identification" (ISTH, II, 1, p. 68 [77]). Such a form of reasoning through an immediate intuition of reality represents human's highest capability and is the true form of intellectualism. It is the kind of intellection that occurs in God and angels, and in humans during the beatific vision (as well as in some rare instances with humans on earth, such as with knowledge of the self, the use of language, the first principles of logic and morality, and poetry) (ISTH, Introduction, pp. 1-2, 6-8; n. 3 on p. 6; n. 5 on p. 7; I, pp. 26, 35; II, 1, p. 52-53; n. 13 on p. 53, 65; II, 2, n. 40 on p. 83; II, 3, n. 1 on p. 91; II, 3, pp. 103-104; Appendix, p. 185; ELK, VII, pp. 226, 244-245; cf. Aquinas, 2a2ae q. 49 a. 5 ad 2-3; 1 q. 58 a. 3; Summa Contra Gentiles, LVII, 8).

Rousselot additionally characterizes the intuitive knowledge acquired through the intellect as a knowledge by way of nature [cognitio per modum naturae] or by connaturality [or variously as a sympathetic knowledge, an affective reaction, or a knowledge by way of love]. For here one knows something by being attuned to it, through an interior experience of attraction or repugnance to something (in a manner similar to how angels would know through a divine idea). Or as Rousselot puts it, with the intellect we know through an "inference as rapid as lightning, based on the bond, known beforehand, between the action and its habitual term" (ISTH, II, 1, pp. 63-64 [71]). Such a connatural form of intellection is quite advantageous, explains Rousselot, as by it a virtuous person can know matters of chastity through the habit of chastity rather than through a course in ethics,[43] a Londoner can know when to say shall or will accurately and without hesitation, a child can know how to use the words right or left, whether a word is pronounced or spelled correctly (due to a habit of orthography), or whether something is within the rules a given game, and finally a French person can know a song, conversation, or anecdote that speaks to the national genius (ISTH, II, 1, pp. 63-67; III, p. 170; ELK, I, p. 80; II, pp. 99, 102, 104-105, 115, 117; III, p. 129; IV, pp. 140, 142-144; n. 9 on p. 143; VII, p. 237; "EF," II, pp. 56-57, 64; II, n. 31 on p. 80).

The lower form of intelligence is the discursive reason [ratio]. Discursive reason is characterized by a primacy of static definitions and deductive reasoning. Such a form of discursive reasoning is only found in humans, and indeed makes up the bulk of human cognition while on earth (ISTH, Introduction, pp. 1-2, 6-8; n. 3 on p. 6; II, 1, p. 52-53; n. 13 on p. 53, 65; II, 2, n. 40 on p. 83; II, 3, pp. 103-104; Appendix, p. 185; ELK, II, pp. 102-103; V, p. 163; VII, pp. 226-227, 240, 245-246; n. 7 on p. 240; cf. Aquinas, 2a2ae q. 49 a. 5 ad 2-3; 1 q. 58 a. 3; *Summa Contra Gentiles*, LVII, 8). While discursive reason is useful to humans, it is not the ideal and measure of intelligent operations, that role is reserved for the intuitive intellect (ISTH, I, p. 29; II, 1, p. 54; II, 6, pp. 146-147; Conclusion, p. 179; ELK, VII, pp. 232-233). Rousselot writes: "Discursive reasoning [*Le raisonnement discursif*], the backbone of science, is so little characteristic of intelligent being that in us it is an effect of sensitive nature: if by intuition we participate in the life of angels, by discursion [*discours*] we touch the successive [*continue*], multiple and relative knowledge of animals" (ISTH, I, p. 39 [38]).

Besides failing to recognize that there is a separate and higher form of intelligence, the intuitive intellect, which escapes its criticisms, Traditionalism and Romanticism also fails to grasp that that there is an analogical hierarchy of intellects (distinguished by increasing immanence, exteriorization, immediacy, and unity) as we pass from corporeal beings, animals, humans, and angels, to finally God. Immanence here refers to the degree that knowledge occurs with a minimal receptivity of elements from without (i.e. the degree to which the knowledge is immanent to the knower). Exteriorization refers to the degree to which one has a grasp of a being external to oneself. Hence in perfect exteriorization "the Reality known by me should be identically the very idea I have of it" (ISTH, Introduction, n. 5 on p. 7 [n. 2 on p. xi]). Immediacy refers to the level of direct intuition that occurs in knowing. Thus the more immediate the knowledge, the more it is non-discursive and is a direct vision of an object. Finally, unity refers to the degree that knowing occurs through fewer acts (or forms or ideas) the higher up the ladder of intellection one is (ISTH, I, pp. 14, 16-20, 23-24, 40; II, 2, p. 89; ELK, I, pp. 64-65; II, n. 32 on p. 113; cf. Aquinas, *Summa Contra Gentiles*, II, 98; IV, 11; *Commentary on the Book of Causes*, 18).

Corporeal beings (rocks) are at the lowest level of intellection and really are only themselves and so have no knowledge of either themselves or other beings. Next come animals which have a sensory awareness of objects in the world but no true knowledge of them (ISTH, I, pp. 19-20). Humans, who are part matter (body) and part spirit (soul), are higher on the scale of intellection and so share in the higher forms of intellect (*intellectio*) found in angels and God. Hence, as we have seen, humans have a limited ability to intuit things in this life (such as in the intuition of self, logical principles, moral values, language use, and poetry) (ISTH, I, p. 31; ELK, II, pp. 99, 103; III, p. 128; V, p. 163). Yet, for the most part humans use a combination of the senses and reason to indirectly abstract the quiddity (essence) of an object, and so the human mind has a lower degree of immanence than that of pure spirits (angels and God). It is also the case that human reasoning only knows the nature of things partially and inexhaustively (with a remainder), and so with a low degree of exteriorization. Finally, humans rely upon a spatial multiplicity of several powers (internal and external senses, reason [*ratio*] and intellect [*intellectus*], and active and passive intellects, as well as upon a temporal succession of acts, in order to know. And with this spatial and temporal duality, humans display a lower degree of unity and immediacy than pure spirits (ISTH, I, p. 29-30; II, 1, pp. 50-52, 59-60; II, 3, pp. 108; III, p. 178;

ELK, I, p. 55; II, p. 92 and n. 8 on p. 92, 96, 112; III, p. 128; IV, p. 138; V, pp. 157, 162; V, n. 35 on p. 170; cf. Aquinas, 1 q. 12 a. 11).

Angels, unlike humans, are pure spirits, separated substances, and so do not possess any material element. Angels then are wholly intuitive spirits, possessing a high degree of immanence, and they know all things through the essential forms coming to them from God [this of course varies with the type of angel: i.e. the angels, archangels, principalities, powers, virtues, dominions, thrones, Cherubim, Seraphim of Ambrose, Gregory the Great, Pseudo-Dionysius, John of Damascus, and Aquinas—angels on the lower end of the scale of intellection require many forms to know things. Others, higher up, know the world through fewer and more universal forms (intelligible species)]. Now in their knowledge through divine forms (through a connaturality or sympathy with their essence) angels grasp things as the really are (with a high exteriorization). Still unlike God, angels do not know things through their own essence but rather through forms coming to them from God (i.e. their ideas are not identical with their substance) and so do not have perfect unity (ISTH, Introduction, p. 9; I, p. 13, 28-29; II, 1, p. 52; II, 2, p. 75; ELK, I, pp. 54-55; III, pp. 127-130; n. 6 on pp. 137-138; V, pp. 156-157; n. 12 on p. 157; V, p. 160; cf. Aquinas, On Truth, q. 8 a. 14 ad 6).

Finally, the highest intellect is God who is Subsistent Intellect. Now God is not only a pure form without matter, but also Pure Act without potency. Hence God's being is identical with God's intellect (as well as with God's love, justice, and mercy). As a consequence all duality disappears in God (God has pure unity in knowledge), and God also knows by pure immanence and immediacy (in a direct vision). For God knows the world through His own essence, through His single substantial form. Finally God knows things exhaustively, knows all that they are, and so with a perfect exteriorization that truly captures the nature of other beings (ISTH, Introduction, p. 9; I, pp. 16-18, 25, 36-37; II, 1, p. 51-52; II, 2, p. 75; n. 8 on p. 95; III, p. 169; Conclusion, pp. 180, 183; ELK, I, p. 57; III, p. 129; n. 18 on p. 129; V, p. 156; n. 12 on pp. 156-157 and n. 13 on p. 157; cf. Aquinas, Summa Contra Gentiles, I, 65; II, 98; IV, 11). Here are some representative quotes of Rousselot on this hierarchy of knowers:

> It follows that the strength of an intelligence will be measured by the expansion, the distention, of the thought self, of its idea, and it will be

all the more powerful, within its class, according as it can concentrate within itself a greater portion of the other without losing its unity. The lowest intellectual beings acquire their ideas only by the impression of material objects since each material object is only itself, and therefore an idea acquired from these beings would not represent many objects. On the other hand, nothing prevents spirits endowed with deeper immanence and whose ideas are consubstantial with them from gathering together into a single mental presence a vast category of objects. ... it is according to the decreasing number of their ideas that we should measure the natural perfection of pure intuitive beings (ISTH, I, pp. 23-24).

Three kinds of intellectual apprehension can be distinguished: grasping, intuition, representation. There is grasping if the intelligible Reality is identical with the very idea one has of it: if God exists, this is how He knows Himself. Physically there is intuition if there is no objective intermediary between the idea and the object, even if the idea is not the same physical reality as the object itself [the way of angels]. ... There is representation when intelligence fabricates in itself an image of the object to be contemplated and considers its object in this image. ... Representation does not reach what is real [the way of humans] (ELK, II, p. 112; cf. Aquinas, *Summa Theologiae*, 1 q. 54 a. 1).

Now due to the fact that human reason involves a combination of powers (senses and intellect), discursion (multiple acts and terms; composing and dividing), and abstraction (the abstracting of a universal form from the sense data), and in addition because our intellectual faculty was wounded by the fall, human reason is quite deficient and defective on earth (ISTH, Introduction, pp. 8-9, 12; I, pp. 25-26; II, 1, pp. 51-52; II, 6, pp. 152-153; Conclusion, pp. 180, 182; "EF," I, n. 28 on p. 42; cf. Aquinas, 1a2ae q. 85 a. 3). Indeed Rousselot is quite harsh on human reasoning. At best discursive reasoning can fabricate a "more or less imperfect resemblance of things," "an image ... of the truth," and we can attain a modest number of verified propositions, a "furtive glance" at essences (ISTH, I, p. 13 and II, 1, p. 59 [4, 66]; cf. ISTH, Introduction, pp. 8, 12; ELK, V, p. 167; "EF," II, p. 71). At worst human knowledge is obscure and uncertain ("deficient, crude, and miserably limited") and we are as "blind as bats in the noonday sun" (ISTH, Introduction, p. 8; I, pp. 25-26; II, 1, p. 50-52 [53]; II, 6, p. 140 [172]; III, p. 175; Conclusion, pp. 180, 182-183; Appendix, pp. 187, 189, 192).[44]

This is not cause for concern, however, or grounds to rebuke reason, as with the Traditionalists, for the entire value and ultimate explanation of discursive reasoning is the simple intuition of God, which is our highest form of reason (ISTH, II, 1, p. 65; Conclusion, p. 183). Or as the mantra of Rousselot has it, intelligence is only the sense of the real as it is the sense of the divine (ISTH, Introduction, pp. 2, 7; ELK, III, pp. 123, 125).

This means, in the first place, that the same faculty that forms our concepts and deductions here below, in another mode, renders us capable of God [capax Dei] (ISTH, I, p. 38 and n. 61 on p. 40; II, 1, p. 59; II, 6, pp. 151-152). In other words, the intelligence, which is capable of a beatific vision of God in the next life as it has an obediential potency or capacity to be enlightened by grace, functions in earthly human life as discursive reason where it grasps God's creation (ISTH, Introduction, p. 7, 12; I, p. 15-16, 26; II, 6, pp. 147-148, 152, 156; III, p. 162; ELK, II, p. 83; III, p. 126; VII, p. 232). Rousselot explains: "The capacity [la possibilité] that we have for the beatific vision, being the only common foundation of the diverse aptitudes of the spirit, defines intelligence itself. Intelligence is only the faculty of being in general because it is the faculty of the Infinite Being. If reason can form judgments of an absolute value, and perceive laws from which not even God can derogate ... the cause of this lies in that potential participation which constitutes intelligence in that capacity for the divine which the beatific vision will fulfill" (ISTH, I, pp. 39-40 [38]). The earthly forms of conceptual knowing are therefore justified as they are the natural operations in a lower world of a spiritual being directed to know God in a higher world through the intuitive intellect (ISTH, Introduction, p. 8). To quote Rousselot once again:

> In effect, for the specification of the intelligence to remain one, and because one cannot find in the power to perceive being in general (or predicamental being) the reason for the power to perceive God, it is necessary to grasp the inverse relationship. We shall say, in the language of the later Scholastics, that we do not have the 'obediential potency' to see God because we have the natural capacity [puissance] to know [connaître] the 'quiddity' of things, but rather vice versa (ISTH, I, p. 40, n. 61 [n. 2 on pp. 38-39]).

Secondly, as humans have a natural desire or appetite for God (for the end of the intellect is to grasp God's being in the afterlife), and as the world participates in God's being and intelligibility, humans also have an attraction to and desire to know the nature of the world (ISTH,

II, 6, pp. 147-149; ELK, III, p. 122; n. 8 on p. 125). As Rousselot remarks, "human intelligence is attracted by being and by the true, as the sole object that charms it, only because its very nature is to be an inclination toward infinite Being insofar as it is the Good of intelligent beings, i.e. insofar as it is the supreme Truth" (ELK, III, p. 122). The conceptual representations that humans form of the world are accordingly animated by an appetition for supreme truth and happiness, they are efforts toward a complete vision of God (ELK, II, p. 118). So humans seek a knowledge of God's creation out of a "muted summons [appels sourds]," "an appetite, an indecipherable obscurity" for God Himself. The soul, in order to find God and gain itself, exercises its faculties of intelligence and plumbs the world here below (ISTH, II, 6, pp. 149, 151-152 [188]). In short, for Rousselot, understanding of reality is founded upon an a priori dynamism toward God ("EF," II, p. 71): "we understand things only insofar as we desire God. ... We ceaselessly pursue the First Truth, and we don't know it. Love for God is solidified in us, as it were, in an unconscious nature" (ELK, III, p. 123 [229]).

An important ramification of Rousselot's epistemology is that ultimately intellect and affection work together. This is evident in that our highest intellectual act, the beatific vision, combines an intellective grasp of God with our personal perfection. Here the intellect attains God in God's nudity, and this intimacy with God's own being constitutes our very end and happiness (ISTH, Introduction, p. 7; I, pp. 31, n. 54 on p. 34-35, 39-40, 43, 46-49; n. 78 on p. 46; n. 84 on p. 49; II, 1, pp. 50, 64, 68; II, 6, p. 160; Conclusion, pp. 180-181; ELK, III, n. 8 on p. 125; V, n. 39 on p. 174; VIII, p. 229; cf. Aquinas, 1 q. 82 a. 3; 1a2ae q. 3 a. 4; On Truth, XXII, 11; Summa Contra Gentiles, III, 39, 59). Moreover, Rousselot argues that even in this life, with respect our connatural acts of knowledge, "perfect knowledge is identical with love" (ELK, III, p. 119). That is to say, knowledge by connaturality combines representation and sympathetic synthesis. For here knowing is defined by love (by an appetite or affective disposition) wherein we have an instinctive sympathy with an object and we vibrate in tune with it through this illuminating sympathization (ELK, II, pp. 86, 90, 117; III, pp. 119-122; n. 1 on p. 119, III, pp. 123, 134; IV, pp. 135-137, 146-147). This is why it is licit to categorize reason as "nothing other than a pure love of Being," for God has made us "naturally sympathetic to being as such" ("EF," II, pp. 52-54; II, n. 21 on p. 77). Rousselot also makes use of these ideas in order to elucidate his influential account of faith.

Rousselot argues that besides the knowledge of God gained through reason, there is a supernatural faith wherein we discover what God has directly revealed to humans. Moreover, this supernatural faith allows us to discover mysteries of the faith such as God being triune that go beyond the scope of reason. Hence the view of the semi-rationalists such as Hermes that reason can provide us with all of the specifications of our faith (albeit after it has studied the Scriptures to determine what it needs to prove) is incorrect ("EF," I, pp. 22-23; n. 3 on pp. 36-37; n. 4 on pp. 36-37; ELK, V, n. 30 on p. 166; VI, n. 47 on p. 222; VII, pp. 230-231, 237-238; ISTH, Appendix, p. 189).[45] Rousselot also rejects what he calls the Scotist, dualistic, or scientific conception of faith, wherein prior to the act of grace there can be a purely rational demonstration of the credibility of the Catholic faith (typically one based on reflection on Scriptural miracles, prophecies, and historical facts about Jesus Christ and the Church, the so-called preambles of the faith).[46] The problem with this scientific view of faith, notes Rousselot, is that while it can safeguard the rationality of faith by showing how one first finds the Catholic faith believable and then believes it, it is hard to see how it safeguards its freedom. For it seems to make faith a necessary product of rational argumentation and does not allow for a freely given 'I do believe.' Moreover it seems to make faith purely natural rather than supernatural ("EF," I, pp. 23-26; II, pp. 45, 47, 63-64; n. 4 on p. 72; n. 5 on p. 73; cf. ELK, VI, p. 183, 199; n. 25 on p. 212; pp. 220-222).

It is not that Rousselot denies the rationality of faith and asserts that faith is blind. For he agrees with other Thomists that "we would not believe unless we saw that we ought to believe" [non crederemus, nisi videremus esse credendum] ("EF," I, pp. 24, 35; cf. Aquinas, 2a2ae q. 1 a. 4 ad 2; 2a 2ae q. 2 a. 4, 5, 10). Consequently for Rousselot a faith altogether lacking the preambles of the faith would be immoral: for all our acts must be reasonable and these preambles help to intellectually justify our assent (ISTH, II, 6, pp. 155-156; n. 37 on pp. 155-156, 158).

Rousselot therefore develops his famous notion of "the eyes of faith" [les yeux de la foi] to resolve all these difficulties, a theory that he finds in part in Augustine (354-430), Thomas Aquinas (c. 1225-1274) [as he interprets him], Cardinal Thomas Cajetan (1469-1534), John of

St. Thomas (1589-1644), Jean-Baptiste Gonet (c. 1616-1681), the Salmanticenses (Seventeenth-Century), and Matthias Joseph Scheeben (1835-1888)] [47] Rousselot argues that faith is rational, i.e. that there are good reasons for believing (the preambles of the faith) and so that grace perfects nature, but that these reasons are only discernable (or at least discernible with a certainty and not a mere probability) through supernatural grace ("EF," I, p. 34; II, p. 62). In Rousselot's own words, "the infused gift of faith, by elevating intelligence, allows it to discern supernaturally the signs of the supernatural world in sensible things" (ELK, VI, n. 10 on p. 193). So while the credibility of faith is rationally demonstrable, this cannot be perceived with certainty without a supernatural light ("ATT," p. 93; cf. Aquinas, *On Truth*, q. 28 a. 4): "[a] certain voluntary disposition produced by grace is indispensably required for every legitimate act of faith and for every certain perception of credibility, not as a perceived internal fact, but as eyes to perceive the external fact" ("EF," I, p. 34; n. 4 on p. 38). On Rousselot's account of faith then, contra the position of Bainvel and others, the perception of credibility is not the fruit of a rational demonstration that precedes faith, but is produced by the light of faith, a grace which "awakens us to a new power of seeing" ("EF," II, p. 64; cf. "EF," I, pp. 32-33; n. 30 on p. 43; II, pp. 61, 68; II, n. 3 on p. 72).

In response to the question of how it can be that there are objective signs for faith in the world (i.e. rational evidence) but they remain ungraspable without a supernaturalized intelligence, Rousselot argues that one needs the right vision and disposition of the will to grasp an external fact as a clue to a larger puzzle (synthesis), i.e. as a clue to a divine revelation ("EF," II, pp. 45, 56, 63-65, 67-68, 70; II, n. 28 on p. 79; "ATT," n. 4 on p. 109; ISTH, II, 5, pp. 128-129; n. 13 on p. 128; ELK, VII, p. 239). So grace "makes us see, within the very ambit of objects we were already attending to, clues to the higher world" ("EF," I, p. 33). Hence by a supernatural illumination (by the light of faith), we are given a new synthetic intelligence (the form) through which we see the object (the matter), and can grasp the connection between external signs and the Catholic faith and assent with a newfound certitude ("EF," I, pp. 26-28; I, n. 4 on p. 38; "ATT," pp. 94-95, 102).[48] In this regard, Rousselot also links his theory of connatural knowledge with his theory of faith. He argues that grace gives us new eyes to see by providing us with a love or an appetite (a connatural inclination or sympathetic intelligence) that imparts its own coloration to perceived objects. Love then makes the object of knowledge appear in a certain way, under this or that color (ELK, II, pp. 86, 90, 117; III, pp. 119-122; n. 1 on p. 119, III, p. 137).[49] Moreover, the love engendered by faith arouses the faculty of knowing and draws it to the object allowing for a better penetration of the object—so with loving vision comes a more perfect knowledge ("EF," II, pp. 49-51, 54-59; n. 7 on p. 73; "ATT," p. 104). In short, "A human in the grip of a passion sees things with new eyes, sees in them a new 'formal object,' as it were" ("EF," II, p. 49). Or at greater length:

> ... love [has] an essential role in the act of faith. ... feeling is not a seducer of intelligence; freedom actually engenders evidence. It is precisely intelligence, corrupted by sin, that is set free by supernatural love. Grace gives intelligence a perfection proper to it, the perfection of seeing. ... love gives us eyes, the very fact of loving makes us see, creates for the loving subject a new species of evidence ("EF," II, pp. 60-61).

Indeed without this life of grace (though we could know of God's existence), all the most rigorous proofs that the Catholic Church is the true Church of God (whether from miracles, the word of God, the holiness of the Church and its members, the history of the Church, or the most exquisite refinements of the moral life) would not raise the assent to Christianity beyond uncertain opinion. Or to put it conversely, what is an ambiguous sign for natural reason can become a reliable sign for supernaturalized reason ("EF," I, pp. 30-32, 34; II, pp. 59-60; II, n. 11 on p. 75; ELK, VI, p. 183; n. 1 on p. 183; VI, pp. 185-186, 189; n. 10 on p. 193; pp. 202, 208-209, 211, 213, 216; n. 36 on p. 217-220; n. 41 on p. 220; pp. 222-224; VII, pp. 238-239; ISTH, II, 5, p. 130-131; cf. Aquinas, 1a 2ae q. 62 a. 3 ad 2; 1a 2ae q. 112 a. 5 ad 32a 2ae q. 1 a. 5 ad 1; 2a 2ae a. 1 a. 4 ad 3; 2a 2ae q. 2 a. 9 ad 3; 2a 2ae q. 5 a. 2; Quodlibetum, II, 6; On Truth, q. 10 a. 10 ad 1; Commentary on Boethius on the Trinity, q. 3 a. 1 ad 4; Commentary on the Sentences, Prologue, III, 3). It is worthwhile examining three quotes of Rousselot on this matter:

> Grace can make us see, it does not just add objective instruction or subjective affective impulsion, but grace can cause someone to perceive, with an objective and true certitude, reasons that would only be probable for natural intelligence left to its own resources ("EF," I, p. 41).
> ... the light of grace, when falling on a sign which in the eyes of natural reason is only probable, makes of it an instrument of certain assent, then

we realize that the faith of the uneducated can be intellectually as certain while being rationally less communicable than the faith of the educated, and that there are not just five or six in the Church who possess reasons for belief that are objectively valid (ELK, VI, pp. 221-222).

And if for the proofs of faith the second element is necessarily a super-natural light, there is no contradiction in saying both that these proofs have an objective value that is fully satisfactory, and that grace is nevertheless required to perceive and affirm them. It is exact to say that 'they call for the assent of every reasonable human' but only because it is exact to add that a truly reasonable judgment about Christ, the Church, the Scriptures can be made only with the help of God's grace. ... they are both absolutely legitimate and undeniably inefficacious if God does not open the soul's eyes ("EF," II, p. 63).[50]

Besides having many supporters in France (Rousselot) and Belgium (Maréchal), Transcendental Thomism also was prominent in Austria and Germany. Its rise coincided with the defeat of National Socialism which allowed the Catholic Church to blossom in Austria and Germany. Hence in Austria the Vienna Catholic Academy was founded in 1945 and Concordats of 1957, 1960, 1962, 1964, and 1968 restored church property seized by the Nazis and instituted a state tax to support the Austrian Catholic Church (including private Catholic schools) and stipulated the teaching of religion in state schools (freedom of religion was established in Austria in 1961 for Protestants and in 1967 for the Orthodox). In Germany Catholics increasingly gained political power through the rule of the Catholic Konrad Adenauer (1876-1976) and his Christian Democratic Union (1950-1966). Accordingly, the Pulpit Laws of the Kulturkampf were finally repealed in 1953, and the Catholic charitable organizations Misereor (1958) and Adveniat (1961) were founded, as well as the Christian Trade Union (1959). More recent times have seen the rise of the Catholic University of Eichstätt (1980) and the Gustav-Siewerth Academy in Weilhelm-Bierbronnen (1988), as well as the 1999 Joint Declaration on the Doctrine of Justification between Catholics and Lutherans (later joined by the Methodists in 2006). Incidentally, the Gustav-Sierwerth Academy was founded by the theologian Joseph Ratzinger who became Pope Benedict XVI in 2005, the first German pope since the Middle Ages.

The most famous Catholic theologian of the twentieth century is perhaps the German **Karl Rahner, S.J. (1904-1984)**.[51] Karl Rahner was born in 1904 in Freiburg, Germany. In 1922 he entered the Jesuit novitiate at Feldkirch in Vorarlberg, Austria following in the footsteps of his older brother Hugo. He then engaged in philosophical studies at Feldkirch and Pullach from 1924-1927 where he came under the influence of the Belgian Jesuit Joseph Maréchal. After studying theology at Valkenburg in the Netherlands from 1929 to 1933 he was ordained a priest in 1932. Rahner then pursued advanced philosophical studies at the University of Freiburg from 1934-1936 where he attended lectures given by Martin Heidegger. Rahner, however, never received an advanced degree in philosophy as his dissertation on Aquinas was rejected by his doctoral director Martin Honecker as being too unfaithful to Aquinas. He thus switched to theological studies at Innsbruck from 1936 to 1937 and received his habilitation in theology in 1937. Rahner started his teaching career as a lecturer in theology at Innsbruck from 1937 to 1939. After the University of Innsbruck was shut down by the Nazi's he undertook some pastoral work in Vienna and Bavaria for the next five years. He returned to academia at the Pullach Theologate from 1945 until 1948 when he went back to Innsbruck and taught there for the next sixteen years. In 1962 he became subject to preliminary censorial regulations from Rome but nothing came of it and indeed he was prominent at the Second Vatican Council as an expert [*peritus*].[52] In 1962 he also entered into a relationship with the German novelist and Green Party politician Luise Rinser (1911-2002), and though they had pet names for each other and exchanged over 2000 letters there is no evidence their relationship went beyond a Platonic level. From 1964 to 1967 he became professor at the University of Munich, taking over the chair held by Romano Guardini, and from 1967 to 1971 at the University of Münster. He finished his career as emeritus professor at Munich (1971-1981) and Innsbruck (1981-1984). Rahner died in 1984 in Innsbruck, Austria and is buried in the Jesuit Church of the Trinity there.

Rahner received numerous accolades throughout his career including an appointment to the International Theological Commission in 1969, the Père Marquette Discovery Award (1979), and around fifteen honorary degrees at such places as the University of Chicago (1974), Georgetown (1974) and Fordham (1980). There are also various societies dedicated to his study such as the Philosophy and Theology Society (1986-) at Marquette University and the Karl Rahner Society (1991-) which is currently hosted at St. John's Seminary in Camarillo, California. Journals dedicated to Rahner include *Philosophy and Theology* (1985-) and the *Karl Rahner Society Bulletin* (1992-).

Karl Rahner's key philosophical work is his *Hearer of the Word* [*Hörer des Wortes*] [HW] (1941; 1963; 1971 [revised by his student Johannes Baptist Metz]).[53]

Although gaining his fame as a theologian, Karl Rahner as we noted started off as a philosopher, and indeed his theology is directly tied to his philosophy, a philosophy influenced by Georg Wilhelm Friedrich Hegel, Pierre Rousselot, Joseph Maréchal, and Martin Heidegger.

Rahner, following Heidegger, claims that the nature of the human is to be a questioning being. Hence philosophy should begin with an analysis of the human spirit as it seeks to know the world, that is to say, with a transcendental reflection upon the *a priori* conditions of human knowing. For, as Rahner metaphorically puts it, by knowing the properties of a keyhole we can know what kind of key can fit in it (HW, I, pp. 3-4, 9; II, pp. 11, 15-16; III, pp. 26-27; VI, pp. 55, 58-59; SPW, Introduction, pp. 19, 21; I, pp. 57-59; FCF, Introduction, p. 19; TI, IX, 2, pp. 28-45; XI, 3, pp. 84-101; XIII, 10, p. 163).

In developing his transcendental approach to philosophy Rahner turns to Aquinas and asserts that in knowledge I first observe the world through my senses and form an image (phantasm) of the object observed. The next step of knowing occurs when I go on to abstract a universal concept from this phantasm. In this way I grasp a singular object under a universal concept (essence; quiddity); or conversely, I refer a universal concept to a 'this' (for example referring the universal concept 'dog' to this dog here 'Fido'). Therefore in an act of abstraction I come to know the essence or quiddity of a particular sense object and moreover that this essence may be detached from that particular object and applied to others as well. In sum, to abstract is to grasp that the quiddity given in an individual object is unlimited and can determine various objects (HW, V, pp. 45-46; SPW, III, pp. 120-124, 139). Secondly, as a knowing spirit I subsist in myself, and yet I also exist in a world of objects which I oppose to myself. For in a judgment I posit an object as known but yet distinct from myself. So in knowing even though I grasp myself as a subject standing apart from the object of my judgment, at the same time I become this object in some way (HW, IV, pp. 42-44; SPW, Introduction, pp. 20, 40-41, 51, 54; I,

p. 75; III, pp. 117-118, 133; TI, v. VI, XII, pp. 153-177). Given this inventory of the steps of knowing, Rahner asks what transcendental conditions allow for such acts of knowledge.

According to Rahner, what allows for knowledge of this sort to occur is the operation of our agent intellect, specifically in terms of what he calls our pre-apprehension [*Vorgriff*; literally anticipation]. Rahner characterizes this pre-apprehension as a reaching beyond individual objects [*excessus* (transgression)] toward [*Woraufhin* (wither)] the absolute range of all possible objects (toward being as such, and ultimately toward God as we will see). The *Vorgriff* then is "the a priori power given with human nature. It is the dynamic movement of the spirit toward the absolute range of all possible objects [i.e. of all being]" (HW, V, p. 47); or again it is "[the] unthematic but ever-present knowledge of the infinity of reality" (FCF, I, p. 33). So according to Rahner humans have an antecedent comprehension of being in its totality and this is a precondition for knowledge.

Rahner, in arguing for the existence of this pre-apprehension of total being, appeals to the fact that knowing involves grasping that a quiddity is in this case limited to a singular sense object. Now the fact that one is aware of this limitation is in itself significant. For in order for a limit to be known as a limit, one must have gone beyond the limit, reached out to something more, indeed to the unlimited as such. So in order to know the limited and the finite, one must have a pre-apprehension of unlimited and infinite being (indeed the very fact that one can ask about being shows one already knows about being in its totality).

Rahner consequently draws the conclusion that the abstraction of a concept occurs due to an intellectual dynamism of the human intellect which places the phantasm against the horizon of Absolute Being. For the human intellect is constantly reaching beyond individual objects and seeking the absolute range of all possible objects, and this allows it to apply a universal concept to our sense-datum and grasp that this concept is realizable in other similar beings. Moreover, when we experience the limit of a singular object, we experience it as an obstacle that we want to get beyond. We grasp it as a particular stage of a larger finality (a stage on our way to pure being). In this way we profile or set the object against the backdrop of the absolute range of all knowledge, against the horizon of unlimited being, and so oppose it to ourselves and see it as objective (HW, III, pp. 32-33; V, pp. 46-48, 50; VIII, p.

78; X, pp. 100-102, 104, 106; XII, p. 119; XIII, pp. 130-131; XIV, pp. 140-141; cf. SPW, Introduction, pp. 21, 23; n. 8 on p. 26; pp. 44-46, 48, 52-54; I, pp. 61-63, 66-68; II, pp. 79-81; III, pp. 140-145, 156-156, 169-170, 183-187, 202, 216, 220-226, 231; IV, pp. 237-241, 267, 280-286, 292-296, 298, 313, 319, 379-383; Conclusion, n. 9 on p. 390; pp. 390-391, 394-400, 402-404; FCF, Introduction, p. 20; I, p. 33; TI, XVIII, 5, pp. 95-97). Rahner thus states:

> [the agent intellect] is the spontaneity of the human spirit, which spontaneity is dynamically ordered to the totality of possible objects and as such already anticipates [vorwegnimmt] in its dynamic orientation the totality of all objects according to their most universal metaphysical structure ... Thus the agent intellect apprehends the individual determination of sensibility (phantasm) in its dynamic orientation to the totality of all possible objects, to esse [being]. ... Insofar as it apprehends this material of sensibility within its anticipatory dynamism to esse [being], it illuminates this material, gives it those metaphysical structures of being which were expressed in the first principles; its actuality becomes that of the actually intelligible, and thus lets the universal be known in the sensible (SPW, III, p. 225).
>
> By preapprehension [Vorgriff] we mean the a priori power, given with the very nature of the spirit, to represent to oneself the single quiddities brought up by the receptive sense knowledge in a dynamic a priori reaching out of the spirit for the absolute range of its possible objects. ... Thus from the start an object is always already seen under the horizon of the last end of the spirit as such (HW, XII, pp. 121-122).

Now to say that objects are grasped as moments of an unending movement of the spirit to absolute being, is just to say that knowledge is possible as our agent intellect is dynamically directed to unlimitedness and infiniteness as such, i.e. to God (HW, V, pp. 51-52, 54; IX, p. 92). Human knowledge then is a continual process of reaching beyond limited finite objects to that which is fully knowable and perfect in itself, God. Hence all knowledge is based on a pre-reflective awareness of God, the absolute and perfect being who is the source of all exemplifications of being (HW, pp. 53-54; FCF, Introduction, p. 21; SPW, III, p. 179-181; TI, IV, 7, pp. 178-179; VI, 16, p. 244). Rahner proclaims:

> ... the illuminating anticipation [Vorgriff] toward Being in general and thus to the absolute self-illumination of Being in the being which possesses Being absolutely is the preceding condition even of the first con-

ceptual knowledge, so that in this latter God is implicitly known (HW, VIII, p. 85).

As suggested by the above quote, God is thus implicitly and unthematically known (pre-apprehended) in every act of knowledge, not as an object, but as the necessary and always already fulfilled condition of all knowledge and action. God is co-affirmed as absolute and infinite being with every item of knowledge (HW, V, pp. 51-52; FCF, Introduction, pp. 21-22; II, pp. 52-54, 57-58; NG, II, p. 84; III, pp. 110-114; SPW, Conclusion, p. 388; DYBG, V, pp. 67-69, 74). To quote Rahner "the Vorgriff aims at God. Not as if it intended God so immediately that it should immediately represent the absolute being in its own self, as an object, and make this being immediately known in itself. The Vorgriff intends God's absolute being in this sense that the absolute being is always and basically co-affirmed by the basically unlimited range of the Vorgriff" (HW, V, p. 51).

The weighty conclusion Rahner draws from this is that God is present in each human soul at each instant and not just on special occasions. God is the absolute being known implicitly in all that we know (as the infinite and unlimited being and perfect fulfillment toward which we are striving). God is the intimate infinite always already there, to use a neologism of Heidegger (HW, VI, pp. 61-62; VIII, pp. 82-84; SPW, III-IV, pp. 195, 284; Conclusion, pp. 406-407). We thus are on the way to God and in fact reach the eternal idea of the True, Good, and Beautiful God at every moment of our existence (as Rahner nicely phrases it "every land is the holy land and every time the fullness of time") (HW, I, pp. 4, 7; DYBG, V, pp. 67-69, 74).

It can even be said, following Blondel, that human nature is always graced to some degree. Or in one of Rahner's favorite expressions, humans possess as a fundamental structure a "supernatural existential" [übernatürliche Existential], a superformed nature wherein a pre-apprehension of God as their infinite and good creator and blessed end occurs (TI, II, 1, p. 1-88; X, 2, pp. 33-35; FCF, IV-V, pp. 127-133, 170-172; DYBG, I, pp. 6-8; NG, V, pp. 119-120, 129-137; TI, I, 9, pp. 311-316; IV, 7, pp. 178-179). As Rahner puts it: "Even prior to justification by sanctifying grace ... the human already stands under the universal, infralapsarian salvific will of God ... it of course supervenes through grace upon the human's essence as nature, but in the real order is never lacking to it. ... all humans permanently stand under the offer of grace really operative in them. This permanent and ever-present offer is always accepted in their moral activity, unless they shut themselves to it by their own moral guilt" ("Existence, Theological," *Sacramentum Mundi*, II, p. 306).

Indeed, according to Rahner, members of other religious confessions, and agnostics and atheists, have an implicit and unthematic knowledge of God and so in a sense are "anonymous Christians" [*Die anonymen Christen*] (that is, if they do not reject the divine). For, as we have seen, it belongs to the fundamental human makeup to be oriented towards absolute and unlimited being, and so all human spirits are always already open to the absolute and Trinitarian being of God, even if they are unaware of it (HW, V, pp. 52, 54; VII, pp. 67-68; VIII, p. 77).[54] Rahner expounds:

> To be a human is to be a spirit, to live life while reaching ceaselessly for the absolute, in openness toward God ... we are always already on the way to God, whether or not we know it expressly, whether or not we will it. We are forever the infinite openness of the finite for God (HW, V, p. 53).

Furthermore, if atheists implicitly accept God and the moral good in their judgments and free acts to the extent that they are capable, they can be saved: "The person who accepts a moral demand from his conscience as absolutely valid for him and embraces it as such in a free act of affirmation, no matter how unreflected, asserts the absolute being of God" ("Atheism and Implicit Christianity," TI, IX, p. 153; cf. TI, V, 1, pp. 10-12, V, 6, pp. 97-134; VI, 23, pp. 390-298; IX, 9, pp. 145-164; IX, 11, pp. 169-184; X, 2, pp. 30-49; X, 17, pp. 318-349; XI, 7, pp. 166-184; XIV, 17, pp. 280-294; XVI, 4, pp. 52-59; XVI, XIII, pp. 199-224; XVIII, 17, pp. 288-295; XXI, 12, pp. 171-184; FCF, VI-VII, pp. 311-313, 343-345).

Still even though God and God's grace are present in all humans, the God known by preapprehension (*Vorgriff*) is in many ways inaccessible. For in pre-apprehension we only affirm the infinite as the unthematized whither [*Woraufhun*] of the movement of the spirit beyond the finite to the infinite. God is therefore not grasped as an object, nor even conceptualized, as God is always at the perimeter or horizon of our thinking. God manifests Himself to us instead in an implicit and non-representational manner. It is not even too much of a stretch to consider God as the great unknown to natural reason, since there is an essential hiddenness and mysteriousness of infinite being (HW, I, p. 9; VI, pp. 58-60, 63; VII, pp. 70-71; XIV, p. 141; FCF, II, pp. 60-63, 65-66, 73; SPW, III, p. 182; Conclusion, pp. 401, 408; TI, XI, 6, pp. 149-165; XIII, 8, pp. 122-132; XVI, 14, p. 238; XVIII, 5, pp. 91-92). So Rahner remarks: "Humanity stands before God as before one who is at least for a time unknown. For God is the Infinite, whom we can know as infinite only by denying the finite and referring to that which lies beyond any finiteness. ... God remains hidden in the positive content of divine infinity" (HW, VI, p. 64). Again he asserts "transcendental experience as such, an experience in which He whom we call 'God' encounters the human in silence, encounters him as the absolute and the incomprehensible, as the term of his transcendence which cannot really be incorporated into any system of coordinates ... the holy mystery" (FCF, Introduction, p. 21).

This being the case, philosophy must be ready to complete itself with theology according to Rahner. For we can recognize the possibility that the unknown or partially known God would desire to grant us a more complete knowledge of Himself. That is to say, besides granting us our basic preapprehension or openness to God, God can also freely choose, through a special divine Revelation, to make Himself more than a mere hiddenness or unknown absolute, or the final whither of our transcendence (HW, III, p. 28; IV, p. 36, 40-41, 44; V, pp. 53-54; VI, p. 64; VII, pp 68-70, 72; VIII, pp. 76-77; IX, p. 94; XIV, pp. 140-141; X, pp. 106-107; XI, p. 112; XIII, pp. 132-135; XIV, pp. 139-140, 146-149; SPW, Conclusion, p. 408). Rahner thus follows Blondel's model of Christian Philosophy wherein philosophy points beyond itself and invites us to listen with reverent attention for an eventual supernatural revelation of God (HW, II, pp. 16-20; FCF, I, pp. 24-25; TI, XIII, 4, pp. 61-79; IX, 3, pp. 46-63; IX, 6, pp. 71-81). Rahner hence writes "the true philosophy of religion is in final analysis nothing but the command given to humanity to listen into history whether God's Word has not resounded in it" (HW, II, p. 21; cf. HW, I, pp. 5-8; II, pp. 11, 19; III, p. 23). Necessarily, such a revelation would take a historical form, for it cannot be permanently coexistent with all moments in history or this removes God's freedom. Rahner thus calls humans to the task of becoming "Hearers of the Word," to search history for signs of God's self-communication (special revelation) and be ready to graciously welcome the depths of God found therein (HW, I, pp. 5, 9; II, pp. 16, 21-22; V, pp. 53-54; VI, p. 55). In Rahner's words:

We are the beings of receptive spirituality, who stand in freedom before the free God of a possible revelation, which, if it comes, happens in our history through the Word. We are the ones who, in our history, listen for the Word of the free God (HW, XIV, p. 142).

Ultimately Rahner finds that such a revelation has occurred in the person of Christ.[55]

Another Transcendental Thomist was the Canadian Bernard Lonergan, about whom *Time* magazine wrote in 1970, "Canadian Jesuit Bernard J.F. Lonergan is considered by many intellectuals to be the finest philosophic thinker of the 20th century" ("The Answer is the Question," *Time Magazine*, April 20, 1970).[57] Such a quote shows the heights to which Catholic Transcendental Thomists ascended in the Twentieth Century.

Bernard Lonergan, S.J. (1904-1984) amazingly had the same birth and death year as Rahner. Lonergan was born in Buckingham, Quebec, Canada in 1904. He attended the Jesuit-run Loyola College in Montreal from 1918-1922 and entered the Society of Jesus himself in 1922. He then completed classical studies at Guelph, Ontario, from 1922 to 1926, and philosophy at Heythrop College in England, receiving a bachelor's degree in philosophy in 1929 (after which he studied language and math at the University of London for a year). In 1930, Lonergan returned to Canada where he taught at his old school of Loyola College. His initial foray into teaching was brief, however, and in 1933 Lonergan was sent to the Gregorian University in Rome to pursue graduate theological studies. He was ordained in 1936 and attained his S.T.D. in theology in 1940. Lonergan went back to Canada for a second time and taught theology first at l'Immaculée-Conception Seminary in Montreal from 1940 to 1946 and then at Regis College in Toronto from 1947 to 1953. In 1953, however, once again he found himself in Rome where he taught at the Gregorian University until 1965 when he was diagnosed with lung cancer. He garnered much fame in theology and was appointed an expert (*peritus*) at the Second Vatican Council. In 1965 he reseated himself at Regis College, Toronto where he taught until 1975 (with a one-year stint as a Stillman Professor at Harvard in 1971-1972). Lonergan had struggled with alcoholism throughout his life and sought treatment at Guest House in Rochester, Minnesota in 1973 but continued to have problems thereafter. Lonergan ended his teaching career at Boston College beginning in 1975 and retiring in 1983. He died in 1984 of colon cancer at a Jesuit Infirmary in Pickering, Ontario.[58]

Lonergan received 19 honorary doctorates, was named to the International Theological Commission (1969), received the Aquinas Medal of the American Catholic Philosophical Association (1970), and was made Companion of the Order of Canada (1971), and Fellow of the British Academy (1975). Lonergan's influence is readily apparent and there are Bernard Lonergan Archives at Marquette University and the Gregorian University in Rome; a Lonergan Centre for Ethical Reflection at Concordia University, Montreal, Canada; a Lonergan Centre at St. Paul University, in Ottawa, Canada; a Lonergan Institute at Boston College; a British Lonergan Association; the Lonergan Communications Center in Cebu City, Philippines and a Lonergan Center in Manila, Philippines; an Asian Lonergan Association; a Dublin Lonergan Centre; a now defunct Lonergan Center at Santa Clara University (1982-1995); a Lonergan Centre in Sydney, Australia; a Lonergan Institute in Seton Hall; a Lonergan Research Institute at Regis College, Toronto, Canada; a Lonergan Institute at St. Anselm's Abbey, Washington, D.C.; and a Los Angeles Lonergan Center at Loyola Marymount University. There are also several journals dedicated to Lonergan studies: Lonergan Workshop Journal (1973-), Lonergan Studies Newsletter (1980-), Method: Journal of Lonergan Studies (1983-), The Lonergan Research Institute Bulletin (1984-), Lonergan Review: A Multidisciplinary Journal (1992-), and Journal of Macrodynamic Analysis (2000-). Finally Lonergan's philosophy influenced the founder of Montessori schools in 1948 in England and the United States, namely, Phyllis Wallbank.[59]

Lonergan's key works are Insight: A Study of Human Understanding [IN] (1957; 1958; 1970; 1978; 1992) and Method in Theology [MT] (1972).[60]

Lonergan, influenced by the epistemological writings of John Henry Newman and Joseph Maréchal, considered himself a 'methodologist.' He can also be classified as a Transcendental Thomist in that his Thomism focuses on epistemology and the subject as opposed to metaphysics, though there are important differences between his Thomism and that of the other Transcendental Thomists.

As indicated by the subtitle of his sizeable work Insight (1957), Lonergan wanted to explore human understanding, and answer the question: What am I doing when I am knowing? In particular, he wanted to work out a transcendental method reflecting the cognitional operations occurring in all acts of knowing, i.e. the conditions of the possibility of knowing any object (MT, I, p. 13; n. 4 on pp. 13-14; C, X, pp. 152-155; SC, XII, p. 207; S, pp. 2-5; PTPII, X, pp. 189-190; XII, pp. 246-248; XV, p. 294; XXI, pp. 393-395; XXII, pp. 430-431; V, V, pp. 222-224). Or as Lonergan phased it, he wanted to develop, not a set of rules for a dolt, but "a normative pattern of recurrent and related operations yielding cumulative and progressive results" (MT, I, p. 4; cf. MT, Introduction, pp. xi-xii; I, pp. 4-5, 13-14, 20, 24). In this way he hoped to develop a methodical, critical, and comprehensive philosophy as well as to "assist the reader in effecting a personal appropriation of the concrete dynamic structure immanent and recurrently operative in his own cognitional activities" for all cognitional processes at bottom share the same pattern (IN, Introduction, p. 11; cf. IN, Introduction, pp. 6, 13-14, 16-17, 22-23; III, p. 97; Epilogue, p. 753; MT, I, p. 13; IV, p. 125).

Such a method is valuable for study of the invariant dynamic pattern of human knowing reveals not just how we understand but also sets limits to all that can be understood (IN, Preface, pp. 3-4, 6-7; Introduction, pp. 12, 16-17, 20; II, p. 57; IV, pp. 139-140; XIV, pp. 424-425; XIX, p. 708; Epilogue, p. 754; MT, I, p. 25; III, p. 83; IX, pp. 212-213, 219; X, p. 261; XII, pp. 297, 316; PTPI, II, p. 31). Hence Lonergan's famous turn of phrase: "Thoroughly understand what it is to understand, and not only will you understand the broad lines of all there is to be understood but also you will possess a fixed base, an invariant pattern, opening upon all future developments of understanding" (IN, Introduction, p. 22; cf. IN, Epilogue, pp. 769-770).

Now according to Lonergan the key invariant pattern of cognition is that all acts of understanding occur through an insight. That is to say, knowledge involves not just adverting to data, nor even combining data together, but a special act of understanding going beyond this called 'insight.' With this in mind, Lonergan defines insight as a "distinct activity of organizing intelligence that places the full set of clues in a unique explanatory perspective" (IN, Preface, p. 3; cf. V, I, pp. 27-28, 38; MT, VIII, pp. 179, 186, 188, 190; IX, p. 213; XIII, p. 345; PTPI, II, p. 32; X, pp. 216-220; UB, II, pp. 38-43; THC, IX, p. 141). Now Lonergan considers an insight to be *a priori* as "it goes beyond what is merely given to sense or to empirical consciousness"

(IN, Preface, p. 5; cf. IN, Preface, p. 3; MT, III, p. 77; XI, p. 293). Yet it is also synthetic because "it adds to the merely given an explanatory unification or organization" (IN, Preface, p. 5). An insight then begins with observations but goes beyond them in framing an explanatory organization for them; it "grasps in given or imagined presentations an intelligible form emergent in the presentations" (IN, IX, p. 300). In simpler terms, an insight seeks to uncover intelligible patterns (intelligible organizations) present in sense-data (IN, XII, p. 347; MT, I, p. 10; III, p. 92). To have an insight then in Lonergan's words is "to get the point, to have a clue, to catch on, to see things in a new light, to grasp how things hang together, to come to know why, the reason, the explanation, the cause" (IN, XI, p. 348; cf. IN, I, p. 44; VI, p. 196, 209, 213, 224; VII, p. 268; VIII, pp. 293-295).

Lonergan gives four examples of insights: 1) The reader who finally puts together the clues to a murder in a mystery novel;[61] 2) Archimedes who recognized that he could tell whether a crown was made of pure gold or not by putting it in a pot of water and seeing how much water was displaced [the hydrostatic principle];[62] 3) Recognizing, as "every schoolboy knows," the definition of a circle as "a locus of coplanar points equidistant from a center"; 4) Recognizing the sequence of positive integers as $n+1$; i.e. 1, 2, 3, 4, etc.[63] Yet insight occurs in all walks of life—in farmers, craftsmen, employers, workers, doctors, lawyers, politicians, in industry and commerce, finance, journalism, public relations, in the homeyard, in sport, in the arts (IN, VI, p. 196; XV, p. 483).

Now study of such insights allows us to gain "an insight into insight." It allows us to see that insights presuppose data (Lonergan is thus an empiricist): either sense perceptions (experience) or mental images. For example, in order to formulate the insight of a circle we need to imagine a center (hub) with equal radii (spokes) extending to an edge (rim). These experiences or images then give rise to a question (Why?) due to our drive to know (what Lonergan also calls our wonder, eros, or "detached and disinterested desire to know"). From the question we get a hint, clue, suspicion, or suggestion as to its solution. Finally we formulate an insight (abstraction) through an inner cognitional process (which occurs frequently in the intelligent and rarely in the stupid notes Lonergan). These insights yield concepts (such as i.e. the first hydrostatic principle, or the concept of a circle), and so pivot between the concrete (sensation or imagination) and the abstract (i.e. the concept, an abstract principle applicable to diverse situations such as the principles of displacement and specific gravity). We now possess an act of understanding (a conceptual insight) which we may judge true or false, necessary or probable (IN, Preface, pp. 4, 6, 8; Introduction, pp. 34-35, 43; I, pp. 28-30, 33-34; II, pp. 58, 60, 69, 71; III, p. 116; VI, p. 196; XI, p. 357; XIV, p. 418; XVI, p. 555; MT, I, p. 18, 22). He writes:

> This primordial drive, then, is the pure question. It is prior to any in-sights, any concepts, any words; for insights, concepts, words have to do with answers, and before we look for answers we want them; such want-ing is the pure question. On the other hand, though the pure question is prior to insights, concepts, and words, it presupposes experiences and images. Just as insight is into the concretely given or imagined, so the pure question is about the concretely given or imagined (IN, I, p.34).

Ultimately, says Lonergan, we find that the invariant pattern of hu-man knowing takes the form of a fourfold level of human conscious-ness. First there is the empirical consciousness [level of presentations or attention]. Here we make observations of data, i.e. experience, perceptions, and images (either data of sense such as colors, shapes, sounds, etc., or data of consciousness such as seeing, hearing, tasting, smelling, touching, perceiving, imagining, inquiring, understanding, formulating, reflecting, judging). This level of consciousness is thus that of observing or imagining and supplies raw material (data) to the next levels.

Next there is the intelligent consciousness [level of understanding]. Here one grasps an immanent intelligent form in the data (either we grasp a thing, what Lonergan calls a unity-identity-whole, or we grasp an intelligible pattern or law). Hence we have an insight into the data and formulate a concept based on this insight. This then constitutes the level of conceiving, defining, thinking, supposing, and considering.

Thirdly is the rational consciousness [level of reflection]. Here we use our reason to verify our conceptual formulations. This yields judg-ments that are true or false, certain or probable. This is the level of affirming or denying, assenting or dissenting.

Finally there is the responsible or moral consciousness [level of de-liberation, evaluation, or decision]. Here we grasp moral values and make moral decisions for which we are responsible. And at its high-est peak we experience being-in-love (IN, Introduction, pp. 13, 20;

III, p. 100, 106, 122; IV, p. 139; VIII, pp. 277-278, 282, 295; IX, pp. 296-302; X, p. 334, 346-348; XI, p. 360; XII, pp. 381, 389; XIII, p. 399, 407; XIV, p. 410; XII, p. 423, 425, 426, 441; XV, p. 467; XVI, p. 522-523, 542-545; XVII, p. 558, 581-585; XVIII, p. 634; XIX, p. 667, 697-698; XX, pp. 725-726, 732; Epilogue, p. 757; MT, I, pp. 11-14, 16, 18, 20, 22, 24; II, p. 35; III, pp. 73-74, 86, 90, 93-94; IV, pp. 102-106, 115, 120-121; V, p. 141; VII, pp. 157, 167; VIII, pp. 178, 181, 185, 187-188, 190; IX, pp. 202, 213; X, pp. 243, 264; XI, pp. 268, 285-286; XII, p. 316; XIII, p. 340, 348; XIV, pp. 358, 364; V, I, pp. 47-49; II, pp. 60-61, 71-78, 93-94; VI, pp. 192-196; PHL, Appendix, pp. 322-323; UB, I, pp. 14-17, VII, pp. 163-169; C, X, pp. 158-164; XIV, pp. 222-224; SC, IX, p. 127; THC, IX, pp. 131-133, 142-144; XIII, pp. 205-206; PTPII, XXI, pp. 396-398, 400; S, pp. 13-15, 20-21).[64] To quote Lonergan in his delineation of the cognitional structure:

> Experiencing is only the first level of knowing: it presents the matter to be known. Understanding is only the second level of knowing: it defines the matter to be known. Knowing reaches a complete increment only with judgment, only when the merely experienced has been thought and the merely thought has been affirmed. ... Experience is for inquiring into being. Intelligence is for thinking out being. But by judgment being is known, and in judgment what is known is known as being (IN, XII, p. 381).
>
> There is the empirical level on which we sense, perceive, imagine, feel, speak, move. There is the intellectual level on which we inquire, come to understand, express what we have understood, work out the presuppositions and implications of our expression. There is the rational level on which we reflect, marshal the evidence, pass judgment on the truth or falsity, certainty or probability, of a statement. There is the responsible level on which we are concerned with ourselves, our own operations, our goals, and so deliberate about possible courses of action, evaluate them, decide, and carry out our decisions (MT, I, p. 9).

Since Lonergan asserts that knowing is a three-stage process (involving observation, formulation of insights, and the determination of the correctness of the insights) he criticizes the radical empiricism of Hume which asserts that knowing is merely a matter of acquiring sense impressions and then combining them. For this ignores the other levels of consciousness. Besides observation, one has to have a conceptual insight into the significance of the sense-data and, as it were, add a set of intelligible relations to the elements of experience (abstraction). Finally one needs to judge the truth of the abstracted concept. Knowing is thus not merely "taking a look" or experiencing, but beyond this understanding (grasping an intelligible pattern in the data) and judging (IN, Introduction, p. 12; VI, p. 206; XII, pp. 383, 396-397; XIV, pp. 437, 441, 449-450; XV, p. 465; XVI, pp. 529, 552; XIX, pp. 669, 675, 683; MT, I, p. 16; III, p. 76; IX, pp. 213-214; C, XIV, pp. 232-236; PTPI, II, p. 39, IX, p. 199). He writes: "Knowing, accordingly, is not just seeing; it is experiencing, understand, judging, and believing. The criteria of objectivity are not just the criteria of ocular vision; they are the compounded criteria of experiencing, of understanding, of judging, and of believing. The reality known is not just looked at; it is given in experience, organized and extrapolated by understanding, posited by judgment and belief" (MT, X, p. 238).

So too Lonergan is anti-Kantian. Rather than insights being purely *a priori* generations of the human mind, they are detections of real patterns in data; they are uncoverings of immanent intelligibilities. Insights then while they go beyond the data are not pure creations of the mind, rather they reveal the nature of external reality (IN, XIV, p. 439; XIX, p. 664; MT, X, p. 264; PTPI, X, pp. 231-234).[65]

As knowing is not taking a look, reality cannot be limited a priori to what is sensible or known in the extroverted biological consciousness, i.e. to material bodies, or what Lonergan calls the "already out there now real." Rather what is real is whatever can be verified by the threefold process of human cognition: experience, insight, and verification. In other words, the real is not identifiable with the ocular but the verifiable. Therefore we can know not just observable entities such as Fido the dog or a tree (proportionate being), but also scientific entities which we do not directly observe but which we can postulate in terms of observables such as an electron or an element in the periodic table, as well as spiritual entities such as human souls and God (transcendent being) (IN, III, pp. 95, 123; VII, p. 260; VIII, pp. 271-283, 291-295; XI, p. 362; XIII, pp. 383, 399-404; XIV, pp. 410-411, 413-417, 448-450; XV, pp. 456, 465; XVI, pp. 513, 519, 523-525, 529, 540; XIX, pp. 656-658, 663-665, 708; Epilogue, p 760; MT, I, pp. 15016; IX, pp. 238-239; X, pp. 262-264; XII, p. 303; SC, IX, pp. 123-124; UB, IV, pp. 103-108; PTPI, IV, pp. 90-93; SC, IX, pp. 124-127, 129-130; PTPII, XII, p. 249).[66]

Furthermore, as we have seen, humans have a detached and disinterested desire to know, a restless dynamism of the mind. In fact humans desire to know all that is real. Thus the eros of the mind, the drive to understand (see why and explain), which is just as much a part of our nature as is eating, sleeping, talking, or loving, is an unrestricted demand for intelligibility. We seek to know everything about everything (IN, Introduction, p. 20; I, p. 28, 34; II, p. 91; III, p. 113; VI, pp. 198, 208; VII, pp. 247, 255; XI, p. 354, 356; XII, pp. 389-390; XV, pp. 483, 498; XVIII, p. 619; XIX, pp. 699, 701, 707-708; XX, pp. 723, 749; MT, I, pp. 10, 13; II, pp. 35-36; III, p. 84; C, V, pp. 84-85; X, p. 157; XII, pp. 198-199; UB, Appendix, pp. 266-270, 370; PHL, IV, pp. 111-114). On account of our detached, disinterested, and unrestricted desire to know we humans reject any obscurantism no matter how slight. Rather than eliminating questions (let's forget it), we must seek to answer them (IN, Introduction, p. 23; XIX, pp. 659, 661-662, 697-698, 705-706; MT, I, p. 12). Lonergan asserts: "The rejection of any and every partial obscurity is the demand that no question whatever is to be met arbitrarily, that every question is to be submitted to the process of intelligent grasp and critical reflection" (IN, XIX, p. 661).

In light of this, Lonergan develops a unique argument for God in his *Insight*, one of the first new arguments for God since the Middle Ages—what is now called an argument from intelligibility (IN, XIX, pp. 695; Epilogue, p. 765; PTPII, I, pp. 4-9). Formally the argument is:

Minor Premise: The real is completely intelligible
Major Premise: If the real is completely intelligible God exists
Conclusion: God exists

Let us examine each premise in turn. The minor premise says that the real is completely intelligible. Now Lonergan defines being as the objective of the detached, disinterested, and unrestricted desire to know, and so its limit is found in answering every intelligent question. Being, in other words, is what is to be known by the totality of true judgments; it is the totality of all that is (IN, XII, p. 372-374, 376-378, 382, 384-385, 387, 393, 396, 398; XIV, p. 416; XVI, pp. 523-525, 539, 544-546; XVII, pp. 573-576; XIX, pp. 662, 665-668; UB, VI, pp. 146-149).

Moreover, as this desire to know is unrestricted—as it is a desire to know everything about everything—being itself must be unrestricted and completely intelligible (otherwise our unrestricted desire to know will be frustrated). So the real is completely intelligible (IN, XII, pp. 373-374, 376; XVI, pp. 523-525, 539, 545-546; XVII, pp. 573-576; XIX, pp. 668, 674-678; 695-696; UB, VI, pp. 146-149).

The major premise postulates that if the real is completely intelligible then God exists. This is so because if complete intelligibility exists then it must occur as an omniscient spiritual act (for it would be an intelligibility that knows everything about everything and which is intrinsically independent of any empirical residue). That is to say, if the real is completely intelligible, then there must exist not just an unrestricted desire of understanding (i.e. a human intellect), but an unrestricted act of understanding (a divine intellect). Moreover, if we restrict knowledge to proportionate being alone, we allow for mere matters of fact without explanation which is unintelligible. We must then appeal to a transcendent formally unconditioned being (i.e. a necessary being; versus the virtually unconditioned being of knowledge) to explain the occurrence of conditioned proportionate beings (i.e. contingent beings) (IN XIX, pp. 696-697; SC, III, pp. 40-42). Lonergan summarizes his proof from intelligibility thusly:

> The first element is the process that identifies the real with being, then identifies being with complete intelligibility, and finally identifies complete intelligibility with the unrestricted act of understanding that possesses the properties of God and accounts for everything else. In this process the expansive moment is first: for if the real is being, the real is the objective of an unrestricted desire to understand correctly; to be such an objective, the real has to be completely intelligible, for what is not intelligible is not the objective of a desire to understand, and what is not completely intelligible is the objective, not of an unrestricted desire to understand correctly, but of such a desire judiciously blended with an obscurantist refusal to understand (IN, XIX, p. 698).

Perhaps the best way to understand Lonergan's argument from intelligibility for God is to see it as appealing to the facts that humans seek to exhaustively understand reality, that the world is found to be intelligible (in the sciences for instance), and that in order to fully understand the world's intelligibility we must posit a God, an unrestricted act of understanding, who creates the world. Nor should such an attempt at ultimate explanation seem excessive as it is analogous to the positing of the law of falling bodies by Galileo. For all Galileo possessed was a large aggregate of acts of observing (i.e. that objects of different masses seemed to fall at the same rate). Yet he went on to unify them in terms of a concept (the law of falling bodies or that all bodies fall at the same rate no matter what their mass) through the insight that all bodies would fall at the same rate if they fell in a perfect vacuum (and so without air resistance) even though this could only be experimentally approximated. Again this postulation of God resembles the mathematical postulation of all positive integers or the postulation of absolute zero in physics. So if we allow our detached and disinterested desire to dominate, then we cannot deny that the real is being, that being is completely intelligible, and that it is founded upon (and in some way ultimately identical with) the unrestricted act of understanding and formally unconditioned being who is God (IN, (IN, II, p. 58; XIX, pp. 664-669, 694-698, 701-705; Epilogue, XX, p. 711, 765-768; MT, III, p. 88). Or put more succinctly, ultimately the world cannot be mediated by questions for intelligence if it does not have an intelligent ground. That is to say, the very fact that we can understand the world shows it is the creation of a divine intellect. For we have a drive to know what, why, and how, and we can reach intellectually satisfying answers that reveal the nature of reality, and this intelligibility cannot occur in the absence of an intelligent ground, God (MT, IV, p. 101; XIII, p. 342).[67]

When it comes to developing his theology, Lonergan follows Blondel in holding that natural theology (general transcendent knowledge) and our natural desire for God, manifest the need for theology (special transcendent knowledge). For science and philosophy show that humans are imperfect knowers and doers. And in order to remedy this and secure sustained development of knowledge and morality, humans have need of the supernatural. Hence we can characterize Lonergan's philosophy as a reversal of the traditional view of Anselm: instead of faith seeking understanding (*fides quaerens intellectum*), we have intellect seeking faith (*intellectus quaerens fidem*). For our own immanent necessities, the exigences of our unrestricted desire to know and to be good, call us to be more than human, and so to submit to divine grace and its accompanying faith and acceptance of God's revelation (IN, XVI, pp. 550-552; XX, pp. 742, 749-750; Epilogue, pp. 753-755, 763-767; MT, IV, p. 103; SC, I, p. 8; IX, p. 123; PHL, Appendix, pp. 348-355). In the end then we cannot affirm reason at the expense of faith, nor faith at the expense of reason. Rather we are to live by faith as well as by reason, by feeling and by definitions and theorems, by the Trinity honored and by the Trinity of learned discourse, by feeling compunction and by defining it, by the God of the philosophers as well as by the God of piety, the God of Abraham, Isaac, and Jacob (IN, XX, pp. 745, 749; Epilogue, p. 755; MT, IV, pp. 114-115; V, pp. 139-140; VI, p. 150; XI, pp. 273-276; XII, pp. 329-330; SC, IX, pp. 131-132; THC, XV, pp. 239-243; PTPII, V, pp. 77-81).

Now the supernatural faith and grace we receive helps insure an untrammeled unfolding of our detached, disinterested, and unrestricted desire to understand through bestowing on us additional knowledge from divine revelation. In this way we can grasp that God is a Trinity, that He enters into the world through Christ (the Incarnation or outer word of God), that He reveals His love for us in Christ crucified, dead, and risen, and finally that He offers us a beatific vision (IN, XX, pp. 746-748; Epilogue, pp. 756, 767; MT, IV, p. 113, 119; XI, pp. 283, 291; XII, pp. 295-296, 298; XIV, pp. 360-362; PTPII, V, p. 83).

And faith helps us perfect our human nature and acquire a solution to the problem of evil other than through social engineering and totalitarian control (IN, Epilogue, pp. 766-768). For grace introduces new conjugate forms or habits into the human person, namely the habits of faith, hope, and charity (the inner word of God) added respectively to our intellect, sensitivity, and will. These allow for conversion to a faith in God as a good creator, hope for a future world where we acquire God more directly, and a supernatural love of others.[68] Faith additionally brings a joy that can remain despite humiliation, failure, and pain, and a radical peace the world cannot give (MT, III, p. 84; IV, p. 105). So by supernatural grace, with its conjugate forms of faith, hope, and love, we can become collaborators with God and the Church (God's institution capable of making needed judgments about morals and doctrine) in the project of overcoming evil and safeguarding the faith (IN, XX, pp. 708, 710-711, 716, 718-726, 740-748; Epilogue, pp.761-765; MT, II, pp. 39, 55; III, p. 57; IV, pp. 103, 105-109, 112-120; X, p. 266; XI, pp. 278, 283, 289-291; XIV, pp. 364-365; SC, IX, p. 129; THC, VIII, pp. 124-127; IX, pp. 133-134; X, p. 161; XI, p. 175; XIII, pp. 208-209; XIV, p. 217; PTPII, II, pp. 12-13, 27; III, p. 38-43; XI, p. 204; XVII, pp. 325-326).

Let us conclude with some quotes of Lonergan who asserts that the supernatural solution "not only meets a human need but also goes beyond it to transform it into a point of insertion into human life of truths beyond human comprehension, of values beyond human estimation, of an alliance and a love that, so to speak, brings God too close to man" (IN, XX, p. 747). Or again: "The purification of our mind is principally the work of God, who illumines our intellects to understand what we had not understood and to grasp as unconditioned what we had repudiated as error, who breaks the bonds of our habitual unwillingness to be utterly genuine in intelligent inquiry and critical reflection by inspiring hope that reinforces the detached, disinterested, unrestricted desire to know and by infusing the charity, and love, that bestows on intelligence the fullness of life" (IN, XX, p. 751). In this manner faith, as it were, gives us a "dispassionate, unrelenting at-oneness with all the true, real, and good, that outlasts the fire-ball of the atom bomb and immeasurably exceed its power to change the living of man" (IN, Editorial Notes, note 751 on p. 806 showing wording from earlier edition of *Insight*).[69]

4

PERSONALISM

1920-2000 in Austria, France, Germany, & the United States

After the Germans conquered France during World War I, they established a Vichy Regime in the south of France. While the Vichy Regime was favorable to Catholicism, as we will see in the next chapter, nonetheless several Catholics joined the famous French Resistance Movement on account of the anti-Jewish practices of the Vichy Regime and a desire for self-rule. Among the Catholic members of the French Resistance were Gaston Fessard, S.J., Raymond Leopold Bruckberger, O.P., Robert-Ambroise-Marie Carré, O.P., Abbé Pierre, and the personalist Emmanuel Mounier (after a falling out with the Vichy Regime).

Personalism holds that what is of central philosophical importance is the person, who is a self-conscious and free moral agent. As such each person is a unique center of value that must be respected and loved. And this is best accomplished when we form relationships with other persons based on the moral law of the supreme person, i.e. God. Personalism, accordingly, rejects attempts to reduce all reality, including human beings, to the material realm. We must hold that self-conscious and virtuous persons (humans and God), not unconscious physical particles in motion, are the fundamental and foundational components of ultimate reality.

The founder of Catholic personalism was **Ferdinand Ebner (1882-1931)** who was born into a Catholic family in Weiner Neustadt, (Lower) Austria in 1882, but became an atheist as a teenager. Ebner would not remain outside the Catholic Church for long, however, and so in 1903, prompted by the memory of his pious father who had just passed away, he returned to theism and "Catholicism" although he remained distant from the institutional Catholic Church (especially in its authoritarian and more ostentatious forms). Ebner chose education as his profession and taught at the Austrian Gymnasiums of Waldegg from 1902-1912 and Gablitz from 1912-1923. Yet a wearisome stint as principal of the latter Gymnasium led him to fall into depression and twice attempt suicide in 1923. Ebner came out of his depression later that year and married a fellow school-teacher, Maria Mizera, but all was not rosy as he had to retire from teaching due to poor health (tuberculosis). Ebner consequently switched full-time to a literary career (which he had commenced in 1919), contributing regularly to the journals *Der Brenner* and *Die Fackel* and writing books. He died in 1931 in Gablitz (Vienna), Germany, having reconciled with the Church on his deathbed.[70]

The key writing of Ebner was his *The Word and the Spiritual Realities* [*Das Wort und die geistigen Realitäten*] [WSR] (1921; 1952) [found in his *Schriften*, vol. I].[71]

This work proved very influential [such as with the Jewish thinker Martin Buber (1878-1965)] due to its assertion that the incipient and fundamental relationship for a human is that of an 'I' [*Das Ich*] to a 'Thou' [*Das Du*]. Ebner, in other words, formulates the view that the primary reality of humans is dialogue, a relation between spiritual realities [knowledge of which Ebner calls a pneumatology]. For I exist as a conscious spiritual life open to another person, to a Thou (*Schriften*, vol. I, WSR, I, pp. 84-85; *Schriften*, vol. I, PLW, I, pp. 645-650; *Schriften*, vol. I, AOF, pp. 800-819; *Schriften*, vol. II, *Journal*, Entries of June 1912 and January 1913, pp. 94, 103). Ebner writes: "The I and the Thou are the spiritual realities of life. ... the I exists only in its relation to the Thou and not outside of it" (*Schriften*, vol. I, WSR, I, p. 85; translation based on that in *The Worlds of Existentialism*, p. 293).

Moreover, as dialogue between spiritual realities presupposes language (the Word [*Das Wort*] or the *Logos*), we can at another level say that the Word (especially as speech) is constitutive of our existence (i.e. what makes us human and separates us from animals is the fact that we can speak). The Word is what gives life to humans in the first place as language allows for a life of dialogue. For the human person is fundamentally the capacity for speaking and being spoken to and one cannot really be an 'I' without a 'Thou.' Language (the Word; Logos) additionally permits thought and reason to take root in our being. And this thought and reason in turn permits us to grasp and express our own existence as an 'I am' or person (our objective relation), and permits us as well to be a hearer and grasp the nature of the world (our objective relation again), and then a doer and act in the world (our subjective relation) (*Schriften*, vol. I, WSR, II, V, VII, pp. 87-89, 124, 154-156). The Word by giving humans language and thought thus lets them enter into relations of dialogue and love ('I-Thou' relations) and realize themselves. Ebner writes: "Personality in turn is unthinkable without reference to the Word. In the Word it is first 'objectively' given as the capacity in the human—because the human being has the Word—for expression in general, and in particular for asserting its own existence in the word 'I' of the statement 'I am.' Through this assertion self-consciousness becomes objective. Personality is therefore the capacity for being the one speaking as well as the corresponding capacity for being the one spoken to—the Thou—again because the human has the Word and is sensitive to the Word" (*Schriften*, vol. I, WSR, II, p. 87; translation based on "Word and Personality," pp. 233-234).

Now possession of the Word, of language, is a gift of God ['In the beginning was the Word' as the Gospel of John says (Jn 1:1)]. For, argues Ebner, humans could not have invented language by themselves. This is because without language there would have been no thought or reason and so no need for language in the first place (indeed no needs whatsoever). That is to say, the Word of God awakens the very life and self-consciousness of the human spirit along with its awareness of the world and its needs. Language then rather than being a form of natural life is supernatural, and it appears in humans after God creates their speaking faculty. Humans fundamentally exist in a "dialogue with God" [*Dialog mit Gott*] wherein God literally speaks humans into being (*Schriften*, vol. I, WSR, II-V, VII, X, XII-XV, pp. 87-95, 105-106, 109-123, 126-130, 154-161, 187-197, 239-240, 267, 281; cf. *Schriften*, vol. I, AOR, II, pp. 746-799; *Schriften*, vol. I, APH, V, pp. 950-963).[72] Ebner interpolates: "The word must have come to life from God, for life itself was not capable of finding the way to the word which creates and awakens the life of the spirit in the human being" (*Schriften*, vol. I, WSR, II, p. 90; translation based on "Word and Personality," p. 235).

The way to God for Ebner is accordingly dialogic, a personal encounter mediated through other humans. We cannot prove God through logic (or metaphysically investigate how God created the world) as such proofs isolate us in our solitude. Nor do such proofs touch the real existence of God as they only demonstrate God as an object and not as a personal being. Rather, we meet God in communion with a human thou, we meet God in the neighbor (1 Jn 4:20) (*Schriften*, vol. I, WSR, III, VII, XIV, XV, pp. 97-98, 155-156, 254-258, 274-283; cf. *Schriften*, vol. I, OUJ, pp 35-36). Ebner expounds his position as follows: "God is near to us not only spiritually but also physically, near to us in everyone, and above all in the human next to us, the neighbor, in everyone who is suffering. God is near to us in the human whom we, emerging from our I-aloneness, make the true Thou of our I" (*Schriften*. vol. I, WSR, XIV, p. 268; translation based on that in *Irish Theological Quarterly*, p. 152). Ultimately it is through our encounters with our neighbors whereby we acquire faith in a personal God, a "humble trust in Him, the trust of the I in the Thou that comes to meet it" (*Schriften*, vol. I, WSR, II-III, XVI-XVII, pp. 90, 98-99, 103, 304-305, 311-321; translation from *The Worlds of Existentialism*, p. 293). And in turn this faith-based encounter with our Eternal Thou allows us to further relate to the thou who is our neighbor.

Ebner, as one can surmise, lays great stress on this personal nature of God. God in the end is best thought of not in the third person [*dritt Person*], as a 'He'—this is God outside of a personal relationship to us. Indeed such a conception of God is overly anthropomorphic as it comes from human imagination; it is an idol, a metaphysical abstraction unworthy of God (*Schriften*, vol. I, WSR, III, XIV, XV, pp. 96-98, 254-257, 274-283). God is rather to be thought of in the second person as a 'Thou' since God is a being with whom we have a genuine interpersonal relationship. Hence "The human's relation to God takes the form of this I-Thou relationship. ... just because it is and shall be a 'personal' one it can be no other than the relation of the I to the Thou. In the last ground of our spiritual life God is the true Thou of the true I in the human" (*Schriften*, vol. I, WSR, I, p. 86; translated based on that in *The Worlds of Existentialism*, p. 293).

Unfortunately this 'I-Thou' dialogic relation can suffer disintegration [*Entwerdung*] and degenerate into a monologue of self-isolation [*Icheinsamkeit*; literally I-aloneness]. In truth this is a form of insanity [*Wahnsinnigkeit*] as it involves a turning away from communion with other humans and God into an self-centered worship of such things as art, literature, philosophy, or false religion (a turning from *pneuma* [spirit] to *psyche*). As Ebner puts it "The human being finds its true spiritual life in realizing the relation of the I to the Thou, not where the human pretends to see it, in dreaming about spirit [*Traum vom Geiste*] in poetry and art, in philosophy and in mythical religion, even though these may be the work of genius. All culture has been and will be nothing else than a dream of the spirit, dreamt by the human being in the I-aloneness of its existence, outside the spiritual realities of life, whose inner law comes to it principally in the conception of the idea'" (*Schriften*, vol. I, WSR, II, p. 89; translation based on "Word and Personality," pp. 234-235; cf. *Schriften*, vol. I, WSR, II, IV, VI, VII, IX, X, pp. 84, 90, 114, 120-121, 144-146, 155-159, 175-179, 181-186, 191-195). Unfortunately this degeneration is a constant possibility due to the fact that humans have fallen through original sin and can forget about God (even if they still retain a spark of divine love).

Yet Christ, the Creative Word of God, can come to redeem us from this monologue. God becomes flesh in Christ in order to give us the true content of faith, God Himself as our personal Thou (Jesus is the Word who allows us to speak God as it were). And as God's Word breaks through our isolationist shell, and as we discover the eternal Thou, we receive an opening to God and other humans and monologue becomes dialogue. Hence according to Ebner Christ the Word of God is the ultimate ground of the relation between the I and the Thou, whether this Thou is another human or God (*Schriften*, vol. I, WSR, II-III, V, VII, XVI, pp. 90-91, 93, 96-97, 126, 154-159, 295-304).

God's Word is thus potentially present to humans both as the Word of pneumatology (the natural Word of God), the Word of language and thought and communion given to all humans, and as the Word of dogmatics (the supernatural Word of God) wherein through the historical incarnation of Christ a human can become an "absolute unique existence" [*absoluter Einzenfall sein*] and show forth divine love (*Schriften*, vol. I, WSR, XIV, pp. 254-273; *Schriften*, vol. I, RC, II, V, VII, VIII, pp. 383-401, 482, 529, 629-637).

Catholic Personalism was initiated in France by **Emmanuel Mounier (1905-1950)**. Mounier was born in 1905 in Grenoble, Isère, Rhône-Alpes, France to devout Catholic parents. After a failed attempt at studying medicine in Paris from 1924-1925 (following in the footsteps of his pharmacist father), he trained in philosophy, first at the University of Grenoble under the Catholic philosopher Jacques Chevalier from 1924 to 1927, and then at the Sorbonne in Paris from

1927-1928 where he received his *agrégation*. Mounier's famous concern for the working classes and the poor was already evident in his university days and he joined the L'association catholique de la jeunesse Française (ACJF) [founded in 1886 by the Catholic socialist Albert de Mun], and the society of St. Vincent de Paul.

Mounier initially supported himself by teaching philosophy at the Lycée Sainte-Marie de Neuilly (1930-1931), the Lycée St. Omer (1931-1932), and the French Lycée in Brussels (1933-1939). He also was an active participant in the Cercle Thomiste of Jacques Maritain at Meudon during these times (1928-1933). Yet he discovered his true profession and vocation in 1932 when he founded the journal *Esprit* (with the assistance of the like-minded Catholics André Déléage, Georges Izard, Jacques Maritain, and Louis-Émile Galéry). This journal was to become the main instrument for the promulgation of his personalistic and socialistic teachings and his critique of the "established disorder"—in the words of Charles Maurras. Shortly thereafter Mounier married Paulette Leclercq in 1935 with whom he had three daughters.

After the commencement of the Second World War, Mounier joined the French Army in 1939, whence he was captured and briefly imprisoned in 1940 [he had also helped to launch the journal *Le voltigeur* to speak out against anti-Semitism]. Upon his release he taught at the École Nationale des Cadres at Uriages from 1940-1941 where the diplomats of the newly-formed Vichy régime were educated (he also taught philosophy at the Lazarist school in Lyon, the Lycée Robin in Vienne/Dauphiné, and had close connections with the Lycée du Parc in Lyon). At first cooperative with the Vichy government, Mounier became more and more disillusioned with its agenda. On account of his questionable allegiances (Mounier had begun associating with the French Resistance as early as 1940), as well as the growing influence of the right-wing Action Française group, publication of his journal *Esprit* was suspended in 1941 and Mounier himself was arrested in 1942. After a two-week hunger strike and eight months in the prisons of Clermont-Ferrand, Vals, and Saint-Paul, Lyon, Mounier was acquitted and granted his release. He then moved to Beau Vallon (Montélimar), Dieulefit, Drôme where he lived and wrote under the name of Leclercq.

At the close of the war in 1945 Mounier returned to Paris and resumed publication of his journal *Esprit*. He also worked to heal the now profound German-French rift with the creation in 1948 of the *Comité français d'échanges avec l'Allemagne nouvelle* and its journal *Allemagne* (1949-1967). Mounier died from a heart attack in 1950 in Châtenay-Malabry, France.[73]

Mounier's name has grown ever more illustrious after his death. He received official recognition by the French government for his role in the French Resistance, and the Association des amis d'Emmanuel Mounier (1950) [with its journal *Bulletin des amis d'Emmanuel Mounier* (1952-)], the Lycée Mounier in Grenoble (1963), and the Instituto Emmanuel Mounier in Madrid (1984-) were named in his honor. There is also a Quai Mounier in Grenoble and Rues Emmanuel Munier in Aussillon, Blaye-les-Mines, Crolles, Orléans, Plaisir, and Villepinte (Paris), France.[74]

Mounier's key works are his *Manifesto in the Service of Personalism* [*Manifeste au service du personnalisme*] [MSP] (1936) and *Personalism* [*Le Personnalisme*] [PERS] (1949) which, as the names suggest, set forth a personalist philosophy, under the influence of Pascal, Malebranche, Lotze, Marx, Scheler, Blondel, Marcel, and Maritain.[75]

Mounier insists that the term personalism "will never be a system or a political machine," rather it is employed "to designate a certain perspective on human problems, and in order to accentuate certain requirements which are not always given their proper worth in the solution to the crisis of the twentieth-century" (WP, Introduction, p. 111 [7-8]; cf. WP, I, p. 113 [9]; PERS, Introduction, p. xv; MSP, I, pp. 1-2, 7-8). Personalism then for Mounier is less a system than a perspective, method, or exigency. As a perspective personalism opposes idealism (an abstract examination of the person) and materialism (a pseudo-scientific naturalism which treats the human as a physiological or psychological specimen). It instead puts forward a spiritual realism that examines "the whole meaning of the human" and studies the human being in all its material, inner, and transcendental dimensions (from the lowest biological and economic conditions to the highest moral and spiritual possibilities) (PERS, I, 1, pp. 5, 9; I, 3, p. 42; WP, Introduction, p. 112 [8]; I, p. 113; VII, p. 171; VIII, pp. 182-183, 186, 190). As a method personalism rejects the abstract deductive method of dogmatic idealism and the crude empiricism of materialism, both of which generalize and objectify and lose touch with the person and its various dimensions. Rather truth is known in the living engagement of a person with the world and other persons, one that involves both rational technique and "conversion to existence" (*metanoia*) (PERS, Introduction, pp. xxi, xxiii [12-13]; I, 6, pp. 74-75; WP, III, pp. 130-132; VII, p. 171; VIII, pp. 180-181). Finally as an exigency personalism rejects solitary complacency and idealistic evasions and, in opposition to this, demands an engagement in society and "the defense of the person against the oppression of apparatuses" (PERS, I, 1, pp. 5, 9; I, 3, p. 42; WP, Introduction, p. 112 [8]; I, p. 113; VII, p. 171; VIII, pp. 182-183, 186, 190; IX, pp. 193-194).

A personalistic philosophy asserts therefore that the human person is the key ingredient in reality, the highest achievement of the universe (PERS, Introduction, p. xvi-xviii; I, 1, p. 8; MSP, I, p. 1; see I, p. 4, IV, p. 47, 53, 55; V, pp. 83-4; VII, pp. 103-104 [91-92]; WP, I, p. 114; PCR, I, 1, p. 14). So, says Mounier, "We call every doctrine and every civilization personalist which affirms the primacy of the human person above the material necessities and above the collective institutions which sustain its development" (MSP, I, p. 1 [7]). This significance extends to each and every person who is an independent spirit of dignity, value, and worth; no person can be duplicated or repeated (the hero in the heart of battle, a lover giving him or herself to another, a creative artist absorbed in work, a saint inspired by love for God, each is unique) (PERS, I, 2, p. 29; I, 3, pp. 41-42; I, 4, p. 46; I, 5, pp. 54-57; MSP, I, pp. 1, 6-7 [7, 11-12]; IV, pp. 44-56 [42-53]). Or to quote Mounier: "... every person has a significance such that it cannot be replaced in the position it occupies in the universe of persons. Such is the majestic grandeur of the person, which gives it the dignity of a universe; and yet its humility for every person is equivalent to it in this dignity, and persons are more numerous than stars" (PERS, I, 3, p. 41 [60]).

Now according to Mounier the person is characterized by five fundamental aspects: 1) Embodiment [Incarnation] (including Self-Awareness and Action); 2) Liberty; 3) Communion; 4) Transcendence [Vocation]; 5) Integration with Singularity (MSP, V, pp. 70-88 [64-80]; PCR, II, p. 70). Mounier encapsulates these five aspects in his definition of the person (though he holds that in the end the person escapes exact delimitation as a thousand photographs will not amount to the walking person): "A person is a spiritual being, constituted as such by a manner of subsistence and of independence in its being. It maintains this subsistence by its adhesion to a hierarchy of values, freely adopted, assimilated and lived, by a responsible engagement and a constant conversion. It thus unifies all of its activity in freedom and in addition, by means of creative acts, develops the uniqueness of its vocation" (MSP, V, p. 68 [63]; cf. PERS, Introduction, p. xvii-xviii, xxi, xxviii; I, 2, p. 23; I, 3, p. 35; WP, VIII, pp. 175-176; MSP, I, pp. 1-2 [7-8], 9-10 [13-15]; IV, pp. 52, 65 [49-50, 55]; WP, VI, p. 152).

The human person in the first place then has an intimate presence to itself, a self-awareness, an inward subjective life (it is an 'I') (PERS, Introduction, xii; I, 1, p. 11; I, 3-5, pp. 35, 50-51; MSP, V, pp. 68-69 [63-64]; TC, III, pp. 54-58 [282-288]; VII, pp. 192-194 [538-540]; PCR, II, pp. 67-70).

Yet Mounier rejects an idealistic or even dualistic account of the person wherein the human self floats free of its body and the world. Though the human self does transcend the body (it is immeasurably more than the tangible body) it is also incarnate in the body and so becomes a part of nature, a carnal spirit (a union of heaven and earth) (PERS, Introduction, p. xxii; I, 1, pp. 3-5, 8-9, 10-11; I, 3, pp. 36, 39; WP, II, pp. 115, 118; MSP, I, pp. 5, 7 [10, 12]; V, pp. 72-73, 77-78, 81 [71-72, 74]; TC, III, pp. [117-123]). As Mounier puts it: "The human being is a body by the same right that it is spirit, wholly body and wholly spirit. Its most primal instincts: eating, reproducing, it has made subtle arts: cuisine and the art of loving. Yet a headache checks the great philosopher and St. John of the Cross would vomit in his ecstasies. ... There is nothing which is in me that is not mixed with earth and blood" (PERS, I, 1, p. 3 [19-20]). Indeed in acknowledgement of the incarnate condition of the self, I should think of myself as a "me-now-here [moi-ici-maintenant]," indeed as a "me-here-now-like this-among these humans-with this past" (WP, III, p. 127 [26]; cf. TC, III, pp. 69-85 [307-331]).

This incarnation of the spirit in the body is even essential to one's personality as the body is "the omnipresent mediator of the life of the spirit" (PERS, I, 1, p. 11 [29]); and so a human "being which is not objective is not a being ... [however] a being which was nothing but objective would lack this full achievement of being, the personal life" (PERS, I, 1, p. 11 [29]). For the body allows one to escape from one's private life and reveal oneself to the world and others: "I cannot think without being or be without my body; I am exposed through it—to myself, to the world, to another" (PERS, I, 1, p. 11 [29]). Or as Mounier asserts at greater length:

The human being is a being-in-the-world. Its condition can only be grasped without being immediately grasped as an incarnate and inserted condition. Just as it does not live or exist independently of others, the person does not live or exist independently of nature. So it must realize itself in a hand-to-hand manner as much as through the inner life. There is not a spiritual gesture which is not founded on a movement and which is not expressed by a movement. There is not a creation that is not also a pro-duction. There is not, therefore, for the human any life of the soul sundered from the life of the body, any moral reform without technical management, any spiritual revolution without material revolution (WP, VII, pp. 159-160 [64]; see WP, VII, p. 157).

A third key aspect of the human person is the free will. Such freedom cannot be seen or proven (the physical world with its laws has no place for freedom), but it can be lived and experienced (PERS, Introduction, p. xvi; I, 3, p. 35 [53]; I, 5, pp. 54-56; I, 6, p. 73; MSP, V, p. 68 [63]). As humans are free they are not determined by their environment, history, society, nor are automatisms of habit and instinct, although these can certainly have an influence on our lives. So even if humans belong to nature (and dwell in various factual conditions), they can also transcend and master nature with their freedom of choosing this or that (as a convict can choose to overcome his upraising and choose a better path) (PERS, I, 1, pp. 6, 12-13; I, 3, p. 35; I, 4, pp. 50-51; I, 5, pp. 57-59, 61-62; I, 6, pp. 75-76, 79; I, 7, pp. 83-84, 88; MSP, XI, p. 167; PERS, I, 5, pp. 57, 62-63; TC, I, pp. 1-2 [38-39]; IX, pp. 272-273 [708-711]).

In fact the person is ever called to a freely-chosen act of self-creation for Mounier. In such a creative decision I break the chain of probabilities or fatalities, brave the intimidating play of forces, and upset all calculations: I create a new order and intelligibility through my incessant creation of new situations, life-patterns, and institutions (PERS, Introduction, pp. xvi-xviii, xxi; I, 1, pp. 5-8, 11-13; I, 2, pp. 23, 29-30; I, 3, pp. 35, 41-42; I, 4, pp. 51-53; I, 5, pp. 46, 51, 54-58; I, 5, p. 63; I, 6, pp. 69-70; II, 1, pp. 118-119; WP, III, pp. 126-127; IV, pp. 135, 141; V, p. 146; VII, p. 161; MSP, V, p. 69; PCR, IV, p. 12). Hence the person is "a living activity of self-creation, of communication and of adhesion, that grasps and knows itself in its act as a movement of personalization" (PERS, Introduction, xviii [8]). Mounier therefore states that the character of a person takes the form of a movement directed to the future. It is what I can be rather than what I am, my availability rather than my possessions, the hope that is still left rather then the achievements left behind (TC, I, pp. 14-16 [58-60]).

It would accordingly not be wrong, notes Mounier, to say that human existence is about action (PERS, I, 3, p. 44; I, 4, p. 51; I, 7, pp. 83, 91-93; II, 1, p. 102; WP, Introduction, p. 111; III, pp. 126, 128-129; IV, pp. 138-139; MSP, XV, pp. 267-272 [226-230]; XVI, pp. 277-280 [234-236]; PCR, I, 6, pp. 32-36). As Marx saw, we must not just analyze the world but also engage in active service and seek to humanize humanity and transform society (PERS, Introduction, p. xix, xxi; I, 2, p. 25; I, 7, p. 86; MSP, III, p. 31; V, p. 73; WP, III, pp. 125-133; IX, p. 194; VII, p. 165; TC, I, p. 7; V, pp. 122-136). Mounier states:

> Personalism is the demand of engagement both total and conditional. Total engagement, for there is only a valid lucidity which is realized and which does not let itself be diverted into a simple critique. We have indeed the passion for the human, but it is an effective passion for us: we seek to understand the human being in order to better transform it. Conditional engagement, for if we do not keep the reins firmly in hand, the internal disaccord of the human will periodically upset the equilibrium of its civilizations, shifting them sometimes towards solitary complaisance, sometimes towards collective folly, sometimes towards idealistic evasions (WP, IX, p. 194 [102]; cf. WP, V, p. 145).

So the primary end of our action should be to create and sustain a community of human persons, a mutually enriching communal life in which we share each other's tasks, troubles, values, and joys (PERS, I, 2, pp. 17, 19, 21-23, 29; I, 3, pp. 36, 38; I, 6, pp. 70, 79; I, 7, pp. 84-86, 90; MSP, VI, p. 95; WP, VII, pp. 167, 169-170; VIII, pp. 176, 185-186; PCR, I, 8, pp. 42-53; II, pp. 75-76; III, 1, pp. 78-92). As Mounier puts it: "We thus find communion implanted in the heart itself of the person, an integrating factor of its very existence" (MSP, V, p. 88 [80]). Hence though the person manifests an individualism whereby it has its own life and character, it also finds integration in joining with other humans in a community.

And there is no better and more integrating community than one founded upon love. Indeed, remarks Mounier, the one irrefutable truth is not the Cartesian "I think, therefore I am," but rather "I love, therefore I am." For to be means to exist with the other, for the other, and in the other (as suggested by the Latin prefix 'ex' [meaning 'out'] in the word exist, to be is to go out of oneself toward another) (PERS, I, 2, pp. 20-21, 29; WP, I, p. 113; V, pp. 149-150). In such a love we treat others as indefinable and inexhaustible subjects with a liberty of their own instead of as objects or instruments. Love is thus a gratitude and a will toward others precisely because they are other than oneself. Love wills another's realization as a person, whatever his or her gifts or disadvantages [and with such a love one is on a pathway going beyond the hero to the saint] (PERS, I, 2, pp. 21-23, 29; I, 3, p. 33; MSP, V, pp. 87-88 [79-80]; TC, III, pp. 85-86 [332-334]; IX, pp. 293-295, 311-312 [744-745, 768]). In this vein Mounier writes:

> If there is one affirmation common to all the personalist philosophies to which we are related ... it is that the essential bearing of a world of persons is not the isolated perception of self (*cogito*) nor the egocentric concern for self, but the communication of consciousnesses ... we should prefer to say, the communication of existences, the existence with another, perhaps we should write it as 'co-existence' (*Mitsein*). The person is not opposed to the 'we' (*nous*) which establishes and nourishes it, but to the irresponsible and tyrannical 'one' (*on*). Not only is it not defined by incommunicability and withdrawal, but rather, of all the realities of the universe, it is the only one which is truly communicable, which is *towards the other*, and even *in the other, towards the world* and *in the world* before being *in itself*. The adult, like the child, obtains itself in its relation to another and to things, in work and comradeship, in friendship, in love, in action, in encounter, and not in its relation to itself [*quant-à-soi*] (WP, VI, pp. 149-150 [52-53]).
>
> The living force of the personal impulse is ... generosity or gratuity, that is to say, ultimately the gift without measure and without hope of return. The economy of the person is an economy of gift [*don*], not of compensation or calculation (PERS, I, 2, p. 22 [40]).

Yet while the person is free, as we have seen, to choose between one act or another, it is not the case that the person is completely free to create him or herself as Sartre claimed (PERS, I, 2, pp. 29-30; III, pp. 41-42; I, v, pp. 54-58; WP, I, 3, pp. 126-127; I, 5, p. 146). For there is at least a common human nature (a universality) that we do not invent (to be fair Sartre recognized this). Nor do we invent our own values (which Sartre did not recognize). Rather we find a secret voice calling out to us, an appeal, a vocation (for this reason it is better to say that each person is free to adopt the means to realize a vocation, than that each person is free to adopt a vocation). That is to say, we find transcendent and objective values that direct our liberty (PERS, I, 3, pp. 41-42; I, 5, pp. 54-58, 61-62; I, 6, pp. 75-77; I, 7, pp. 88, 90; II, 1, pp. 97, 120; WP, I, p. 114; IV, pp. 137-138; MSP, V, p. 85 [77-78]).

Indeed if there were no objective values then there would be no reason to avoid acting as an animal and seeking to fulfill all our desires ("the intense life"), or to be a tyrant with Caligula (PERS, I, 5, p. 58 [76]; I, 7, p. 85). Mounier thus asserts:

> ... human freedom is the freedom of a person, and of this person, thus constituted and situated in itself in the world and in the presence of values (PERS, I, 5, p. 59 [77]).
>
> Our freedom is the freedom of a situated person, it is also that of a person who has realized values [valorisée]. I am not free solely by the act of exercising my spontaneity; I become free if I incline this spontaneity into the sense of a liberation, that is to say, of a personalization of the world and myself. ... Thus I am not disposed in the arbitrariness of my freedom, although the point at which I espouse it may be buried in my heart. My liberty is not only springing, it is ordered, or better yet called. This call gives it its vital force [force d'élan] (PERS, I, 5, p. 61 [79]).

In other words, true freedom is the freedom to choose the good (to give oneself to something greater than oneself), lest one only be free to choose between the plague and cholera (PERS, I, 2, p. 19; I, 5, pp. 63-64; WP, VII, p. 165). Indeed paradoxically we can say that "we are truly free only in the measure that we are not entirely free" (WP, III, pp. 127-128 [26]). The human person then is called to renounce itself and its interests, to go forth and lose itself (wherein it will find itself again; for it is by denying what we are statically that we discover what we are prospectively, says Mounier) (PERS, I, 3, pp. 40-41; TC, XI, pp. 289, 292 [739, 742]). Indeed at times I may even be called upon to accept suffering and death (heroic sacrifice) so as to not betray the values I find ["... wanting to live at any price is, one day, to accept living at the price of the reasons for living"] (PERS, I, 6, p. 71 [90]; cf. PERS, I, 6, pp. 66-67, 80-81). So as Mounier notes: "Personal being is generosity. ... Life within us, especially in the face of danger, asks only to adapt itself to the cheapest price. ... The person risks and spends without regard to the price" (PERS, I, 6, p. 67 [85]).

This call within the interior of the human, with its demand to transcend ourselves and embrace goodness, also reveals the existence of a supreme being (PERS, I, 2, pp. 31-32; MSP, V, pp. 78-79 [71-72]; TC, IX, pp. 284-285 [734-735], 312-313). For in acting, as we have seen, humans are required to give-way and give themselves over to values and other persons and so surpass themselves: the person one could say is a "power of infinite expansion" [envergure infinie] (PERS,

I, 6, pp. 66-67, 80-81; MSP, VI, p. 101 [90]; TC, IX, pp. 302-303 [755-756]; PCR, I, 9, pp. 54-58; II, p. 75; IV, p. 121; XIX, pp. 370-374). Further reflection also reveals that what here draws us out of ourselves is the appeal of eternal values, "a metaphysical response to a metaphysical call, an adventure in the order of the eternal, proposed to each human being in the solitude of its own choice and of its own responsibility" (MSP, I, p. 6 [11]; cf. PERS, I, 3, p. 35; I, 6, pp. 68-70; MSP, I, p. 6; IV, pp. 52-53; WP, IV, p. 135). Hence the call to the good life lets humans grasp a power outside of themselves (a non-sensible reality superior to theirs in its quality of being). As Mounier writes suggestively "the movement that constitutes the person does not remain enclosed within itself, but it indicates a transcendence which lives among us, and which does not escape all attempts to describe it [denomination]" (PERS, VI, p. 65 [83]).

Furthermore, as humans in the end can only really give themselves over to another person rather than to the impersonal force of a value, ultimately the human person is directed toward a personal God, a generous God who offers a relation of unique intimacy to each person (an illimitable interchange of love) (PERS, Introduction, p. xviii; I, 6, pp. 65, 80; II, 1, p. 121). Indeed by supernatural faith—"the confidence or the supreme and obscure intimacy of the person with the transcendent Person" (PERS, I, 6, p. 80 [99]; cf. TC, IX, pp. 309-310 [763-764])—we comprehend that God has taken on the human form of the incarnate Christ in a further gift of His person to us (PERS, Introduction, p. xxi-xxii; I, 2, p. 30; I, 6, p. 80; MSP, V, p. 69 [64]; TC, IX, pp. 282-284 [730-733]). And with this faith we acquire a joyous assurance that good in the end will prevail in our climate of struggle; i.e. we embrace what Mounier calls a "tragic optimism" (PERS, I, 1, pp. 15-16 [34]; I, 2, pp. 18, 24; I, 6, p. 82; WP, V, pp. 147, 151-152; VIII, pp. 184-185; SF, III, pp. 90-92, 105-106).

Ultimately then for Mounier God is found in leading a life rather than through proofs or conceptual systems. For, as he describes it, one grasps God in a face-to-face meeting with spiritual fact (du face à face avec le fait religieux), in the most intimate part of one's intimacy (au plus intime de son intimité) (TC, IX, pp. 312-313 [768-769]). More specifically, one discovers God in one's heart, in a contact with a real presence, when one leads a life of love and virtue. Mounier thus asserts: "People will ask for proofs of transcendence, of the value of values. Belonging to the universe of freedom, transcendence is not an object of proof. Its certitude appears in the plenitude of the personal life" (PERS, I, 6, p. 68 [86]). Or again, "We gain it [the hidden Absolute] through the effort we make towards it more than through the always faltering, even grotesque representations we give to ourselves about it. A conceptual system may underline with precision what it is not, it only grasps what it is in a mediocre manner" (WP, II, p. 119 [18]; cf. PERS, I, 6, p. 71).

Another developer of personalism was **Maurice-Gustave Nédoncelle (1905-1976)** who was born in Roubaix, Nord, France in 1905 where his father was a professor. He joined the Sulpician order in 1922, attended the Seminary of Saint-Sulpice in Paris (1922-1926) and the Sorbonne (1926-1929) where he received a licentiate in philosophy and was ordained a year later in 1930. He then continued his studies at the Sorbonne and was awarded a doctorate in philosophy and letters in 1943. Nédoncelle taught at the Collège Albert-de-Man in Nogent-sur-Marne, France (1930-1943), at the Catholic Institute of Lille (1943-1945), and at the University of Strasbourg (1945-1976) [he also found the time to complete a doctorate in theology there in 1945 and serve as Dean of the Human Sciences from 1956-1967]. Nédoncelle died in Strasbourg in 1976. He received an honorary doctorate from the University of Louvain, was inducted into the Légion d'honneur, became a monsignor and church canon, and was president of the Association des professeurs de philosophie des Facultés de France.[76]

The key works of Nédoncelle are his *Reciprocity of Consciousnesses* [*La réciprocité des consciences*] [RC] (1942; 1962) and *Towards a Philosophy of Love and the Person* [*Vers une philosophie de l'amour et de la personne*] [PLP] (1946; 1957).[77] In these works Nédoncelle shows the influence of John Henry Newman, Friedrich Von Hügel, Maine de Biran, Maurice Blondel, Gabriel Marcel, Louis Lavelle, and René Le Senne.

Nédoncelle provides a more systematic account of personalism than did Mounier (what he calls a metaphysics of the person). According to Nédoncelle personalism designates "every doctrine that attributes to persons an important place in reality or, more radically, that regards them as the sole reality ... personalism consists in demanding respect for the human person in moral action and the organization of society" (PLP, Conclusion, XIII, p. 209 [235]; cf. RECC, Part Three, I, 187,

189, pp. 223-224, 225-226; PLP, Preface, p. ix-x; I, 3, p. 60; CL, Preface, p. 7; HPN, 2nd edition of 1963, Preface, p. 11).

Persons are the "sole reality," in the first place, as they are the only beings who possess self-awareness and free will. For to be a person is to have an awareness of oneself (intersubjectivity). One cannot eliminate the subject of reflection that all thought begins with; I am born in a thought which stirs up my thoughts in the words of Nédoncelle. The person then has an intimate center of consciousness, an 'I,' a self-presence (RECC, Preface, pp. 8-9, Part One, II, 43, 46, pp. 58, 61-62; Conclusion, 269, p. 319; PLP, I, 1, n. 1 on p. 36; III, 9, pp. 158-159; Conclusion, XIII, p. 213; HPN, IV, 45, pp. 88-89; CL, I, 1, pp. 21-22; I, 8, pp. 164-166, 168). The person is also free to become what it wants. One could say then that the only necessity that governs the person is the necessity of determining one's own being by one's choice. For freedom means that one can break away from one's causes and past and create oneself (RECC, Part Two, I, 119, p. 152; Part Three, III, 229, 238, 241, 244, pp. 270, 274-275, 278-282, 285-286; PLP, I, 1, pp. 16-17; II, 4, p. 101; II, 5, pp. 104-106; II, 6, pp. 115, 120; III, 8, p. 154).

Yet the defining characteristic of a person for Nédoncelle is what he terms "reciprocity of consciousnesses," the reciprocal relationship between an 'I' [moi] and a 'thou' [toi] which is one's original being. Communication of consciousnesses, in other words, is a primitive fact [fait primitif], the cogito has a reciprocal character from the get go (RECC, Part One, Preface, 2, pp. 8-9; Part One, I, 4-5, p. 11; Part One, I, 8, pp. 16; Part One, I, 14, p. 22; Part One, III, 74, p. 101 and n. 1 on p. 101; Part Two, IV, 166, 169, pp. 200-202; Part Three, II, 201, pp. 236-237; Part Three, III, 247, p. 290; Conclusion, 269, p. 319; PLP, II, 4, pp. 94-96; III, 8, p. 143; Conclusion, XIII, pp. 213, 219; HPN, I, 1-2, p. 6; CL, I, 1, pp. 23-25; TDC, II, pp. 13-15; HPDP, I, 4-5, pp. 36-47, 51-53).

First, I have become what I am through the numerous influences of other persons since the cradle. Thus I owe a debt to countless benefactors including my parents, siblings, friends, teachers, and various societal members (PLP, Conclusion, p. 219): "The act by which I am is the act by which another makes me be," as Nédoncelle puts it concisely (PLP, II, 4, p. 93).[78]

Second, the very perception of another person reveals a "minimum of reciprocity." For another person can only be perceived if the person

has offered him or herself to the world and to me (and so, at least obscurely, wants to be known); and I can only perceive the other person
if I have accepted that offer (RECC, Part One, I, 8-9, pp. 16-17; Part
One, II, 52, 55, pp. 72, 76; Conclusion, 269, p. 319; PLP, II, 4, pp. 94-
95; HPN, I, 1-2, pp. 1-6; HPN, 2nd edition of 1963, Preface, pp. 9-11).
Meeting with another, says Nédoncelle, involves a first gift of "radiance [*rayonnement*] which makes another known and loved without
his knowledge, in brief his coming and his presentation to existence.
Then it is the voluntary gift which he makes of his proper substance
and which brings him to receive in himself the act of the other as the
stimulation to which he freely consents or responds" (RECC, II, 34,
pp. 48-49; cf. PLP, I, 3, pp. 73-75; HPDP, I, 4, pp. 36-46, 49-50). So
just to exist is to be a minimum of goodness to another, a gift of presence (PLP, I, 1, p. 20; III, 8, p. 138). Nédoncelle expands this point as
follows:

> To be in the world is to be a minimum of goodness offered in public. Hu-
> man consciousnesses are well hidden from attentions by the cosmic mas-
> querade; but there is an aspect under which they cannot do otherwise
> than give themselves as a spectacle and communicate their share in excel-
> lence to those who contemplate them. ... To be in the world is to be able
> to dissimulate and to wreak havoc; but it is first of all, before the ugliness
> sets in, to open one's soul to other souls and to bring them an initial pres-
> ence which is a blessing [*bienfait*]. A countenance [*visage*] that appears is
> a reality that is yielded, a secret that is cautiously unveiled, a value which
> is diffused and is not taken back. ... It is always this initial moment which
> love lies in wait for and that is why it is born in reciprocity even though
> it must often sink into solitude" (PLP, I, 1, p. 20 [29-30]).

Third, as suggested by the above quote, our very first encounter with
another person is "immaculate." Our initial lighting upon another person is filled with curiosity, a desire to know more about the person, an
initial openness on our part. So from the very first there is an acceptance of another person, a desire to dialogue with and invite the other
into our own existence (even a desire to devote oneself to the other)
(RECC, Part One, Preface, 1, p. 7; Part One, I, 8, p. 16; Part One, II,
34, p. 48; PLP, II, 4, pp. 92, 94, 100; III, 8, pp. 137-139; Conclusion,
XIII, pp. 214, 217-218; HPN, I, 1-2, pp. 1-6).[79] So a mere exchange
of regards, words, or services, immediately generates a metaphysical
community between two people, a solidarity of their personal essences
(RECC, Part One, I, 8, 14, pp. 17, 22-23; Conclusion, 269, p. 319).

With this in mind Nédoncelle can assert that "there is at the beginning of every personal consciousnesses a benevolence which is at the same time received and accorded, that is to say a germ of reciprocity. Personal love has from the first an interpersonal core, not only in the act which wants the other, but in the knowledge which has the intuition of its presence" (RECC, Part One, I, 8, p. 16). Ultimately, however, one is obliged to go beyond this initial, often unacknowledged, reciprocity with others to enter into true acts of love.[80]

Now love, according to Nédoncelle's metaphysics of charity, is an affective, conscious, and active generosity (giving) to another person. In love I will the self for the sake of the other, that is to say I love the other for him or herself as the other is an end equal or superior to myself [Nédoncelle will even say, much like Levinas, that I here have an infinite responsibility for the beloved placed on my shoulders] (RECC, Part One, I, 13-14, pp. 21, 23; Part Two, II, 137, pp. 172-173; Part Three, II, 212-213, 217, pp. 246-249, 251-252; Three, IV, 268, pp. 315-316; PLP, Introduction, p. 6; I, 1, pp. 8-10, 12, 24; I, 3, pp. 64, 68; II, 4, p. 85).[81]

Yet such a love must be reciprocal since love seeks a communion of consciousnesses: the gift offered calls for a gift received (the unilateral generosity of certain saints is thus incomplete) (RECC, Part One, I, 4, pp. 11-12; Part Three, I, 185, pp. 222-223; Part Three, II, 219-221, 223, pp. 255-259; PLP, I, 1, pp. 13, 15-16; III, 9, p. 164). In fact, Nédoncelle favorite definition of love is "the will toward mutual promotion" [la volonté de promotion mutuelle] (RECC, 269, p. 319; PLP, I, 1, p. 13; I, 3, p. 77; III, 8, p. 155; Conclusion, XIII, p. 215), that is to say, "the will to promote a thou and be promoted by him [or her]" in turn (PLP, II, 7, p. 132 [154]). For the essence of love is found in existing in and for one another (as with God in the Trinity) (RECC, Part One, II, 38, p. 53; Part One, II, 57, n. 1 on p. 81). True love is witnessed wherever there is a bond of "a self to a thou of such a sort that they are one for the other and each in willing the other wills him or herself" (RECC, Part One, I, 30, p. 42). Ideally in such a reciprocal love, I will the thou and the thou wills me in an act uniting the discovery, education, creation, and mutual and perfect advancement of two persons (RECC, Part One, I, 29-30, pp. 41-42; PLP, I, 1, pp. 20-25, 29-30; II, 5, p. 111-112; III, 9, p. 165; Conclusion, XIII, p. 217).

Nédoncelle notes four ways in particular in which lovers can advance and promote each other. Love first of all wills the continued existence

of the beloved thou. For the other enriches me by his or her very presence: I am rewarded by the fact that the other merely is (RECC, Part
One, II, 34, p. 49; PLP, I, 1, pp. 19-20; I, 3, pp. 60-63). Secondly, love
wills the originality or uniqueness of the other. It regards the other,
the thou, as having its own subjectivity (alterity), autonomy, desires,
and plans which it must respect (RECC, Part One, I, 31, p. 44; PLP,
I, 1, pp. 8, 32-33; I, 2, p. 49; I, 3, pp. 60-63; II, 4-5, pp. 92, n. 3 on p.
102, and pp. 111-112). Love thus wants to give the beloved the solid-
ity of its singular personality and the liberty of its unfettered being
(PLP, I, 1, pp. 18, 22; Conclusion, XIII, p. 218; PE, I, 9, pp. 85, 88-
89). Thirdly, love seeks to affect the beloved for the better. It seeks to
develop the being of the beloved, perfect its growth of character and
vocation (RECC, I, 8, p. 16; I, 27-28, pp. 35-37, II, 55, p. 76; PLP,
I, 1, pp. 8, 12-13, 18-22; I, 2, pp. 38-39; I, 3, pp. 60-64; IO, XII, pp.
128-132 [148-153]; CL, Preface, p. 8). So "to love another is to seek
to render him loving, or if he is this, it is to rejoice that he should be
this" (RECC, Part One, II, 60, p. 84). Love in short is a commitment
to making the other and oneself utterly loving and lovable (PLP, I, 1,
pp. 18, 22-24; I, 3, pp. 59-60; PE, I, 9, pp. 85, 88-89). He queries:

> What does it mean to give oneself to another? It is to commit oneself
> to be concerned about the other, to make the other exist more fully. But
> the lover would deny the worth of its love did it not desire the beloved
> to share it and be loving in its turn. To will that the other be loving is
> to will that the other love in me this by which I can and will to love the
> other; it is to will that the other love me. 'I belong to you' means: depend
> on me for yourself, I consecrate myself to you. ... It also means: I depend
> on something in you to help me in being worthy of you and capable of
> being useful to you. Help me to help me. I want you to be such that I
> can in my turn place myself in your hands and that you would give me a
> greater value. By the fact that I attach myself to you, I make you able to
> transform me for yourself... my love is an invocation that I address to you
> and that I address to me (PLP, I, 1, pp. 22-23 [32]).

Lastly, such a will to promote the other also involves a willingness to
enter into self-sacrifice [dévoûment] for the other, i.e. heroism (RECC,
Part One, I, 11, 13, pp. 19, 21; Part Two, III, 150, pp. 185-186; PLP,
I, 1, pp. 9-10, 12, 25; I, 2, pp. 37-38, 43-44). Hence in a way to love
another means giving this other the power to make oneself unhappy
(RECC, Part Three, II, 219, pp. 255-256). Yet this is not the last word,
as one finds fulfillment and joy in giving one's all to the beloved [for

love is its own reward] (RECC, Part One, I, 13, p. 21; Part One, II, 36, p. 51; Part Three, II, 214, p. 249; PLP, I, 3, p. 61; II, 4, pp. 95-96; CL, Preface, p. 9; but cf. PLP, I, 1, p. 12). We can thus say [contra the Lutheran theologian Anders Nygren] that there is an *eros* of *agape*, a desire to find the soul in losing it (i.e. in helping others) (PLP, I, 1, pp. 18-19). Nor must we must forget that the best love is reciprocal, while I am sacrificing for and enhancing the thou, the thou in turn is doing the same for me (PLP, I, 1, pp. 24, 27-28).

Now love at its peak, a love that displays these four means of promotion, creates what Nédoncelle calls a "heterogeneous identity" [*l'identité hétérogène*]. Here two lovers retain their uniqueness and originality (heterogeneity; singularity) all the while giving themselves to the other and becoming one (identity; universality). Or in slightly different terms, love places two immaculate and immanent beings (with consciousnesses of self for self and by self) in communion with each other (with a will of other for other) (RECC, RECC, Part One, I, 29-30, pp. 39-43; Part One, II, 34, p. 49; Part One, II, 55-57, pp. 75-76, 79-80; Part Three, II, 220-221, 223, pp. 257-259; Conclusion, 269, pp. 319-321; PLP, I, 1, pp. 32-35; I, 3, pp. 60-63; II, 5, p. 104; II, 7, p. 132; III, 8, pp. 137-138; Conclusion, XIII, pp. 218, 233; HPN, I, 4, pp. 9-11; PE, I, 9, pp. 86-88). Nédoncelle asserts:

> I become the other, to the degree that I promote the existence of the other, and am wanted by the other. Through this will, the two subjects become one, and this cannot happen except in the measure in which they are different (PLP, I, 1, p. 33 [44]).
>
> Personality is the condition of the self that obliges it to seek its progressive fulfillment by itself, according to a perspective at once unique and universal (PLP, I, 3, p. 60 [74-75]; cf. RECC, Part One, III, 79, p. 109; RECC, Part Two, I, 118, p. 151; PLP, II, 7, p. 132; Conclusion, XIII, p. 217).

So in the end reciprocity of consciousnesses creates what Nédoncelle calls a dyad or a 'we' [*nous*] (RECC, Part One, I, 18-19, pp. 27-29; II, 37, 55-57, pp. 52, 75-76, 78-80; Conclusion, 269, pp. 319-321; PLP, Preface, p. viii; Introduction, p. 5; I, 7, p. 124; III, 12, pp. 189-190; TDC, II, pp. 15-18; IO, IX, p. 89 [102]). For in the intimate communion of two people (an I and a thou) there arises a consciousness of oneself in another and another in oneself wherein what is intimate in oneself lodges in another stream of life, and the two people now live and grow together (RECC, Part One, I, 24, 26, pp. 33-34; Part One, II, 43, p. 58; PLP, I, 1, pp. 30-32; I, 2, p. 56). In this way, two human lovers incorporate each other's values and purposes into their own being (endosmosis or introception), and so each is transformed by the other (RECC, Part Three, II, 218, p. 254; PLP, II, 5, pp. 109-110).

Nédoncelle goes on to develop his ethics on the basis of this reciprocity of consciousnesses. For in order to generate a true love, an efficacious dyad, a reciprocal communion, one must embrace what Nédoncelle terms the "ideal self" [le moi idéal] as opposed to the "empirical self" [le moi empirique]. The empirical self is the awareness of one's unique living self which is irreducibly original, but also temporal and fragmentary (RECC, Part One, I, 6, p. 15; Part One, III, 74, 82, 88, 91, pp. 102, 112-113, 118, 121; PLP, II, 5, pp. 106-107; III, 8, p. 139; Conclusion, XIII, p. 218). The ideal self, on the other hand, is the self that I strive to be, my best and deepest self, my true essence, and it occurs within my conscience *sub specie bonitatis meae* (under the form of my goodness). Ultimately the ideal self, as we will see, is the self God wants me to be (an intimate divine tribunal), or better God's active presence or creative will in me (RECC, Part One, II, 52-53, pp. 72-73; Part One, III, 65, 69-70, 74, 76-77, 82, 88, 91, 93, pp. 90-91, 94-95, 102-103, 106, 112-113, 118, 121, 123; Part Two, II, 54, p. 74; Part Two, III, 147, pp. 183-184; IV, 162, p. 197; Part Three, I, 183-184, pp. 220-221; Part Three, IV, 260, 263-264, 266-267, pp. 305, 309, 312, 314-315; Conclusion, 269, p. 321; PLP, I, 2-3, pp. 47, 61, 70; II, 4-5, pp. 100, 102-105, 108, 111-112; II, 7, pp. 132-133; III, 8, p. 153; Conclusion, XIII, p. 218; HPN, I, 3-4, pp. 6-11; IV, 46-47, pp. 89-90; VII, 80, pp. 140-141; IO, I, pp. 4-9, 13 [11-15, 23-24]). Let us now look at a few passages of Nédoncelle in regard to this ideal self:

> Communication [is] ... a primitive fact, but it would lose all its meaning if it did not have as a correlative an intimate vocation, a freedom of choice and adhesion, a self-formation of character, and attachment to a transcendent source which places each human being above the conditioning forces of nature and society. The tension and the surpassing [of oneself] thus manifest a call and a grace (PLP, Conclusion, XIII, pp. 211-212 [238]).
>
> In order to conquer myself, I must then enter with the universe into a relationship of reciprocal knowledge and action. ... Each expression of myself in time [la durée] presupposes a positive self that aims at an ideal

value, and an ideal value that requires my positive self. I am an active
freedom by my absolute vocation (PLP, III, 8, pp. 153-154 [177]).

... every perception of another implies a minimum of reciprocity; every reciprocity is initially and essentially allied to love; all personal love
is at the same time the sentiment, knowledge, and will to promotion;
finally, every will to promotion involves a continuity of the world of spirits and even a heterogeneous identity of the I and thou, since the ideal I
and thou are then intermingled in the loving act (PLP, II, 4, p. 92 [109]).

At its apex the ideal self also reveals a path of natural reason to God.
It does so through a reflection on the intimate interior of oneself: "In
order to go to God we must have reason, but we must also have an-
tennas" (CL, I, 6, p. 135; cf. ITCP, Introduction, pp. 9-11; I, p. 17).[82]
Here Nédoncelle takes a three-pronged approach. First there is a "way
of access to the divine" through the values (transcendentals) of truth,
goodness, and beauty.[83] The fecundity of math, the goodness of moral
heroism (wherein we may be led to do what is right against our will),
the beauty of art and music (such as in Bach and Handel) show us
the existence of an order of reality superior to nature and ourselves.
Values give us the conviction of crossing a frontier, of discovering an
autonomous source of gracious and disinterested nobility, a spiritual
authority. As Nédoncelle sees it, no one can look into the eyes of a
child, or at a great work of art, without feeling at some level that a
divine charity is present and that it is capable of bearing my burdens
(RECC, Part Three, III, 242, pp. 282-283; cf. RECC, Part One, III,
76, 79, pp. 104-105, 109; Part Three, I, 174, 188, pp. 212, 224-225;
Part Three, IV, 268, pp. 315-316; PLP, II, 4, pp. 90, 99; Conclusion,
XIII, pp.231-232; CL, I, 5-6, pp. 117-118, 120-126, 139-142; HPDP,
II, 1, pp. 70-75; PE, I, 4, pp. 56-60; TDC, VI, pp. 58-59; HPN, II, 8,
pp. 21-23).

Yet while the existence of values shows us that a divine being exists (that mercy is the first principle of reality and that perfection and
complete unification is realized somewhere), it gives us an incomplete
perception of God, a God who is veiled. It falls short of revealing a
personal God (or as Nédoncelle puts it, values give us a consciousness
of God, but not a consciousness of God living in us) (RECC, Part
One, I, 14, p. 22; Part One, II, 54, p. 74; Part One, III, 76, 79, pp.
104-105, 109; Part One, III, 90-91, pp. 119-121; Part Three, I, 174,
177-178, 182, 186, 191, 195-196, pp. 213-216, 219, 222-223, 227,
230-231; Part Three, II, 202, pp. 237-238; PLP, II, 4, p. 93; Conclu-

sion, p. 223; HPDP, II, 7, pp. 148-160; Epilogue, p. 178; CL, I, 6, pp. 123, 127-138).

There is accordingly, for Nédoncelle, an additional "way of access," not just "to the divine," but "to God," wherein one can discover a more personal God through reflection on the origin, vocation, and destiny of the human person. For as we have seen, the human has the task of being both a unique person (originality) as well as embracing a universal perspective (unity). Said differently, the human is called to retain its individual autonomy, yet, all the while, to enter into a 'we' with another human, a union where there is real reciprocity and mutual influence and moreover the potential for unlimited development. We could thus say that a human receives, as a task and a promise (indeed as a promise that precedes me), a call to the total accomplishment of itself within a total communication of consciousnesses, a call to find the fullness of its being in a harmonious union of beings.

Yet these demands exceed the resources of nature and myself. I, with my limited resources, certainly could not bring such a promise into being. Nor can nature, which returns me to myself, ensure an indefinite growth in my identity (interiority) by entering into a harmony of consciousnesses (exteriority). I am doomed to frustration if I try to erect the promise of an ongoing (even infinite) career of continuity, yet one with continued innovation (wherein something new and original is created), on such scant foundations (RECC, Part One, II, 56, p. 79; Part One, III, 64-66, 84, 86-88, 90, pp. 88-92, 114, 116-120; Part Three, II, 218, pp. 253-254; Part Three, III, 234, p. 269; PLP, I, 3, pp. 65, 79; II, 5, pp. 112-114; III, 8, pp. 155-156; Conclusion, pp. 221, 223; CL, Preface, pp. 9-10; I, 6, pp. 127-130, 134-138).

In order to explain how such a task and promise can arise, we consequently need to posit a Divine Thou [*Toi Divin*] who is the creator and unlimited promotor [*promotor indefini*] of the human being. God is a person whose grace gives me the power to be simultaneously faithful to my essence and to the development of a spiritual harmony with others, the power to preserve my identity as well as enact the universal perfection of the 'we' (RECC, Part One, III, 67-72, 91, pp. 92-98, 121; PLP, II, 4-5, pp. 93, 112-114; Conclusion, pp. 221-222; CL, Preface, pp. 9-10, I, 6, pp. 128-131; HPN, VII, 85-91, pp. 146-153). For God gives me an end, a direction to my life, a vocation (a deep immanent law of my development) toward a connection of spirits—one which I cannot give to myself. God additionally is a great personal consciousness that envelops me (roots me) and gives me the strength to perfect myself and others (in other words, God always accompanies me along the way). I grasp God then as this anterior power granting me the possibility of attaining a harmonious reciprocal love and simultaneously spiritually invent myself. Finally, in God, I perceive myself as preceded, as wanted, by a being who is the voluntary source of myself and the extramundane infinite energy of charity. The God of Charity [le Dieu-Charité], the Infinite Good, is therefore an ever vigilant and victorious charity that my will finds beyond itself and which invites me to constitute myself for others (RECC, Part One, III, 63, 66, 68-70, 74, 76-79, 93-95, pp. 88-89, 92-94, 101, 105, 107-110; PLP, Preface, p. ix; I, 3, pp. 69, 80; Conclusion, XIII, pp. 222, 231).

God is hence the incessant grace, always present in nature, through which I think and act,[84] the eternal Thou that precedes, achieves, and completes my creative acts ["I think, thus I am thought; I will, thus I am willed"] (PLP; II, 4, p. 93 [110]; cf. PLP, I, 3, p. 75; RECC, Part One, I, 8, p. 17; Part One, I, 19-29, pp. 29-39; Part One, I, 30-32, pp. 41-46; Part One, III, 64, 66-71, pp. 86-87, 92-98; Part Three, II, 224-225, pp. 259-260; Part Three, IV, 251, 268, pp. 294-295, 316-317; CL, II, 1, pp. 166-167; II, 3, pp. 205-206; Conclusion, pp. 228-231; "FTP," pp. 24-25). Nédoncelle writes:

> The invincible absolute can only be a charity. For it then supports all things ... It communicates to each consciousness in order to achieve this. By knowing all knowledge, it introduces identity there, by attaching itself to all love it provokes and ratifies diversity ... finally by wanting all wanting it announces universality, because its wanting is infinitely good. ... Thus it is at the same time giving an imperative [imperation] and liberation, beginning and end" (RECC, Part One, III, 92, p. 122).

> In the initial purity of the conscience and in its call to an unlimited development, we can recognize the necessary presence of a being which is not nature and which gives us our personhood. That such a being would be a subsisting charity is what has appeared to us as a certitude. That this charity should be worthy of being called personal or rather superpersonal, is, in the limit of a rational demonstration, the best way that we have and the most sure of expressing ourselves. Exigent mercy, absolute authority, and elevating love: God is this or He is nothing (RECC, Part One, III, 76, p. 103).

> [Love] does not even fear to aspire to the conquest and explanation of all realities: the task it gives itself is to take the universe as it is and to transform it according to its own law. It is the ideal that, under penalty

of destroying itself, recoils before nothing. ... It undertakes to acquire the fullness of the real if it does not yet possess it. It is a voracious and agile value that must not leave anything without relation to itself, and for which it is indispensable to be able to distribute all the destinies. It alone claims to bear the weight of the world, and it is obliged to do so by virtue of its primitive impulse [élan]. ... Reason, however, urges that love would stop midway and render itself irrational if it were not itself a living consciousness in which ours find their source, their support, and their end. No obstacle can forbid this assertion, and all the indications [indices] of our experience suggest that we accept it (PLP, I, 3, pp. 65, 76 [80-81, 94]; cf. PLP, I, 3, p. 66-67, 72).

Lastly, Nédoncelle allows, as a legitimate path to God, the "intuition of a donor," or the knowledge of God through personal experience. He argues that throughout life, especially in times of crisis, we can have a personal contact with God as a protector and friend. And some humans can further attain a supernatural mystical experience of God (RECC, Part One, III, 76, p. 103; CL, Preface, p. 10; I, 6, pp. 134-138; HPDP, II, 7, pp. 151-160).[85]

In a similar manner we can show (with at least some degree of probability) that the soul is immortal, for Nédoncelle, through our experience of love. For love is not a will for annihilation but for the continued prolongation of two personal consciousnesses [love wishes for an immortal community of beloveds]. And love, which requires a sacrifice of oneself, seeks the unlimited development of the dyad of lover-beloved, something which is unattainable in this life. Hence love awaits another life and gives us reason to believe in the immortality of the soul wherein love will be perfected and one will regain what one has sacrificed (RECC, Part Three, II, 224-225, pp. 259-260; Part Three, IV, 248, 251, 259-260, 266, pp. 292, 299, 304-306, 314). Finally we also recognize that something of eternal value is elaborated in the irreversible course of our decisions, that we bear a responsibility for the creation of ourselves and of loving relationships. This then suggests the existence of a place of judgment, a place of reward (heaven) for those who display love and a place of punishment (hell) for those who do not (though we need not take the sensible image of hell as burning fire literally). In short, it suggests that we collaborate in the creation of our destiny. Some thinkers have of course rejected the existence of hell (i.e. universalists) as it would indicate a divine cruelty. However, the divine cannot be indifferent to a rejection of itself, and it would be far worse of God to give out what is not merited (this would mean that God rewards those who refuse to respond to a generous divine solicitation, those who are carried along by the love of God but don't advance it) (RECC, Part Three, IV, 263, p. 308).[86]

5

EXISTENTIALISM

1930-1970 at its Peak (Continuing on into 2000) in Belgium,
England, France, Germany, Italy, Mexico, Spain, & the United States

In 1940, with the establishment of the Vichy Regime (1940-1944), a Catholic served as the French Minister of Education for the first time in almost twenty years, the classical philosopher Albert Rivaud (1876-1955), who was followed by another Catholic philosopher Jacques Chevalier from 1940-1941 [Chevalier was later sentenced to hard labor after the fall of the Vichy Regime], and the Catholic existentialist Louis Lavelle was appointed Inspector General for Public Education from 1940-1941. The Vichy Regime also set up the École Nationale des Cadres at Uriages (1940-1942) where its diplomats were educated and where such Catholic thinkers as Henri de Lubac, S.J. (1896-1991), Jean Lacroix (1900-1986), Emmanuel Mounier (1901-1950), Jean Guitton (1901-1999), and Jean-Marie Domenach (1922-1997) taught (indeed Guitton was banned from university teaching from 1946-1950 on account of his pro-Vichy writings).

Hence ironically, at the same time as the Nazis were working to overturn the Christian religion in Germany, for political reasons they instituted the decidedly pro-Catholic Vichy Regime in Southern France during World War II (1939-1945).[87]

So in 1940-1942 the Vichy Regime, headed by the French Action proponent Marshal Pétain, the Catholic Pierre Laval, and the Catholic Minister of Justice Raphaël Alibert, officially legalized the presence of all religious orders in France (since 1901 the presence of non-sanctioned religious orders was merely tolerated) and allowed them to teach in private and state schools. Religious education was again made the norm in state schools (though limited after 1942), and a temporary school bond program was established to fund private Catholic schools. In addition much of the property of the Catholic Church that had been seized during the Third Republic was returned. As the Catholic poet Paul Claudel (1868-1955) wrote: "France is delivered after sixty years of slavery under the radical and anti-Catholic party (professors, lawyers, Jews, and Free Masons). The new government invokes God and renders the Grand Chartreuse to the religious, hope of being delivered from universal suffrage and parlementarism" (Journal Entry of July 6, 1940).

The Vichy Regime was also unfortunately a pawn of the Nazi's and hence in 1940 passed laws excluding Communists, Freemasons, Gypsies, Homosexuals, Immigrants, and Jews from public office, the press, and teaching (and Jews had to register their status with the local government). In addition in 1940 around 15,000 people (40% of whom were Jews) had their French nationality revoked. Then beginning in 1942 75,000 French Jews (out of around 350,00 Jews in France) were rounded up and deported to the French internment camps of Beaune-la-Rolande, Drancy, and Pithiviers, and then to Germany and Poland (only around 2500 of whom survived the war after they fell prey to neglect and the Nazi labor and death camps—historians debate the degree to which the French authorities knew the ultimate fate waiting for the Jews under the hands of the Nazis, nonetheless Pierre Laval was later executed and Philippe Pétain imprisoned for life).

In 1995 the French government apologized for collaboration with the Nazis and in 1997 the French Catholic hierarchy apologized for the same reason. Lest we forget, several French bishops had spoken out against the Jewish deportations (and in some cases the anti-Jewish laws as well) such as Jean Delay of Marseille, Pierre-Marie Gerlier of Lyon who founded the L'Amitie Chretienne (1941-), Jean Géraud Saliège of Toulouse, and Pierre-Marie Théas of Montauban, as well as the Catholic poets Paul Claudel and Charles Péguy, the Catholic novelist Léon Bloy, the Catholic intellectuals Étienne Borne, Claude Bourdet who wrote for Combat (1944-), Fr. Pierre Chaillet, S.J., Henri Daniel-Rops who edited Les Juifs (Paris: Plon, 1937) [with essays by Maritain and others], Oscar de Ferenzy who edited Les juifs et les chrétiens (1936-1940) and wrote Les Juifs et nous chrétiens (Paris: Flammarion, 1935), Bruno De Solages, Rector of the Catholic Institute of Toulouse, the Oratorian Marie-André Dieux, Gaston Fessard, S.J. who founded the resistance review Cahier du Témoignage Chrétien (1941-) [and solicited contributions from François Mauriac, Henri Chambre, S.J., and Stanislas Fumet who also edited Temps présent

which was banned in 1941 for criticizing anti-Semitism], Victor Fon-
toynont, S.J., who wrote "Le sens chretienne de l'histoire," *Rencontre* 4
(1942), Charles Journet who edited *Israel et la foi chretienne* (Fribourg:
Luf, 1942) [with contributions by Joseph Chaine, Joseph Bonsirven,
Louis Richard, and Henri de Lubac] and wrote the article "Antisemi-
tisme," *Nova et Veta* (1941), Gabriel Marcel whose articles were censored in 1942 by the Vichy Regime, Jacques Maritain, the Sulpician
Canon Louis Richard, who wrote "La question juive et la foi chretienne" for the *Chronique social de France* in 1942 which was censored
and not published until 1952 and his *Israel et le Christ* (Fribourg: Luf,
1942), and Auguste Valensin, S.J., as had the Vatican itself in 1942.
We can also mention the Seelisberg Conference on Jewish-Christian
Relations in Switzerland (1947).

Nor should we forget those French Catholics who risked imprisonment and death in order to help Jews escape the country such as the
Capuchin Pierre-Marie Benoît in Marseilles, Pierre Chaillet, S.J., Fr.
Joseph Folliet, founder of the Compagnons de Saint François, the Jewish convert Fr. Alexandre Glasberg, Mother Marie of Notre Dame de
Sion in Melun, Edmond Michelet who became Minister of Justice in
1959-1961 (who also arranged for the flight of Dietrich von Hildebrand as we have seen), and Abbé Pierre the founder of Emmaus.

In fact around 1942 many Catholics began to turn against the Vichy
Regime when they witnessed the reversal of some pro-Catholic educational policies, its unwillingness to grant a new Concordat, its increasing anti-Semitism and deportations of French Jews, and the forced
departure of French youth to labor in Germany, including former supporters such as Cardinal Alfred-Henri-Marie Baudrillart, Rector of
the Catholic Institute of Paris, Cardinal Emmanuel Célestin Suhard
of Paris, Henri Frenay who edited *Verités* (1941-) and wrote for *Combat* (1944-), and Emmanuel Mounier (1905-1950) and his journal *Esprit* which was banned in 1941 for its critique of anti-Semitism.

Four of the French figures mentioned above, Chevalier, Guitton,
Lavelle, and Marcel, were involved in the philosophical movement of
existentialism. Existentialism was a philosophical movement that held
that thought must begin by examining the concrete existential situation of the human being. Existentialists accordingly placed stress on
the overall meaning of human existence, the freedom to choose how
one acts, and the incorrectness of an abstract and disinterested approach to philosophy and life. So too if theistic they emphasized expe-

riential paths to God; for existentialism came in both atheistic (Heidegger and Sartre) and theistic flavors (Kierkegaard, and the various
Catholic Existentialists).

One of the founders of French Existentialism [or what he called the
Philosophy of the Spirit] was **Louis Lavelle (1883-1951)**.[88] Lavelle
was born in 1883 in Saint-Martin-de-Villéreal, Lot-et-Garonne,
Aquitaine, France. Deciding against attending the École Normale Supérieure, he studied at the University of Lyon with Arthur Hanne-
quin from 1906-1909, and was involved with the libertarian movement there, attaining his license to teach in 1909. From 1909 to 1914
Lavelle attended graduate school in philosophy at the Sorbonne in
Paris (studying with Octave Hamelin, Léon Brunschvicg, and Henri
Bergson at the nearby Collège de France) and taught in various lycées
throughout France, including the Lycée of Laon (1906-1907), the Lycée of Neufchateau (1907-1909), the Lycée of Vendôme (1909-1911),
and the Lycée of Limoges (1911-1914). Lavelle married Julie Bernard
in 1913 (with whom he had three daughters, each of whom became a
professor, as well as a son who developed a painful bone condition and
whom Lavelle cared for; and indeed one of his grandsons is the trea-
surer of the L'Association Louis Lavelle). After World War I broke out
in 1914, Lavelle voluntarily entered the French Army and took part in
battles at Aisne, Somme, and Verdun in 1915. During an engagement
on the Western Front in 1916, Lavelle was captured and confined to
a prisoner of war camp for the duration of the war. Quite amazingly,
Lavelle was able to complete his major dissertation for the Sorbonne
while he was a prisoner and he taught a course on Pascal to his fellow
prisoners.

After World War I ended in 1918, Lavelle was released. He completed his doctorate in philosophy from the Sorbonne in 1922 (under André Lalande, Léon Brunschvicg, and Étienne Gilson) and continued to teach at lycées throughout France until 1932 including the
Lycée Fustel-de-Coulanges in Strasbourg (1919-1925) where he also
helped organize the Alsace-Lorraine schooling system, the Lycée de
Saint-Louis in Paris (1924-1925), and the Lycées Condorcet, Victor
Duruy, Louis-le-Grand, and Henri IV (1925-1940).

Lavelle himself became a professor of philosophy at the Sorbonne
in 1932 and held the position of chargé d'enseignement there from
1934-1936. In 1934 Lavelle founded the movement and book series

"Philosophy of the Spirit" with René Le Senne.[89] As we have seen, with the rise of the pro-Catholic Vichy Regime in 1940, Lavelle was appointed Inspector General for Public Education in 1940, serving under his friend Jacques Chevalier who was the new Minister of Education. At the pinnacle of his fame and influence, Lavelle was elected into the prestigious philosophy position at the Collège de France in Paris in 1941 (replacing Édouard Le Roy who had replaced Henri Bergson; Lavelle himself was to be succeeded by Maurice Merleau-Ponty). Lavelle went on to found the philosophy journal Logos (1939-), write a history of philosophy series, Chroniques philosophiques, for the journal Le Temps (1930-1942), and participate in the Centre catholique des intellectuels français (1949). Lavelle died in Parranquet, Lot-et-Garonne, France in 1951. Lavelle was elected into the Academy of Moral and Political Sciences in 1947, into the Academy of the Peloritana in Messina, and into the Academy of Sciences of Bologna in 1950; he was also a member of the Legion of Honor. Lavelle Colloquia were held in 1983 and 1985, and an Association Louis Lavelle was founded in 1989 along with its Bulletin (1989), and a journal Études Lavelliennes has been promised to appear soon. Lavelle was described by his fellow faculty member at the Collège de France, Maurice Halbwachs, as a "nice, sweet, distinguished, and friendly man, a little dull."

Lavelle's key works are his On Act [De l'Acte] [OA] (1937) and The Error of Narcissus [orifessor] [EN] (1939), written under the influence of Plato, Descartes, Malebranche, Nietzsche, Bergson, Maine de Biran, and Hamelin.[90]

The key to reality, for Lavelle, is the human act. Now an act is a putting into play of a movement that only I can accomplish; it depends on my initiative alone (OA, I, 1, pp. 42-43; I, 4, p. 62; I, 8, p. 100; I, 9, pp. 114-115; CS, V, pp. [93-95]; VI, pp. [117-122]). For in acting, I experience my own self-causation, my initiative from within, a pure efficacy ever present and available by which I break from the laws of phenomenal nature (even if I am also affected by nature and habit to a degree) (OA, I, 1, pp. 43-45; I, 7, p. 84; II, 18, p. 165; EN, I, 11, p. 36; VII, 10, p. 134).

So by focusing my attention on the inner act by which I constitute my personal life, I can grasp my freedom of the will, an "internal experience of the act in its initiative and in its accomplishment" (OA, I, 1, p. 52 [21]). For instance I recognize the power within me of being able to move my little finger (OA, I, 1, pp. 42-44; I, 4, p. 65; I, 7, pp.

[120-125]; I, 8, p. 100; OSI, p. [282]). Indeed this is the only way I can do so, for those who seek freedom in the zone of the observable will not find it, and, in fact, will be left wondering how freedom could ever insert itself there] (OA, II, 11, pp. 126, 133; II, 12, p. 145; III, 25, pp. [455-479]; OBG, Introduction, pp. [9, 22]; OHS, III, 10, 13, pp. [237-264, 317-342]; TV, vol. I, II, 3, pp. [413-431]; PS, III, 9, pp. [139-162]; CRO, I, 3, pp. [20-22]; III, 4, pp. [55-57]; VI, pp. [111-113]; "SSI," pp. 70-78). As Lavelle writes:

> Scientific laws help me not at all to know the individual now before me. I focus my attention upon him; I know he must obey these laws ... However what I am looking for as I watch him is not the external things which influence him and which he cannot change, for these express what he is not, rather than what he is; I am looking for the freedom which he exercises, sometimes without knowing it, for were it not for this I would relegate him to the domain of things, and would cease to consider him, in both senses of the word. The rule which we apply to our knowledge of other people, namely never to stop at words or acts, but to penetrate to meanings and intentions, clearly shows where, in every domain, we must seek the truly real. In all things, as here, it resides in their inwardness and their spirituality, of which we see nothing but the appearance—an appearance which often distorts the truth, but which is nearly always as far as we go (EN, XII, 2, pp. 209-210).

An act then is a putting into play of the potentialities within my being (OA, I, 1, pp. 42-43; I, 8, p. 100; EN, VII, 3, pp. 126-127; TP, II, pp. 22, 25; OHS, Introduction, p. 215; I, 1, pp. 239-240). For the self, in a way, is "nothing but a possibility waiting to be realized, and never completely made, it is never done making itself" (EN, II, 1, p. 43), it is a "pure potentiality, just insofar as it has not yet been exercised" (EN, I, 5, p. 29). What is more, with my freedom I can choose to actualize these powers and constitute my being, or to leave them in a state of potency and let them wither away (EN, I, 5, p. 29; III, 7, 10-11, pp. 66, 70-71; X, 3, p. 178; OA, II, 11, pp. 133-134; II, 12, pp. [200-216]; II, 17, p. [289]; OHS, II, 5, pp. [115-138], Conclusion, pp. [539-556]; CRO, X, 1, pp. 181-183; ES, II, 5, pp. 111-115; PBTW, p. 268). Lavelle states:

> Our self is nothing more than a bundle of virtualities: it is for us to realize them. ... And it is quite conceivable that one should miss it, whether through laziness or through fear, or because one finds it easier or more expedient to yield to public opinion and to renounce oneself, letting

oneself be dragged unresistingly down the slope of social conformity. ... Sincerity is at once the attention which arouses our potentialities, and the courage which gives them form, without which they would be nothing. ... Sincerity consists not merely, as is imagined, of examining with pitiless lucidity one's own secret thoughts; it compels this same inner being to cross its own frontiers, to take its place in the world, and there to manifest what it is (EN, III, 11, p. 71).

The anguish of existence and the secret of responsibility reside at that precise point at which, before the eyes of the world, we convert into an act which leaves an indelible trace upon the world, a possibility which previously had no existence except for us (EN, III, 5, p. 64).

The whole art of living consists in preventing our intermittent good impulses from going to waste and withering away. We must take hold of them, set them to work, and make them bear fruit. The essential sin is, without any possible doubt, the sin of negligence (EN, X, 3, p. 178).

In a way then in an act I wrench myself from becoming and create my being. For the act precedes my being and determines it, and every word I say and every thing I do add to what I am. In acting, as it were, I consent to release one of various options that can become my own, and in so doing I consent to what I wish to think, say, produce, and be (OA, I, 1, p. 43; I, 9, pp. 106, 111; I, 11, pp. 129-130; II, 18, p. 151; TP, I, p. 7; II, pp. 25, 27; EN, I, 8, p. 34; II, 8, pp. 43-44; III, 10-11, pp. 70-71; OBG, I, p. [47]; FS, V, p. 100; OHS, II, 9, pp. [210-235]; IONT, II, 1, p. 81; "IO," p. 182). Acting is thus a form of self-creation, for I am nothing if not what I make of myself (EN, I, 5, p. 29; II, 9, p. 53; OA, I, 1, pp. 44, 51, 53; I, 4, pp. 61, 67; I, 7, p. 84; I, 11, pp. 120, 126-127; II, 12, pp. 138, 148; OHS, I, 1, pp. 227, 240-241; OTE, II, 4, p. 176; III, 7, p. 189; "IPB," p. 47). To again quote Lavelle here:

The function of consciousness is to force me to take possession of myself. And this taking possession resembles a creation, since it consists in giving reality to a potential being which has, so to say, been put at our disposal. But to remain as a potentiality is not to be. I can then, if I choose, not be; I can refuse to accept the existence which is ceaselessly offered me (EN, III, 6, p. 65).

It is the case that there is no other inside than the act itself by which, in consenting to be, I create my own being and I inscribe within the totality of being a mark that eternally subsists (OA, I, 4, p. 71).

What shall I do with existence during the long interval of time which, I always tend to imagine, still separates me from death—this stretch of time, in which everything will depend on what may be given me, but still more on the way I receive it? There is a fundamental rule which I must keep ever before my eyes, namely, that my life's every action, my mind's every thought, my body's every movement should be, as it were, a commitment and a creation of my being, an expression of a decision taken, and of my determination to be what these proclaim. This must also be true of every sentence I speak or write, whereas so often I am content merely to describe a memory or to designate an object. For every man invents himself unceasingly, though he does not know what the end will be. As soon as he stops inventing, he changes into a thing (EN, IV, 11, pp. 89-90).

Indeed only in the act can we show ourselves as we truly are. For only by facing obstacles that test our mettle and our commitment to various ideals, and staying the course, can we provide testimony of our true character. And so we never become entirely ourselves "until we go out from ourselves to act, until we leave the domain of pure vitality to take our place in the world" (EN, IV, 1, p. 77). As Lavelle asks: "What is an interior disposition unattested by any act? In this sense I am what I do, and not what I am capable of; the latter is merely what I think I could do" (EN, IV, 10, pp. 87-88). Lavelle here even anticipates Sartre in asserting that we first possess existence, and only later by acting manifest our essence (OA, I, 6, pp. [92-97]; II, 12, pp. 136-140, 148; II, 18, pp. 150, 158; EN, III, 10-11, pp. 70-71; OSI, pp. 70-71; IONT, I, 2, pp. 33-39; OHS, II, 9, pp. [210-236]).

Yet contrary to Sartre, for Lavelle the act is a duty to be fulfilled, a task to be realized. That is to say, it is only by participation in being, and, moreover, in the essence and secret initiative that it holds out for us, that we can truly create ourselves. For the creation of ourselves is only viable, in the end, if we enter into a relation with eternal actuality, with the Absolute (i.e. God), receiving a possibility it proposes to us (OA, I, 1, p. 44, 46-48; I, 4, p. 69; I, 7, pp. 77, 79, 83-85; I, 8, pp. 94, 98; II, 11,18, pp. 139, 168; II, 12, p. 203; III, 19, pp. [337-344, 352]; III, 22-23, pp. [397-428]; OBG, Introduction, pp. [18-20]; 8, p. [239]; EN, III, 10, p. 70; V, 6, p. 100; OHS, I, 2, pp. 45-64; "IPB," pp. 43-44, 50-52; "SSI," pp. 79-80). We cannot then just choose to be anything, rather we must choose to live in accordance with our deepest essence or true and better self—with the values that God has instantiated in us—and body them forth (EN, II, 1, 6, pp. 44, 65; OA, I, 1, pp. 45, 56; I, 4, p. 62). In fact in realizing myself I also must draw upon a transcendent source and power beyond the I, a power which supports and sustains me, and which I make my own (OHS, Introduction, p. 212; OA, I, 4, pp. 58, 68-70; I, 8, p. 91; I, 11, pp. 133-134; II, 12, p. 135; EN, III, 12, p. 72; IV, 11, pp. 89-90; VII, 8, p. 131)—an absolute being which is *partout présent tout entier* [everywhere wholly present]), in Lavelle's notable words.[91] It is worthwhile here to peruse some of Lavelle's formulations of this idea:

> There is an inwardness which no eye can see but it is reality's ultimate bedrock, beyond which it is impossible to go and which one cannot reach without passing through all the superficial layers which vanity, easy conformism, or habit have wrapped around it ... It is indeed as many believe the remotest point of solitude. But also, the moment we discover it, we are no longer alone. A world opens out which is within us but into which every being can be invited (EN, II, 2, p. 44).
>
> It seems that consciousness has been given to us less that we might choose to be what we would like to be, than to discover what we already are. We are only truly free when the revelation has been vouchsafed to us of what we are of necessity. Until then, we think we are free, but, in reality, we are the sport of each isolated whim; we merely drift from one beginning to another, from one disillusionment to another, forever unsatisfied, a mere spectator of ourselves. Can it be said that there is no worse slavery than to be imprisoned in one's essence? But the man who could argue thus is the living proof that he has not found his essence. The truth is that we have the incomparable privilege of seeking it, of coming to understand it, and of being faithful to it; failing which, it remains nothing, like a talent unused. ... and which is for us not so much to know as to realize (EN, VII, 2, pp. 124-126).

Lavelle does not hesitate to make use of the theological notions of destiny and vocation here (OA, II, 11, pp. 130-134; II, 12, p. 147; EN, VII, 3, pp. 126-127). For to constitute my essence, I must participate in the call of the divine, embrace a model God never ceases proposing to me, a model which is there for me to discover and to will (OA, II, 18, pp. 168-170; EN, II, 7, p. 51; VII, 11, pp. 135-136). More specifically, our vocation is what we are called to do [*devoir-être*] (our true essence, the design God has for us), what we are good at, what brings us a sense of peace and joy and ease, and what rings true (EN, VII, 2, pp. 124-126; TP, I, pp. 14-16; II, pp. 34-35; V, pp. 97-98, 145-146; OHS, IV, 13, pp. [453-476]; OA, III, 9, pp. [353-362]; FS, I, pp. 15-16; CS, VI, p. [123]). In Lavelle's words:

> And so my vocation is my response to the voice of my most intimate and secret being ... It is at first nothing more than a possibility which

is offered me; the original character of my spiritual life consists in making this possibility mine. Then it becomes my true essence. ... A vocation has no distinguishing mark; we are given no extraordinary sign that we are objects of election; our vocation remains invisible, although it transfigures the humblest tasks of our daily lives. Yet because it brings the sense of a correspondence between what we have to do and the talents we have been vouchsafed, it lightens our path and supports us on our way. When he finds it, each of us is born to the spiritual life, and ceases to feel isolated and useless. It does not absolve us from the obligation to decide and to act, as one might imagine; the contrary is true. It lays an immense burden on our shoulders, calling us to be ready to accept some new duty, to commit ourselves—never to stand idly by ... This we may call the design which God has for each of us, and which we may, indeed, never realize. In that case our life has failed; it has slipped by outside us as it were, and without our participation; it has never emerged from the world of appearance, and day by day and moment by moment it has passed into oblivion with them (EN, VII 5, 7, pp. 128-131).

Lavelle in this regard appeals to a beautiful metaphor and asserts that the human task is to create a spiritual self-portrait, with the world as our canvas or material (i.e. our template), our actions as our paint or chisel (i.e. our media), and values as our reference. For we must forge our being by our acts and in so doing leave for the world a beautiful work of art, or if we have painted or sculpted badly, purge ourselves of our ill-considered acts and start anew (EN, III, 2, p. 61; OA, II, 18, p. 168; OHS, I, 1, p. 229). Here it is worth reproducing two more quotes of Lavelle's:

The progressive formation of our inner being resembles the work both of the painter and the sculptor. The painter's art consists in the accumulation of successive touches of color. These innumerable individual touches outlast the movement of the artist's hand which applied them. In the same way, the soul seems to create itself, little by little, like a spiritual painting. But forgetting resembles sculpture, and its more abstract, severer procedure. It is the action of the sculptor's chisel, chipping fragments of marble away, that lays bare the form beneath. In the same way, the self must forget the events through which it has passed, together with the feelings it has experienced, and finally stand forth in its essential nudity. For without forgetting, purification and renunciation, forgiveness, and sleep, and death, are all inconceivable; it is always present in them all, though unable by itself to produce them. Forgetting is an essential element of all the notable forms of renunciation by means of which our being recollects itself, in the solitude of its essence and its truth (EN, VI, 9, pp. 119-120).

Forgetting is the mark of our weakness and our wretchedness, since it means that the individual is perpetually losing something of himself; but it is also the mark of our strength. It shows that our minds have the power to destroy comparable to the power to create, a power which is, in a sense, superior to the other. Further, it is a means of continual self-purification and rebirth. It gives us the presence of what is, by taking away from us the presence of what has ceased to be. It has an annihilating and liberating function which detaches us from every preoccupation which would impede us, enabling us to begin our lives all over again at every moment. ... there is a spiritual forgetting, which is positive, by means of which I commit, as it were, the whole of my past to God, so as to put all my confidence in his present gift of grace (EN, VI, 7, pp. 116-117).

Lavelle also develops his idea of vocation by introducing the apt distinction between real being and manifest being. My real being or inner being is my ideal being, the person I should be, i.e. my true essence. My manifest being or outer being is the being I show to the world, which often is a far cry from my true self (OA, II, 12, p. 48; EN, III, 3, p. 62; cf. III, 1-2, pp. 60-61; IV, 8, pp. 84-85; IONT, II, 3, pp. 110-115; TV, vol. I, II, 3, pp. [362-378]). Lavelle writes: "The whole problem of vocation therefore consists in knowing the distinction I should make between the very essence that God proposes to me, and which is always in my depths as the best and ideal part of myself so to speak, and the very essence I manage to realize and succeed in making an effective possession" (OA, II, 18, p. 168 [332]). Or as Lavelle observes at greater length:

[Other people] are concerned with my realized being more than with the act which calls it into being. They see in me the man already revealed, he who differs from everyone else in his character and in his weaknesses, and not the man I want to be, he who is forever seeking to transcend his nature and cure his imperfections. I am vaguely aware of the presence in myself of a power as yet unused, a hope as yet not disappointed. Another, observing me, sees nothing but the being I can show him, whereas what I am conscious of is the being I can never show. Unlike him, my eyes are always fixed on what I am not rather than on what I am, my ideal rather than on my present state, on the goal of my desires rather than the distance by which I am separated from it (EN, II, 7, pp. 50-51).

True sincerity does not consist in considering as real and our own all the obscure impulses, the unformed desires, the vague temptations which flit across our minds. They are not ours until we have begun to dwell upon them and to give them some consistency. True sincerity is to pass through them, to descend into the depths of ourselves, there to discover what we want to be (EN, III, 2, p. 60-61).

To be sincere is to descend into the depths of our selves, and there to find the gifts which are ours, and yet which are nothing except by the virtue of the use we make of them. It is refusing to let them lie unused. It is preventing them remaining buried within us, in the darkness of the realm of possibility. It is bringing them forth into the light of day, so that, in the view of all, they increase the wealth of the world, by being, as it were, a revelation which continually enriches it. Sincerity is the act by which, at one and the same time, a man knows himself and makes himself. It is the act by which he shows himself to be what he is, and consents to contribute, according to the measure of his strength to the work of creation (EN, III, 6, pp. 65-66).

For the key to living out our vocation is to display sincerity, i.e. to allow no distinction between our real being and our manifest being, to show ourselves to others exactly as we are (EN, III, 10, 12, pp. 70-72; IX, 6, pp. 163-164; CRO, V, 7, pp. 101-104; PS, IV, 14, pp. [254-278]; CS, VII, 5-7, pp. [152-162]; VIII, 10, pp. [186-189]). In his words, "sincerity is an attempt to abolish all the distinction between our real and our manifest selves. ... It demands of us that we should penetrate below and beyond all the superficial layers of consciousness, the domain of fleeting impressions, into that mysterious region where are born those deep desires which we acknowledge as our own, and which are our life's contact with the absolute" (EN, III, 7, p. 66).

The problem with Narcissus and humans of the same ilk is that they are primarily concerned with the image or spectacle they offer to the world (i.e. their image in the pool), an image that represents not so much what they are, nor even what they would like to be, but more what they wish people to believe they are. Sincere individuals, on the other hand, do not imagine that such an image exists, or if it exists that it is different from what they are. They hide nothing of what they are, admit no duplicity, evasion, or dissembling, ensuring that their being does not differ from their appearance, and only show forth the perfection of their nature (EN, I, 3, pp. 27-28; III, 5, 7-8, 12, pp. 64, 66, 68, 72; IV, 8-9, pp. 85-87; XII, 8, p. 216). Sincere people then follow the sage advice of Lavelle, revealed in one of his most famous quotes: "If I am what I ought to be within, I will also be so without. ... But, in solitude, it is necessary to act as if one were seen by all people, and when one is seen by all people, to act as if one were alone" (EN, III, 8, p. 67). Hence for Lavelle:

> A friend is someone in whose presence we hold nothing back; we show ourselves as we are; there is no difference between what we are and the impression we wish to create. And in him also there is abolished the difference, characteristic of our relations with all other men, between the within, which is only real for us, and the without, which is the appearance we offer to the world (EN, IX, 12, p. 171).
>
> Sincerity liberates us from every preoccupation with public opinion or with the effect we are producing. It brings us back to our own origin, showing us to ourselves as we were when we left the Creator's hands, when life first flashed forth, and before outer appearances had begun to seduce us, or we had learned the art of pretending (EN, III 12, p. 72).

In particular we are called to manifest love in all our will acts (OA, I, 1, pp. 50, 55; I, 8, pp. 97-98; I, 11, pp. 122-125; III, 27, pp. [522-536]; TP, II, p. 33; EN, II, 2, 4, pp. 45, 47; III, 6, p. 58; VII, 3, pp. 126-127; IONT, II, 2, pp. 95-109; OHS, II, 8, pp. [188-209], Conclusion, pp. [553-556]; PS, IV, 13, pp. [233-253]; CS, IX, 17, pp. [190-223]; PBTW, p. 264; FS, V, pp. 96-98, 100; TV, vol. I, II, 2, pp. [312-345]): "a human should have no other idea than to go out from himself into the world, to find something to know, or someone to love" (EN, I, 8, p. 33).

Here firstly we must love others for themselves and not as mere objects to describe or tool to use (EN, I, II, 7, p. 51; IX, 4, p. 161; CRO, X, 1-2, pp. [181-185]; XI, 4-6, pp. [214-225]; REL, XII, p. 85; XX, pp. 115-118; ES, III, 1-2, pp. 117-123).

Secondly, we must love others for what they can be (and help them to realize it) and not just for what they are, i.e. love them for their real being and not only their manifest being. Regrettably, while we see our own potentialities and make allowances for ourselves if we should falter, oftentimes we only see the bare actions of others and are quick to judge them and statuefy their characters (EN, II, 7, pp. 50-51). Lavelle expounds:

> There is no deep relationship between humans that is not founded on gentleness. ... Gentleness is not the same as indulgence for the faults of another; rather it is the recognition of his existence and his presence in the world. With the practice of gentleness, his mere existence ceases to be an offense to us; we no longer try to thwart him or destroy him; we accept him; we are happy that he

should be. We enjoy his existence, so to say, with him. We see it as an invitation to a spiritual cohabitation, physical cohabitation being no more than an image of this. Gentleness is active good will towards other men, not for what they are only, but for what they might be. It enables us to see many possibilities which a rougher hand would force underground or blight, and which, perhaps, would never come to the light of day and bear fruit were it not for the attention and confidence we have shown (EN, X, 7, pp. 182-183).

Thirdly, in love or charity, which Lavelle defines as "pure attention to the existence of another person" (EN, IX, 7, p. 165), we must be present to others, bestow our attention and affection upon them, show an interest in them, whether in act, word, questioning, or even silence (EN, II, 9-10, pp. 53-54; IV, 7, 9, pp. 84, 87; VI, 2, p. 111; ES, II, 3, pp. 104-107; IV, 1, pp. 135-139; CRO, II, 4-6, pp. [38-45]). That is to say each person is to be treated as a potential friend (CRO, X, 11-12, pp. [196-200]; ES, III, 5, pp. 131-133; FS, I, p. 3). Otherwise those whom we meet in life become "a passer-by of no more importance for us than the stones along the wayside" (EN, III, 5, p. 48). In the grand words of Lavelle [one's quite different from those of the atheist existentialist Sartre who said 'hell is other people' (Huis Clos)]:

> ... all those about us, all those we meet along the way are, for us, opportunities and challenges. We have no right to reject them. And so what we are left with is less the choice of people among whom we live, than the discovery of the precise point of contact between their destiny and ours which will lead us to mutual enrichment rather than to separation or enmity (EN, IX, 11, p. 169).
> There is a form of indifference which is holy. It consists in making no distinctions among the people who cross our path, bestowing on each our undivided presence, answering faithfully and exactly the appeal which each is making to us. ... Its sole law is that we should offer everyone the same luminous welcome. We must hold the scales even between them all, allowing no prejudice or predilection to tilt the beam. Then we become able to make the necessary subtle adjustments in our dealings with them, while at the same time giving each what he is hoping for, and asking for, and what he needs. The most perfect justice here becomes identical with the purest love; one cannot say whether it has abolished all preferences, or whether each individual has become the object of a preferential love. ... It is to adopt the point of view of God himself, who looks upon all beings with single-minded impartiality. ... it is the eye of love, which distinguishes the precise need of every individual, the word which will touch his heart, and the treatment he deserves (EN, VI 5, p. 114).

Fourthly, like God, we must help other humans become self-sufficient and exercise their own initiative (OA, 1, 11, p. 125; ES, III, 3-5, pp. 124-134; IV, 2-4, pp. 139-152). Lavelle's form of the Golden Rule is thus: We must do to others what God has done for us (OA, 1, 11, p. 125). We should raise ourselves and others to the highest peak by mutual help ("each for all"), each of us like a rung of the ladder to support each other (EN, II, 9, 11, pp. 53, 55-56; VIII, 6, p. 145; IX, 7, p. 165; CRO, V, 6-7, pp. [69-88]; X, 13, pp. [200-204]). Lavelle writes:

> I cannot free myself from the desire to advise others, to change their ideas and improve their behavior, to make them agree with me; I cannot help desiring to make them feel and think as I do. And this is in part, doubtless, because I want to dominate them, and to make them the confirmation and extension of myself. But it is also because I know that all individuals are really one, struggling to find the same truth and the same good (EN, IX, 7, p. 165). ·
>
> The most difficult thing in our relations with others is what may appear the simplest: namely to recognize in them that individual existence by which they resemble us and yet are different from us, that presence in them of a unique and irreplaceable individuality, of an initiative and liberty, of a vocation which is their own and which we must help them to realize, instead of feeling jealous of it, or seeking to bend it in the hopes of making it serve ours. For us, this is the first command of charity, and perhaps also the last (EN, II, 7, p. 51).
>
> Two persons are not in the world as two boxers, one of whom is destined to win, and the other to be beaten. Rather, they are two mediators, seeking a common good; and what either finds is profitable to the other (EN, X, 6, pp. 181-182).

God then for Lavelle, as for Augustine, is found within. God, though He transcends the participated realm, is the ever present and immanent source, end, and enrichment of the self (OA, I, 9, pp. 105-110, 116; EN, XII, 11, p. 221; SPWR, IV, 3, pp. 148-153): "To seek the absolute in oneself and not outside oneself in the most intimate, profound and personal experience" (IL, p. [48]). So by going interiorly I can discover the mystery of my advent—a divine understanding, love, will, and efficacy infinitely greater than words can describe (OA, I, 1, p. 42; I, 4, pp. 66, 70; I, 8, p. 99; TP, I, pp. 10, 13-16; II, pp. 29, 33; TV, vol. II, III, 4, pp. [479-400]; Appendix, pp. [536-538]; FS, II, pp. 36-37; III, pp. 63-64, 67-70; V, p. 100; CS, VII, 8, pp. [160-162]). Nor should it be surprising that the key to reality is found within me, for all being is univocal, and so pure act is personal and possesses a perfect interiority

like me, it is an I calling me by name from its depths (indeed only by
it am I the power to be an I) (OA, I, 1, pp. 55-56, 61, 68; I, 8, pp. 92,
97, 99-102; II, 13, pp. [223-224]; TP, I, p. 18; OBG, Introduction, pp.
[10, 19-23, 28]; I, pp. [43-54, 61-64, 72]; II, pp. [77, 83-84]; IV, pp.
[101-132]; VI, p. [165]; VII, p. [248]; TV, vol. I, II, 2, p. [325] vol. II,
III, 4, pp. [464-479]; OTE, IV, 12, p. [429]; "IPB," pp. 43, 52; "IO," p.
187). Lavelle claims that "a human's aim is to go deeper into himself by
discovering in the depths of his finite essence an infinite destination" (EN,
XI, 8, p. 198), and so "this divine secret is closer to one than one is to
oneself; it is the intimacy of pure Being. ... It discloses itself to none
but a purely spiritual apprehension" (EN, II 1, p. 43). So too by going
within I find the law with which I must collaborate to craft my destiny.
For as I descend more deeply into myself, I see that Being is one with
Value and Goodness, and acquire a revelation of the Absolute in a call
of meaning, duty, and beauty (OA, I, 4, pp. 59, 61, 72; I, 7, pp. 82, 86;
I, 8, pp. 93, 97-98; I, 11, p. 138; II, 18, p. 150).

Lavelle is even willing to call this an "ontological argument" for God,
even though it takes a slightly different form from that of Anselm. For
my self is a possibility that must be put into play to create itself. And
the very power of producing this self is grounded in the infinity of an
act that is eternal cause of itself. In other words my limited thinking is
a possibility that is realized by way of penetrating into the intimacy of
pure being and universal thinking; the cogito is a putting into play of a
possibility I find in myself which is given to me by God in His absolute
creative efficacy. So I think therefore God is, God who has existence as
His essence, fullness of essence and pure existence at once (OHS, I, 4,
pp. 243-248, 252-256, 258; OBG, VI, pp. [170-172]; VIII, p. [232];
IONT, I, 1, pp. 16-24; II, p. 71; EN, XI, 10, p. 202).

Still it is probably best to consider it a moral argument for God as
morality is the primary intermediary between humans and God for
Lavelle. For the call to love others places us before God (OA, I, 8, p.
102; EN, III, 9, pp. 68-69; IV, 8, p. 85; IX, 5, p. 163; XII, 10, p. 219;
CS, III, pp. [60-61]; CRO, XII, 1-2, pp. [223-227]): "the touch of that
very love which makes us conscious of our divine origin" (EN, VI 2, p.
110) or "in the act of love [is found] ... the indissoluble bond between
pure act and participation" (OA, III, 27, p. [530]. He remarks:

All that is most noble and beautiful in the world that my imagination can
conceive—all *that* is my deepest intimacy; and when I run away from it,

excusing myself as unworthy or incapable, I run away from myself. The most superficial things or the basest, which beckon to me or hold me captive, are distractions drawing me away from myself; it is not so much that I cannot bear the sight of what I am, but that I lack the courage to exercise the powers I have at my disposal, or to satisfy the demands whose voice I hear within me. ... We cannot discover that our being is to be found in this secret intimacy, wherein none penetrates but ourselves, without having recourse to introspection" (EN, II 1, p. 43).

Sincerity is the act by which I put myself under the eye of God; there is no other sincerity. For of God alone may it be said that outward appearance is as though it were not. He is himself the pure presence of everything that is. When I turn to Him, everything in me but what I am ceases to count.

For God is not only the ever-open eye, from whom I can hide nothing of what I know about myself; but He is also the light which pierces the darkness, revealing me to myself as I have always been without knowing it. Self-love which hid me from myself is a garment which suddenly drops off. Another love folds about me, one which makes my soul itself transparent. ...

To be sincere, we must not merely think of God as a witness: we must take Him as a model. For sincerity does not consist merely in seeing ourselves in His light, but in making ourselves in conformity with His will. What am I but what He wishes me to be? And yet, there immediately appears before me an infinite disparity between what I do and this power within me, which, in spite of everything, it is my one aspiration to exercise (EN, III 13, p. 73).

Finally, by going within I can affirm that the soul, with its awareness, intelligence, freedom, initiative, and activity, is anchored in absolute being and survives all the vicissitudes of the temporal realm, even the corruption of the body (OA, II, 18, pp. 151-152; OHS, Introduction, pp. 214-215). Still the existence of the soul cannot be logically demonstrated, and much like with our knowledge of freedom, one who tries to grasp the soul in the same way as the body will never find it. For there is no soul object one can observe and so no rejoinder to the materialist who says he or she has never encountered the soul (none except to try and show the materialist that the very fact the mind can think itself subjected to the body shows it has an independence from it, and that we can be human only on the condition we choose to be human and not animal or material) (EN, I, 3, 9, pp. 28, 35; OHS, Introduction, pp. 217-221; ES, I, p. 85; CRO, I, 5, pp. [23-25]).

Lavelle though has a very unique view of the afterlife in that he holds that our future state is not a continuation of our temporal existence on earth, nor the sempiternity of Aquinas, but rather a participation in divine eternity to a degree. So we cannot identify the afterlife with a perception that lasts forever, a spatialized eternity, a freezing of our essence. The nature of the spirit is rather to do away with differences of past and future, to dwell in an eternal present never broken off. Such a state will resemble certain peak experiences in this life where we pass from becoming to a self-conscious duration or even a semblance of eternity (OHS, Introduction, pp. 215-216; I, 4, pp. 257-258, 260-261; III, 14, pp. 263, 268, 274; IV, 19, pp. [477-513]; CS, XI, 1-10, pp. [283-285]; FS, I, pp. 18-21; "IPB," pp. 58-62; "NA," pp. 50-52).

Possession of such an eternal life is ever a possibility for us as long as we live (as our essence is only full constituted, our act of creation completed, by death), for by the virtuous actions that we perform we put a stamp on reality, we choose eternity over becoming, and raise ourselves up to heaven (OA, II, 12, p. 146; II, 18, pp. 168-170; EN, I, 5, p. 30; OTE, IV, 12, pp. 192-195, 200-202, 204-206, n. 22 on p. 200; FS, I, pp. 16-17; CS, XI, pp. [256-283]). Thus our use of the soul determines what we will one day be, and we receive only what we have in some sense given to ourselves (OA, p. [95]; OHS, Introduction, p. 215; II, 14, pp. 274, 281-282; EN, V, 4, p. 97; X, 2, pp. 177-178): With the same resources, some raise themselves up to Heaven, others fall down to Hell (EN, XI, 1, p. 192; cf. V, 3, p. 96). Lavelle writes:

> As long as life remains in us, we nurse the hope that we can change what we are, or conceal it. But once it is threatened or near its end, nothing counts but what we are. One is only perfectly sincere in the presence of death, because death is irrevocable, and, by terminating our existence confers upon it the character of the absolute. That is what is expressed in the picture of the judge whose eye misses nothing, and who, at the moment of our death, sees into the remotest corners of our soul. What is the truth behind this idea of the Divine Eye? Is it not that it is now impossible for us to add anything to what we have made, to escape from ourselves into any future, and to continue to make a distinction between our real and manifested being? And since this is the moment when the will loses its power, it is now impossible to avoid confronting the spectacle of our being in its finished state, our being, which, up to this moment, had been nothing more than a rough sketch, susceptible of endless additions and corrections? (EN, III, 13, p. 73).

At birth, my personal existence enters the immense universe, to enable my liberty to exert itself, and, so to say, to choose what I shall be.
But how shall I have used this liberty? I shall not know the answer until
death, which is the hour of every restitution, when my solitude is consummated, and when I cannot carry away with me anything but what
I have given to myself (EN, IV, 11, p. 90; cf. EN, X, 2, pp. 177-178).[92]

In conclusion then Lavelle's philosophy represents a response to
the atheistic positivism dominant in France in the early 1900s. For
he argues that human existence goes beyond the purely physical and
biological and tries to reintroduce the importance of a spiritual reality
and the ideas of the conscious human self or spirit, free will, value, and
God. To quote his companion in the founding of the Philosophy of
the Spirit, Le Senne, who describes the motivation of he and Lavelle,
"In naming it Philosophy of the Spirit, our dominant desire was to put
spirit in its place, which seemed to us to be first place, whether from
the point of view of knowledge or the point of view of value" ("La Philosophie de l'esprit," I, p. 110; cf. "La Philosophie de l'esprit," pp. 107,
109-110, 112; "NA," pp. 37-39). Or in a final quote:"... when a person
declares that one should live to seek truth, discover beauty, bestow
charity, do good, he implies by this declaration, that truth, beauty, the
good, and love are *not mere appearances*, but that they must gradually
reveal themselves as manifesting the Absolute" ("La Philosophie de
l'esprit," p. 116) [emphasis mine].

The most prominent French Catholic existentialist—one greatly
influenced by World War II, namely by his time spent with the Red
Cross where he saw at firsthand the threat of dehumanization and the
turning of humans into numbers and statistics (see PE, IV, p. 121)—
was the lay philosopher **Gabriel Honoré Marcel (1889-1973)**. Marcel was born in 1889 in Paris, France. Sadly, he lost his mother at the
age of three and he was raised by his father and his aunt, whom his
father had remarried in 1896. His father, a government official (at first
a Ministre Plénipotentiaire and later Director of the Beaux-Arts, the
Bibliothèque Nationale, and Museums; who also authored a book on
painting, *La peinture francaise au XIXe siecle* in 1905), was an agnostic
(influenced by Renan, Spencer, and Taine) and bestowed this viewpoint upon his only child. Yet similar to the path taken by Maritain,
Marcel attended the Sorbonne from 1906-1910 where he studied
with the Catholic philosopher Victor Delbos and Lucien Lèvy-Bruhl,

as well as the nearby Collège de France where he studied with Bergson, and he was increasingly drawn to the views of romanticism, idealism, and theism from 1909-1912 (influential here as well was reflection on the music of Bach, Beethoven, Brahms, Mozart, Schubert, Schumann, on love, and on his deceased mother). Marcel left the Sorbonne in 1910 after he earned his agrégation but before completing his doctorate on Spinoza.

Marcel settled on a career of teaching philosophy, and so instructed at the Lycée de Vendôme (1911-1913) and at a private school above Lake Geneva (1912-1913) until the start of the war. During the First World War, as we have seen, Marcel served in the Red Cross where he was responsible for informing families of the loss of their soldier sons. After World War I ended Marcel resumed his philosophy career at the Lycée Condorcet in Paris (1915-1918) and the Lycée de Sens (1919-1922) where he married Jacqueline Boegner in a Lutheran Church in 1919 (they adopted a son in 1922). From 1916-1917 he also engaged in a metapsychical seance with the help of an ouija board, and this séance seemingly revealed information about a dead soldier that later proved accurate and so convinced him of the existence of an afterlife.

Marcel soon moved to Paris where he turned his attention to a budding literary career, writing plays and becoming an author for the *Nouvelle Revue Française* and the *L'Europe Nouvelle* from 1923-1939 (where he discovered the Catholic author Georges Bernanos). It was in Paris as well where Marcel encountered François Mauriac, Charles Du Bos, Robert Garric, and Louis Massignon, and through their influenced converted to Catholicism in 1929 (his wife converting in 1947 just before she died). In 1933 Marcel became active in the Oxford Group (founded in 1931 by the Lutheran physician Frank Buchman and in 1938 rechristened the Moral Rearmament Movement) with its four absolutes of honesty, purity, unselfishness and love and its five C's of confidence, confession, conviction, conversion, and continuance. Marcel left the movement, however, after a few years and before the Vatican condemned it in 1952 for advocating morality without religious faith, authority, or dogma. Marcel also hosted Friday gatherings at his home on the Rue de Tournon with Emmanuel Levinas, Louis Lavelle, René Le Senne, Jean Wahl, Paul Ricoeur, and others.

Marcel returned to academia in the midst of the Second World War and taught at the famous Lycée Louis-le-Grand in Paris (1939), and the Lycée of Montpellier (1941). After World War II, Marcel found himself in the unenviable position of serving on a committee whose purpose was to examine and possibly censure for treason those writers who had supported the Vichy Regime. Marcel resigned in 1945, however, when his push for leniency over vengeance was ignored (indeed his former student Robert Brasillach was executed later that year). Marcel later became a drama critic for *Nouvelles Littéraires* from 1945-1969 when he went nearly blind. He also wrote musical compositions from 1945-1946 and served as a delegate at the UNESCO conference in Beirut in 1948. Marcel died in 1973 in Paris. One of his granddaughters later taught philosophy at the Lycée de Havre.

Marcel delivered the famous Gifford Lectures in 1949-1950 in Aberdeen, Scotland (he later gave the William James Lectures at Harvard University in 1961 as well); he received the Grand Prize of Literature from the French Academy in 1949 for his plays and was elected to the Académie des sciences politiques et morales in 1952. Marcel was also awarded the Hanseatic Goethe Prize from the University of Hamburg in 1956, the French National Grand Prize for Literature in 1958, the Osiris Prize in 1963, the Peace Prize of the German Booksellers [Börsenverein des Deutschen Buchhandels] in Frankfurt in 1964, the Grand Prize of the City of Paris in 1968, the legion of Honor and the Erasmus Prize in Rotterdam in 1969, and the Grand Cross of the National Order of Merit in 1969. Marcel also received honorary doctorates from the Universities of Tokyo, De Paul, and Salamanca. There is a Présence de Gabriel Marcel in Paris (1975-) and a Gabriel Marcel Society (1986-) at Le Moyne College, a Gabriel Marcel Collection at the Harry Ransom Center of the University of Texas at Austin, and a Fonds Gabriel Marcel at the Bibliotheque Nationale in Paris.[93]

Marcel is primarily known for his *The Mystery of Being* [*Le mystère de l'être*], 2 vols. [MOB] (1949-1950).[94]

The proper method of philosophy, according to Marcel, is a phenomenological description of our inner life experiences, rather than a demonstrative deduction of select propositions from a set of others. It is a reflection upon these experiences in minute detail in order to circumscribe them, throw more light upon them, understand them more fully, and follow the clues where they lead (MOB, vol. I, Introduction, pp. 2-4; III, pp. 49-59, 64-68; IV, p. 74; V, pp. 109-110; VII, pp. 171, 180-181; X, pp. 242, 262; vol. II, I, pp. 6-9; VII, p. 134; VIII, p. 142; TWB, I, pp. 3-7; XIV, pp. 209-213; BH, I, pp. 103, 115; PF, III, pp. 102-105; HV, VI, p. 136; CF, Introduction, p. 7; I, pp. 14-15, 22-25;

VI, p. 121). Thus philosophy for Marcel must take a concrete rather than an abstractive approach, and philosophize in the here and now (MOB, vol. I, VI, p. 143; VII, pp. 172, 175; IX, p. 235; vol. II, I, p. 3; III, pp. 55, 57; IV, p. 70; VI, pp. 104-105; VIII, p. 143; IX, p. 172; X, pp. 188, 199-202; PE, IV, pp. 104-105, 120, 126; CF, Introduction, p. 4; I, pp. 12-13; III, pp. 61, 63-66; HV, VI, p. 137; EBHD, Introduction, pp. 10-14; VIII, p. 148; MMS, II, 3, pp. 153-162). As Marcel has it "I believe that our point of reference can be based only upon experience itself, treated as a massive presence which is to be the basis of all our affirmation. ... a concrete approach to being" (MOB, vol. II, IV, p. 59).[95]

Understanding the human situation then requires going beyond the method of science which treats something as a problem (through primary reflection), to the method of philosophy which treats something as a mystery (through secondary reflection).

A problem, known in primary reflection, is something that can be solved by a technique. It can be clearly defined, is amenable to investigation, and can be verified by observations of objective data. A problem thus lies before me as something to be looked at (to be approached disinterestedly, objectively, and as a spectator), analyzed, and critically dissected. As such the solution to a problem can schematized in universal terms and become the property of all; it possesses "the privilege of [the] universality of thinking [of] scientists or technicians whose method is that of a series of operations which can be carried out by anybody else in the world who is placed in the same setting and can make use of similar tools" (MOB, vol. I, Introduction, p. 11). Primary reflection, dealing with problems, is thus analytic, reductive, objective, universal, and empirically verifiable.

Such problems make up the bulk of everyday reasoning and science. For instance a mechanic can try to understand why a motorcycle is no longer functioning by taking it apart. A police office can try to determine when and why a car accident happened (ironically Marcel was to suffer a very horrible automobile accident himself in 1953, or just a few years after he wrote this). A chemist can try to develop a process for synthesizing a substance. Or a businessman determine where he put a missing watch (MOB, vol. I, Introduction, pp. 5-9, 11; II, p. 25; II, pp. 45-56; V, p. 97; VII, p. 155; X, pp. 260-265; vol. II, IV, p. 73; VIII, p. 158; PE, I, pp. 17, 29; BH, I, p. 100).

A mystery, on the other hand, which is known in secondary reflection, is a particular situation in which I find myself involved, that presses on me from the inside. Hence I cannot stand outside of a mystery as an onlooker (this would be to stand outside the human condition). Nor can a mystery in its singularity be summed up, broken up, or integrated into a system (rather it must be seen in its unity). Nor can I determine in advance what are the conditions for resolving a mystery. There is no roadmap or manual I can turn to, but rather only a line of direction upon which I can move to find illumination (that is to say, a mystery resembles an orchestral score which I can recognize expresses an inner necessity and whose elements I can follow along to allow its hidden meaning to more and more filter through, even if its whole meaning is not strictly speaking logical or completely graspable). Secondary reflection, dealing with mysteries, is therefore synthetic, non-reductive, personal, concrete, and confirmable only in private experience (and so empirically unverifiable).

Mysteries, in fact, represent an encounter of deep spiritual significance in the deepest part of my being, the inward reality of a presence that infinitely transcends all possible verification. Such mysteries form the main enigmas of philosophy and life and include such things as the appreciation of art or a great vintage of wine, the trust one has for a lover, the mechanic fixing one's motorcycle, the police officer at the door, the love of the person caring for an accident victim, birth, death, the self and what I should live by, etc. (MOB, vol. I, Introduction, pp. 6-12, 16-17; II, p. 46; V, pp. 101-103; VII, pp. 162-165; IX, p. 210; X, pp. 260-269; vol. II, I, pp. 11, 13; IV, pp. 74-75; V, p. 103; VIII, pp. 154-160; TWB, I, pp. 9, 14-15; III, p. 39; CF, I, p. 14; VI, p. 135; VII, p. 141; PE, I, pp. 15-22, 30; IV, p. 128; HV, VIII, p. 182; BH, I, p. 117). Here is how Marcel draws his famous distinction between a problem and a mystery:

> A problem is something which I meet, which I find complete before me, but which I can therefore lay siege to and reduce. But a mystery is something in which I am myself involved, and it can therefore only be thought of as a sphere where the distinction between what is in me and what is before me loses its meaning and its initial validity. A genuine problem is subject to an appropriate technique by the exercise of which it is defined: whereas a mystery, by definition, transcends every conceivable technique. It is, no doubt, always possible (logically and psychologically) to degrade a mystery so as to turn it into a problem (BH, I, p. 117).

A problem is something which one runs up against, which bars the way. It is before me in its entirety. A mystery, however, is something in which I find myself involved, whose essence therefore, is not to be completely before me ... Ultimately, any attempt to problematize implies the notion of a certain continuity of experience which must be preserved. But the experience which concerns us in this context, whatever scientific interpretation we give it, is really *my* experience, *my* system, the extension however remote, of an original datum which in the final analysis, is my body. In the case of a mystery, however, I am by definition led beyond a 'system for me.' I am involved *in concreto* [concretely] in an order which by definition can never become an order or a system for me, but only for a mind which transcends and includes me, and with which I cannot even ideally identify myself. The terms *beyond, transcendence*, here take on their full meaning (CF, III, pp. 68-69).

Now the great temptation (a temptation which deserves a study of its own) is to reduce a mystery to a problem, to look at human life in purely scientific and objective terms (as with certain biologists, neuroscientists, psychologists, sociologists, and Marxists), rather than viewing it from within its own depths, and opening oneself up to its full significance. Yet such an arbitrary and dictatorial act of reduction mutilates the life of the spirit at its core (MOB, vol. I, VI, pp. 148-153; X, pp. 250-251; BH, I, pp. 100-101, 111, 119-120; II, p. 171; PE, I, pp. 12-15, 20). For it turns the human being into what Marcel calls a functionalized self.[96]

Functionalization (a broken world) is the reduction of a person to an agglomeration of functions (Mr. 'so and so'), it is a summing up of a person's identity in terms of a few ready-made adjectives, as in the compilation of a dossier by a state official: name, place of residence, occupation, religious affiliation, party membership, education, etc. (MOB, vol. I, II, pp. 26-39; III, pp. 66-67; V, pp. 103-105; IX, pp. 225-226; CF, I, p. 33; PI, VIII, p. 230). Thus instead of forming intimate relations with other concrete and creative persons, we interact with humans who have become abstract and depersonalized functions: i.e. the door operator, ticket puncher, trade union member, banker, doctor, patient, voter, etc. (MOB, vol. I, II, pp. 35-36, 38-39, 41; PE, I, pp. 10-11; MMS, I, 3, pp. 37-75; SCH, IV, pp. 62-63). Marcel here was greatly influenced by his experiences working for the Red Cross in World War I where there was a tendency to replace a deceased French soldier's name with a number and talk about him in numerical terms, i.e. soldier number 98 [Marcel also puts before our imagination other instances where a number becomes the identity of a human being—the inmate of Cell Block C329, the occupant of room number 55] (MOB, vol. I, V, pp. 105-109; EBHD, II, pp. 35-36). At its worst functionalization views a woman as a mere mechanism for bringing children into the world or for cooking food, a patient as someone who pays the bills, whom I am occupied with only during my shift and whom I may leave in the lurch after it is over, or even as a subject for experimentation, and a worker as a job to be done, a return to be produced (MOB, vol. II, III, p. 42-46, 50; X, pp. 207-208; vol. II, IV, p. 61; TWB, V, pp. 86-87). Indeed this is the path to forced labor and cremation camps, to forced euthanasia of the old, sick, and deformed (MOB, vol. II, IX, pp. 165, 182-185).

Yet something in the human protests against the violation and debasement that is the functionalized self. Marcel writes "Life in a world centered on function is liable to despair because in reality this world is empty, it rings hollow" (PE, I, p. 12; cf. HV, III, p. 61; VI, p. 145; BH, IV, p. 208; MOB, vol. I, III, pp. 53-55; IX, p. 228; X, p. 268). For humans are not reducible to outer garments. They are more than objects or even somebodies; they are unique beings with their own inwardnesses, dignity, and value, sacred and created in the image of God (MOB, vol. I, II, p. 41; V, pp. 103-109; VII, p. 169; vol. II, IX, pp. 165, 182-185; HV, I, pp. 23-24; TWB, VII, pp. 107-112, 117; PE, I, p. 42). Contrary to treating people as objects, numbers, functions (as someone who is there for our information, service, or convenience, i.e. an 'in order to'), possessions (what Marcel labels a state of 'having'), or passer-bys, we must treat them as real living, breathing persons, as centers of value, as a 'thou' as Ebner and Buber would have it.

True love then is not possessive and self-centered but oblative and other-directed. Its motive is not a desire to be well-thought of by others, nor gain, utility, or self-satisfaction (as it would be with someone who used a beneficiary's gratitude to secure a hold over him or her), but a will to participate in the life of another, to give oneself to another for his or her own sake (MOB, vol. I, VI, pp. 140-144, 152-153; VII, p. 154; vol. I, IX, pp. 222, 231; vol. II, III, p. 51; VI, p. 109; VII, pp. 132-135; PI, VIII, pp. 235-237; HV, VI, pp. 138, 141; CF, VII, pp. 143-146). So though a husband may first consider his wife primarily in terms of sensual enjoyments, or as a cook and charwoman, he is (ideally) led to discover that she has a value of her own and treat her as a beloved (MOB, vol. I, III, pp. 59-60, 67-68). Nor does love treat a sinner as the judge of an accused man in the dock would, rather it is willing to forgive a friend who disappoints or a wife who reveals she has been unfaithful and that one's daughter is not one's own. For by such acts of forgiveness we help others regain their souls (MOB, vol. I, V, pp. 98-99; VIII, pp. 188-189).

Love, in fact, is characterized by three main traits for Marcel: availability, commitment, and sacrifice. In availability [disponibilité] we are not shut up in our own selves, preoccupied with our concerns and business, but are present to others, willing to give them the time of day, to respond to their requests for aid or companionship (MOB, vol. I, VIII, p. 201; IX, pp. 251-253; EBHD, II, pp. 39-41; VII, p. 130; HV, I, pp. 23-25; II, p. 39; VI, p. 146; CF, Introduction, p. 10; I, pp. 12, 32-34; II, pp. 39-40, 52-54; III, pp. 72, 77; VIII, pp. 149, 154-156; MMS, II, 5, pp. 193-210; BH, I, pp. 69, 83-84, 106-107, 144-154; II, pp. 155-162, 167; PE, I, pp. 38-41). For in availability rather than seeing other humans as things that belongs to me, I instead belong to them; I give, commit, and consecrate myself to them, place myself at their disposal, open an unlimited credit account in their name ('you can do with me what you want') and freely put myself in their hands (CF, II, pp. 39-40; IV, pp. 97-101; HV, I, p. 23; V, p. 133; PI, VIII, pp. 236-240; PE, I, p. 43; III, p. 102). It is worth quoting Marcel on this commendable notion of love as availability and presence:

> Total spiritual availability, that is to say of pure charity ... It is an undeniable fact, though it is hard to describe in intelligible terms, that there are some people who reveal themselves as 'present'—that is to say, at our disposal—when we are in pain or in need to confide in someone ... The person who is at my disposal is the one who is capable of being wholly with me when I am in need of him; while the one who is not at my disposal seems merely to offer me a temporary loan raised on his resources. For the one I am a presence; for the other I am an object (PE, I, pp. 39-40).

In availability then, by a tone of voice, by a look, by a smile (rather than in stereotyped formulas), by listening, even by a silence, I am a radiance of charity that lights up other people's solitude, refreshes them, meets them at a level of inwardness and creative development, and makes a contribution to their lives, however small (MOB, vol. I, III, p. 51; IV, p. 64; VII, pp. 170-172; IX, pp. 218-222, 230-231, 238-239; X, pp. 252-256; vol. II, III, p. 49; HV, V, pp. 126, 131; EBHD, IV, pp. 66-68; PE, I, pp. 40, 42). As Marcel describes this: "What happens is, in a word, that the stranger has started off by putting himself, as it were, ideally in my shoes. He has come within my reach as a person. It is no longer a mere matter of his showing me the way as a guide-book or a map might, but of his really giving a helping hand to somebody who is alone and in a bewildered state. This is nothing more than a sort of spark of spirituality, out as soon as it is in; the stranger and I part almost certainly never to see each other again, yet for a few minutes, as I trudge homewards, this man's unexpected cordiality makes me feel as if I had stepped out of a wintry day into a warm room" (MOB, vol. I, IX, pp. 220-221).

Love also involves a commitment to another (fidelity) despite the inevitable lapses of interest, disappointments, and setbacks on both the lover's and beloved's part. In other words, love is a giving of one's entire being to another, an unconditional promise to be true to and be there for the beloved no matter what: 'I'll come,' 'I'll take care of you if you are sick or invalid,' 'I'll always love you,' etc. (MOB, vol. II, VII, pp. 136-139; VIII, p. 153; X, pp. 243, 245, 248-249; PE, III, pp. 93-95; EBHD, IV, pp. 69-74). In fidelity I open up an unlimited credit line to another as it were. Hence fidelity can seem naïve and impossible to the bystander (CF, VI, pp. 133-135; VIII, pp. 152-154, 158-166; BH, pp. 47-48, 75-76).

Finally, love can demand great sacrifices of oneself, even the sacrifice of one's life (MOB, vol. I, VIII, pp. 202-203; HV, VI, p. 144; PI, VIII, pp. 232-235).[97] Marcel writes: "There is no shared ground on which common sense and the hero or martyr could meet; they are like two axes that can never intersect. In itself, sacrifice seems madness; but a deeper reflection, the secondary and recuperative reflection of which we spoke earlier on, enables us, as it were, to recognize and to approve it as a worthy madness. We understand that if a man were to shirk from such madness, he would be falling below himself" (MOB, vol. I, VIII, p. 204). Such a willingness to sacrifice one's life springs from a call coming from one's inner depths (MOB, vol. I, VIII, pp. 205-209; IX, p. 211). For "the person who is carrying the act out has, without any doubt at all, the feeling that through self-sacrifice he is reaching self-fulfillment; given his own situation and that of everything dear to him, he realizes his own nature most completely, he most completely is, in the act of giving his life away" (MOB, vol. I, VIII, p. 205).

Now it is precisely in the elucidation of our higher modes of experience (spiritual data), such as love, with its traits of fidelity and sacrifice, and hope, that Marcel finds the basis for belief in God (MOB, vol. I, III, p. 49; BH, I, pp. 118-121; CF, Introduction, pp. 6-7; VIII, pp. 173-174; IX, p. 182; XII, p. 218; PF, IV, pp. 106-125; HV, V, p. 132; PE, I, p. 46; II, p. 88).[98] Let us examine each of these in turn.

In the first place, love, with its call to total commitment and sacrifice, ultimately reflects a call coming from somewhere other than my own life; it is a call rising up from being (the ontological mystery), one that betokens the presence of God (CF, I, pp. 35-36).[99] For in pledging fidelity and sacrificing for another I recognize reality's hold over me, indeed that the ground of what I am and do is an Absolute Thou (even if unconsciously) (MOB, vol. II, V, pp. 90-93; CF, VIII, pp. 170-171; BH, pp. 50-56; PE, I, pp. 35-36; HV, II, p. 50; V, pp. 125, 130; VI, p. 145); "fidelity reveals its true nature which is to be an evidence, a testimony ... a desire for the unconditional which is the requirement and the very mark of the Absolute in us" (HV, V, p. 134). In the words of Marcel:

However strange it may seem to our minds, it is possible for there to be an unconditional love of creature for creature—a gift which will not be revoked. Whatever may occur, whatever disappointment experience inflicts on our hypotheses, our cherished hopes, this love will remain constant, this credit intact. ... love is faith itself, an invincible assurance based on Being itself. It is here and here alone that we reach not only an unconditioned fact but a rational unconditional as well; namely that of the absolute Thou ... such a love is perhaps like a prenatal palpitation of faith (CF, VI, pp. 136-137).

What does it really mean to swear fidelity? and how can such a promise be made? The question cannot be asked without giving rise to an antinomy. The promise in fact is made on the basis of some present inner disposition. However: Can I affirm that the disposition, which I have just at the moment that I commit myself, will not alter later on? No doubt there are certain states of exaltation which are associated with an awareness of their own perenniality. But don't both reflection and experience indicate that it is my duty to question the validity of this awareness, i.e., this affirmation? All I have the right to affirm is that it certainly seems to me that my feeling or inner disposition cannot change. *It certainly seems to me.* ... But it is sufficient for me to say *it seems to me* in order to find it necessary to add as though *sottovoce* [under my breathe]; but I can't be sure of it. It is then impossible for me to declare: I swear that my inner disposition will not change. This immutability no longer is the object of my allegiance. What is more, we may observe that the being to whom I swear fidelity can change in turn; he can become something which gives

me the right to say: 'This is not the man I committed myself to; he has
changed so much that my promise is null and void.' ...
   This, however, seems to be a vicious circle only to the mind of the bystander who views fidelity from without, all fidelity seems incomprehensible, impracticable, a wager, and scandalous too: How, it will be asked
could this man be faithful to that coarse person with the flat nose, or
to that cadaverous old woman, or to that blue-stocking? ... Hence this
ground of fidelity which necessarily seems precarious to us as soon as
we commit ourselves to another whresorto is unknown, seems on the
other hand unshakable when it is based not, to be sure, on a distinct apprehension of God as someone other, but on a certain appeal delivered
from the depths of my own insufficiency *ad summam altitudinem* [to the
highest altitude]; I have sometimes called this the absolute resort. This
appeal presupposes a radical humility in the subject; a humility which is
polarized by the very transcendence of the one it invokes. Here we are as
it were, at the juncture of the most stringent commitment and the most
desperate expectation. It cannot be a matter of counting on oneself, on
one's own resources, to cope with this unbounded commitment; but in
the act in which I commit myself, I at the same time extend an infinite
credit to Him to whom I do so; Hope means nothing more than this
(CF, VIII, pp. 158, 163, 167).
   The person who gives up his life for a cause is aware of giving all, of
making a total sacrifice; but even if he is going to a certain death, his act
is not a suicide, and there is, metaphysically speaking, a gap between
the act of sacrificing his life and that of killing himself. Why? Here we
must introduce the notions of availability and unavailability. Doubtless,
the person who gives up his life gives up everything, but he does it for
something else that he asserts means more, that is worth more; he puts
his life at the disposal of that higher reality; he extends to the ultimate
that availability which is exemplified in the fact of dedicating oneself to a
person, to a cause. In so doing, he has, if I may say so, proved that he has
placed or situated his being beyond life. There is not and cannot be any
sacrifice without hope, and hope is suspended in the ontological realm
... Whether or not he actually believes in eternal life, the person who
sacrifices himself acts as if he believed (CF, III, p. 77).

   In a famous exchange about immortality at the 1937 International
Philosophy Convention in Paris, Léon Brunschvicg argued that Marcel cared about Marcel's immortality more than Brunschvicg cared
about Brunschvicg's immortality. Marcel retorted that this was incorrect, for what he cared about was the immortality of those he loved.
For in love we hope that the beloved will get better and will not die.
In fact, to love someone (such as a mother a son) is to say 'you will not

die,' [*Aimer un être, c'est lui dire: Toi, tu ne mourras pas!*], i.e. you will
not ever die (MOB, vol. II, IV, pp. 68-70; HV, II, p. 65; VI, p. 147;
EBHD, VIII, pp. 142-145; PI, VIII, pp. 231, 241-244; cf. Marcel's
play *Le mort de demain*, II, 6, where the phrase first originated). For
we grasp in the light of love (in the depths of our being, in an intercon-
nection with reality) that death is not the ultimate reality (HV, II, pp.
29, 31, 34-35, 41, 44, 48; VI, pp. 147, 153). Hope then is an absolute
confidence that a cure will be found, death will be avoided (where one
transcends all possible disappointment and doesn't worry about the
how). Hope is a looking upon the death of a beloved with love, for it is
a trust in the creative power of being and its resources, in the Absolute
Thou and the Love it bears for us (MOB, vol. II, IX, pp. 168-169, 174;
HV, II, pp. 46-48, 53, 55, 67; BH, I, pp. 77-80; PE, I, pp. 26-28; PF,
III, pp. 92-102; TWB, XIV, pp. 212-213). Marcel states:

> Hope consists in asserting that there is at the heart of being, beyond
> all data, beyond all inventories and calculations, a mysterious principle
> which is in connivance with me, which cannot but will that which I will,
> if what I will deserves to be willed and is, in fact, willed by my whole
> being. We have now come to the centre of what I have called the onto-
> logical mystery ... To hope against all hope that a person whom I love
> will recover from a disease which is said to be incurable is to say: It is
> impossible that I should be alone in willing this cure, it is impossible
> that reality in its inward depth should be hostile or so much as indif-
> ferent to what I assert is in itself a good. It is quite useless to tell me of
> discouraging cases or examples: beyond all experience, all probability, all
> statistics, I assert that a given order shall be re-established, that reality is
> on my side in willing it to be so. ... hope rises to a plane which transcends
> the level of all possible empirical disproof—the plane of salvation as op-
> posed to that of success in whatever form (PE, I, p. 28).

Thus through the experiences of sacrificial love, fidelity, and hope,
we can come to see the meaning of life, its bearing and relevance, and
so reject the view of atheistic existentialism that life has come into my
hands by accident, like a briefcase that one happens to find dropped
on the pavement (MOB, vol. I, IX, pp. 211-215; MOB, vol. I, III, pp.
58-59, 67-68; PE, I, p. 46). For in these spiritual experiences we get a
glimpse of a reality greater than ourselves, an invisible presence which
surrounds us, carries us along with its current, and is inseparable from
our own vocation, indeed which is more truly us than we ourselves are
(MOB, vol. I, VI, pp. 140-144, 152-153; VII, p. 154; vol. II, I, pp. 7-8,

11, 19; III, pp. 37-38; V, p. 89; IX, p. 174; X, pp. 208-210; CF, Introduction, p. 10; I, pp. 32-34; II, pp. 39-40; III, p. 72; VIII, p. 165; BH,
I, pp. 54, 106-107, 151-154; II, p. 167; HV, Preface, pp. 8-9; I, p. 25).
In sacrificial love, fidelity, and hope, we assert that solitude is not the
last word of things, that we are not condemned to live and die alone,
that being is not ultimately hostile to what is most important to us,
that being is not indifferent to value but is goodness itself (MOB, vol.
I, IX, pp. 236-237; vol. II, III, pp. 46-47, 49, 51-52; IV, p. 68; VIII, p.
149; IX, pp. 178, 184; HV, II, pp. 57-58; VI, pp. 141-142; PF, III, pp.
83-91; TWB, VI, p. 101; PH, I, pp. 43-45; PE, III, pp. 97-98; IV, p.
12; CF, Introduction, p. 8; I, pp. 21, 31; VIII, pp. 151-152).

In Spain Catholic Existentialism was well-represented by **Xavier
Zubiri y Apalátegui (1898-1983)** who was born in Donostira-San
Sebastián, Guipuscoa, in the Basque region of Spain, in 1898. Zubiri studied with and was influenced by José Ortega y Gasset (as well
as with García Morente, Julio Rey-Pastor, Julio Palacios, Angel Amor
Ruibal, and Juan Zaragüeta) at the University of Madrid from 1918-
1920. He then went on to study with the Thomists Cardinal Désiré
Mercier and Léon Noël at the University of Louvain from 1919-1920,
receiving a licentiate in philosophy in 1921, and then at the Gregorian
University in Rome from 1920-1921. He received a doctorate in theology from the Gregorian in 1920 and in philosophy from the University of Madrid in 1921. Not yet satisfied with his education, he trav-
eled throughout Europe from 1928-1931 where he studied philology
with Werner Jaeger; philosophy with Edmund Husserl and Martin
Heidegger; quantum physics with Louis De Broglie, Eugen Goldstein,
and Ernst Schrödinger; biology with Richard Goldschmidt, Otto
Mangold, Hans Spemann, and von Geluchten; and mathematics with
Charles de La Vallée-Poussin, Julio Rey-Pastor, and Ernst Zermelo.
    Zubiri became a professor at the University of Madrid from 1926-
1936, but he left Spain during the Civil War (1936-1939) and taught
at the Catholic Institute in Paris and studied Eastern and Semitic
Languages at the Biblical Institute in Rome and at the Sorbonne with
Émile Benveniste, Anton Deimel, Édouard Dhorme, O.P., and René
Labat. Upon the conclusion of the war Zubiri married a former student, Carmen Castro (the daughter of the author Américo Castro)
and returned to Spain to a position at the University of Barcelona from
1940-1942. He, however, soon left academia and gave private weekly

seminars (*cursos*) in Madrid from 1945-1976 at his Sociedad de Estudios y Publicaciones (with a year stint at the Gregorian in 1973) and
also translated scientific and philosophical works for the remainder of
his life. He also helped to found the journal *Realitas* (1973-). Zubiri
died in Madrid in 1983.

Zubiri received an honorary doctorate from Duestro University in
1980 and won the prize Ramón y Cajal in 1982. There is a Fundación
Xavier Zubiri in Madrid (1989-), and a Xavier Zubiri Foundation
of North America (1997-). An International Congress on Zubiri was
held in Madrid in 1993 and a second one in 1998 [with subsequent
ones in 2005-2006] and there is a *Xavier Zubiri Review* (1998-).[100]

In contrast to his meager output, Zubiri's influence on Spanish philosophy has been immense, his major influence being through his *Nature, History, God* [*Naturaleza, Historia, Dios*] [NHG] (1942; 1963;
1974) [a collection of essays from 1932-1944].[101]

Zubiri, showing the influence of his Thomist teachers over his phenomenological ones, begins his philosophy not from the mental phenomena of Husserl, the vital being of Ortega, or the understanding
of Heidegger, but from the apprehension of a thing. For the mind is
sentient and so intellection (noology) is formally the apprehension of
reality, the actualization of the real (noematic) in intelligence (noetic)
(SI, I, 1, pp. 9-11; I, 4, pp. 31-35; "HDH," pp. 11-12; HG, I, pp. 34-
38, 42; II, p. 67; III, p. 105). Truth then is reality actualizing intellect
in conformity with itself. The human does not so much as possess the
truth as become possessed by it. As such it yields the patency of a real
thing in all the richness of its notes, the fact that a thing is and oper-
ates in accordance with the being of its notes (SI, I, 7, pp. 83-87; II,
7, pp. 193-217, 219-220; NHG, I, 1-3, pp. 12, 21-22, 33-35, 38, 43,
46-48, 50, 60, 73; OE, VIII, pp. 135-154; HG, I, p. 34; IV, pp. 144,
160-161, 182-187; V, pp. 228-229).[102]

Now as knowing is an "attending modestly" to the reality of things
(NHG, I, 2, p. 44-45), in grasping reality, we apprehend a thing in
its own right (*en propio*) or of its own (*de suyo*) (SI, I, 5, pp. 44-47;
Appendix, 4, pp. 48-49; I, 8, pp. 92-96; III, 3, pp. 256-265, 273-275;
III, 6, pp. 303-308; OE, IX, pp. 354-365). In this way we can grasp
the "essence" of a thing, its quidditative nature (or variously, its what-
ness, content, structure, totality of notes, properties, or characteristics—such as the color, shape, and size of a table). In fact, the essence
of something, according to Zubiri, is a substantivity [*la sustantividad*]

(similar to but going beyond contemporary trope theory), rather than a substantiality [la sustancialidad], as is normally understood. The substantivity of a thing is a closed, particular, and total system of constitutional notes, wherein each note implies the others. Hence there is an interdependency, unity, and sufficiency of the system, and altering even one of the notes would preclude the others (OE, VII, pp. 166-167, 175-183, IX, pp. 246-247, 281-282; HG, I, pp. 24-27). That is to say, there is but one single and self-same activity of the system occurring in each and every one of its notes, a coherential unity of substantivity (HG, I, p. 40). This is in contrast to the classical theory of the subtantiality of a thing, as with Aristotle, Locke, or Spinoza, where a thing is a subject that is independent of its properties, a substantial subject in which properties inhere. For real things are not substantial subjects, but substantive systems, integrated collections of accidents or notes. And notes in turn are not properties inhering in a subject, but coherent notes that rest upon themselves and unite in a system (HG, I, pp. 26-27).

Indeed the essence for Zubiri is also what makes something real. The essence is the principle of reality of a thing (its transcendentality). Thus the notes of silver are not just properties but the argentuous reality itself. The notes and existence are both part of the ownness of a thing, moments of its content in its own right (de suyo) (OE, II, pp. 51-52; VI, pp. 121-122, 124-125; VII, pp. 127-131; VIII, pp. 164-185; IX, pp. 187-189, 195-202, 256-267, 319-320, 329-342, 389, 408-410, 429-436; DSR, I, pp. 23-26; SI, I, 6, pp. 70, 73-75, 78-81; II, 7, pp. 222-225; HG, I, pp. 24-27, 30, 37, 48; II, p. 77).

In this regard Zubiri is more Aristotelian than Thomist. Contra Aquinas "essence" is not just an aptitude for existence, a concept which may exist, but the fact that the notes of a dog or a man belong to an object in its own right (de suyo), and so the thing really is, of itself, a dog or a man. Reality then gives itself in being, actualizes itself, in specific notes, a power to act in virtue of its notes: essence appears as existent (OE, IX, pp. 354-365, 366-373). Essence (de suyo) then for Zuburi is prior to suchness (aptitude for existence) [Thomistic essence] and existence (actuality), as both suchness and existence are moments of something that is real and from itself (de suyo) (OE, IX, pp. 354-373, 412-417; HG, I, p. 29; III, pp. 104-105). So being or existence is a further act of the reality of a thing insofar as it is, and is grounded in its reality. It is the mundane activity (worldly actuality, physical presence, being here and now, the way a real thing manifests itself in the world) of the real (OE, IX, pp. 296-297, 373-378, 391-393; "HDH," pp. 11-14, 67-69; HG, I, pp. 29, 48). And contra Heidegger reality (*de suyo*) (act [*acto*], actuity [*actuidad*]) comes before being (actuality [*actualidad*]) which is the actuality of a real thing. Reality, in order to be in actuality, begins as a system of notes in act (OE, IX, pp. 395-407).

Zubiri is perhaps best known for his concept of religation [*religación*; from the Latin term *religare*—to tie or bind—which also forms the root of the word religion] (NHG, III, 1, pp. 310-311; III, 4, p. 322).[103] Now the human being is religated, implanted in existence (versus the throwness of Heidegger), linked to what antecedently makes it be (NHG, I, 1-2, pp. 24, 33-34; III, 1, 4, pp. 312, 324-329). Reality enables and impels the human being, captures it. For the human being is taken hold of by the power of the real which is its ground. Indeed reality is ultimate, possibilitating and impelling, it is a power that supports the human being, moves it, and allows it to be a person, an 'I' in all its richness (HG, II, pp. 69, 75-79, 85; III, pp. 91, 99-104; IV, pp. 137, 145; VII, p. 266).

Thus human existence is one that is relatively absolute [*relativamente absoluta*]. For I need to be religated to reality, to the power of the real, to make my absolute being. I am restless (*inquietud*) in the sense that I can only develop myself when living in a reality among things and other humans which open up possibilities for me to choose and adopt (to make something of and realize myself). I acquire my being then by confronting reality as such, by being hurled by the power of reality (NHG, Introduction, p. xii; III, 4, pp. 343-344; HG, I, pp. 53-55; II, pp. 80-86; III, pp. 102, 105-112; IV, p. 209; VII, pp. 265-266; Conclusion, p. 273). Zuburi writes: "Each human finds itself hurled towards the ground of the power of the real, in the inexorable physical forcefulness to choose for a form of reality" (HG, Conclusion, p. 273).

Moreover, the very fact that things can affect me (in knowledge and action) shows that the reality of a thing does not exhaust itself in that which it is, but exceeds and transcends it. Or as we could put it, being real in a thing is more than being this or that thing. So there is an expansion of the real character of each thing beyond what it concretely is. Each real thing bears a power not exhausted in the reality of the concrete thing; besides a thing's immersion in itself, what it is in and by itself (in front of me), it also has an expansion to more than itself, it is its ownness and the presence of reality itself (happening in me).

And it is this presence of reality itself, reality simpliciter, that determines my personal being (HG, III, pp. 105-112; IV, pp. 170-172). As a consequence, the power of the real is given in real things (and its properties) but is not to be identified with things. Things are merely intrinsic vectors of this power by being real as such, by their constitution of reality (HG, Conclusion, p. 273). Therefore the reality in which the power of the real is ultimately grounded is not a concrete real thing, none of which is a reality in itself, but an absolutely absolute [absolutamente absoluta] reality, i.e. God, the theological dimension of our being. God is the ultimate and radical depth from which the reality of each human emerges (NHG, Introduction, pp. viii-ix; III, 4, p. 346; HG, III, p. 102; IV, pp. 170-171; V, pp. 223-227, 239; VI, pp. 240-241; "OM," pp. 74-75). As Zubiri puts it:

> The personal life of a human being consists in possessing itself, and through religation makings its own I, its own being. This being is an acquired absolute being and therefore is relatively absolute... It is acquired by means of the physical determination of the power of the real as something ultimate, possibilitating and impelling. ... As a moment of things and determinant for the I, the power of the real is more than reality, and therefore more than the power of each real concrete thing. ... But the power of the real is grounded essentially in the nature of reality itself. Hence, this power is grounded on an absolutely absolute reality, distinct from real things, formally constituting them as real things by virtue of that absolutely absolute reality. This reality, then, is God (HG, III, p. 114).

This ensures that Zubiri has very unique conception of God. God, as absolutely absolute reality, the power of the real, is formally present in the concrete reality of each thing, constituting it as its own irreducible reality (versus being a cause of an effect) (HG, III, pp. 112-115). God is immanent and present in each being as the very ground of its being, God is each thing's own reality and presence of reality (HG, III, pp. 113-114). Conversely, things give me God in His very reality when they give me their reality. Real things manifest the deity of God who is in them, formally constituting them as a divine configuration (HG, III, p. 118; IV, p. 136).

All the same, God is not identical with things, God is a transcendent font *in* them (not *to* them), God is a formal concretion in things, a fontanality, constituting them as real in and of themselves (HG, III, pp. 102, 130-132; IV, p. 140; V, pp. 223-225, 239). So the power of the real in each thing is more than its particular reality, it is a transcendence of God not beyond but in things (HG, VII, p. 253). Applied on the human level, a human has its being-in-God without being-God. God is formally in human realty causing this reality to make itself in the divine reality (as a finite manner of being God, being dei-fored) without being the divine reality (HG, VII, pp. 257-259; Conclusion, pp. 277-278).

So God is best not conceived of as infinite, necessary, or perfect, as Thomists or Scotists do, but as the *ens fundamentale* [fundamental being] who grounds us (NHG, III, 1, 4, pp. 301-302, 330-333). So too, based on Zubiri's metaphysics, God is the supreme reality, not the supreme subsistent being [*ipsum esse subsistens*; self-subsistent being] of Aquinas, or the infinite being of Scotus (which would be an entification of reality and a making of God an entity). For reality is prior to being (things are real prior to being worldly entities). God is then beyond being as Plato, Pseudo-Dionysius, Meister Eckhart, Marius Victorinus, and Cajetan grasped. For in God "there is" (*haber*) surpasses "is" (*ser*), God is pure essentiality rather than formal identity of suchness and existence. God is fullness in His own right and by Himself, plenary reality *de suyo* [of Himself] or *a se* [from Himself] (NHG, III, 4, pp. 337-338; HG, Introduction, p. 19; I, p. 48; III, pp. 101-102, 125-134; OE, IX, pp. 391, 417-418).

Moreover, humans ultimately have a threefold encounter with God; or put differently there are three moments of the theological dimension of humans (whether they know it or not) (NHG, III, 4, pp. 328-329, 332; HG, IV, p. 151-152; V, pp. 224-225, 237-239; Conclusion, pp. 272-276). For God is not just the reality-ground (ultimate) towards which we are constitutively hurling, but also possibilitating and impelling. In other words, God is our ground, as well as the foundation of all the possibilities according to which we can live, and the strength to achieve them. Or in Zubiri's words, God is an absolutely absolute reality which is ultimate, possibilitating, and impelling (ground of the compulsion to be my particular I, and the support of my being) (HG, I, p. 49; II, pp. 87-88; III, pp. 115-118; IV, pp. 190-191; V, pp. 229-231, 237-238; VII, p. 253; Conclusion, p. 271). God thus has a naked presence in things and is experienced by humans. God announces His presence in things by a kind of knocking of the knuckles at the human door, as it were, an intimation of Himself, as the "towards" of the religating power of the real, as the transcendent font of what I am, and as the support of my being (HG, IV, pp. 137-138, 142-145; V, pp. 228-231; VII, pp. 266-267).

As God is not an object, nor a necessary being, but a ground, things also give us God as a person—one that is living, intellectual, and volitional (NHG, III, 1, pp. 301-302; HG, III, pp. 120, 123; IV, p. 140). God is living auto-possession and absolutely His ownness in that He fully possesses Himself, and God is intelligent and volitional in that he is the absolute actuality of His own transparent reality and sufficient to Himself (HG, III, pp. 125-134): "God is a reality absolutely personal, in a dynamism of absolute life, auto-actual in intelligence and volition" (HG, III, p. 129). Indeed God's thouness is an inconceivable Thou, prior to the I-Thou relation of humans (HG, IV, p. 141).

So the God of philosophy is the God of religion once divorced of Greek notions. For as the ground of the power of the real, God is not just a first cause, but a God whom we can address in prayer and supplication (HG, III, p. 100-102). Indeed here we go beyond the four causes of Aristotle (matter, form, agent, end) and have a personal causality, a cause that is friend, companion, counselor, lover, a form of person-person causality based on the ecstatic and diffusive love of God that is not reducible to psycho-physical causation and its terms of collision or pressure (NHG, III, 4-5, pp. 372, 382-383, 389-390; HG, IV, pp. 154-156; VII, pp. 255-256). Hence Zubiri's motto of 'Dios nos tenga de su mano' [May God hold us in His hand].[104]

Now besides knowing God in intellect as ground of my being, by faith I can go beyond this and make a surrender [la entrega] to God, placing myself in the hands of God. In faith I go beyond the inchoate relegation to God which comes as attraction, solicitation, insinuation, or suggestion, to surrender and firmly adhere to the personal reality of God (for the human does not just drift in the current but must row to fully reach God) (HG, IV, pp. 164-165). Knowledge and faith are hence different even if both can be ways to each other and both are usually connected in an encounter with God: for the mysteries of Christianity cannot be demonstrated, and moreover God is known as Maker, Omnipotent, Provident, and Merciful by faith alone as Scotus recognized (HG, III, p. 116; IV, pp. 157-161, 174-181, 207-215; V, p. 232; VII, pp. 260-264). And as God is the ground of reality as ultimate (finality), the possibility of possibilities (possibilitating), and destination (impellence), a supernatural surrender to God allows for 1) veneration (acquiescence) and worship of God as unfathomable and

ultimate plenitude (patency; manifest; Father), giving us faith; 2) supplication of God as supreme possibilitator of our lives (firmness; faithful; Son), giving us hope; and 3) a refuge in God as the very strength
of our lives (facticity; indisputable; Holy Spirit), giving us love (HG,
IV, pp. 147-149, 162). Lastly God comes to humans as Christ (HG,
V, pp. 232-235, 240-248; VII, pp. 260-264). Zubiri explains;

> In God, as effusive love, His ecstasy leads to the production of a per-
> sonal life in which the pure act of His nature subsists; this is the Trinity.
> His effusive being tends to exteriorize itself freely in two forms. First
> naturally producing things distinct from Him; this is creation. Later
> supernaturally deifying His entire creation by means of a personal In-
> carnation in Christ and a sanctifying communication in man through
> grace. Through this deification, which in some way affects the whole of
> creation, creation returns to associate itself with God's intimate life, but
> in a different way; in Christ, through a true circumincession of human
> nature in the Divine; in man, through an extrinsic but real presence of
> God; in the visible elements, through a glorious transfiguration (NHG,
> III, 5, p. 419).[105]

We have seen how Zubiri applied his unique metaphysics to the
doctrine of the Trinity. Now let us look at how he applies it to the
Eucharist. Zuburi as a Catholic accepts the real presence of Christ
in the consecrated bread (and so it is not a mere metaphor or symbol), though not as a physico-chemical reality. Indeed Christ is present
here and now (*estar* versus *ser*) in the Eucharist as spiritual food (from
transformed material food), as principle of life.

Classical metaphysics, with the Fourth Lateran Council and Aquinas, here appealed to notions of substance and accident (i.e. there is a
transubstantiation or change in substance from bread to the body of
Christ during the mass, though the accidents remain the same). Yet as
we have seen for Zubiri the real is fundamentally substantivity (things
are systems of properties that adhere or cohere to each other in an intrinsic unity) not substantiality (where properties inhere in a subject).

So in the consecration of the host what happens is a transsubstanti-
vation rather than a transubstantiation. Here the substantivity of the
bread changes without changing any of its properties. For the bread
retains its naked reality as bread (a reality-thing) but takes on a new
meaning (meaning-thing) as spiritual food, its substantivity is opened

up to a higher unity [just as a chair is a physical object with a new meaning of something for sitting, or a cave is a geological object with a new meaning of something to dwell in]. Christ leaves the naked reality of the bread intact to confer a new condition upon it, making it a superior unity of Himself. So material substantivity is converted into spiritual substantivity.

So too, as we have seen, reality (act or actuity, that it is, *estar en acto*) comes before being (actuality or worldly being, what it is, *ser actual*). So with the Eucharist Christ is present in bread not just as act but as actuality, as actual presence for humans. And again this actuality is acquired without the least change in the properties of the bread or in Christ (unlike with actuity). So the Eucharist is not a matter of a change in substance with retention of accidents—this would equate transformation with a reality, an act or actuity, and so it would equate the reality of Christ in the bread with the reality of Christ in heaven. Rather Christ is actualized in the bread; Christ has a real and physical presence in bread (which retains its own naked reality), even if this presence is not identical with Christ's naked reality. So we have a transactualization of the consecrated host ("TRE," pp. 39-59; HG, I, pp. 24-25).[106]

6

ANALYTICAL PHILOSOPHY

1950-2000 in Canada, England, France, Germany, Norway, Poland, Scotland, & the United States

The religious equivalent of the Nobel Prize is the Templeton Prize, worth a cash value of 1.6 million dollars. The 2007 recipient was the Catholic Analytic philosopher Charles Taylor (other Catholic philosophers who have won the prize include Stanley Jaki, O.S.B., Michael Novak, Fr. Michael Heller, and Francisco Ayala).

Analytical Philosophy arose in the early twentieth-century as American, Austrian, English, German, and Polish philosophers—including Gottlieb Frege (1848-1925), Alfred North Whitehead (1861-1947), Bertrand Russell (1872-1970), George Edward Moore (1873-1958), Moritz Schlick (1882-1936) [logical positivist, who as we have seen was a supporter of von Hildebrand and was murdered by a former student], Ludwig Wittgenstein (1889-1951) [logical positivist], Hans Reichenbach (1891-1953) [logical positivist], Rudolf Carnap (1891-1970) [logical positivist], Gilbert Ryle (1900-1976), Alfred Tarski (1901-1983) [Catholic], John Langshaw Austin (1911-1960), Willard Van Orman Quine (1908-2000), Alfred Jules Ayer (1910-1989) [logical positivist], and Wilfrid Sellars (1912-1989)—turned to an analysis of language as their preferred method for doing philosophy. For proponents of this system of philosophy held that the careful, logical, and rigorous analysis of language, including the use of symbolic logic, would help to clarify and solve (or dissolve) philosophical problems. Though initially many analytical philosophers were hostile towards metaphysics and religion (exceptions being Frege, Whitehead, Wittgenstein, and the Catholic Tarski), over time analytic philosophers grew more supportive of these endeavors. One of these was the lay Catholic philosopher Elizabeth Anscombe.

Gertrude Elizabeth Margaret Anscombe (1919-2001)[107] was born in Limerick, Ireland in 1919 where her father, an English army officer, was stationed. She returned to England to be educated, however, and attended Sydenham High School from 1931-1934 where she developed a voracious appetite for poring over theological works. On account of her reading, and further inquiries with the Dominicans of Blackfriars College, Oxford, Anscombe was swayed by Catholicism and converted to that religion in 1938. Anscombe had begun her higher education at St. Hugh's College, Oxford the previous year and received a First in Greats in 1941. The year of 1941 was also significant for Anscombe as that was the year she married a fellow Catholic convert and philosopher, Peter Geach, whom she had met at Blackfriars College (they eventually had seven children together one of whom would became a Dominican nun).

Anscombe relocated to the other famous English university in 1942, becoming a research fellow at Newnham College, Cambridge. While at Cambridge Anscombe met and befriended the analytical philosopher Ludwig Wittgenstein and indeed became his literary executor and translator of his works after his death in 1951 (along with Rush Rhees and Georg Herbert von Wright). Anscombe subsequently returned to Oxford, however, where she taught at Somerville College for over twenty years (1946-1970). It was in Oxford in 1948 where she held a famous debate with C.S. Lewis at the Socratic Club (besides her debates at the Socratic Club, which existed from 1942-1972, Anscombe also participated in Catholic philosophical discussions held at the Spode House Conference Center at the Hawkesyard Priory, Staffordshire from 1954-1987). Lewis admitted Anscombe had gotten the better of him and hence rewrote portions of his book *Miracles* (1948) in its second edition of 1960. Indeed the large-statured and fierce-in-debate Anscombe received the moniker "Dragon Lady" and was known to sport a monocle, to smoke cigars (she would blow smoke rings at her opponents in debate), to swear like a sailor (she once gave a paper where she said one of the things that brings intrinsic pleasure is going to the bathroom although she used a considerably less refined word for this), and unless you were the pope to refuse to wear a dress as opposed to her normal attire of pants.[108]

The year 1970 saw Anscombe return to Cambridge at New Hall where she taught philosophy until 1995 when she transferred to the University of Lichtenstein. Active in intellectual matters until the end of her life, in 1988 Anscombe worked with Dr. Hymie Gordon to found the Program in Human Rights and Medicine at the University of Minnesota. Anscombe also was active in more practical concerns, and in the 1990s Anscombe, along with her daughters, was twice arrested for protesting in front of abortion clinics throughout England (the fellow Catholic convert and lawyer John Finnis defended her). Anscombe died in 2001 while reciting the rosary and singing the Salve Regina with her family gathered around her bed.

Anscombe received many awards throughout her life: in 1967 she became a fellow of the British Academy; in 1978 she received the Austrian Ehrenkreuz Pro Litteris et Artibus; in 1979 she became a foreign honorary member of the American Academy of Arts and Sciences; in 1982 she received the Aquinas Medal from the American Catholic Philosophical Association; in 1983 she received the Forschungpreist Alexander von Humboldt Stiftung; in 1987-1989 she received honorary degrees from Notre Dame University and the Catholic University of Louvain; and in 1999 she received a Papal medal pro Ecclesia et Pontifice (along with her husband Peter Geach). An Anscombe Society dedicated to the promotion of abstinence from pre-marital sex on college campuses, was founded at the University of Princeton in 1995 by the Catholic philosophy professor Robert George and the convert historian Elizabeth Fox-Genovese, and now exists at M.I.T. and elsewhere.

The lay Catholic philosopher Anscombe has been praised as "the undoubted giant among women philosophers, a writer of immense breadth, authority, and penetration" (Mary Warnock), "simply the most distinguished, intellectually formidable, original, and troublesome philosopher in sight" (J.M. Cameron), and as having written "the most important treatment of action since Aristotle" (Donald Davidson).[109] These claims are made not without reason, for Anscombe's two great works *Intention* [INT] (1957; 1963; 2000) and "Modern Moral Philosophy" (1958) helped to launch action theory (the philosophy of action) and contemporary virtue ethics, respectively, and impacted the thought of Catholic and non-Catholic alike including some of the "luminaries" of recent analytic philosophy such as Robert Brandom, Donald Davidson, Cora Diamond, Michael Dummett [Catholic], Philippa Foot, John Haldane [Catholic], Sir Anthony Kenny [a former Jesuit and now agnostic], Iris Murdoch, Thomas Nagel, Hilary Putnam, Roger Scruton, Charles Taylor [Catholic], Judith Jarvis Thompson, and Crispin Wright.

Anscombe herself was influenced by her friend and mentor Wittgenstein and consequently approached philosophy in an analytical manner, i.e. through the careful and deliberate reflection on language and logic. As she notes: "Analytical philosophy is more characterized by styles of argument and investigation than by doctrinal content. It is thus possible for people of widely different beliefs to be practitioners of this sort of philosophy. It ought not to surprise anyone that a seriously believing Catholic Christian should also be an analytical philosopher" (FHG, VIII, p. 66).

Anscombe's first major work *Intention* [INT] (1957) is, as indicated by the title, an analytical exploration of intentions and how they can be distinguished from non-intentions.[110] According to Anscombe, unconscious bodily actions (i.e. biological processes which are known only by external observation) are not intentional acts—for instance, the peristaltic movement of the gut, or a jerk of the body when falling asleep. Nor are conscious involuntary actions (which can be known by internal experience apart from observation, i.e. with one's eyes closed) intentional acts—namely, tics, a reflex response to a kick of the knee, a gasp, being startled, an idle stroke of one's beard, a scratch of one's head, or tripping (INT, 6-8, pp. 9-15; 17, p. 25; 20, p. 32; "MME," p. 38).[111] This even applies to those conscious involuntary actions that take the form of "mental causes," that is to say, sensations, feelings, images, or ideas that automatically lead to an action—such as the hearing of a knock which immediately causes one to go open the door without any desire or forethought, or responding to what another person says in pure anger and without a reason for doing so (INT, 10-11, pp. 16-18; 12, pp. 18-19; 14, p. 23; MPM, VIII, pp. 76-81). Following the terminology of Aquinas, Anscombe considers all of these acts to be *actus hominis* (acts of the human), rather than *actus humanus* (human acts) or truly intentional acts ("AIDE," pp. 12-14, 17).

This is because intentional acts or intentions—which like conscious involuntary actions are grasped in an inner experience and not merely by an external observation of one's bodily movements (in this case a practical knowledge of an action)—deal with the future, according to Anscombe. They are reports of future actions taking the basic form: 'I am going to do such-and-such' (for instance, 'I am going to take a walk,' 'I am going to get my camera,' or 'I am seeing my dentist'). All the same, it must be recognized that intentions are not predictions about the future (about what is likely to happen), but rather reasons for acting, ones that give an answer to the question 'Why?' in regard to future actions (INT, 1-2, pp. 1-5; 5, p. 9; 9, p. 13; 15, p. 23; 22, 24, pp. 34-35, 42; 29, pp. 51-52; 32, p. 57; 48-50, pp. 87-90). Hence with an intention one acts on the basis of a significance that one dwells on, something at which one aims, an 'in order to' or a 'because'—such as 'to open a window,' 'a desire for gain,' 'to release him from this awful suffering,' or 'to get rid of the swine' (i.e. the hated person) (INT, 15, p. 23; 16, p. 24; 47, p. 85). For example, someone may 'intentionally' hang up one's jacket after being told to do so out of a desire to please the host or to keep one's jacket clean, safe, or easily accessible, or someone may kill another person because this other person killed one's father (INT, 12-13, pp. 18-21). Anscombe writes:

> ... intentional actions are a sub-class of the events in a man's history which are known to him not just because he observes them. In this wider class is included one type of involuntary actions, which is marked off by the fact that mental causality is excluded from it; and mental causality is itself being characterized by being known without observation. But intentional actions are not marked off just by being subject to mental causality, since there are involuntary actions from which mental causality is not excluded. Intentional actions, then, are the ones to which the question 'Why?' is given application (INT, 16, p. 24).

Anscombe additionally argues that intentional actions involve a different direction of fit than non-intentional actions. This is so because intentional actions introduce changes *into* the world whereas with non-intentional actions one is changed *by* the world. Consequently, my writing of a shopping list (or of a book) is different from the approach taken by a detective or historian trying to reconstruct these things. For if I notice a discrepancy between the list and my basket I work to rectify this by adding an item to the basket, but a detective who finds the same discrepancy fixes it by altering the list (INT, 32, pp. 56-57).

Importantly, and very influentially, Anscombe argues that there are different "descriptions" for one and the same human act, and that an act can be intentional under one description but unintentional under another (INT, 6, p. 11; 19, pp. 28-29; 43, p. 80; "AIDE," p. 12). She gives the example of a man pumping water at a well, his hand grasping a metal bar which it is moving up and down. As it turns out, the person pumping the water is also seeking to poison the occupants of the house who are Nazis. Now here one level of description is at the level of science (preintentional movement) wherein one notes that certain substances are getting generated in nerve fibers causing certain muscles to contract and relax. Similar physical levels of description would involve saying that one is wearing away the soles of one's shoes, sweating, or making a disturbance in the air. Yet these descriptions are not intentional since, as we have noted, an intention is an answer to the question 'Why?' in regard to an action. Thus intentional descriptions of this action, of which again there are several, would be such things as 'He's pumping,' 'He's getting water,' 'He's poisoning the inhabitants,' or 'He's saving the Jews' (INT, 23, pp. 37-39; 30, p. 53). In fact these intentional descriptions are increasingly broad, and a means to an end to the final description, which in some sense is the ultimate intention [similarly, one's intention at one level could be 'He is making a table' for the ultimate intention of 'He is earning a living'] (INT, 1, p. 1; 4, p. 9; 26, p. 46; ERP, IX, p. 86; "CCH," pp. 14-18).[112]

Anscombe stresses that though an intention (i.e. a reason for action) precedes an action, and can be said to explain it, it does not cause or determine the action. For humans have the freedom to choose which intentions to act under (INT, 3, p. 7; 5, pp. 9-10; 12, p. 19; 14, p. 22; 15, p. 24; 29, p. 52). Anscombe is thus a convinced critic of compatibilism (soft determinism), or the view that while someone is not free to walk if tied up (i.e. if there are external factors preventing one from acting), someone is free if determined by internal conditions alone (i.e. if only internal factors prevent someone from acting differently than one does, or as it is normally put, if one is able to do what one wants even if what one wants is predetermined). She argues that this betrays an inconsistency on the part of the compatibilists (indeed a dogmatic slumber). For if my actions are in the end predetermined by processes I do not control, then my freedom is illusory, even if I am only here being determined by my inner conditions (i.e. by my brain states or desires). In other words, there is no way to make sense of a notion of freedom which holds in the face of physical impossibility. Actions then can only be truly voluntary if performed under the command of reason but not determined by it [this is why for Anscombe intentions must be defined in terms of the questions that they answer and not the psychological processes which precede them]. Consequently, the laws of nature resemble the rules of chess or of a card game which limit our moves within a game but do not predetermine them as one has the freedom to choose one more over another (MPM, XIII, pp. 145-147; XV, pp. 165-167, 172; HLAE, IX, pp. 89-108; FHG, VIII, p. 68 n. 15-16).[113] Anscombe writes:

> Ever since Kant it has been a familiar claim among philosophers that one can believe in both physical determinism and 'ethical' freedom. The reconciliations have always seemed to me to be either so much gobble-degook, or to make the alleged freedom of action quite unreal. My actions are mostly physical movements; if these physical movements are physically predetermined by processes which I do not control, then my freedom is perfectly illusory ... For freedom at least involves the power of acting according to an idea (MPM, XIII, p. 146).

Anscombe's other major work, her 1958 essay on "Modern Moral Philosophy," is perhaps the most misunderstood essay in twentieth-century philosophy. Interpreters claim that in this paper Anscombe argues for the importance of virtue ethics and moral psychology to moral philosophy. And this is indeed true and Anscombe is rightly credited with reinstating virtue ethics (which goes back to Plato, Aristotle, Ambrose, Augustine, and Aquinas). Yet many of these same interpreters argue that Anscombe's paper also rejects a natural law theory of ethics (that is, it substitutes virtue ethics for natural law). And this is incorrect. For a reading of some of Anscombe's other ethical works shows that she maintains a theory of natural law throughout her writings (although to be honest her wording at times in "Modern Moral Philosophy" lends itself to this faulty interpretation).[114]

In reality the point Anscombe is trying to make in her "Modern Moral Philosophy" is that virtue ethics is a form of ethics about which Catholic and non-Catholic ethicists can come to a consensus, while someone who rejects a notion of God must also reject an ethics of natural law (not that Anscombe herself favored this latter view). That is to say in a secular culture there can at least be an agreement between believers and non-believers about virtues and vices and their contribution to human flourishing; and this constitutes a basis for an objective ethics in which virtues and vices are assessable as good or bad insofar as they contribute to human well-being. In other words, Anscombe's point is that one can do ethics apart from Christian belief, following the example of Aristotle, where instead of appealing to the notion of 'wrong,' one can appeal to those of 'untruthful, unchaste, and unjust.' Anscombe is additionally making the point that moral philosophers, whatever their views on religion, can and should mutually agree upon the need to develop an adequate moral psychology before taking up an ethical philosophy, i.e. the importance of first developing an account of action, intention, pleasure, and desire before doing ethics proper (ERP, IV, pp. 26, 29, 32-33, 38; cf. ERP, IX, p. 91).

Let us now retrace Anscombe's arguments for this position in her essay "Modern Moral Philosophy." Anscombe notes that the "law-conception" of ethics, with its notions of duty, obligation, and moral ought, historically arose after the virtue ethics of Aristotle, due to the influence of the Stoics, the Jewish Torah, and Christianity, and in particular their notion of a divine moral law. And she, not surprisingly, argues that the notions of moral duty and obligation also conceptually depend upon that of a natural law (cosmic and/or divine) and cannot be detached from it. For the notions of should, need to, ought to, or must, make reference to being obliged or bound or required to do something, i.e. being subject to a moral law. So, argues Anscombe, if you cease to believe in a God who is a lawgiver (contra the Stoics, Jews, and Christians), then you should also give up the conception of moral obligation (ERP, IV, pp. 30-31, 38, 42; n. 2 on p. 31, pp. 37-38, 42; cf. INT, 41, n. 1 on p. 78; HLAE, XIV, pp. 194-206; FHG, XIII, p. 116).

Unfortunately, states Anscombe, modern moral philosophers such as David Hume, John Stuart Mill, Henry Sidgwick, George Edward Moore, Patrick Nowell-Smith, and Richard Mervyn Hare try to retain the notions of ought, duty, right, and obligation, and so a law-conception of ethics, outside the context of a divine legislator. Yet such notions then lose all "reasonable sense," only retaining a mesmeric force as a vacuous hangover from a Judeo-Christian lawgiver ethics [which is why modern thinkers often try to ground norms through additionally appealing to a psychologically compelling force] (ERP, IV, pp. 30-32, 37, 40-41; cf. INT, 41, p. 78; FHG, XIII, pp. 113-116). Anscombe writes "the concepts of obligation, and duty—*moral* obligation and *moral* duty, that is to say—and of what is *morally* right and wrong, and of the *moral* sense of 'ought,' ought to be jettisoned if this is psychologically possible; because they are survivals, or derivatives from survivals, from an earlier conception of ethics which no longer generally survives, and are only harmful without it" (ERP, IV, p. 26;

cf. ERP, IV, pp. 26-27) [we can see how this language could lead to a misinterpretation of her thought].

Still the main problem with modern moral philosophy for Anscombe is that it all too often embraces a utilitarian point of view [that is to say it is consequentialistic, a term Anscombe herself coined]. In other words, most modern moral philosophers hold that the prohibition of harmful acts, whether one is taking about lying, or harming or killing innocent persons, are useful rules of thumb, rules which can and should be violated at times as a means to certain ends. For according to utilitarianism (at least the act-utilitarianism found in Bentham and others) what makes an action good or bad is solely whether or not it leads to the greater good. Hence actions that harm a minority but aid a majority are morally justifiable, even praiseworthy (ERP, IV, pp. 33-34; cf. ERP, VII, p. 71; "AIDE," p. 21; "CCH," pp. 20-24; "MME," pp. 38, 46).

An essential feature of Christian ethics, on the other hand, is the moral principle that "there are certain things forbidden whatever consequences threaten, such as: choosing to kill the innocent for any purpose, however good; vicarious punishment; treachery (by which I mean obtaining a man's confidence in a grave manner by promises of trustworthy friendship and then betraying him to his enemies); idolatry; sodomy; adultery; making a false profession of faith" (ERP, IV, p. 34). So under no circumstance can a Christian do evil for the greater good, whether it be committing adultery, apostasy, lying, or murder—as in the classic utilitarian example wherein one imprisons or murders an innocent person to placate an angry mob set on destructive vengeance (or in Anscombe's updated examples wherein one executes an innocent man to avert a nuclear bomb strike, or boils a baby to avoid a frightful disaster befalling a thousand or even a million people) (ERP, IV, pp. 39-40, 42; n. 6 on p. 40; VI, pp. 58-59; VII, pp. 64-65, 71; HLAE, XXI, pp. 261-277; FHG, VIII, n. 8, 13-14 on pp. 67-68; XII, pp. 234-238; "MME," pp. 38-40, 45-47; "AIDE," p. 21; cf. Rom 3:8). For it is always wrong "to commit sin that good might come; and we may not commit any sin, however small, for the sake of any good, however great, and if the choice lies between our total destruction and the commission of sin, then we must choose to be destroyed" (ERP, VIII, p. 79; cf. ERP, IV, pp. 35-36; "AIDE," pp. 16-17). Consequently, the just individual "habitually refuses to commit or participate in any unjust actions for fear of any consequences, or to obtain any advantage, for himself or anyone else" (ERP, IV, p. 40).[115] These prohibitions are bedrock then, says Anscombe, even if there is a large area of ethics wherein what is just is determined partly by a prudent weighing up of consequences.

This is why Anscombe spared no ink in condemning the "utilitarian" actions that occurred during the Second World War, both on the part of the Axis and the Allies. In the first place, the Nazis did horrible things to numerous innocent people (i.e. the death camps), and they "terror-bombed" British cities from 1940-1944, initially with conventional bombs and later with V-1 and V-2 rockets (ERP, VII, pp. 66). Yet the manner in which the allies prosecuted the war was not itself without fault. For the English and its allies also engaged in the "obliteration bombing" (i.e. area bombing versus target bombing) of various German cities from 1942-1945 in order to undermine the morale of the Germans. In so doing they directly or indirectly killed numerous people, most of whom were innocent, in the cities of Aachen, Berlin (2000 deaths), Bochum, Cologne, Dortmund, Dresden (25,000 deaths), Düsseldorf, Essen [Ruhr], Hamburg (50,000 deaths), Kassel, Mainz, and Pforzheim (ERP, VI, pp. 58-59; VII, pp. 62-63; VIII, p. 76). Anscombe also criticized the bombing of the Westkapelle dyke in Zeeland, Netherlands by the British in 1944. Bombing of this dyke released a torrent of water that made it easier for the British forces to capture the Nazi-occupied city of Walcheren. Unfortunately the rushing water also knowingly drowned around 180 innocent civilians (ERP, VII, p. 66; VIII, p. 79). Even greater casualties resulted when the American president Henry Truman ordered atomic bombs to be dropped on the Japanese cities of Hiroshima (c. 75,000 deaths) and Nagasaki (c. 60,000 deaths) to avoid a costly (in terms of casualties) land invasion of Japan (ERP, VII, p. 64). Anscombe even went so far as to publicly protest the nomination of Truman for an honorary degree at Oxford in 1956, arguing against those holding that "a couple of massacres to a man's credit are not exactly a reason for not showing him an honor" (ERP, VII, p. 65) [her actions forced a vote regarding the merits awarding the degree to Truman, a vote that came out in favor of Truman].

Anscombe argues that such actions show a false belief that one must harm the innocent out of defense of one's country or church, and along with it a mistrust of God's promises (ERP, VI, pp. 60-61). It is as though one here retorted to God 'We had to break your law lest your church fail. We could not obey your commandments, for we did not believe your promises' (ERP, VI, p. 61).

One reason for the prevalence of the flawed ethical theory of utilitarianism according to Anscombe is the common denial of the doctrine of double effect; for, reasons Anscombe, if one rejects the doctrine of double effect all that is left is the utilitarian weighing up of evils (ERP, VI, pp. 54, 58; "MME," pp. 24-36). The doctrine of double effect—formulated by Aquinas (c. 1225-1274), the Salmanticenses [the Spanish Carmelites] (1665-1715), and Jean-Pierre Gury, S.J. (1801-1866)—or what Anscombe calls the principle of side-effects, asserts that though one can never engage in an intrinsically evil action (i.e. do evil either as an end or as a means to an end), one can on occasion perform actions that have both a good effect and a bad effect (i.e. a double effect), namely, if one does not intend but merely foresees the bad effect, if the good effect is not directly attained by means of the evil effect, and if there is a proportionate reason (a sufficient goodness) for allowing the incidental bad effect to occur ("AIDE," p. 21; ERP, VI, pp. 54, 58, 66; VII, p. 68; VIII, pp. 77-79; cf. Aquinas, *Summa Theologiae*, 1a2ae q. 20 a. 5; 2a2ae q. 64 a. 7). For instance, by the doctrine of double effect, it is permissible to kill an attacker in self-defense in default of a non-lethal way to escape. Here one does not intend the death of attacker, but rather it is a side effect of action taken to ward off the attack. So too one can legitimately bomb a military target such as a munitions factory or a naval dockyard even if there may be collateral damage and nearby innocents are killed (ERP, VI, p. 66; VIII, pp. 78-79; "AIDE," p. 18). Again one can build rail, sea, and air transportation systems, and race tracks, or in emergencies open flood-gates or close fire-doors, foreseeing that doing so may result in the death of some people ("AIDE," p. 22; HLAE, XXI, p. 265, 274-275; XXIII, pp. 285-291; "MME," p. 48). Turning to the field of medicine, by the doctrine of double effect, a doctor may attempt a dangerous surgery or give a pain-relieving drug to a patient with a mortal illness (palliative medicine), knowing full well that such actions may hasten the patient's death, as here the doctor does not intend the patient's death but only foresees its possibility (ERP, VI, pp. 54-55; "MME," n. 1 on p. 38, pp. 39, 48). To take a last example, a woman can take an anovulant pill (i.e. a birth-control pill; assuming here that it functions solely by stopping ovulation and is not an abortifascent) to check the painful condition of dysmenorrhea (or endometriosis) during her monthly cycle, as she only incidentally intends to not get pregnant ("CCH," pp. 14-17).[116]

Anscombe had the good fortune to be born into an England in which Catholicism was prospering, and in which Catholics could attend the Universities. It had not always been so. For though beginning with the "Second Spring" of Catholicism in Britain (1818-1852), Catholicism only flourished in Britain (with the exception of Northern Ireland) after the English Catholic Relief Acts of 1791, 1793, and 1829; after the Jesuit Stonyhurst College and St. Patrick's College, Maynooth, and the Benedictine Downside Abbey and Ampleforth Abbey were founded from 1794-1802; after the hierarchy was re-established in England in 1850 and in Scotland in 1878; after Catholics were allowed back into the Universities of Cambridge, Oxford, and Dublin, universities they founded, with the passing of English University Test Acts in 1871-1873 (and the subsequent permission of the English bishops in 1895) and the Irish Universities Act of 1908; and after almost all anti-Catholic legislation was removed with the English Catholic Relief Act of 1926. These measures allowed and encouraged the re-establishment of many Catholic Institutions of Higher Education including the Jesuit-founded University College, Dublin (1883) [after the failure of Newman's Catholic University of Ireland], Milltown Institute, Dublin (1889), Campion Hall, Oxford (1895), Heythrop Hall, Oxford (1926) [becoming Heythrop College, University of London in 1970]; the Dominican-founded Hawkesyard, Staffordshire (1894) and Blackfriars, Oxford (1921); the Benedictine-founded Benet's Hall, Oxford (1897) and Glenstal Abbey, Ireland (1927); the Franciscan-founded Greyfriars, Oxford (1910) and International Study Centre, Kent (1974); as well as St. Peter's College, Glasgow (1874), St. Edmund's House, Cambridge (1896) [becoming a College in 1996], a Chair of Scholastic Philosophy at Queen's University, Belfast in 1908 [set up to appease Irish Catholics], Plater College, Oxford (1921-2005), Ushaw College, Durham (1968), the Catholic Linacre Centre for Health Care Ethics, London (1969), the Catholic Maryvale Institute, Birmingham (1980), St. Andrew's College, Scotland (1981), the Von Hügel Institute, Cambridge (1987), the Margaret Beaufort Institute, Cambridge (1994), and the Marian Study Centre, Durham (1996).

Many societies for the defense or preservation of English Catholicism also sprung up such as the Catholic Truth Society (1868), Newman Society, Oxford (1878), Catholic Social Guild (1909), Catholic Evidence Guild (1918), PAX Peace Society (1936-1971), Spirit of the Sword Movement (1940), Spode House Conference Centre for Catholic intellectual discussions, Hawkesyard Priory, Staffordshire (1954-1987), St. Dismas Society for the homeless in Southampton (1962), Catholic Theological Association (1984), Cardinal Hume Centre (1986), the ecumenical Churches Together in Britain and Ireland (1990), and the World Community for Christian Meditation founded by John Main, O.S.B. (1991).

Indeed recently memorials for the Catholic Martyrs of Britain have appeared at Tinburn Tree, London and Hollywell Street, Oxford (2006-2009), in 2006 Aidan Nichols became the first Catholic holder of a chair of theology in Oxford since the Reformation, in 2007 the former Prime Minister Tony Blair (1997-2007) converted to Catholicism, in 2008 Louise Richardson became the first Catholic Rector of the University of St. Andrews in Scotland since the Reformation (a university where the Catholic philosopher John Haldane is Director of its Center for Ethics and who was appointed Consultor to the Pontifical Council for Culture in 2005), in 2009 Lewis Ayres assumed the Bede Chair in Catholic Theology at the University of Durham, and in 2009 Ireland passed a blasphemy law which criminalized "publishing or uttering matter that is grossly abusive or insulting in relation to matters sacred by any religion, thereby intentionally causing outrage among a substantial number of adherents of that religion." Let us now shift our attention to another country, Canada, a country strongly influenced by England in its language and thought.

The leading Canadian Catholic philosopher, indeed perhaps the leading Canadian philosopher altogether, is **Charles Margrave Taylor (1931-)**. Charles Taylor was born in 1931 in Montreal, Canada and completed a bachelor's degree at McGill University in 1952. Winning a Rhodes Scholarship, he attended the University of Oxford where he received a bachelors in politics in 1955, a master's degree in philosophy in 1960, and a doctorate in philosophy in 1961 (under Isaiah Berlin and Elizabeth Anscombe). He then became a teaching Fellow of All Soul's College, Oxford, in 1956 and held that position until 1961. Taylor returned to Canada to teach at McGill University in 1961 and has taught there except for a brief stint from 1976 to 1983 at Oxford where he was Chichele Professor of Social and Political Theory (succeeding his teacher Isaiah Berlin). He has also recently become a professor at Northwestern University.

Besides his philosophical scholarship, Taylor is also famous for his political involvement. He helped to found the socialistic New Democratic Party in Quebec and was Vice President of this party from 1965 to 1973. He even unsuccessfully ran for the position of Canadian Prime Minister in 1962-1965.

Taylor has received numerous honors the past few years. In 1991 he was appointed to the the the Conseil de la langue française, in 1995 he was made a companion of the order of Canada, in 1996 he received the Marianist Award from the University of Dayton, in 1998-1999 he gave the Gifford Lectures in Edinburgh, Scotland (and again at Glasgow from 2008-2009), in 2000 he was made a Grand Officer of the National Order of Quebec, in 2003 he received the Social Science and Humanities Research Council of Canada Gold Medal Award, in 2007 he was appointed to the Rapport de la Commission de Consultation sur Les Practiques d'Acommodement Reliées aux Différences, in 2007, as we noted above, he received the Templeton Prize, and in 2008 he received the Kyoto Prize in philosophy. He is also a member of the Canadian Royal Society.[117]

Taylor's key works are his *Sources of the Self* [SOS] (1989) and *Varieties of Religion Today* [VRT] (2003) [representing the Institute for Human Sciences Lectures in Vienna of 2000].[118] Charles Taylor has been influenced by and combines both analytic and Continental (Romanticism, Hegelianism) approaches to philosophy. He is also greatly influenced by the Augustinian tradition.

In his epistemology Taylor rejects both relativism and the correspondence theory of truth and instead favors a notion of "epistemic gain" under the influence of Heidegger, Wittgenstein, Polanyi, and MacIntyre. Admittedly, says Taylor, humans are inescapably linked to their particular frameworks, and so cannot completely disengage themselves from their history, situation, desires, and values. Yet humans can also articulate a rational account of their beliefs, that is, humans can "distinguish and lay out the particular features of the matter in a perspicuous order" ("RAT," p. 90). Moreover, this very ability to articulate one's beliefs in a perspicuous manner allows for transcultural judgments of superiority, or "epistemic gain," as certain views are better able to account for experiences, reduce errors, and resolve confusions and contradictions ("RAT," pp. 87-92, 99-105; "FFT," pp. 152-

83; SOS, III, p. 72; XXV, p. 514; PHA, I, pp. 7-19; III, pp. 39-60; HAL, I, pp. 36-39; "RC," pp. 205-206).

Taylor is perhaps most famous, however, for his ethics, for exploring what viewpoint has the highest epistemic gain in regard to explaining moral agency and personal identity (or relatedly, what are their transcendental conditions). In particular Taylor distinguishes between a weak and a strong evaluation and argues that the human self primarily finds its identity in the latter.

Weak evaluation involves a quantitative comparison of desires wherein one considers each of one's desires as *ipso facto* something to be pursued, all the while seeking to determine which combination of desires leads to the greatest overall satisfaction. For example, one might survey one's current desires to eat and to swim to see how they can be combined most satisfactorily. What is significant then about weak evaluation is that every desire is considered valuable as such. Strong evaluation, on the other hand, involves a qualitative comparison of desires in order to determine which of these desires are higher and more noble and which lower and more base. Strong evaluation involves "discriminations of right or wrong, better or worse, higher or lower, which are not rendered valid by our own desires, inclinations, or choices, but rather stand independent of these and offer standards by which they can be judged" (SOS, I, p. 4). Thus in strong evaluation some desires are found to be superior and others inferior in and of themselves, and not just because of their conflict with other desires. For instance, one might consider one's desires for family, care for others, universal justice, world peace, or religion as most important, and one's desire for drugs or sex as lowest (SOS, I, p. 14; III, pp. 50, 53, 75; HAL, I, pp. 16-19). As a result there is a great difference between weak and strong evaluation: "Whereas for the simple weigher [of weak evaluations] what is at stake is the desirability of different consummations, those defined by his *de facto* desires, for the strong evaluator reflection also examines the different possible modes of being of the agent. Motivations or desires do not only count in virtue of the attraction of the consummations but also in virtue of the kind of life and kind of subject that these desires properly belong to" (HAL, I, p. 25).[119]

Significantly, Taylor argues that going beyond weak evaluation and engaging in strong evaluation is essential to being a human self. For our very identity is bound up with the forms of life that we assert are of ultimate importance and of most value, whether what matters to us is being a Catholic, Protestant, socialist, or Freudian (SOS, II, p. 33; HAL, I, pp. 28, 33-34). As Taylor puts it "My identity is defined by the commitments and identifications which provide the frame or horizon within which I can try to determine from case to case what is good, or valuable, or what ought to be done, or what I endorse or oppose. In other words, it is the horizon within which I am capable of taking a stand" (SOS, II, p. 27; cf. SOS, II, pp. 26-29, 34-35, 41). So strong evaluations, by virtue of the qualitative distinctions they incorporate, are what provide an orientation or a framework of meaning for our lives (SOS, II, pp. 30-32, 42-44, 47-48, 51-52; III, p. 68; HAL, II, 45-76). As Taylor sees it then:

> ... we come here to one of the most basic aspirations of human beings, the need to be connected to, or in contact with, what they see as good, or of crucial importance, or of fundamental value. And how could it be otherwise, once we see that this orientation in relation to the good is essential to being a functional human agent? The fact that we have to place ourselves in a space which is defined by these qualitative distinctions cannot but mean that where we stand in relation to them must matter to us. Not being able to function without orientation in the space of the ultimately important means not being able to stop caring where we sit in it (SOS, II, p. 42).
>
> You cannot help having recourse to these strongly valued goods for the purposes of life: deliberating, judging situations, deciding how you feel about people, and the like. The 'cannot help' here is not like the inability to stop blinking when someone waves a fist in your face, or your incapacity to contain your irritation at Uncle George sucking his dentures, even though you know it's irrational. It means rather that you need these terms to make the best sense of what you're doing. By the same token these terms are indispensable to the kind of explanation and understanding of self and others that is interwoven with these life uses: assessing his conduct, grasping her motivation, coming to see what you were really about all these years, etc. (SOS, II, p. 59).

Taylor goes on to inquire into what moral ontology best articulates (has the highest epistemic gain for) these strong moral evaluations. He asks "What is the picture of our spiritual nature and predicament that makes sense of our [moral] responses? 'Making sense' here means articulating what makes these responses appropriate: identifying what makes something a fit object for them and correlatively formulating more fully the nature of the response as well as spelling out what all this presupposes about ourselves and our situation in the world" (SOS, I, p. 8).

Of course, many modern ethical theories are naturalistic and, rejecting any notion of moral transcendentalism, assert that moral standards (including any strong evaluations if admitted) arise from humans themselves (or from the natural world). Such theories take diverse forms. Humeans reduce morality to a set of instinctive sentiments or natural reactions found in humans (David Hume; Alain Renault). Projectivists argue that humans project values onto a value-neutral universe (whether it be the Relativism of Jean-Paul Sartre and Albert Camus; the Quasi-Realism of John Mackie, Simon Blackburn, and David Wiggins; or the Sociobiology of E.O. Wilson and B.F. Skinner). Again Rationalists avoid all qualitative distinction and ontology, and instead identify the moral view with that of the impartial spectator (as does Enlightened Egoism; Kantianism; Pragmatism; the Utilitarianism of Jeremy Bentham and John Stuart Mill; and the Proceduralism of Richard Hare and Jürgen Habermas) (SOS, I, pp. 22-23; II, pp. 31-32; III, pp. 53-55, 75-79, 85, 93, 98, 103; XXV, pp. 495-505; SA, XV, pp. 543, 581).

Yet, contrary to these naturalistic theories, the best account we can give of our moral practices (the manner in which we actually argue, reason, and deliberate in our moral lives), argues Taylor, is to treat values as something we encounter, i.e. to assert a moral realism or objectivism (SOS, III, pp. 53-55).

In the first place, contra Humeanism and Sociobiology, our responses to values occur in a manner differing from that of a taste for sweets or an aversion to odors, i.e. from a biological instinct. For in encountering a good we sense that we are moved by what is valuable in it rather than it having value solely because of our reaction. To take one example, we defend a universalism in regard to respecting human life and integrity, not just because we have such reactions, or even find them useful to the human race (utilitarianism), but because, perceiving the dignity of persons, we believe it would be utterly wrong and unfounded to draw the boundaries any narrower than the whole human race. This moral realism is buttressed by the fact that we can and do argue over what is a fit object of moral respect (i.e. whether something merits our reaction), and we can additionally scrutinize our moral intuitions for their consistency, but it would make no sense to argue whether something is a fit object of nausea or whether someone is being inconsistently nauseated (which are mere brute facts). Thus it is that we find problematic any attempt to distinguish the value of human beings based on characters having to do with skin color or physical traits. All of which goes to show that our moral intuitions discriminate real properties of things (which can be discovered, carefully observed, and better delimited) and are not just visceral reactions (SOS, I, pp. 5-8, 15-19; III, pp. 55-57, 74-77; SA, XV, pp. 589-591).

Secondly, our moral claims (especially those involving strong moral evaluations wherein we distinguish good and evil, noble and base, virtuous and vicious, higher and lower) command our allegiance and override our needs for self-esteem, recognition, sexuality, money, etc. They hence make requisite an ethics of self-transcendence, self-denial, and generous action. Now it is difficult to explain this sense that something incomparably important is involved here without impoverishment, if it is only the human self or nature and not a transcendent ontology that accords moral demands their status (SOS, II, p. 26; III, p. 60; XXV, p. 517; SA, VIII, pp. 312, 338; XV, pp. 543-545, 555, 581-582; XVII, p. 642; XVI, pp. 606-609; XVII, p. 641; XVIII, pp. 693-694; XIX, p. 712, 726; XX, p. 744). Nor is it apparent how a naturalistic moral theorist could respond to someone who asked why one should be moral or strive to be ethically mature (especially to the point of extending one's concern to universal human prosperity), other than by appealing to one's prudent interest, in which case it is not at all clear why one should not confine one's concern to one's own material welfare, family, or immediate milieu (SOS, III, pp. 87, 89-90; SA, VIII, p. 310; XV, pp. 562, 572).

Thus asserts Taylor, on the whole, moral realism makes more sense of our moral lives and has a higher epistemic gain than moral naturalism. In fact, there is an inescapable understanding of some form of the good with its notes of being meritorious, reasonable, incomparably higher, and demanding sacrifice in our moral horizon. And the terms indispensable for explaining how we lead our life, those we can't help having recourse to, are real. For what is real is precisely what we have to deal with, what won't go away even if it doesn't fit in with our prejudices (indeed we cannot know if humans can be completely explained in a scientific and naturalistic manner until we have first explained the life they live in its own terms) (SOS, III, pp. 58-60, 68, 73-74, 76; SA, VII, p. 286; "RC," pp. 206-209, 213).[120]

Taylor, as suggested by the title of his major work, also develops an argument for moral realism (and for theism) based on an examination of the moral sources—"goods reflection on which morally empowers us"—required by our modern ethical ideals (SOS, XV, p. 264). This argument begins with the recognition that humans today, despite differences of theological and metaphysical belief, agree surprisingly well about the demands of justice and benevolence (such as a concern for the welfare of all humans, and the inappropriateness of judicial torture, mutilation for crimes of theft, or an openly-declared racism), even if there are rare disagreements such as with the propriety of abortion. Moreover, some commitments to benevolence and justice are stringent and far-reaching (such as need to help a stranger outside the gates or someone in danger) and so can exact a high cost upon the moral agent. Indeed a moral agent may even believe that there are things worth dying for (SOS, XXV, pp. 500-505, 518; ACM, I, pp. 28-34; VI, p. 120).

Hence the pressing need to find a moral source (a motivation that has the power to inspire and strengthen our resolve in moral matters and overcome the obstacles that lie upon the way) that can support our lofty moral ambitions, i.e. Doctors without Frontiers, G8 initiatives to aid Africa, and environmental crusades; for high standards need strong sources.

Now it is here not enough, argues Taylor, to be moved by the feelings of guilt or shame arising from not meeting these moral ideals, nor by the mental high of self-satisfaction, nor even by a sense of our own worth and honor, in doing good (as with Hobbes, Bentham, De Vigny, Camus, and Derrida) (SOS, XXV, p. 515; VRT, II, p. 79). For though these motives may suffice for a time, without stronger moral sources there is the danger that one will eventually slacken in one's resolve. Indeed such motivations make philanthropy vulnerable to the shifting fashions of media attention and feel-good hype, i.e. the cause of the month (this famine, this war), and something to be forgotten about when it drops off the news screen. Furthermore, when faced with the disappointments of human performance (how refractory humans typically fall short of their potential), and the vastness of the situations needing remediation, one could easily become angry, feel futile, or take on contempt, hatred, and aggression towards those who fall short. Indeed one may even fall prey to a political extremism and engage in the ruthless use of force, despotism, and tutelage, in one's flaming indignation against injustice (SOS, XXV, p. 516; MSI, XIII, pp. 192-193; ACM, I, pp. 28-34; VI, p. 120; SA, XVII, p. 639; XVIII, pp. 694-697). Such inadequate moral sources hence can quickly lead, observes Taylor, "from dedication to others to self-indulgent, feel-good responses, from a lofty sense of human dignity to control powered by contempt and hatred, from absolute freedom to absolute despotism, from a flaming desire to help the oppressed to an incandescent hatred for all those who stand in the way" (ACM, I, p. 34).

The question then really becomes how to have the greatest degree of philanthropic action with the minimum of hope in mankind and what moral source can allow for this. In fact, if we found that we were living beyond our means in holding allegiance to standards of justice and benevolence that exceeded our moral sources, it would be more honest and prudent to moderate and scale down our moral ambitions than to try and live them out (SOS, XXV, pp. 517-521; SA, XVII, pp. 639-640).

This being said, according to Taylor, the only moral source capable of solidly founding human solidarity is a sense of the objective dignity and value of human beings coupled with a belief in a theistic perspective (SOS, II, p. 26; III, pp. 55-57, 73-76, 88; XV, pp. 510-518; SA, XVI, pp. 606-609; XVIII, pp. 693-694; XIX, p. 712, 726; XX, p. 744). For only a recognition of the intrinsic value of human life, an ineradicable bent toward some good beyond life, and an affirmation of the divine goodness of creation, can prop up our far-reaching, burdensome, and self-sacrificial moral commitments to benevolence and justice (SOS, XXV, pp. 515-521; "MMR," pp. 70-75; ACM, I, p. 27). So too a theistic view can most help us escape being drawn toward a negation of life and violence in the pursuit of moral endeavors. For such a view stresses the importance of forgiveness and reconciliation wherein we forgo any satisfaction of retribution and renounce the right of the innocent to vindictively punish the guilty (out of a grasp of the common flawed nature of humans and that we are all to blame) (SA, XVIII, pp. 701, 706-710).

Furthermore, theism, particularly in its Christian form, offers us a vision of love based on what we as humans most profoundly are—beings created in the image of God. And it was this agapic Christian vision that allowed Mother Teresa and Jean Vanier (and we could mention Catherine of Genoa, Camillus of Lellis, Vincent de Paul, Father Damien, and Abbé Pierre) to extend help to the irremediably broken, the useless and handicapped, the sick, those dying without dignity, fe-

tuses with genetic defects. For they grasped that the Christian is called
to a love and compassion that is unconditional, one not based on what
a recipient has made of him or herself, but rather on the fact that they
reflect their Creator (SOS, XXV, p. 517; SA, XVIII, pp. 677-684;
ACM, I, pp. 31-35). So summing up Taylor writes:

> We are meant to be concerned for the life and well-being of all humans
> on the face of the earth; we are called on to further global justice between
> peoples; we subscribe to universal declarations of rights. Of course, these
> standards are regularly evaded. Of course, we subscribe to them with a
> great deal of hypocrisy and mental reservation. It remains that they are
> the publicly accepted standards. And they do from time to time galva-
> nize people into action-as in the great television-inspired campaigns for
> famine relief or in movements like Band-Aid.
>
> To the extent that we take these standards seriously (and that var-
> ies from person to person), how are they experienced? They can just be
> felt as peremptory demands, standards that we feel inadequate, bad, or
> guilty for failing to meet. No doubt many people, probably almost all
> of us some of the time, experience them this way. Or perhaps we can
> get a 'high' when we do sometimes meet them, from a sense of our own
> worth or, more likely, from the momentary relief from the marginal but
> oppressive sense we usually have of failing to meet them. But it is quite
> a different thing to be moved by a strong sense that human beings are
> eminently worth helping or treating with justice, a sense of their dignity
> or value. Here we have come into contact with the moral sources which
> originally underpin these standards. ... The original Christian notion of
> agape is of a love that God has for humans which is connected with their
> goodness as creatures (though we don't have to decide whether they are
> loved because good or good because loved). Human beings participate
> through grace in this love. There is a divine affirmation of the creature,
> which is captured in the repeated phrase in Genesis I about each stage
> of the creation 'and God saw that it was good.' Agape is inseparable from
> such 'seeing-good' (SOS, XXV, pp. 515-516).[121]

All of which is to say that Clifford and others are incorrect in asserting that religious beliefs are based upon an absence of evidence, i.e. a
blind faith. For although Taylor asserts the limited viability of the traditional proofs for God,[122] he grants that there can be an epistemic gain
(or what he calls a "supersession argument") in taking up a religious
position (that is to say, a theological perspective can eliminate various
errors and make a whole range of phenomena more tractable) ("PP,"
pp. 340-342; PHA, III, pp. 41-47). For, as we have seen, our sense of
something greater and higher, of our deep nature, of important moral

matters, of objective goods, of the moral meaning of the universe, of a fullness of love, of a current running through all things, of a healing power, are best made sense of from a theistic perspective (SA, IX, p. 350; XVII, p. 638; ACM, I, p. 27; "PP," p. 342). Our aesthetic experiences can also open us up to something higher. For we can grasp that the beauty of nature and art (Dante, Bach, Rembrandt, Chartes) is a force that interpellates us and tells us something about reality, and so cannot be explained away as merely a triggering of certain reactions in our brain when we see a painting or landscape (SA, VII, p. 288; XV, pp. 554-555; XVI, pp. 595-599, 605-609; XVII, p. 622; XVIII, pp. 693-694). Only then by invoking transcendence can we make sense of a world full of beauty, meaning, warmth, moral action, and a horizon of self-transformation (SA, XV, p. 592; XVI, p. 594).[123]

In the end, however, Taylor admits that this notion of a Christian moral source and objective moral goodness is not so much a matter of guarantee as it is a matter of faith (a hunch, an anticipatory confidence)—a faith that one can stand among others in a stream of love which is in fact God's very life and which transforms us beyond a merely human perfection (SA, Introduction, pp. 7-10, 15-20; I, p. 84; II, p. 143; XV, pp. 550-551; XVI, p. 592; XVII, p. 655; XVIII, pp. 701-703; XX, p. 768). As Taylor concludes, "There is a large element of hope, a hope implicit in Judaeo-Christian theism (however terrible the record of its adherents in history), and in its central promise of a divine affirmation of the human, more total than humans can ever attain unaided" (SOS, XXV, p. 521).

None of this should this be considered problematic, since, as Augustine and William James noted, some truths are hidden unless one goes halfway toward meeting them. For instance in order to know whether someone likes one or not (or to grasp the atmosphere at a party, the full range of what someone is trying to communicate, the nature of prayer, or the existence of God) one cannot adopt a stance of maximum distance and suspicion, but rather must be open to the relationship or phenomenon. In such situations then, where what one experiences has to do with and depends upon one's disposition, orientation, bent of life, and one's openness to deeper realities, a fact cannot fully come forth unless a preliminary faith exists in its coming.

With this in mind, it is apparent that the principle of William Clifford—that it is wrong always and everywhere to accept something on insufficient evidence (and that desires are obstacles to the truth)—

really becomes the principle 'better risk loss of truth than chance of error.' For if we strictly keep our willing nature out of play, we risk adopting a rule of thinking that prevents us from acknowledging certain kinds of truth that are really there, i.e. we close ourselves off from various truths (indeed those who claim to keep passion out of their beliefs altogether are suffering from a false consciousness). In fact contrary to Clifford who rejects views insofar as they attract us, this is precisely what justifies the believer's interest in them as it is hint of something important that the believer needs to explore (VRT, II, pp. 45-52, 54-57; "PP," pp. 349-353; SA, IX, p. 332; XX, pp. 729-730). Augustine and William James then are right to assert that our very longing for a religious and transformative perspective, our desire for eternity, our being moved by the life of St. Francis, can reveal God to us; our deep desire for religious matters is a hint as to their reality, that we have encountered them on some level (SA, XII, pp. 433-436; XIV, pp. 510, 515, 530-533).

Though rather rare in France,[124] one Frenchman who has embraced the analytic tradition in philosophy is the Catholic thinker **Francis Jacques (1934-)** who was born in Strasbourg in 1934. Jacques studied mathematics and physiology at the University of Paris Sud (Orsay) and philosophy at the Sorbonne from 1952-1955 and received his agrégation (license to teach) in 1958. Jacques subsequently taught at the Lycée St. Louis from 1961-1964 and at the Lycée Chaptal from 1965-1966 as well as getting married to Elaine Martin in 1962. It was at the University of Rennes from 1967-1986, however, where Jacques achieved prominence as a teacher (he additionally pursued further studies and received a doctorate in philosophy from the University of Paris-Nanterre in 1975 under Paul Ricoeur and Jules Vuillemin). He was also active in the Centre Catholique des Intellectuels Français at this time. Jacques went on to serve as professor of philosophy nearly simultaneously at the Catholic Institute of Paris from 1986-2000 (he also received a doctorate in theology there in 2000) and at the Sorbonne Nouvelle, Paris-III from 1985-2001, where he was director of the Centre de Recherches de Philosophie du Langage.

Among Jacques's honors are his being named Laureat of Concours Général in 1952, Laureat of the French Academy in 1983, Laureat of the French Institut in 1986, a French representative to the International Federation of Philosophy in 1988-1998, and a commander of the Palmes Académiques in 1993. Moreover, in 1996 Jacques was appointed a consultant to the Pontifical Academy of the Sciences, in 2000 he was elected into the Académie d'Education et de Sciences Sociales, and from 2002-2003 he occupied the Chair Étienne Gilson at the Catholic University of Paris. He has also been past president of the Association des philosophes chrétiens. L'Association de philosophie Francis Jacques (AFPJ), a society dedicated to the study of his thought, was formed in 2002.[125]

Francis Jacques's key work is his *Difference and Subjectivity* [*Différence et subjectivité: Anthropologie d'un point de vue relationnel*] [DS] (1982) [winner of the prix Broquette-Gonin from the French Academy].[126]

Jacques, following Wittgenstein, is critical of what he calls a "metaphysics of subjectivity," or the view, found in Augustine, Montaigne, Pascal, Descartes, Maine de Biran, Rousseau, Lavelle, Kant, Kierkegaard, and Husserl, that the person is a permanent center of awareness, a substantial self, an 'I', that is the subject of all thoughts (DS, Preface, pp. xxv-xxix; Introduction, p. 3; I, pp. 16, 20, 24-29, 43; IV, pp. 162-170; Conclusion, p. 319).[127]

Firstly, notes Jacques, historically before a child exists for itself, it exists for others, i.e. for a family; and before a child speaks, it is spoken about. Indeed a child is, in order, first a 'he/she' (who is discussed by others), then a 'you' (who names other persons and things), and only lastly an 'I' (who names and identifies itself).

Secondly, a child's existence has already been determined in significant ways before it comes into world: for instance, the child is assigned a place in the family, its surname identifies it with its forebears, and it is given a language and a community (DS, I, pp. 17-18, 45-50).

Thirdly, a subject's identity is established through communication with others. Early on a child gains its identity by learning how others address it, and by distinguishing itself from others (particularly its mother and father). So too throughout life, the subject creates itself in a linguistic exchange with other persons, listening and responding to them, borrowing terms, beliefs, characteristics, even its differences from them (DS, II, pp. 45-57, 104-110; VI, pp. 306-312; Conclusion, pp. 318, 331). More technically then, Jacques argues that there is a discourse, a mutual interlocutive relation [what Jacques calls a primary relation (*primum relationis*)] that precedes and creates personal identities (DS, Preface, xiv; Introduction, pp. 9-10; II, p. 100; III, pp.

117-118, 122-123, 125-126, 160-161; VI, p. 275; Conclusion, pp. 317, 332-334).

Self-identity consequently is less a matter of having an immediate self-consciousness, than something acquired through a slow and steady process of construction. Far from being a Cartesian substantive reality, the self is produced, it is a trans-agential function (DS, I, pp. 22, 27-28, 44; III, p. 127). Jacques writes:

> Specifically it is impossible to conceive the self as a pure presence to oneself. We have just grasped that the self is not a being which would possess its personal identity through nature or through the awareness of a spiritual substance residing within or intimately linked to it, as though it would suffice for finding itself to enter into itself. ... For the self is a being that sometimes manages and sometimes fails to constitute itself as one and the same, through all the engagements in which it occupies a formal position or an institutional place of communication. ... *ego adsum* [I am present]. The self truly discovers itself or on the contrary ... slips away and conceals itself in communicative activity. ... Decidedly the certitude of the self is not primary. If we want to talk about our experience of the self, we will say that it is discursive before being existential (DS, I, p. 55 [76-77]).

More specifically, and representing Jacques's unique contribution to philosophy, I can only construct my self-identity if I integrate all three poles of the communicative act: 1) locution (utterance)—speaking to others while calling myself an 'I'; 2) allocution—being spoken to by others as a 'you'; and 3) delocution—being spoken about by others as a 'him' or a 'her.' So in addition to the two traditional relations or roles in conversation, the 'I' who speaks to another (the self, speaker, locutor, utterer), and the 'you' present before me to whom I speak (the allocutee)—both of which are echoed in the I-Thou relationship of personalists such as Ebner and Buber—Jacques introduces a third relation, the 'he' or 'she,' or the absent or distant third party about whom we speak (the delocutee) (DS, Preface, pp. xv-xvi, xxi-xxii; Introduction, pp. 11-12; I, pp. 30-33; VI, pp. 275-282; Conclusion, p. 318; DIA, I, pp. 5-27; II, 2, pp. 97-102). Jacques comments: "Schematically, the subject will succeed in constructing its self-identity to the extent that it manages ... to integrate the three poles of any communication act: by speaking to others and saying I, by being spoken to by others as you, or by being spoken of by others as a he/she that the subject would accept as appropriate" (DS, Preface, p. xv).

This is not to say with Hume, the structuralists Lévi-Strauss and Lacan, or Freud that subjectivity is an illusion: subjectivity is real, it is just that it is secondary and derived (for it follows the primordial relation or the a priori communicational relationality that originates co-utterers). As we have seen, I am constituted as a person by my relations to others as expressed in and through language. Hence I grasp my 'self' and develop a personal identity with "sameness" and "permanence" in the course of relating to and distinguishing myself and my thoughts from others and their thoughts (DS, Preface, pp. xii, xx-xxii, xxiv-xxviii; Introduction, pp. 6-7, 11-12; I, pp. 38-41, 55; II, pp. 76, 90-99, 113-114; IV, pp. 175-176, 179-182, 185; V, pp. 187-190; Conclusion, p. 332; BKF, V, pp. 319-326). For through interpersonal relations the ego repeatedly identifies itself at times as an 'I' who is speaking and at other times as a 'you' who is spoken to, as another person's other or differential pole (DS, Introduction, pp. 2-3; II, pp. 100-102; V, p. 231). Moreover, the need for mutual understanding forces me to assume numerous propositional attitudes (beliefs, feelings), listen to what is said, and occupy the various possible worlds implied in a discourse. In this way the 'I' is formed as a concretion of beliefs, a constant renewal of certain mental states, engendered in the course of communicational relations with others (DS, II, pp. 100-102; V, p. 241-242). Jacques writes: "The utterer is a subject in the measure where speaking consists for it in identifying itself during and through the communications in which it happens to take part" (DS, Preface, p. xxviii [18]).

So too self-awareness (self-reflection; interiority) comes after and through relationality, it is a late and derivative product and not the essence of the person (DS, II, p. 62; IV, pp. 162-165; Conclusion, pp. 324-325). This is because, for Jacques, self-consciousness is merely a communication of self to itself, a speaking to oneself as though to a second self, a consciousness that thinks, reflects back upon its thinking, and utters 'I think' (DS, II, p. 98; V, pp. 190-194, 244). Furthermore, this communication of self to itself, this back-referencing, is grounded upon a long history of communication with and by others—i.e. a language game—wherein I gain access to language and to propositional attitudes (beliefs; feelings) (DS, IV, pp. 162-165, 170; V, pp. 213-216; VI, pp. 280-282). So I come to know myself not through a reflexive turning inward (auto-representation), but through a sedimentation of communicational habits (DS, I, p. 47). Or in Jacques's pithy phrase, self-knowledge is a "recycling of discourse with the self" (DS, V, pp. 199-200 [229]). Less pithily Jacques writes:

> The discourse of the ego with itself presupposes ... its insertion in a speaking community. When it speaks to itself, the ego is not a full and complete person, which is expressed before itself. It is inasmuch as it is linked to a you that the I is then capable of being in relation with itself thanks to the you. The I is linked to the you as to someone who in its turn is in a relation with me. The ego comes back to itself by means of the you, it experiences itself as the you of a you. The silent discourse of self-consciousness cannot precede communicative activity. Rather to the contrary, it presupposes it. A relations with another is constitutive both of the interiority of the subject and of the situation of speech (DS, V, p. 200 [230-231]).
>
> [The] person ... does not stand on its own. ... In the beginning is the relation, on the basis of which alternating and cooperating persons appear who diverge and become decentered in their difference. There is no absolute presence or back-reference to oneself, no primordial glance turned toward itself in its intimate innermost being. The person only becomes conscious in its act of interdiscursive confrontation with another, prior to experience. ... For the person, existing, i.e. having reality, can only mean seizing oneself without possessing oneself in all of the different relations that have been present and real to us. Reflecting can only mean entering for a time, and with a seriousness unequally shared by all human beings, into the provisional loop of discourse with oneself (DS, Conclusion, p. 325 [364]).

Ultimately for Jacques the self is best thought of as a "seat of a communicative competence" (DS, Conclusion, pp. 317, 320-321 [360]), in other words, a pragmatic competence or an internalizing of the rules of syntax and semantics and a common framework, that makes one capable of intercepting and interacting discursively with what goes on in a network of ideal communication (DS, Introduction, pp. 5-8; II, pp. 100-102; V, pp. 229, 241-242, 248; DIA, II, 4, pp. 134-150; III, 1, 4, pp. 179-184, 248-254; V, pp. 287-295). He asserts: "the personal self cannot be regarded as a sufficient and solitary subjectivity constituting its own reality, but rather as the seat of a certain number of powers, abilities, and relational checks: meeting the other in a creative interspace [*entre-deux*], maintaining itself in relation with the other, or on the contrary closing up on itself or grasping itself" (DS, III, p. 124 [151]). So in place of the Cartesian *Cogito, ergo sum* (I think, therefore I am), Jacques substitutes a *Loqueris, ergo sum* (You speak, therefore I am) (DS, II, p. 57; V, pp. 208-213). For while 'I think' can accompany all my statements, their origin or founding agency is an interlocutive relation (DS, Conclusion, pp. 330-331; BKF, V, pp. 314-316).

Jacques develops an interesting ethics on the basis of this communicational relationality that founds persons. He argues that the Cartesian notion of the self as a cogito with its own inner contemplation makes it hard to avoid viewing others as inferiors, threats, or rivals (as with Hegel or Sartre) and entering into a battle to death between consciousnesses. For if my own self is the basis of my relation with others, I first must assert myself over others, seek to possess them, and understand them on the basis of "the same" (i.e. myself) (DS, Preface, pp. xxii; III, p. 154-155; Conclusion, pp. 323, 327). Yet if before I act, speak, and take consciousness, I am already linked with others in a primary communicational relation, and indeed am powerless to be without them, then I need not privilege the same (self) over the other (you) (DS, Preface, p. xvii; III, pp. 116, 125, 135, 159-160; VI, p. 255).[128] Furthermore, as I can only define myself by occupying an ideal speaker-listener position within a socially constituted canonical communication system, I must immediately recognize others as *persons*, i.e. partners in a dialogue in which the meaning of our words and our references to things in the world will be regarded as our common property (DS, Introduction, p. 6; III, pp. 144-145, 150-154; VI, pp. 255-259). This rules out my trying to unilaterally influence the conversational direction to my own advantage, or using the other as a means to my centrifugal self, which would be to treat the other as an object and not a person. Rather I must relate to "the other" in accordance with a principle of non-violence (DS, VI, pp. 300-306; Conclusion, p. 324). Hence Jacques's unique phrasing of the moral maxim is: Treat the person of the other, in the discourse that you have about him or her, always at the same time as a possible allocutee [i.e. a possible 'you'] (DS, II, p. 111 [136]).

All the same, the interlocutive relation can confirm each person in a positive difference, one not subordinated or assimilated to sameness. For in interlocution each person is both same and other, speaker and listener, a self that is for the other and not just for the same, involved in a communication of two parties with individual differences (DS, Preface, p. xxi; III, pp. 129-130, 14 4-145, 151, 155-157; VI, pp. 250-252, 259-262, 270-274; Conclusion, pp. 317, 320-323; LSI, I, pp. 45-50). Thus discourse creates persons that are equal but distinct. For

instance in one relation of positive difference a father is engendered as
a father by a son whom he has engendered as son (DS, VI, pp. 263-
267, 277).[129]

Jacques, not surprisingly, appeals to his notion of three communicational poles in working out a theory of the Trinity. He argues that
the Absolute is not a substance, state, or system, but instead a living
relationality. And just as a human person, the very model of the divine, can take on three linguistic roles—I, you, or he/she—so too can
God in God's Trinitarian being. God the Father is the I that allocu-
tively engenders the Son as his You (His allocutee), and the Son in
turn gives his you the name of Father. And the Holy Spirit is the gift
of love between Father and Son, and from both Father and Son, the
delocutive He of their relationality. For the Absolute consists of a relational unity—a unity of operations—of three divine persons that
manifest themselves separately (paternity, filiation, procession) but act
jointly (when one divine person acts, all three act; for instance the Son
primarily makes Himself visible in the Incarnation even if this is the
work of all three persons in unison), and which achieve their identity
and differentiation by relating to each other (DS, II, pp. 63-73; III, p.
127; n. 16 on p. 352; V, pp. 232-236, 263-267).[130]

7

POSTMODERNISM

1970-2000 in Belgium, Canada, France, & the United States

Beginning in the 1950s French academia reversed its course and once again became highly secularized, its philosophy departments dominated by atheists. Recently, however, there has been a famous "turn to theology" [*le tournant théologique*] in France, commencing around 1980.[131] So as the philosopher Michel Serres put it in 1984 "In the years 1967-1970 when I wanted to interest my students I spoke to them of politics and if I wanted to make them laugh I spoke of religion. Today it is exactly the opposite." This movement has been spearheaded by Jewish thinkers such as Emmanuel Levinas (1906-1995), Protestants such as Paul Ricoeur (1913-2005), and Catholics such as Fr. Stanislas Breton (1912-), Michel Henry (1922-2002), Jean-François Courtine (1944-), Jean-Luc Marion (1946-), and Jean-Louis Chrétien (1952-); and a notable turn of interest toward theology has even been found in the works of more secular thinkers.[132] Notable too and quite surprising is that this revival happened in the midst of a philosophical movement that at first glance seems highly antagonistic to theology in general—postmodernism.

Postmodernism is a fairly recent development in philosophy (dating from the late 1960s)—launched by thinkers such as Jean-François Lyotard (1924-1998), Gilles Deleuze (1925-1995), Michel Foucault (1926-1984), Jean Baudrillard (1929-2007), and Jacques Derrida (1930-2004)—which represents a critique of the Enlightenment view of modernity. Postmodernism in particular rejects the modernist view that human reason can discover objective essences, order, realities, or truths (and that human history and society can progress). It has thus been variously described as a "skepticism toward all metanarratives" (Lyotard), i.e. all large-scale justificatory accounts of the nature of things; or a rejection of the "metaphysics of presence" (Derrida), i.e. a rejection of the view that reality can be transparently represented by a knowing subject. Postmodernism then is a contemporary version of skepticism and is at once anti-realist, repudiating the view that human reason is capable of understanding the nature of reality, anti-foundationalist, disavowing the view that human reason can find objective grounds and reasons for belief; and anti-metaphysical.

An influential student of Derrida, one of the most famous living French philosophers, **Jean-Luc Marion (1946-)**, took his teacher's postmodern thought in a decidedly Catholic direction. Marion was born in 1946 in Meudon (Paris). He attended the University of Nanterre and the Sorbonne from 1964-1968, where he received his licentiates in letters and philosophy, and the École Normale Supérieure from 1967 to 1970, where, in the midst of various student uprisings, he attained his agrégation in 1971. It was at the École Normale where Marion met and was influenced by the aforementioned Jacques Derrida (1930-2004), the founder of postmodernism, as well as the lapsed Catholic Marxist Louis Althusser (1918-1990) [who was eventually institutionalized for murdering his wife]; Marion also met Corinne Nicolas there whom he married in 1970 (and with whom he had two sons). After receiving his agrégation in 1971, Marion attended the Sorbonne from 1973-1981 and received his doctorate in philosophy in 1981 under the philosopher Ferdinand Alquié (1906-1985).

Marion began his teaching career at the Sorbonne (1973-1981), and continued on at the University of Poitiers (1981-1988), the University of Paris X, Nanterre (1988-1995), and again at the Sorbonne (1995-) where he served as department chair (1995-2000) as well as director of the Centre d'études cartésiennes (1996-). In 1994 Marion also became a professor at the University of Chicago's School of Divinity.

Marion's honors include receiving the *Grand Prix de Philosophie de l'Académie Française* in 1992; an honorary doctorate from the University of Utrecht in 2005; and the Karl-Jaspers Preis and election into the French Academy in 2008.[133]

The key works in which Marion sets forth his Catholic postmodernism, are *God without Being [Dieu sans l'être]* [GWB] (1982; 2002) [winner of the Prix Henri Desmarest in 1982] and *Being Given: Toward a Phenomenology of Givenness [Etant donné: Essai d'une phénénologie de la donation]* [BG] (1997) [Part II of his Triptych on Phenomenology].[134]

Marion, influenced by both phenomenology and postmodernism, as well as by Pseudo-Dionysius, argues that the reductions and first principles of phenomenology (developed by Husserl) must be rethought and expanded·in light of postmodernism (developed by Levinas and Derrida).

To Husserl's eidetic reduction—wherein we ignore all accidental diversity in order to conceptualize the essences of objects that intuitively appear to us in experience—and his more idealistic transcendental reduction—wherein we further reduce the meanings of objects to their constitution by a transcendental consciousness—we need to add a third reduction: the reduction of all things to pure unconditioned givenness (BG, Preface, p. ix; Introduction, pp. 2-3, 11-12; I, p. 18; III, p. 177; IV, pp. 234, 245; Conclusion, p. 320; RG, Introduction, p. 3; I, pp. 35-39; II, pp. 65-76; Conclusion, p. 204; "EPR," p. 99).

On a related note, instead of basing phenomenology on the Husserlian first principles of "So much appearing, so much being," and "Back to the things themselves," or even his so-called principle of all principles "everything that offers itself originarily to us in intuition [i.e. experience] must simply be received for what it gives itself," we must ground it on a new first principle: "So much reduction, so much givenness" [*Autant de réduction, autant de donation*] (BG, Preface, pp. ix-x [7]; Introduction, pp. 3; I, pp. 11-12, 14, 16, 18, 38; II, p. 73; IE, Forward, p. xxi; I, pp. 16-17, 25; II, p. 47; RG, I, pp. 32-39; Conclusion, pp. 203-205; "PCG," pp. 122-123; "EPR," p. 100).

The addition of this new reduction and this new first principle is necessary because, prior to the intuition of objects, whether physical or mental (i.e. phenomenal experience), prior to intentionality (i.e. conceptualization), indeed prior to Heideggerian being, is givenness. So if we want to remain true to the stated goal of phenomenology, namely to reduce things to the pure immanence of appearing (and so rid ourselves of any unnecessary accretions, i.e. semblances, presuppositions, theories, transcendencies), then we must focus our attention on the mere fact of something being given [*étant donné*] in lived experience, rather than on its being visible or conceivable, or its act of being (BG, Introduction, pp. 3, 5, 15-16; I, p. 20-21, 27, 38-39; II, p. 118; III, pp. 120-121, 122, 125; IE, I, pp. 19-20; IV, pp. 106, 108). Moreover, in so doing, we avoid unwittingly excluding a wide variety of phenomena (non-objective phenomena), that give themselves without intuition or being—what Marion will call the saturated phenomenon (BG, I, pp.

17, 32, 38-39, 55; III, p. 120). For as Marion puts it, while what gives itself shows itself (i.e. all things are given in auto-manifestation), all that gives itself does not show itself (i.e. not all things give themselves as objects or by being) (BG, I, p. 59; III, pp. 119, 158; IV, pp. 221-222, 227; Conclusion, p. 322; IE, I, p. 19; II, pp. 30, 44, 47; "EPR," p. 87).

Such a widening of the scope of phenomenology allows Marion to categorize three different kinds of phenomena. First is what he calls the common-law phenomenon, i.e. material beings and technological products. These are visible phenomena which are poor in intuition and so have a shortage of givenness. Or in phenomenological terms, here intentionality exceeds intuitive givenness. That is to say, these phenomena are grasped through a mental concept (intention; signifi-·cation; noesis) which exceeds what can be experienced (intuition; fulfillment; noema) and so awaits future fulfillment. For example, books, cubes, or tables are conceptualized in a mental intention as six-sided objects. Yet they physically occur in such a way that they can never present all of their six sides to us at once. We at most simultaneously see three of their sides (albeit we can walk around these objects and experience their other sides and in this way achieve a fulfillment of the intention) (BG, I, pp. 24-27, 31; III, p. 126; IV, pp. 185-187, 191-192, 196; V, p. 263; IE, II, p. 53; III, pp. 62-63; IV, p. 112; V, pp. 104-107; "SP," pp. 214-215; "EPR," p. 91; "BS," pp. 383-385, 400-406). On account of this, the appearance of a common-law phenomenon is foreseeable (non-surprising), reproducible, and it lends itself to an exhaustive knowability (BG, IV, pp. 203, 207, 223-224, 241-242; V, pp. 305-306, 308, 311).

Second, comes the ideal phenomenon, i.e. mathematical or logical phenomena. These are barren or empty of intuition (they have a miniscule or "degree zero" of phenomenality) and so occur as a pure vision of essences or idealities, i.e. as a concept or intention alone. Yet this complete lack of intuition or objectified phenomenality, this minimum of givenness, ensures that truths in mathematics and logic are known with certainty (BG, IV, pp. 180, 191, 195, 222; V, pp. 263-264, 311; IE, II, p. 53; IV, p. 112; "SP," p. 214).

Third, is Marion's unique contribution to phenomenology, the saturated phenomenon. These are phenomena wherein the intuition exceeds intention, where there is a saturation, addition [le surcroît], or excess [l'excès] of intuition over conceptualization, a phenomenality of full givenness (BG, Preface, p. x; Introduction, p. 4; IV, p. 197;

V, pp. 264, 308, 313-314; Conclusion, pp. 321-322; IE, Foreword, p. xxi). On account of this excess of intuition over concept, the saturated phenomenon transcends the Kantian categories of quantity, quality, relation, and modality. Specifically the saturated phenomenon is 1) unseekable according to quantity (amazing)—it continually adds to and surpasses the sum of its parts and so is immeasurable and cannot be aimed at [*invisible*; from *viser*, to aim at]; 2) unbearable according to quality (bedazzling)—it gives too intensely for our gaze to see or conceive it; 3) absolute according to relation—it is an absolutely unique, unconditioned, and unforeseeable [*imprévisible*] coming forward, one not analogous to or explainable by any other happening with which we are familiar; and 4) irregardable according to modality—it appears with an indescribable plurality of excess that annuls all effort at comprehension and reproduction (BG, IV, pp. 199-227; n. 56 on p. 364; "SP," pp. 103-124). As the saturated phenomenon is too rich to be conceived, measured, anticipated, or contained, it overwhelms our thought and leaves us in a state of amazement and bedazzlement: it is a *mysterium fascinans et tremendum* [an enchanting and awesome mystery] in the words of Rudolf Otto (IE, VI, p. 159). Or looked at from another angle, the saturated phenomenon as indeterminate is conceptually inexhaustible. It overflows with a plurality (indeed infinity) of meanings, each of which is legitimate (IE, IV, p. 112; "FRI," pp. 400-401, 403-405). In short for Marion:

> To the phenomenon that is supposed to be poor in intuition [e.g. material objects] can we not oppose a phenomenon saturated with intuition? … a phenomenon where intuition would give more, indeed immeasurably more, than intention ever would have aimed at or foreseen? (BG, IV, p. 197 [276-277]).
>
> … the saturated phenomenon is characterized as such by the excess of intuition in it, which subverts and therefore precedes every intention that it exceeds and decenters. The visibility of the appearing henceforth arises against the flow of [*contre-courant*] the intention—following a para-dox, a counter-appearance, a visibility counter to the aim (BG, V, p. 267 [368-369]).

Marion thus likens the appearance of the saturated phenomenon, with its superabundance of intuition, to a too intense light, one that blinds us like the sun (BG, IV, pp. 203-205). And just as an excess of light is not seen directly on a piece of photographic paper, but is inferred from its overexposure, i.e. from the smudge that it makes, so too the saturated phenomenon cannot be clearly made out but appears as a "perturbation of the visible"—or in the various metaphors of Marion as a blurred image coming through a too narrow aperture, a too short lens, or a too cramped frame; as a fast moving object seen in its motion blur; or as the noise of a poorly communicated message (BG, IV, pp. 215-216). He writes "Intuition is no longer exposed in the concept; it saturates it and renders it overexposed—invisible, unreadable not by lack, but indeed by an excess of light" (BG, IV, p. 198 [279]; IE, II, p. 53; IV, p. 112; "SP," pp. 195-197), so "The eye perceives not so much the apparition itself of the saturated phenomenon as the perturbation that it produces in person within the common conditions of experience" (BG, IV, pp. 215-216 [301]).

The saturated phenomenon therefore is a wholly new kind of phenomenon. It does not appear as an object, for it gives us nothing to see (BG, IV, p. 216; V, p. 244). Nor does it appear as possessing being. Rather, it is a sheer appearing of the givenness of intuition, that is to say, a call to which we must respond (BG, I, pp. 52-58; IV, p. 199; V, pp. 284, 286-289, 297-299; RG, Conclusion, p. 204).

Now the saturated phenomenon, comments Marion, occurs in various forms and can manifest itself in the phenomena of birth, death, time (internal time consciousness), beauty (aesthetic experiences; the sublime), music, poetry, film, dance, the infinite, friendship, as well as giving ones word (oath-making), giving one's time, life (sacrifice), death (martyrdom), peace, or meaning (BG, I, pp. 52, 57-58; IV, pp. 207, 216, 219-220, 246; V, pp. 289-290, 300-303; n. 82 on p. 336; n. 87 on p. 337; n. 47 on p. 348; n. 6 on p. 350; IE, II, pp. 37-40; MPC, V, pp. 112-115; MEP, VI, p. 37; XXI, pp. 101-105; XXXVIII, pp. 195-202; "OG," pp. 74-75; "IN," pp. 39-41; "EPR," pp. 97-98; "FRI," pp. 409-410; "IMG," p. 32; "BS," pp. 393-397). Marion though focuses on five special types of saturated phenomenon, the event, idol, flesh, icon, and revelation (which incorporates each of the four previous types).

Let us examine each of these five special types of saturated phenomenon in turn. The first key kind of saturated phenomenon is the event which is an historical phenomenon such as a political revolution, a battle (such as the battle of Waterloo), a sporting or cultural performance (such as a soccer game, concert, or an academic lecture), and birth or death. The event saturates the Kantian category of quantity and so is "unforeseeable, irreversible, unrepeatable as such, immediately past and devoid of cause or reason" (IE, II, p. 41 [49]; cf. IE, II, pp. 38-43). Moreover, as it rises up from causes unknown or non-assignable, i.e. with a surplus of effects over causes, we cannot predict the event, or assign to it a unique cause or exhaustive explanation. Hence the event yields to an infinite hermeneutic and can be explained in terms of a plurality of horizons (for instance one could assign the cause of the battle of Waterloo to military, diplomatic, political, economic, or ideological reasons) (BG, IV, pp. 228-229; V, p. 267; IE, II, pp. 31-36, 41-43; "TRH," p. 146).

The second key type of saturated phenomenon is the idol, a visible object (a first visible) whose splendor stops my intentionality and gaze at itself. With an idol then my gaze [le regard] "is fixed in it, and far from passing beyond [transiter], remains facing what becomes for it a spectacle to re-spect" (GWB, I, p. 11 [20]). The idol can even be likened to an "invisible mirror" which sends the thrust of the gaze back upon itself. Hence, the idol, which saturates the category of quality, bedazzles me with its splendor, reflects my gaze, and limits the scope of my aim making it ultimately unseekable [invisible] (GWB, I, pp. 7, 9-12, 13-14, 19-21; II, pp. 25-26; III, p. 57; IV, p. 111; VI, p. 168; BG, IV, pp. 200-201, 205, 229-230; V, pp. 267, 293; IE, II, pp. 51-52; III, pp. 54-55, 59; CV, I, pp. 12-13, 15-19; II, pp. 25-33, 35-38, 44-45).

An example of an idol is the painting. The painting is a pure visible that swallows up my gaze and hoards its admiration. It is a maximum of intuitive intensity that sight cannot pierce (BG, I, pp. 39-40; IE, III, pp. 60-62; "BS," pp.391-394). As such, the painting does not manifest itself as an object or with beingness (in what Heidegger would call a present-to-hand manner). For we could replace its pigments one by one, and so change its substance entirely, yet the painting would still be visible (BG, I, p. 41). Moreover, unlike an object such as a flower pot, the painting of a flower pot has no missing sides (no lack of intuition). It is a pure visible without remainder, one which offers a new, irrepeatable, and unsubstitutable meeting at each glance. It is ever an "I know not what" and incomprehensible (IE, III, pp. 63-64, 66-68, 70-72, 76; III, p. 158; IV, p. 180). Similarly, the painting goes beyond pleasure, monetary value, utility, and commerce (what Heidegger would call the ready-to-hand) (BG, I, pp. 42-45). The painting then, while it occurs in a physical frame with pigments (it is subsisting) and can be sold (it is useful), has a phenomenality beyond objectness, beingness, and utility. It ultimately reduces to the ascent into visibility itself, the appearing in the raw, of a beautiful, meaningful, and passionate artwork, an ochre serenity (BG, I, pp. 46-51).

Regrettably and inappropriately, philosophy has often sought to turn God into an idol as well. This is particularly true of attempts to develop a metaphysics of God, i.e. to develop what Heidegger terms an ontotheology—a metaphysical theology which considers God as the ground of all beings (onto-logy), and as the highest being which accounts for everything (theo-logy). For in so doing, metaphysics tries to include God within presence by assigning to God a proper name and an essential definition. Yet this is to limit God to earthly catego-ries, to consign God to the measure of the human gaze, to what is in fact a low-water mark of the divine. A metaphysical picture of God as an idol thus silences and fails to reach God: it acts like a mirror that reflects our gaze back upon ourselves rather than upward to God. In effect metaphysics substitutes "God" for the true God by fixing and freezing human aspirations on a limited image or worldly expression of God, squeezing the infinite into a finite framework, instead of be-holding God in a manner adequate to what He Himself is (GWB, I, pp. 7, 9-14, 16, 18, 20; II, pp. 27-30; III, pp. 55-56; IV, p. 111; VI, p. 168; n. 28 on p. 231; IE, VI, pp. 150, 152-153; RG, I, pp. 3-9; II, pp. 32-33). Marion complains:

> For the concept, when it knows the divine in its hold, and hence names "God," defines it. It defines it, therefore also measures it to the dimen-sion of its hold. Thus the concept ... measures the divine as a function of itself; the limits of the divine experience of Dasein [human existence] provoke a reflection that turns it away from aiming at, beyond, the invis-ible, and causes it to freeze the divine in a concept, an invisible mirror (GWB, II, p. 29 [44]).

For example, in a first idolatry, an ontic idolatry, Cartesian meta-physics speaks of God as self-caused [causa sui], as substance [ousia], and as the ultimate ground of the world [onto-theology]. Yet this is to consider the being of God as abstract and in univocity or identi-ty with the being of other creatures [ens commune (general being)]. Hence it fails to allow for a personal, transcendent, and mysterious God (GWB, Preface, p. xvi; I, p. 16; II, pp. 33-34; III, p. 64, 69, 82, 94, 106; n. 19 on p. 207; BG, III, pp. 161-162; "FRI," pp. 410-411).[135] As Marion expounds:

In thinking "God" as *causa sui* [self-caused], metaphysics gives itself a
concept of "God" that at once marks the indisputable experience of Him
and His equally incontestable limitation; by thinking "God" as an efficiency so absolutely and universally foundational that it can be conceived
only starting from the essence of the foundation, and hence finally as
the withdrawal of the foundation into itself, metaphysics constructs for
itself an apprehension of the transcendence of God, but under the figure
alone of efficiency, of the cause, and of the foundation. ... The *causa sui*
[self-caused] offers only an idol of "God," so limited that it can neither
aspire to a worship and an adoration or even tolerate them without immediately betraying its insufficiency (GWB, II, p. 35 [54-55]).

Even the Thomistic view of God as *ens* [(pure) being] or *ipsum esse
subsistens* [self-subsistent being], as well as the Heideggerian conception of God as the Being of beings [Being/being; ontological differ-
ence] represent an idolatry, this time a second or ontological idolatry.
For these views still fixate our gaze on a conceptualization or representation of God; they interpret God in terms of a presence (a beingness),
one which precedes and determines God in advance (GWB, English
Preface, p. xxi-xxii; II, pp. 25, 30-32, 34, 39-45, 49-50, 52, 58-59; III,
pp. 64, 66, 69-70, 80-82; n. 67 on pp. 217-218; BG, I, p. 7; V, p. 266;
RG, Introduction, p. xxxv; I, pp. 1-3; "IMG," p. 22).

Indeed for Marion any attempt to reason about God or prove His
existence is blasphemous and idolatrous: "Every proof, in fact, however demonstrative it may appear, can only lead to the concept. ... equiv-
alence to a concept transforms God into "God" ... human discourse
determines God" (GWB, II, p. 32 [50-51]; cf. GWB, II, p. 35-36, 44)

The third singular saturated phenomenon is the human flesh. This
is not flesh in its physicality, but in its agony, anxiety, desire, grief, joy,
orgasm, pleasure, or sickness. The flesh consequently cannot be seen
or appear at all (unlike an object, or even the event or the idol). Rather
my taking flesh is a passivity or receptivity that allows me to feel and
sense myself (I am my flesh), and through my feelings and sensations
makes the world appear. Flesh is thus with Michel Henry auto-affec-
tion, it affects itself in itself by being affected by nothing other than itself—neither the body, mind, world, nor another person. Consequently, the flesh, which saturates the category of relation, escapes reason.
So, for instance, I cannot foresee my pain with an intentional aim, i.e.
organize it or want it. Rather pain eludes all relation (there is nothing
like it or equal to it) and is a unique and incommunicable occurrence

(BG, IV, pp. 231-232; V, p. 267, 293; V, pp. 299, 311-312, 316, 318; IE, IV, p. 82, 87-88, 91-92, 94-100; MEP, XXIII, pp. 112-120).

The fourth special type of saturated phenomenon is the icon, one example of which is the face of the other [l'autrui]. Now the face of the other person is not an object, it does not offer a spectacle to look at, but is irregardable: it literally consists of two black holes, i.e. the pupils. In fact, the icon of the face functions exactly opposite of the idol. The face is a counter-intentionality, a gaze which weighs on me, subverts my gaze with its own, and so reverses the intentionality (BG, I, p. 40; IV, pp. 232-233, 243; V, pp. 267, 293, 318; n. 88 on pp. 366-367; IE, IV, p. 100; CV, I, pp. 1-2, 19-23; IV, pp. 70-75, 85-87; MEP, XX, pp. 97-101). Moreover, in envisaging me and reversing my intentionality, the face addresses me with its call and says to me 'Thou shalt not kill.' I must accordingly renounce my mastery over the other's face, a face which cannot be possessed, and instead submit myself to its point of view [hence Marion claims that artistic portraits of the human face murder the human by trying to make it a visible idol] (BG, II, p. 88; III, p. 158; IE, III, pp. 77-79; IV, p. 112, 115-117, 119-121; V, p. 267; MPC, VII, p. 167). The face, as a phenomenon which saturates the category of modality, also, like the event, offers an infinite hermeneutics to us. For the various features, expressions, and movements of the face cannot be conceptually explicated and delimited, but rather possess an infinity of meanings at each moment, an endless flux of significations (IE, IV, pp. 120-121, 123; "BS," p. 395).

Finally, the fifth and ultimate saturated phenomenon, one which combines the previous four types of saturation—e.g. a saturation of saturation which is given at once as historical event, idol [if in a proper form], flesh, and icon (face) [particularly this latter]—is the revelation of God. For God manifests Himself as an overflowing or excess of intuition that completely saturates our intention. Our experience of God and His revelation thus takes the form of a stupor, a blindness of bedazzling glory, a luminous darkness (GWB, III, pp. 74-78, IV, pp. 108, 117; IE, VI, pp. 160-162; BG, III, pp. 160; IV, pp. 204, 210, 242-245; "IMG," pp. 20-23).

As God manifests Himself to us in an excessive manner, He overwhelms our faculties and gives more than we could ever put into words. As a result God is incomprehensible and inconceivable (GWB, II, pp. 46, 50; III, p. 55; IE, VI, p. 154; RG, I, p. 24; IV, pp. 148-158; "IN," p. 36; "FRI," pp. 400, 403-407, 412; "IMG," pp. 21-22). Marion writes: "God Himself in order to be thought ... must be thought ... as that which surpasses [outrepasse], detours, and distracts [affole] all thought, even non-representational. By definition and decision, God, if He must be thought, can meet no theoretical space for His measure [mesure], because His measure exerts itself in our eyes as unmeasurable [démesure]" (GWB, II, p. 45 [71]).

This divine excessiveness also makes God unnamable.[136] For none of the divine names exhaust God. Divine names, in truth, most manifest the distance that separates all names from God, and mark God's absence, anonymity, and withdrawal from the world (as Marion points out, in French 'name' [nom] and 'no' [non] sound the same). Or looked at from the opposite end of the spectrum, God in fact summons an infinity of nominative horizons and admits and surpasses/refuses all names at once.

God, who lies outside of any univocal relation to the finite or causality, should thus be conceived of in a postmodern fashion and freed from metaphysics (onto-theology) with its conceptualization of God as the ground of being. Otherwise we risk conceiving of God as an object or a being and depersonalizing God. Indeed such a God alone is the God before whom we can pray, as Heidegger recognized (GWB, English Preface, p. xxi; II, p. 45; III, p. 810).

Marion famously asserts that we must also go beyond the Heideggerian God of ontological difference, God as the Being of beings, and even cease thinking of God in terms of being altogether, so as to "think God without any condition, not even that of Being" (GWB, II, p. 45 [70]; cf. GWB, Introduction, p. 2; II, pp. 41, 44-45, 52; III, pp. 60-62, 69-70, 106; IE, VI, p. 147; RG, IV, p. 189, V, pp. 202-215, 231-233; "IN," pp. 30-33; "TAOT," n. 57 on p. 73; "IMG," pp. 19-20, 25-26). For as Marion asks: "Does Being define the first and the highest of the divine names? When God offers Himself to be contemplated and gives Himself to be prayed to, is He concerned primarily with Being? When He appears as and in Jesus Christ, who dies and rises from the dead, is He concerned primarily with Being? No doubt, God can and must in the end also be; but does his relation to Being determine Him as radically as the relation to his Being defines all other beings? Under the title God without Being, I am attempting to bring out the absolute freedom of God with regard to all determinations, including, first of all, the basic condition that renders all other conditions possible and even necessary—for us, humans—the fact of Being" (GWB, English Preface, p. xx).

Marion's God then is a God "otherwise than being" (under the obvious influence of Levinas), nay a God "without being" [*sans l'être*] (GWB, II, p. 45; IE, VI, pp. 147-148).[137] He writes:

> Hence it follows that God is expressed neither as a being nor as Being, nor by an essence. ... We are in the process of discovering, as much through Denys the Mystic as through Nietzsche, that it is not self-evident that an *ousia* [being] or that a concept should be able to determine in what way this might be God. It remains to be glimpsed, if not with Heidegger, at least in reading him, and, if really necessary, against him, that God does not depend on Being/being, and even that Being/being depends on distance. Depend on: neither abolition, nor continuation, but a resumption that surpasses and maintains" (GWB, III, p. 106 [153-154]).

Beyond being, beyond presence, beyond name, God is accordingly best characterized, says Marion, as the self-communication of love or as pure gift (GWB, III, pp. 97, 105-106; IV, p. 108; BG, Preface, pp. x, xx, xxiv; IE, I, p. 2; RG, I, p. 24; IV, pp. 158-162; MEP, Introduction, pp. 5-6; ID, IV, pp. 177-178; V, pp. 251-252; "MCP," p. 263; "IMG," p. 38). Marion proclaims: "Because God does not fall within the domain of Being, He comes to us and as a gift ... God saves the gift precisely inasmuch as He is not, and does not have to be. For the gift does not have first to be, but to pour out in an abandon that, alone, causes it to be; God saves the gift in giving it before being" (GWB, p. 3 [12]).[138] Or again: "God can give Himself to be thought without idolatry only starting from Himself alone: to give Himself to be thought as love, hence as gift; to give Himself to be thought as a thought of the gift. Or better, as a gift for thought, as a gift that gives itself to be thought" (GWB, II, p. 49 [75]).

Marion therefore suggests that we cross the word God when writing it out, i.e. place an 'x' through it: G̶o̶d̶ This crossing of God reflects both the fact that God is beyond being and that God reveals Himself as an unreserved love who dies on the cross for humans without any expectation of return (GWB, II, pp. 46-47; III, pp. 61-63, 71-72; IV, p. 108; VII, p. 193). Marion expounds:

> The unthinkable forces us to substitute the idolatrous quotation marks around "God" with the very G̶o̶d̶ that no mark of knowledge can de-

marcate; and, in order to say it, let us cross out ~~God~~, with a cross, provisionally of St. Andrew [a cross which rested on two legs, not just one, on the ground], which shows the limit of the temptation, conscious or naive, to blaspheme the unthinkable in an idol. The cross does not indicate that ~~God~~ would have to disappear as a concept, or intervene only in the capacity of a hypothesis in the process of validation, but that the unthinkable enters into the field of our thought only by rendering itself unthinkable there by excess, that is, by criticizing our thought. To cross out [*raturer*] ~~God~~, in fact, indicates and recalls that ~~God~~ crosses out our thought because he saturates it; better, he enters into our thought only in obliging it to criticize itself (GWB, II, p. 46 [72]).

No doubt we will name it ~~God~~, but in crossing ~~God~~ with the cross that reveals Him only in the disappearance of his death and resurrection. For the other term of distance, ~~God~~, rightly does not have to be, nor therefore to receive a name of being, whatever it may be. ... ~~God~~ who crosses Being/being only in submitting the first to the cross in which is signed the hyperbolic agape "which surpasses all knowledge" (Eph 3:19) (GWB, III, pp. 105-106 [152-153]).

Now as God is an excess of saturation, without being, and equivocal with the world, in the end the only sure path to God is to let God speak for Himself, to come to us in a divine revelation (GWB, II, p. 48; IV, p. 109; V, p. 139; MPC, III, p. 70; n. 10 on p. 70). So rather than seeking to comprehend the incomprehensible God philosophically (that is to say, idolatrously on the basis of world, cause, or concept), we must receive God through a gift of His own excessiveness, a gift without cause, antecedent, condition, or ground (GWB, II, pp. 36-37; III, p. 70; BG, IV, pp. 195, 198, 211, 235, 241-247; IE, II, p. 53; "OG," pp. 69-70; VR, I, pp. 1-4; "TRH," p. 152).

And the chosen form of self-revelation, on the part of the invisible, unseeable, excessive, and inconceivable God, is to inscribe Himself in and saturate visible icons that manifest His face (GWB, I, pp. 17-23; MPC, IV, pp. 78-87, 93-98; VII, pp. 164-168; "IMG," pp. 28-29, 33-35). Such icons manifest the infinite intentionality of the divine face, and so open up the invisible to the envisioning of our gaze and veneration. In other words, we here become a visible mirror of an invisible gaze that summons us face to face, person to person, a mirror saturated beyond itself due to the glory of God (GWB, I, pp. 7-9, 20-22; RG, I, pp. 25-26; V, pp. 178-180; V, pp. 252-253). Or as Marion puts it, the divine icon "summons the gaze to surpass itself by never freezing on a visible, since the visible only presents itself here in view of the invisible. The gaze ... must always rebound upon the visible, in order to remount the infinite stream of the invisible. ... The icon opens up in a face [le visage] that gazes at our gazes in order to summon them to its depth. ... The opening up of a face where the human gaze is engulfed, invited to see the invisible" (GWB, I, pp. 18-19 [29-31]).

In particular, God, according to Marion, has chosen to use the visible icons of the bishops of the Catholic Church, the Eucharist, the Confession of Faith, the Scriptures, and the Incarnation of Christ to reveal Himself.

Let us discuss these in reverse order. God, incomprehensible and transcendent, becomes incarnate in Christ (GWB, III, p. 107; CV, III, pp. 57-58, 62-63; MPC, V, pp. 120-123; "FRI," pp. 405-406). And Christ as incarnate God lets Himself be spoken by the Father as His Word [the Said], and in so doing allows the unspeakable and silent to come in language to meet us (GWB, V, pp. 140-144). Marion explains "Our language will be able to speak of God only to the degree that God, in his Word, will speak our language and teach us in the end to speak it as He speaks it—divinely, which means in all abandon" (GWB, V, p. 144).

God's Word is also present in the Bible which abolishes the gap between speaker, sign, and referent. With the Bible then we do not aim at the text (sign) but through the text aim at the referent, the Word, which explains itself with the text. For the Bible, saturated with the unspeakable Word, escapes the world, and lets us be outside of the text [hors-texte]. Indeed through the Bible we let the Word speak us in docile abandonment (GWB, V, pp. 143-144, 147-149, 156; VII, pp. 196-197; n. 54 on p. 216).

In the gift of the Eucharist the Word of God is made flesh, forms one body with our own, and so summons our gaze, attention, and worship. Hence the Eucharist delivers us from our distance with respect to God and allows us to speak the Word (GWB, English Preface, p. xxiv; Introduction, pp. 3-4; V, pp. 150-153; VI, pp. 161, 168-182; n. 19 on p. 202; n. 14 on p. 228; MPC, VII, pp. 137-145; "PG," pp. 208-210; "PS," pp. 89-102). The Eucharist in other words offers us a non-idolatrous presence of God and indeed "the only correct hermeneutic site where the Word is said in person" (GWB, V, p. 153 [215]).

Lastly, the bishop is invested with Christ and teaches His Word. Hence the bishop alone truly merits the title of theologian, and theo-

logians are well-advised to theologize in agreement with their bishops
(GWB, V, pp. 153-154, 158).

Marion then quite radically separates theology from philosophy, almost reverting to a fideistic position.[139] He states: "Theology does not
then have to do with "God," in whatever sense one understands Him.
It has to do with the fact ... of faith in the Crucified, a fact that faith
alone receives and conceives: it secures its scientificity only by fixing
itself on the positive fact of faith, namely, the relation of the believing human to the Crucified" (GWB, III, p. 65 [98]). Or again "We
can only fully subscribe to the position, which admits ... the irreducible heteronomy [of] ... thought [and] ... revelation ... The God who
reveals Himself has nothing in common (at least in principle, and at
least as He does not condescend to it) with the "God" of the philosophers, of the learned, and ... of the poet" (GWB, II, p. 52 [80]).

In a way theology must even look upon philosophy as foolishness, or
rather become foolish in the eyes of philosophy. For faith and reason,
when it comes right down to it, are irreconcilable, and so we can only
corrupt Christianity by making use of Greek thought (GWB, III, pp.
62-64, 68, 90-91, 93). This is why a theology which abandons its own
foundation in faith alone [la foi seule], faith in faith deferred until the
end of time, and attempts to make use of philosophy, can in the best
of cases only recognize a "square circle" or "wooden iron," not the risen
Christ. So theology must ever remain the "ontic science of Christianity and of believing existence" and cannot become a matter of scientific
certainty and objectivity (GWB, III, p. 67 [102]; VII, pp. 183, 196;
IE, IV, p. 124; BG, IV, p. 234; "TRH," pp. 145-146).

Still in the end Marion avoids a pure fideism in arguing that faith is
necessary, not because we lack intuitions that would allow us to validate our theological concepts, but because there is an excess of intuition in relation to these concepts (GWB, V, pp. 157-158; VI, p. 163;
"TRH," pp. 145-146). So faith is not irrational, but rather a way of
understanding through a reason higher than our own, the Logos or
Word of God. Faith gives us the Logos, which in turn gives us the concepts necessary to think that of which we already have the intuition; in
a way then the Logos lets us see God's interpretation of our intuitions
(VR, VIII, pp. 145-154; "TRH," pp. 150-151). Hence Marion, borrowing a conception from Rousselot writes: "What we lack in order
to believe is quite simply one with what we lack in order to see. Faith
does not compensate, either here or anywhere else, for a defect of vis-

ibility: on the contrary, it allows reception of the intelligence of the phenomenon and the strength tó bear the glare of its brilliance. Faith does not manage the defect of evidence—it alone renders the gaze apt to see the excess of the pre-eminent saturated phenomenon, the Revelation" ("TRH," p. 150). Just as one sees nothing in a game of chess if one doesn't know the rules, or hears nothing in a conversation if one is ignorant of the language, so too only faith gives us the concepts to let the intuitions of Christ burst forth in their true glory. So lacking faith, and the intelligence and concepts it supplies, one might have before oneself all the facts and evidences of the Scriptures about Christ, but nonetheless be unable to properly make them out and understood them ("TRH, pp. 147-149).

Another postmodernist is **Jean-Yves Lacoste (c. 1948-)** who was born around 1948 in France.[140] He attended the École Normale Supérieure from 1968-1972 and was ordained a priest around 1975. Lacoste then attended the University of Poitiers c. 1985-1988 where he received a doctorate in philosophy under Jean-Luc Marion in 1988. Lacoste has taught at Clare Hall, Cambridge (1990-), the College of Blandings (1998-), the University of Chicago (2001-2005), and the Catholic Institute of Paris (2001-).

Lacoste's key work is his *Experience and the Absolute* [*Expérience et absolu*] [EA] (1994).[141]

Lacoste constructs his philosophy under the influence of Heidegger whom he takes to have correctly set forth the basic manner of human existence. According to the early Heidegger humans exist in a "place" [*lieu; localité*] or topology—understood not as a geometrical coordinate, but as a coordinate of life or existence, a here or a there (EA, I, pp. 7-9). This place constitutes our world or horizon (inherence; being-in-the-world). It is an opening or disclosure of beings—an inaccessible, non-circumscribable, and distant horizon, that allows for things to be nearby, accessible, usable (ready-to-hand), or comprehensible (present-at-hand), as they stand out from and offset this horizon (EA, I, pp. 8-9; II, p. 23; VIII, p. 155; IX, p. 169).

Now human existence (*Dasein*) in the world is fundamentally a not-being-at-home, a foreignness or uncanniness. For the world is something that we cannot abstract ourselves from, it is always already there as the horizon of every manifestation. And the world has already taken possession of ourselves as something we have not wished for, something which preexists and outlives us—it is a form of house arrest, as it were, to which we must submit. Thus the fundamental emotion the world brings is anxiety, though this anxiety can be masked as we absorb ourselves in our daily tasks. Additionally, as we grasp that our worldly existence is mortal, we also come to live with an emotion of care about the future, about our being-to-death (EA, I, pp. 10-13, 16; III, p. 40; V, p. 82; IX, pp. 170-172; LNT, II, p. 102; LNT, VI, pp. 145-152).

Yet Heidegger's thought underwent a famous turn in 1934, and besides the world (the opening of the field in which the real things manifest themselves, the light in which beings appear) he introduced the notion of the earth (EA, I, p. 14). The earth is a dwelling place which shelters and protects us, and so is where we feel at home. Here our daily deeds do not mask another reality but are our reality. Accordingly, joy and serenity now replace anxiety as our fundamental mood and we dwell peacefully in the present (EA, I, pp. 15-18).

Lacoste combines these two modes of being, and argues that the fundamental or initial human state is a going back and forth between world (foreignness, anxiety) and earth (dwelling, serenity). So our place, our here and there, transitions between the world in which we are not at home and the earth which is our homeland (EA, I, pp. 19-22; II, p. 26; III, p. 43).

Unfortunately both world and earth draw a veil between humans and God; God exists in them as a chiaroscuro, a non-evident (EA, I, p. 17; III, pp. 41, 45-46; V, p. 87; LNT, II, pp. 87-89, 94-96, 100-102). For the world is secular and so God is dead in the world, or at the very least hidden and unknown. And while the earth is sacred, this sacredness ensures that any god which appears there is other than God. Thus while the earth may reveal an immanent sacred, a pagan god, it is devoid of the transcendent and personal God of theism (EA, Introduction, p. 2; I, p. 18; III, p. 43; VI, p. 102-105, 108-109; VIII, p. 147, 159; IX, p. 168, 170-171; WAW, I, pp. 5-11; LPG, V, p. 132; "LPP," p. 397). Consequently neither world nor earth allows humans to meet God face to face, to meet the Lord of Being, an absolute someone who promises a relation with us (EA, I, pp. 18, 21).

Yet humans are not doomed to atheism or paganism according to Lacoste because, besides world and earth, there is a third realm of human existence, one not recognized by Heidegger, the liturgy (EA, III, p. 40; VI, pp. 145, 155-162; WAW, I, pp. 16-17, 21-22; LNT, III, pp.

67-72). Liturgy typically takes the form of prayer, a translating of our veneration of God into the carnal language of the flesh (such as crossing ourselves, opening or raising our hands, or kneeling down), but is also understood more generally by Lacoste as any form of relating to God, whether through a Church service or a more isolated contemplation (EA, Introduction, p. 2; I, pp. 21-22; II, p. 37; VIII, p. 156; n. 17 on p. 197; "SK," p. 147). So liturgy, following Littré, can be defined as the "order and ceremonies of the divine worship" (EA, Introduction, p. 2 [2]). Lacoste therefore takes as his task, the development of a phenomenology of liturgy.

Liturgy is a form of existence that is able to institute a non-place (or rather overdetermine a place, as strictly speaking there is no exemption from place) that subverts our topology and transgresses the world and earth. Hence through liturgy we no longer have to define ourselves as either inhering in the world or dwelling on the earth (EA, I, p. 22; II, pp. 24-26; III, pp. 32-34, 36, 40-42; V, pp. 87, 96; VI, p. 101; VIII, p. 161; IX, p. 177). Moreover, by bracketing the profane world and the numinous earth, by refusing to let them interpose themselves between us and the divine (even if we still continually exist in terms of being there and dwelling), liturgy allows us to give a new significance to our lives, to show that we are about more than just living (EA, II, pp. 33-34, 38-42; III, pp. 41, 52, 54; IV, p. 64; V, pp. 79, 87, 89-90, 95; VIII, p. 166; IX, pp. 174-175; "LCA," p. 98). In particular, liturgy lets us redefine our being-in-the-world, our being-there [être-là], as being-before-God [coram Deo; être devant Dieu], as face-to-face with God (EA, II, pp. 24-26, 28-29; III, pp. 41, 44; V, p. 98; IX, pp. 178, 185; WAW, I, pp. 18-21). Liturgy is thus "the deliberate gesture of one who ordains one's being-in-the world a being-before-God, and who does violence to the former in the name of the latter" (EA, II, p. 39 [48]).

Still liturgy, according to Lacoste, is limited in its ability to unite us with God. In fact liturgy is more a presence to God—an exposition of ourselves to God (or abnegation to God following De Bérulle)—than the presence of God (EA, IV, p. 63). The Absolute then is not available to us in the liturgy, but instead remains at an infinite distance, in the night, a hidden God (EA, II, p. 35; IV, pp. 55, 63-65; VII, pp. 124-125; VIII, pp. 148, 152; LNT, II, pp. 133-140; "PTEG," p. 16; "SK," pp. 144-146; "TGLH," pp. 247, 267-270; LPG, III, pp. 81-85; IX, pp. 205-210, 220-227). As Lacoste remarks:

In the chiaroscuro of the world and history, liturgy ... is that experience
in which consciousness confronts a veiled [*inévident*] Absolute and cannot take leave, except with a perpetual ambiguity, at least of the necessities of a perpetual discernment to which no infallibility is guaranteed.
No one enters into [*fait l'expérience*] liturgy without wishing for God
to visit. Yet no one has an experience of liturgy without comprehend-
ing that God is never there present to consciousness in a fully evident
manner. We know God is present. We even pretend to assimilate his
presence to a Parousia. But we know just as surely that in the immanent
sphere of consciousness we can develop the proof of our attention, but
not the apodeictic proof of a visitation (EA, IV, p. 63 [76-77]).

This means that fundamentally, and for the most part, liturgy is a
non-vision, non-encounter, non-feeling, non-fruition, and "non-expe-
rience" of God: "... inexperience, greater than any experience, [is that]
which indicates the relation of the human to the Absolute" (EA, III,
p. 53 [64]). Liturgy rests therefore on a bare faith in God, a putting
ourselves before an unexperienced, unfelt, and unfamiliar God (not
surprisingly its fundamental moods are boredom and the joy of humiliation) (EA, VIII, pp. 145-148, 150, 156-157; IX, pp. 191-194; n.
3 on p. 203; n. 3 on p. 204; "WCA," p. 91; "LCA," pp. 100, 103).

This is not to say God is totally unknown to us, for faith must at
least be based on a thought [*savoir*] of God as the one to whom we address our praise, on a named God: "God is known only in the element
of faith" ("IA," p. 66). Yet in liturgy we have no personal knowledge
[*connaissance*] of God, no proximity to, interiority of, or familiarity
with God (EA, III, p. 48; VIII, p. 141).[142] Lacoste writes:

> Our presence to God and the expectation of God—by definition—open
> up the field of liturgy. But the expectation can be frustrated, on the one
> hand (the Absolute cannot come to conscious experience, which we will
> acknowledge to be the daily bread of prayer), and it gives me on the other
> hand no right over whatever I am expecting. ... The one who prays does,
> of course, know in principle to whom one addresses one's praise or one's
> requests: liturgy is instituted in the element of knowledge. But knowl-
> edge and inexperience do not contradict each other. It is not, therefore,
> senseless to hold that the transcendence of the human toward God can
> have no other experiential content than that which the human manifests
> of itself there, and that the proximity of a known God [*Dieu connu*] does
> not itself come to experience—or if one prefers, that knowledge [*savoir*]
> is the only experience to which liturgy can ordinarily commend itself

and the only one to which it absolutely must commend itself (EA, III, pp. 47-48 [58]).

Hence liturgy can be likened to a kenotic existence in imitation of Christ who died humiliated on a cross for us: in liturgy we exist as fools-in-Christ, accepting a knowledge [savoir] of God alone, without experience or affect, embracing a will-to-powerlessness (contra Nietzsche), and putting ourselves at the mercy of God (EA, VIII, pp. 163-167; IX, p. 179-181, 189-190, 193-194).

This is so in the first place for Lacoste because we cannot tell God what to do. We cannot place demands or limits on God's power. God's unveiling then cannot be mandated. We can only offer ourselves to God and hope for God's manifestation as a gift, not a payment of a debt (whether by a natural knowledge or grace) (EA, III, p. 46; V, p. 91; VI, p. 107, 109-110; VIII, p. 137, 139, 146-148, 150; "EEKG," p. 859).

In the second place, God is not an object, and so is not the sort of thing with which we should wish to maintain an experiential relation (EA, I, p. 22; II, p. 26; "PTEG," pp. 1, 14; "EEKG," pp. 845-846). In fact, were we to experience or feel God, there is every possibility that what we experienced or felt was not actually God (EA, V, p. 92; "PTEG," p. 14; "EEKG," pp. 847-848).[143] More technically, Lacoste argues that God appears with an irreducible phenomenality, i.e. a phenomenality that forbids a reduction to an essence. Instead what we are left with is a faith-based belief in God's existence ("IA," pp. 60-67).

In the third place, to demand conceptual mastery over God before entering into a relationship with Him would make praying impossible for the child or simple person [le charbonnier—literally the coal burner] (EA, IX, pp. 182-185). Yet if liturgy is a matter not of speaking about God (conceptually knowing God), but of speaking to God (relating to God and being before God) this becomes possible for everyone ("SK," pp. 147-148).

In the fourth place, liturgical overdetermination is precarious and fragile, and in the end, unless one is a saint or in heaven, the modes of world and earth come to reassert themselves covering up God. Or rather, as we have seen, in this life we can never completely extricate ourselves from inherence in the world or dwelling on the earth; we are always integrated into a place or topology (EA, I, p. 22; II, pp. 24-26, 28-29, 34; V, pp. 97-98; "LCA," p. 100; "LPP," pp. 397-398). Consequently, even in prayer God occurs to us in an ambiguous manner, in a chiaroscuro [clair-obscure] of world and earth (EA, II, pp. 26, 30-31, 36-37; III, pp. 43, 46, 48; IV, pp. 59, 62, 66-69, 72; V, pp. 84. 91; VIII, pp. 139-140, 143, 161-162; IX, pp. 186-186; n. 9 on pp. 200-201; n. 1 on pp. 204-205; LNT, XIII, pp. 337-338; "PTEG," pp. 17-18; "SK," pp. 149-152; "EEKG," p. 860).

Intimate knowledge [connaissance] of God must thus await the end of our lives (EA, VI, p. 107, 109-110; VIII, p. 137, 139). For situated as we are in a pre-eschatological state, it is too soon for us to know God; instead we must await a God who comes in the next life, in an eschatological event, in the Parousia, in order to acquire an unambiguous presence of God. Or as Lacoste puts it "We are free to offer [God] our hospitality ... but on the other hand history situates us away from the eschatological reversal where the Absolute will offer us a definitive hospitality" (EA, V, p. 93 [112-113]). Liturgy then looks forward to the presence of God in the Parousia, the eschaton, the second coming of Christ. It is a hope-filled prayer that a veiled God will eventually come and proffer proof of His presence (LNT, XIII, pp. 337-338; see Mt 24:3-39; 1 Cor 15:23; 1 Thes 2:19, 3:13, 4:15, 5:23). Liturgy is thus "the expectation or desire for Parousia in the certitude of the non-parousiacal presence of God" (EA, III, p. 45 [55]).[144] Or at greater length:

> Liturgy imitates the Parousia while acknowledging the non-parousiacal presence of God, and no experience that necessarily figures in liturgical grammar will annul the distance that separates us in the world from the Parousia. The conjunction of knowledge and inexperience ... cannot be overturned. The human wishes to see God but everything then disappoints the human regard (EA, VIII, p. 143 [173]).
>
> And the fact that the heart may feel both God's presence and absence, and always a greater absence, is the cornerstone of all hermeneutics of so-called religious experiences. God is unfelt more than He is felt. Anticipations of his eschatological presence, that is, of his Parousia, may very well be granted to privileged witnesses. But in the everydayness proper to our experience of God, we have to be satisfied with sheer non-eschatological presence ("PTEG," p. 18; cf. "PTEG," pp. 18-19).

As such, patience becomes our privileged mode of relating to the Absolute (EA, V, pp. 91, 93; VIII, pp. 156-157; IX, pp. 193-194). In Lacoste's words:

the liturgical relation … of the human with God [is] governed by a logic of inexperience, and … the liturgical vigil is not the time in which the human enjoys his theological knowledge [*connaissance*], but the one in which the human awaits the coming of the morning when the experiential will ratify the conceptual content of knowledge [*connaissance*]. … Patience is therefore for consciousness, if we must speak of it, a major liturgical virtue. The patient consciousness knows that its attention [*attention*] and expectation [*attente*] give it no hold over God. It is a confession of powerlessness (EA, V, p. 91 [111]).

Still while liturgy cannot actually achieve the Parousia, it is a power to consign to irrelevance what separates us from the Parousia, to bracket world, history, and earth, and so nullify the distance separating us from the eschaton. For liturgy allows us to inchoately (symbolically) subvert our topology by living in constant expectation of God's coming, orienting our being continually toward the eschaton, indeed to live as if the Parousia were already here. So liturgy is a non-place wherein we can rethink our initial being and bring it closer to its origin or accomplishment, wherein we can manifest another horizon or dimension of our existence, namely our highest possibility, "the place of a fragile anticipation" of God's coming (EA, Introduction, p. 2; II, pp. 25, 33-39 [45]; III, pp. 41-45, 47-48, 51, 53; IV, pp. 57-59, 61-62; V, pp. 83-84, 87-90, 94-98; VI, pp. 103, 105-110; VII, pp. 131, 137-139; VIII, pp. 162-163, 166; LNT, II, pp. 73-77, 119-122, 128-129; III, pp. 155-158, 177-180, 187-202, 209-214; WAW, III, p. 101; LNT, XIII, pp. 334-335; LPG, VI, pp. 149-157; VIII, pp. 200-204; IX, pp. 212-219; "PA," pp. 26-33; "LPP," p. 395; "MHLS," pp. 265-266, 280-282; "KG," p. 868). In liturgy then we grasp that our true nature is found at the end of the world, that the Good Friday experience will give rise to Easter, and so we intertwine our inherence in the world and our dwelling on the earth with our being before God (EA, IV, pp. 67-68; VIII, p. 138). As Lacoste puts it:

> Liturgy in fact conjoins expectation with the recognition of a presence. The world is the kingdom of the non-Parousia, and it wishes for the Parousia. On the other hand, the delimitation of the liturgical non-place offers itself to interpretation as the bracketing [*mise entre parenthèses*] of world and history. Liturgy does not, of course, bring about the Parousia. It does, however, represent a certain power of putting out of play everything which separates the human from the Parousia, or to say it differ-

ently, of living in a presence as if – but only *as if* – this presence were the
Parousia (EA, IV, p. 58 [71]).

Moreover, in Lacoste's mind, liturgy in the strict sense, i.e. the mass
with its Eucharist, is the closest we can come to an inkling of God's
presence pre-eschatologically. For when the faithful enter into praise,
chant, meditative silence, or love for God in the mass, God is most felt
and seen as present, indeed the anonymous Absolute becomes God
the Father ("SK," pp. 152-153; LNT, VII, pp. 185-191). Additionally
the mass contains the Eucharist, a memorial that is contemporaneous
with God's body and blood, and so in it past, present, and future are
bracketed. What is more in the Eucharist God becomes present in the
flesh, and this very presence of God can be taken in and praised, such
as with an act of genuflection before the tabernacle and communion
(EA, II, p. 36; V, p. 92; VIII, p. 147; n. 4 on p. 203; LNT, III, pp. 72-
83; IV, p. 96; XIII, pp. 325-326, 336; see also LNT, II, pp. 115-117;
III, pp. 169, 197-201; "PAFF," pp. 218-221, 223-225, 231; "LPP," p.
397; "WCA," p. 91; "SEE," pp. 227-228).

Let us close this book with a discussion of the thought of **William
Desmond (1951-)** who was born in 1951 in Cork, Ireland. He attended the National University of Ireland from 1968-1974, receiving
a bachelors in English and Philosophy in 1972 and a Masters in philosophy in 1974. He then came to the United States where he attended Pennsylvania State University from 1974-1978 where he received
a doctorate in philosophy in 1978. Desmond has taught philosophy
at St. Bonaventure University (1978-1979), University College, Cork
(1979-1980), St. Patrick's College, Maynooth (1981-1982), Loyola
College (1982-1994) [Chair of the Department from 1986-1994],
the Catholic University of Louvain (1994-), and the National University of Ireland, Maynooth (2008-).[145]

Desmond has also been president of the Hegel Society of America
(1990-1992), the Metaphysical Society of America (1994-1995), and
the American Catholic Philosophical Association (2007-2008). He
gave Aquinas Lectures at John Carroll University in 2002 and at the
National University of Ireland, Maynooth in 2003.

The key work of William Desmond, at least in terms of his natural theology, is his *God and the Between* [GB] (2008).[146] In this work,
Desmond declines the moniker postmodernism for his thought. Still

his work has many affinities with postmodernism, and if we decide to not label his philosophy postmodernist, we can at least consider him a pre-modernist. For Desmond rejects and wants to move beyond modern ways of thinking, in order to return to earlier ways of thought (GB, II, p. 39; n. 3 on p. 53; "NDR," pp. 37-45).

Desmond argues that humans have traditionally tried to understand the reality surrounding them in three main ways—univocal, equivocal, or dialectical. Yet while each of these ways is useful, and can deliver a partial truth, they culminate in a more complete fourth way, Desmond's metaxological way (GB, XIV, pp. 281, 284).

The objective univocal way seeks to uncover a "sameness" or "intelligible determinacy" in the multiplicity or overdeterminacy of beings, and represents the approach taken by Parmenides, Plato, Descartes, Spinoza, Leibniz, and John Craig (GB, III, pp. 49-53, 55-56, n. 9 on p. 61, 65-67; BB, II, pp. 47-80; EB, II, pp. 51-77; PU, I, p. 12; DDO, Introduction, p. 6; III, pp. 68-69). These thinkers hold "To be is to be intelligible; to be intelligible is to be determinate; and to be determinate is to be univocal" (GB, III, p. 50). And so the univocal way appeals to the importance of an ordered, clear, methodical, and publicly communicable understanding of the world.

The univocal way is quite useful in seeking for a logical coherence, intelligible determination, or geometrical exactness in matters of common sense, science, and math. Yet at its extreme it can degenerate into a "postulatory finitism," a reductionistic faith that there is nothing in excess of determination, i.e. besides the finite realm (GB, III, p. 50), based on what Desmond calls a *mathesis* or mathematizing of nature, wherein what doesn't conform to one's strict criterion of the determined intelligible is cast off as unreal (GB, III, p. 50; cf. BB, I, p. 17; II, pp. 49, 70-73; III, pp. 95-102; IV, pp. 159-160; ISTH, I, pp. 37-43, 61-62, 64; II, p. 79; PU, V, pp. 191-197). Consequently, we here end up with a scientism wherein science is said to answer all the essential questions or promises to do so, and so it is claimed that issues currently reserved for philosophy and religion will ultimately cede their mystery to scientific determination (GB, III, p. 70). This in fact is the way of modernity which stresses science, technological control, the secularization of everyday life, the desacralization, devaluation, and instrumentalization of nature, as well as human self-responsibility (autonomy), an alleged maturing of rational humanity, and a self-intoxicated will to power (GB, Introduction, pp. 2, 5; I, n. 1 on p. 18; I, pp. 19, 21; VI, p. 136; XII, p. 252). Modernity thus proposes that humans live between a worthless beginning and a purposeless end; they are a purposing in the face of the purposelessness of other-being (GB, I, pp. 20-21; III, pp. 61, 63; IV, p. 87; VI, p. 119; "BR," pp. 212, 218-219). Modernity then in seeking to determinate everything, and to omit what cannot be defined mathematically, can all too easily ignore the manyness, unpredictable otherness, overdetermined inexhaustibility, wonder, perplexity, mystery, and astonishing glory and value of the world (GB, III, pp. 49-52, 61, 63, 66; IV, p. 75; V, p. 106).

Even if a univocal approach should deem that God exists, it tends to make God the highest determinate intelligibility and so reduces him to the level of creation. It thus yields the God of the philosophers (a counterfeit double of God)—either God as *causa sui* or a self-effecting power with Descartes, God as *Deus sive natura* or a pantheistic God or nature with Spinoza, a moralistic God with Kant, or God as the mathematical master or mechanical watch maker with Paley (GB, Introduction, pp. 9-10, 13; III, pp. 49-50, 62, 66, 68; IV, p. 88; VI, p. 117; X, pp. 216-218; IST, I, p. 41; IV, pp. 146-164; V, pp. 177-181; EB, XIV, p. 432). So it fails to be true to God as the inexhaustible and surplus origin of being (GB, III, pp. 50, 66, 68).

The subjective equivocal way, followed by Heraclitus, Augustine, Pascal, Kierkegaard, Nietzsche, and Deconstructionists such as Derrida, focuses on the transience (becoming, flux) and differences found in nature. As such it is alive to the richness of reality, what cannot be determinately fixed, ambiguous difference, and unmediated manyness. Yet it can at times neglect the lasting constancies and interconnections of reality and so devolve into a pluralism and skepticism where being is indeterminate, unknowable, absurd, or incommunicable. And though it helps us see God as beyond the finite and unmasterable (and so is attune to the chiaroscuro of the divine), it also can leave God completely unknowable (GB, Introduction, pp. 9-10, 13; III, pp. 49-50, 52, 54; IV, pp. 73-74, 86, 88-89; V, pp. 93, 95, 102; VI, p. 117; BB, III, pp. 85-88; IV, pp. 131-132; EB, III, pp. 79-115; PU, I, pp. 12-13; V, p. 181; DDO, Introduction, p. 6; III, pp. 68-69).

The transobjective and transsubjective dialectical way of Kant and Hegel attempts to do justice to the dynamic interplay of sameness (unity) and otherness (difference), by advocating a togetherness of opposites, holding that what stands in opposition also stands in relation. Yet in the end it tends to merely privilege a more ultimate identity,

a more subtle speculative sameness, a transcendental-speculative univocity (the self-mediation of thought thinking itself) (GB, Introduction, pp. 9-10, 13; III, p. 49; V, pp. 91-92, 103; VI, p. 117; BB, IV, pp.
131-136, 143-145, 154-164, 173; V, p. 187; IX, p. 364; XII, p. 484;
EB, IV, pp. 117-129; PU, I, p. 13; DDO, Introduction, pp. 6-7; IV, pp.
118-124; V, pp. 124-128; VI, pp. 130-134). So like the univocal way, it
too produces a counterfeit double of the living God, and reduces God
to a pantheistic self-mediation or self-determination that is closed in
on itself (GB, V, pp. 92, 104, 106, 109; VI, p. 117).

Desmond hence champions a fourth pre-modern metaxological
way (from the Greek term *metaxu*—between). The metaxological way
grasps that humans exist in "the between" [*metaxu; medias res*], that is
to say, in an intermedium of being between origin and end, singularity
and community, constancy and impermanence (flux), unity and multiplicity, finitude and infinitude (i.e. in a being that continually comes
into and passes out of existence), time and eternity, birth and death,
and nature (immanence) and divinity (transcendence)[147] (GB, Introduction, pp. 2-3, 6-11; IV, pp. 74, 89, 92; V, p. 96; VI, pp. 119, 141;
XIV, pp. 284-287, 294, n. 8 on p. 29, 332, 335, 337; BB, Preface, p. xi;
I, pp. 44-46; IX, p. 333; X, p. 380; XII, pp. 470-471; PU, I, pp. 1-2;
III, pp. 87-92; IV, p. 115; V, pp. 167-168; VI, pp. 199-211, 233-234;
"BSP," pp. 14-15; IST, Introduction, pp. 21-24; II, p. 79; X, pp. 343-
344; PO, I, p. 33). As he writes, we humans "come to ourselves in the
midst of things, between an origin and an end we cannot completely
determine" (GB, VI, p. 118).

As existing in the middle, our basic state as humans is one of a
"porous medium of passing" wherein we are open (porous) to what
is other than ourselves and to what eludes, exceeds and transcends
us (GB, III, pp. 60-66; IV, pp. 87, 89; V, p. 107; VI, pp. 123-125;
VII, pp. 164-165; XIV, pp. 301-302, 305; BB, V, pp. 177-194; EB,
Introduction, pp. 4-9, V, pp. 163-169, 177, 209-220; see "BDD," pp.
26-33; PO, Introduction, pp. 3-6; I, pp. 60-61; III, pp. 131-146; IV,
pp. 187-207; V, pp. 223-229; VI, p. 266; IST, I, pp. 65-66; DDO,
Introduction, pp. 1-2, 4-5; IV, pp. 99-103; PU, I, p. 16; "BSP," pp. 15-
16). In the metaxological way then we respect the over-determinacy
of being, what cannot be conceptually mastered. In so doing we grasp
that reality is a rich complex of plurivocal happenings, a community
of voices, each with its own singularity and integrity. We also refuse
to omit as real what cannot be determinately and intelligibly articu-

lated in a complete manner, and are open to the transcendent spaces of otherness found in the between (GB, Preface, pp. xi-xii; Introduction, pp. 10-11, 13; V, p. 104; VI, p. 117; BB, I, p. 33; V, pp. 177, 190, 201; VIII, pp. 322-323; IX, pp. 348, 355; XII, pp. 463-466, 480-485, 494; XIV, p. 325; "BSP," pp. 30-32, 35; "NDR," pp. 37, 47-49; IST, IV, pp. 145-148). In light of this multiplicity of meaning, truth cannot be exhausted by any one finite determinacy, rather it is overdetermined and plurivocal, and there is need for chastened epistemic claims and retention of metaphysical mystery (BB, V, pp. 200-201). Thus the way of metaxology is an intermediating way beyond the univocity that reduces transcendence into sameness, the equivocity that disperses difference, and the dialectical path that sublates unity and difference by a facile reconciliation into a dialectical-speculative whole (GB, III, p. 49; XIV, p. 323; PU, I, pp. 10-11, 14-16; V, pp. 173-178; DDO, Introduction, pp. 7-8; V, pp. 124-128; VI, pp. 130-134, 137-144).

The metaxological way also lets us achieve a proper view of the divine transcendence and its reserves (its over-determination). By its approach we grasp that God outstrips every categorical determination and so can't be intellectually mastered (GB, II, p. 45; VI, pp. 117, 123-124, 127). In a metaxological approach then, rather than knowing God through demonstrative proofs, we know God through what Desmond labels "ways," "probes," or "hyperboles of being," which are overdeterminate signs or pointers to ultimate transcendence found in immanence, "happenings in immanence that are not determined by immanence alone" (GB, XIV, p. 313), or an "excess of inwardness that is not of inwardness" (GB, VI, p. 146), even tugs or knocks of the divine (GB, Introduction, p. 4, 8, 10; III, pp. 58-59, 71, 76; IV, p. 90; V, pp. 106, 114-115; VI, pp. 118, 121-122, 127, 140; VII, p. 169; XIV, pp. 284-286, 309, 313; IST, I, pp. 64-69; "GEW," pp. 75-78; "BSP," pp. 22-27).[148] For God, according to Desmond, is known in the heart beyond reason, in astonishment, perplexity, and mystery: with a primal ethos or reverence for the overdetermination and excess of being, with a spirit of finesse or poetics and not just geometry, i.e. with a porosity (GB, Preface, p. xi; Introduction, pp. 3-4, 10-11; I, pp. 17-19; II, pp. 35-37; III, pp. 62-63, 66-67; VI, pp. 127-128; "BR," pp. 222-230; IST, Introduction, pp. 2, 5; II, pp. 95-96; VIII, p. 268; "BDD," pp. 736-742; "MAC," pp. 232-236, 239-241). He thus remarks "Yes, yes: we do need more determinate articulation . ... [But also] a further turn towards the primal ethos, in mindfulness of a fuller feel for the being-there of being and beings" (GB, II, p. 45).

Now according to Desmond there are four hyperboles of being. The first hyperbole (the existential way to God) is the idiocy of being, the sheer 'that it is' of finite being (GB, Introduction, pp. 9, 11; II, p. 32; VI, p. 107; BB, VI, pp. 225-265; XIV, p. 337; IST, IV, pp. 63-67; PU, III, pp. 55-70). For the astonishing thereness or givenness of be-ings—the perplexity of their existence which is not self-explanatory (for it is transient and a coming into being and a passing away)—is a too muchness or excess of what is given to be. And so it puts us in mind of a more original source of beings, something that gives them to be before they can give themselves (something which determinate being presupposes to be at all), an overdeterminate generosity of being or God (GB, III, pp. 52, 55; VI, pp. 118, 129-131, 165-167; XII, p. 251; XIV, pp. 284-285, 296; PU, Preface, pp. ix-x; II, pp. 45, 52; III, pp. 55-57, 98-101; V, pp. 167-173, 186-190; VI, pp. 199, 228-229, 250; DDO, VIII, pp. 183-196; BB, I, pp. 15-17, 39; II, p. 71; IX, pp. 339-340; EB, p. 170; IST, Introduction, p. 31; I, pp. 38, 49; PO, pp. 32-33).

The second hyperbole (the aesthetic way to God) is the aesthetics of happening, the glory and beauty of the world (GB, Introduction, p. 11; II, pp. 38-39; XIV, pp. 314, 336; IST, IV, pp. 67-68). Here we are im-pressed not just with the fact that something is, but what it is, its sin-gular and determinate character (its thisness). For there is a sweetness and sheer goodness of the being of things (shown in our spontaneous shunning of death which invokes the goodness of our source) (GB, II, pp. 32-35, 38; V, p. 100; VI, pp. 124, 131, 154). And there is as well a marvelous intricacy of order and beauty to the world, an abundant, rich, and colorful variegation of life, and an integral harmony with the community of others (i.e. a manyness with togetherness); in short, a feast of being. On account of the excessive and overdeterminate this-ness of things we are filled with longing and peace and carried beyond to the transfinite glory, sublimity, and power of the creator (GB, I, p. 18; II, p. 44; IV, p. 75; VI, pp. 134-138; VII, p. 165; BB, VII, pp. 159-162, 168-169; PU, I, pp. 2-3; DDO, VII, pp. 154-163).

Desmond, in presenting the second way to God, movingly notes how the divine is manifested in the sweetness and beauty of such things as a glint of sun through a shutter, a starry night, the squall of a sudden rain, the roll of the ocean, a spring morning after a storm; a

mustard seed, the fall of a yellow leaf, a flower dangling outside a sky-
light, hatched chicks freshly scattered in the spring, a crow cawing or a
blackbird singing on a twilight tree; a drink of pure water, the comfort
of fire on a bitter day, a glass of wine on an oak table; a smile, a song,
playing a game, running a race, a child holding one's hand, a sleeping
child, a face, the uninsistent aid of an agapeic servant, the last visit
with a dying man, the bawl of a baby being born; the music of Bach
or Mozart (GB, IV, p. 76; VII, pp. 135-138; XIV, pp. 300, 337-340;
BB, VII, pp. 164-165, 169). Indeed it is worth looking directly at Desmond's poetic words:

> The glory of the morning, the lark on high, the wind in the summer
> trees, the day's heat on the meadow, those swans there gliding on the
> lake, the glint of light on the wave, the sudden squall at sea, a golden
> voice, and effortless runner, the comic first step of a child, or just having
> a laugh, or bidding farewell, or biding with the dying, helpless to com-
> fort but being there, these and much, much more, all speak the glory of
> finitude; and yet there is a transcending that is still more. Whoever says
> the desire for God springs up only from the deficient is blind to the mad
> longing that arises out of fullness itself (GB, II, p. 40).

The third hyperbole (comprising the exigent way to God) is the
erotics of selving. It is based on the fact that humans are self-surpass-
ing beings, for they possess a primal porosity to what exceeds their
own determination, a desire to be [conatus essendi] (GB, Introduction,
p. 12; VI, pp. 141, 146; XIV, p. 336; IST, IV, p. 68). Moreover, it
turns out that nothing determinate ultimately satisfies human self-
surpassing, not the delights of the flesh, nor the sublimities of the
spirit. Only something beyond us and beyond the determinate finite,
only the overdeterminate plenitude of being, can satisfy our restlessness and want. For we have a desire or eros for a life beyond our own,
beyond death. So impelled by our own lack we reach out to God (GB,
II, pp. 41-42; III, p. 58; V, pp. 101-102, 111-115; VI, pp. 141-145;
PU, IV, pp. 113-118; VI, pp. 211-215; DDO, I, pp. 17-34; BB, X, pp.
395-406; XI, pp. 438-448; EB, X, pp. 323-345).

The fourth hyperbole (the ethical and religious ways to God), is the
agapeics of community (an agapic selving). Here we do not act out of
lack, in contrast with the last way, but go beyond ourselves in a compassion of being [compassio essendi], giving ourselves over to another
in a surplus of generosity (and loving others for themselves). This is

motivated by an incontrovertible call of the good that we don't produce: a charge laid upon us, a summons of the unconditional good
that is not just our good. Moreover, this ethical life calls us to be in
solidarity with all other humans, who are ends in themselves and of
infinite value, including the poor, hungry, sick, bereft, tormented, and
leper. Hence all social conventions fall by the wayside in the face of
the overdeterminate appeal of other. Indeed we are even called to sacrificial love, to lay down our lives for another. Now this ethical reality
with its unconditional requirement, this solidarity and surplus of giving, cannot be accounted for by appealing to human nature (contra
Iris Murdoch); for we become ethical through this ethos and do not
originate it ourselves. Hence ethics only makes sense by invoking the
overdeterminate goodness of God (GB, Introduction, pp. 6-7, 12; II,
pp. 43-44; V, pp. 97-99, 111; VI, pp. 141-147, 151, 155-157; VII, pp.
166-169; XIV, p. 336; BB, VII, p. 166; X, pp. 406-415; XI, pp. 448-
461; EB, I, pp. 18, 28, 33-39, 44-47; II, pp. 62-65, 75; III, p. 91, 114-
115; IV, pp. 121-122, 151-158; V, pp. 167, 201, 207, 217, 219; XI, pp.
347-364; IST, IV, pp. 68-69; PU, IV, pp. 118-126; V, pp. 199-200; VI,
pp. 211-215, 221-232, 237-241, 253-258; DDO, VII, pp. 163-175;
"GEW," pp. 72-75).

Now the God known hyperbolically has ten main characteristics
for Desmond. God is 1) over-being—God is not a being or a thing,
but agapeic being and beyond being (but not without being contra
Marion); God is surplus excess (hyperousia; an overdetermined and
inexhaustible origination), unconditional in itself (God's that it is cannot not be) and absolving in letting creation be irreducibly other; 2)
over-one and over-whole—God is absolutely singular, a unique and
hyperbolic One, beyond the whole, yet also a dynamic constancy of
activity and transcending plenitude to what is other; 3) eternal—God
is a surplus pluperfect origin prior to time and coming to be; 4) incor-
ruptible—God as an exceeding surplus has no lack and so is immutable (constant fidelity and reliability), yet is also an agapeic upholding
of the otherness of creation in its freedom, releasing the gift of being
and letting it be for itself even to the point of failure; 5) impassible—
God needs nothing outside of Himself and is self-sufficient, but yet is
not autarkic (not utterly utter, thinking only of itself as with Aristotle's god); God is rather an asymmetrical overflow of love and agapeic
service to the other as well as constant availability and intimacy to
humans (indeed the cry and joy of creatures enters God's heart); 6)

absolute—God is self-defining (nothing but God is God), infinite reserve, plenitude, and promise, yet willing to empty Himself in abdica-
tion to live in the dirt and ash heap (mixing with the filth of creation)
and die in love for the other; 7) infinite—God is over-determinate, beyond form and potency, an infinite excess, undiminished reserve, and
so generous, yet without being any the less for it (like a parent who
gives to a child or a teacher to a student), an endless resource of spend-
ing; 8) God is overall-power[149]—God is above power, unlimited self-
expression, unconstrained by anything, yet an empowering that is not
the dominating power of a master or king or the mechanistic power of
a machine but more like the restless power of the sea that releases and
lets others go in a creative possibilizing; 9) God is overall-minding—
God knows all but not by a knowledge of determinate states of affairs
or unsurpassable quantities of information in a data bank, but by a
creative and responsive knowing, creating and dwelling with the other
even as it is genuinely other; 10) God is too good—God is a hyperbolic good, agape, good beyond measure, comprehension, and being.
For God's goodness is excessive, pluperfect, overfull, and overdetermined. God, as we have seen, is an agapeic servant who wills to be as
nothing, a kenotic love always outside of itself in the midst of singulars
loved singularly and without reserve, giving for the pure good of the
recipient who may not even comprehend that it is a recipient, seeking
no reward, fanfare, flattery, recognition ('It was nothing'). Yet all the
same, God's goodness is beyond good and evil, a generosity in excess
of the measure of our moralities, a forgiving agape, a mercy beyond
justice, as it is a giving that offers no why, and indeed can look like
a reckless disregard for justice (such as when Jesus gave those who
worked a full day and those who didn't the same pay—see Mt 20:1-
16) (GB, Introduction, pp. 6-8; I, p. 23; III, p. 58; V, pp. 93, 99-100,
103, 107-109, 112-113; VI, pp. 123-128, 131, 139, 147, 150; VII,
pp. 163-164; XII, pp. 253-255 and n. 3 on p. 242; XIII, pp. 269-270;
XIV, pp. 282-308, 312-330, 333, 335, 338-340; n. 10 on p. 302; n. 18
on p. 311; IST, Introduction, p. 27; IV, pp. 151-153; V, pp. 192-199;
"MMN," pp. 115-118; BB, VII, pp. 159-164, 168-169; IX, p. 201;
XII, pp. 236-238; XIII, pp. 262-263; EB, Introduction, pp. 6, 9; I, p.
26; IV, pp. 117, 132, 158; V, p. 163; XVI, pp. 501-514). Desmond
thus writes of God's goodness, "One does nothing to merit it, and no
payment is exacted, for it offers itself simply as the life of the good, a
life we are to live" (EB, V, p. 217).[150]

CONCLUSION

Apart from examination of Scripture, theologians have often appealed to another principle in order to arrive at an inventory of theological doctrine.

This is the Canon of St. Vincent of Lerins (c. 380-445) who argued that the true Catholic faith is that which is universal, antique, and based on consent [*universitatem, antiquitatem, consensionem*], or in his famous words that which has been believed "everywhere, always, and by all [*quod ubique, quod semper, quod ab omnibus*]" (*Commonitorium*, 4). More specifically, for Vincent of Lerins, that which is universal is what has been confessed by everyone throughout the whole world [*tota per orbem terrarum*], that which is antique is what has been held by the holy ancestors and fathers [*sanctos majores ac patres*], and that which is based on consent are those definitions and positions held by all (or at least almost all) of the priests and doctors of the Church [*omnium vel certe pene omnium sacerdotum pariter et magistrorum definitiones sententiasque*].

Similar ideas gained traction in the Renaissance with the formulation of probabilism (and its variants aequiprobabilism and probabiliorism) by Thomas Cajetan (1469-1534), Bartolome de Medina, O.P. (1527-1581), Luis Molina, S.J. (1528-1581), Domingo Bañez, O.P. (1528-1604), Francisco Suarez, S.J. (1548-1617), Leonard Lessius, S.J. (1554-1623), Thrysus Gonzalez, S.J. (1624-1705), Alphonsus de Liguori (1696-1787), and others. For these moral theologians argued that in the situation of a moral dilemma one could follow one's conscience and act contrary to a law (what was called the "unsafe" option) if one's view was shared by a consensus of moral theologians [even if one's opinion was less probable than the alternative for probabilism, only if one's opinion was as probable as the alternative for aequiprobabilism, and only if one's opinion was more probable than the alternative with probabiliorism].[151]

I wish to do something similar for Catholic philosophy, and based on my surveys of nineteenth and twentieth century Catholic philosophy, the positions of the Patristic (especially Augustine), Medieval (especially Aquinas), Renaissance, and Modern Catholic philosophers, as well as Official Statements of the Magisterium (Councils, Encyclicals, Catechisms, etc.), come up with a philosophical canon or *sensus rationis* [sense of reason] or *consensus philosophiae* [philosophical consensus]. Now it might be too strong to say that these are the fundamental principles of any Catholic philosophy worthy of the name, and so that to the extent one deviates from these positions one may be a philosopher but is not a Catholic philosopher. Still these beliefs represent the philosophical principles that have received the common consent or concurrence of support of the vast majority of Catholic philosophers, and so are a pointer to a Catholic philosophy; and one who rejects them retreats at their own peril from the secure position afforded by the tradition of Catholic philosophy. Here then is a *sensus rationis* [sense of reason] based on two thousand years of Catholic philosophy and Magisterial pronouncements.

Twelve Focal Principles of Catholic Philosophy:

1) Foundational Empiricism: Experience is the foundation of scientific and philosophical knowledge.

2) Elaborative Rationalism: While knowledge begins in experience, the intellect is actively involved in developing truths and principles of science and philosophy.

3) Epistemological Realism [Correspondence Theory of the Truth]: The intellect is able to grasp the nature of reality to a degree.

4) Metaphysical Libertarianism: Humans possess a free will which is a power to choose one action or another in a given set of circumstances (see DH 622, 1486, 1554-1555, 1939, 2003; *Libertas*, nn. 1-6; CCC, 1730-1749, 1861).

5) Mental Dualism [Non-materialism]: While the mind is deeply integrated into the body (and brain), it goes beyond and escapes its physical embodiment to a degree.

6) Collaboration of Faith and Reason: Faith and reason are in concord in the development of philosophical and theological truths (DH 2776, 3004; *Fides et Ratio*, Prologue).

7) Natural Theology [Metaphysics is Prior to Science]: Reason can show God exists and determine His nature to some degree (that is to say there is an evidential basis for belief in God) (DH 3026; *Humani Generis*, n. 29; CCC, 31-49).

8) Spiritual Immortality: The human soul can be shown to be immortal (DH 1440; CCC, 366).

9) Moral Objectivism [Natural Law]: Moral values are part of the fabric of reality and known by all humans at least in part.

10) Three-Font Principilism: Human acts are to be judged right or wrong based on the act itself, the circumstances and consequences of the act, and the intentions (motives) of the agent, and there are some acts that are intrinsically evil and never to be done (*Veritatis Splendor*, nn. 75-82, 95-97; CCC, 1749-1761).

11) Agapic Harmonism: Love requires self-sacrifice and other-regard and yet yields the happiness of the lover (*Deus Caritas Est*, nn. 3-8).

12) Axiological Personalism: The human person possesses intrinsic value and must be loved for its own sake.

This is not to say there is one single philosophical system that all Catholic philosophers must hold to in all matters. Rather only that there should ideally be an agreement in regard to some main principles. For repeating what John Paul II asserts, "The Church has no philosophy of her own [*suam ipsius philosophiam non exhibet Ecclesia*] nor does she canonize any one particular philosophy in preference to others" (*Fides et Ratio*, 49). Thus while there are central principles which represent a consensus, and which a Catholic philosopher is wise to retain, there may be legitimate divergences of thought on the peripheries.

Now if I were to personally advocate the most fruitful course for Catholic Philosophy in the Twenty-First Century, I would recommend a constructive blending and engagement of Neo-Thomism, Romanticism, Personalism, Phenomenology, Existentialism, and Analytical Thought, with select insights from other movements incorporated for good measure (though of course history does not always meander along the straightest path, nor humans along the most sensible one). For while there was perhaps too much of a focus on and hegemony of Thomism in the past, to the extent that the valuable contributions of non-Thomistic thinkers were sometimes obscured, nowadays there has been too quick of an abandonment of Thomism by Catholic philosophers. Yet the importance of Thomism to Catholic philosophy cannot be ignored and those thinkers who ignore it do so at their own peril. For Aquinas generated a solid foundation and platform for Catholic philosophy, one that is unfortunately increasingly overlooked or misinterpreted. Lastly, Catholic philosophy will have to engage modern science, yet it must recognize that philosophy introduces principles that are prior to science, and that while it must reconcile itself with science, this can only be the legitimate achievements of a well-grounded science, not those of speculative thinkers who create theories more in the light of their own philosophical beliefs even if they make use of scientific data (indeed the science with which religion must be reconciled is not the science of today, nor the science of a thousand years from now, nor even a million years from now, but the science of the year infinity, i.e. the science known to the mind of God).

Of course while Catholic philosophy is very much alive and active at the close of the twentieth-century, Catholicism as a practiced faith is in a more tentative position at least in Europe and parts of the Americas due to secularization, and is at one of its lowest points in terms of public opinion. Yet a new millennium awaits.

ABBREVIATIONS

ACM—*A Catholic Modernity?* (1999)

ACP—See Swindal (2005)

"ACP"—"Abt Christian Philosophy" (1960)

"AI"—"Appearing and Irreducible" (2010)

"AIDE"—"Action, Intention, DE" (1982)

AG—*Approaches to God* (1953)

AOF—*Attempt at Outlk for Future* (1930)

AP—*The Acting Person* (1969)

APH—*Aphorismen* (1931)

AS—*Art and Scholasticism* (1920)

ATH—See Dulles (1994)

"ATT"—"Answer to Two Attacks" (1914)

BB—*Being and the Between* (1995)

BBKL—See Bautz (1990-2010)

"BDD"—"Being, Det. and Dialectic" (1995)

BDTC—See Brown (1996)

BG—*Being Given* (1997)

BH—*Being and Having* (1935)

BHP—See Bréhier (1967-1969)

BKF—*Belief, Knowledge, and Faith* (2005)

"BR"—"Betrayals of Reverence" (2000)

"BS"—"The Banality of Saturation" (2007)

BSP—*Being and Some Philosophers* (1949)

"BSP"—"Btwn System and Poetics" (2007)

BT—*Belief Today* (1964)

BTCT—See Knasas (2003)

C—*Collection* (1968)

CA—*Centesimus Annus* (1991)

CAHP—See Baldwin (2003)

CAP—See Ariès (1955)

"CARM"—"Carmel" (1989)

CC—*Christian Confrontation* (1945)

CCC—See Duquin (2003) [or see below]

CCC—*Catechism of the Catholic Church*

"CCH"—"Contraception & Chastity" (1972)

CCP—See Critchey (1998)

"CDG"—"Religious Imagination ..." (2002)

CE—*Christian Ethics* (1953)

CEP—See Bocheński (1961)

CEWP—See Urmson (1989)

CF—*Creative Fidelity* (1940)

CHAD—See Jacquemet (1948-2000)

CHP—See Copleston (1953-1974)

CL—*Consciousness and Logos* (1961)

CM—*Cartesian Meditations* (1977)

CMCT—See Carey (1960)

"CNL"—"Contraception/Nat. Law" (1965)

CP—See Coreth (1987-1990)

"CPC"—"Christian Phil. & Charity" (1992)

CRHP—See Mascia (1957)

CRO—*Conduct in Regard ... Other* (1957)

CRPH—*Christianity and Philosophy* (1936)

CS—*The Consciousness of the Self* (1933)

CT—See Bacik (1989)

"CT"—"Consecrated Thought" (2005)

CTE—See Nichols (1998)

CTF—See Benrubi (1926)

CTIC—See Herr (1985)

CV—*The Crossing of the Visible* (1991)

DDO—*Desire, Dial. and Otherness* (1987)
DENZ—See Denzinger (2002)
DH—See Denzinger (1999)
DIA—*Dialogics* (1979)
DK—*The Degrees of Knowledge* (1932)
DP—See Huizman (1993)
DPR—See Reese (1996)
DS—*Difference and Subjectivity* (1982)
DSR—*The Dyn. Struct. of Reality* (1989)
DTC—See Vacant (1903-1950)
DTCB—See Brown (2005)
DYBG—*Do You Believe in God* (1969)
EA—*Experience and the Absolute* (1994)
EB—*Ethics and the Between* (2001)
EBHD—*Exist. Backgd of Hum. Dign.* (1963)
EC—*Ethics and Community* (1999)
ECP—*Elem. of Christian Philosophy* (1960)
ECHP—*Essay on Christ. Philosophy* (1955)
EE—*Existence and the Existent* (1947)
"EEKG"—"Exp. Ev. Know. of God" (1984)
EEP—See Embree (1997)
EF—See Melchiorre (2006)
"EF"—"The Eyes of Faith" (1910)
EJ—*Experience and Judgment* (1975)
EL—*Ethics of Liberation* (1998)
ELK—*Essays on Love and Know.* (2008)
EMCT—See McGrath (1995)
EMFT—See Murray (2004)
EN—*The Error of Narcissus* (1939)
EP—See Bochert (2005)
"EPR"—"Event, Phen. & Revealed" (2003)

ER—See Jones (2004)
ERP—*Ethics, Religion, and Politics* (1981)
ES—*Evil and Suffering* (1940)
EV—*Evangelium Vitae* (1995)
FCF—*Foundations of Christ. Faith* (1976)
FEB—*Finite and Eternal Being* (1950)
"FFT"—"Foucault on Free. & Truth" (1984)
FKCT—See McEnhill (2004)
FHG—*Faith in a Hard Ground* (2008)
FMA—*Fundamental Moral Attitudes* (1966)
FPTC—See Gutting (2001)
FR—*Fides et Ratio* (1998)
"FRI"—"Form. Reason ... Infinite" (2004)
FS—*Four Saints* (1951)
FT—See Hudson (1992)
"FTP"—"Fund. Theo. & Philosophy" (1966)
FUP—See McCool (1989), pp. 114-160;
GB—*God and the Between* (2008)
"GEW"—"God, Ethos, Ways" (1999)
GF—See Jonkers (2005)
GI—*Graven Images* (1957)
"GKL"—"God Knowable as Lovab." (2007)
GP—*God and Philosophy* (1941)
GPE—*God and the Perm. of Evil* (1963)
GR—*A Gilson Reader* (1957)
GWB—*God without Being* (1982)
HA—See Dulles (1971)
"HA"—"Husserl and Aquinas" (1929)
HAL—*Human Agency and Language* (1985)

"HC"—"Humanity at the Crossr." (1948)

HCEC—See McBrien (1995)

"HDH"—"Hist. Dim. of Human B." (1974)

HG—*Human and God* (1984)

HHP—See Hirschberger (1958-1959)

HLAE—*Human Life, Act., and Ethics* (2005)

HPDP—*Human Prayer, Divine Pray.* (1962)

HPN—*Human Person and Nature* (1943)

HT—See Hocedez (1947-1952)

HW—*Hearers of the Word* (1941)

HWP—See Caponigri (1963-1971)

HTL—*Hist. and Theol.of Liberation* (1976)

HV—*Homo Viator* (1944)

HYP—See Passmore (1966)

IA—*Invention of the Americas* (1998)

IC—*Individual and Community* (1922)

ICEA—See Colin (1997)

ICP—*Intro. to Christ. Philosophy* (1960)

ICS—*An Invest. concerning the State* (1925)

ID—*The Idol and Distance* (1977)

IE—*In Excess* (2001)

IEC—See Pizzardo (1948-1954)

ID—*Ideas* (1931)

IH—*Integral Humanism* (1936)

IL—*Inaugural Lesson* (1942)

"IMG"—"The Impossible for Man" (2007)

IMA—*The Idea of Moral Action* (1916)

IN—*Insight* (1957)

"IN"—"In the Name" (1999)

INT—*Intention* (1957)

IO—*Intersubjectivity and Ontology* (1974)

"IO"—Introduction to Ontology" (1965)

IONT—*Introduction to Ontology* (1947)

IP—*An Introduction to Philosophy* (1962)

IPB—"In the Presence of Being" (1960)

IST—... *A Sabbath for Thought?* (2005)

ISTH—*The Intellect. of St. Thomas* (1908)

ITCP—... *A Christian Philosophy?* (1956)

JD—*Jaws of Death* (1990)

"KG"—"Knowledge of God" (2005)

"KTB"—"Knowledge, Truth, Being" (1932)

"LCA"—"Liturgy and Coaffection" (2005)

LCN—See Ledure (1984)

LI—*Logical Investigations* (1970)

LNT—*Notes on Time* (1990)

LP—*Liturgy and Personality* (1933)

LPG—*The Phenomenality of God* (2008)

"LPP"—"Presence and Parousia" (2001)

LR—*Love and Responsibility* (1960)

LSI—*Logical Space of Interlocution* (1985)

LTK—See Kasper (1993-2001)

"MAC"—"Metaphys. after Critique" (2005)

MAP—See Shook (2005)

"MCHH"—"Christian Philosophy" (1999)

MCT—See Livingston (2000)

MEP—*The Erotic Phenomenon* (2003)

MHP—See Marías (1967)

"MHLS"—"More Haste Less Speed" (2007)

MJ—*Metaphysical Journal* (1927)

MKMV—*Mor. and Know. Mor. Val.* (1922)

"MME"—"Murder and Moral. Euth." (1982)

"MMN"—"Maybe, Maybe Not" (2003)

"MMR"—"Modern Moral Ration." (1997)

MMS—*Man against Mass Society* (1952)

MOB—*The Mystery of Being* (1949-1950)

MOR—*Moralia* (1980)

MP—*Moral Philosophy* (1960)

MPC—*Prolegomena to Charity* (1986)

MPL—*Method for a Phil. Liberation* (1974)

MPM—*Metaphy. & Philos. of Mind* (1981)

MPV—"Modes of Particip. in Value" (1961)

MR—*Methodical Realism* (1936)

MSI—*Modern Social Imaginaries* (2004)

MSP—*Manifesto ... Serv. Personal.* (1936)

MT—*Method in Theology* (1972)

MTCJ—See Bird (1967)

"NA"—"Negation and Absence" (1993)

NCE—See Marthaler (2003)

"NDR"—"N. Deconst. or Reconst." (2000)

NCS—See McCool (1989)

NG—*Nature and Grace* (1964)

NHG—*Nature, History, God* (1942)

NL—*The Nature of Love* (2009)

NLW—*Natural Law* (1986)

NT—See McCool (1994)

NTB—*The New Tower of Babel* (1953)

OA—*On Act* (1937)

OB—See Mascall (1971)

OBG—*On Being* (1928)

"OBHM"—"Behalf of Handmaid" (1968)

OCF—*Our Christian Faith* (1980)

OE—*On Essence* (1962)

"OG"—"On the Gift" (1999)

OGP—See Honderich (2005)

OHS—*On the Human Soul* (1951)

OHYP—See Shanley (2001)

OHYT—See Brezik (1981)

"OM"—"The Origin of Man" (1967)

OPE—*On the Problem of Empathy* (1917)

OSI—*On Spiritual Intimacy* (1955)

OTE—*On Time and Eternity* (1945)

OUJ—*Out of the Journal* (1916-1917)

OUP—*On the Use of Philosophy* (1961)

PA—*Potency and Act* (1998)

"PA"—"Phenom. of Anticipation" (2009)

PAF—See Aubert (1958)

"PAFF"—"Presence and Affection" (2001)

PAMP—See Drummond (2002)

PBTW—*Fr. Phil. btw the Two Wars* (1942)

PC—*Psychical Causality* (1922)

"PCG"—"Sketch Phil. Conc. of Gift" (1999)

PE—*The Philosophy of Existence* (1949)

PEC—*The Person and Community* (1994)

PCB—*Phil. Constants of Being* (1983)

PCHP—See Popkin (1999)

PCR—*Pers. & Comm. Revolution* (1935)

PDG—See Lavelle (1942)

PE—*Personalist Explorations* (1970)

PERS—*Personalism* (1949)

PF—*Philosophical Fragments* (1961)

PFA—See Deledalle (1963)

PFPM—See Theau (1977)

PG—*The Peasant of the Garonne* (1966)

"PG"—"The Present and the Gift" (2009)

PH—*Problematic Man* (1967)

PHA—*Philosophical Arguments* (1995)

PHL—*Phenomenology and Logic* (2001)

PHP—See De la Torre (1988)

"PHT"—"Phil. Handmaid of Theo.?" (1965)

PI—*Presence and Immortality* (1959)

PL—*Philosophy of Liberation* (1975)

PLMA—*Love in the Middle Ages* (1908)

PLP—*Love and the Person* (1946)

PLW—*Problem of Languag. & Word* (1926)

PM—See Spiegelberg (1960) [or see below]

PM—*A Preface to Metaphysics* (1939)

PN—*Philosophy of Nature* (1935)

PO—*Philosophy and Its Others* (1990)

PP—*Presence and Parousia* (2006)

"PP"—"A Philosopher's Postscript" (2005)

PPF—See Lacroix (1966)

PS—*The Powers of the Self* (1948)

"PS"—"Phenom. of the Sacrament" (2010)

"PSP"—"Paganism, Superst. & Phil." (1985)

PT—*The Philosopher and Theology* (1960)

PTCW—See Sciacca (1964)

"PTEG"—"Perc. Trans. & Exp. God" (2008)

PTPI—*Phil. & Theol. Papers* I (2004)

PTPII—*Phil. & Theol. Papers* II (2007)

PTRD—See Schaub (1928)

PU—*Perplexity and Ultimacy* (1995)

"PV"—"Phenomenology of Values" (1966)

PWW—See Tymieniecka (2002)

"RAT"—"Rationality" (1982)

RC—*The Reality of Christ* (1920-1927)

"RC"—"Reply to Commentators" (1994)

RCSM—See Auvergne (1938)

RECC—*Recip. of Consciousnesses* (1942)

REL—*Rules of Everyday Life* (2004)

REP—See Craig (1998)

RG—*Reduction and Givenness* (1989)

"RG"—"The Reason of the Gift" (2005)

ROG—"Die Rolle des obj. Gutes ..." (1930)

RP—See Gilson (1966)

RPC—See Duméry (1956)

RPF—See Guitton (1968)

RPFR—See Wolf (1999)

"RPP"—"Rel. & Poverty of Phil." (2004)

RR—*Reason and Reasons* (1948)

RT—*Ransoming the Time* (1941)

S—*The Subject* (1968)

SA—*A Secular Age* (2008)

SC—*A Second Collection* (1974)

SCH—*Searchings* (1967)

SCT—See Schoof (1970)

"SEE"—"Sacr., Ethics, Eucharist" (1984)

SF—*Small Fear of the 20th Cent.* (1948)

SH—*The Sacred Heart* (1955)

SHP—See Thonnard (1955) [or see below]

SHP—*Struct. of the Human Person* (1994)

SHT—See Cessario (2005)
SI—*Sentient Intelligence* (1980-1983)
SIP—*Introduction to Philosophy* (1991)
"SK"—"Silent Knowledge" (2002)
SMP—*Spirit of Medieval Philosophy* (1932)
SOS—*Sources of the Self* (1987)
"SP"—"The Saturated Phenomenon" (1996)
SPC—See Souilhé (1934)
SPI—See Inglis (1998)
SPW—*Spirit in the World* (1939)
SPWR—*Speech and Writing* (1942)
"SSI"—"Sci. of Spirit. Inwardness" (1941)
ST—*The Spirit of Thomism* (1964)
SW—*Science and Wisdom* (1935)
TC—*Treatise of Character* (1946)
TCCT—See Kerr (2007)
TCFC—See Brosman (1995)
TCFP—See Matthews (1996)
TCP—See Delfgaauw (1969)
TIC—*Transformation in Christ* (1940)
TCRT—See Macquarrie (1988)
TCT—See Ryan (1965)
TD—*On the Theology of Death* (1958)
TDC—*Temp. Dyn. Consciousnesses* (1997)
TE—See Riet (1963-1965)
TELAL—*Ethics Lat. Am. Liberation* (1973)
TEP—See Winquist (2000)
"TGLH"—"Thinking about God ..." (1987)
THC—*A Third Collection* (1985)
TI—*Theological Investigations* (1954-1992)
TLE—*Theo. of Liberation and Ethics* (1975)
TMC—*True Morality & Counterfeits* (1955)

"TOAT"—"Th. Aq. & Onto-Theol." (2003)
TP—*Total Presence* (1934)
TPC—See Huisman (1967)
TPE—*St. Thomas & Permiss. of Evil* (1963)
"TPR"—"Transform. Phil. of Rel." (2006)
TR—*Thomist Realism & Crit. Know.* (1983)
"TRE"—"Theol. Refl. on Eucharist" (1981)
"TRH"—"They Recognized Him" (2002)
TS—See John (1966)
TT—See Shanley (2002)
TV—*Treatise of Values* (1951-1955)
TWB—*Tragic Wisdom and Beyond* (1968)
TWFP—See Schrift (2006)
TYT—See Berkhof (1989)
UA—*Untrammeled Approaches* (1978)
UB—*Understanding and Being* (1980)
UHF—See Urdanoz (1998)
V—*Verbum* (1967)
VR—*The Visible and the Revealed* (2005)
VRT—*Varieties of Religion Today* (2006)
VS—*Veritas Splendor* (1993)
WAW—*World and Absence of Work* (2000)
"WCA"—"Work & Comp. Appear." (2003)
WE—See Friedman (1991)
WIH—*What Is the Human* (1994)
WIP—*What Is Philosophy?* (1960)
"WKG"—"Ways to Know God" (1940)
WP—*What is Personalism?* (1947)
WPR—See Long (2003)
WSR—*Word & Spirit. Realities* (1921)

NOTES

1 Let me thank some of my students who read through and made suggestions for improving earlier versions of these chapters: Enrique ("Rick") Alonso, Luis Espinoza, Gerardo Pantoja, Jeremiah Riley, and Joseph ("Joe") Starkweather. Thanks also to the librarians Patricia Lyons and Jeannine MacAller for all their help.

2 Among the more than 600 Catholic political philosophers of the Twentieth-Century we can number:

Socialists [including Marxists]: Albert de Mun (1841-1914); Henri Savatier (1855-1952); Fr. John A. Ryan (1865-1945); Fr. Luigi Sturzo (1871-1959); the poet Charles Péguy (1873-1914) [who converted to Catholicism and died in the First World War]; Marc Sangnier (1873-1950), who founded Le Sillon (1894-1910); Peter Maurin (1877-1949) [who founded the Catholic Worker Movement (1933)]; Eric Gill (1882-1940); Theodor Steinbüchel (1888-1949); Gabriel Le Bras (1891-1970); Ammon Hennacy (1893-1970); the death-bed convert Arnaud Dandieu (1897-1933), founder of L'Ordre Nouveau (1930-); Louis-Joseph Lebret, O.P. (1897-1966) who founded Économie et humanisme (1942); Maurice Laudrain (c. 1900-1985), founder of the journal Terre Nouvelle (1935-); Jean Lacroix (1900-1986); André Cruiziat (1904-1998), founder of La Vie Nouvelle (1947-); the Jewish convert Alexandre Marc (1904-2000), founder of L'Ordre Nouveau (1930-); Emmanuel Mounier (1905-1950), who founded Esprit in 1931; Mikolaus Monzel (1906-1960), at the University of Munich; Heinrich Mertens (1906-1968); Étienne Borne (1907-1993); Henri Chambre, S.J. (1908-1994); Stefan Kisielewski (1911-1991), founder of Znak (1956-1976); the Canadian convert Marshall McLuhan (1911-1980); Walter J. Ong, S.J. (1912-2003); the convert John C. Cort (1913-2006); Roger Garaudy (1913-) [a convert who has recently converted to Islam]; Henri Desroche, O.P. (1914-1994); René Rémond (1918-); Franco Rodano (1920-1993); Jean-Marie Doménach (1922-1997), editor of Esprit; Charles Davis, O.P. (1923-1999) [who left the Catholic Church]; the Slovenian Bishop Vekoslav Grmic (1923-2005); Michel de Certeau, S.J. (1925-1986); Fr. Giulio Girardi (1926-); Fr. Ivan Illich (1926-2002); the Pole Leszek Kolakowski (1927-2009) [who grew closer to Catholicism at the end of his life]; Jean-Yves Calvez, S.J. (1927-); Michael Harrington (1928-1989); Laurence Bright, O.P. (c. 1928-); the Englishman Brian Wicker (1929-) who founded New Left Catholicism in England; Arthur F. McGovern, S.J. (c. 1935-); Terry Eagleton (1943-), who founded Slant (1964-1970); Guy Coq (c. 1955-), editor of Esprit; Marc-Olivier Padis (c. 1955-), editor of Esprit.

The noted Catholic liberation theologians are also socialistic in outlook such as: Gunter Rodolfo Kusch (1922-1979); Arturo Roig (1922-); the Peruvian Augusto Salazar Bondy (1925-1974); Juan Luis Segundo, S.J. (1925-1997); Gustavo Gutierrez, O.P. (1928-); Johann Baptiste Metz (1928-); Ignacio Ellacuria, S.J. (1930-1989) [assassinated]; Franz Hinkelammert (1931-); Hugo Assmann, S.J. (1933-2008); Fernando Cardenal, S.J. (1934-); Enrique Dussel (1934-); Virgilio Elizondo (1935-); Leonardo Boff, O.F.M. (1938-); Juan Carlos Scannone, S.J. (c. 1938-); John Sobrino, S.J. (1938-); Pedro Trigo, S.J. (1942-); Horacio Cerutti-Guldberg (1950-); Osvaldo Ardiles (1952-); Anibal Fornari (c. 1957-); Gerhard Kruip (1957-).

Liberals: Lord John Acton (1834-1902); Bernard Vaughan, S.J. (1847-1922); Franz Hitze (1851-1921); Damián Isern y Marco (1852-1914); Andrea Cappellazzi (1854-1932); Fr. Heinrich Brauns (1868-1939); Friedrich Wilhelm Foerster (1869-1962); Angel Amor Ruibal; Karl Otto Petraschek (1876-1950); Fr. Ignaz Seipel (1876-1932); Yves de la Briere, S.J. (1877-1941); Maurice Defourny (1878-1953); Francesco Carnelutti (1879-1965); Emil Erich Holscher (1880-1935); Joseph Vialatoux (1880-1970); Leonardo Coimbra (1883-1936); Götz Briefs (1889-1974); Oswald von Nell-Breuning, S.J. (1890-1991); Paul Jostock (1895-1965); Stanislas Fumet (1896-1983); Gaston Fessard, S.J. (1897-1979); Louis-Joseph Lebret, O.P. (1897-1966); John Francis Cronin (c. 1898-1970); Ignatius Theodore Eschmann, O.P. (1898-1968); Anton Hilckman (1900-1970); Franz Hermann Mueller (1900-1994); the convert Waldemar Gurian (1902-1954), who founded the Review of Politics (1939); Eberhard Welty, O.P. (1902-1965); the Austrian Eugen Kogon (1903-1987) [imprisoned under the National Socialists]; François Perroux (1903-1987), at the College de France; Luis Recasens Siches (1903-1977); John Courtney Murray, S.J. (1904-1967); the Spaniard Louis Legaz Lacambra (1906-1980) [Department of Education from 1962 to 1968]; the Spaniard Jose Luis Lopez Aranguren (1909-1996); Fr. Jose Maria Diez Alegria (1911-); the convert Ernst Friedrich Schumacher (1911-1977); the Mexican Leopoldo Zea (1912-2004); Joaquin Ruiz-Gimenez Cortes (1913-2009) [Spanish Minister of Education from 1951-1956]; the Spaniard Jose Todoli Duque, O.P. (1915-1999); René Rémond (1917-2007) [member of the French Academy; Pontifical Academy of Social Sciences]; Gabriel Bowe, O.P. (1923-); the Australian Alan Donagan (1925-1991); Manfred Hättich (1925-2003); the Spaniard Victorino Rodríguez y Rodríguez, O.P. (1926-); Adriano Bausola (1930-); Pietro Giuseppe Grasso (1930-); Fr. Jozef Tischner (1931-2000); the English-Canadian politician Charles Taylor (1931-) [a founder of Communitarianism]; the Czech Nikolaus Lobkowicz (1931-); Alain Besançon (1932-); the Spaniard Fr. Joseph de Torre (1932-), Opus Dei; Jacques Garello (c. 1934-); Helmut Peukert (1934-) [former priest; Pragmatism]; Herbert Schambeck (1934-); Fr. Patrick de Laubier (1935-); Francesco Gentile (1936-); John Aloysius Coleman, S.J. (1937-); R. Bruce Douglass (c. 1937-); Mary Ann Glendon (1938-), at the University of Harvard; Thomas De Koninck (c. 1940-); John Langan, S.J. (1940-); Jean-Marie Donegani (1948-); Robert Kraynak (1949-); Pierre Manent (1949-); Fr. J. Bryan Hehir (c. 1950-), at the University of Harvard; John F. Kavanaugh, S.J. (c. 1950-); Patrick Riordan (1950-); Christopher Wolfe (c. 1950-) [also Natural Law Theorist]; Fr. Robert Sirico (1951-), who founded the Acton Institute; Jean-Marc Trigeaud (1951-); Eugene James Dionne (1952-); Edmund Arens (1953-) [Pragmatism]; John P. Hittinger (c. 1954-); Gregory M.A. Gronbacher (c. 1955-); Paul J. Weithman (1959-); Vittorio Hösle (1960-); Flavio Felice (c. 1965-), founder of the Centro Studi Tocqueville-Acton; the Australian Samuel Gregg (c. 1965-), of the Acton Institute (1990-).

Natural Law Theorists: Theodor Meyer, S.J. (1821-1913), Hieronymus Noldin, S.J. (1838-1922); the Belgian Auguste Castelein, S.J. (c. 1840-1915); Santo Schiffini, S.J. (1841-1906); Georg von Hertling (1843-1919) [Prime Minister of Bavaria]; Albert Maria Weiß, O.P. (1844-1925); Viktor Cathrein, S.J. (1845-1931); Joseph Rickaby, S.J. (1845-1932); the Cardinal Louis Billot, S.J. (1846-1931); Manuel Polo y Peyrolón (1846-1918); Heinrich Pesch, S.J. (1854-1926); the Sulpician Adolphe Tanquerey (1854-1932); Anton Koch (1859-1915); Joseph Mausbach (1861-1931); Antonin-Gilbert Sertillanges (1863-1948) [member of the Academy of Moral and Political Sciences]; Dominikus Prümmer, O.P. (1866-1931); Marie-Benoît Schwalm, O.P. (1866-1908); Otto Schilling (1874-1956); Giorgio Del Vecchio (1878-1970); Auguste Valensin, S.J. (1879-1953); Odo Lottin, O.S.B. (1880-1965); Jacques Maritain (1882-1973); Alfred O'Rahilly, S.J. (1884-1969); Gallus Manser (1886-1950); the Belgian Canon Jacques Leclercq (1891-1971); the Austrian Johannes Messner (1891-1984); Heinrich A. Rommen (1897-1967); Yves Simon (1901-1961); Felice Battaglia (1902-1977); John Cuthbert Ford, S.J. (1902-1989); Thomas Gilby, O.P. (1902-1975); Alessandro Passerin d'Entreves (1902-1985); Fr. Osvaldo Lira (1904-1996); John Courtney Murray, S.J. (1904-1967); Vernon J. Bourke (1907-1998); Gustave Ermecke (1907-1987); Ismael Quiles, S.J. (c. 1907-1995); Joseph Fuchs, S.J. (1912-2005) [Proportionalist]; Philippe Delhaye (1912-1990); Michel Villey (1914-1988), at the Sorbonne; Jean-Marie Aubert (1916-); Cardinal Cahil Daly (1917-2009); the Spaniard Juan Vallet de Goytisolo (1917-); Giovanni Ambrosetti (c. 1920-); Sergio Cotta (1920-2007); Mieczyslaw Albert Maria Krapiec, O.P. (1921-2008); Pietro Piovani (1922-1980); William E. May (1928-) [New Natural Law]; Rudolf Weiler (1928-); Germain Grisez (1929-) [New Natural Law]; Alasdair MacIntyre (1929-) [Communitarian]; Ralph McInerny (1929-); Charles E. Rice (1931-); the Austrian Wolfgang Waldstein (c. 1934-); Franz Böckle (c. 1935-); Reginaldo M. Pizzorni (c. 1935-); Lloyd Weinreb (1936-), at the University of Harvard; Stephen Theron (1939-); John Finnis (1940-), at the University of Oxford [New Natural Law]; Alfonso Gómez-Lobo (1940-); Joseph Boyle (1942-) [New Natural Law]; Anthony J. Lisska (c. 1943-) [Analytical Thomist]; Philip E. Divine (1944-); Josef Seifert (1945-); Rocco Buttiglione (1948-); Russell Hittinger (1949-); Fr. Michael

Bertram Crowe (c. 1950-); the Swiss convert Martin Rhonheimer (1950-), Opus Dei; Janet E. Smith (1950-); the convert from atheism Jay Budziszewski (1952-); Eberhard Schockenhoff (1953-); Howard Kainz (c. 1954-); the convert Jay Budziszewski (c. 1955-); Robert P. George (1955-), at the University of Princeton [New Natural Law]; Patrick de Laubier (1935-); Francesco D'Agostino (1946-); Jean Porter (1955-); Douglas Kries (1958-); Domingo Basso, O.P. (c. 1960-); Anthony Battaglia (c. 1961-); Miguel Ayuso Torres (1961-); Bebhinn Donnelly (c. 1965-); Matthew Levering (1971-); Graham McAleer (c. 1965-); Mark Murphy (c. 1968-); Ana Marta González (1969-); Christopher Kaczor (1969-); Fulvio Di Blasi (c. 1970-).

Conservatives: Bishop José Torras y Bages (1846-1916); Charles Stanton Devas (1848-1906); Hippolyte Gayraud, O.P. (1856-1911) [known for his anti-Semitic political platform; Neo-Thomist]; the Spaniard Marcelino Menéndez y Pelayo (1856-1912); Juan Vázquez de Mella (1861-1928) [Neo-Thomist]; Vincent McNabb, O.P. (1868-1943) [Catholic Land Movement]; Hillaire Belloc (1870-1953) [Catholic Land Movement]; Albert Jay Nock (1873-1945); the convert Gilbert Keith Chesterton (1874-1936) [Catholic Land Movement]; Arthur Joseph Penty (1875-1937) [Catholic Land Movement]; Jacques Bainville (1879-1936); the Portuguese Alfredo Pimenta (1882-1950); the convert Henri Massis (1886-1970); Carl Schmitt (1888-1985) [excommunicated]; the convert poet Allen Tate (1889-1979) [Agrarian]; the British convert Christopher Dawson (1889-1970); Leo R. Ward, C.S.C. (1893-1984); Richard Nikolaus von Coudenhove-Kalergi (1894-1972); Léon de Montaigne de Poncins (1897-1976) [anti-Semitic writer]; Wilhelm Röpke (1899-1966); Friedrich von Hayek (1899-1992 [Nobel Prize in Economics]; the Hungarian convert Aurel Kolnai (1900-1973); the convert Marxist spy Whittaker Chambers (1901-1961) [who famously implicated Harry Dexter White and Alger Hiss as soviet spies]; the convert Francis Graham Wilson (1901-1976); Eric Voeglin (1901-1985); the convert Ross J.S. Hoffman (1902-1979); the convert Christopher Hollis (1902-1977); the convert Mortimer J. Adler (1902-2001); Bertrand de Jouvenal (1903-1987); Josef Pieper (1904-1997); the Belgian Marcel de Corte (1905-1994); the Spaniard Jose Corts Grau (1905-1995); Fr. Julio Meinvielle (1905-1973) [Anti-Semitic]; Jean de Fabregues (1906-1983); Robert Brasillach (1909-1945) [student of Marcel who was executed after World War II for his work with the Vichy Regime]; the convert Willmoore Kendall (1909-1968); the death-bed convert Frank Meyer (1909-1972); the Austrian-American Erik Maria von Kühnelt-Leddihn (1909-1999); Augusto Del Noce (1910-1989); Ernest vanden Haag (1914-2002), at Fordham University; Barbara Ward (1914-1981); Pierre Boutang (1916-1998); Rafael Calvo Serer (1916-1988), Opus Dei; Peter Robert Edwin Viereck (1916-2006) [Pulitzer Prize]; Francisco Elias de Tejada y Spinola (1917-1978); Juan Vallet de Goytisolo (1917-); the convert Russell Kirk (1918-1994), founder of Modern Age (1957-); Francis P. Canavan, S.J. (1918-2009); Harry V. Jaffa (1918-); Jean Madiran

(1920-); Rafael Gambra Ciudad (1920-2004); Marcel Clément (1921-2005); the Hungarian Thomas Molnar (1921-); Stephen J. Tonsor (1923-); Frederick D. Wilhelmsen (c. 1923-); William F. Buckley (1925-2008) who founded National Review (1955-); the convert Leo Brent Bozell (1926-1997) who founded Triumph (1966-); Judge John T. Noonan (1926-); William Marra (1928-1998); James V. Schall, S.J. (1928-); George Francis McLean (1929-); Pietro Giuseppe Grasso (1930-); the convert Jeffrey Hart (1930-); James McFadden (c. 1931-1999) who founded Human Life Review (1975-); Robert Novak (1931-2009); Ellis Sandoz (1931-); George Westcott Carey (1933-); Michael Novak (1933-); Melvin E. Bradford (1934-1993); Medford Stanton Evans (1934-); Garry Wills (1934-); Francesco Gentile (1936-); the convert Richard John Neuhuas (1936-2009) who founded First Things (1990-); George Panichas (c. 1937-); Dale Vree (c. 1940-), founder of New Oxford Review (1977-); Giancarlo Giurovich (1943-2000); Claes Gösta Ryn (1943-); the Canadian Richard Bastien (1944-); George H. Nash (1945-); the convert M. Joseph Sobran (1946-); Chantal Delsol (1947-); William Donohue (1947-), of the Catholic League; Rocco Buttiglione (1948-); E. Michael Jones (1948-); Allan C. Calrson (1949-) [Agrarian]; Peggy Noonan (1950-); Peter Augustine Lawler (1951-); George Weigel (1951-); Roger Kimball (1953-); Bruce Frohnen (c. 1955-); James Kalb (c. 1955-); Remi Fontaine (1956-); the Canadian Jean Renaud (1957-); Denis Sureau (1958-); Joseph Bottum (c. 1960-); Dinesh D'Szousa (1961-); Sean Hannity (1961-); the Dutch scholar Andreas Kinneging (1962-); Thomas E. Woods (1972-).

3   Other Nazi critics include the prominent Catholic Action proponents Fritz Gerlich (1883-1934) and Erich Klausener (1885-1934) who were put to death during the even earlier purge of the Night of the Long Knives in 1934; as well as the Catholic philosophers and theologians Friedrich Wilhelm Foerster (1869-1962); Arnold Rademacher (1873-1939); Bernhard Lichtenberg (1875-1943) [who died on the way to a concentration camp]; Wilhelm Neuss (1880-1965); Laurentius Siemer, O.P. (1888-1956) [who was imprisoned]; Erich Przywara, S.J. (1889-1972); Romano Guardini (1885-1968); Fr. Georg Moenius (1890-1953); Ignatius Eschmann, O.P. (1898-1968) [who was imprisoned in a concentration camp]; Anton Hilckman (1900-1970) [who was imprisoned]; Gertrud Luckner (1900-1995); Aurel Kolnai (1900-1973); and Eugen Kolgon (1903-1987) [who was imprisoned in a concentration camp].

4   Translation from Moran, Dermot, *Introduction to Phenomenology* (London: Routledge, 2000), p. 127. Other paginations are from Edmund Husserl, *Ideas* [ID] (London: Collier, 1931), *Logical Investigations* [LI], 2 vols (London: Routledge, 1970), *Experience and Judgment* [EJ] (Evanston: Northwestern University Press, 1975), and *Cartesian Meditations* [CM] (New York: Kluwer, 1977).

5   For information on the life and thought of Edith Stein see: DTC (1939), Tables générales, p. 4076; IEC (1953), v. IX, pp. 1314-1315; PM (1960), v. I,

pp. 223-224; CP (1988), v. II, pp. 650-665; DP (1993), v. II, pp. 2700-2701;
HCEC (1995), p. 1223; BDTC (1996), p. 749; EEP (1997), pp. 679-683;
ICEA (1997), pp. 477-492; BBKL (1999), v. XV, pp. 1318-1340; LTK (2000),
v. IX, p. 1946; OHYP (2001), pp. 142-144, 215; PAMP (2002), pp. 451-474;
PWW (2002), pp. 232-239, 648-656; NCE (2003), v. XIII, pp. 505-506;
ACP (2005), pp. 350-356; EP (2005), v. IX, pp. 239-241; EF (2006), v. XI,
pp. 11073-11075; her autobiography *Life in a Jewish Family: 1891-1916* [*Aus
dem Leben einer jüdischen Familie (1965; 1985)*], tr. Josephine Koeppel (Wash-
ington: ICS Publications, 1986); and also Graef, Hilda, *The Scholar and the
Cross: The Life and Works of Edith Stein* (Westminster, Maryland: Newman
Press, 1955); Collins, James, *Three Paths in Philosophy* (Chicago, Illinois: Henry
Regnery, 1962), pp. 85-105; Elders, Leo, ed., *Edith Stein: Leben, Philosophie,
Vollendung* (Würzburg: Naumann, 1991); Herbstrith, Waltraud, *Denken
im Dialog: Zur Philosophie Edith Steins* (Tübingen: Attempt Verlag, 1991);
Matzker, Reiner, *Einfühlung: Edith Stein und die Phänomenologie* (Frankfurt:
Peter Lang, 1991); Herbstrith, Waltraud, *Edith Stein: A Biography*, tr. Bernard
Bonowitz (San Francisco: Ignatius Press, 1992); Müller, Andreas, *Grundzüge
der Religionsphilosophie von Edith Stein* (Freiburg: Alber, 1993); Bejás, Andrés,
*Vom Seienden als solchen zum Sinn des Seins: Die Transzendentalienlehre bei
Edith Stein und Thomas von Aquin* (Frankfurt: Peter Lang, 1994); Sculz, Peter,
Edith Steins Theorie der Person (Freiburg: Alber, 1994); Hecker, Herbert;
Phänomenologie des Christlichen bei Edith Stein (Würzburg, Echter, 1995);
Waithe, Mary, ed., *A History of Women Philosophers*, ed. Mary Ellen Waithe
(Dordrecht: Kluwer, 1995), v. IV, pp. 157-187; McAlister, Linda, ed., *Hypatia's
Daughters: Fifteen Hundred Years of Women Philosophers* (Bloomington: Indi-
ana University Press, 1996), pp. 267-279, Baseheart, Mary Catherine, *Person
in the World: Introduction to the Philosophy of Edith Stein* (Dordrecht: Kluwer,
1997); Herbstrith, Waltraud, *Edith Stein: Etappen eines philosophischen Werde-
gangs* (Munich: Neue Stadt, 1997); Sawicki, Marianne, *Body, Text, and Science:
The Literacy of Investigative Practices and the Phenomenology of Edith Stein* (Dordrecht: Kluwer, 1997); Herbstrith, Waltraud, ed., *Never Forget: Christian and
Jewish Perspectives on Edith Stein*, tr. Susanne Batzdorff (Washington, D.C.:
ICS Publications, 1998); Kavunguvalappil, Antony, *Theology of Suffering and
the Cross in the Life and Works of Blessed Edith Stein* (Frankfurt: Peter Lang,
1998); Petermeier, Maria, *Die Religiöse Entwicklung der Edith Stein* (Frankfurt:
Peter Lang, 1998); Fisher, Linda, ed., *Feminist Philosophy* (Dordrecht: Kluwer,
2000), pp. 213-235; Ales Bello, Angela, and Daniel Martino, eds., *The Phi-
losophy of Edith Stein* (Pittsburgh: Duquesne University Press, 2001); Oben,
Freda, *The Life and Thought of St. Edith Stein* (New York: Alba House, 2001);
Quito, Emerita, *Phenomenology: Edmund Husserl and Edith Stein* (Malate: De
La Salle University Press, 2001); Reichardt, Mary, *Catholic Women Writers: A
Bio-Bibliographical Sourcebook* (Westport: Greenwood Press, 2001), pp. 362-
368; Wulf, Claudia, *Freiheit und Grenze: Edith Steins Anthropologie und ihre
erkenntnistheoretischen Implikationen* (Vallendar: Patris Verlag, 2002); Borden,

Sarah, *Edith Stein* (London: Continuum, 2003); Beckmann-Zöller, Beate, and Hanna Gerl-Falkovitz, *Die unbekannte Edith Stein: Phänomenologie und Sozialphilosophie* (Frankfurt: Peter Lang, 2006); MacIntyre, Alasdair, *Edith Stein: A Philosophical Prologue, 1913-1922* (Lanham: Rowman & Littlefield, 2006); Calcagno, Antonio, *The Philosophy of Edith Stein* (Pittsburgh: Duquesne University Press, 2007); Maskulak, Marian, *Edith Stein and the Body-Soul-Spirit at the Center of Holistic Formation* (Frankfurt: Peter Lang, 2007); *American Catholic Philosophical Quarterly* 82:1 (2008) [Special Edition on Stein]; Sharkey, Sarah Borden, *Thine Own Self: Individuality in Edith Stein's Later Writings* (Washington: Catholic University of America Press, 2009).

6   Other philosophical writings of Stein are *On the Problem of Empathy* [*Zum Problem der Einfühlung*] [OPE] *(1917); An Investigation concerning the State* [*Eine Untersuchung über den Staat*] [ICS] [written 1921] (1925); *Introduction to Philosophy* [*Einführung in die Philosophie*] [IP] [written 1920-1931] (1991); *The Structure of the Human Person* [*Der Aufbau der menschlichen Person*] [SHP] [Münster Lectures of 1932-1933] (1994); *What Is the Human?: A Theological Anthropology* [*Was ist der Mensch? Eine theologische Anthropologie*] [WIH] [written 1933] (1994); *Women's Education and Occupations* [*Frauenbildung und Frauenberufe*] [written 1928-1933] (1949; 1959); her major Scholastic work *Finite and Eternal Being* [*Endliches und ewiges Sein*] [FEB] (written in 1936-1937; published in 1950); *World and Person* [*Welt und Person*] [WP] (1962); *Potency and Act: Studies toward a Philosophy of Being* [*Potenz und Akt: Studien zu einer Philosophie des Seins*] [PA] [written 1931] (1998); *The Woman: Reflections and Questions* [*Die Frau. Reflexionen und Fragestellungen*] (2000); *Education and Development of Individuality* [*Bildung und Entfaltung der Individualität*] [Essays of 1926-1933] (2001); and *Contributions to Phenomenology and Ontology* [*Beiträge zu Phänomenologie und Ontologie*] (2009).

Stein's philosophical writings have been translated as *On the Problem of Empathy* [OPE], tr. Waltraut Stein (Washington: ICS Publications, 1989); *Essays on Women*, tr. Freda Mary Oben (Washington: ICS Publications, 1996); *Philosophy of Psychology and the Humanities* [translation of *Psychical Causality* [PC] and *Individual and Community* [IC], tr. Mary Catherine Baseheart and Marianne Sawicki (Washington: ICS Publications, 2000)]; *Finite and Eternal Being* [FEB], tr. Kurt Reinhardt (Washington: ICS Publications, 2002); and *An Investigation concerning the State* [ICS], tr. Marianne Sawicki (Washington: ICS Publications, 2006). These translations form part of *The Collected Works of Edith Stein* (CWES), 11 vols. (Washington: ICS Publications, 1986-) and are made use of here.

Philosophical essays written by Stein include:"Was ist Phänomenologie?" in *Wissenschaftliche Beilage zur Neuen Pfälzischen Landes-Zeitung* 5 (May 15, 1924);"Husserls Phänomenologie und die Philosophie des hl. Thomas von Aquino," *Jahrbuch für Philosophie und phänomenologische Forschung Erganzungsband.* (1929), *pp*. 315-338 [translated as "Husserl and Aquinas"

["HA"] in *Knowledge and Faith* (Washington: ICS Publications, 2000), pp. 8-61]; "Was ist Philosophie?: Ein Gespräch zwischen Edmund Husserl und Thomas von Aquino" [1929] in ESW, vol. 15 (1993), pp. 19-48; "Aktuelles und ideales Sein—Species—Urbild und Abbild" [1931] in ESW, vol. 15 (1993), pp. 57-63; "Erkenntnis, Wahrheit, Sein" [1932] in ESW, vol. 15 (1993), pp. 49-56 [translated as "Knowledge, Truth, Being," ["KTB,"] in *Knowledge and Faith* (Washington: ICS Publications, 2000, pp. 65-73]; "La Phénoménologie," *Journée d'études de la Société thomiste de Juvisy* (1932), v. I, pp. 75, 88, 101-109; "Die deutsche Summa," *Die christliche Frau* 32 (August-September, 1934), pp. 245-252 and (October 1934), pp. 276-281; "Martin Heideggers Existentialphilosophie" [1935-1936 Appendix to *Endliches und ewiges Sein*], in ESW, vol. 6 (1962), pp. 69-135; "Entwurf eines Vorworts zu *Endliches und ewiges Sein*" [1935-1936], in ESW, vol. 15 (1993), pp. 63-64; "Wege der Gotteserkenntnis: Die symbolische Theologie des Areopagiten und ihre sachlichen Voraussetzung," [1940-1941] in ESW, vol. 15 (1993), pp. 65-127 [translated as "Ways to Know God," ["WKG"] in *Knowledge and Faith* (Washington: ICS Publications, 2000), pp. 83-114]. Many of these essays have been translated as *Knowledge and Faith*, tr. Walter Redmond (Washington: ICS Publications, 2000).

The complete writings of Edith Stein are collected in the *Edith Steins Werke* [ESW], 18 vols. (Freiburg: Herder, 1950-1998) and *Edith Stein Gesamtausgabe* [ESGA], 25 vols. (Freiburg: Neyer, 2000-2009).

Finally Stein authored various poems, prayers, and hymns: indeed her German version of Psalm 61 ("Erhör o Gott mein Flehen") was made a part of the official German Prayer Book, the *Gotteslob* (1975; 1996), hymn #302.

7   Stein in fact gives a quite detailed phenomenological description of human freedom. She argues that an indisputable fact of self-consciousness is that human persons possess a free will wherein the will is the final determiner of an action (hence she often calls the will the 'fiat' [let it be done] of decision-making). That is to say, when one acts one experiences the "switching on of the machine," the initiation of the process of willing (OPE, III, p. 55 [61]; FEB, VII, 3, p. 372; VIII, 3, p. 504; PC, III, 4, p. 52; WIH?, II, pp. 52-74; ICS, I, 2, pp. 68-72; PA, V, 8, pp. 141-143). Stein comments: "if we take a look at the inception of action (or, of a mere doing), the 'fiat!' with which the action is set into motion, we see that it belongs necessarily to each genuine doing—even if it be a purely mental doing—as an inner jolt. Going out from the jolt, the doing starts to run its course" (PC, III, 4, p. 57; cf. PC, III, 4, pp. 58, 60; IV, 4, pp. 70, 73).

Stein was not unaware of the fact that humans are bodily creatures and so that their behavior can be affected by: a) various pre-existing inclinations [aspirings; stances] (a wanting to do something); b) resolves (a resolving to do something whether one wants to or not); and c) rational motives (reasons)

(PC, III, 3-4, pp. 51, 56; IV, 1, p. 61; IV, 3-4, pp. 69-71; V, 4, pp. 88, 91-92; IC, I, 3, p. 171; IV, 4, p. 269). Yet she argues that in the end, as creatures with a free will, humans always have the freedom to choose for or against a given inclination/resolve/motive (to declare one's allegiance to it, to give oneself over to it, to let it take possession of oneself). So for instance one can use one's will to accept the wish (inclination) to take a recreational trip or to resolve to overcome a hesitancy to take an examination. If this is the case inclinations, resolves, and motives limit (or delimit) our behavior without determining it. (PC, III, 3-4, pp. 49-50, 52; IV, 1, pp. 61, 64; IV, 3, p. 69; IC, IV, 4, p. 269; OPE, III, p. 55 [61]). Stein comments:

> "... suppose I have made up my mind to make an important communication to someone at an opportune moment. I get together with him, and in the course of the conversation the 'favorable moment' presents itself. As soon as that becomes clear to me, I say to myself 'now!' and start my communication. Saying now is not the renewal of a resolve with which I was 'brimming over' the whole time; rather, it's the 'fiat!' that leads from the resolve to the performance. ... Perhaps I see someone haul off to take a punch at someone else, and I seize him by the arm. The action is produced out of the stance 'that shouldn't be!' without any further ado. ... Yet you can still detect a jolt the action initiates. ... Insofar as the ego comes into consideration at all as a radiation point of required acts and does not degenerate into the blind tool of someone else's will, you can still detect the jolt that initiates any doing; otherwise we've got no doing at all. Free acts for us are synonymous with the 'doing' of the ego, and we can define the realm of free acts by the fact that they, and they alone, can emerge out of a resolve and must be initiated by a 'fiat!'" (PC, III, 4, pp. 57-58).

And while some philosophers have argued that "free choice" is an illusion as it is really only a matter of the stronger inclination (or motive) winning out, Stein argues that ultimately it is the will which determines which of two competing inclinations (in what Stein calls a Buridan's ass situation) wins out, that is to say the will chooses which inclination to make the stronger one. Hence one can have an inclination to go on a hike but suppress it with the will due to one's having made up one's mind to finish one's work, and so make the latter inclination the stronger one (PC, IV, 4, pp. 72-73; V, 4, p. 91). In a similar manner I might know that I could cheer up a sick individual by reassuring him of his imminent recovery but refuse to do so by choosing to follow a counter motive to not say what I am not convinced of (PC, III, 4, p. 55; V, 5, p. 96; FEB, VII, 5, pp. 401-402; OPE, IV, p. 97 [108]). It is here worthwhile looking at some longer passages of Stein regarding conflicts of motivation:

> "... with inclinations ... we have to distinguish between voluntariness, and the freedom to accept them or refuse them, to allow them to become operative within us or to renounce them. Suppose I accept an inclination. That means I give myself over to it, I allow it to take possession of me. That is not yet to say that the

inclining leads to a doing, or that it converts into a willing. For example, the wish awakens in me to make a recreational trip. I accept it as a wish, I don't shut it out, I give it room, and it develops into an intense desire for relaxation for the beauty of the countryside, for fresh air and sunshine. However, alongside of this desire there exists in me the firm resolve to deal first with the work that I've begun, and the desire is not allowed to arrive at its natural consequence. I do not will the trip, and I do not carry it out" (PC, IV, 1, pp. 61-62).

... if I'm stuck in the struggle of conflicting motives, if I'm placed before a decision, still I am the one to whom the decision falls. The decision does not impose itself automatically, as the tipping of the scales toward the side of the 'weightier' motive indicates. Rather, I make up my mind in its favor *because* it is weightier. Even if more can be said for the doing than for the abstaining, the doing still requires my '*fiat*!'. I can grant it according to the 'weightiness,' but I can also grant it without carrying out any weighing of motives or, finally, when the motives look equally weighty to me. Thus, free acts presuppose a motive. But besides that, they require an impulse that is not motivated itself" (PC, III, 4, p. 55; cf. PC, III, 4, p. 59; IV, 1, pp. 61-62, 64; IV, 3-4, pp. 70-73; IC, I, 3, pp. 193-194).

8   Mention should also be made of Stein's *Finite and Eternal Being* (1950) wherein Stein discusses a "pointing of the visible world beyond itself as a natural revelation of God" ("WKG," Appendix, p. 126; cf. "WKG," II, 4, pp. 112-113; Appendix, pp. 125, 128; FEB, II, 7, p. 59; SHP, I, pp. 32; III, pp. 60-61, 65; VII, p.150; WIH?, II, pp. 40-52; V, pp. 174-223) [Stein here uses the German word for pointing [*Verweisung*] in contrast to the Thomistic notion of a proof [*Beweis*] for God and in contrast to Scheler's notion of a disclosure [*Aufweis*] of God].

One such pointing is a dim awareness of another being who is the support and ground of my own unsupported and groundless being. For I can experience the feeling of being secure in the world which counteracts the anxiety that comes by grasping my own nothingness (FEB, II, 7, pp. 56, 59; VI, 4, p. 344). Here is how Stein encapsulates this "referring" to God's existence: "The nullity and transiency of its own being becomes clearly manifest to the ego once its thinking seizes upon its own being and seeks to lay bare its deepest roots. But the ego also touches upon these depths of its own being prior to all reflective and retrospective existential analysis in the experience of anxiety [*Angst*] ... this anxiety or dread is the fear of being no more, and it is thus the experience of anxiety which 'brings people face to face with nothingness.' ... The undeniable fact that my being is limited in its transience from moment to moment and thus exposed to the possibility of nothingness is counterbalanced by the equally undeniable fact that despite this transience, I am, that from moment to moment I am sustained in my being, and that in my fleeting being I share in enduring being. In the knowledge that being holds me, I rest securely. This security, however, is not the self-assurance of one who under her own power stands on firm ground, but rather the sweet and blissful security of a child that is lifted up and carried by a strong arm. ... In my own being, then, I encounter another kind of being that is not mine but that is the support and ground of my own unsupported and groundless being. ... The ground and support of my being—as of all finite being—can ultimately be only one being which is not some received being (as is all human being). It must be a necessary being, i.e., it must differ from everything that has a beginning in that it alone cannot not be. Because the being of this existent is not received being, there cannot be any separation between what it is (and what could or could not be) and its actual existence: It must be its very act of existing. ... Everything temporal is as such fleeting and therefore needs an eternal hold or support. ... The security which I experience in my fleeting existence indicates that I am immediately anchored in an ultimate hold and ground (notwithstanding the fact that there may also be some mediate supports of my being). But this experience is a rather dim and indefinite feeling that can hardly be called knowledge" (FEB, II, 7, pp. 57-59; cf. FEB, III, 12, pp. 105-106, 109-111, 119; VI, 4, p. 354; "HA," II, p. 21).

In this work, Stein also discusses two ways in which Revelation can aid philosophy. First, Revelation can help correct the ideas generated by philosophy as revelation is the measure of all truth [Stein calls this the formal dependence of philosophy on faith] (FEB, Introduction, 2, 4, pp. 5, 12-13, 21, 23, 25, 28-29; "HA," II, pp. 17-19; "WKG," II, 4, pp. 107, 109). Second, Revelation can supply new content for philosophy to ponder [Stein calls this the material dependence of philosophy on faith] (FEB, Introduction, 4, pp. 13, 21-23; "HA," II, pp. 17-19; "WKG," II, 4, pp. 107, 109; SHP, II, pp. 49-51; VII, pp. 161-162). For revelation (faith) supplies reason with the notions of the Incarnation (Christ is the incarnate God and is one person with two natures), the Trinity (God is one nature with three persons), original sin, redemption, supernatural perfection, and the Eucharist, notions reason by itself is incapable of discovering (FEB, Introduction, 2, 4, pp. 2-3, 21-23; III, 12, p. 119). And revelation can also supply philosophy with new content for incorporation that it has not yet been able to grasp by its own resources even though philosophy possesses the ability do so, such as the notions of creation and the origin of the soul (FEB, Introduction, 4, pp. 23, 25-26; III, 12, p. 120; V, 13, p. 308): "certain tasks which they [philosophers] would never have envisaged without this additional theological knowledge" (FEB, Introduction, 4, p. 23; cf. FEB, Introduction, 2, 4, pp. 5, 12-13, 23, 25, 28-29; SHP, IV, p. 73). Stein speaks of this twofold dependency of philosophy upon theology as follows: "Grace purifies and strengthens the human intellect, making it less vulnerable to error. ... Christian doctrine also enriches philosophy with certain concepts (such as that of creation) which actually remained foreign to it as long as it did not draw from this source (though it was never intrinsically impossible for it to discover them)" (FEB, Introduction, 4, p. 21; cf. "HA," II, p. 17). Stein thus affirms a "Christian philosophy" following Maritain wherein philosophy "in order to arrive at a more comprehensive knowledge of things that are ... appropriates for itself the answers given by Christian theology" (*Finite and Eternal Being,*

Introduction, 4, p. 24 and n. 18 pp. 548-550). So we need not fear a corruption of philosophy by revelation, as, following Przywara, "philosophy reaches its perfection with the aid of theology, not by being itself transformed into theology" [durch Theologie, nicht als Theologie; literally 'through theology, not as theology'] (FEB, Introduction, 4, p. 25).

As example of an area in which theology has perfected philosophy is that of the Trinity. Stein argues that once we possess the idea of the triune God from Scripture, we can go on to recognize the image of the Trinity (wherein the effect is a representation of the cause) in both humans and in nature [contra Aquinas who held that nature displayed only a vestige of the Trinity (wherein the nature of the cause can merely be inferred from the effect)] (FEB, VII, 9, p. 464; n. 1 on p. 596; n. 88 on p. 604).

Humans manifest an image of the Trinity in several ways. First, they are made up of body (or a circumscribed and outward expression of their essence; the Son), a soul (or a life-source or well-spring that molds itself into the body; the Father), and a spirit (or a free self-transcending being; the Holy Spirit) (FEB, VII, 7, pp. 422-423; VII, 9, pp. 434, 462-464). Second, following Augustine, the soul itself consists of mind [Father], knowledge [Son], and love [Holy Spirit] (or in another conception of memory, intellect, and will) (FEB, VII, 9, pp. 449-450, 452, 456). And, following Haecker, our soul possesses thinking, feeling, and willing components, as well as knowledge [receiving], love [affection], and service [responsive activity] (FEB, VII, 9, pp. 450, 455-456, 465, 467). The natural world possesses several images of the Trinity as well. First, matter is divided into liquid, solid, and gaseous forms (FEB, VII, 7, pp. 423, 465). Secondly, the living realm of nature is divided up into plants, animals, and humans (FEB, VII, 9, pp. 426, 462-463, 465). Stein additionally mentions a more metaphysical image of the Trinity found in inanimate, animate, and human beings wherein they have a potent force (primordial source) [Father], with a unity of meaning or essence [Son], that unfolds with a vital radiation into a structural carrier of the essence [Holy Spirit] (FEB, VII, 7, p. 423 (FEB, VII, 8-9, pp. 424, 427, 467). For instance in the human the soul stands upon itself, is filled with meaning and power, and forms itself in accordance with its meaning (FEB, VII, 7, 9, pp. 423, 448, 464).

9   For information on von Hildebrand's thought see: PM (1960), v. I, p. 222-223; CHAD (1962), v. VI, pp. 738-739; BBKL (1990), v. II, pp. 845-846; CP (1990), v. III, pp. 172-200; DP (1993), v. I, pp. 1351-1352; LTK (1996), v. V, p. 104; ICEA (1997), pp. 471-476; OHYP (2001), pp. 142-143; PAMP (2002), pp. 475-496; PWW (2002), pp. 61-74; CCC (2003), pp. 39-48; NCE (2003), v. VI, pp. 830-831; EF (2006), v. VI, pp. 5293-5294; his autobiographies "Self-portrait of Dietrich von Hildebrand," in The Book of Catholic Authors, ed. Walter Romig (Grosse Pointe-Michigan: W. Romig, 1962), pp. 206-215 and Von Hildebrand, Alice, The Soul of a Lion: Dietrich von Hildebrand [Memoiren und Aufsätze gegen den Nationalsozialismus, 1933-1938 (1993)]

(San Francisco: Igantius Press, 2000); as well as Teed, Dexter, "A Price on His Head," *New York Post* (December 3, 1943), p. 7; Schwarz, Balduin, "Dietrich von Hildebrand on Value," *Thought* 24, 1949, pp. 655-676; Schwarz, Balduin, ed., *The Human Person and the World of Values: A Tribute to Dietrich von Hildebrand* (New York: Fordham University Press, 1960); Schwarz, Balduin, *Wahrheit, Wert und Sein: Festgabe für Dietrich von Hildebrand* (Regensburg: Habbel, 1970); Laun, Andreas, *Die naturrechtliche Begründung der Ethik in der neueren katholischen Moraltheologie* (Vienna: Dom-Verlag, 1973), pp. 160-230; *Aletheia* 1 (1977) [Special Issue on von Hildebrand]; Nielsen, Eileen, "Dietrich von Hildebrand, RIP," *National Review* 29 (March 18, 1977), pp. 316-317; *Aletheia* 5 (1992) [Special Volume on Von Hildebrand]; Gooch, Augusta, "Value Hierarchies in Scheler and Von Hildebrand," *Southwest Philosophical Studies* 15 (1993), pp. 19-27; Husserl, Edmund, "Urteil über Hildebrands Doktorarbeit," in Husserl, Edmund, *Briefwechsel* (Dordrecht: Kulwer, 1993), v. III, pp. 125-126; Dunlop, Francis, "Truth and Value: The Philosophy of Dietrich von Hildebrand," *Journal of the British Society for Phenomenology* 25:3 (1994), pp. 312-313; Fedoryka, Maria, "Dietrich von Hildebrand on Max Scheler as Philosopher and Personality: Toward an Understanding of Phenomenological Method," *Aletheia* 6 (1994), pp. 321-339; Tallon, Andrew, "Affection, Cognition, Volition: The Triadic Meaning of Heart in Ethics," *American Catholic Philosophical Quarterly* 68 (1994), pp. 211-232; Arjonillo, Rolando, *Conjugal Love and the Ends of Marriage A Study of Dietrich von Hildebrand and Herbert Doms in the Light of the Pastoral Constitution Gaudium et Spes* (Frankfurt: Peter Lang, 1998); Seifert, Josef, *Dietrich von Hildebrand's Kampt gegen den Nationalsozialismus* (Heidelberg: C. Winter, 1998); Thomas, Howard, "A Portrait of Dietrich von Hildebrand," *Crisis* 18 (2000), pp. 21-26; Jordan, Michael, "The Theological Axiology of Dietrich von Hildebrand," *Logos* 4:2 (2001), pp. 66-77; Waldstein, Michael, "Dietrich von Hildebrand and St. Thomas Aquinas on Goodness and Happiness," *Nova et Vetera* 1:2 (2003), pp. 403-464; Mager, Michael, *Begründung sittlicher Freiheit: eine Untersuchung zur philosophischen Grundlegung sittlicher Freiheit bei Victor Cathrein, Dietrich von Hildebrand, und Romano Guardini in Auseinandersetzung mit Immanuel Kant* (Münster: Lit, 2004); Von Hildebrand, Alice, "Debating Beauty: Jacques Maritain and Dietrich von Hildebrand," *Crisis* 22:7 (2004), pp. 38-41; Crosby, John, "The Witness of Dietrich von Hildebrand," *First Things* 168 (2006), pp. 7-9; Laun, Andreas, "Dietrich von Hildebrand's Struggle against German National Socialism," *Logos* 9:4 (2006), pp. 132-144.

10   This work has been translated as *Christian Ethics* [CE] (New York: David McKay, 1953). Von Hildebrand's ethical philosophy is also spelled out in such works as *The Idea of Moral Action [Die Idee der sittlichen Handlung]* [IMA] (1916; 1969); *Morality and the Knowledge of Moral Values [Sittlichkeit und ethische Werterkenntnis]* [MKMV] (1922; 1969); *Metaphysics of Community [Metaphysik der Gemeinschaft]* (1930); *Catholic Professional Ethics [Das katholische Berufsethos]* (1931); *Fundamental Moral Attitudes [Sittliche*

Grundhaltungen] [FMA] (1933); The Moral Foundation of the Community [Die sittlichen Grundlagen der Völkergemeinschaft] (1946) [a collection of essays]; True Morality and its Counterfeits [TMC] (1955) [written in collaboration with his wife Alice Jourdain and reissued as Morality and Situation Ethics (1966)]; Graven Images: Substitutes for True Morality [GI] (1957) [also written with his wife]; The Sacred Heart: An Analysis of Human and Divine Affectivity [SH] (1965) [reissued as The Heart (1977)]; The Essence of Love [Das Wesen der Liebe] (1971) [partially translated as "The Essence of Love" in Aletheia 1 (1977), pp. 1-15, and fully translated by John Crosby as The Nature of Love [NL] (South Bend: St. Augustine's Press, 2009)], Situation Ethics and Other Writings [Situationsethik und kleinere Schriften] (1973); Aesthetics [Ästhetik], 2 vol. (1977, 1984); Moralia [MOR] (1980). He also wrote several works on marriage and sexual ethics. I use these translations throughout.

Von Hildebrand delved into other areas of philosophy as well in his Timely Questions in the Light of Eternity [Zeitliches im Lichte des Ewigen] (1932) [a collection of essays]; The Meaning of Philosophical Inquiry and Knowledge [Der Sinn Philosophischen Fragens und Erkennens] (1950) [translated as What Is Philosophy? [WIP] (London: Routledge, 1960)]; On Death [Über den Tod] (1980) [reissued as Jaws of Death: Gate of Heaven [JD] (1990)]; Dictation of the Truth [Diktat der Wahrheit] (1991) [a collection of his texts]. He is also known for his theological writings which are often critical of an overly-liberal Catholicism such as his Liturgy and Personality [Liturgie und Persönlichkeit] [LP] (1933); Transformation in Christ [Die Umgestaltung in Christus] [TIC] (1940) [written under the pseudonym Peter Ott]; The New Tower of Babel (1953) [a collection of essays]; Humanity at the Crossroads [Die Menschheit am Scheideweg] (1954) [a collection of essays]; and Trojan Horse in the City of God: The Catholic Crisis Explained (1967).

Von Hildebrand's main philosophical articles were his: "Die ethische und moralpädagogische Bedeutung der weltlichen und religiösen Motive," Jahrbuch des Vereins für Erziehungswissenschaft 15 (1922), pp. 65-90;"Die Unsterblichkeit der Seele" ["On the Immortality of the Soul"], Münchener Neueste Nachrichten (1926); "Die Rolle des objektiven Gutes für die Person innerhalb des Sittlichen," ["ROG"] in Philosophia Perennis: Festgabe für Josef Geyser zum 60, ed. von Rintelin, Fritz-Joachim (Regensburg: Josef Habbel, 1930), v. II, pp. 973-995;"Men as Instruments," Commonweal 33 (1941), pp. 643-648;"The World Crisis and the Human Person," Thought 16 (1941), pp. 457-462;"The Dethronement of Truth," Proceedings of the American Catholic Philosophical Association 18 (1942), pp. 3-16; "Humanity at the Crossroads," ["HC"], Thought 22 (1948), pp. 447-462;"Zum Problem der Schönheit des Sichtbaren und Hörbaren," in Mélanges Joseph Maréchal, ed. Joseph Maréchal (Brussels: Desclée de Brouwer, 1950), v. I, pp. 180-191;"Transformation of Man's Nature," Proceedings of the American Catholic Philosophical Association 25 (1951), pp. 16-25;"Beauty and the Christian," Journal of Arts and Letters

3:2 (1951); "The Role of Affectivity in Morality," *Proceedings of the American Catholic Philosophical Association* 32 (1958), pp. 85-95; "Technology and its Dangers," in *Technology and Christian Culture*, ed. Robert Mohan (Washington: Catholic University of America Press, 1960), pp. 72-98; "The Modes of Participation in Value," [MPV] *International Philosophical Quarterly* 1 (1961), pp. 58-84; "Dangers in Constructing a Contemporary Christian Philosophy," in *Christian Philosophy in the College and Seminary*, ed. George McLean (Washington: The Catholic University of America Press, 1966), pp. 14-19; "Phenomenology of Values in a Christian Philosophy," [PV] in *Christian Philosophy and Religious Renewal*, ed. George McLean (Washington: The Catholic University of America Press, 1966), pp. 3-19; "Belief and Obedience: The Critical Difference," *Triumph* 5 (1970), pp. 11-14; "Edith Stein Remembered," in *Never Forget: Christian and Jewish Perspectives on Edith Stein*, ed. Waltraud Herbstrith (Washington: ICS Publications, 1998), p. 238; "Henri de Lubac über dessen Buch Surnaturel 1946," in *Mein Schriften in Rückblick*, ed. Henri de Lubac (Einsiedeln: Johannes Verlag, 1996), p. 99; "Beauty in the Light of the Redemption," *Logos* 4:2 (2001), pp. 78-92.

For a bibliography of von Hildebrand see Schwarz, Balduin, "Bibliography of Dietrich von Hildebrand's Works," in *The Human Person and the World of Values*, ed. Balduin Schwarz (New York: Fordham University Press, 1960), pp. 195-210 and Preis, Adolf, "Hildebrand Bibliographie," *Aletheia* 5 (1992), pp. 363-430. Von Hildebrand's works have been collected as *Gesammelte Schriften*, 10 vols. (Regensburg: J. Habbel, 1971-1984).

11 In his *Nature of Love*, von Hildebrand similarly characterizes love as possessing the traits of affective value-response, superactuality, delight in beloved, union ('I am yours'), benevolence, self-gift [*Hingabe*], commitment, happiness, reciprocity, affirming other as individual, advancing credit to other and seeing best of the other (NL, II, pp. 43-57; III, pp. 66-76).

12 For more on the life and thought of Dussel see: CP (1990), v. III, pp. 696-702; EF (2006), v. IV, p. 3170; Morkovsky, Mary, "Bergson and Dussel on Creating New Societies," in Cauchy, Venant, ed., *Philosophy and Culture* (Montreal: Montmorency, 1988), v. II, pp. 568-573; Batstone, David, et al., eds., *Liberation Theologies, Postmodernity, and the Americas* (London: Routledge, 1997); Barber, Michael, *Ethical Hermeneutics: Rationalism in Enrique Düssel's Philosophy of Liberation* (New York: Fordham University Press, 1998); Alcoff, Linda Martin, and Eduardo Mendieta, eds., *Thinking from the Underside of History: Enrique Dussel's Philosophy of Liberation* (Lanham: Rowman and Littlefield, 2000); Mendieta, Eduardo, ed., *Latin American Philosophy: Currents, Issues, Debates* (Bloomington: Indiana University Press, 2003); *Listening* 43:1 (2008) [Special Volume on Dussel].

13 These works have been translated as *Philosophy of Liberation* [PL], tr. Aquilina Martínez and Christine Morkovsky (Maryknoll: Orbis Books, 1985)

and *Ethics and the Theology of Liberation* [TLE], tr. Bernard McWilliam (New York: Orbis Books, 1978) and are used by myself in this book.

Other well-known works on the philosophy of liberation by Dussel are *Caminos de la liberación* (1972) [translated as *History and the Theology of Liberation* [HTL], tr. John Drury (Maryknoll: Orbis Books, 1976)]; *Towards an Ethics of Latin-American Liberation* [*Para una ética de la liberación latinoamericana*] [TELAL], 5 vols. (1973-1980); *Method for a Philosophy of Liberation* [*Método para una filosofía de la liberación*] [MPL] (1974; 1991); *Introduction to the Philosophy of Liberation* [*Introducción a la Filosofía de la Liberación*] (1977); and *Ethics of Liberation* [*La Ética de la Liberación*] [EL] (1998).

Dussel has written numerous other books on philosophy, history, politics, and theology, as well as over seventy papers, including: *Ética communitaria* [EC] (1986) [translated as *Ethics and Community* (New York: Orbis, 1989)]; *1492: El encubrimiento del Otro* (1992) [translated as *The Invention of the Americas* [IA], tr. Michael Barber (New York: Continuum, 1998)]; *Apel, Ricoeur, Rorty y la Filosofía de la Liberación* (1993) [translated as *The Underside of Modernity: Apel, Ricoeur, Taylor, and the Philosophy of Liberation*, tr. Eduardo Mendieta (New Jersey: Humanities Press, 1996)]; *Debate en torno a la ética del discuso de Apel* (1994); *Etica della comunicazione* (2001) [with Karl-Otto Apel]; *Beyond Philosophy: History, Marxism, and Liberation Theology* (2002); *20 tesis de política* (2006) [translated as *Twenty Theses on Politics* (Durham: Duke University Press, 2008)];

14   Dussel accordingly says that philosophy employs the analectical method [*el método analítica*] wherein we see the other as beyond (*ana*) the comprehended horizon of the world through a meeting with the other's face and voice (PL, V, 3, pp. 158-159; TLE, II, pp. 38-41; EL, III, 4, pp. 90-94; VI, 1-2, pp. 193-213; MPL, III, pp. 101-106; V, pp. 186-188; HTL, I, p. 2).

15   Among the nearly 150 Catholic Phenomenologists we can mention: Fr. Franz Brentano (1838- 1917) [who later broke with the Catholic Church]; Fr. Anton Marty (1847-1914) [who later left the priesthood and Church]; Alexius Meinong (1853-1920); Max Scheler (1874-1928) [who married Von Hildebrand's previous fiancée in his second marriage which cost him his position at Munich; subsequently Scheler left the Church after his third marriage]; Gaston Rabeau (1877-1949) [also a Transcendental Thomist]; Anna Reinach (1884-1954), convert and wife of phenomenologist Adolf Reinach]; the Spaniard Manuel Garcia Morente (1886-1942); Erich Przywara, S.J. (1889-1972), of the seminary in Pullach [also an Augustinian, Integralist, and Thomist]; the Jewish convert Siegfriend Hamburger (c. 1889-1980); the Pole Roman Ingarden (1893-1970), of Jagiellonian University [though his Catholicism was questioned by some]; August Brunner, S.J. (1894-1985); the convert nun Adelgundis Jaegerschmid, O.S.B. (c. 1895-1996) [who was a student of Husserl and took care of his wife in her last days]; Gaston Berger

(1896-1960) [Director General of Higher Learning for the French Ministry of Education (1953-1960)]; the convert Aurel Kolnai (1900-1973); Balduin Schwarz (1902-1993); Dominic De Petter, O.P. (1905-1971); Stephen Strasser (1905-1991); Sofia Vanni-Rovighi (1908-1990); Herman Leo Van Breda, O.F.M. (1911-1974) [who was the founder of the Husserl Archives and helped sneak Husserl's papers out of Germany and convert Husserl's wife to Catholicism]; Alphonse de Waelhens (1911-1981); Bernard Delfgaauw (1912-1993); Henry Duméry (1920-) [who was removed from the priesthood and four of whose works were placed on the Index of Forbidden Books in 1958]; Milan Komar (1921-2006); Antonio Millán-Puelles (1921-2005); Fr. Antoon Vergote (1921-); William Luijpen (1922-); Alice Jourdain [von Hildebrand] (1923-) [the pupil and later wife of Dietrich von Hildebrand]; the Pole Anna Teresa Tymieniecka (1923-); Manfred Frings (1925-2008); Louis Dupré (1925-); Robert Spaemann (1927-); William Marra (1928-1998) [whose daughter was imprisoned for harboring an antiabortion criminal fugitive]; Jacques Taminiaux (1928-); Ghislaine Florival (1929-); Adriaan Peperzak (1929-); the Pole Fr. Jozef Tischner (1931-2000); the Brazilian Carlos Cirne-Lima, S.J. (1931-); Dagfinn Follesdal (1932-); Alphonso Lingis (1933-); Quentin Lauer, S.J. (c. 1935-); Fr. Robert Sokolowski (c. 1936-); Patrick de Laubier (1935-); the Pole Karol Tarnowski (1937-); Angela Ales Bello (c. 1940-); John Crosby (1944-) [also a Personalist]; Hanna-Barbara Gerl-Falkovitz (c. 1944-); Bernard Sichere (1944-); Josef Seifert (1945-); Claudie Lavaud (c. 1949-); Fr. Philippe Capelle (1954-); Emmanuel Gabellieri (1957-); the Pole Tadeusz Gadacz (1955-); the Dutchman Ruud Welten (c. 1958-); Emmanuel Falque (1963-).

Phenomenology has greatly influenced many Catholic theologians as well, such as the German Fr. Karl Adam (1876-1966); Romano Guardini (1885-1968); Edward Schileebeeckx, O.P. (1914-); Fr. Enda McDonagh (1930-); and Fr. Louis-Marie Chauvet (1942-).

Phenomenology, as we will see, has also significantly influenced French Catholic postmodernists such as Michel Henry (1922-2002); Fr. Jean-Yves Lacoste (1923-); Jean-François Courtine (1944-); Jean-Luc Marion (1946-), of the Sorbonne; and Jean-Louis Chrétien (1952-), of the Sorbonne.

16   In 1950, after completing a talk at Notre Dame University, Gilson was shocked to find out that one of its faculty, Waldemar Gurian had published "Europe and the United States: An Open Letter to Etienne Gilson," *Commonweal* 53 (December 15, 1950) [reprinted in French in *Le Figaro*] which accused Gilson of timidly fleeing Europe for the safer confines of North America during the Second World War and of being soft on Soviet Communism. Because of this attack the Collège de France refused Gilson any honorary status and he was pillorized by the French press in the so-called l'affaire Gilson [see "L'Affaire Gilson," *Esprit* 178 (1951), pp. 590-596; "Une lettre de M. Étienne Gilson," *Le Monde* (February 22, 1951), pp. 1-4; "M. Étienne Gilson répond

à M. Waldemar Gurian," *Le Monde* (March 8, 1951), p. 4; and "M. Étienne Gilson rompt le silence," *Le Figaro* (February 17, 1951), p. 4)]. Gilson later received an apology from Gurian who had written the article based on inaccurate second-hand information (see the rebuttal of John Corbett in *Le Figaro* of December, 1950) and Gilson in a nice gesture had masses offered for Gurian prior to and upon his death.

17 For more on Gilson's bio and oeuvre see: CTF (1926), pp. 196-197; CAP (1955), pp. 92-93; DTC (1959), Tables générales, pp. 1814-1815; CRHP (1957), pp. 471-472; CMCT (1960), pp. 495-506; CHAD (1962), vol. VI, pp. 26-28; TE (1963), vol. I, pp. 153-174; PTCW (1964), pp. 544-546; TCT (1965), pp. 59-87; TS (1966), pp. 32-54; RPF (1968), pp. 52-54, 156; TCP (1969), p. 39; HA (1971), pp. 220-221; HWP (1971), vol. V, pp. 129, 136-138; OB (1971), pp. 92-105, 230-231; CHP (1974), vol. IX, pp. 260-264; PFPM (1977), pp. 122-137; OHYT (1981), pp. 28-44; CTIC (1985), pp. 195-201; PHP (1988), p. 322; TCRT (1988), pp. 287-289; CEWP (1989), p. 120; CP (1989), vol. II, pp. 519-545; FUP (1989), pp. 161-199; NCS (1989), pp. 253-255; FT (1992), pp. 83-90, 169-184; BBKL (1993), vol. XXII, pp. 418-436; DP (1993), vol. I, pp. 1131-1132; NT (1994), pp. 137-154; HCEC (1995), p. 561; LTK (1995), vol. IV, pp. 653-654; BDTC (1996), pp. 275-277; ICEA (1997), pp. 458-479; CTE (1998), pp. 102-103; SPI (1998), pp. 193-214; UHF (1998), vol. VIII, pp. 448-462; PCHP (1999), p. 712; RPFR (1999), pp. 75-85; MCT (2000), vol. II, p. 215; FPTC (2001), pp. 94-97; OYHP (2001), p. 265; TT (2002), pp. 7, 10-12, 41, 79; BTCT (2003), pp. 64-66, 224-231; NCE (2003), vol. VI, pp. 227-228; WPR (2003), pp. 343-345; EMFT (2004), pp. 256-259; ER (2004), vol. V, pp. 3491-3492; ACP (2005), pp. 339-344; EP (2005), vol. IV, pp. 91-93; OGP (2005), p. 340; SHT (2005), pp. 88-89; EF (2006), vol. V, pp. 4742-4744; TWFP (2006), pp. 131-132; Jolivet, Regis, *Le thomisme et la critique de la connaissance* (Paris: Descleïe, de Brouwer, 1933); Renard, Alexandre, *La querelle sur la possibilité de la philosophie chrétienne* (Paris: Éditions école et collège 1941); Maritain, Jacques, ed., *Étienne Gilson, philosophe de la chrétienté* (Paris: Cerf, 1949); Savaria, Madeleine Gabrielle, *Étienne Gilson's Concept of the Nature and Scope of Philosophy* (Washington: Catholic University of America Press, 1951); Casey, Joseph, *The Notion of Being in Recent Works of Etienne Gilson* (Rome: Gregorian University Press, 1953); Owens, Joseph, ed., *Etienne Gilson Anniversary Studies* (Toronto: Pontifical Institute of Medieval Studies, 1958); O'Neil, Charles, ed., *An Etienne Gilson Tribute* (Milwaukee: Marquette University Press, 1959); Edie, Callistus, ed., *Mélanges offerts à Étienne Gilson* (Paris: J. Vrin, 1959); Nédoncelle, Maurice, *Is There a Christian Philosophy?* (New York: Hawthorn, 1960), pp. 85-106; Cardahi, Choucri, *L'Academie francaise devant la foi* (Paris: Éditions de la Source, 1964), pp. 340-350; Wippel, John, *Twentieth-Century Thinkers* (New York: Alba, 1965), pp. 59-87; Livi, Antonio, *Étienne Gilson: Filosofia cristiana e idea del limite critico* (Pamplona: Ediciones Universidad de Navarra, 1970); Quinn, John, *The Thomism of Étienne Gilson:*

A *Critical Study* (Villanova: Villanova University Press, 1971); Kopaczynski, Germain, *Linguistic Ramifications of the Essence-Existence Debate* (Washington: University Press of America, 1979), pp. 12-15, 54-92, 150-187; D'Alverny, Marie-Thérèse, and Monique Couratier, eds., *Etienne Gilson et nous* (Paris: J. Vrin, 1980); Shook, Laurence, *Étienne Gilson* (Toronto: Pontificial Institute of Medieval Studies, 1984); Schmitz, Kenneth, *What Has Clio to Do with Athena?: Etienne Gilson, Historian and Philosopher* (Toronto: Pontifical Institute of Medieval Studies, 1987); Guillet, Jacques, *La théologie catholique en France de 1914 à 1960* (Paris: Médiasèvres, 1988), pp. 18-26; Madiran, Jean, *Gilson: Chroniques philosophiques* (Maule: Editions Difralivre, 1992); Gouhier, Henri, *Étienne Gilson: Trois essais* (Paris: Vrin, 1993); Prouvost, Géry, ed., *Revue Thomiste* 94 (1994), pp. 355-553 [Special Issue on Gilson]; Jeauneau, Édouard, *Translatio Studii, the Transmission of Learning: A Gilsonian Theme* (Toronto: Pontifical Institute of Medieval Studies, 1995); Bloomer, Matthew, *Judeo-Christian Revelation as a Source of Philosophical Reflection according to Étienne Gilson* (Rome: Apollinare Studi, 2001); Hart, Trevor, ed., *Dictionary of Historical Theology* (Grand Rapids: Authentic Media, 2001), pp. 227-229; Kerr, Fergus, *After Aquinas* (London: Blackwell, 2002), pp. 12-13, 80-85; Redpath, Peter, ed., *A Thomistic Tapestry: Essays in Memory of Etienne Gilson* (Amsterdam: Rodopi, 2003); Di Ceglie, Roberto, *Étienne Gilson: Filosofia e rivelazione* (Naples: Edizioni Scientifische Italiane, 2004); Murphy, Francesca, *Art and Intellect in the Philosophy of Étienne Gilson* (Columbia: University of Missouri Press, 2004).

18   The former work has been translated as *The Spirit of Medieval Philosophy* [SMP], tr. A.H.C. Downes (New York: Charles Scribner's, 1940)]; and the second as *Methodical Realism* [MR], tr. Philip Trower (Front Royal: Christendom Press, 1990). I make use of these and other translations of Gilson throughout.

Other philosophical works of Gilson include: *Christianity and Philosophy* [*Christianisme et philosophie*] [CRPH] (1936) [translated as *Christianity and Philosophy*, tr. Ralph MacDonald (1939)]; *The Unity of Philosophical Experience* (1937) [William James Lectures at Harvard University of 1937]; *Reason and Revelation in the Middle Ages* (1938) [Richards Lectures at the University of Virginia in 1937]; *Being and Essence* [*L'être et l'essence*] (1948; 1952) [translated as *Being and Some Philosophers* [BSP] (Toronto: Pontifical Institute of Medieval Studies, 1949; 1952)]; *Elements of Christian Philosophy* (1960) [ECP]; *Introduction to Christian Philosophy* [*Introduction à la philosophie chrétienne*] [ICP] (1960) [translated as *Christian Philosophy*, tr. Armand Maurer (Toronto: Pontifical Institute of Medieval Studies, 1993)]; *The Philosopher and Theology* [*Le philosophe et la théologie*] [PT] (1960) [translated as *The Philosopher and Theology* (New York: Random House, 1962)] [autobiographical]; *The Spirit of Thomism* [ST] (1964); *Linguistics and Philosophy* [*Linguistique et Philosophie*] (1969) [one of the earliest Thomistic accounts of the philosophy of language; translated as *Linguistics and Philosophy*, tr. John Lyon (Notre Dame: University of Notre Dame Press, 1988)]; *Difficult Atheism* [*L'athéisme difficile*] (1979); *Philosophical Constants of Being* [*Constantes philosophiques de l'être*] [PCB] (1983); *Thomist Realism and the Critique of Knowledge* [*Réalisme thomiste et critique de la connaissance*] [TR] (1983) [translated as *Thomist Realism and the Critique of Knowledge*, tr. Mark Wauck (San Francisco: Ignatius Press, 1986)]; *Three Quests in Philosophy* (2008) [a collection of lectures]. I make use of the English translations of Gilson throughout this book. He also wrote several books on art and politics.

Gilson was primarily known, however, for his many books on the history of philosophy, especially his works on Augustine, Bonaventure, and Aquinas, namely: *Le Thomisme: Introduction au système de saint Thomas* (1919; 1922; 1927; 1942; 1944; 1986) [translated as *The Philosophy of St. Thomas Aquinas*, tr. Edward Bullough (Cambridge: Heffner and Sons, 1924; 1941; 1944) and *The Christian Philosophy of St. Thomas Aquinas*, tr. Laurence Shook (New York: Random House, 1956)]; *Études de philosophie médiévale* (1921); *La philosophie au moyen-âge*, 2 vols. (1922; 1944); *Saint Thomas d'Aquin* (1925; 1931; 1941) [translated as *Moral Values and the Moral Life*, tr. Leo Ward (St. Louis: Herder, 1931)]; *Wisdom and Love in Saint Thomas Aquinas* (1951); *Saint Thomas et nous* (1954; 1966) [translated as *Thomas Aquinas and our Colleagues* (Princeton: Princeton University Press, 1953)]; *History of Christian Philosophy in the Middle Ages* (1955); *Saint Thomas Aquinas and Philosophy* (1961) [with Anton Pegis; representing the McCauley Lectures at Georgetown University in 1960]; *Modern Philosophy* (1963) [with Thomas Langan]; *In Search of Saint Thomas Aquinas* (West Hartford: Saint Joseph College, 1966) [with Anton Pegis; representing the McAuley Lectures at Georgetown University of 1966]; *Recent Philosophy* (1966) [with Thomas Langan]; *From Aristotle to Darwin and Back* [*D'Aristote à Darwin et retour*] (1971); *Études médiévales* (1983); *Saint Thomas the Moralist* [*Saint Thomas moraliste*] (1974); *Pourquoi Saint Thomas a critiqué Saint Augustin* (1986).

Gilson additionally wrote over 300 articles including: "Sur le positivisme absolu," *Revue Philosophique de la France et de l'Etranger* 68 (1909), pp. 63-65; "Le système de Thomas d'Aquin," *Revue des cours et conférences* 22 (1913), pp. 223-230, 352-359, 429-436, 572-580 and 22 (1913), pp. 42-53, 249-272, 788-797; "La religion et la foi," *Revue de Métaphysique et de Morale* 29 (1922), pp. 359-371; "Pourquoi saint Thomas a critiqué saint Augustin," *Archives d'histoire doctrinale et littéraire du moyen âge* 1 (1926), pp. 5-127; "Intervention dans la discussion de La querelle de l'athéisme," *Bulletin de la Société française de la philosophie* 28 (1928), pp. 56-61, 66-69; "Philosophie religieuse," *Revue Philosophique de la France et de l'Etranger* 108 (1929), pp. 448-455; "Le réalisme méthodique," Geyser, Joseph, ed., *Philosophia perennis* (Regensburg: J. Habbel, 1930), vol. I, pp. 745-755; "Réflexions sur la controverse S. Thomas—S. Augustin," in Mandonnet, Pierre, ed., *Mélanges Mandonnet* (Paris: Vrin, 1930), vol. I, pp. 371-383; "La notion de philosophie chrétienne," *Bulletin de la Société française de la philosophie* 31 (1931), pp. 37-49, 52-59, 72, 77-82, 84-85; "Le problème de la philosophie chrétienne," *Vie intellectuelle* 12 (1931), pp. 214-232 [translated as "The Problem of Christian Philosophy," *Hound and Horn* 5 (1932), pp. 433-451]; "Sur Auguste Comte," *Vie intellectuelle* 12 (1931), pp. 245-249; "La tradition francaise et la chrétienté," *Vigile* 1 (1931), pp. 53-87 [translated by Denis Hawkins as "Christendom and the French Tradition," *Arena* 1 (1938), pp. 262-281]; "Réalisme et méthode," *Revue des sciences philosophiques et théologiques* 21 (1932), pp. 161-186; "Autour de la philosophie chrétienne," *La Vie Intellectuelle* 21 (1933), pp. 404-424 [translated as "Concerning Christian Philosophy," in Klibansky, Raymond, ed., *Philosophy and History* (Oxford: Clarendon Press, 1936), pp. 61-76]; "Intervention dans la discussion de La philosophie chrétienne," in *Journées d'études de la société thomiste* 2 (1933), pp. 63-67, 69-71, 139-142; "La specificité de l'ordre philosophique," *Vie Intellectuelle* 21 (1933), pp. 404-424 [translated as "The Distinctiveness of the Philosophic Order," tr. D.A. Patton, in Klibansky, Raymond, ed., *Philosophy and History* (Oxford: Oxford University Press, 1936), pp. 61-76]; "Sur quelques difficultés de l'illumination augustinienne," *Revue Philosophique de la France et de l'Etranger* 36 (1934), pp. 321-331; "La méthode réaliste," and "Vade-mecum du débutant réaliste," *Revue de Philosophie* 5 (1935), pp. 97-108, 289-301 [the latter of which has been translated as "Vade-mecum of a Young Realist," in Houde, Roland, et al., eds., *Philosophy of Knowledge* (Philadelphia: Lippincott, 1960), pp. 385-394]; "L'intelligence au service du Christ-Roi," *Vie intellectuelle* 41 (1936), pp. 181-203 [translated as "The Intelligence in the Service of Christ the King," in Caponigri, Aloysius, *Modern Catholic Thinkers* (New York: Burns and Oates, 1960), pp. 495-506]; "Le christianisme et la tradition philosophique," *Revue des Sciences Philosophiques et Théologiques* 30 (1941), pp. 249-266; "Le thomisme et les philosophies existentielles," *Vie intellectuelle* 13 (1945), pp. 144-155; "Egypte ou Grèce?," *Mediaeval Studies* 8 (1946), pp. 43-52; "Existence and Philosophy," *Proceedings of the American Catholic Philosophical Association* 21 (1946), pp. 4-15; "Les intellectuels dans la chrétienté," *Travaux et documents* (May-June 1947), pp. 3-15; "Doctrinal History and Its Interpretation," *Speculum* 24 (1949), pp. 483-492; "On Faith, Science, and Philosophy," *Christianity and Crisis* 9 (1949), pp. 167-168; "Situation des philosophes actuels devant la foi," *Samaine des Intellectuels Catholqiues 1949* (Paris: Éditions du Flore, 1949), pp. 34-55; "Nature et portée des preuves de l'existence de Dieu," in Maréchal, Joseph, *Mélanges Joseph Maréchal* (Paris: L'Édition Universelle, 1950), vol. II, pp. 378-395; "La preuve du De ente et essentia," *Doctor Communis* 3 (1950), pp. 257-260; "Les recherches historico-critiques et l'avenir de la scolastique," in *Scholastica ratione historico-critica instauranda* (Rome: Pontificum Athenaeum Antonianum, 1951), pp. 503-516 [translated as "Historical Research and the Future of Scholasticism," *Modern Schoolman* 29 (1951), pp. 1-10]; "Science, Philosophy, and Religious Wisdom," *Proceedings of the American Catholic Philosophical Association* 26 (1952), pp.

5-13; "Theology and the Unity of Knowledge," in Leary, Lewis, ed., *The Unity of Knowledge* (New York: Doubleday, 1955), pp. 35-46; "Where Is Christendom?," *Temoignage* (January 1, 1956), pp. 29-30; "The Spirit of Thomism," in Pegis, Anton, ed., *The Gilson Reader* (New York: Doubleday, 1957), pp. 247-275; "What is Christian Philosophy," in Pegis, Anton, ed., *A Gilson Reader* (New York: Image Books, 1957), pp. 177-191; "La possibilité philosophique de la philosophie chrétienne," *Revue des Sciences Religieuses* 32 (1958), pp. 168-196; "Can the Existence of God Still Be Demonstrated," in Pegis, Anton, ed., *St. Thomas and Philosophy* (West Hartford: St. Joseph College, 1961), pp. 1-14 [McAuley Lectures of 1960]; "De la connaissance du principe," *Revue de Métaphysique et de Morale* 66 (1961), pp. 373-397; "Réflexions sur le catéchisme," *Carmel* 4 (1961), pp. 286-302; "The Spirit of Medieval Philosophy," in McGill, Frank, ed., *Masterpieces of World Philosophy* (New York: Collins, 1961), vol. II, pp. 946-952; "Trois lecons sur le problème de l'existence de Dieu," *Divinitas* 5 (1961), pp. 23-87; "L'être et Dieu," *Revue Thomiste* 62 (1962), pp. 181-202, 398-416; "God: Existential Act," and "Laws of Metaphysical Experience," in Drennan, D.A., ed., *A Modern Introduction to Metaphysics* (New York: Free Press, 1962), pp. 42-49, 656-661; "Notes pour l'histoire de la cause efficiente," *Archives d'histoire doctrinale et litteraire du moyen âge* 29 (1962), pp. 7-31; "La possibilité de l'athéisme," *Il problema dell'atteismo* (Brescia: Morcelliana, 1962), pp. 39-42; "God and Contemporary Thought," in Dommeyer, Frederick, ed., *In Quest of Value* (San Francisco: Chandler Publishing Company, 1963), pp. 313-328; "Prolégomènes à la Prima Via," *Archives d'histoire doctrinale et litteraire du moyen âge* 30 (1963), pp. 53-70; "Lettra sul pluralismo," *Sapienza* 18 (1965), pp. 439-440; "Suis-je schismatique?," *France Catholique* (July 2, 1965), p. 1; "Trois lecons sur le thomisme et sa situation présente," *Seminarium* 17 (1965), pp. 682-737; "On the Art of Misunderstanding Thomism," in Pegis, Anton, ed., *In Search of St. Thomas Aquinas* (West Hartford : St. Joseph College Press, 1966), pp. 33-44 [The McAuley Lectures of 1966]; "Catholicisme et philosophie," *Itinéraires* 1:5 (1967), pp. 38-70; "Christianisme et philosophie," *Itinéraires* 1:3 (1967), pp. 39-65; "On Behalf of the Handmaid," ["OBHM"], in Shook, Laurence, ed., *Theology of Renewal* (Montreal: Palm, 1968), vol. I, pp. 236-249; "The Twofold Certitude," in Macquarrie, John, ed., *Contemporary Religious Thinkers* (New York: Harper and Row, 1968), pp. 167-180; "The Idea of God and the Difficulties of Atheism," *Philosophy Today* 13 (1969), pp. 174-205; "Darwin dans l'évolution," *Revue des Deux Mondes* 37 (1970), pp. 264-282; "Eléments d'une métaphysique thomiste de l'être," *Archives d'histoire doctrinale et litteraire du moyen âge* 40 (1973), pp. 7-36; "Propos sur l'être et sa notion," in Piolanti, Antonio, ed., *San Tommaso e il pensiero moderno* (Rome: Pontificia Accademia Romana di S. Tommaso d'Aquino, 1975), pp. 7-17; "La filosofia cristiana a la luz de Aeterni Patris," *Scripta Theologica* 11 (1979), pp. 661-681; "On Some Difficulties of Interpretation," in Joos, Ernest, ed., *La scolastique: Certitude et recherche* (Montreal: Bellarmin, 1980), pp. 1-26; "The Corporeal World and the Efficacy of Second Causes," in Owen, Thomas, ed., *God's Activity in the World* (Chico: Scholars Press, 1983), pp. 213-230; "Remarks on Experience in Metaphysics," in Russman, Thomas, ed., *Thomistic Papers*, V (Houston: Center for Thomistic Studies, 1990), pp. 40-48. Gilson also wrote several popular articles on education, literature, philosopy, politics, and religion for *L'Aube*, *Le Monde*, *Sept*, and other journals. A few of these articles have been collected in Pegis, Anton, ed., *A Gilson Reader* [GR] (Garden City: Image Books, 1957), and Courtine, Jean-François, ed., *Autour de saint Thomas* (Paris: J. Vrin, 1983). For a bibliography of Gilson see McGrath, Margaret, *Étienne Gilson: A Bibliography* (Toronto: Pontifical Institute of Medieval Studies, 1982); and Harding, John, "Etienne Gilson, 1884-1984," *New Blackfriars* 65 (1984), pp. 232-233.

19   These Cartesian and Wolffian-influenced Thomists include Joseph Valla (c. 1740-1790) [with his Philosophia Lugdunensis], Andres de Guevara y Basoazabal (c. 1748-1830), Narcisse Cacheux (1789-1869), Jaime Balmes (1810-1848), Matteo Liberatore, S.J. (1810-1882), Gaetano Sanseverino (1811-1865), Josef Kleutgen, S.J. (1811-1883), Salvator Tongiorgi, S.J. (1820-1865), Michael Rosset (c. 1820-1873), Antonio-Maria Bensa (fl. 1855), A. Dupeyrat, S.S. (1826-1905), Domenico Palmieri, S.J. (1829-1909), Tommaso Maria Zigliara, O.P. (1833-1893), Michaele de Maria (1836-1913), Tillman Pesch, S.J. (1836-1899), Franz Egger (1836-1918), Cardinal Giuseppe Prisco (1836-1923), Alberto Lepidi, O.P. (1838-1925), Giovanni Battista Rastero (c. 1840-1897), Maximilian Limbourg (c. 1841-1895), Girolamo Maria Mancini, O.P. (1842-1924), Pierre-Marie Brin, S.S. (1843-1894), Vincent Remer, S.J. (1843-1910), Jean Baptiste Van der Aa, S.J. (c. 1843-1900), Juan Jose Urraburu, S.J. (1844-1904), Élie Blanc (1846-1927), John Rickaby, S.J. (1847-1927), Pierre Vallet, S.S. (fl. 1878-1899), Pio de Mandato, S.J. (1850-1914), Cardinal Desire Mercier (1851-1926), Bishop Benedetto Lorenzelli (1853-1915), Carl Frick (1856-1931), Joseph Gredt, O.S.B. (1863-1939), Sebastian Reinstadler, S.J. (1864-1935), the Cistercian J.S. Hickey (1865-1933), Gabriel Picard, S.J. (c. 1876-1940), Pedro Descoqs, S.J. (1877-1946), Reginald Garrigou-Lagrange, O.P. (1877-1964), Léon Noël (1878-1953), Roland-Gosselin, O.P. (1883-1934), Charles Boyer, S.J. (1884-1980), and Régis Jolivet (1891-1966).

20   Gilson here arguably does not accurately represent the whole of Aquinas's thought. For while it is true that at times Aquinas stresses how God's essence exceeds a human's ability to understand it and so it is better to say that we know what God is not rather than what God is, on other occasions Aquinas seems to believe a positive theology in which we describe the perfections of God such as goodness and beauty is possible (see *Summa Theologiae*, I q. 4-6, 8, 13, 18-21). Indeed Aquinas's *Summa Theologiae*, I q. 13 a. 6 explicitly states: "When it is said 'God is good,' [sometimes] this means nothing other than that 'God is the cause of the creature's goodness'; ... Hence 'good' would

be said primarily of the creature rather than of God. But ... these names in some way are said not only of God causally but also essentially [*huiusmodi nomina non solum dicuntur de Deo causaliter, sed etiam essentialiter*]. For when it is said that 'God is good,' or 'wise,' not only is it signified that He is the cause of wisdom or goodness, but that these exist in Him in a more eminent way" [*Cum enim dicitur Deus est bonus, vel sapiens, non solum significatur quod ipse sit causa sapientiae vel bonitatis, sed quod haec in eo eminentius praeexistunt*] (see also *Summa Theologiae*, I q. 4 a. 1 and 3; I a. 5; I. q. 6 a. 1-4; I q. 39 a. 8).

21   Gilson's position on Christian philosophy has also been defended by Franz Ehrle, Régis Jolivet, Antonin Sertillanges, O.P., Antoine Motte, O.P., André-Jean Festugière, O.P., Aimé Forest, Germain Grisez, Joseph Owens, C.S.S.R., Yves Floucat, and Ralph McInerny, and we can add the encyclical *Fides et Ratio* of 1998, nn. 75-76: "The term Christian philosophy includes those important developments of philosophical thinking which may [would] not have happened without the direct or indirect contribution of Christian faith.... Revelation clearly proposes certain truths which may [would] never have been discovered by reason unaided, although they are not of themselves inaccessible to reason" [*Cum de philosophia christiana sermo fit, omnes comprehendi debent praestantes illi progressus philosophicae disciplinae, qui numquam contigissent nisi opem directe vel oblique christiana fides attulisset ... lucide quasdam exhibet veritates Revelatio, quas tametsi attingere potest ratio, nunquam tamen easdem repperisset si suis unis viribus innixa esset*] (*Fides et Ratio*, n. 76). Hence *Fides et Ratio* supports Gilson's position but is not quite identical with it, unless we translate the ambiguous Latin subjunctives as 'would' instead of 'may' or 'might,' i.e. as supporting Gilson over Maritain.

22   The position that philosophy to be true to itself must be completely autonomous and separate itself from theology was also held by several notable Catholics, especially Thomists from Fribourg and Louvain, including: Cardinal Désiré-Félicien-François-Joseph Mercier (1851-1926), Pierre Mandonnet, O.P. (1858-1936), Belgian Maurice de Wulf (1867-1947), the Oratorian Gaston Rabeau (1877-1949), Léon Noël (1878-1953), Daniel Feuling, O.S.B. (1882-1947), Marie-Dominique Chenu, O.P. (1895-1990), Fernand Van Steenberghen (1904-1993), Stefan Swiezawski (1907-2004), Georges Van Riet (1916-), Fr. Edward Augustus Sillem (c. 1930-), and Fr. John F. Wippel (c. 1935-).

23   Something also reflected in the fact that God's chosen name is Yahweh [*ehyeh*] which seems to have roots deriving from the Hebrew word for being.

24   Indeed Gilson's presentation of the difference between essence and existence in Aquinas [under the influence of Boethius, Avicenna, and William of Auvergne] garnered him great fame (ST, III, pp. 63-68; BSP, II, pp. 63-64; III, pp. 74; VI, p. 195-202; GR, XV, pp. 233-245; ICP, X, pp. 120-123). Gilson in this regard argued that the key Thomistic metaphysical doctrine is that of the

real distinction between essence and existence. In other words, a fundamental truth of reality is that a finite being has two metaphysical principles, its essence and an act of being through which it exists (i.e. that we can metaphysically distinguish between a being [ens], what the being is [essentia] and the act which causes a thing to be and to be what it is [esse]). For all that does not belong to the concept of an essence must come to it from without, and I can conceive of an essence without knowing whether or not it exists such as a Phoenix [a large monstrous bird that appeared every 500-1000 years in Egypt]. Thus the essence of a finite being does not contain the cause of its being, instead a finite being owes its being to God who is pure being and whose essence is to exist.

Now with this crucial distinction, claims Gilson, Aquinas went beyond Aristotle for whom form (substance) is being. That is to say, for Aristotle it is the same thing for something to be what it is and to exist, whereas for Aquinas substance refers to an essence which may or may not exist but being refers to the existence added to the essence. For the form of a horse makes it be a horse but it does not make it be. Moreover, Gilson argues, as we have seen, that Aquinas was able to here go beyond Aristotle on account of Christian Revelation. Or in a pithy phrase of Gilson's, philosophers did not infer the supreme existentiality of God from knowledge of the existential nature of things but rather from the self-revelation of God as a pure act of existing (and not just knowing as with Aristotle) they realized the existential nature of things (GP, II, pp. 64-66). In fact, Gilson controversially interprets Aquinas as saying that while we can know with unaided reason that the existence of finite beings is distinct from their essence, and that therefore essence and existence coincide in God, revelation alone can show us that God is pure being itself.

For, claims Gilson, Aquinas nowhere tries to prove by reason that divine esse [being] is also the supreme perfection and actuality of being; for in order to do this he needed to further argue that necesse esse [necessary being] is ipsum esse [being itself], i.e. that God is not just pure essence as Augustine held, which Aquinas does not attempt to do. Scotus and Suarez rejected any argument of this sort in any case (ICP, III, pp. 30-31; VI, pp. 56-63; ECP, V, p. 131; GP, II, pp. 63-66, 70-71; BSP, I, pp. 1-5; II, pp. 48-49; III, pp. 90-91; V, pp. 155-160, 165-168, 174-176; VI, pp. 214-215; see Aquinas, On Being and Essence, 4). Gilson writes: "A finite being does not possess its existence from itself. In order to be it must receive being from necessary being which is God. But this is in no sense a proof that in order to confer actual existence on a finite being God must concreate within it an essence endowed with an act of being which, though distinct from it, forms with it a being (ens) or that-which-has being" (ICP, V, p. 63). So concludes Gilson, these truths were discovered by Aquinas due to the graced happening that a fully-informed metaphysician happened also to be a theologian fully conversant with Scripture and so could arrive at the idea of things being a participated image of the pure Act of Being (ECP, V, pp. 131-132).

25   Maritain had a humorous sign hanging over his cell at the Toulouse monastery which read:"Here lives an old hermit arrived at the end of his life. If his head is no longer worth anything, as well leave him to his dreams. If you believe he still has something to accomplish then have the charity to observe the rule imposed by his work: Not more than a half-hour of conversation!"

26   For more on the life and thought of Maritain see his wife's biography, Maritain, Raïssa, *We Have Been Friends Together* [*Les grandes amitiés*, 2 vols. (1941; 2000)] (New York: Longmans, Green, and Company, 1942)] and see: CTF (1926), pp. 196-197; PTRD (1928), pp. 201-202, 227; SPC (1934), pp. 138-139; RCSM (1938), pp. 37-46; PDG (1942), pp. 41-44; DTC (1950), Tables générales, p. 3147; CAP (1955), pp. 90-92; SHP (1955), p. 1007; CRHP (1957), pp. 472-473; CMCT (1960), pp. 328-350; CEP (1961), p. 238; PFA (1963), pp. 24-37; TE (1963), vol. I, pp. 315-339; PTCW (1964), pp. 541-544; TCT (1965), pp. 89-106; RP (1966), pp. 352-354, 789-792; TS (1966), pp. 16-31; RPF (1968), pp. 77-79, 155; TCP (1969), pp. 39-41; HA (1971), pp. 220-221; HWP (1971), vol. V, pp. 137-139; OB (1971), pp. 242-245; CHP (1974), vol. IX, pp. 254-260; PFPM (1977), pp. 122-137; CHAD (1979), vol. VIII, pp. 684-693; OHYT (1981), pp. 45-60; CTIC (1985), pp. 201-206; PHP (1988), pp. 322-326; TCRT (1988), pp. 285-287; CEWP (1989), p. 191; CP (1989), vol. II, pp. 493-518; CT (1989), pp. 221-234; FUP (1989), pp. 114-160; NCS (1989), pp. 252-253; WE (1991), pp. 157-160, 352-357; FT (1992), pp. 39-50, 65-76, 161-184, BBKL (1993), vol. V, pp. 829-835; DP (1993), vol. II, pp. 1932-1935; NT (1994), pp. 75-96; EMCT (1995), pp. 359-360; HCEC (1995), p. 816; TCFC (1995), pp. 226-227; BDTC (1996), pp. 513-515; TCFP (1996), pp. 40-51; LTK (1997), vol. VI, p. 1386; CTE (1998), pp. 100-102; REP (1998), vol. VI, pp. 101-105; UHF (1998), vol. VIII, pp. 417-447; PCHP (1999), pp. 712-713; MCT (2000), vol. I, p. 352 and vol. II, p. 215; FPTC (2001), pp. 94-98; OHYP (2001), p. 253; TT (2002), pp. 6, 41-42, 99-100, 107-108, 136-137, 215-217; BTCT (2003), pp. 61-65, 107-114, 131-133; CAHP (2003), pp. 463-466; CCC (2003), pp. 26-33; NCE (2003), vol. IX, pp. 177-181; WPR (2003), pp. 338-343; EMFT (2004), pp. 458-460; ER (2004), vol. VIII, pp. 5712-5713; ACP (2005), pp. 330-338; EP (2005), vol. V, pp. 712-718; OGP (2005), p. 555; SHT (2005), pp. 88-89; EF (2006), vol. VII, pp. 7020-7024; TWFP (2006), pp. 165-166; Phelan, Gerald, *Jacques Maritain* (London: Sheed & Ward, 1937); Hook, Sidney, *Reason, Social Myths, and Democracy* (New York: Humanities Press, 1940), pp. 76-104; *Thomist* 5 (1943) [Special Volume on Jacques Maritain]; *Revue Thomiste* 49 (1949) [Special Issue on Jacques Maritain]; Allen, Edgar, *Christian Humanism: A Guide to the Thought of Jacques Maritain* (London: Hodder and Stoughton, 1950); Doolan, Aegidius, *The Revival of Thomism* (Dublin: Clonmore & Reynolds, 1951), pp. 38-46; Fecher, Charles, *The Philosophy of Jacques Maritain* (Westminster: Newman Press, 1953); *Commonweal* 60 (June 11, 1954) [Special Issue on Maritain]; Croteau, Jacques, *Les fondements thomistes du personnalisme de Maritain* (Ottawa: Éditions de l'Université

d'Ottawa, 1955); Fumet, Stanislas, *Jacques Maritain* (Paris: A. Fayard, 1957); Bars, Henry, *Maritain en notre temps* (Paris: B. Grasset, 1959); Evans, Joseph, *Jacques Maritain: The Man and His Achievement* (New York: Sheed and Ward, 1963); Sampaio, Laura, *L'intuition dans la philosophie de Jacques Maritain* (Paris: J. Vrin, 1963); Smith, Colin, *Contemporary French Philosophy* (London: Methuen, 1964), pp. 265-267; Daly, Mary, *Natural Knowledge of God in the Philosophy of Jacques Maritain* (Rome: Officium Libri Catholici, 1966); Nottingham, William, *Christian Faith and Secular Action: An Introduction to the Life and Thought of Jacques Maritain* (St. Louis: Bethany Press, 1968); *New Scholasticism* 46 (1972), pp. 18-31 [Special Issue on Jacques Maritain]; Evans, Joseph, *Jacques Maritain: A Biographical Memoir* (Washington: National Academy of Education, 1973); Griffin, John, *Jacques Maritain: Homage in Words and Pictures* (Albany: Magi Books, 1974); Amato, Joseph, *Mounier and Maritain: A French Catholic Understanding of the Modern World* (University of Alabama Press, 1975); Smith, Brooke, *Jacques Maritain: Antimodern or Ultramodern* (New York: Elsevier Scidentific Publishing Company, 1976); Daujat, Jean, *Maritain, un maître pour notre temps* (Paris: Téqui, 1978); Dunaway, John, *Jacques Maritain* (Boston: Twayne Publishers, 1978); *Thomist* 42 (1978) [Special Issue on Maritain]; Henle, Robert, et al., eds., *Selected Papers from the Conference-Seminar on Jacques Maritain's The Degrees of Knowledge; Aquinas* 25 (1982) [Special Volume on Maritain]; *Giornale Metafisica* 4 (1982) [Special Volume on Maritain]; Shannon, Marie, *Jacques Maritain* (London: Catholic Truth Society, 1982); Doering, Bernard, *Jacques Maritain and the French Catholic Intellectuals* (Notre Dame: University of Notre Dame Press, 1983); Floucat, Yves, *Pour une philosophie chrétienne: Éléments d'un débat fondamental* (Paris: Téqui, 1983); Ramsey, Paul, *Nine Modern Moralists* (Lanham: University Press of America, 1983), pp. 209-256; Allard, Jean-Louis, *Jacques Maritain, philosophe dans la cité* (Ottawa: Éditions de l'Université de Ottawa, 1985); Hudson, Deal, *Understanding Maritain* (Macon: Mercer University Press, 1987); Guillet, Jacques, *La théologie catholique en France de 1914 à 1960* (Paris: Médiasèvres, 1988), pp. 14-18; Knasas, John, *Jacques Maritain: The Man and His Metaphysics* (Notre Dame: American Maritain Association, 1988); Bars, Henry, Bernard Hubert, and Yves Floucat, *Jacques Maritain et ses contemporains* (Paris: Desclée, 1991); Lacombe, Olivier, *Jacques Maritain* (Paris: Téqui, 1991); Prouvost, Géry, *Catholicité de l'intelligence métaphysique: La philosophie dans la foi selon Jacques Maritain* (Paris: Téqui, 1991); Arraj, James, *Mysticism, Metaphysics, and Maritain* (Chiloquin: Inner Growth Books, 1993); Floucat, Yves, *Jacques Maritain, ou La fidélité à l'éternal* (Paris: FAC, 1996); McCamy, Ronald, ed., *Out of a Kantian Chrysalis: A Maritainian Critique of Fr. Maréchal* (New York: Peter Lang, 1998); Chenaux, Philippe, *Entre Maurras et Maritain: Une génération intellectuelle catholique* (Paris: Cerf, 1999); Gross, Raoul, *L'être et la beauté chez Jacques Maritain* (Fribourg: Éditions Universitaires Fribourg, 2001); Ollivant, Douglas, ed., *Jacques Maritain and the Many Ways of Knowing* (Washington: American Maritain Association,

2002); Dougherty, Jude, *Jacques Maritain: An Intellectual Profile* (Washington: Catholic University of America Press, 2003); McInerny, Ralph, *The Very Rich Hours of Jacques Maritain: A Spiritual Life* (Notre Dame University of Notre Dame Press, 2003); Trapani, John, ed., *Truth Matters: Essays in Honor of Jacques Maritain* (Washington: American Maritain Association, 2004); Belley, Pierre-Antoine, *Connaître par le coeur: La connaissance par connaturalité dans les oeuvres de Jacques Maritain* (Paris: Téqui, 2005); De Thieulloy, Guillaume, *Le chevalier de l'absolu: Jacques Maritain entre mystique et politique* (Paris: Gallimard, 2005); Barré, Jean-Luc, *Jacques and Raïssa Maritain: Beggars for Heaven* (Notre Dame: University of Notre Dame Press, 2006); Chenaux, Philippe, *Humanisme intégral de Jacques Maritain* (Paris: Cerf, 2006); De Thieulloy, Guillaume, *Antihumanisme intégral?: L'Augustinisme de Jacques Maritain* (Paris: Téqui, 2006); Aucante, Vincent, et al., eds., *Jacques Maritain, philosophe dans la cité* (Paris: Parole et Silence, 2007); *Revue des sciences religieuses* 81:3-4 (2007), pp. 301-521 [Special Issues on Maritain]; Valadier, Paul, *Maritain à contre-temps* (Paris: Desclée de Brouwer, 2007); Oppy, Graham, ed., *The History of Western Philosophy of Religion* (Oxford: Oxford University Press, 2009), vol. V, pp. 105-118.

27   These books have been translated as *Distinguish to Unite: Or, The Degrees of Knowledge* [DK], tr. Gerald Phelan (New York: Scribner, 1959) and *Approaches to God* [AG], tr. Peter O'Reilly (New York: Harper, 1954) and I make use of these and other translations of Maritain throughout.

Among Maritain's other works of philosophy are: *Elements of Philosophy* [*Eléments de Philosophie*, 2 vols.] (1920-1923) [translated as *An Introduction to Logic* (1937), *Formal Logic* (1946), and *An Introduction to Philosophy* [IP], tr. Edward Ingram Watkin (New York: Sheed & Ward, 1962)]; *Antimodern* [*Antimoderne*] (1922); *Saint Thomas d'Aquin* (1923); *Reflections on Intelligence* [*Réflexions sur l'intelligence et sur sa vie proper*] (1924); *The Angelic Doctor* [*Le Docteur angélique*] (1930) [translated as *The Angelic Doctor* (New York: The Dial Press, 1931) and as *St. Thomas Aquinas* (London: Sheed & Ward, 1933; 1958)]; *On Christian Philosophy* [*De la philosophie chrétienne*] (1932) [translate as *An Essay on Christian Philosophy* [ECHP] (New York: Philosophical Library, 1955)]; *Seven Lessons on Being and the First Principles of Speculative Reason* [*Sept leçons sur l'être et les premiers principes de la raison speculative*] (1934) [translated as *A Preface to Metaphysics: Seven Lectures on Being* [PM] (London: Sheed & Ward, 1939)]; *Wijsheid en praktijk* (1934); *Philosophy of Nature* [*La Philosophie de la nature*] [PN] (1935); *Science and Wisdom* [*Science et sagesse*] [SW] (1935) [Lectures at the Angelicum of 1934; *Integral Humanism* [*Humanisme intégral*] [IH] (1936) [translated as *True Humanism*, tr. Margot Adamson (New York: Charles Scribner's Sons, 1938)]; *Toward a Philosophy of the Human Person* [*Para una filosofia de la persona humana*] (1937); *Four Essays on the Spirit in its Carnal Condition* [*Quatre essais sur l'esprit dans sa condition charnelle* (1939); *Saint Thomas and the Problem of Evil*

[TPE] (1942) [Aquinas Lecture at Marquette University in 1942]; *Étienne Gilson* (1945); *Short Treatise on Existence and the Existent* [*Court Traité de l'existence et de l'existant*] [EE] (1947) [translated as *Existence and the Existent* (New York: Pantheon, 1948)]; *The Significance of Contemporary Atheism* [*La signification de l'athéisme contemporain*] (1949); *Nine Lessons on the First Notions of Moral Philosophy* [*Neuf Leçons sur les notions premières de la philosophie morale*] (1951) [translated as *An Introduction to the Basic Problems of Moral Philosophy* (Albany: Magi Books, 1990)]; *The Sin of the Angel: An Essay on a Reinterpretation of Some Thomistic Positions* (1959); *Man's Approach to God* (1960) [Wimmer Lecture of 1960 at Saint Vincent College, Latrobe]; *Moral Philosophy* [*La Philosophie morale: Examen historique et critique des grands systèmes*] [MP] (1960); *On the Use of Philosophy* [OUP] (1961) [Lectures of 1960 at Princeton University]; *God and the Permission of Evil* [*Dieu et la permission du mal*] [GPE] (1963) [1962 lectures to the Little Brothers of Jesus in Toulouse].

Maritain is also well-known for his many writings on art and politics including *Art and Scholasticism* [*Art et scolastique*] [AS] (1920). He also wrote several theological works, especially towards the end of his life, including: *Confession of Faith* [*Confession de foi*] (1941); *The Life of Prayer* [*La vie d'oraison*] (1943) [with Raïssa Maritain; translated as *Prayer and Intelligence* (New York: Sheed & Ward, 1943)]; *On the Grace and Humanity of Jesus* [*De la Grâce et de l'humanité de Jésus*] (1967); *The Peasant of the Garonne* [*Le Paysan de la Garonne*] [PG] (1966); and *On the Church of Christ: The Person of the Church and Her Personnel* [*De l'Eglise du Christ: La Personne de l'Eglise et Son Personnel*] (1970).

Among his 700 or so essays are: "La science moderne et la raison," *Revue de Philosophie* 6 (1910), pp. 575-603; "L'intuition: Au sense de connaissance instinctive ou d'inclination," *Revue de Philosophie* 23 (1913), pp. 5-13; "Einstein et la notion du temps," *Revue Universelle* 2 (1920), pp. 358-364; "L'intelligence et le règne du coeur," *Revue Universelle* 1 (1920), pp. 623-629; "De l'humanisme chrétien," *Revue Universelle* 4 (1921), pp. 107-113; "L'église et la philosophie de Saint Thomas," *Revue des Jeunes* 11 (1921), pp. 130-163; "Spiritisme et spiritualisme expérimentale," *Revue Universelle* 5 (1921), pp. 689-695; "Connaissance de l'être," *Revue Universelle* 11 (1922), pp. 109-118, 243-248, 655-664; "De la métaphysique des physiciens ou de la simultaneité selon Einstein," *Revue Universelle* 10 (1922), pp. 426-445; "De la verité," *Revue Universelle* 9 (1922), pp. 652-664;. "L'idée thomiste de l'intelligence et nature humaine," *Revue Universelle* 13 (1923), pp. 635-645; "Science et contingence," *Revue Fédéraliste* 6 (1923), pp. 372-380;" "Une question sur la vie mystique et la contemplation," *La vie spirituelle* 7 (1923), pp. 636-650; "À propos des Cahiers du R.P. Maréchal," *Revue Thomiste* 29 (1924), pp. 416-425; "Saint Thomas," *Revue des Jeunes* 14 (1924), pp. 461-505; "Le Thomisme et la crise de l'esprit moderne," *Acta Hebdomadae Thomisticae* (1924), pp. 55-79; "La vie propre de l'intelligence et l'erreur idéaliste," *Revue Thomiste* 29 (1924), pp.

268-313; "Grandeur et misère de la métaphysique," *Chroniques* 1 (1925), pp. 139-179; "The Contemporary Attitude towards Scholasticism," in Zybura, J.S., ed., *Present Day Thinkers and the New Scholasticism* (St. Louis: Herder, 1926), pp. 185-195; "De l'obéissance au pape," *Vie Spirituelle* 15 (1927), pp. 755-757; "Expérience mystique et philosophie," *Revue de Philosophie* 35 (1926), pp. 571-618; "Philosophie et science expérimentale," *Revue de Philosophie* 33 (1926), pp. 342-378; "Saint Thomas d'Aquin," in Baumann, Émile, ed., *La vie et l'oeuvre des quelques grands saints* (Paris: Libraire de France, 1926), pp. 237-266; "La doctrine scholastique de la liberté," *La Vie Intellectuelle* 4 (1929), pp. 242-260; "À propos de la renaissance thomiste," *La Vie Intellectuelle* 6 (1930), pp. 314-324; "Catholic Thought and Its Mission," *Thought* 4 (1930), pp. 533-547; "De la notion de philosophie de la nature," in Geyser, Joseph, ed., *Philosophia Perennis* (Regensburg: J. Habbel, 1930), vol. II, pp. 819-828; "Todo y Nada," *Vigile* 1 (1930), pp. 181-212; "De la connaissance métaphysique et des noms divins," *Vigila* 1 (1931), pp. 149-197; "La notion de philosophie chrétienne," *Bulletin de la Société Française de Philosophie* 31 (1931), pp. 37-72; "Notes sur la personalité," in Claudel, Paul, ed., *Les îles* (Paris: Plon, 1931), pp. 177-190; "Saint Jean de la Croix, practicien de la contemplation," *Études Carmélitaines* 16 (1931), pp. 62-109; "Science et philosophie d'après de principes du réalisme critique," *Revue Thomiste* 36 (1931), pp. 1-46; "Le système de Saint Thomas," *Hochschulwoche* 1 (1931), pp. 139-145; "De la notion de philosophie chrétienne," *Revue Néoscholastique de Philosophie* 34 (1932), pp. 153-186; "Du réalisme critique," *Nova et Vetera* 7 (1932), pp. 1-17; "Notes sur la connaissance," *Rivista di Filosofia Neoscolastica* 24 (1932), pp. 13-23; "Autour des Degrés du Savoir: Réponse au R.P. M.D. Roland-Gosselin," *Bulletin Thomiste* 10 (1933), pp. 188-190; "De la philosophie morale adéquatement prise," *Revue de l'Université d'Ottawa* 2 (1933), pp. 105-134; "La philosophie chrétienne," in Gilson, Étienne, ed., *La philosophie chrétienne* (Juvisy: Journées d'Études de la Société Thomiste, 1933), pp. 147, 163-164; "Une philosophie de la liberté," *Nova et Vetera* 8 (1933), pp. 249-295; "La philosophie de la nature," *Vie Intellectuelle* 31 (1934), pp. 228-259; "Philosophie de la nature et sciences expérimentales," *Acta Pontificiae Academiae Romanae S. Thomae Aquinas et Religionis Catholicae* 1 (1934), pp. 77-93; "Science et sagesse," *Nova et Vetera* 9 (1934), pp. 389-407 [translated as "Science and Wisdom," in Anshen, Ruth Nanda, ed., *Science and Man* (New York: Harcourt, Brace, and Company, 1942), pp. 65-96]; "Le Thomisme et le sens du mystère," *Revue de l'Université d'Ottawa* 4 (1934), pp. 149-161; "Deux essais pour un nouvel humanisme," *Esprit* 3 (1935), pp. 88-117; "Notes pour un programme d'enseignement de la philosophie de la nature et d'enseignement des sciences dans une faculté de philosophie," *Bollettino filosofico* 1:2 (1935), pp. 15-31; "Wisdom into Knowledge," *Blackfriars* 17 (1936), pp. 86-92; "De la connaissance poétique," *Deuxième Congrès International d'Esthétique et de Science de l'Art* 3 (1937), pp. 168-170 [translated as "On Poetic Knowledge," *Blackfriars* 26 (1945), pp. 51-54]; "D'un nouvel humanisme ou d'un humanisme intégral,"

Bulletin de l'Union pur la Vérité 44 (1937), pp. 359-418; "Le discernement médical du merveilleux d'origine divine," Études Carmélitaines 22 (1937), pp. 95-104; "Idée de la personne," Temps Présent 1 (December 24, 1937), p. 2; "Philosophie et Science," Acta Pontificiae Academiae Romanae S. Thomae Aquinatis 3 (1937), pp. 250-266, 270-271; "Réflexions sur la nécessité et la contingence," Angelicum 14 (1937), pp. 281-295 [translated as "Reflections on Necessity and Contingency," in Brennan, Robert, ed., Essays in Thomism (New York : Sheed and Ward, 1942), pp. 25-37]; "L'expérience mystique naturelle et le vide," Études Carmélitaines 23:2 (1938), pp. 116-139; "Freudisme et psychanalyse," Revue Thomiste 44 (1938), pp. 712-734 [translated as "Freudianism and Psychoanalysis," Cross Currents 6:4 (1956), pp. 307-324]; "L'intelligence et la vie," Études Carmélitaines 23 (1938), pp. 42-45; "Individu et Personne," Temps Présent 2 (January 14, 1938), p. 2; "Men and Morals," Blackfriars 19 (1938), pp. 717-725; "Notes sur le Freudisme," Études Carmélitaines 23 (1938), pp. 128-139; "War and the Bombardement of Cities," Commonweal 28 (1938), pp. 460-461; "Contre le naturalisme," Temps Présent 3 (June 2, 1939), p. 3; "I Believe," in Fadiman, Clifton, ed., I Believe (New York: Simon and Schuster, 1939), pp. 197-210; "L'idée thomiste de la liberté," Revue Thomiste 45 (1939), pp. 440-459; "Integral Humanism and the Crisis of Modern Times," Review of Politics 1 (1939), pp. 1-17; "La juste guerre," Temps Présent 3 (September 29, 1939), p. 1 [translated as "Just War," Commonweal 31 (1939), pp. 199-200]; "Qui est mon prochain?," La Vie Intellectuelle 65 (1939), pp. 165-191 [translated as "Who Is My Neighbor?," Homiletic and Pastoral Review 40 (1939), pp. 166-167]; "Surnaturalisme," Temps Présent 3 (May 26, 1939), p. 1; "The Conquest of Freedom," in Anshen, Ruth, ed., Freedom: Its Meaning (New York: Harcourt, Brace, and Company, 1940), pp. 631-649; "Contemorary Renewals in Religious Thought," in Randall, John Herman, ed., Religion and the Modern World (Philadelphia: The University of Pennsylvania Press, 1940), pp. 1-20; "Good Will in Science," The New York Times (August 4, 1940), IV, p. 7; "The Conflict of Methods at the End of the Middle Ages," Thomist 3 (1941), pp. 527-538; "Hope in Christianity," English Catholic Newsletter 97 (1941), pp. 3-4; "L'humanisme de saint Thomas," Medieval Studies 3 (1941), pp. 174-184 [translated as "The Humanism of St. Thomas Aquinas," in Runes, Dagobert, ed., Twentieth Century Philosophy (New York: Philosophical Library, 1943), pp. 295-311]; "The Immortality of Man," Review of Politics 3 (1941), pp. 411-427; "Religion Is the Best Defender of Personal Freedom," The New World (January 17, 1941), p. 7; "Science, Philosophy, and Faith," Religion in Life 10:1 (1941), pp. 3-20; "Atonement for All," Commonweal 36 (1942), p. 509; "Christian Humanism," Fortune 25 (1942), pp. 106-107; "Il faut parfois juger," Pour la Victoire (December 19, 1942), pp. 1-2; "The Natural Law," Commonweal 36 (1942), pp. 83-85; "Natural Law and Human Rights," The Dublin Review 210 (1942), pp. 116-124; "Spontanéité et indépendence," Medieval Studies 41 (1942), pp. 23-32; "Aspects contemporains de la pensée religieuse," Fontaine 6 (1943), pp. 18-33, 151-160; "Humanism and the Dignity of Man," in Ryan, John, ed., *Democracy: Should It Survive?* (Milwaukee : Bruce, 1943), pp. 137-146; "L'immortalité de l'âme," *La Nouvelle Relève* 3 (1943), pp. 1-18 [translated as "The Immortality of Man," in Compton, Arthur Holly, ed., *Man's Destiny in Eternity* (Boston: Beacon Press, 1949), pp. 21-41]; "Sur la doctrine de l'aséité divine," *Medieval Studies* 5 (1943), pp. 29-50; "A Catholic View of the Crucifixion ["L'enseignement chrétien de l'histoire de la crucifixion"]," *Jewish Frontier* 11 (1944), pp. 14-15; "A Reply to Professor Mercier," *Thought* 19 (1944), pp. 573-575; "Poetic Experience," *Review of Politics* 6 (1944), p. 4; "La dialectique immanente du premier acte de liberté," *Nova et Vetera* 20 (1945), pp. 218-235; "Saint Thomas d'Aquin et le problème du mal," *Vie Intellectuelle* 13 (1945), pp. 30-39; "L'immortalité," *Archivio di Filosofia* 15 (1946), pp. 73-95; "Personne et individu," *Acta Pontificiae Academiae S. Thomae Aquinatis* 12 (1946), pp. 3-33; "A New Approach to God," *Science of Culture* 4 (1947), pp. 280-297; "L'existentialisme de St. Thomas," *Acta Pontificiae Academiae S. Thomae Aquinitatis* 13 (1947), pp. 40-64; "From Existential Existentialism to Academic Existentialism," *Sewanee Review* 56 (1948), pp. 210-229; "Les chemins de la foi," *Nova et Vetera* 24 (1949), pp. 97-112; "De la connaissance humaine," *Travaux du Congrès International de Philosophie consacré au Problemes de la Connaissance* (Port-au-Prince: L'Imprimerie de l'État, 1944), pp. 105-120 [translated as "On Human Knowledge," *Thought* XXIV (1949), pp. 225-243]; "L'obligation morale," *Revue Thomiste* 49 (1949), pp. 508-522; "On the Meaning of Contemporary Atheism," *The Review of Politics* 11 (1949), pp. 267-280; "Science, Materialism, and the Human Spirit," *Catholic Mind* 47 (1949), pp. 417-420; "Is Science to Blame?," *Commonweal* 52 (1950), pp. 557-558; "Les jugments de valeur," *Nova et Vetera* 25 (1950), pp. 116-134; "Religion and the Intellectuals," *The Partisan Review* 17 (1950), pp. 93-98; "The Angelic Doctor," *Proceedings of the American Catholic Philosophical Association* 25 (1951), pp. 4-10; "On Knowledge through Connaturality," *Review of Metaphysics* 4 (1951), pp. 473-482; "The Problem of Means," *Commonweal* 53 (1951), p. 415-421; "Western Civilization and Religious Faith," *The Library Journal* 76 (1951), pp. 1284-1289, 1380-1385, 1402-1403; "Natural Law and Moral Law," in Anshen, Ruth Nanda, ed., *Moral Principles of Action: Man's Ethical Imperative* (New York: Harper, 1952), pp. 62-76 "La répercussion de l'empiricisme sur la culture," *Nova et Vetera* 27 (1952), pp. 1-14 [translated as "The Cultural Impact of Empiricism," in *Thomist* 14 (1952), pp. 448-466]; "Tolerance and the Absolutes," *Commonweal* 56 (1952), pp. 342-344; "Angoisse et existentialisme," *Nova et Vetera* 28 (1953), pp. 241-248; "The Breviary of Hate," *Social Research* 20 (1953), pp. 219-229; "Philosophy and the Unity of the Sciences," *Proceedings of the American Catholic Philosophical Association* 27 (1953), pp. 34-56; "Une foi par quoi l'on vit," *Nova et Vetera* 28 (1953), pp. 81-86; "The Philosopher in Society," in Leo Baeck, ed., *Essays Presented to Leo Baeck* (London: East and West Library, 1954), pp. 96-105; "Sur la notion de la subsistence," *Revue Thomiste* 54 (1954), pp. 242-256 [translated as "On the Notion of Subsistence," in McWilliams,

J.A., ed., *Progress in Philosophy* (Milwaukee: Bruce, 1955), pp. 29-45]; "The Divine Plan," in Runes, Dagobert, ed., *Treasury of World Philosophy* (New York: The Philosophical Library, 1955), pp. 786-789; "Una Sexta Via," *Ad Ordem* 53 (1955), pp. 119-126; "Christianity and Philosophy," in *Man in Contemporary Society* (New York: Columbia University Press, 1956), vol. II, pp. 823-838; "Le péché de l'Ange," *Revue Thomiste* 56 (1956), pp. 197-239; "Confession of Faith," in Burnett, Whit, ed., *This is My Philosophy* (New York: Harper and Brothers, 1957), pp. 86-101]; "Language and the Theory of Sign," in Anshen, Ruth Nanda, ed., *Language: An Enquiry into Its Meaning and Function* (New York: Harper and Brothers, 1957), pp. 86-101; "Natural Law," in Utley, Thomas, ed., *Documents of Modern Political Thought* (Cambridge: Cambridge University Press, 1957), pp. 181-189; "Philosophy and the Unity of the Sciences," in *Studi sul pensiero di Giuseppe Zamboni* (Milan: Marzorati, 1957), pp. 705-722; "Philosophy and Experimental Science," and "The Philosophy of Nature," in Koren, Henry, ed., *Readings in the Philosophy of Nature* (Westminster: The Newman Press, 1958), pp. 50-61, 83-87; "Theocentric Humanism," in Koch, Adrienne, ed., *Philosophy for a Time of Crisis* (New York: E.P. Dutton, 1959), pp. 199-214; "About Christian Philosophy," in Schwartz, Balduin, ed., *Human Person and the World of Values* (New York: Fordham University Press, 1960), pp. 1-10; "The Natural Law and the Human Person," in Murphy, J. Stanley, ed., *Christianity and Culture* (Baltimore: Helicon Press, 1960), pp. 39-48; "A Third Way: By the Contingent and the Necessary," in Kaufman, Walter, ed., *Religion from Tolstoy to Camus* (New York: Harper and Brothers, 1961), pp. 380-382; "Dieu et la science," *Nova et Vetera* 36 (1961), pp. 241-251; "Philosophy of Science," in Beck, Robert, ed., *Perspectives in Philosophy* (New York: Rinehart and Winston, 1961), pp. 73-78; "Amour et amitié," *Nova et Vetera* 40 (1965), pp. 241-249; "Letter sur la philosophie à l'heure du Concile," *Nova et Vetera* 40 (1965), pp. 241-249; "De la grâce et de l'humanité de Jésus," *Nova et Vetera* 41 (1966), pp. 1-23, 161-218; "Vers und idée thomiste de l'évolution," *Nova et Vetera* 42 (1967), pp. 87-136; "Reflexions sur la nature blessée et sur l'intuition de l'être," *Revue Thomiste* 68 (1968), pp. 5-40; "Quelques reflexions sur le savoir théologique," *Revue Thomiste* 69 (1969), pp. 5-27; "Le tenant-lieu de théologie chez les simples," *Nova et Vetera* 44 (1969), pp. 81-121; "Il n'y a pas de savoir sans intuitivité," *Revue Thomiste* 70 (1970), pp. 30-71; "A Proof for Immortality," in Miller, Edward, ed., *Philosophical and Religious Issues* (Encino: Dickenson, 1971), pp. 293-304; "Du savoir moral," *Revue Thomiste* 82 (1982), pp. 533-549.

Some of these essays have been collected in: *Ransoming the Time* [RT] (1941); *Reason and Reasons* [*Raison et raisons*] [RR] (1948) [translated as *The Range of Reason* (New York: Scribner, 1952)]; *Challenges and Renewals* (Notre Dame: University of Notre Dame Press, 1966); *A Maritain Reader* (Garden City: Image Books, 1966); *Untrammeled Approaches* [*Approches sans entraves*] [UT] (1973); *Natural Law* [*La loi naturelle*] [NLW] (1986).

Compilations of Maritain's works are found in Maritain, Jacques, *Oeuvres*, 2 vols. (Bruxelles: Desclée de Brouwer, 1975-1978), Maritain, Jacques, *Oeuvres complètes*, 15 vols. (Fribourg: Éditions Univresitaires, 1982-1999), and Maritain, Jacques, *The Collected Works of Jacques Maritain*, 20 vols. (1995-).

For Bibliographies of the work of Jacques Maritain see: Gallagher, Donald, et al., eds., *The Achievement of Jacques and Raissa Maritain: A Bibliography, 1906-1961* (New York: Doubleday, 1962); Fraga De Almeida Sampaio, Laura, ed., *Intuition dans la philosophie de Jacques Maritain* (Paris: Vrin, 1963), pp. 169-211; Allion, Jean-Marie, ed., *Bibliographie des œuvres de Jacques et Raïssa Maritain* (Kolbsheim: Cercle d'Etudes Jacques & Raïssa Maritain, 1982).

A Maritainian archives is found at the Jacques Maritain Center of the University of Notre Dame and at the Centre d'Etudes Jacques et Raïssa Maritain in Kolbsheim France.

28   Maritain encapsulates the Thomistic theory of knowledge in the following seven theses: 1) There is a vigorous correspondence between knowledge and immateriality; 2) To know is to be in a certain way something other than what one is: it is to become a thing other than oneself (*fieri aliud a se*), to be or become the other as other (*esse seu fieri aliud in quantum aliud*). Thus there is a kind of union, transcending every material union, between knower and known; 3) To know is to the sense and to the intellect as to exist is to the essence or quidditative function. For knowing is an active, immaterial superexistence whereby a subject existing for itself, through its own activity, has an unlimited existence and becomes other things; 4) The act of knowing differs from all of the actions we ordinarily observe around us in the world and is neither an Aristotelian action or passion. For it does not consist in the production of anything, even within the knowing subject, but is an advancing of oneself to an act of supereminent perfection; 5) When it is a matter of knowing something other than God, knowing involves intentional being (*esse intentionale*) [representative existence; the existence of a sign] —which is to say that an object is divested of its proper existence and made present in an immaterial and intentional state (in an abstract and universal way) in one's mind—rather than natural being (*esse naturae*) [entitative existence; the existence of a thing] which is the way a singular and concrete thing exists outside of thought, the being it possesses in its own nature. Thus there are two ways of having existence, one in the subject (immaterial) and one outside of the subject (material); 6) The known is united with the knower through immaterial forms which are likenesses or species (presentative forms) of the known object. This occurs as the external senses receive the impressed species from the thing and the internal senses produce an image (phantasm) of the sensed thing in the imagination and memory. Then in a first intellectual act the active intellect produces an impressed species (presentative form) abstracted from the sensible image by setting free the intelligibility it contains. And in a second intellectual act it produces the expressed species (the elaborated or uttered presentative form)

which is the mental word or concept uttered by the active intellect and stored in the passive intellect; 7) The likenesses or intelligible species (presentative forms), as immaterial forms, are formally vicars of the object, pure likenesses of the object. They allow the soul to acquire an existence not limited to itself alone and gain knowledge (DK, III, pp. 119-126, 131; III, n. 115 on p. 129; UA, XIV, pp. 310-320). Hence a Thomistic noetic is realistic and "recognizes the existence of things outside the mind and the possibility of attaining these things for the mind and of constructing within·itself and by its own activity, beginning with the senses, a true knowledge, or conformity with what is" (DK, II, p. 24 [44-45]; cf. DK, Preface, p. ix; III, pp. 76, 80-83, 109, 114-115; V, p. 226; IP, II, 4, pp. 124-125).

29   In light of his natural theology, Maritain distinguishes three kinds of atheists: 1) the real atheist [true or absolute atheist]—someone who rejects the life of love and the moral good, or who tries to separate the good from the Good (i.e. God) and so has an idol of the good and truly denies the existence of God. For the real atheist mistakenly thinks the casting aside of the ultimate end is enfranchisement and moral maturity. Maritain implies there are very few real atheists, perhaps including only such figures as Proudhon, Feuerbach, Nietzsche, Marx, Hitler, and Picasso (or some of his art); 2) the pseudo atheist – the person who claims to deny God but really only denies a misrepresentation of God (one is here indignant against the Jupiter of this world, the God of the philosophers) due to their upbringing in an atheistic education or a wounding "religious" social environment, or deceived by sophisms and disordered reasons. Yet as this kind of atheist embraces goodness (absolute value and the ultimate end), he or she does know God in some way, even if unconsciously or implicitly (in the dark mirror of the moral good). Said differently one here possesses God as an authentic object of reason and will without knowing it in the choice of the good for the sake of the good (through practical knowledge). Still there is a frailty to this kind of knowledge of God; 3) the practical atheist—someone who claims to believe in God but shows they really don't by how they act. Here one is a theist for the sake of appearance or outward show, or class or family advantage, or background, but one lives on empty formulas as shown by one's denying the gospel of love, despising the poor, out of an interest in oneself, prestige, or possessions. Here one has a decorative but not living faith and indeed is in a lower or just as low state as that of the pseudo atheist (RR, VI, pp. 66-71, 81-85; VII, pp. 91, 96-102; VIII, pp. 103-113; DK, VI, n. 70 on pp. 290-291; VI, p. 292; n. 96 on p. 309; AG, IV, p. 100-103; IH, II, 2, pp. 63-66; OUP, II, p. 41; cf. Aquinas, *Summa Theologiae* 1a2ae q. 89 a. 6 and q. 109 a. 3).

30   Maritain also accepts various intuitive but non-demonstrative ways to God of the practical intellect founded on this connatural knowledge. Indeed as Maritain remarks "there are for the human as many ways of knowing that God exists as there are steps forward for him on the earth or paths to his own

heart. For all our perishable treasures of being and beauty are besieged on all sides by the immensity and eternity of the One Who Is" (OUP, III, pp. 64-65).

Firstly, we can discover God in the beauty of artistic work and creative poetry. For beauty is a transcendental perfection that transcends the things it is in and attests to their kinship with the infinite. In other words beauty is a reflection of the Absolute Spirit from which things proceed (AG, IV, pp. 84-92; DK, I, p. 2). Secondly, there is a moral knowledge of God, grounded in unconditional moral obligations, inalienable rights, and the intrinsic dignity of human person (what Maritain calls the choice of the good in the first act of freedom). For we discover a moral good with its mysterious demand that good ought to be done as it is good [out of *bonum honestum* or pure goodness], i.e. from a formal motive which transcends the whole order of empirical convenience and desire (and similarly that we must avoid evil not out of fear of punishment but because it is wrong). Now this implies an ideal order of our activity, a law of human acts transcending the whole empirical order, a Goodness transcending all empirical experience. For we cannot rationally justify moral obligations without invoking an uncreated Reason from which the world proceeds and which is the subsistent Good itself (AG, IV, pp. 92-100, 103-104; n. 10 on p. 94; n. 11 on p. 97; RR, VI, pp. 68-69). Likewise, we grasp that love is not a passing pleasure or a more or less intense emotion, but a root tendency, the very meaning of our being, and so we grasp a transcendent Love permeating and activating all beings (RR, VII, pp. 91-92, 95; AG, IV, pp. 104-108).

31   In terms of the notion of Christian Philosophy, Maritain presents a similar, though not identical, view to that of Gilson's. Maritain explicates this relationship between philosophy and theology by distinguishing, with regard to philosophy, between an order of specification (its nature in itself) and an order of exercise (its exercise in a concrete life; its historical state) (ECHP, III, p. 17; "ACP," pp. 2-4; SW, III, pp. 79-107, 127-133; EE, V, pp. 141-146). In its order of specification philosophy is independent of faith in terms of its objects, principles, and methods. For it is based on experiential evidence and logical proof and so no reasoning derived from faith touches its inner fabric. Philosophy is thus autonomous in terms of its specification and can through itself grasp various truths (ECHP, II, pp. 11-12, 14-15; III, pp. 29, 31; IV, pp. 35-37; "ACP," pp. 8-10; SW, III, p. 102). Yet in its actual order of exercise philosophical reason is weak and can be aided by grace and revelation. Said revelation does two things for philosophy, it gives it inner subjective strengthening as well as objective endowments (i.e. new content) (ECHP, III, p. 32; IP, I, 7, pp. 77-83; SW, III, p. 82; "ACP," pp. 6-8). Revelation strengthens philosophy as the habit of faith purifies the philosophical *habitus* [habit] and lets the truth shine forth with more vividness and makes the work of philosophy easier, more certain, and more fruitful (ECHP, III, pp. 27-28; IV, pp. 36, 41, 44, 49; AG, II, n. 16 on pp. 67-68; DK, VI, pp. 305-306). Secondly, revelation gives new notional data to philosophy, and in two forms. It supplies reason with concepts that

exceed its scope and abilities—data that unaided reason cannot grasp (such as the ideas of the Trinity—three subsistences of personality identical with the divine essence—and Incarnation of God in the flesh, God as a creating and not just conserving cause, a possible love of friendship of God above all things and for Himself, and the Redemption) (ECHP, I, pp. 10-11; Appendix, p. 60; DK, V, pp. 248-249; VI, pp. 297, 306; AG, II, pp. 70-71). Revelation also supplies reason with notions that even if philosophy is physically capable of grasping, it is morally incapable of doing so. For historically it can often be the case that while certain ideas were not totally unknown to philosophers and there were some conceptual preparations, still prior to revelation they remained unclarified and in the shadows. Here then revelation can supply philosophy with data that it is capable of grasping on its own but which it has failed to do explicitly [so Maritain is not quite as pessimistic as Gilson was about reason's ability to grasp these data apart from revelation. In the first place philosophers had at least a partial grasp of many of these concepts apart from revelation. And secondly, Maritain seems to allow the possibility that philosophy could have more fully grasped them apart from revelation even if it historically didn't, whereas Gilson appears to favor the view that philosophy really did not have the capability of grasping these truths without revelation]. Some of these notions that Christian revelation gives to philosophy, though which are graspable by reason, are the philosophical distinctions between substance and accident, essence and existence, nature and person, and nature and grace, and the ideas of creation, the soul as the object of salvation, sin as an offense against God, God as subsisting being and subsisting love itself, and the Logos (ECHP, III, pp. 18, 21, 23; SW, III, pp. 90-91, 102; PM, V, p. 95; "ACP," pp. 5-8). Let us turn to some quotes of Maritain on Christian Philosophy:

"Christian philosophy is philosophy itself insofar as it is situated in those utterly distinctive conditions of existence and exercise into which Christianity has ushered the thinking subject, and as a result of which philosophy perceives certain objects and validly demonstrates certain propositions, which in any other circumstances would to a greater or lesser extent elude it" (ECHP, III, p. 30).

"In sum, we understand that the state of philosophy has been changed and lifted up by Christianity, not only with respect to the objective material proposed but also with respect to the vitality and deepest dynamism of the intellect. On all these counts it must be affirmed that faith guides or orientates philosophy, *veluti stella rectrix* [as a guiding star], without thereby violating its autonomy; for it is always in keeping with its own proper laws and principles and by virtue of its rational norms alone that philosophy judges things. This is true even of those things which, albeit naturally accessible to reason alone, would not in reality be recognized or preserved by reason without taint of error, if reason had not been at once notified of their existence and fortified in itself through a kind of living continuity with superior lights" (ECHP, III, p. 29)

"We need to distinguish the nature of philosophy from its state. In other words, we need to distinguish the order of specification from the order of exercise. Considered in its pure nature or essence, philosophy, which is specified by an object naturally knowable to reason, depends only on the evidence and criteria of natural reason. But here we are only considering its abstract nature. Taken concretely, in the sense of being a *habitus* [habit] or a group of *habitus* [habits] existing in the human soul, philosophy is in a certain state, it is either pre-Christian or Christian or a-Christian, which has a decision influence on the ways in which it exists and develops. In fact, it receives from faith and from revelation an aid without which theologians have said it is incapable of realizing fully the claims of its true nature; I mean, without too many mistakes. From faith and revelation it receives objective data which deal primarily with revealed truths of the natural order. The highest of these have been regularly missed or misstated by the great pagan philosophers. Moreover, these objective data are also concerned with the repercussions of truths of the supernatural order on philosophical reflection, and here the connections and echoes really extend indefinitely. And from the subjective reinforcements which also extend indefinitely philosophy receives the superior wisdom, theological wisdom and infused wisdom, which rectify and purify in the soul the philosophical habitus with which they maintain a continuity not of essence but of movement and illumination, fortifying them in their proper order, and lifting them to higher levels" (SW, III, pp. 79-80).

This aiding of philosophy by theology is especially evident in morality. Here Maritain distinguishes between a natural morality (in infraposition to theology), a moral philosophy sublated or subalternated to theology (wherein the principles of the subalternated science are made evident by a superior science), and moral theology proper (which is purely supernatural). Now natural morality is based on pure reason with no input from revelation, such as with Plato's cardinal virtues (wisdom, courage, temperance, and justice), Aristotle's virtues, or Aquinas's natural law. It can disclose a few ethical truths but it is based on our fallen nature and lacks a knowledge of the ultimate end. Moreover, here our love for God is based on a love for ourselves.

Moral philosophy in contrast is based on philosophical reasoning done in the light of theology. It hence uses the light of reason but a light completed and perfected by faith. Here, following Cajetan, we want God to be ours not out of love of ourselves but out of love of God (*volo Deum mihi, non propter me* [I want God for myself, not on account of myself]). For grace penetrates the depths of nature and renders it no longer closed in on itself. So too moral philosophy discovers our true supernatural end and beatitude (in the beatific vision of God) as well as the theological virtues of faith, hope, and charity (DK, I, pp. 14-15; ECHP, IV, pp. 39-41; Appendix, pp. 62-65, 67-68, 72-73, 75, 79-80, 86, 88, 92-93; n. 5-6 on p. 100-101; n. 26 on p. 104; IP, II, 9, p. 186; MP, V, pp. 75-91; SW, III, pp. 80-81, 107-127; IV, pp. 137, 152-209; Appendix, pp. 221-241; see Aquinas, *Summa Theologiae*, 2a2ae q. 17 a. 5 n. 8).

Finally there is moral theology, a divine science based directly on the Word of God. Here by revelation we grasp the Decalogue and the New Law of Christ, the code of morality issued from on-high, which we can integrate with our natural ethics. Maritain contrasts moral philosophy (sublated to theology) and moral theology (following from theology) in the following manner:

> "Instead of considering human acts themselves under the intelligible light (*ratio formalis* [formal reason]) of God's intimate life as revealed and communicated, moral philosophy adequately considered envisages even the supernatural end itself under the practical and human light of human acts being capable of regulation by reason (appropriately completed)" (ECHP, Appendix, p. 80).

> "[Moral theology] is specified solely by God as reached through the objective light of revelation. Moral philosophy (adequately considered), on the other hand, ponders human acts in so far as they are capable of being regulated by human reason (suitably completed),—and is specified and limited by this practical object. And, in fact, it is only because the existential conditions of human action are actually tied up with realities about which revelation alone can teach us with certitude that moral philosophy adequately considered must of necessity take revelation into account—and be subalternated to theology" (ECHP, Appendix, p. 76; cf. Appendix, p. 91).

32   For more on the thought of Wojtyła, see: CP (1990), vol. III, p. 815; DP (1993), vol. II, pp. 2959-2961; NT (1994), pp. 157-161; HCEC (1995), pp. 714-715; LTK (1996), vol. V, pp. 979-980; ICEA (1997), pp. 493-500; OHYP (2001), p. 212; PWW (2002), pp. 486-490; BTCT (2003), pp. xviii-xxiv, 30, 307; NCE (2003), vol. VII, pp. 992-1007; Hebblethwaite, Peter, *John Paul II* (Toronto: Gabe Publications, 1979); Lawler, Ronald, *The Christian Personalism of Pope John Paul II* (Chicago: Franciscan Herald Press, 1982); Woznicki, Andrew, *The Dignity of Man as a Person: Essays on the Christian Humanism of His Holiness John Paul II* (San Francisco: Society of Christ, 1987); McDermott, John, ed., *The Thought of Pope John Paul II* (Rome: Gregorian University Press, 1993); Schmitz, Kenneth, *At the Center of the Human Drama: The Philosophical Anthropology of Karol Wojtyła* (Washington: Catholic University of America, 1993); O'Carroll, Michael, *John Paul II: A Dictionary of His Life and Teachings* (Belfast: J.M.J. Publications, 1994); Buttiglione, Rocco, *Karol Wojtyła: The Thought of the Man Who Became John Paul II* (Grand Rapids: Eerdmans, 1997); Curran, Charles, and Richard McCormick, eds., *John Paul II and Moral Theology* (Mahwah: Paulist Press, 1998); DiNoia, Joseph, and Romanus Cessario, eds., *Veritatis Splendor and the Renewal of Moral Theology* (Hungington: Our Sunday Visitor, 1999); Weigel, George, *Witness to Hope: The Biography of John Paul II* (New York: Harper Collins, 1999); Kupczak, Jarosaw, *Destined for Liberty: The Human Person in the Philosophy of Karol Wojtyła* (Washington: Catholic University of America Press, 2000); Reimers, Adrian, *An Analysis of the Concepts of Self-Fulfillment*

and *Self-Realization in the Thought of Karol Wojtyła, Pope John Paul II* (Lewiston: Edwin Mellen Press, 2001); Simpson, Peter, *On Karol Wojtyła* (Belmont: Wadsworth, 2001); Dulles, Avery, *The Splendor of Faith: The Theological Vision of Pope John Paul II* (New York: Crossroad, 2003); Foster, David, ed., *The Two Wings of Catholic Thought: Essays on Fides et Ratio* (Washington: The Catholic University of America Press, 2003); McNerney, John, *Footbridge towards the Other: An Introduction to the Philosophical Thought of John Paul II* (Bristol: Continuum, 2003); Curran, Charles, *The Moral Theology of Pope John Paul II* (Washington: Georgetown University Press, 2005); *John Paul II* (Pleasantville: Reader's Digest, 2005); Dulles, Avery, ed., *Pope John Paul II on the Body* (Philadelphia: Saint Joseph's University Press, 2007); Varghese, Kleetus, *Personalism in John Paul II* (Hindmarsh: ATF Press, 2007); Rhonheimer, Martin, ed., *The Perspective of the Acting Person* (Washington: Catholic University of America Press, 2008); Savage, Deborah, *The Subjective Dimension of Human Work: The Conversion of the Acting Person according to Karol Wojtyła/John Paul II and Bernard Lonergan* (Frankfurt: Peter Lang, 2008); MacIntyre, Alasdair, *God, Philosophy, Universities* (London: Rowman & Littlefield, 2009), pp. 151-172; Barrett, Edward, *Persons and Liberal Democracy: The Ethical and Political Thought of Karol Wojtyła/Pope John Paul II* (Lanham: Lexington Books, 2010).

33   These works have been translated as *Love and Responsibility* [LR] (San Francisco: Ignatius Press, 1993) and the *The Acting Person* [AP], edited by Anna-Teresa Tymieniecka and translated by Andrzej Potocki (Reidel: Dordrecht, 1979). There is some controversy in that the editor of *The Acting Person*, Anna-Teresa Tymieniecka, tended to replace John Paul II's Latin scholastic terms such as *suppositum* with English equivalents such as ontological nucleus, structural basis, etc. (see Buttiglione, p. 117; Weigel, p. 174 and 880, and Simpson, pp. 5-6). Regardless I make use of these translations throughout.

Other philosophical works of Wojtyła include *Evaluation of the Possibility of Constructing a Christian Ethics based on the Assumptions of Max Scheler's System of Philosophy* [*Ocena możliwości zbudowania etyki chrześcijańskiej przy założeniach systemu Maksa Schelera*] (1959) [thesis of 1953]; *Perche l'uomo: Scritti inediti di antropologia e filosofia* (1995); *Lectures from Lublin* (Franfurt: Peter Lang, 2003); *The Theology of the Human Body* (1997) [collection of Wednesday Audience Lectures of 1979-1984]. An anthology of Wojtyła's thought was published as *Toward a Philosophy of Praxis*, ed., Alfred Bloch, et al. (New York: Crossroad, 1980).

We should also mention Pope John Paul II's more philosophical encyclicals: *Redemptor Hominis* (1979); *Laborem Exercens* (1981); *Sollicitudo Rei Socialis* (1987); *Centesimus Annus* [CA] (1991); *Veritatis Splendor* (1993); *Evangelium Vitae* [EV] (1995); and *Fides et Ratio* [FR] (1998).

Karol Wojtyła wrote 190 essays (mostly in Polish) on philosophy, politics, and theology from 1949-2003. One can profitably consult such articles as:

"Slowo konkowe," *Analecta Cracoviesia* n. 5-6 (1973-1974), pp. 243-263 [discussion of his *The Acting Person* (1969)]; "The Personal Structure of Self-Determination," *Tommaso d'Aquino nel suo VII centenario—Congresso Internazionale, Roma-Napoli, 17-24 aprile, 1974* (Naples: Edizioni Domenicane Italiane, 1974), pp. 379-390; "Bishops as Servants of the Faith: The Problem and its Theological Foundations," *The Irish Theological Quarterly* 43 (1976), pp.260-274; "Das Problem der Erfahrung in der Ethik," in *Tomasza z Akwinu, Redakcja Wydawnictw* (Lublin: Catholic University of Lublin Press, 1976), pp. 267-288; "The Intentional Act—the Human Act: That is, Act and Experience," *Analecta Husserliana* 5 (1976), pp. 269-280; "Teoria e prassi nella filosofia della persona umana," *Sapienza* 29 (1976), pp. 377-384; "La verità sull'uomo," *Osservatore Romano* 49 (1976), p. 2; "Participation or Alienation?," *Analecta Husserliana*, VI (1977), pp. 61-73; "Amore fecondo e responsabile," in *Discorso al Congresso del Cisf , 21 giugno 1978* (Milan: Gruppo Periodici Paolini, 1978), pp. 26-34; "Subjectivity and the Irreducible in Man," *Analecta Husserliana* 7 (1978), pp. 107-114; "Teoría y Praxis: Un tema humano y cristiano," *Verbo* 169 (1978), pp. 1191-1204; "Travail et sens de l'homme," *Documetation catholique*75 (1978), pp. 911-913; "Die menschliche Person im Kontext der ehelichen Hingabe und Elternschaft," in Piegsa, Joachim, et al., eds., *Person im Kontext des Sittlichen* (Düsseldorf: Patmos Verlag, 1979), pp. 160-174; "The Person: Subject and Community," *Review of Metaphysics* 33 (1979), pp. 273-308; "The Task of Christian Philosophy Today," *Proceedings of the American Catholic Philosophical Association* 53 (1979), pp. 3-4; "The Transcendence of the Person in Action and Man's Self-Teleology," *Analecta Husserliana* 9 (1979), pp. 203-212; "Die ethische Fibel," in Wojtyła, Karol, *Erziehung zur Liebe: Mit einer ethischen Fibel* (Stuttgart-Degerloch: Seewald, 1980), pp. 63-154; "The Degrees of Being from the Point of View of the Phenomenology of Action," *Analecta Husserliana* 11 (1981), pp. 125-130; "La persona: Soggetto e comunitá," *Il Nuovo Areopago* 5 (1986), pp. 7-52; "La soggetività e l'irriducibilità nell'uomo," *Il Nuovo Areopago* 6 (1987), pp. 7-16; "L'autoteleologia dell'uomo e la trascendenza della persona nell'atto," *Il Nuovo Areopago* (1988), pp. 6-18; "Il disegno di Dio sulla famiglia," *Il Nuovo Areopago* 7 (1988), pp. 5-44; "Evolution and the Living God," in Peters, Ted, ed., *Science and Theology: A New Consonance* (Boulder: Westview Press, 1998), pp. 149-152; "Curriculum Philosophicum," [unpublished autobiographical notice], in Weigel, George, *Witness to Hope* (New York: HarperCollins, 2005), pp. 893-901. Some of these essays have been collected in *I fondamenti dell'ordine etico* (1981); *The Person and Community* [PEC] (1994); *Ethics and Morality* (Frankfurt: Peter Lang, 2004).

He has also written works of autobiography, poetry, spirituality, theology, and theater (see his *Tutte le opere letterarie. Poesie, drammi e scritti sul teatro* (Milan: Bompiani, 2001).

For a bibliography of the writings of Wojtyła see: Kaczyński, E., and B. Mazur, "Bibliografia di Karol Wojtyła," *Angelicum* 56 (1979), pp. 149-164; Tymieniecka, Anna-Teresa, "Bibliography of Philosophical Publications of Cardinal Karol Wojtyła/Pope John Paul II," *Phenomenology Information Bulletin* 3 (1979), pp. 105-111; Gramatowski, W., and Z. Wilińska, *Karol Wojtyła negli scritti* (Vatican City: Libreria Editrice Vaticana, 1980); Schmitz, Kenneth, *At the Center of the Human Drama: The Philosophical Anthropology of Karol Wojtyła/Pope John Paul II* (Washington: The Catholic University of America Press, 1993), pp. 147-163; Girenti, Giuseppe, "Nota Bibliografica," in Wojtyła, Karol, *Metafisica della persona: Tutte le opere filosofiche e saggi integrativi* (Milan: Bompiani, 2003), pp.1581-1596.

34   Proportionalism has been defended by Fr. Louis Janssens (1908-2002); Fr. Franz Scholz (1909-1998); Bernard Häring, C.S.S.R. (1912-1998); Josef Fuchs, S.J. (1912-2005); Fr. Franz Böckle (1921-1991); the Dutchman Cornelius J. Van Der Poel, C.S.S.P. (1921-); Richard A. McCormick, S.J. (1922-2000); Bruno Schüller, S.J. (1925-2007); Walter Kerber, S.J. (1926-2006); John F. Dedek (1929-); the Dutchman William Van Der Marck (1929-); James Keenan, S.J. (c. 1930-); Klaus Demmer, M.S.C. (1931-); Fr. Charles Curran (1934-); David Hollenbach, S.J. (c. 1934-); Franz Furger (1935-1997); Peter Knauer, S.J. (1935-); Garth Hallett, S.J. (c. 1937-); Rudolf Ginters (1939-); Sr. Margaret Farley (c. 1940-); Philip S. Keane, S.S. (c. 1940-); Daniel C. MacGuire (c. 1945-); Maurice de Wachter (c. 1945-); Edward Collins Vacek, S.J. (c. 1948-); Timothy E. O'Connell (c. 1954-); Joseph Selling (c. 1955-); James Walter (c. 1955-); Bernard Hoose (c. 1957-); Richard M. Gula, S.S. (c. 1958-); and Lisa Sowie Cahill (c. 1960-).

35   According to John Paul II what proportionalists fail to see is that intrinsically evil acts are defined in terms of a specifying circumstance. Thus the object of the act includes a primary circumstance. He writes "One must therefore reject the thesis, characteristic of teleological and proportionalist theories, which holds that it is impossible to qualify as morally evil according to its species—its 'object'—the deliberate choice of certain kinds of behavior or specific acts, apart from a consideration of the intention for which the choice is made or the totality of the foreseeable consequences of that act for all persons concerned" (VS, 79; cf. VS, 78; Aquinas, *Summa Theologiae*, 1a 2ae q. 18 a. 10; cf. 1a 2ae q. 18 a. 2, 3, 5, 10-11). With this in mind murder can be defined as the killing of an innocent human (versus an aggressor or criminal), theft as the taking of another's property against the reasonable will of the owner (so one can take the property of another in great need), and lying is defined by some moral theologians as the telling of a falsehood to one who deserves to know the truth. And as such the moral norms here are exceptionless [See Smith, Janet, "Moral Terminology and Proportionalism" in Hibbs, Thomas, ed., *Recovering Nature* (Notre Dame: University of Notre Dame Press, 1999), pp. 127-146 and "Veritatis Splendor, Proportionalism, and Contraception," *Irish Theologi-*

cal *Quarterly* 63: 4 (1998), pp. 307-326; and "Natural Law and Personalism in Veritatis Splendor," in Allsopp, Michael, et al., eds., *Veritatis Splendor: American Responses* (Kansas City: Sheed and Ward, 1995), pp. 194-207].

36 There have been more than 1000 Twentieth-Century Catholic Neo-Thomists including:

American Neo-Thomists: Charles Coppens (1835-1920); Fr. John Gmeiner (1847-1913); William Poland, S.J. (1848-1923); James Conway (1849-1905); Fr. Edward Pace (1861-1938); the Xaverian Joseph Conlan [Brother John Chrysostom] (1863-1917); William Joseph Brosnan, S.J. (1864-1951); William Turner (1871- 1936), at the Catholic University of America; Edward Gregory Lawrence Van Becelaere, O.P. (1872-1946); John F. McCormick; Gerard Esser, S.V.D. (c. 1882-1950); James Aloysius McWilliams (1882-1965); Rudolf Allers (1883-1963); the Capuchin Celestine Nicholas Charles Bittle (c. 1884-1937); Bishop James Ryan (1886-1947); Henry Ignatius Smith, O.P. (1886-1957); Roy Joseph Deferrari (1890-1965); Gerald B. Phelan (1892-1965); Paul Joseph Glenn (1893-1957); Fr. Charles Aloysius Hart (1893-1959); Leo Richard Ward, C.S.C. (1893-1984); Henri Renard, S.J. (1894-1981); Bishop Fulton J. Sheen (1895-1979) [who became a Servant of God in 2002]; Gerard Smith, S.J. (1896-1975); William Humbert Kane, O.P. (1901-1970); Walter Farrell, O.P. (1902-1951); Anton Charles Pegis (1905-1978); Jordan Aumann, O.P (1906-2007); Vernon J. Bourke (1907-1998) [also an Augustinian]; Robert J. Henle, S.J. (1909-2000); James Francis Anderson (1910-1981); George Peter Klubertanz, S.J. (c. 1912-1975); Jean McCall Oesterle (c. 1913-2003); Vincent Edward Smith (1915-1972); John Oesterle (c. 1915-1977); Robert Harvanek, S.J. (1916-1996); James Daniel Collins (1917-1985); Fr. Edward Aloysius Synan (1918-1997); William Wallace, O.P. (1918-); Maurice Holloway, S.J. (1920-2008); Victor B. Brezik, C.S.B. (c. 1920-); James A. Weisheipl, O.P. (1923-1984); James B. Reichmann, S.J. (1923-); James Sadowsky, S.J. (1923-); Fr. Ernan McMullin (1924-); Benedict M. Ashley, O.P. (c. 1925-); Richard J. Connell (c. 1925-); Leo Elders, S.V.D. (1926-) [Congregation for the Doctrine of the Faith]; Joseph Bobik (1927-); Ralph McInerny (1929-); Bernard E. Doering (c. 1930-); Jude P. Dougherty (1930-); David Burrell, C.S.C. (1933-); Raymond Leo Dennehy (1935-); Leonard A. Kennedy, C.S.B. (c. 1935-); Thomas O'Meara, O.P. (1935-); Fr. John F. Wippel (c. 1935-); Leo Sweeney, S.J. (1936-2001); the convert Peter Kreeft (c. 1939-); Bishop Joseph Augustine Di Noia, O.P. (1943-) [Congregation for the Doctrine of the Faith]; Romanus Cessario, O.P. (1944-); the laicized Capuchin Thomas Russman (c. 1948-); Deal Wyatt Hudson (1949-); Alfred J. Freddoso (c. 1950-); Curtis L. Hancock (1950-); John Knasas (c. 1950-); Joseph Koterski, S.J. (c. 1950-); Peter A. Redpath (c. 1951-); Robert J. Spitzer, S.J. (1952-); Mark D. Jordan (c. 1953-); Brian Leftow (1956-); John F. Boyle (1958-); David B. Twetten (c. 1959-); Edward Feser (c. 1960-); Hugh McDonald (c. 1960-); Michael Tkacz (c. 1960-); Steven A.

Long (c. 1960-); Gregory Reichberg (c. 1962-); Mark F. Johnson (c. 1963-); Fr. Philip Larrey (1963-); Michael S. Sherwin, O.P. (1963-); Brendan Sweetman (c. 1963-); Thomas Joseph White, O.P. (c. 1965-); Matthew Levering (1971-) [Ressourcement Thomism].

Australian and British Neo-Thomists: Bernard Boedder, S.J. (1841-1916); Joseph Rickaby, S.J. (1845-1932); John Rickaby, S.J. (1847-1927); Michael Maher, S.J. (1860-1918); the convert George Hayward Joyce, S.J. (1864-1943); the Cistercian J.S. Hickey (1865-1933); Vincent McNabb, O.P. (1868-1943); Francis Aveling (1875-1941); the Irishman Peter Coffey (1876-1943); the convert Leslie Joseph Walker, S.J. (1877-1958); the convert Cyril Charlie Martindale, S.J. (1879-1963); the Swiss convert Edward Bullough, O.P. (1880-1934); Laurence Shapcote, O.P. (c. 1880-1940); the Irish physicist Alfred O'Rahilly, S.J. (1884-1969); Daniel Callus, O.P. (1888-1965); Martin Cyril D'Arcy, S.J. (1888-1976); David Knowles (1896-1974); the Irishman Arthur Little, S.J. (1897-1949); the Capuchin James Edward O'Mahony (c. 1897-1960); the Australian Marist Austin Woodbury (1899-1979); Victor White, O.P. (1902-1960); Thomas Gilby, O.P. (1902-1975); Gerald Vann, O.P. (1906-1963); Mark Brocklehurst, O.P. (1906-1967); Bernard Philip Kelly (1907-1958); the convert Frederick Charles Copleston, S.J. (1907-1994) [who engaged in some famous BBC Debates with the atheists Bertrand Russell and Alfred Jules Ayer]; Conrad Pepler, O.P. (1908-1993); Kenelm Foster, O.P. (1910-1986); Ian Hislop, O.P. (1915-1974); John Coventry, S.J. (1915-1998); Thomas Corbishley, S.J. (c. 1915-); Columba Ryan, O.P. (1916-2009); the Irish Bishop Cahal Daly (1917-); the Australian Bishop Joseph Eric D'Arcy (1924-); Cornelius Ernst, O.P. (1924-); Thomas Gornall, S.J. (c. 1930-); Fr. Edward Sillem (c. 1930-) [also Integralist]; the Irishman Fr. James McEvoy (1943-); Simon Tugwell, O.P. (1943-); the Irishman Patrick Quinn (1944-); the Capuchin Thomas Weinandy (1946-), at the University of Oxford; Aidan Nichols, O.P. (1948-), at the University of Oxford; Francis John Selman (c. 1950-); Vivian Boland, O.P. (c. 1955-); Hugh Bredin (c. 1955-) [who holds a Chair of Scholastic Philosophy at Queen's University, Belfast]; William E. Carroll (c. 1955-); Francesca Aran Murphy (c. 1955-); Simone Gaine, O.P. (c. 1964-).

More recently several British Thomists (joined by some American, Canadian, French, and Italian Thomists) have tried to combine Analytic Philosophy with Thomism and have created what is called Analytical Thomism. It numbers among its adherents: Fr. Denis John Bernard Hawkins (1906-1964); the convert Peter Geach (1916-) [husband of Elizabeth Anscombe]; Barry Miller (1923-); Gerard J. Hughes, S.J. (1924-); Alan Donagan (1925-1991); Herbert McCabe, O.P. (1926-2001); Alasdair MacIntyre (1929-); the convert Christopher John Fardo Williams (1930-1997); Fergus Kerr, O.P. (1931-); James F. Ross (1931-); Stephen Theron (1939-); David Braine (1940-); Timothy McDermott, O.P. (c. 1940-); Thomas D. Sullivan (c. 1940-); Denys

Turner (1942-), of the University of Cambridge and Yale University; Robert Hambourger (c. 1945-); Gareth Moore, O.P. (1948-2002); Kevin L. Flannery, S.J. (1950-); Brian Davies, O.P. (1951-); the Scot John Joseph Haldane (1954-), at the University of St. Andrews [Consultor to the Pontifical Council for Culture]; Scott MacDonald (c. 1955-); the Frenchman Roger Pouivet (1958-); Giovanni Ventimiglia (c. 1959-); Brian J. Shanley, O.P. (c. 1960-); Christopher Martin (c. 1961-); Mark Wynn (1963-); the Australian Hayden Ramsay (1964-); the Australian John R. T. Lamont (1964-); Thomas Crean, O.P. (c. 1965-); John P. O'Callaghan (c. 1965-).

Austrian, Dutch, and German Neo-Thomists: Hugo Hurter (1832-1914); Constantin Gutberlet (1837-1928); Hieronymus Noldin, S.J. (1838-1922); Fr. Ceslaus Schneider (1840-1908); the Austrian Heinrich Joseph Seuse Denifle, O.P. (1844-1905); Albert Maria Weiss, O.P. (1844-1925); Cardinal Franz Ehrle, S.J. (1845-1934); Ernst Commer (1847-1928) [Sodalitium Pianum]; Thomas Esser, O.P. (1850-1926); Fr. Joseph Pohle (1852-1911); Clemens Baeumker (1853-1924); Joseph Mausbach (1861-1931); the Dutchman Joseph Gredt, O.S.B. (1863-1940); the Dutchman Joseph-Théodore Beysens (1864-1945); Johann Baptist Stufler, S.J. (1865-1952); Dominikus Prümmer, O.P. (1866-1931); Joseph Geyser (1869-1948); Heinrich Schaaf, S.J. (c. 1870-1925); Martin Grabmann (1875-1949); Franz Sawicki (1877-1952); Franz Pelster, S.J. (1880-1956); the Dutchman Peter Hoenen, S.J. (1880-1961); Heinrich Lennerz, S.J. (1881-1961); Martin Daniel Feuling, O.S.B. (1882-1947); Siegfried Behn (1884-1970); Alexander Horvath, O.P. (1884-1956); Hans Meyer (1884-1966); Josef Koch (1885-1967); Caspar Nink (1885-1975); Karl Eschweiler (1886-1936) [National Socialist]; Martin Honecker (1888-1941) [who rejected the philosophy dissertation of Karl Rahner]; Theodor Steinbüchel (1888-1949); Erich Przywara, S.J. (1889-1972) [also an Augustinian, Integralist, and Phenomenologist]; the Dutchman Sebastiaan Tromp, S.J. (1889-1975); Gottlieb Söhngen (1892-1971); Alois Dempf (1891-1982); Johannes Messner (1891-1984); August Brunner, S.J. (1894-1985) [also a Phenomenologist]; Caspar Friethoff, O.P. (1897-1974); Michael Schmaus (1897-1993) [National Socialist]; Fritz von Rintelen (1898-1979); Josef de Vries, S.J. (1898-1989); Anselm Stolz, O.S.B. (1900-1942); Eberhard Welty, O.P. (1902-1965); Gustav Siewerth (1903-1963) [also an Existentialist]; Bernhard Lakebrink (1904-1991); Josef Pieper (1904-1997) [National Socialist]; Fr. Ludwig Ott (c 1906-1985); Paul Wilpert (1906-1967); Bernard Welte (1906-1983) [also an Existentialist]; Max Müller (1906-1994) [also an Existentialist]; Arthur Fridolin Utz (1908-2001); Wilhelm Keilbach (1908-1982); the Dutchman Norbert Luyten, O.P. (1909-1986); Ludger Oeing-Hanhoff (1923-1986); the Dutchman Theo Beemer (1927-2003); Max Seckler (1927-); Alma von Stockhausen (1927-); Albert Zimmermann (1928-), at the Thomas-Institut; Heinrich Beck (1929-) [also an Existentialist]; the Hungarian-German Béla Weissmahr, S.J. (1929-2005); Ulrich Horst, O.P. (1931-); Francis Joseph Kovach (c. 1931-); the former Dominican Otto Hermann Pesch (1931-); Walter M. Neidl (c. 1935-); the Dutchman Karl-Wilhelm Merks (1938-); Horst Seidl (1938-); the Dutchman Jan Aersten (c. 1954-), at the Thomas-Institut; David Berger (1968-); the Dutchman Rudi te Velde (c. 1970-); the Dutchman Jörgen Vijgen (1974-).

Belgian, French, and Swiss Neo-Thomists: Edmond Domet de Vorges (1829-1910); the Belgian Auguste Castelein, S.J. (c. 1840-1915); the Antonin Marie Dummermuth, O.P. (1841-1918); Elisée Vincent Maumus, O.P. (1842-1912); Vincent Remer, S.J. (1843-1910); Stéphane Harent, S.J. (1845-1926); Marie-Thomas Coconnier, O.P. (1846-1908); the Sulpician Pierre Vallet (fl. 1878-1909); Joseph Gardair (1846-1911); Bishop Elie Blanc (1846-1927); the Belgian Gustave Lahousse, S.J. (1846-1928); Cardinal Louis Billot, S.J. (1846-1931); Joachim Joseph Berthier, O.P. (1848-1924); the Sulpician Albert Farges (1848-1946); the Belgian Cardinal Désiré Mercier (1851-1926); Alfred Vacant (1852-1901); Eugene Portalié, S.J. (1852-1909); Gaston Sortais, S.J. (1852-1926); Clodius Piat (1854-1918); the Integrist Bernard Gaudeau, S.J. (1854-1925); Xavier- Marie Le Bachelet, S.J. (1855-1925); Jean-Vincent Bainvel (1858-1937); Adhémar d'Ales (1861-1938); the Belgian Pierre Mandonnet, O.P. (1858-1936); the Belgian Désiré Nys (1859-1927); Ambroise Gardeil, O.P. (1859-1931); Ambroise Montagne, O.P. (c. 1860-1940); Marcel Chossat, S.J. (1862-1926); the Belgian Armand Thiéry, O.P. (1868-1955); Antonin-Gilbert Sertillanges (1863-1948) [Academy of Moral and Political Sciences]; the Marist Émile Peillaube (1864-1934); Sebastian Reinstadler, S.J. (1864-1935); Marie-Benoît Schwalm, O.P. (1866-1908); Thomas Pegues, O.P. (1866-1936); the Swiss Gallus Manser (1866-1950); Éduard Hugon, O.P. (1867-1929); the Belgian Maurice de Wulf (1867-1947); the Belgian Simon Deploige (1868-1927); Étienne Hugueny, O.P. (1868-1942); Léonce de Grandmaison, S.J. (1868-1927); Joseph de Tonquédec, S.J. (1868-1962) [the official exorcist of Paris]; Marc de Munnynck, O.P. (c. 1870-1935); Charles-Henri Dehove (c. 1871-1940); Paul Gény, S.J. (1871-1925); Benoît Henri Merkelbach, O.P. (1871-1942); René Jeanniere, S.J. (1873-1917); the reconvert Ernst Bernard Allo, O.P. (1873-1945); Bishop Gabriel Brunhes (1874-1947); Henri Pinard de la Boullaye, S.J. (1874-1958); Marie Stanislas Gillet, O.P. (1875-1951); Ambroise-Marie de Poulpiquet, O.P. (1875-1915); Auguste Pelzer (1876-1958); Joseph De Guibert, S.J. (1877-1942); Edgar Hocedez, S.J. (1877-1948); Réginald Garrigou-Lagrange, O.P. (1877-1964); the Sulpician Hippolyte Ligeard (1878-1916); the Belgian Maurice Defourny (1878-1953); the Belgian Léon Noël (1878-1953); Odo Lottin, O.S.B. (1880-1965); Jean-Marie Hervé (1881-1958); the Belgian psychologist Baron Albert Michotte (1881-1965); Blaise Romeyer, S.J. (1882-1954); the Belgian Nicolas Balthasar (1882-1959); Joseph Le Rohellec, SSPX (1883-1930); Marie-Dominique Roland-Gosselin, O.P. (1883-1934); René Arnou, S.J. (1884-1972); Charles Boyer, S.J. (1884-1980); the Belgian Paul Decoster (1886-1939); Clément Suermondt (1887-1953); Gabriel Théry, O.P. (1891-1959); Régis Jolivet (1891-1966) [also an Existentialist];

the Belgian Canon Jacques Leclercq (1891-1971); Cardinal Charles Journet (1891-1975); André-Charles Gignon, O.P. (1892-1977); Lucien Chambat (c. 1893-1955); the Belgian Canon Fernand Renoirte (1894-1958); Louis de Raeymaeker (1895-1970); Marie-Dominique Chenu, O.P. (1895-1990) [whose book was placed on the Index of Forbidden Books in 1942 and who expelled from Le Saulchior in 1954]; François Joseph Thonnard (c. 1896-1960); Cardinal Henri du Lubac S.J. (1896-1991) [Nouvelle Théologie]; the Belgian Edgar De Bruyne (1898-1959); Antoine Dondaine, O.P. (1898-1987); Aimé Forest (1898-1983) [also an Existentialist]; Henri Gouhier (1898-1994), at the Sorbonne [also an Existentialist; member of the French Academy]; Michel Guerard de Lauriers, O.P. (1898-1998) [traditionalist member of Society of St. Pius X]; Benoît Lavaud, O.P. (c. 1898-1960); Thomas Deman, O.P. (1899-1955); Pierre Boisselot, O.P. (1899-1964) [expelled from Le Saulchoir in 1954]; Léopold Malevez, S.J. (1900-1973); Henri-Dominique Simonin, O.P. (c. 1900-1990) [who later became a Trappist monk]; Louis-Bertrand Gillon, O.P. (c. 1901-1970); the Belgian Fr. Albert Dondeyne (1901-1985); the Belgian Gaston Isaye, S.J. (1903-1984); Marie-Rosaire Gagnebet, O.P. (1904-1983); Louis Gardet (1904-1986); Olivier Lacombe (1904-2001), of the Sorbonne [Academy of Moral and Political Sciences]; the Belgian Fernand Van Steenberghen (1904-1993); Louis Charlier, O.P. (c. 1905-1975); Louis-Bertrand Geiger, O.P. (1906-1983); Marie-Hyacinthe Laurent (1906-1968); Canon Maurice Paissac, O.P. (1906-1994); Jean Daujat (1906-1998); Dominique Dubarle, O.P. (1907-1987); Marie-Joseph Nicolas, O.P. (c. 1906-2000); Raymond-Léopold Bruckberger, O.P. (1907-1998); Marie-Michel Labourdette, O.P. (1908-1990); José De Wolf, S.J. (c. 1909-1950); the Swiss Norbert Luyten, O.P. (1909-1986); the Belgian Clemens Vansteenkiste, O.P. (1910-1997); Jean-Hervé Nicolas, O.P. (1910-2001); the Belgian Fr. Gérard Verbeke (1910-2001); Jean-Dominique Robert, O.P. (1910-); Jan Hendrik Walgrave O.P. (1911-1986) [also an Integralist]; Louis Monden, S.J. (1911-2002); Philippe Delhaye (1912-1990); Marie-Dominique Philippe, O.P. (1912-2006); René-Antoine Gauthier, O.P. (1913-1999); Pierre-Marie Gils, O.P. (1913-); Louis-Jacques Bataillon, O.P. (1914-2009); the Belgian Canon Roger Aubert (1914-); Jean-Marie Aubert (1916-); the Belgian Georges Van Riet (1916-); Marie-Vincent Leroy, O.P. (1917-1994); Fr. Theo Belmans (1922-); Bertrand de Margerie S.J. (1923-2003); Bernard Montagnes, O.P. (1924-); the Belgian Servais Pinckaers, O.P. (1925-); Jean-Pierre Torrell, O.P. (1927-), at the University of Fribourg; Pierre-Marie Émonet (c. 1934-); the Swiss Rudi Imbach (1946-), at the Sorbonne; André Clément (c. 1950-); Yves Floucat (1950-); the Swiss convert Martin Rhonheimer, Opus Dei (1950-); Stéphane-Marie Barbellion (1955-); Gilbert Narcisse, O.P. (1957-) [also Romanticism]; Henry Donneaud, O.P. (1960-); Daniel Ols, O.P. (c. 1960-); Serge-Thomas Bonino, O.P. (1961-); Thierry-Marie Hamonic, O.P. (1961-); the Swiss Charles Morerod, O.P. (1961-); Thierry-Dominique Humbrecht,

O.P. (1962-); Gilles Emery, O.P. (1962-); Géry Prouvost (1964-); Emmanuel Tourpe (1970-).

Canadian Neo-Thomists: the Christian Brother Symphorien-Louis [Stanislas Roberge] (1848-1924); Louis-Adolphe Paquet (1859-1942); Hermas Bastien (1897-1977); Julien Péghaire, C.S.S.P. (1898-1952); Ignatius Theodore Eschmann, O.P. (1898-1968); Louis Lachance (1899-1963); Louis-Marie Regis, O.P. (1903-1985); Charles de Koninck (1906-1965); Joseph Owens, C.S.S.R. (1908-2005); Laurence Kennedy Shook, C.S.B. (1909-1993); Armand Maurer, C.S.B. (1915-2008); André Naud (1925-2002); Jean-Louis Allard (1926-); Lawrence Dewan, O.P. (1932-); Kenneth L. Schmitz (c. 1940-) [also Romanticism]; Louis Brunet (1955-).

Italian Neo-Thomists: Michele De Maria (1836-1913); Alberto Lepidi, O.P. (1838-1925); Girolamo Maria Mancini, O.P. (1842-1924); Salvatore Talamo (1844-1932); Giuseppe Mauri (1849-1932); Pio de Mandato, S.J. (1850-1914); Guido Mattiussi, S.J. (1852-1925) [author of the famous twenty-four Thomistic theses (1914)]; Enrico Buonpensiere, O.P. (1853-1929); Gioacchino Ambrosini, S.J. (1857-1931); Francesco Saverio Calcagno (1867-1939); Giuseppe Zamboni (1875-1950) [who was expelled from the Catholic University of Milan in 1931 due to his views on gnosiology]; Agostino Gemelli, O.F.M. (1878-1959); Emilio Chiocchetti (1880-1951); Amato Masnovo (1880-1955); Giulio Canella (1881-1916 [?]) [known for the famous Bruneri/Canella amnesia case]; Mariano Felice Cordovani, O.P. (1883-1950); Fr. Francesco Olgiati (1886-1962); Giuseppe Capograssi (1889-1956); Umberto Antonio Padovani (1894-1968) [also an Existentialist]; Vincenzo La Via (1895-1982); Carlo Giacon, S.J. (1900-1984) [founder of the Gallarate Movement in 1945]; Cardinal Paolo Dezza, S.J. (1901-1999); Gustavo Bontadini (1903-1990); Romano Amerio (1905-1997) [Traditionalist]; Marino Gentile (1906-1991); Sofia Vanni Rovighi (1908-1990); Luigi Bogliolo, S.D.B. (1910-1998); Giovanni Di Napoli (c. 1910-1985); Nicola Petruzzellis (1910-1988); Augusto Del Noce (1910-1989); Cornelio Fabro, C.P.S. (1911-1995); Antonio Piolanti (1911-2001); Roberto Busa, S.J. (1913-) [editor of the Index Thomisticus]; the Passionist Enrico Zoffoli (1915-1996) [a critic of the Neo-Catechumenal movement]; Dario Composta, S.D.B. (1917-2002); Umberto Degl'Innocenti (c. 1918-); Fr. Brunero Gherardini (c. 1924-); Battista Mondin, S.X. (1926-); Dalmazio Mongillo, O.P. (1928-2005); Vittorio Possenti (c. 1935-) [also a Personalist]; Antonio Livi (1938-); Carmelo Vigna (1940-); Luciano Malusa (1942-); Bishop Marcelo Sanchez Sorondo (1942-); Giuseppe Abba (1943-); Umberto Galeazzi (c. 1945-); Mario Enrique Sacchi (1945-); Tomas Tyn, O.P. (1950-1990) [Servant of God]; Angelo Marchesi (c. 1955-); Giuseppe Barzaghi, O. P. (1958-); Marco D'Avenia (c. 1960-); Fr. Guido Mazzotta (c. 1960-); Adriano Oliva, O.P. (1964-); Roberto Di Ceglie (c. 1970-); Maria Antonietta Mendosa (c. 1970-); Enrico Maria Radaelli (c. 1970-).

Portuguese and Spanish Neo-Thomists: José Mendive, S.J. (1836-1906); Alejandro Pidal y Mon (1846-1913); Manuel Polo y Peyrolón (1846-1918); Juan Muncunill, S.J. (1848-1928); Antonio Hernández Fajarnés (1851-1909); Norberto del Prado, O.P. (1852-1918); Manuel Antonio Ferreira-Deusdado (1858-1918); Pedro Maria Lopez Martinez (1861-1934); José Daurella y Rull (1864-1927); Alberto Gomez Izquierdo (1870-1929); Jesús Valbuena, O.P. (c. 1872-1960); the Philippino Francisco Marín-Solá, O.P. (1873-1932); Ramón Orlandis Despuig, S.J. (1873-1958); Juan Zaragüeta y Bengoechea (1883-1974); Manuel Barbado, O.P. (1884-1945); the convert Fr. Manuel García Morente (1886-1942); Santiago Maria Ramírez de Dulanto, O.P. (1891-1967); Pedro Lumbreras (1892-1970); Francisco Muniz, O.P. (c. 1903-1983); Jaime Bofill (1910-1965); Leopoldo Eulogio Palacios (1912-1981); Teófilo Urdánoz Aldaz, O.P. (1912-1987); Manuel Úbeda Purkiss (1913-1999); Adolfo Munoz Alonso (1915-1974); Jose Todoli Duque, O.P. (1915-); Angel González Alvarez (1916-1991); the Portuguese Arnaldo de Miranda Barbosa (1917-); Rafael Gambra Ciudad (1920-2004); Antonio Millán-Puelles (1921-2005), Opus Dei; Francisco Canals Vidal (1922-2009); Jesús García López (1924-2005); Abelardo Lobato Casado, O.P. (1925-); Leonardo Polo Barrena (1926-); Victorino Rodríguez, O.P. (1926-1997); Jorge Pérez Ballestar (1926-); Alfonso López Quintás (1928-), Opus Dei [also an Existentialist]; Carlos Cardona (1930-1993); Juan Cruz Cruz (1940-); Fr. Lluís Clavell (1941-); Alejandro Llano Cifuentes (1946-); Fernando Ocáriz (1944-); Ángel Luis González (c. 1945-); Eudaldo Forment (1946-); Rafael Alvira (c. 1948-); Jose Antonio Izquierdo Labeaga (c. 1950-); Enrique Alarcón (c. 1955-); Lorenzo Vicente Burgoa (1955-); Marcus F. Manzanedo (c. 1960-); Ignacio Guiu Andreu (1963-); Juan Fernando Sellés (c. 1964-). There have also been many Thomists from Poland and South America (Argentina, Brazil, Chile, and Mexico in particular) in the twentieth-century.

We should also mention other Scholastic thinkers such as the Bonaventurans Ephrem Longpré, O.F.M. (1890-1965), Patrice Robert, O.F.M. (1904-), Zachary Hayes, O.F.M. (1932-), and the Capuchin Camilo Bérubé (c.1955-); the Scotists Alois von Schmid (1825-1910), Parthenius Minges (1861-1926), Joseph Déodat de Basly (1862-1937), Léon Veuthey, O.F.M. (1896-1974); Allan Bernard Wolter, O.F.M. (1913-2006), the convert Walter Höres (1928-), and Bernardino Bonansea (c. 1934-); the Ockhamist Philotheus Boehner, O.F.M. (1901-1955); and the Suarezians Domenico Palmieri, S.J. (1829-1909), Santo Schiffini, S.J. (1841-1906), Max Limbourg (1841-1920), Juan José Urrábu, S.J. (1844-1904), Victor Cathrein, S.J. (1845-1931), Christian Pesch, S.J. (1853-1925), Joseph Hontheim, S.J. (1858-1929), Josef Donat, S.J. (1868-1946), Gabriel Picard, S.J. (c. 1876-1940), Pedro Descoqs, S.J. (1877-1946), Nicolao Monaco, S.J. (c. 1880-1940), the Spaniard José Hellin, S.J. (1883-1973), Joseph Santeler (1888-1968), Maximilian Rast (1892-1973), Jesús Iturrioz, S.J. (c. 1902-1985), Ramon Cenal Lorente, S.J. (1907-1977), Jesús Munoz Pérez Vizcaíno, S.J. (1908-1996), José Maria de

Alejandro (c. 1910-1970), Fr. Jose Ignacio Alcorta Echevarria (1910-1983), Juan Roig Gironella, S.J. (1912-1980), Ismael Quiles (c. 1925-), Antonio Puigcerver Zanon (c. 1930-), the Cuban Jorge J.E. Garcia (1942-).

37   Though most of the priests served in a non-combative role, it appears several, such as Pierre Rousselot, S.J. (1878-1915), were more actively involved in the combat. For Rousselot mentions that he was the Sergeant of his trench and sometimes ferried orders to his Captain and that the Sergeant who commanded the next trench over was a Trappist monk (so in his words, 'O penetration clericale!'). His fellow Jesuits Pierre Teilhard De Chardin and Henri de Lubac meanwhile served as stretcher-bearers [see De Chardin's, *The Making of a Mind: Letters from a Soldier-Priest, 1914-1919* (New York: Harper, 1961)].

Others besides Rousselot who ended up losing their lives in World War I were the Catholic poets Charles Péguy (1873-1914) and Ernest Psichiri (1883-1914), the grandson of the deist Renan, and the Catholic novelist Alain Fournier (1886-1914). In addition Catholic thinkers such as Étienne Gilson, Louis Lavelle, and Raymond-Léopold Bruckberger, O.P. were imprisoned during the First World War, the Belgian Cardinal Désiré Mercier worked on behalf of the Belgian people during this time, and Gabriel Marcel served in the Red Cross.

38   Around 30,000 French priests served in the military during the First World War and over 4500 of them gave their lives (including around 1450 Assumptionists, Benedictines, Brothers of the Christian Schools, Capuchins, Dominicans, Fathers of the Holy Ghost, Jesuits, Lazarists, Little Brothers of Mary, Redemptorists, Society of Foreign Missions, and Trappists).

39   Here Transcendental Thomists appeal to various texts of Aquinas (texts which critics charge are interpreted incorrectly and taken out of context—and in this they seem correct—it of course being a different question whether the views of the Transcendental Thomists have merit or not):

> "The truth by which the soul passes judgment on all things is the first truth; for, just as from the truth of the divine intellect there flow into the angelic intellects those innate species by which they know all things, so does the truth of the first principles by which we pass judgment on everything proceed from the truth of the divine intellect into our intellect as an exemplar [*exemplariter*]. And since we cannot judge by means of it unless it is a likeness [*similitudo*] of the first truth, we are hence said to pass judgment on everything according to the first truth" (*On Truth*, q. 1, a. 4 ad 5).

> "All cognitive beings also know God implicitly in any object of knowledge. Just as nothing has the note of appetibility except by a likeness to the first goodness, so nothing is knowable except by a likeness to the first truth" (*On Truth*, q. 22 a. 2 ad 1).

"And so it is necessary to say that the human soul knows all things in the eternal exemplars [*in rationibus aeternis*]; by participation in these exemplars we know all things. For the intellectual light itself, which is in us, is nothing else than a participated likeness [*participata similitudo*] of the uncreated light, in which are contained the eternal exemplars [*rationes aeternae*]" (1 q. 84 a. 5)

"The intellect becomes actual through the intelligible species by which it is informed. But if the intellect is in act, it is knowing itself" (I q. 84 a. 7; cf. *On Truth*, q. 1 a. 9; cf. I q. 16 a. 6; 1 q. 88 a. 3; *Commentary on the Metaphysics*, IV, 6; *Commentary on the Sentences*, I, d. 3 q. 4 a. 5).

40 The French Minister Combes who had written the initial laws expelling the religious orders from France made no bones about his position: "I don't want two Frances, clerical France and modern France. I desire the extinction of clerical France, the complete triumph of modern France."

41 For more on the life and thought of Pierre Rousselot see: SPC (1934), pp. 142-145; DTC (1939), vol. XIV, pp. 134-138 and Tables générales, p. 3928; HT (1947), vol. III, pp. 270-272; IEC (1953), vol. X, p. 1416; CAP (1955), p. 100; SHP (1955), p. 1006; PAF (1958), pp. 452-511; TE (1965), vol. II, pp. 295-299; RP (1966), pp. 350-351, 787; SCT (1970), pp. 189-193; HA (1971), pp. 210-212; HWP (1971), v. V, p. 140; CHP (1974), v. IX, p. 264; CP (1989), v. II, pp. 437-452; FUP (1989), pp. 38-86; NCS (1989), pp. 250-251; ATH (1994), pp. 110-112, 213-214; NT (1994), pp. 97-116; HCEC (1995), p. 1139; CTE (1998), pp. 95-96; SPI (1998), pp. 182-183; UHF (1998), vol. VIII, pp. 474-475; LTK (1999), vol. VIII, pp. 1333-1334; MCT (2000), vol. II, p. 200; BBKL (2003), vol. XXII, pp. 1165-1169; BTCT (2003), pp. 168, 211; NCE (2003), vol. XII, pp. 394-395; TT (2003), pp. 23-24; ACP (2005), pp. 312-317; EF (2006), vol. X, p. 9878; Tonquédec, Joseph de, "Pierre Rousselot," *Revue critique des idées et des livres* 26 (1919), pp. 603-606; Broux, Alexandre, *Les Jésuites morts pour la France* (Tours: A. Mame, 1921), pp. 57-58; De Grandmaison, Léonce, "Pierre Rousselot," in Rousselot, Pierre, *L'intelletualisme de Saint Thomas* (Paris; Beauchesne, 1924), pp. [v]-[xl]; Marty, Elie, *Le témoignage de Pierre Rousselot, S.J., 1878-1915: D'après ses écrits et sa correspondance* (Paris: Beauchesne, 1940); Tilliette, Xavier, "Le Père Pierre Rousselot," *Messager du Coeur de Jésus* 117 (1942), pp. 264-272; Harper, Ralph, "Two Existential Interpretations," *Philosophy and Phenomenological Research* 5 (1945), pp. 392-397; De Wolf, José, *La justification de la foi chez saint Thomas d'Aquin et le Père Rousselot* (Brussels: Edition universelle, 1946); Harper, Ralph, *Existentialism: A Theory of Man* (Cambridge: Harvard University Press, 1948), pp. 108-131; Durand, Alexandre, "The Certainty of Faith," *Downside Review* 67 (1949), pp. 247-259; Nédoncelle, Maurice, "L'influence de Newman sur les Yeux de la foi de Rousselot," *Revue des sciences religieuses* 27 (1953), pp. 321-332; Scott, Frederick, "Maurice Blondel and Pierre Rousselot," *The New Scholasticism*, 36:3 (1962), pp. 330-352; *Recherches de Science Religieuse* 53 (1965) [Special Issue on Rousselot]; Kunz, Erhard,

Glaube, Gnade, Geschichte: die Glaubenstheologie des Pierre Rousselot (Frankfurt: J. Knecht, 1969); hilippe, Marie-Dominique, *Une philosophie de l'être est-elle encore possible?* (Paris: Téqui, 1975), vol. V, pp. 46-60; McDermott, John, *Love and Understanding: The Relation of Will and Intellect in Pierre Rousselot's Christological Vision* (Rome: Gregorian University Press, 1983); Pottier, Bernard, "Les yeux de la foi après Vatican II," *Nouvelle Revue Théologique* 106 (1984), pp. 177-203; Sheehan, Thomas, "Pierre Rousselot and the Dynamism of Human Spirit," *Gregorianum* 66:2 (1985), pp. 241-267; McCool, Gerald, "History, Insight and Judgment in Thomism," *International Philosophical Quarterly* 27:3 (1987), pp. 299-312; McDermott, John, "Sheehan, Rousselot, and Theological Method," *Gregorianum* 68 (1987), pp. 705-717; Sheehan, Thomas, *Karl Rahner: The Philosophical Foundations* (Athens: Ohio University Press, 1987), pp. 55-73; Weiher, Charles, "Knowing and Symbolic Functions," *New Scholasticism* 62 (1988), pp. 412-437; O'Meara, Thomas, "Karl Rahner: Some Audiences and Sources for His Theology," *Communio* 18:2 (1992), pp. 237-251; Bellandi, Andrea, "Les yeux de la foi di Pierre Rousselot," *Vivens homo* 6:2 (1995) 279-313; Colin, Pierre, ed., *Intellectuels chrétiens et esprit des années 20* (Paris: Cerf, 1997), pp. 107-108; McDermott, John, "De Lubac and Rousselot," *Gregorianum* 78:4 (1997), pp. 735-759; Tallon, Andrew, *Head and Heart: Affection, Cognition, Volition as Triune Consciousness* (New York: Fordham University Press, 1997), pp. 253-255, 260-262, 279-283; Zielinski, Slawomir, *Se gagner soi-même et gagner Dieu* (Fribourg: Editions universitaires, 1997); McCamy, Ronald, *Out of a Kantian Chrysalis?: A Maritainian Critique of Fr. Maréchal* (Frankfurt: Peter Lang, 1998), pp. 18-21; Tallon, Andrew, "Doctrinal Development and Wisdom: Rousselot on Sympathetic Knowing by Connaturality," *Philosophy & Theology* 15:2 (2003), pp. 353-383; Tourpe, Emmanuel, "Au principe de Surnaturel: Le thomisme de Pierre Rousselot, 1879-1915," *Revue des sciences religieuses* 77:2 (2003), pp. 166-182; Lacoste, Jean-Yves, ed., *Encyclopedia of Christian Theology* (London: Routledge, 2005), vol. II, pp. 947-955; Boersma, Hans, "A Sacramental Journey to the Beatific Vision. The Intellectualism of Pierre Rousselot," *Heythrop Journal* 49 (2008), pp. 1015-1034; St. Hilaire, Robert, "Desire Divided: Nature and Grace in the Neo-Thomism of Pierre Rousselot," *Harvard Theological Review* 101 (2008), pp. 507-525.

42   The first work has been translated as *The Intellectualism of Saint Thomas*, tr. James O'Mahony (New York: Sheed and Ward, 1935), and as *Intelligence: Sense of Being, Faculty of God* [ISTH], tr. Andrew Tallon (Milwaukee: Marquette University Press, 1999), and the second work as *The Eyes of Faith*, tr. Avery Dulles and Joseph Donceel (New York: Fordham University Press, 1990). I use these translations here.

Rousselot also wrote the ethical treatises *Contributions to the History of the Problem of Love in the Middle Ages* [*Pour l'historie du problème de l'amour au Moyen-Age*] [PLMA] (1908; 1933) [translated by Alan Vincelette as *The Prob-*

lem of Love in the Middle Ages [PLMA] (Milwaukee: Marquette University Press, 2001)]; Quaestiones de conscientia (1937).

His philosophical and theological articles include: "Amour spirituel et synthèse aperceptive," Revue de philosophie 16 (1910), pp. 225-240; "Lettre à M. Laberthonnière [Discussion]," Annales de Philosophie Chrétienne 159 (1910), pp. 393-397, 524-527; "L'être et l'esprit," Revue de philosophie 16 (1910), pp. 561-574; "Métaphysique thomiste et critique de la connaissance," Revue néoscolastique de philosophie 17 (1910), pp. 476-509; "La religion chrétienne," Etudes 125 (1910), pp. 593-628, 128 (1911), pp. 721-744, 129 (1911), pp. 32-56 [with Joseph Huby; republished in Huby, Joseph, ed., Christus: Manuel d'histoire des religions (Paris: Beauchesne, 1912), pp. 641-1017 with Alexandre Brou, Joseph Huby, Léonce de Grandmaisonm; and translated as Huby, Joseph, ed., The Life of the Church (London: Sheed and Ward, 1932)]; "Les yeux de la foi," [translated as the "The Eyes of Faith" in The Eyes of Faith (New York: Fordham University Press, 1990)] ["EF"], Recherches des sciences religieuses 1 (1910), pp. 241-259, 444-475; "L'esprit de saint Thomas d'après un livre récent," Études 128 (1911), pp. 614-629; "Vérité et probabilit: Une théorie nouvelle," Recherches de science religieuse 3 (1912), pp. 495-496; "Remarques sur l'histoire de la notion de foi naturelle," Recherches des sciences religieuses 4 (1913), pp. 1-36; "Intellectualisme," in D'Ales, Adhémar, ed., Dictionnaire apologétique de la foi catholique (Paris: Beauchesne, 1914), vol. II, pp. 1066-1081; "Intorno all'atto di fede," Rivista di apologia cristiana 11 (1914), pp. 55-56; "Réponse à deux attaques," Recherches des sciences religieuses 5 (1914), pp. 57-69 [translated as "Answer to Two Attacks" [ATT] in The Eyes of Faith (New York: Fordham University Press, 1990)]; "Note sur le développement du dogme," Recherches des sciences religieuses 38 (1950), pp. 113-120; "Théorie des concepts par l'unité fonctionnelle suivant les principes de saint Thomas," Archives de philosophie 23 (1960), pp. 573-607; "Petite théorie du développement du dogme," Recherches des sciences religieuses 53 (1965), pp. 355-390; "Idéalisme et Thomisme," Archives de philosophie 42 (1979), pp. 103-126.

Several of Rousselot's articles have been translated in Essays on Love and Knowledge [ELK], tr. Andrew Tallon, Pol Vandevelde, and Alan Vincelette (Milwaukee: Marquette University Press, 2008).

See the bibliographies of Rousselot in L'intellectualisme de Saint Thomas (Paris: Beauchesne, 1924), pp. [xli]-[xliii]; Recherches de Science Religieuse 53 (1965), pp. 340-342; McDermott, John, Love and Understanding: The Relation of Will and Intellect in Pierre Rousselot's Christological Vision (Rome: Gregorian University Press, 1983), pp. 303-309; and in Rousselot, Pierre, Intelligence (Milwaukee: Marquette University Press, 1999), pp. 232-236. Pierre Rousselot's manuscripts are housed in the Jesuit Archives of Vanves (Paris), France.

43   Here is how Aquinas writes in regard to a connatural knowledge of virtue"... the virtuous person, through the habit of the virtue, has a proper

judgment about those things which are in agreement with [*conveniunt*] virtue" (2a2ae q. 2 a. 3 ad 2; cf. 2a2ae q. 45 a. 2; ISTH, II, 1, p. 63; II, 3, p. 99). So too there is a connatural knowledge of logical principles for Aquinas: "All knowledge where true science is in question is possible in virtue of returning to first principles immediately present to the intellect" (*On Truth*, XIV, 9; cf. *Commentary on the Posterior Analytics*, I, 19; ISTH, II, 1, p. 66).

44   As Rousselot rather strongly remarks "The best images, the official images, we should even say, of our intellectual conceptions in the Thomist system, are those blurred visions [*visions troubles*] that let us roughly describe a distant object without being able to make out its exact shape" (ISTH, II, 2, p. 81 [94]; Aquinas 1 q. 85 a. 3). Later on Rousselot admitted that he had exaggerated the irrealism of conceptual knowledge (ELK, II, p. 118).

45   While the dogmas of religion are unreformable truths [contra the Modernists] according to Rousselot—for a dogma is not a purely human product but arises from divine revelation (ISTH, I, p. 192; II, 5, p. 127; Conclusion, p. 182)—still God and the divine realm cannot be completely encapsulated in static definitions and dogmas. So though we can use particular philosophical terms and concepts to express dogmas, such a philosophical elaboration of dogma is neither exhaustive of the divine nor the only one imaginable. For instance Platonism and Aristotelianism are both valid forms of the elucidation of dogmas, and there are other philosophical forms that could be used as well. For that matter, the common non-philosophical ideas of ordinary people suffice to give an approximate idea of the whole of theology, even if they are ultimately less adequate and refined than those of learned philosophers (ISTH, Introduction, pp. 8-10; n. 7 on p. 9; II, 5, pp. 128-129; n. 13 on p. 128; ELK, V, p. 157; cf. Aquinas, 1 q. 1 a. 5 ad 2; 1 q. 42 a. 5 ad 1; 3 q. 75 a. 4 ; 3 q. 63 a. 2; *On Truth*, XXVII, 2, 7; XXI, 2, 3; *On the Trinity*, I, 4, II, 3; *Summa Contra Gentiles*, II, 98). So though on occasion humans can grasp truths in a definitive and unrevisable way, for the most part we only have an imperfect representation of things and there are different ways of elucidating these truths (ISTH, II, 1, pp. 56, 60; II, 1, n. 35 on p. 65; Appendix, p. 189, 192).

46   This scientific conception of faith (especially popular up until around 1950) is in actuality found in two slightly different forms.

Francisco Suárez, S.J. (1548-1617), following Alexander of Hales. O.F.M. (1183-1245); Raymond Martin, O.P. (d. 1261); Albert the Great, O.P. (c. 1193-1280), Thomas Aquinas (c. 1225-1274), John Capreolus, O.P. (c. 1380-1444), Melchior Cano, O.P. (1525-1560), Domingo Bañez, O.P. (1528-1604), Juan de Maldonato, S.J. (1533-1583), Francisco de Toledo, S.J. (1533-1596), Cardinal Robert Bellarmine, S.J. (1542-1621), Gregory of Valencia, S.J. (1546-1603, Gabriel Vasquez, S.J. (1549-1604), and Leonhard Lessius, S.J. (1554-1623), argued that faith is preceded by a natural judgment of its credibility based on objective signs (i.e. miracles, prophecies, testimony of martyrs, church teachings, etc.) which makes faith rational (for by these signs we can grasp that God has spoken to humans). This natural judgment of credibility is, however, followed by a willed assent to God's scriptural testimony based purely on the authority of God and made in the light of supernatural grace. Suárez's position was adopted by Giles de Coninck, S.J. (1571-1633), John of St. Thomas, O.P. (1589-1644; Rodirgo de Arriaga, S.J. (1592-1667); Jean-Baptiste Gonet, O.P. (1616-1681); Bishop Jacques-Bénigne Bossuet (1626-1704); the Salmanticenses (Carmelites of Salamanca) [Seventeenth-Century]; Domenico Viva, S.J. (1648-1726); Charles René Billuart, O.P. (1685-1757); St. Alphonsus de Liguori (1696-1787) [Doctor of the Church]; Heinrich Kilber, S.J. (1710-1783) [Theologia Wirceburgensis]; Nicholas Sylvestre Bergier (1718-1780); Ignatius Neubauer, S.J. (1726-1795); Marian Dobmayer, O.S.B. (1753-1805); Giovanni Perrone, S.J. (1794-1876); Marie-Ange Chastel (1804-1861); Bishop William Ullathorne (1806-1889); Cardinal Henry Manning (1808-1892), Franz Hettinger (1813-1890); Wilhelm Wilmers, S.J. (1817-1889); Heinrich Denzinger (1819-1893); G.M. Jansen (1828-1900); Cardinal Tommasso Zigliara (1833-1893); Cardinal Camillo Mazzella, S.J. (1833-1900); Bernhard Tepe, S.J. (1833-1904); Fr. Paul de Broglie (1834-1895); Matthias Joseph Scheeben (1835-1888); José Mendive, S.J. (1836-1906); Constantin Gutberlet (1837-1928); Bishop Charles François Turinaz (1838-1918); Jules Didiot (1840-1903); Paul von Schanz (1841-1905); Santo Schiffini, S.J. (1841-1906); Fr. Thomas Bouquillon (1842-1902); Albert Maria Weiss (1844-1925); Stéphane Harent, S.J. (1845-1926); Victor Cathrein, S.J. (1845-1931); Gustave Lahousse (1846-1928); Louis Billot, S.J. (1846-1931); Johannes Vincentius de Groot O.P. (1848-1922); Henri De Brouwer (c. 1850-1900); Pio de Mandato, S.J. (1850-1914); Paul Mannens (c. 1850-1920); Alfred Vacant (1852-1901); Eugène Portalié, S.J. (1852-1909); Anton Straub, S.J. (1852-1931); Christian Pesch, S.J. (1853-1925); the Integrist Bernard Gaudeau, S.J. (1854-1925); the Sulpician Adolphe Tanquerey (1854-1932); Hippolyte Gayraud, O.P. (1856-1911); Bishop Giuseppe Ballerini (1857-1933); Joseph Hontheim, S.J. (1858-1929); Jean-Vincent Bainvel. S.J. (1858-1937); Marie-Benoî Schwalm, O.P. (1860-1908); Josef Nienhaus (c. 1860-1920); Gerard Cornelius Van Noort (1861-1946); Blazio Beraza, S.J. (1862-1936); the mathematician Jean-Armand de Séguier, S.J. (1862-1937); Hilaire de Barenton; O.F.M. (c. 1864-1950); Édouard Hugon, O.P. (1867-1929); the Capuchin Hilarin Felder (1867-1951); Étienne Hugueny, O.P. (1868-1942); Vincent McNabb, O.P. (1868-1943); Joseph de Tonquédec, S.J. (1868-1962); Fr. Cyrille Labeyrie (c. 1870-1910); Auguste Lefebvre, O.S.B. (c. 1870-1930); Francis Aveling (1875-1941); the Suarezian Pedro Descoqs, S.J. (1877-1946); Réginald Garrigou-Lagrange, O.P. (1877-1964); the Sulpician Hippolyte Ligeard (1878-1918); Cesare Manzoni (c. 1880-1930); Giuseppe Maria Petazzi, S.J. (c. 1880-1940); Jean-Marie Hervé (1881-1958); Heinrich Lennerz, S.J. (1881-1961); Ignaz Ottiger (1882-1891); Marie Dominique Roland-Gosselin, O.P. (1883-1934);

Alexander Horvath (1884-1956); René Compaing, S.J. (c. 1885-1920); Karl Eschweiler (1886-1936); Martin Cyril D'Arcy, S.J. (1888-1976); Léopold Malevez, S.J. (1900-1973); Marie-Michel Labourdette, O.P. (1908-1990); José De Wolf, S.J. (c. 1909-1950); Louis Monden, S.J. (1911-2002); Marie-Dominique Chenu, O.P. (1895-1990); André Lyonnet (c. 1910-1970); Jean-Hervé Nicolas, O.P. (1910-2001); Marie-Dominique Philippe, O.P. (1912-2006); the Belgian Canon Roger Aubert (1914-), of the University of Louvain; Albert Sohier, S.J. (c. 1915-1975).

Cardinal Juan de Lugo, S.J. (1583-1660), following Ramon Llull (1232-1315), John Duns Scotus, O.F.M. (c. 1265-1308), and Raymond de Sabunda (d. 1436), develops an even more scientific system of faith. He argues that the motive itself of faith is partially based on a logical syllogism that divine revelation is probable and that God cannot deceive us (based on various objective signs). Grace merely lets us perceive the voice of God Himself in these signs and elevates our natural assent into a supernatural one. De Lugo's position was adopted by Caspar Hurtado, S.J. (1575-1647); Juan de Ripalda, S.J. (1595-1648); Cardinal Sforza Pallavicini (1607-1667); Miguel de Elizalde, S.J. (1616-1698); Gilles Extrix, S.J. (1624-1694); Thyrsus Gonzalez de Santalla, S.J. (1624-1705); François Lamy, O.S.B. (1636-1711); Claude François Alexandre Houtteville (1686-1742); François Para du Phanjas, S.J. (1724-1797); L. de Marabail (c. 1750-1810); Georg Hermes (1775-1831); Julius August Ludwig Wegschneider (c. 1785-1849); Josef Kleutgen, S.J. (1811-1883); Johan Baptist Franzelin, S.J. (1816-1886); Marc Antoine Marie François Duilhé de Saint-Projet (1822-1896); Ferdinand Stentrup (1831-1898); Hugo Hurter (1832-1914); Bishop Franz Egger (1836-1918); Ambroise Gardeil, O.P. (1859-1931); Henri Pinard de la Boullaye (1874-1958); Ambroise-Marie de Poulpiquet, O.P. (1875-1915); Anselm Stolz, O.S.B. (1900-1942).

47   Rousselot's theory of the eyes of faith proved influential on such theologians as Bishop Gabriel Brunhes (1874-1947), Karl Adam (1876-1966), Pierre Boisselot, O.P. (1899-1964), the phenomenogist Jean Mouroux (1901-1973), Karl Rahner, S.J. (1904-1984), Hans Urs von Balthasar (1905-1988), the existentialist Thomist Bernard Welte (1906-1983), and Avery Dulles, S.J. (1918-), in addition to his immediate followers such as Guy De Broglie, De La Taille, Huby, Lebreton, Malmberg, Masure, and Tiberghien.

48   Rousselot argues more technically that there is an identity and reciprocal priority between the judgment of the credibility of faith and the belief in that faith. That is to say, the perceptive knowledge (faith) both precedes and follows the perceived knowledge (credibility) ("EF," I, p. 32; "ATT," p. 98). Or put differently, judgments of credibility don't really precede but are simultaneous with the initial act of faith ("EF," II, p. 51). For we perceive a fact (clue) and its related law (synthesis) at once: the law is seen through the clue but it is only in seeing the law that the clue is seen as clue. That is to say, perceiving the clue as clue requires perceiving that to which it is the clue, i.e. its connection with the

law. So in a way it is true to say that the clue is the cause of the assent we give to the conclusion, yet it is just as true to say that it is the perceived conclusion that sheds light on the clue and endows it with a meaning ("EF," I, pp. 29-31). For instance though I have read Hamlet many times, I may take up the play again and gasp 'I've got it! That's it!' as I grasp a clue simultaneous with a perception of Hamlet's character as a whole. Logically the clue comes first, but from another point of view it follows upon the understanding ("EF," I, p. 30). Indeed the perceived clue both precedes the assent insofar as it is rational, and follows upon the assent insofar as it is supernatural ("EF," I, pp. 31-32).

49   An internal committee of Jesuits in 1920 examined and concluded that Rousselot's theory was too divorced from safe opinion to be followed by the Jesuits. The Superior Generals of the Jesuit Order Wlodimir Ledochoswki and John Baptist Janssens subsequently forbade Rousselot's teachings on faith to be taught or defended by the Jesuits in 1920 and 1951, respectively. See Letter of Wlodimir Ledochowski of July 15, 1920 in *Acta Romana Societatis Iesu* (Rome: Typis Polyglottis Vaticanis, 1919-1923), vol. III, pp. 229-233; Letter of February 11, 1951 of John Baptist Janssens in *Acta Romana Societatis Iesu* (Rome: Typis Polyglottis Vaticanis, 1951), vol. XII, pp. 72-94, especially p. 77. However, Avery Dulles among others has questioned whether these past prohibitions are currently binding on Jesuits (see Rousselot, Pierre, *The Eyes of Faith* (New York: Fordham University Press, 1990), Appendix, p. 113).

50   In order to support his theory of the eyes of faith Rousselot proffers four lines of evidence. He first asserts that only his theory, and not that of proponents of a scientific view of faith (such as Bainvel), allows us to understand how a Catholic and a non-Catholic can examine the same data but one comes to believe in the truth of the Catholic faith while the other does not. For Rousselot's theory allows us to explain the difference in that the former individual had the eyes of faith whereas the latter did not. Just as two scientists or two detectives may observe the same phenomena or crime scene but only one arrive at the proper conclusion—the one who perceives it as a clue pointing to a conclusion or law (the one who synthesizes and sees a connection)—believers and non-believers may differ not in representational notes (i.e. mental contents), but in the power of intellectual activity; for the believer alone is given a new faculty of perception whereby facts are seen as clues in relation to larger truths ("EF," I, pp. 27-29, 34; II, pp. 56, 67; II, n. 32 on p. 80). As Aquinas puts it: "For of those seeing one and the same miracle or hearing the same sermon, some believe and some do not believe. And so it is necessary to put forth another internal cause, which moves a human internally to assent to those things which are of faith ... And thus faith, in regard to the assent, which is the chief act of faith, is from God moving humans internally by grace" (2a 2ae q. 6 a. 1). Or again, "Infidels have ignorance concerning matters of faith, for they neither see or know them in themselves nor do they know that they are credible. But the faithful have knowledge of them in this way, not by

demonstration, but insofar as they see that they are to be believed through the light of faith" (2a 2ae q. 1 a. 5 ad 1; cf. 1 q. 1 a. 5 ad 1; cf. "ATT," pp. 97, 99).

Secondly, Rousselot claims that his view of faith better accounts for the faith of children, the unlearned, and the immediate convert (ELK, VI, p. 221). For faith equally can be found in the little child after baptism, uneducated peasants, as well as in the clever theologian (ISTH, II, 6, pp. 155-156; n. 37 on pp. 155-156, 158 ("ATT," n. 12 on p. 110). Yet Bainvel and others have a hard time accounting for how an act of true faith can occur before the preambles of the faith are distinctly and explicitly known. For it is hard to see how children and the unlearned (for instance a young villager brought up on the Catechism, or a native taught by a missionary), could have a scientifically-justified faith [proponents of the view of a scientific faith make appeal here to various respective certitudes, reflex practical principles, subjective preferences, probabilities, or trusts in teachings of pastor or parents: yet these seem inadequate to give a scientific faith and could also occur in a Moslem, Buddhist, Shintoist, as well as in Socrates or an unbeliever, and so would give no reason for preferring one religion to another, or for preferring the homilies of a pastor over the lectures of a schoolteacher] ("EF," I, pp. 24-25; n. 12 on p. 40; II, p. 61). Here too Bainvel's view seems to imply the faith of the unlearned is superficial and undeveloped. Yet for Rousselot the faith of the peasant (*charbonnier*), who may not be able to express his whole faith in an explicit manner, is just as reasonable as that of the historian or academic or medieval doctor of theology ("EF," I, n. 29 on pp. 42-43; II, pp. 61-62; II, n. 23 on p. 78 and n. 28 on p. 79). Again mothers do not begin educating their children in the faith by saying 'You know, there is a good God who has told us that Jesus exists' [and there are various miracles, fulfilled prophecies, etc.]. In other words, they don't expound a philosophical and theological argument for the credibility of faith to their children. Rather, they just tell them 'Ask the little Jesus to make you a good boy' ("ATT," p. 106). Lastly, with the immediate convert faith occurs through a direct, rapid, and supernatural induction (an infused intuition), and so is not temporally preceded by any demonstration of credibility, as with the centurion who uttered, 'my Lord and my God' ("EF," I, pp. 32-33; "ATT," pp. 105-106; ISTH, II, 6, pp. 155-156; n. 37 on pp. 155-156, 158; cf. Mk 15:37-39).

Thirdly, Rousselot argues that the external signs that make someone come to the faith are quite varied. In actuality, people have come to the faith through a whole variety of signs: the holiness of a good priest or a Christian woman, the healing of a sick person, the marvelous effect of receiving Holy Communion, the impression produced by a religious feast, the recognition of Catholic Rome as civilizing, reflection on the life of Christ or the history of Israel, seeing the life of the Church, witnessing miracles, etc. ("EF," I, p. 33; n. 30 on p. 43; II, pp. 61, 68; II, n. 3 on p. 72). Indeed grace allows us to see manifest signs of Catholicism in everything: in a blade of grass, in world history, in the most commonplace word or face (for, adds Rousselot, the lover recognizes the beloved by a single hair of her neck) ("EF," I, pp. 35-36).

Fourthly Rousselot claims that the unhealed intellect needs grace to perceive the sufficiency of reasons for belief. Without grace, we do not have the triumphant confidence that our reason can clarify being. For after the fall our reason lacks full perfection in functioning (ELK, VII, pp. 237-238; "ATT," pp. 94, 103).

51   For more on the life and philosophical thought of Karl Rahner see: DTC (1950), Tables générales, pp. 3854-3856; CMCT (1960), pp. 138-176; TS (1966), pp. 167-179; SCT (1970), pp. 126-131; OB (1971), pp. 67-74, 233-242; HA (1971), pp. 227-229; HWP (1971), v. V, pp. 142-144; CTIC (1985), pp. 247-259; PHP (1988), pp. 327-330; TCRT (1988), pp. 381-382; CP (1989), v. II, pp. 600-608; CT (1989), pp. 13-25; FUP (1989), pp. 225-230; NCS (1989), pp. 260-263; TYT (1989), pp. 241-252; DP (1993), v. II, p. 2408; ATH (1994), pp. 151-153, 172-174, 215-217, 266-268; NT (1994), p. 160; HCEC (1995), pp. 1077-1078; BDTC (1996), pp. 646-647; LTK (1997), vol. VII, pp. 805-808; CTE (1998), pp. 142-145; REP (1998), v. VIII, pp. 35-39; PCHP (1999), p. 715; MCT (2000), v. II, pp. 205-214, 476-479; OHYP (2001), pp. 138-141; TT (2002), pp. 14, 83-91, 124-126, 166-178, 217-227; BTCT (2003), pp. 100-102; NCE (2003), v. XI, pp. 892-895; WPR (2003), pp. 351-354; ER (2004), v. XI, pp. 7600-7602; FKCT (2004), pp. 188-192; ACP (2005), pp. 373-379; EP (2005), v. VIII, pp. 231-234; SHT (2005), pp. 87-88; EF (2006), v. X, pp. 9371-9373; TCCT (2007), pp. 87-104; BBKL (2009), v. XXX, pp. 1123-1127; Baker, Kenneth, *A Synopsis of the Transcendental Philosophy of Emerich Coreth and Karl Rahner* (Spokane: Gonzaga University Press, 1965); Vorgrimmler, Herbert, *Karl Rahner: His Life, Thought, and Works* (Glen Rock: Paulist Press, 1965); Röper, Anita, *The Anonymous Christian* (New York: Sheed and Ward, 1966); Muck, Otto, *The Transcendental Method* (New York: Herder and Herder, 1968), pp. 181-204; Donceel, Joseph, *The Philosophy of Karl Rahner* (Albany: Magi Books, 1969); McCool, Gerald, *The Theology of Karl Rahner* (Albany: Magi Books, 1969); Branick, Vincent, *An Ontology of Understanding: Karl Rahner's Metaphysics of Knowledge in the Context of Modern German Hermeneutics* (St. Louis: Marianist Communications Center, 1974); Carr, Anne, *The Theological Method of Karl Rahner* (Missoula: Scholar's Press, 1977); Rolwing, Richard, *A Philosophy of Revelation according to Karl Rahner* (Lanham: University Press of America, 1978); Tallon, Andrew, ed., *Personal Becoming* (Milwaukee: Marquette University Press, 1982); Vass, George, *Understanding Karl Rahner, I: A Theologian in Search of a Philosophy* (London: Continuum, 1985); Vass, George, *Understanding Karl Rahner, II: Mystery of Man and the Foundations of a Theological System* (Westminster, 1985); Kerr, Fergus, *Theology after Wittgenstein* (Oxford: Blackwell, 1986), pp. 7-14; Vorgrimler, Herbert, *Understanding Karl Rahner: An Introduction to His Life and Thought* (New York: Crossroads,

1986); Bonsor, Jack, *Rahner, Heidegger, and Truth* (Lanham: University Press of America, 1987); Bridges, James, *Human Destiny and Resurrection in Pannenberg and Rahner* (New York: Peter Lang, 1987); Scheehan, Thomas, *Rahner: The Philosophical Foundations* (Athens: Ohio State University Press, 1987); Murphy, Marie, *New Images of the Last Things: Karl Rahner on Death and Life after Death* (New York: Paulist Press, 1988); Phan, Peter, *Eternity in Time: A Study of Karl Rahner's Eschatology* (Selinsgrove: Susquehanna Univerisity Press, 1988); Ford, David, ed., *Modern Theologians* (Oxford: Blackwell, 1989), pp. 183-204; Nichols, Aidan, *From Newman to Congar* (Edinburgh: T. & T. Clark, 1990), pp. 214-235; *Communio* 18 (1991) [Special Issue on Rahner]; Duffy, Stephen, *The Graced Horizon: Nature and Grace in Modern Catholic Thought* (Collegeville: Liturgical Press, 1992), pp. 85-114; Dych, William, *Karl Rahner* (Collegeville: Liturgical Press, 1992); Sullivan, Francis, *Salvation Outside the Church?: Tracing the History of the Catholic Response* (New York: Paulist Press, 1992), pp. 171-181; Tallon, Andrew, ed., *Philosophy and Theology* 7 (1992), pp.113-243 [Special Issue on Rahner]; Conway, Eamonn, *The Anonymous Christian—A Relativised Christianity?: An Evaluation of Hans Urs von Balthasar's Criticisms of Karl Rahner's Theory of the Anonymous Christian* (Frankfurt: Peter Lang, 1993); Marshall, Molly, *No Salvation Outside the Church?* (Lewiston: Edward Mellen Press, 1993), pp. 115-154; Guenther, Titus, *Rahner and Metz: Transcendental Theology as Political Theology* (Lanham: University Press of America, 1994); Latourelle, René, ed., *Dictionary of Fundamental Theology* (New York: Crossroads, 1994), pp. 804-806; Schiavone, Christopher, *Rationality and Revelation in Rahner* (New York: Peter Lang, 1994); Worthing, Mark, *Foundations and Functions of Theology as Universal Science: Theological Method and Apologetic Praxis in Wolfhart Pannenberg and Karl Rahner* (Frankfurt: Peter Lang, 1996); Purcell, Michael, *Mystery and Method: The Other in Rahner and Levinas* (Milwaukee: Marquette University Press, 1998); Carey, Patrick, et al., eds., *Biographical Dictionary of Christian Theologians* (Westport: Greenwood Press, 2000), pp. 427-431; Dych, William, *Karl Rahner* (London: Continuum, 2000); Fields, Stephen, *Being as Symbol: On the Origin and Development of Karl Rahner's Metaphysics* (Washington: Georgetown University Press, 2000); Hastings, Adrian, *The Oxford Companion to Christian Thought* (Oxford: Oxford University Press, 2000), pp. 591-593; Losinger, Anton, *The Anthropological Turn: The Human Orientation of the Theology of Karl Rahner* (New York: Fordham University Press, 2000); Ludlow, Morwenna, *Universal Salvation: Eschatology in the Thought of Gregory of Nyssa and Karl Rahner* (Oxford: Oxford University Press, 2000); Pasquini, John, *Atheism and Salvation: Atheism from the Perspective of Anonymous Christianity in the Thought of the Revolutionary Mystic and Theologian Karl Rahner* (Lanham: University Press of America, 2000); Peters, Carmichael, *A Gadamerian Reading of Karl Rahner's Theology of Grace and Freedom* (Lanham: Catholic Scholars Press, 2000); *Philosophy & Theology* 12 (2000) [Special Issue on Rahner]; Pandiappallil, Joseph, *Jesus the Christ and*

Religious Pluralism: Rahnerian Christology and Belief Today (New York: Crossroad, 2001); Burke, Patrick, *Reinterpreting Rahner* (New York: Fordham University Press, 2002); Klein, Terrence, *How Things Are in the World: Metaphysics and Theology in Wittgenstein and Rahner* (Milwaukee: Marquette University Press, 2003); *Philosophy & Theology* 15:1 (2003) [Special Issue on Rahner]; Kilby, Karen, *Karl Rahner: Theology and Philosophy* (London: Routledge, 2004); *Louvain Studies* 29 (2004) [Special Issue on Karl Rahner]; MacEnhill, Peter, et al., eds., *Fifty Key Christian Thinkers* (London: Routledge, 2004), pp. 221-226; Crowley, Paul, ed., *Rahner beyond Rahner* (Lanham: Rowman & Littlefield, 2005); Fischer, Mark, *The Foundations of Karl Rahner* (New York: Crossroads, 2005); *Gregorianum* 86:2 (2005), pp. 235-396 [Special Rahner Issue]; Marmion, Declan, et al., eds., *The Cambridge Companion to Karl Rahner* (Cambridge: Cambridge University Press, 2005); Marion, Declan, et al., eds., *Christian Identity in a Postmodern Age: Celebrating the Legacies of Karl Rahner and Bernard Lonergan* (Dublin: Veritas, 2005); *Philosophy & Theology* 71 (2005) [Special Issue on Rahner]; Grieco, Eileen, *Love and Knowledge in Modern Thomism* (Frankfurt: Peter Lang, 2006); Ibekwe, Linus, *The Universality of Salvation in Jesus Christ in the Thought in the Thought of Karl Rahner* (Würzburg: Echter, 2006); Bosco, Mark, and David Stagaman *Finding God in All Things: Bernard Lonergan, John Courtney Murray, and Karl Rahner* (New York: Fordham University Press, 2007); Kilby, Karen, *Karl Rahner: A Brief Introduction* (New York: Herder and Herder, 2007); O'Meara, Thomas, *God in the World: A Guide to Karl Rahner's Theology* (Collegeville: Liturgical Press, 2007); Conway, Padraic, *Karl Rahner* (Oxford: Peter Lang, 2010).

52   In 1962-1963 Rahner had to submit everything he wrote to Rome for prior censorship. In 1951 Rahner was also forbidden to discuss the notion of concelebration by the Holy Office (see *Acta Apostolicae Sedis* 46 (1954), pp. 668-670).

53   Quotations are modifications of the translation of this work by Joseph Donceel and published as *Hearer of the Word* [HW] (New York: Continuum, 1994).

Rahner's other philosophical works are his *Spirit in the World* [*Geist in Welt*] [SPW] (1939; 1957 [revised by his student Johannes Baptist Metz]) and his *Theologische und philosophische Zeitfragen im katholischen deutschen Raum* (written in 1943; published in 1994).

His major work in theology *Grundkurs des Glaubens* (1976) [translated as *Foundations of Christian Faith* [FCF] (New York: Crossroad, 1978)] also includes some philosophical elements. Rahner also wrote many other works of theology and spirituality including: *Zur Theologie des Todes* [TD] (1958) [translated as *On the Theology of Death* (New York: Herder, 1961); *Das Problem der Hominisation* (1961) [translated as *Hominisation: The Evolutionary Origin of Man as a Theological Problem* (New York: Herder and Herder,

1965)]; *Nature and Grace* (New York: Sheed and Ward, 1964); *Alltägliche Dinge* [BT] (1964) [translated as *Belief Today* (New York: Sheed and Ward, 1967)]; *Offenbarung und Überlieferung* (1964) [with Joseph Ratzinger] [translated as *Revelation and Tradition* (New York: Herder and Herder, 1966)]; *Intellektuelle Redlichkeit und christlicher Glaube* (1966); *Religionsfreiheit* (1966); *Glaubst du an Gott?* [translated as *Do You Believe in God?* [DYBG] (New York: Newman Press, 1969)]; *Gnade als Freiheit* (1968) [translated as *Grace in Freedom* (London: Burns & Oates, 1969)]; *Ist Gott noch gegragt?* (1973); *Was sollen wir noch glauben?* (1980) [with Karl-Heinz Weger] [translated as *Our Christian Faith: Answers for the Future* [OCF] (New York: Crossroads, 1980)]; *Theologie in Freiheit und Verantwortung* (1981) [with Heinrich Fries]; *Horizonte der Religiosität* (1984).

Rahner has also helped to edit (and contribute articles to) some of the most well-known encyclopedias of Catholic thought in Germany including: *Enchiridion Symbolorum* (Freiburg: Herder, 1952-1955); *Lexikon für Theologie und Kirche*, 14 vols. (Freiburg: Herder, 1957-1968); *Kleines Konzilskompendium* (1966); *Sacramentum Mundi: An Encyclopedia of Theology*, 6 vols. (London: Burns and Oates, 1968-1970); *Herders theologisches Taschenlexikon* (Freiburg: Herder, 1972); *Encyclopedia of Theology: The Concise Sacramentum Mundi* (London: Burns and Oates, 1975); *Dictionary of Theology* [*Kleines Theologisches Wörterbuch* (1961)] (New York: Crossroad, 1965; 1981; 1985). He has also edited several books.

His philosophical, spiritual, and theological essays have been collected in *Theological Investigations* [*Schriften zur Theologie*], 23 vols. [TI] (1954-1992). See in particular Rahner's various philosophical essays including: "The Theological Concept of Concupiscence," TI, I, 3, pp. 347-382; "Concerning the Relationship between Nature and Grace," TI, I, 9, pp. 297-318; "Some Implications of the Scholastic Concept of Uncreated Grace," TI, I, 10, pp. 319-346; "On the Resurrection of the Body," TI, II, 6, pp. 203-216; "On the Question of a Formal Existential Ethics," TI, II, 7, pp. 217-234; "The Dignity and Freedom of Man," TI, II, 8, pp. 235-264; "Reflections on the Experience of Grace," TI, III, 6, pp. 86-90; "Nature and Grace," TI, IV, 7, pp. 165-188; "The Hermeneutics of Eschatological Assertions," TI, IV, 13, pp. 323-346; "The Life of the Dead," TI, IV, 14, pp. 347-354; "Thoughts on the Possibility of Belief Today," TI, V, 1, pp. 3-22; "Christianity and the Non-Christian Religions," TI, V, 6, pp. 115-134; "The Commandments of Love in Relation to the Other Commandments," TI, V, 17, pp. 439-459; "The Man of Today and Religion," TI, VI, 1, pp. 3-20; "Small Question Regarding the Contemporary Pluralism in the Intellectual Situation of Catholics and the Church," TI, VI, 2, pp. 21-30; "Reflections on Dialogue within a Pluralistic Society," TI, VI, 3, pp. 32-42; "Ideology and Christianity," TI, VI, 4, pp. 43-58; "Philosophy and Theology," TI, VI, 6, pp. 71-81; "A Small Fragment on the Collective Finding of Truth," TI, VI, 7, pp. 82-88; "Theology of Freedom," TI, VI, 13, pp. 178-196;

"Reflections on the Unity of the Love of Neighbor and the Love of God," TI, VI, 16, pp. 231-252; "Anonymous Christians," TI, VI, 23, pp. 390-398; "Being Open to God as Ever Greater," TI, VII, 2, pp. 24-56; "Intellectual Honesty and Christian Faith," TI, VII, 3, pp. 47-71; "The Scandal of Death," TI, VII, 11, pp. 140-144; "On Truthfulness," TI, VII, 22, pp. 229-259; "On Christian Dying," TI, VII, 26, pp. 285-293; "Theology and Anthropology," TI, IX, 2, pp. 28-45; "Philosophy and Philosophizing in Theology," TI, IX, 3, pp. 46-63; "The Historicity of Theology," TI, IX, 4, pp. 64-82; "Observations on the Doctrine of God in Catholic Dogmatics," TI, IX, 8, pp. 127-145; "Atheism and Implicit Christianity," TI, IX, 9, pp. 145-164; "Church, Churches, and Religions, TI, X, pp. 30-49; "The Church and Atheism," TI, XXI, pp. 137-150; "Fragmentary Aspect of a Theological Evaluation of the Concept of the Future," TI, X, 12, pp. 235-241; "The Theological Problems Entailed in the Idea of the New Earth," TI, X, 14, pp. 260-272; "Immanent and Transcendent Consummation of the World," TI, X, 15, pp. 273-289; "Reflections on Methodology in Theology," XI, 3, pp. 68-114; "The Experience of God Today," TI, XI, 6, pp. 149-165; "Theological Considerations on Secularization and Atheism," TI, XI, 7, pp. 166-184 [see also his "Theological Reflections on the Problem of Secularization," in Shook, Laurence, ed., *Theology of Renewal, Vol. I: Renewal of Religious Thought* (New York: Herder and Herder, 1968), pp. 167-192]; "Theological Observations on the Concept of Time," TI, XI 13, pp. 288-308; "Theological Considerations on the Moment of Death," TI, XI, 14, pp. 309-321; "Anonymous Christianity and the Missionary Task of the Church Today," TI, XII, 9, pp. 161-178; "On Recognizing the Importance of Thomas Aquinas," TI, XIII, 1, pp. 3-12; "Thomas Aquinas on Truth," TI, XIII, 2, pp. 13-032; "The Current Relationship between Philosophy and Theology," TI, XIII, 4, pp. 61-79; "Experience of Self and the Experience of God," TI, XIII, 8, pp. 122-132; "Ideas for a Theology of Death," TI, XIII, 11, pp. 169-186; "Observations on the Problem of the Anonymous Christian," TI, XIV, 17, pp. 280-294; "The Foundation of Belief Today," TI, XVI, 1, pp. 3-23; "Religious Enthusiasm and the Experience of Grace," TI, XVI, 3, pp. 35-51; "Anonymous and Explicit Faith," TI, XVI, 4, pp. 52-59; "Faith between Rationality and Emotion," TI, XVI, 5, pp. 60-78; "The Acceptance in Faith of the Truth of God," TI, XVI, 10, pp. 169-176; "The One Christ and the Universality of Salvation," TI, XVI, 13, pp. 199-224; "The Hiddenness of God," TI, XVI, 14, pp. 227-243; "An Investigation of the Incomprehensibility of God in St. Thomas Aquinas," TI, XVI, 15, pp. 244-254; "Jesus Christ in the Non-Christian Religions," TI, XVII, 5, pp. 39-50; "The Theological Dimension of the Question about Man," TI, XVII, 6, pp. 53-70; "The Body in the Order of Salvation," TI, XVII, 7, pp. 71-89; "On Bad Arguments in Moral Theology," TI, XVIII, 4, p. 74-85; "The Human Question of Meaning in Face of the Absolute Mystery of God," TI, XVIII, 5, pp. 89-104; "Experience of Transcendence from the Standpoint of Christian Dogmatics," TI, XVIII, 11, pp. 173-188; "Faith as Courage," TI, XVIII, 13, pp. 211-225; "Christian Dying," TI, XVIII, 14, pp. 226-256; "On the Importance of the Non-Christian Religions for Salvation," XVIII, 17, pp. 288-295; "Foundations of the Christian Faith," TI, XIX, 1, pp. 3-15; "Brief Theological Observations on the State of Fallen Nature," TI, XIX, 4, pp. 39-53; "Eternity from Time," TI, XIX, 13, pp. 169-178; "Why Does God Allow Us to Suffer?," TI, XIX, 15, pp. 194-208; "Justifying Faith in an Agnostic World," TI, XXI, 8, pp. 130-136; "The Church and Atheism," TI, XXI, 9, pp. 137-150; "The Act of Faith and the Content of Faith," TI, XXI, 10, pp. 151-161; "The Specific Character of the Christian's Concept of God," TI, XXI, 13, pp. 185-195; "The Question of Meaning as a Question of God," TI, XXI, 14, pp. 196-207; "Conscience," TI, XXII, 1, pp. 3-13.

See also his philosophical essays: "Religionsphilosophie und Theologie," *Salzburger Hochschulwochen* 10 (1937), pp. 24-32; "Introduction au concept de philosophie existentiale chez Heidegger," *Recherches de science religieuse* 30 (1940), pp. 152-171; "Der Gesetzesbegriff in der christlichen Offenbarung" *Alpbacher Tagung* (1948), pp. 247-254; "Krankheit der christlichen Philosophie?," *Wort und Wahrheit* 7 (1952), pp. 401-402; "Der Neothomismus und die Sprache der Zeit," *Wort und Wahrheit* 7 (1952), pp. 85-92; "Theoretische und reale Moral in ihrer Differenz," *Handbuch der Pastoraltheologie* (Freiburg: Herder, 1966), pp. 153-163; "Über das Experiment im christlich-kirchlichen Bereich," in Rahner, Karl, ed., *Chancen des Glaubens* (Freiburg: Herder, 1971), pp. 238-247; "Fe anónyme y fe explicita," *Razón y Fe* 888 (1972), pp. 141-148; "Anonymes Christentum und Student," *Image* 7 (1976), pp. 8-11; "Expérience de l'Esprit et choix existentiel," in Schillebeeckx, Edward, ed., *L'expérience de l'Esprit* (Paris: Beauchesne, 1976), pp. 173-186; "Bemerkungen zur Logik der existentiellen Erkenntnis," *Geist und Leben* 59 (1986), pp. 241-247.

Finally see Rahner's articles "Existence, Theological" "Philosophy and Theology" and "Potentia oboedentialis," in *Sacramentum Mundi* (New York: Herder, 198-1970), II, pp. 306-307, V, pp. 20-24, 65-67; "Existential," *Herders Theologisches Taschenlexikon* (Freiburg: Herder,, 1972), vol. II, pp. 272-273; "Philosophie und Theologie," "Pluralismus," *Herders Theologisches Taschenlexikon* (Freiburg: Herder, 1973), vol. VI, pp. 37-43, 61-63; "Anonymer Christ," *Handbuch der Pastoraltheologie* (Freiburg: H erder, 1972), vol. V, pp. 19-20; "Existential, übernatürliches," *Lexikon für Theologie und Kirche* (Freiburg: Herder, 1959), vol. III, p. 1301; "Präexistentianismus," *Lexikon für Theologie und Kirche* (Freiburg: Herder, 1963), vol. VIII, pp. 674-675.

His archives are housed at the University of Innsbruck.

For a bibliography of Rahner see: Bleistein, Roman, et al., eds., *Bibliographie Karl Rahner 1924-1974*, 2 vols. (Freiburg: Herder, 1969-1974); Tallon, Andrew, ed., *Personal Becoming* (Milwaukee: Marquette University Press, 1982), pp. 179-223; Pedley, C.J., "An English Bibliographical Aid to Karl Rahner," *Heythrop Journal* 25 (1984), pp. 319-365; Pekarske, Daniel, *Abstracts of Karl Rahner's Theological Investigations 1-23* (Milwaukee: Marquette Univer-

sity Press, 2002); Pedley, C.J.,"An English Bibliographical Aid to Karl Rahner,"
Heythrop Journal 26:3 (2007), pp. 319-365; Pekarske, Daniel, *Abstracts of Karl
Rahner's Unserialized Essays* (Milwaukee: Marquette University Press, 2009).

54   In this way Rahner professes to avoid the extrinsicism wherein grace is
a mere superstructure added to nature. Rather grace, he says, is a constitutive
part of our being and as such is always modifying our nature (FCF, IV, pp.
123-124; TI, I, 9, pp. 298, 302-303; IV, 7, pp. 165-188; XVI, 1, p. 10; "Potentia
Oboedientialis," *Sacramentum Mundi*, V, p. 66).

55   Rahner, somewhat notoriously, has advanced a philosophical and
theological pluralism. He argues that even in the past the Catholic Church
has tolerated different schools of thought (i.e. Augustinianism, Thomism,
Scotism, Suarezianism, etc.). And this pluralism is exaggerated today due to
the vast amount of scholarly material and different viewpoints (with their
own presuppositions). Hence we are stuck with a pluralism of sorts. This
is not to say that we should not work to minimize divergences and that the
Church has no right to reject heterodox views (TI, II, 7, pp. 217-234; II, 8,
p. 236; VI, 2, pp. 21-30; VI, 3, pp. 32-42; VI, 7, pp. 82-88; XI, 1, pp. 4-6,
13-14; "Pluralismus," in LTK (1963), vol. VIII, pp. 566-567). Hence Rahner
writes "But the theologies remain multiple, because the whole of present-day
theology, with its various disciplines, terminologies, approaches, problems, and
audiences, cannot be even approximately grasped by the individual" (Theology,"
in *Sacramentum Mundi* (1960), vol. VI, p. 240.

Rahner, like Lavelle as we will see, has an interesting view of the afterlife
wherein the next life will be a form of eternity similar to that of God's, i.e. an
existence beyond time. He thus rejects the view that the afterlife will be as
though we only change horses and ride on, to use the expression of Feuerbach
(FCF, IX, p. 436; TI, IV, 13, pp. 323-354; VII, 11, pp. 140-144; VII, 26, pp.
285-293; X, 12, pp. 235-241; X, 14-15, pp. 260-289; XI, 14, pp. 309-321;
XIII, 11, pp. 169-186; XVIII, 14, pp. 226-256; XIX, 13, pp. 169-177; TD,
I, pp. 24-39; II, pp. 46-54).

56   Catholicism had been outlawed, and the Jesuits and Augustinians expelled, along with 10,000 French Catholic Acadians, followed English takeover
of Canada in 1763.

57   *Time* had earlier published another article on Lonergan: "Understanding Understanding," *Time Magazine* (January 22, 1965).

58   For more on the life and thought of Lonergan see: MTCJ (1967), pp.
126-151; HWP (1971), v. V, pp. 146-149; OB (1971), pp. 84-90; CHP
(1974), v. IX, p. 268; CHAD (1975), v. VII, pp. 1058-1060; CTIC (1985),
pp. 260-264; PHP (1988), pp. 327-330; TCRT (1988), pp. 379-380; CP
(1989), v. II, pp. 753-770; CT (1989), pp. 27-38; FUP (1989), pp. 225-230;
NCS (1989), pp. 260-263; FT (1992), pp. 109-122, 161-168; ATH (1994),
pp. 153-155; NT (1994), p. 160; HCEC (1995), pp. 792-794; BDTC (1996),

pp. 470-471; DPR (1996), pp. 425-426; LTK (1997), v. VI, pp. 1046-1047;
CTE (1998), pp. 182-185; REP (1998), v. V, pp. 822-825; OHYP (2001), p.
265; TT (2002), pp. 14-15, 123-124; BTCT (2003), pp. 102-107; NCE
(2003), v. VIII, pp. 772-775; WPR (2003), pp. 354-357; ER (2004), v. XI,
pp. 5510-5511; ACP (2005), pp. 380-389; SHT (2005), p. 88; EF (2006), v.
VII, pp. 6775-6777; TCCT (2007), pp. 105-120; Continuum 2 (1964) [Spe-
cial Issue on Lonergan]; Muck, Otto, The Transcendental Method (New York:
Herder and Herder, 1968), pp. 255-284; Di Norcia, Vincent, Inquiry and
Development in Bernard Lonergan's Insight (Toronto: University of Toronto
Press, 1969); Tracy, David, The Achievement of Bernard Lonergan (New York:
Herder and Herder, 1970); Vertin, Joseph, Critical Realism: Cognitional Ap-
proach and Ontological Achievement according to Bernard Lonergan (Washing-
ton: Theological College Publications, 1970); Donahue, Eugene, Study-Guide
to Bernard Lonergan's Insight (Omaha: Creighton University Press, 1972);
Tyrell, Bernard, Bernard Lonergan's Philosophy of God (Notre Dame: Univer-
sity of Notre Dame Press, 1974); Corcoran, Patrick, ed., Looking at Lonergan's
Method (Dublin: Talbot Press, 1975); Meynell, Hugo, An Introduction to the
Philosophy of Bernard Lonergan (New York: Barnes & Noble, 1976); Lamb,
Matthew, History, Method and Theology: A Dialectical Comparison of Wilhelm
Dilthey's Critique of Historical Reason and Bernard Lonergan's Meta-Methodol-
ogy (Missoula: Scholars Press, 1978); Nilson, Jon, Hegel's Phenomenology and
Lonergan's Insight (Meisenheim: Hain, 1979); Crowe, Frederick, The Lonergan
Enterprise (Cambridge: Cowley, 1980); Crowe, Frederick, Method in Theology:
An Organon for Our Time (Milwaukee: Marquette University Press, 1980);
McKinney, Ronald, The Role of Dialectic in the Thought of Bernard Lonergan
(New York: Fordham University Press, 1980); O'Callaghan, Michael, Unity
in Theology: Lonergan's Framework for Theology in Its New Context (Washing-
ton: University Press of America, 1980); Lamb, Matthew, Creativity and
Method: Essays in Honor of Bernard Lonergan, S.J. (Milwaukee: Marquette
University Press, 1981); Religious Studies and Theology 5:2 (1985) [Special
Issue on Lonergan]; Meynell, Hugo, The Theology of Bernard Lonergan (At-
lanta: Scholars Press, 1986); Danaher, William, ed., Lonergan and You: River-
view Reflections 1985 (Pymble: Lonergan Workshop Committee, 1987);
Falcao, Nelson, Knowing according to Bernard Lonergan (Rome: Urbaniana
University Press, 1987); Fallon, Timothy, ed., Religion and Culture: Essays in
Honor of Bernard Lonergan, S.J. (Albany: State University of New York Press,
1987); Melchin, Kenneth, History, Ethics, and Emergent Probability: Ethics,
Society, and History in the Work of Bernard Lonergan (Lanham: University
Press of America, 1987); Braio, Frank, Lonergan's Retrieval of the Notion of
Human Being (Lanham: University Press of America, 1988); Fallon, Timothy,
et al., eds., Religion in Context: Recent Studies in Lonergan (Lanham: Univer-
sity Press of America, 1988); Gregson, Vernon, ed., The Desires of the Human
Heart: An Introduction to the Theology of Bernard Lonergan (New York: Paulist
Perss, 1988); Matustik, Martin, Mediation of Deconstruction: Bernard Loner-

gan's *Method in Philosophy* (Lanham: University Press of America, 1988); Crowe, Frederick, *Appropriating the Lonergan Idea* (Washington; Catholic University of America Press, 1989); Ford, David, ed., *The Modern Theologians* (Oxford: Blackwells, 1989), vol. I, pp. 205-216; McEvenue, Sean, et al., eds., *Lonergan's Hermeneutics* (Washington: Catholic University of America Press, 1989); Boly, Craig, *The Road to Lonergan's Method in Theology* (Lanham: University Press of America, 1991); Oko, Dariusz, *The Transcendental Way to God according to Bernard Lonergan* (Frankfurt: Peter Lang, 1991); Rende, Michael, *Lonergan on Conversion* (Lanham: University Press of America, 1991); Crowe, Frederick, *Lonergan* (Collegeville: The Liturgical Press, 1992); Kinberger, Mary, *Lonergan on Conversion* (Frankfurt: Peter Lang, 1992); Mooney, Hilary, *The Liberation of Consciousness: Bernard Lonergan's Theological Foundations in Dialogue with the Theological Aesthetics of Hans Urs von Balthasar* (Frankfurt: J. Knecht, 1992); Tekippe, Terry, *Lonergan and Thomas on the Will* (Lanham: University Press of America, 1992); Danaher, William, ed., *Australian Lonergan Worshop* (Lanham: University Press of America, 1993); Liddy, Richard, *Transforming Light: Intellectual Conversion in the Early Lonergan* (Collegeville: Liturgical Press, 1993); Shute, Michael, *The Origins of Lonergan's Notion of the Dialectic of History* (Lanham: University Press of America, 1993); Liddy, Richard, *Transforming Light: Intellectual Conversion in the Early Lonergan* (Collegeville: Liturgical Press, 1993); Sala, Giovanni, et al., eds., *Lonergan and Kant* (Toronto: University of Toronto Press, 1994); Stebbins, J. Michael, *The Divine Initiative: Grace, World-Order, and Human Freedom in the Early Writings of Bernard Lonergan* (Buffalo: University of Toronto Press, 1995); Doorley, Mark, *The Place of the Heart in Lonergan's Ethics: The Role of Feelings in the Ethical Intentionality Analysis of Bernard Lonergan* (Lanham:University Press of America, 1996); Stewart, William, *Introduction to Lonergan's Insight* (Lewiston: Edward Mellen Press, 1996); Tekippe, Terry, *What is Lonergan Up to in Insight?* (Collegeville: Liturgical Press, 1996); Flanagan, Joseph, *Quest for Self-Knowledge: An Essay in Lonergan's Philosophy* (Toronto: University of Toronto Press, 1997); Naickamparambil, Thomas, *Through Self-Discovery to Self-Transcendence: A Study of Cognitional Self-Appropriation in Bernard Lonergan* (Rome: Gregorian University Press, 1997); Melchin, Kenneth, *Living with Other People: An Introduction to Christian Ethics based on Bernard Lonergan* (Toronto: Novalis, 1998); Meynell, Hugo, *Redirecting Philosophy: Reflections on the Nature of Knowledge from Plato to Lonergan* (Toronto: University of Toronto Press, 1998); Cronin, Brian, *Foundations of Philosophy: Lonergan's Cognitional Theory and Epistemology* (Nairobi: Consolata Institute of Philosophy Press, 1999); Jonsson, Ulf, *Foundations for Knowing God: Bernard Lonergan's Foundations for Knowledge of God and the Challenge from Antifoundationalism* (Frankfurt: Peter Lang, 1999); Carey, Patrick, et al., eds., *Biographical Dictionary of Christian Theologians* (Westport: Greenwood, 2000), pp. 324-329; Hastings, Adrian, et al., eds., *The Oxford Companion to Christian Thought* (Oxford: Oxford University Press, 2000), pp. 393-394;

Ormerod, Neil, *Method, Meaning, and Revelation: The Meaning and Function of Revelation in Bernard Lonergan's Method in Theology* (Lanham: University Press of America, 2000); Berchmans, Robert, *A Study of Lonergan's Self-Transcending Subject and Kegans' Evolving Self* (Lewiston: Edward Mellen Press, 2001); Coelho, Ivo, *Hermeneutics and Method: The Universal Viewpoint in Bernard Lonergan* (Toronto: University of Toronto Press, 2001); McPartland, Thomas, *Lonergan and the Philosophy of Historical Existence* (Columbia: University of Missouri Press, 2001); Ogilvie, Matthew, *Faith Seeking Understanding: The Functional Specialty Systematics in Bernard Lonergan's Method in Theology* (Milwaukee: Marquette University Press, 2001); Rusembuka, Muhigirwa, *The Two Ways of Human Development according to Bernard Lonergan* (Rome: Gregorian University Press, 2001); Kanaris, Jim, *Bernard Lonergan's Philosophy of Religion* (Albany: State University of New York Press, 2002); Ogilvie, Matthew, et al., eds., *Australian Lonergan Workshop II* (Drummoyne: Novum Organum Press, 2002); Baker, Deane-Peter, ed., *Explorations in Contemporary Continental Philosophy of Religion* (New York: Rodopi, 2003), pp. 65-79; Saracino, Michele, *On Being Human: A Conversation with Lonergan and Levinas* (Milwaukee: Marquette University Press, 2003); Tekippe, Terry, *Bernard Lonergan: An Introductory Guide to Insight* (New York: Paulist Press, 2003); Tekippe, Terry, *Bernard Lonergan's Insight: A Comprehensive Commentary* (Lanham: University Press of America, 2003); Crowe, Frederick, et al., eds., *Developing the Lonergan Legacy* (Toronto: University of Toronto Press, 2004); Fitzpatrick, Joseph, *Philosophical Encounters: Lonergan and the Analytic Tradition* (Toronto: University of Toronto Press, 2005); Marmion, Declan, et al., eds., *Christian Identity in a Postmodern Age: Celebrating the Legacies of Karl Rahner and Bernard Lonergan* (Dublin: Veritas, 2005); Mathew, William, *Lonergan's Quest: A Study of Desire in the Authoring of Insight* (Toronto: University of Toronto Press, 2005); Teevan, Donna, *Lonergan, Hermeneutics and Theological Method* (Milwaukee: Marquette University Press, 2005); Berger, David, et al., ed., *Thomistenlixikon* (Bonn: Nova & Vetera, 2006), pp. 388-399; Cronin, Brian, *Value Ethics: A Lonergan Perspective* (Nairobi: Consolata Institute of Philosophy Press, 2006); Snell, Russell, *Through a Glass Darkly: Bernard Lonergan and Richard Rorty on Knowing without a God's-Eye-View* (Milwaukee: Marquette University Press, 2006); Beards, Andrew, *Method in Metaphysics: Lonergan and the Future of Analytical Philosophy* (Toronto: University of Toronto Press, 2007); Bosco, Mark, et al., eds, *Finding God in All Things: Celebrating Bernard Lonergan, John Courtney Murray, and Karl Rahner* (New York: Fordham University Press, 2007), pp. 15-79, 199-204; Liddy, Richard, *Startling Strangeness: Reading Lonergan's Insight* (Lanham: University Press of America, 2007); Liptay, John, ed., *The Importance of Insight* (Toronto: University of Toronto Press, 2007); Beards, Andrew, *Method in Metaphysics: Lonergan and the Future of Analytical Philosophy* (Toronto: University of Toronto Press, 2008); Bell, Ian, *The Relevance of Bernard Lonergan's Notion of Self-Appropriation to Mystical-Political Theol-*

ogy (Frankfurt: Peter Lang, 2008); Braman, Brian, *Meaning and Authenticity: Bernard Lonergan and Charles Taylor on the Drama of Authentic Human Existence* (Toronto: University of Toronto Press, 2008); Fitterer, Robert, *Love and Objectivity in Virtue Ethics: Aristotle, Lonergan, and Nussbaum on Emotions and Moral Insight* (Toronto: University of Toronto Press, 2008); Savage, Deborah, *The Subjective Dimension of Human Work: The Conversion of the Acting Person according to Karol Wojtyła/John Paul II and Bernard Lonergan* (Frankfurt: Peter Lang, 2008); Walmsley, Gerard, *Lonergan on Philosophic Pluralism* (Toronto: University of Toronto Press, 2008); Beards, Andrew, *Insight and Analysis* (London: Continuum, 2010); Crowe, Frederick, *Lonergan and the Level of Our Tine* (Toronto: University of Toronto Press, 2010); Halse, Scott, *Bernard Lonergan's Methodology and the Philosophy of Religion* (Lewiston: Edwin Mellen Press, 2010); Lambert, Pierrot, *Bernard Lonergan* (Vancouver: Axial, 2010); McPartland, Thomas, *Lonergan and Historiography* (Columbia: University of Missouri Press, 2010); Shute, Michael, *Lonergan's Discovery of the Science of Economics* (Toronto: University of Toronto Press, 2010).

59   See Wallbank's article "The Philosophy of International Education," *Divyadaan* 12:2 (2001), pp. 193-209.

60   Lonergan's other key philosophical works are his *Verbum: Word and Idea in Aquinas* [V] (1967; 1997); *The Subject* [S] (1968); *Philosophy of God and Theology: The Relationship between Philosophy of God and the Functional Speciality, Systematics* (1973); *Understanding and Being* [UB] (1980; 1990); *Phenomenology and Logic* [PHL] (2001). He also wrote several theological works including: *Grace and Freedom: Operative Grace in the Thought of St. Thomas Aquinas* (1941; 1971; 2000); *Doctrinal Pluralism* (1971). Lonergan is also known for his works on pedagogy and economics.

Lonergan's philosophical articles include: "True Judgment and Science," *Blandyke Papers* 291 (1929), pp. 195-216; "The Form of Inference," *Thought* 18 (1943), pp. 277-292; "The Concept of Verbum in the Writings of Saint Thomas Aquinas," *Theological Studies* 7 (1946), pp. 349-392; 8 (1947), pp. 35-79, 404-444, 10 (1949), pp. 3-40, 359-393; "The Natural Desire to See God," *Proceedings of the Eleventh Annual Convention of the Jesuit Philosophical Association* (April 18, 1949), pp. 31-43; "Isomorphism of Thomist and Scientific Thought," *Sapientia Aquinatis* 4 (1955), pp. 119-127; "Insight: Preface to a Discussion," *Proceedings of the American Catholic Philosophical Association* 32 (1958), pp. 71-81; "Philosophic Difference and Personal Development," *The New Scholasticism* 32 (1958), p. 97; "Appropriation of Truth," in Carron, Malcolm, et al., eds., *Readings in the Philosophy of Ecucation*. 3rd ed. (Detroit: University of Detroit Press, 1963), pp. 41-44; "Metaphysics as Horizon," *Gregorianum* 44 (1963), pp. 307-318; "Cognitional Structure," in Crowe, Frederick, ed., *Spirit as Inquiry: Studies in Honor of Bernard Lonergan* (Chicago: St. Xavier College, 1964), pp. 230-242; "Subject and Soul," *Philippine Studies* 13 (1965), pp. 576-585; "The Dehellenization of Dogma," in Baum,

Gregory, ed., *The Future of Belief Debate* (New York: Herder and Herder, 1967), pp. 69-91; "The Transition from a Classicist World View to Historical Mindedness," in Biechler, James, ed., *Law for Liberty: The Role of Law in the Church Today* (Baltimore: Helicon, 1967), pp. 126-133; "The Absence of God in Modern Culture," in Mooney, Christopher, ed., *The Presence and Absence of God* (New York: Fordham University Press, 1968), pp. 164-178; "Natural Knowledge of God," *Catholic Theological Society of America Proceedings* 23 (1968), pp. 54-69; "Philosophy and Theology," *American Catholic Philosophical Association Proceedings* 44 (1971), pp. 19-30; "The Origins of Christian Realism," *Theology Digest* 20 (1972), pp. 292-305; "Dimensions of Meaning," in McShane, Philip, ed,. *Introducing the Thought of Bernard Lonergan*. (London: Darton, Longman, and Todd, 1973, pp. 46-61; "Merging Horizons: System, Common Sense, Scholarship," *Cultural Hermeneutics* 1 (1973), pp. 87-99; "Aquinas Today: Tradition and Innovation," *The Journal of Religion* 55 (1975), pp. 165-180; "Natural Right and Historical Mindedness," *American Catholic Philosophical Association Proceedings* 15 (1977), pp. 132-143; "The Human Good," *Humanitas* 15 (1979), pp. 113-126; "A Post-Hegelian Philosophy of Religion," in Lawrence, Fred, ed., *Lonergan Workshop*, v. 3 (Chico: Scholars Press, 1982), pp. 179-197; "The Original Preface to Insight," Method: Journal of Lonergan Studies 3 (1985), pp. 3-7; "Lonergan's Own Account of Insight," *Lonergan Studies Newsletter* 12 (1991), pp. 22-24; "The Human Good: Two Fragments," *Lonergan Studies Newsletter* 13 (1992), pp. 18-19; "Philosophy and the Religious Phenomenon," *Method: Journal of Lonergan Studies* 12 (1994), pp. 121-146.

Lonergan has also written several theological articles including "St. Thomas' Thought on Gratia Operans," *Theological Studies* 2 (1941), pp. 289-324 and 3 (1942), pp. 69-88, 375-402, 533-578; "Humble Acknowledgement of the Church's Teaching Authority," *The Canadian Messenger of the Sacred Heart* 62 (1952), pp. 5-9; "Theology and Understanding," *Gregorianum* 35 (1954), pp. 630-648; "Openness and Religious Experience," *Atti del XV convegno del centro di studi filosofici tra professori universitari Gallarate* (Brescia: Morcelliana, 1961), pp. 460-462; "Belief: Today's Issue," *Canadian Messenger* (June 1968), pp. 8-12; "Theology in its New Context," in Shook, Laurence, ed., *Theology of Renewal, Vol. I: Renewal of Religious Thought* (New York: Herder and Herder, 1968), pp. 34-46; "Functional Specialties in Theology," *Gregorianum* 50 (1969), pp. 485-504; "The Future of Christianity," *The Holy Cross Quarterly* 2 (1969), pp. 5-10; "Theology and Man's Future," *Cross Currents* 19 (1969), pp. 452-461; "Revolution in Catholic Theology," *Catholic Theological Society of America Proceedings* 27 (1973), pp. 18-23; "The Ongoing Genesis of Method," *Studies in Religion/Sciences Religieuses* 6 (1976-1977), pp. 341-355; "Theology and Praxis," *Catholic Theological Society of America Proceedings* 32 (1977), pp. 1-16; "Religious Experience," in Dunne, Thomas, et al., eds., *Trinification of the World* (Toronto: Regis College Press, 1978), pp. 71-83; "Religious Knowledge," in Lawrence, Fred, ed., *Lonergan Workshop*, v. 1 (Missoula: Montana:

Scholars Press, 1978), pp. 309-327; "The Dimensions of Conversion," in Conn, Walter, ed., *Conversion: Perspectives on Personal and Social Transformation* (New York: Alba House, 1978), pp. 15-21; "Prologomena to the Study of the Emerging Religious Consciousness of Our Time," *Studies in Religion/Sciences Religieuses* 9 (1980), pp. 3-15; "Reality, Myth, Symbol," in Olson, Alan, ed., *Myth, Symbol, and Reality* (Notre Dame: Notre Dame University Press, 1980), pp. 31-37; "The Gratia Operans Dissertation," *Method: Journal of Lonergan Studies* 3:2 (1985), pp. 9-46; "Letter on Contraception and the Natural Law," *Lonergan Studies Newsletter* 11 (1990), pp. 7-8; "Method in Catholic Theology," *Method: Journal of Lonergan Studies* 10:1 (1992), pp. 3-23; "Moral Theology and the Human Sciences," *Method: Journal of Lonergan Studies* 15 (1997), pp. 5-18; "The Scope of Renewal," *Method: Journal of Lonergan Studies* 16 (1998), pp. 83-101; "Variations in Fundamental Theology," Method: Journal of Lonergan Studies 16:1 (1998), pp. 5-24; "Analysis of Faith," *Method: Journal of Lonergan Studies* 20 (2002), pp. 125-154.

Most of these articles have been collected in *Collection* [C] (1967; 1988); *A Second Collection* [SC] (1974); and *A Third Collection* [THC] (1985); *Philosophical and Theological Papers 1958-1964* [PTPI] (1996); *Philosophical and Theological Papers 1965-1980* [PTPII] (2004); *Shorter Papers* (2007).

His works are being collected as Collected Works of Bernard Lonergan, 25 vols., ed., Doran, Robert, and Frederick Crowe (Toronto: University of Toronto Press, 1988-2015); and an abridged edition of his works has appeared as *Introducting the Thought of Bernard Lonergan* (London: Darton, Longman, and Todd, 1973) and Mark, Morelli, and Elizabeth Morelli, eds., *The Lonergan Reader* (Toronto: University of Toronto Press, 1997). Lonergan's Archives are housed at the Gregorian University in Rome.

For an Index to Lonergan's works one can see Fallon, Timothy, et al., eds., *Combined Lonergan Indices* (Santa Clara: Santa Clara University, 1987). For a bibliography of Lonergan see Crowe, Frederick, "Bibliography of the Writings of Bernard Lonergan," *Continuum* 2:3 (1964), pp. 543-549; Crowe, Frederick, ed., *Lonergan Bibliography: Primary Sources* (Falls Church: Lonergan Studies Newsletter, 1983); and O'Callaghan, Michael, et al., *Lonergan Bibliography* (Covington: St. Joseph Abbey, 1982); and Tekippe, Terry, *Primary Bibliography of Lonergan Sources* (New Orleans: Notre Dame Seminary Press, 1988).

61   Lonergan notes that a reader may be given all the clues in a detective story yet fail to spot the criminal. Hence insight into solving the crime demands going beyond the clues through a supervening act of organizing intelligence (IN, Preface, pp. 3-4).

62   The Greek mathematician Archimedes (287-212 B.C.) was given the problem of determining whether a crown constructed for king Hiero was made of pure gold, or whether the goldsmith had mixed in cheaper silver with the gold and kept the extra gold for himself. Moreover, as the crown was holy and to

be placed on the statue of a god it could not be disturbed by cutting it open to find out. Archimedes in a well-known tale was taking a bath when he shrieked 'Eureka!' (I have found it) and ran naked through the streets of Syracuse, as he had just discovered an insight, no doubt stimulated by his own taking of a bath, that helped him solve the problem. Archimedes's insight was that an object of greater mass would displace more water than one of lesser mass and that silver (10.6 grams/cubic centimeter) was less dense than gold (19.3 grams/cubic centimeter). Hence a crown of mixed silver and gold would be larger than one of pure gold of the same weight and displace more water. Archimedes then made a mass of gold equivalent in weight to the crown and found that it indeed displaced less water than the crown in issue did when placed in a bowl filled to the brim with water. He thus showed that the king had been cheated by the goldsmith who was summarily put to death (IN, I, pp. 27-30; V, I, p. 25; see Vitruvius, *The Ten Books of Architecture*, IX; Archimedes, *On Floating Bodies*, I, 7). Here again insight goes beyond the data as many frequented the baths of Syracuse without formulating the principles of hydrostatics.

63   We could imagine similar examples wherein the mathematical sequence 2, 4 ... is unknown until more data is revealed and we either have the mathematical relation n+2 (2, 4, 6, 8), nx2 (2, 4, 8, 16), or n^2 (2, 4, 16, 256).

64   This fourth level of consciousness comes out more in Lonegan's *Method in Theology* than in his *Insight*, at least in an explicit form. Some commentators consider loving a fifth level of consciousness in Lonergan.

Interestingly, Lonergan derives four transcendental precepts from this four-fold scheme of human consciousness: 1) Be attentive (empirical consciousness); 2) Be intelligent (intelligent consciousness); 3) Be reasonable (rational consciousness); and 4) Be Responsible; Be in Love (moral consciousness) (MT, I, p. 20; II, pp. 53, 55; IX, p. 231; XI, p. 268; XII, p. 302; PTPII, IV, p. 75).

65   Lonergan lastly is opposed to skepticism and relativism. He argues that a proper understanding of the human process of knowing, and especially the third level of rational consciousness (judgment), shows knowledge is possible. For a judgment occurs when the conditions for something being known are fulfilled (where we have what Lonergan terms a virtually unconditioned) (IN, X, p. 304-307, 312, 340-341; XI, p. 355, 360-362; XII, p. 398; XVII, p. 573-575; XIX, p. 676; XX, p. 729; MT, III, p. 75; IV, p. 102; XIII, p. 351; PHL, III, pp. 71-77; Appendix, pp. 339-340; UB, V, pp. 112-120). And there are types of cognition for which there are a limited number of conditions for knowing that need to be fulfilled, where one can attain mastery over a situation. For in such cases one can acquire knowledge of a given phenomenon to such a degree that there are no further pertinent questions that could arise (and so there is nothing which could give rise to a new perspective on the matter at hand and reveal the unsatisfactoriness of our initial viewpoint and force its revision). So in situations where there a "mind that is alert, familiar with the

concrete situation, and intellectually master of it" (IN, X, p. 312, 318), humans can attain the virtually unconditioned, and achieve invulnerable insights and certain knowledge (here one hits the bull's eye or the nail on the head). While such situations are extremely rare for Lonergan (dealing with the existence of concrete phenomena), he does say that we can know such things as the following for certain: 1) a typewriter here exists; 2) I am here speaking to you now (or reading or writing); 3) a fire happened (or at least 'something happened') when one leaves a tidy home and returns home to find the windows broken, smoke in the air, and water on the floor (IN, Preface, p. 5; I, p. 37; X, pp. 306-313, 321, 324, 327, 340; XI, pp. 348, 359, 366-371; XII, pp. 379-380; XIV, p. 437; SC, IX, p. 125; PTPII, VII, p. 129; PHL, III, pp. 73-74; UB, V, pp. 120-125). For we can know that a typewriter exists no matter what the rest of the universe may prove to be (i.e. no matter what else I may come to know about the typewriter and its chemical composition, construction, economic background, etc., or whether one even knows how to define a typewriter) [indeed these further judgments depend on me knowing that this is a typewriter] (IN, XI, pp. 368-370, 380; XIII, p. 400-401). Lonergan also asserts that logical and mathematical propositions can be known for certain (their truth depends on the mere postulation of syntactical rules and defining terms subject to these rules) (IN, X, p. 329-330, 334-335, 339, 387; XIV, pp. 428-430, 434; XIX, p. 663; MT, III, pp. 75-76; XII, p. 316; PHL, I, pp. 4-16; II, pp. 38-40; III, pp. 68-71, 77-78; UB, V, pp. 12y6-130; Appendix, pp. 252-256).

With regard to most matters, however, certain knowledge is not possible and we are left with only probable knowledge. For even though we may think we have grasped the issue properly there may be further unknown relevant questions (IN, II, p. 90; III, pp. 112-114, 117; X, p. 309, 327; XI, p. 359; XIV, p. 437; MT, VII, pp. 167, VIII, pp. 191-192; PHL, XI, p. 265). Still even here one can learn more and more about an object and gain a perspective that approaches or converges upon the truth (and one can add that as far as one knows the questioning is closed). And while there is always the possibility one's views will later have to be revised, one can minimize this possibility by: 1) making sure the problem is accurately defined; 2) allowing further relevant questions to arise; 3) avoiding rashness of decision; 4) allowing one's pure and disinterested desire to know to win out over one's interested and attached drives, connations, desires, fears, appetites, and interests; and 5) reviewing one's sources and motives for the belief, one's supporting judgments, and the consequences of the belief (which is just what the God of truth demands of us) (IN, IX, p. 297; X, pp. 310, 324-329; XI, pp. 368, 370; XII, p. 372; XIII, pp. 404-408; XIV, pp. 444, 447, 453-454; XX, pp. 723, 727-728; 730, 736-739; MT, I, p. 19; II, pp. 43-47; VI, p. 149; VII, p. 159; SC, III, p. 36; PTPI, II, pp. 38-41; X, pp. 226-230).

Most importantly, we can enter into what Lonergan calls the self-correcting process of learning. Here we examine the presuppositions, implications, and applications that serve as the background of a given area of knowledge and see how they fit in coherently with the presuppositions and implications of other insights; that is to say here we engage in the gradual acquisition and accumulation of a large body of insights which refine and correct prior insights. In this manner we use each new part to fill out, complement, qualify, and correct the understanding reached in earlier parts. Eventually we can achieve a convergence of multitudinous evidence and find that the components reveal a picture (MT, III, p. 81; VII, p. 158-159, 161-167; IX, pp. 208-209; XIII, pp. 401-402). An example of the self-correcting process of learning would be the recognition that water is H_2O and then that there are heavy and ordinary forms of water, or that the earth is flat in our view but not in the integration of views (IN, III, p. 98; VI, p. 197; VII, p. 259-260; IX, p. 303; X, pp. 312-314, 322-323, 333, 340, XI, p. 370; XV, p. 503; MT, III, pp. 71-72).

66   Lonergan gained notoriety in his later years for his supporting a historicist notion of culture over a classicist notion of culture. As he defines the terms, a classicist notion of culture is one wherein there is one culture that is universal, fixed, permanent, and normative. Here there are immortal works of art, a perennial philosophy, a permanent theology, unchanging laws, and an abstract and unchanging human nature and unchanging terminology (MT, Introduction, p. xi; II, p. 29; IV, pp. 123-124; XII, pp. 301, 326; THC, III, p. 52; SC, XIV, pp. 232-236; PTPII, V, pp. 73-76; XI, pp. 199-203).

A historicist (empirical or modern) notion of culture on the other hand holds that the meanings and values that inform a way of life may slowly develop. Here there are real differences of culture, theology is an ongoing process, science and worldviews vary from time to time and place to place, and the nature of a human being develops over time. We can think of the difference between the four Greek elements and the modern elements in the periodic table as an example (MT, Introduction, p. xi; I, p. 11; II, p. 29; III, p. 81; IV, pp. 123-124; VII, p. 154; IX, pp. 215-220, 223-224, 226; XI, pp. 270, 279-281, 293; XII, pp. 300-301, 305, 310, 312, 315, 328; SC, I, p. 3; PTPII, V, pp. 95-102; XV, pp. 283-287; S, p. 10).

In shifting from classical to historical consciousness then we move from logic to method, Aristotelian science (necessity) to modern science (probabilistic, correlative), from the metaphysics of soul to self-appropriation, from the human with a constant human nature to the human as historical (cultural change), from first principles to transcendental method (SC, IV, pp. 50-53; X, pp. 137-141; XIV, pp. 197-200, 207-208; MT, XI, p. 280; XII, p. 315; PTPII, V, pp. 84-85). Or in the words of Lonergan, one's horizon (one's total field of concern, maximal field of vision, one's object of interest and knowledge) can vary over time due to one's milieu, social background, education, personal development, or conversion (MT, IV, p. 104; VII, p. 154; IX, pp. 235-237; XI, p. 269; PHL, VIII, pp. 198-203, 209-215; XIII, pp. 280-284, 288-289; XIV, pp. 298-300, 310-317; C, XIII, p. 213; THC, II, pp. 16-17; XI, pp. 170-171;

XV, pp. 245-247; PTPII, II, pp. 10-11). Lonergan writes: "There is the emergence of method. It consists in the transposition of systematic meaning from a static to an ongoing dynamic context. Originally systems were constructed to endure. They aimed at true and certain knowledge of what is necessarily so. But in modern times systems express, not what necessarily is so, but what intrinsically is hypothetical and in need of verification. Again, they express, not what is expected to be permanent, but what is expected to be revised and improved as further data are uncovered and better understanding is attained" (MT, XII, pp. 304-305). So what we currently believe to be true in science, philosophy, and theology is merely what is currently known (it is merely provisional; de facto, tentative, the best available option) and may be revised in the future (SC, XIV, p. 197-200, 207-208; XV, p. 236; PTPII, V, pp. 72-73; PTPII, VI, p. 115; XV, p. 283; XIX, p. 356).

Hence, says Lonergan, we have to recognize that in theology the issues vary over time and we can't merely advert to the early Church and preach to ancient Athens, Corinth, or Rome. Instead theology must meet the questions of the day for the people of the day. For doctrines are interpretable from different contexts, can be better understood over time, and what is more must be preached to different cultures. What is permanently true then is a doctrine in the context in which it was defined, not the doctrine isolated from its context (MT, IV, pp. 112, 114, 118; V, p. 150; XI, pp. 271, 276; XII, pp. 296-298, 320, 323-326; XIII, p. 347, 349; PTPI, IX, pp. 205-206). For instance, the notion of a person in theology has been defined in different ways by Boethius, Richard of St. Victor, Aquinas, and the phenomenologists and personalists, and so is best thought of as a heuristic notion (SC, XIV, p. 200; PTPII, XI, pp. 210-211). Lonergan asserts: "What seems the key task in current Catholic theology? My answer has been a contrast between a rigid logical ideal alone fit to house eternal truths in a permanent synthesis and, on the other hand, the concrete, ongoing, cumulative process guided by method. Only a theology structured on method can assimilate the somewhat recently accepted hermeneutic and historical methods and it alone has room for developing doctrines and developing theologies. The key task, then, in contemporary Catholic theology is to replace the shattered thought-forms associated with eternal truths and logical ideals with new thought-forms that accord with the dynamics of development and the concrete style of method" (SC, XIV, p. 202).

This is not to say that Lonergan embraced a conceptual relativism. In the first place he argued that there is some constancy in that our dynamic structure of cognition (our method of inquiry with its empirical, intellectual, and rational consciousness), as well as our moral being, is not open to radical revision (for any revision would occur through this structure of consciousness itself) (MT, Introduction, p. xii; I, pp. 19-20, 22; III, p. 81). Secondly, there is some stability in our basic descriptions and scientific data and so revisions will still account for the old data albeit in a new way (and there are even genuine achievements of the past where things fit together nicely and our views approach the truth). Thus in a historicist culture there is conceptual constancy with conceptual variation. For example, fire remained the same thing in terms of familiar elements but was explained as an element by Aristotle, phlogiston by early chemists, and oxidation by Lavoisier (IN, XIX, p. 705; Epilogue, pp. 759-760, 762; MT, XI, p. 287; XII, p. 313; SC, XVI, p. 278). Additionally, Catholic doctrine is based on revelation (the word of God) and so is not a mere word or symbol (although it is necessary to communicate this revelation differently to different audiences and so by diverse conceptualizations and expressions) (IN, XX, p. 743; Epilogue, p. 761-762). Finally there is a normative structure of being-in-love with God which is a bond uniting all humans despite cultural differences (MT, I, pp. 11-12; XI, pp. 282-284, 292; XII, pp. 302-303; 326-327, 333; XIII, pp. 341, 351-352; XIV, pp. 362-363; SC, IX, p. 128).

67   Lonergan later comes to modify his blanket advocacy of proofs for God's existence. Not that he completely rejects such proofs. He continues to argue that seeking proofs for God is a legitimate enterprise, and indeed that his proof found in *Insight* is a valid one. Yet he now argues that few humans initially come to believe in God's existence through examining a proof. Rather, typically humans first believe in God and then later on construct proofs for God's existence (or as he puts it, love of God normally proceeds knowledge of God). Hence Lonergan comes to think that conversion is more important than proof (temporally and ontologically) in knowing God.

Indeed Lonergan comes to argue that only someone subject to divine grace can readily grasp a proof for God. That is to say a proof for God is only rigorous when placed in a systematically formulated horizon, and this occurs most easily on account of a conversion. For knowledge of God requires differentiation of consciousness (recognizing the complementarity of common sense, theory, interiority, and transcendence), personal leisure, good moral habits and existential decisions, and resistance to personal evil and bad examples. Thus most people (especially the unlearned) by grace first attain a person-to-person loving relation with God and then through the eyes of faith gain a new horizon whereby they can discern God's hand in nature (and prove God) and his message in revelation (MT, XIII, pp. 337-339; SC, IX, p. 133; XIII, p. 224; XIV, p. 237; XVI, p. 277; PTPII, IX, pp. 172-173, 175-177; X, pp. 189-191, 195). Lonergan remarks: "I do not think that in this life people arrive at natural knowledge of God without God's grace, but what I do not doubt is that the knowledge they so attain is natural" (SC, IX, p. 133). And he writes: "Proof always presupposes premises, and it presupposes premises accurately formulated within a horizon. You can never prove a horizon. You arrive at it from a different horizon, by going beyond the previous one, because you have found something that makes the previous horizon illegitimate. But growth in knowledge is precisely that. There are proofs for the existence of God. I formulated them as best I could in chapter 19 of *Insight*, and I'm not repudiating that at all. But I say it is not a matter of comparing the two; it is using the resources of both [proofs and conversion]" (PTPII, X, p. 195). And finally: "Basically the issue is a transition from the abstract logic of classicism to the concreteness of method. On the former view what is basic is proof. On the latter view what is basic is conversion. Proof appeals to an abstraction named right reason. Conversion transforms the concrete individual to make him capable of grasping not merely conclusions but principles as well" (MT, XIII, p. 338).

Lonergan even argues that canon 2, n. 1 of Vatican Council I (1869-1870) merely asserts the possibility of a rational knowledge of God (made in the light of grace) and not that the natural light of reason is sufficient for fallen humans to come to such a knowledge. For Lonergan claims that the *Acta* explicitly envisage this as a question not of fact but of right (possibility) and he argues that the words *ab homine lapso* [by the lapsed human] were once part of the decree but later removed. Hence according to Lonergan Vatican Council I merely asserts that in principle there is a valid and certain argument accessible to the human mind that concludes with an affirmation of God's existence. Moreover he claims that this canon is perhaps best understood as referring here to the state of pure nature. That is to say, according to Lonergan, Vatican I asserts that humans can know God by reason only if grace has healed their current nature corrupted by the Fall (MT, XIII, pp. 338-339; SC, IX, pp. 117-118; PTPII, XI, p. 204; cf. Hermann Joseph Pottmeyer, *Der Glaube vor dem Anspruch der Wissenschaft: Die Konstitution Dei Filius des 1. Vatikanischen Konzils* (Freiburg: Herder, 1968), pp. 168-204; Mansi, Giovan Domenico, ed., *Sacrorum Conciliorum Nova et Amplissima Collectio* 53 (Graz: Akademische Druck, 1927), p. 168; Vacant, Jean-Michel-Alfred, *Études théologiques sur les constitutions du Concile du Vatican* (Paris: Delhomme et Briguet, 1895, vol. I, pp. 7-15, 282-337, 570-695). See, however, my rejection of Lonergan's interpretation in favor of the claim that Vatican I asserts that humans can come to a rational knowledge of God both in the state of pure nature and in the state of fallen nature (see my *Recent Catholic Philosophy: The Nineteenth Century,* Milwaukee: Marquette University Press, 2009), n. 40, pp. 263-264.

68 It is worth mentioning that for Lonergan conversion (self-transcendence) is a radical change in one's views, one's horizon. It involves having an about-face or new beginning which reveals a greater depth of things, a moving from one set of roots to another, from one horizon to another. Now there are three kinds of conversion: 1) Intellectual conversion—the radical clarification and elimination of myth concerning reality and human knowing. Here one rejects that knowing is seeing (as it also involves understanding and judging), that the real is what is out there now to be looked at. For here one engages in self-appropriation and knows oneself as an empirical, intelligent, and rational consciousness; 2) Moral conversion—a changing of one's criterion of decisions from satisfaction to value. Here one opts for true goods even for values against satisfaction where they conflict; one seeks what is truly good, worthwhile, and

valuable; 3) Religious conversion—here one fully embraces God in faith and hope, and one loves God with one's whole heart, mind, soul, and strength in charity (being-in-love). It is true, says Lonergan, that just as the arm spontaneously protects the head (or we spontaneously reach out to save another from falling), we aspire to the good of the whole and spontaneously love the beloved, with a self-sacrificing or self-surrendering love. Yet by charity we can have a love without limits, qualifications, conditions, or reservations, an unrestricted love of another that manifests itself in acts of kindness, goodness, fidelity, gentleness, and self-control. One is here held, possessed, and owned by a total and other-worldly love, and because of this one finds a new basis for valuing, a cosmic context and purpose, and a power to accept the suffering involved in undoing the effects of decline (MT, IV, p. 114; V, p. 150; VII, p. 161; IX, p. 217; X, pp. 237-244, 249; XI, pp. 267, 270-271, 273, 292; XII, pp. 298, 302, 312, 330-331; XIII, p. 352; XIV, pp. 356-357, 361; THC, XI, p. 179; XV, pp. 247-249; PTPII, XIX, p. 362; V, pp. 86-88; XVII, pp. 316-331; XX, pp. 389-390). Lonergan writes: "Intellectual conversion is to truth attained by cognitional self-transcendence. Moral conversion is to values apprehended, affirmed, and realized by a real self-transcendence. Religions conversion is to a total being-in-love as the efficacious ground of all self-transcendence, whether in the pursuit of truth, or in the realization of human values, or in the orientation man adopts to the universe, its ground, and its goal" (MT, IX, p. 241).

69   Transcendental Thomism (whose proponents number more than 175) was particularly popular in the Jesuit order, especially in the years 1920-1970, and we can number among the Transcendental Thomists: Pierre Scheurer, S.J. (1872-1957); the Oratorian Gaston Rabeau (1877-1949) [also a Phenomenologist]; the Belgian Joseph Maréchal, S.J. (1878-1944); the Dutchman Peter Hoenen, S.J. (c. 1880-1960); Canon Pierre Tiberghien (1880-1963); Canon Fr. Eugene Masure (1882-1958); Charles Lemaître, S.J. (1883-1957); Engelbert Wingendorf (c. 1909-1980); Guy de Broglie, S.J. (c. 1889-1975); Auguste Grégoire (1890-1949); André Marc, S.J. (1892-1961) [also an Existentialist]; Joseph Defever, S.J. (1899-1964); Jean Marie Le Blond, S.J. (1899-1973); the convert Basil Christopher Butler, O.S.B. (1902-1986); the Dutch Felix Malmberg, S.J. (1903-1979); Gaston Isaye, S.J. (1903-1984); Johannes Baptist Lotz, S.J. (1903-1992); Léopold Malevez, S.J. (1904-1973); Joseph de Finance de Clairbois, S.J. (1904-2000); Walter Brugger, S.J. (1904-1990); André Hayen, S.J. (1906-1988) [also a Blondelian Augustinian]; Joseph Donceel, S.J. (1906-1994); Alfred Delp (1907-1945) [put to death by the Nazis]; Henri Bouillard, S.J (1908-1981) [also a proponent of Nouvelle-Théologie and a Blondelian Augustinian]; William Norris Clarke, S.J. (1915-2008); Gerald McCool, S.J. (c. 1918-2005); Austrian Emerich Coreth, S.J. (1919-2006); Ludger Oeing-Hanhoff (1923-1986); the Spaniard José Gómez Caffarena, S.J. (1925-); Joseph Flanagan, S.J. (1925-) [Lonerganian]; William Ryan, S.J. (1925-) [Lonerganian]; the Spaniard Leonardo Polo (1926-);Richard Schaeffler, S.J. (1926-);Johannes Baptist Metz (1928-); the Austrian Otto Muck, S.J.

(1928-); George Vass, S.J. (1928-); Bernard Sesboüé, S.J. (1929-);Herbert Vorgrimler (1929-) [Rahnerian]; Virgilio Melchiorre (1931-); Hans Waldenfels, S.J. (1931-) [Rahnerian]; Karl-Heinz Weger, S.J. (1932-) [Rahnerian]; the Canadian Frederick Crowe, S.J. (c. 1933-) [Lonerganian]; Bernard Tyrrell, S.J. (1933-) [Lonerganian]; David Burrell, C.S.C. (c. 1934-) [Lonerganian]; Erhard Kunz, S.J. (1934-); Thomas Franklin O'Meara, O.P. (1935-) [Rahnerian]; the convert Hugo Meynell (1936-) [Lonerganian]; Jörg Splett (1936-); Hansjürgen Verweyen (1936-); Eberhard Simons (1937-2005); Robert Doran, S.J. (1939-) [Lonerganian]; Fr. Terry Tekippe (1940-2005) [Lonerganian]; Thomas Sheehan (1941-) [Rahnerian]; Andrew Tallon (c. 1943-) [a former Jesuit]; Fr. Jack Bonsor (1944-) [Rahnerian]; Albert Raffelt (1944-) [also an Augustinian]; Paul Gilbert, S.J. (1945-); John McDermott, S.J. (c. 1945-); Patrick Byrne (1947-) [Lonerganian]; Giovanni Sala, S.J. (c. 1951-) [Lonerganian]; Neil Omerod (c. 1955-) [Lonerganian]; Andrew Beards (1957-) [Lonerganian]; Roman Siebenrock (c. 1965-) [Rahnerian]; Declan Marmion (c. 1970-) [Rahnerian].

Among the many critics of Transcendental Thomism are: Benedict Ashley, O.P., Canon Robert Aubert, David Berger, Maurice Blondel, Vernon Bourke, Charles Boyer, David Braine, Bishop Gabriel Brunhes, Auguste Brunner, S.J., David Burrell, Giovanni Cavalcoli, O.P., Romanus Cessario, O.P., Yves Congar, Eamonn Conway, Charles Davis, Thomas Deman, O.P., Dominic De Petter, O.P., Ambroise-Marie de Poulpiquet, O.P., Pedro Descoqs, Josef de Vries, S.J., Leslie Dewart, José De Wolf, S.J., Maurice de Wulf, Joseph Augustine Di Noia, O.P., Avery Dulles, Leo Elders, Cornelio Fabro, John Finnis, Francis Fiorenza, Ambroise Gardeil, O.P., Réginald Garrigou-Lagrange, O.P., Étienne Gilson, Jean Griesch, Germain Grisez, Stéphane Harent, S.J., Denis John Bernard Hawkins, Robert Henle, S.J., William Hill, Walter Höres, Stanley Jaki, Bernard Jansen, S.J., Renato Jeanniere, S.J., Walter Kasper, Fergus Kerr, John Knasas, Hans Küng, Lucien Laberthonniere, Marie-Michel Labourdette, O.P., Bernard Lakebrink, Hippolyte Ligeard, Antonio Livi, Gallus Manser, Jacques Maritain, Paul Molnar, Aidan Nichols, Jean-Hervé Nicolas, O.P., Caspar Nink, Helmut Ogiermann, S.J., Heinrich Ott, Fr. Joseph Owens, Anton Pechhacker, S.J., Helmut Peukert, Marie-Dominique Philippe, Winfred George Phillips, Josef Pieper, Mark Pontifex, Jean Porter, Erich Przywara, S.J., Joseph Ratzinger, J.B. Reichman, Andrew Reck, Marie-Dominique Roland-Gosselin, O.P., Leo Scheffczyk, Kenneth Schmitz, Piet Schoonenberg, Max Seckler, Anselm Stolz, O.S.B., Leo Sweeney, S.J., Adolphe Tanquerey, Illtyd Trethowan, Canon Georges Van Riet, Canon Ferdinand Van Steenberghen, René Virgoulay, Hans Urs von Balthasar, Dietrich von Hildebrand, William Wallace, Frederick Wilhelmsen.

70   For more on the life and thought of Ebner see: CP (1990), v. III, pp. 129-146; DP (1993), v. I, pp. 886-887; LTK (1995), v. III, p. 433; BBKL (1999), v. XV, pp. 496-507; OHYP (2001), pp. 142, 151; EF (2006), v. IV,

pp. 3178-3178; Johnston, William, *The Austrian Mind: An Intellectual and Social History*, 1848-1939 (Berkeley: University of California Press, 1976), pp. 217-220; Horwitz, Rivka, "Ferdinand Ebner as a Source of Buber's Dialogic Thought," in Haim, Gordon, and Jochanan Bloch, eds., *Martin Buber: A Centenary Volume* (Beersheva: KTAV, 1984), pp. 121-134; Von Balthasar, Hans Urs, *Theo-Drama: Theological Dramatic Theory* (San Francisco: Ignatius Press, 1988), v. I, pp. 639-644; Bergman, Samuel, and Arnold Gerstein, *Dialogical Philosophy from Kierkegaard to Buber* (Albany: SUNY, 1991), pp. 157-161; Kunszt, Gyorgy, "The Word as Ultimate Reality: The Christian Dialogical Personalism of Ferdinand Ebner," *Ultimate Reality and Meaning* 20 (1997), pp. 93-98; Chapel, Joseph, "Why Confess Our Sins Out Loud?: Some Possibilities Based on the Thought of Ferdinand Ebner and Louis-Marie Chauvet," *Irish Theological Quarterly* 66:2 (2001), pp. 141-156.

71   Portions of this work have been translated as "Word and Personality" [translation of Fragment 2], tr. William Kramer, *Philosophy Today* 11:4 (1967), pp. 233-237; and "The Word and Spiritual Realities" in Friedman, Maurice, ed., *Worlds of Existentialism* (Atlantic Highlands: Humanities Press, 1991), pp. 292-298, which I use throughout.

Ebner also wrote: *Aphorismen zu einer Philosophie des Lebens* (1910-1911); *Aphorismen zur Ethik* (1912); *The Reality of Christ [Die Wirlichkeit Christi]* [RC] (1920-1927); *Die Sinnhaftigkeit des Wortes* (1922-1923); *On the Problem of Language and the Word [Zum Problem der Sprache und des Wortes]* [PLW] (1926); *Attempt at an Outlook for the Future [Versuch eines Ausbllicks in die Zukunft]* [AOF] (1930); *Aphorismen* [APH] (1931); *Wort und Liebe* (1935); *The Word is the Way [Das Wort ist der Weg]* (1949; 1983); *Fragmente, Aursaetze, Aphorismen* (1963); *Das Wunder des Wortes* (1965), *Out of the Journal [Aus Dem Tagebuch, 1916-1917]* [OUJ] (2007), amongst other works. His complete works have been collected as *Schriften*, 3 vols. (Munic: Kösel-Verlag, 1963-1965).

72   Ebner was influenced here by Johann Peter Süßmilch (1707-1767) and Johann Georg Hamann (1730-1788), and echoes Louis de Bonald (1754-1840), who have a similar notion of the divine origin of language.

73   For more on Mounier see: RCSM (1938), pp. 77-91; IEC (1952), vol. VIII, pp. 1490-1491; CAP (1955), pp. 98-99; CMCT (1960), pp. 200-221; PPF (1966), pp. 100-108; MHP (1967), p. 439; TCP (1969), pp. 113-118; HWP (1971), v. V, p. 249; CHP (1974), v. IX, pp. 311-316; CHAD (1982), v. IX, pp. 809-810; LCN (1984), pp. 127-155; CP (1990), v. III, pp. 438-448; BBKL (1993), v. VI, pp. 211-213; DP (1994), v. II, pp. 2062-2067; TCFC (1995), pp. 126, 249; BDTC (1996), pp. 550-551; TCFP (1996), pp. 41-46; LTK (1998), v. VII, p. 507; UHF (1998), v. VIII, pp. 363-388; NCE (2003), v. X, pp. 30-31; WPR (2003), pp. 224-227; EMFT (2004), pp. 490-491; EF (2006), v. VIII, pp. 7656-7659; EP (2005), v. VI, pp. 415-416; TWFP

(2006), pp. 169-170, 258; Grevillot, Jean Marie, *Les grands courants de la pensée contemporaine: existentialisme, marxisme, personnalisme chrétien* (Paris: Vitrail, 1947), pp. 164-274; Coates, John Bourne, *The Personalism of Emmanuel Mounier* (London: Personalist Group, 1948); *Esprit* 18 (1950) [Special Edition on Mounier]; Zaza, Noureddine, *Étude critique de la notion d'engagement chez Emmanuel Mounier* (Paris: Droz, 1955); Copleston, Frederick, "The Human Person in Contemporary Society," in *Contemporary Philosophy* (London: Burns & Oates, 1956), pp. 109-115; Calbrette, Jean, *Mounier le mauvais esprit* (Paris: Nouvelles Éditions latines, 1957); Clément, Marcel, *Mounier* (Paris: Itinéraires, 1959); Moix, Candide, *La pensée d'Emmanuel Mounier* (Paris: Éditions du Seuil, 1960); Guissard, Lucien, *Emmanuel Mounier* (Paris: Éditions universitaires, 1962); Charpentreau, Jacques, and Louis Rocher, *L'Esthétique personnaliste d'Emmanuel Mounier* (Paris: Les Editions ouvrieres, 1966); Conilh, Jean, *Emmanuel Mounier, sa vie, son oeuvre, avec un exposé de sa philosophie* (Paris: Presses Universitaires de France, 1966); Roy, Pierce, *Contemporary French Political Thought* (London: Oxford University Press, 1966), pp. 49-88; Hervé, Chaigne, *Emmanuel Mounier ou le combat du juste* (Paris: Guy Ducros, 1968); De Smedt, Marc, and Bruno Lagrange, eds., *Mounier* (Paris: Le nouveau planète, 1970); *Esprit* 4 (1970) [Special Edition on Mounier]; Lafosse, Francis, ed., *L'homme et son message: Mounier* (Paris: Le nouveau planète, 1970); Blázquez Carmona, Feliciano, *Emmanuel Mounier* (Madrid: E.P.E.S.A., 1972); Borne, Étienne, *Emmanuel Mounier; ou, Le combat pour l'homme* (Paris: Seghers, 1972); Doménach, Jean-Marie, *Emmanuel Mounier* (Paris: Éditions du Seuil, 1972); Rauch, Rufus, *Politics and Belief in Contemporary France: Emmanuel Mounier and Christian Democracy, 1932-1950* (The Hague: Nijhoff, 1972); Roy, Jean Marie, *Mounier aux prises avec son siècle* (Paris: Beauchesne, 1972); Cantin, Eileen, *Mounier: A Personalist View of History* (New York: Paulist Press, 1973); Doménach, Jean-Marie, *Mounier según Mounier* (Barcelona: Editorial Laia, 1973); Amato, Joseph, *Mounier and Maritain: A French Catholic Understanding of the Modern World* (Birmingham: University of Alabama Press, 1975); Kedward, Harry, *Resistance in Vichy France* (Oxford: Oxford University Press, 1978), pp. 196-209; Kelly, Michael, *Pioneer of the Catholic Revival: The Ideas and Influences of Emmanuel Mounier* (London: Sheed and Ward, 1979); Boyer, Régis, *Actualité d'Emmanuel Mounier* (Paris: Cerf, 1981); Hellman, John, *Emmanuel Mounier and the New Catholic Left, 1930-1950* (Toronto: University of Toronto Press, 1981); Collot-Guyer, Marie-Thérèse, *La cité personnaliste d'Emmanuel Mounier* (Nancy: Presses Universitaires de Nancy, 1983); D'Astorg, Bertrand, ed., *Le Personnalisme d'Emmanuel Mounier* (Paris: Seuil, 1985); Kedward, Harry, and Roger Austin, eds., *Vichy France and the Resistance: Culture & Ideology* (London: Croom Helm, 1985), pp. 171-189; Arnaud, Paul, *Le personnalisme et la crise politique et morale du XXe siècle: Vie et oeuvre d'Emmanuel Mounier 1905-1950* (Nanterre: Paul Arnaud, 1988); Lurol, Gérard, *Mounier* (Paris: Éditions Universitaires, 1990); Judt, Tony, *Past Imperfect: French Intellectuals,*

1944-1956 (Berkeley: University of California Press, 1992), pp. 86-90; Bergès, Michel, *Vichy contre Mounier* (Paris: Economica, 1997); Hellman, John, *The Knight-Monks of Vichy France* (Montreal: McGill-Queen's University Press, 1997), pp. 33-37, 142-145; Lurol, Gérard, *Emmanuel Mounier*, 2 vols. (Paris: Harmattan, 2000); Petit, Jean-François, *Penser avec Mounier: une éthique pour la vie* (Lyon: Diffusion Sofedis, 2000); Hughes, Henry, *The Obstructed Path: French Social Thought in the Years of Desperation, 1930-1960* (Piscataway: Transaction, 2001), pp. 96-98; Calvez, Jean-Yves, *Chrétiens, penseurs du social: Maritain, Mounier, Fessard, Teilhard de Chardin, de Lubac, 1920-1940* (Paris: Cerf, 2002); Padis, Marc-Olivier, *Esprit: Une revue dans l'histoire 1932-2002* (Paris: Ed. Esprit, 2002); Coq, Guy, ed., *Emmanuel Mounier: L'actualité d'un grand témoin*, 2 vols. (Paris: Parole et silence, 2003-2006); Boudic, Goulven, *Les Métamorphoses d'une revue: Esprit 1944-1982* (Paris: IMEC, 2005); Petit, Jean-François, and Rémy Valléjo, eds., *Agir avec Mounier: Une pensée pour l'Europe* (Lyon: Chronique sociale, 2006), Petit, Jean-François, *Philosophie et théologie dans la formation du personnalisme d'Emmanuel Mounier* (Paris: Cerf, 2006).

74   Mounier's work has additionally influenced several groups including: the Amis d'Esprit (1933-); the Catholic Worker Movement [founded in 1933 by Dorothy Day and the French philosopher Peter Maurin]; the journal *Terre Nouvelle* (1935-) founded by Maurice Laudrain; *Cahiers Suise Esprit* (1945-); *La Vie Nouvelle* (1947-) founded by André Cruiziat and Pierre Goutet [with its journal *Citoyens 60* (1960-)]; *Znak* in Cracow, Poland (1956-1976) founded by Stefan Kisielewski, Tadeusz Mazowiecki, and Jerzy Zawieyski; and Le Club Jean Moulin (1958-1970).

75   These works have been translated as *A Personalist Manifesto* [MSP], tr. the Monks of St. John's Abbey (London: Longmans, Green, and Company, 1938) and *Personalism* [PERS], tr. Philip Mairet (London: Routledge and Kegal Paul, 1952).

His other personalist philosophical works are his *Personalist and Communal Revolution* [*Révolution personnaliste et communautaire*] [PCR] (1935) [a collection of essays]; *Christian Confrontation* [*L'Affrontement chrétien*] (1945) [translated as *The Spoil of the Violent*, tr. Katharine Watson (London: Harvill Press, 1955)]; *What Is Personalism?* [*Qu'est-ce que le personnalisme?*] [WP] (1947) [translated as "What is Personalism?," tr. Cynthia Rowland, in Mounier, Emmanuel, *Be Not Afraid* (Sheed and Ward, 1954), pp. 111-196]; *The Small Fear of the Twentieth Century* [*La Petite Peur du XXe siècle*] (1948) [translated as "Studies in Personalist Sociology," [SF], tr. Cynthia Rowland, in Mounier, Emmanuel, *Be Not Afraid* (Sheed and Ward, 1954), pp. 3-108]; and *Present Tasks of a Thought of Personalist Inspiration* [*Taches actuelles d'une pensée d'inspiration personnaliste*] (1949) [translated as *The Present Tasks of Personalism*, tr. London Personalist Group (London: London Personalist Group, 1949)]; *L'Engagement de la foi* (1968) [a collection of his writings]; *Treatise of Character* [*Traité de caractère*] [TC] (1946) [written during his imprisonment under the Vichy Regime and issued in an abridged translation as *The Character of Man* tr. Cynthia Rowland (Rockcliff, 1956). Mounier also wrote several works on the history of philosophy and politics.

Mounier's most important philosophical articles are: "Refaire la renaissance," *Esprit* 1 (1932), pp. 5-51; "Les équivoques du personnalisme," *Esprit* 20 (1934), pp. 317-318; "Nos positions: Primauté du spirituel," *Esprit* 20 (1934), pp. 2-5; "Pour une technique des moyens spirituels," *Esprit* 26 (1934), pp. 182-198, 27 (1934), pp. 400-421, 29 (1935), pp. 733-767; "Qu'est-ce que le personnalisme?," *Esprit* 27 (1934), pp. 357-367; "Révolution communitaire," *Esprit* 28 (1935), pp. 548-580; "Pluralisme chrétien," *Esprit* 32 (1935), pp. 284-285 "Pour une enquête permanente sur la vie et l'homme contemporains," *Esprit* 35-36 (1935), pp. 674-676; "Notre humanisme," *Esprit* 37 (1935), pp. 1-24; "Chrétiens dans la Cité," *Esprit* 41 (1936), pp. 797-800; "Lignes de positions: Chrétiens et incroyants," *Esprit* 41 (1936), pp. 1-12; "La femme aussi est une personne," *Esprit* 45 (1936), pp. 291-297; "La femme chrétienne dans la pensée chrétienne," *Esprit* 45 (1936), pp. 396-407; "Manifeste au service du personnalisme," *Esprit* 49 (1936), pp. 7-216; "Propriété capitaliste et propriété humaine," *La vérité aux Françaises* (February, 1937), pp. 112-120; "Bilan spirituel," *Esprit* 66 (1938), pp. 873-890; "Semaine sociale et personnalisme," *Esprit* 68 (1938), pp. 201-215; "Appel à un rassemblement pour une démocratie personnaliste," *Esprit* 75 (1938), pp. 424-432; "Observations on the Tradition of French Personalism," *The Personalist* 20 (1939), pp. 280-287; "L'enjeu des valeurs judéo-chrétiennes: Personnalisme catholique," *Esprit* 89 (1940), pp 220-246, *Esprit* 90 (1940), pp. 395-405, and *Esprit* 91 (1940), pp. 57-72; "Études carmelitains: Les hommes sont-ils égaux?," *Esprit* 94 (1941), pp. 45-50; "Les devoirs du pluralisme," *Esprit* 99 (1941), pp. 361-367; "L'école et les réalistés spirituelles," *Esprit* 99 (1941), pp. 426-429; "Personne et communauté," *Temps nouveaux* (February 21, 1941); "Pour un humanisme français," *Journées d'études d'Uriage* (1941); "Personalism in France," *Transformation* 4 (Autumn, 1946), pp. 49-52; "Personnalisme et socialisme," *Cité soir* 1 (August, 1945); "Les dialogue Marxisme-Existentialisme," *Servir* 16 (April 18, 1946); "Où la liberté se cherche une place," *Servir* 20 (May 16, 1946); "Situation du Personnalisme," *Esprit* 118 (1946), pp. 4-25 and 120 (1946), pp. 432-547; "Existence," *Esprit* 121 (1946), pp. 652-653; "Pour une action personnaliste," *Esprit* 119 (1946), pp. 161-163; "Entretien sur la fin du monde," in Spender, Stephen, et al., *Les Conférences de l'UNESCO* (Paris, Fontaine, 1947), pp. 11-28 [includes talk of Mounier given at the first UNESCO Sorbonne Conference in November-December, 1946; translated as "Reflections on an Apocalyptic Age," in Spender, Stephen, ed., *Reflections on Our Age* (London: Wingate, 1948), pp. 19-38]; "Quelques réflexions sur le personnalisme," *Synthèses* 4 (1947), pp. 25-30; "Ma mauvaise querelle de l'Esprit," *Le Populaire* (July 19, 1947); "Le réel n'est à personne," *Esprit* 130 (1947), pp. 206-213; "Les équivoques du personnalisme," *Esprit* 129 (1947), pp. 265-282; "Optimisme et pessimisme chrétiens," *Esprit* 131 (1947), pp. 483-485; "L'incroyance des croyants," *Esprit* 134 (1947), pp. 1094-1095; "Aux avant-postes de la pensée chrétienne," *Esprit* 137 (1947), pp. 436-444; "Perspectives existentialistes et perspectives chrétiennes," in Pontalis, Jean-Bertrand, ed., *Pour et contre l'existentialisme* (Paris: Atlas, 1948), pp. 129-164; "Le christianisme et l'idée de progrès," in Siegfried, André, ed., *Progrès technique et progrès moral* (Neuchâtel: Office de publicité, 1948), pp. 181-223; "Cheminements du personnalisme," *Esprit* 141 (1948), pp. 12-13; "L'homme et la technique," *Esprit* 142 (1948), pp. 344-348; "Réponse à quelques critiques," *Esprit* 143 (1948), pp. 457-461; "Tâches actuelles d'une pensée d'inspiration personnaliste," *Esprit* 150 (1948), pp. 679-708; "Foi chrétienne et civilisation," in *Foi en Jésus-Christ et monde d'aujourd'hui* (Paris: Flore, 1949), pp. 56-96 [translated as "Christian Faith and Civilization," tr. Erwin Geissman, *Crosscurrents* 1:1 (Fall, 1950), pp. 3-23]; "L'observation de la personnalité totale," *Bulletin de l'Association des travailleuses sociales* (1949); "L'homme et l'univers," *Esprit* 155 (1949), pp. 743-747; "De l'esprit de vérité," *Esprit* 161 (1949), pp. 657-660 and 166 (1950), pp. 663-664; "Comme Dieu en France," *Bulletin des amis d'Emmanuel Mounier* 9-10 (1956), pp. 5-8; "L'Athéisme en France," *Bulletin des amis d'Emmanuel Mounier* 9-10 (1956), pp. 17-20 [reprinted in Bastide, Georges, *Les Etudes philosophiques: L'Athéisme* (Paris: Presses Universitaires de France, 1966)]; "Le combat des optimistes et des désespérés," *Bulletin des amis d'Emmanuel Mounier* 12 (1958), pp. 23-25; "Dialogue sur comment les étudiants d'aujourd'hui abordent-ils les problèmes philosophiques," *Bulletin des amis d'Emmanuel Mounier* 15 (1960), p. 18-24 [BBC telecast of philosophical discussion of May 23, 1949 involving Mounier, Alfred Jules Ayer, and Henri Jourdan].

And Mounier's theological essays include: "Catholicisme," *Esprit* 11-12 (1933), pp. 791-792; "Court traité du catholicisme ondoyant," *Esprit* 62 (1937), pp. 282-314; "En interrogeant les silences de Pie XII," *Le Voltigeur* 13 (1939) [a famous essay criticizing Pope Pius XII for his "silence" during the Holocaust; reprinted in *Bulletin des amis d'Emmanuel Mounier* 23-24 (December, 1964)]; "Cléricalisme et anticléricalisme," *Servir* 24 (June 13, 1946); "De l'usage du mot catholique," *Esprit* 155 (194), pp. 710-713 and 159 (1949), pp. 425-531; "L'Avenir de la religion," *Bulletin des amis d'Emmanuel Mounier* 9-10 (1956), pp. 20-23; "Deux débats dans l'Église de France," *Bullletin des amis d'Emmanuel Mounier* 9-10 (1956), pp. 26-28.

Some of these essays have been collected in *Mounier, l'homme et son message* (Paris: Denoël, 1970) [extracts from the journal *Esprit*]; *Ecrits sur le personnalisme* (Paris: Seuil, 2000); *Refaire la Renaissance* (Paris: Seuil, 2000). Mounier also wrote numerous essays on political topics, as well as philosophical book reviews. For an extensive bibliography of Mounier see Mounier, Emmanuel, *Oeuvres, v. IV: Receuils, Posthumes, Correspondance* (Paris: Seuil, 1963), pp. 835-876.

A compilation of Mounier exists as *Oeuvres de Mounier*, 4 vol. (Paris: Seuil, 1961-1963). Mounier's manuscripts and unpublished works reside at the Esprit library of Châtenay-Malabry (Paris), France.

76   For more on Nédoncelle see: DTC (1939), Tables générales, 3289-3290; PM (1960), v. II, p. 591; PTCW (1964), pp. 582-583; PPF (1966), pp. 109-115; CHP (1974), v. IX, pp. 316-317; CHAD (1982), v. IX, pp. 1136-1138; CP (1990), v. III, pp. 479-486; BBKL (1993), v. VI, pp. 549-551; DP (1993), v. II, pp. 2096-2097; BDTC (1996), p. 565; LTK (1998), v. VII, p. 722; UHF (1998), v. VIII, pp. 397-402; RPFR (1999), pp. 34-45; EF (2006), v. VIII, pp. 7803-7804; Grevillot, Jean Marie, *Les grands courants de la pensée contemporaine: existentialisme, marxisme, personnalisme chrétien* (Paris: Vitrail, 1947), pp. 164-274; Liddle, Vincent, "The Foundations of the Moral Philosophy of Maurice Nédoncelle," *Philosophical Studies* 15 (1966), pp. 122-130; Farber, Marvin, ed., *Philosophic Thought in France and the United States* (Albany: State University of New York Press, 1968), pp. 81-82; Rafferty, Kevin, "The Personalist Way to God according to Maurice Nédoncelle," *Philosophical Studies* 19 (1970), pp. 22-50; Nguyen, Van Chien, *La philosophie de la personne et de l'amour chez Maurice Nédoncelle* (Saigon: Editions le temps présent, 1970); Hellman, John, "The Opening to the Left in French Catholicism: The Role of the Personalists," *The Journal of the History of Ideas* 34:3 (1973), pp. 381-390; Braun, Lucien, *La pensée philosophique et religieuse de Maurice Nédoncelle* (Paris: Téqui, 1981); Chadiac, Bakhos, *L'intersubjectivité promotionelle dans le personalisme de Maurice Nédoncelle* (Kaslik: Université Saint-Esprit Kaslik, 1985); Mannath, Joe, "Love as the Key to Understanding the Person: The Personalist Philosophy of Maurice Nédoncelle," *Journal of Dharma* 21 (1996), pp. 94-103.

77   The latter work has been translated as *Love and the Person* [LP], tr. Ruth Adelaïde (New York: Sheed and Ward, 1966) [I use the pagination from this English translation followed by the page numbers of the French edition in brackets: *Vers une philosophie de l'amour et de la personne* (Paris: Aubier, 1957)].

Among Nédoncelle's other philosophical works are his: *Suffering [La souffrance]* (1939; 1950) [translated as *Suffering*, tr. Marjorie Vernon (London: Burns & Oates, 1941) and republished in Butterfield, William, ed., *Be Ye Perfect* (London: Spiritual Book Associates, 1943)]; *The Human Person and Nature [La personne humaine et la nature]* [HPN] (1943; 1963); *On Fidelity [De la fidélité]* (1953); *Existe-t-il une philosophie chrétienne?* (1956; 1964) [translated as *Is There a Christian Philosophy?*, [ITCP], tr. Illtyd Trethowan (London: Burns & Oates, 1959)]; *Consciousness and Logos [Conscience et logos]* [CL] (1961) [a collection of articles; portions of this work, namely the Preface, pp. 9-10 and section I, 6, pp. 128-138 were translated as "Person and/or World as the Source of Religious Insight," in McLean, George, ed., *Traces of God in a Secular Culture* (Staten Island: Alba House, 1973), pp. 187-209]; *Personalist Explorations [Explorations personnalistes]* [PE] (1970) [a collection of articles]; *Intersubjectivity and Ontology* [*Intersubjectivité et ontologie: Le défi personnaliste*] [IO] (1974) [a collection of articles; translated as *The Personalist Challenge*, tr. François Gérard and Francis Burch (Allison Park: Pickwick, 1984)]; *Separative Sensation and the Temporal Dynamism of Consciousnesses* [*Sensation séparatrice et dynamisme temporel des consciences*] [TDC](1977) [a collection of articles]. Nédoncelle also wrote many works of the history of philosophy and theology including: *Human Prayer, Divine Prayer* [*Prière humaine, prière divine*] [HPDP] (1962) [translated as *God's Encounter with Man*, tr. A. Manson (New York: Sheed and Ward, 1964)]; *The Christian Belongs to Two Worlds* [*Le chrétien appartient à deux mondes*] (1970).

Nédoncelle's key philosophical essays are his: "Le silence de Dieu," *La vie spirituelle* 62 (1940), pp. 129-143; "La guérison de Narcisse," *Rencontres* 5 (1941), pp. 129-129; "Amour personnel et dévouement collectif," *Caritas* 52 (1947), pp. 6-10; "La philosophie catholique au XXe siècle," *Ecclesia* 6 (1948), pp. 552-555; "Proposon et persona dans l'Antiquité classique," *Revue des sciences religieuses* 22 (1948), pp. 277-299; "La signification du moi idéal," in *Actes du Xe Congrès international de philosophie* (Amsterdam: North Holland Publishing Company, 1948), v. II, pp. 912-914; "La liberté se communique-t-elle?," in *Actes du IVe Congrès des sociétés de philosophie de langue françaises* (Neuchâtel: Éditions de la baconnière, 1949), pp. 111-116; "Les données de la conscience et le don des personnes," *Giornale di Metafisica* 5 (1950), pp. 70-80; "Existe-t-il une réciprocité des consciences en histoire?," in *Actes du VIe Congrès des sociétés de philosophie de langue française* (Paris: Presses Universitaires de France, 1952), pp. 143-147; "Les faits de conversion devant la réflexion chrétienne," in Nédoncelle, Maurice, and René Girault, eds., *J'ai rencontré le Dieu vivant* (Paris: Editions de la Revue des Jeunes, 1952), pp. 11-40; "La philosophie de l'action et les philosophies de la personne," *Les études philosophiques* 7 (1952), pp. 387-389; "Sur l'évolution de quelques métaphores relatives à la transcendence," in *Actes du XIe Congrè de philosophie* (Louvain: Nauwelaerts, 1953), pp. 97-103; "La philosophie," in Ariès, Philippe, *Cinquante ans de pensée catholique française* (Paris: Fayard, 1955), pp. 85-104; "Les variations de Boèce sur la personne," *Revue des sciences religieuses* 29 (1955), pp. 201-238; "Philosophie de la religion," in Klibansky, Raymond, ed., *Philosophy in the Mid-Century* (Florence: La nuova Italia, 1958), v. III, pp. 189-222; "Chronique de philosophie religieuse," *Revue des sciences religieuses* 33 (1959), pp. 65-82; "Croyance, confiance et foi," *Les études philosophiques* 14 (1959), pp. 163-172; "La notion de personne dans l'oeuvre de saint Anselme," *Specilegium Beccense* 1 (1959), pp. 31-43; "Un chemin philosophique vers Dieu," *Tijdschrift voor Philosophie* 22 (1960), pp. 425-440; "Communication intellectuelle et communication personnelle," *Actes du XIIe Congrès des sociétés de philosophie de langue française* (Florence: Sansoni, 1961), v. IV, pp. 227-231; "Les équivoques de la réflexion philosophique," *Giornale di Metafisica* 16 (1961), pp. 1-16; "De l'expérience esthétique à l'expérience religieuse," in *Atti del XV Convegno del Centro di studi filosofici tra professori universitari Gallarate* (Brescia: Morcelliana, 1961); "Nature et conscience personnelle," *Les études philosophiques* 16 (1961), pp. 238-241; "Rayonnement intellectuel et rayonnement personnel," *Actes du XIIᵉ Congrès international de philosophie de Venise* (Firenze: Sansoni Editore, 1961); "Le sens positif de l'athéisme," *Atti del XVI Convegno del Centro di studi filosofici tra professori universitari Gallarate* (Brescia: Marcelliana, 1962), pp. 397-406; "Simples réflexions sur l'autorité de la conscience," in Todd, John Murray, ed., *Problèmes de l'autorité* (Paris: Le Cerf, 1962), pp. 225-236 [translated as "Reflections on the Authority of Conscience," in John Murray Todd, ed., *Problems of Authority* (Baltimore: Helicon, 1962), pp. 189-198]; "La mutation du pouvoir technique et la problème de la responsabilité morale," *Atti del XVII convegno del Centro di studi filosofici tra professori universitari Gallarate* (Brescia: Marcelliana, 1963), pp. 284-286; "Le moi du Christ et le moi des hommes à la lumière de la réciprocité des consciences," in Bouëssé, Humbert, and Jean-Jacques Latour, eds., *Problèmes actuels de Christologie* (Paris: Desclée et Brouwer, 1965), pp. 201-226; "Remarques sur l'expression de la personne en grec et en latin," *Revue des sciences religieuses* 40 (1965), pp. 34-47; "Théologie et philosophie ou les métamorphoses d'une servante," *Concilium* 6 (1965), pp. 93-102 [translated as "Philosophy, Handmaid of Theology?," ("PHT"), in Metz, Johannes Baptist, ed., *Fundamental Theology: The Church and the World* (New York: Paulist Press, 1965), pp. 93-104]; "Trois approches d'une philosophie de l'Esprit: Lavelle, Le Senne, Nabert," *Filosofia* 16:4 (1965), pp. 717-730; "Réponse à l'enquête sur la philosophie," *Giornale di Metafisica* 21 (1965), pp. 614-617; "La genèse réciproque des consciences et l'éternité," *Atti del XX convegno del Centro di studi filosofici tra professori universitari Gallarate* (Brescia: Morcelliana, 1966), pp. 309-313; "Théologie fondamentale et philosophie" ["Fundamental Theology and Philosophy"] ["FTP"] (1966) [unpublished]; "Démythisation et conception eschatologique du mal," Castelli, Enrico, ed., *Le mythe de la peine* (Paris: Aubier, 1967), pp. 195-222; "Sur quelques conditions d'une ontologie personnaliste," *Giornale di Metafisica* 23 (1967), pp. 213-218; "Le masque et la personne," *Bulletin de l'Association Guillaume Budé* 4:1 (1968), pp. 21-31; "Dialectique et dialogue dans la réciprocité des consciences," *Actes du XIVᵉ Congrès de sociétés de philosophie de langue française* (Paris: P.U.F., 1969), pp. 248-251; "Remarques sur les rapports de présence et de causalité psychiques," in *Omaggio a Vincenzo la Via* (Catania: Tipo dell'Università di Catania, 1969), pp. 219-226; "Les sources sensible et axiologiques de l'affirmation religieuse," (1970) [unpublished]; "La relation à autrui," *Carmel* 5 (1971), pp. 4-18; "Doutes relatifs à l'autonomie philosophique et à l'hétéronomie religieuse," *Atti del XXV Convegno di Centre di Studi filosofici tra professori universitari Gallarate* (Brescia: Morcelliana, 1971), pp. 286-294; "De la foi comme connaissance dans l'histoire de la philosophie occidentale," Giacon, Carlo, ed., *Scritti in onore di Carlo Giacone* (Padova: Antenore, 1972), pp. 583-600; "Le heurt initial dans la rencontre des personnes," in Seckler, Max, ed., *Begugnung* (Graz: Styria, 1972), pp. 23-30; "Groupes et personne," in Metz, René and Jean Schlick, eds., *Les*

RECENT CATHOLIC PHILOSOPHY ❦ THE TWENTIETH CENTURY

groupes informels dans l'Églises (Strasbourg: Cerdic, 1972), pp. 129-147 [translated as "Group and Person," in Metz, René, and Jean Schlick, eds., *Informal Groups in the Church* (Eugene: Pickwick, 1975), pp. 137-158]; "Communication et interprétation du témoignage," Castelli, Enrico, ed., *Le témoignage* (Paris: Aubier, 1972), pp. 279-290; "Communicabilité et communication des consciences," *Giornale di Metafisica* 28:1 (1972), pp. 1-11; "De l'inspiration artistique comme chemin vers la transcendence," *Aisthesis* 7 (1972), pp. 23-34; "De l'être comme relation primordiale des étants," *Rivista di Filosofia neoscolastica* 65:1 (1973), pp. 3-16; "La finitude de la conscience," *Teoresi* 28 (1973), pp. 25-44; "L'être est-il la valeur ultime?," *Atti del XXVII Convegno del Centro di studi filosofici tra professori universitari Gallarate* (Brescia: Morcelliana, 1974); "Les equivoques de la secularisation," in Walgrave, Jan, and Antoine Vergote, eds., *Miscellanea Albert Dondeyne: Godsdienstfilosofie, Philosophie de la religion* (Louvain: Louvain University Press, 1974), pp. 241-249; "La manipulation des esprits," in Robert, Charles, *L'homme manipulé* (Strasbourg: Cerdic, 1974), pp. 53-67 [translated as "The Manipulation of Minds," in Robert, Charles, ed., *Manipulated Man* (Pittsburgh: Pickwick, 1977), pp. 53-67]; "À quoi est due l'apparence impersonnelle de la conscience?," Caramella, Tina, ed., *Miscellanea di Scritti filosofici in memoria di Santino Carmella* (Palermo: Accademia di scienze, lettere e arti di Palermo, 1974), pp. 225-238; "De la pudeur comme source de la sécularisation," *Revue de droit canonique* 25 (1975), pp. 158-167; "Le sacre et la profanation," in Castelli, Enrico, ed., *Prospettive sul sacro* (Padua: CEDAM, 1975), pp. 43-55; "Nature et valeur permanente de l'amour platonique," *International Studies in Philosophy* 8 (1976), pp. 27-38 [and in *Saggi Filosofici* 34 (1977), pp. 27-38]; "The Other and Causality" ["Altérité et causalité"], in Tymieniecka, Anna-Teresa, ed., *The Self and the Other* (Dordrecht: Kluwer, 1977), pp. 101-112; "Simultanéité physique et simultanéité des consciences," *Atti del XXXI Convegno del Centro di studi filosofici tra professori universitari Gallarate* (Brescia: Morcelliana, 1977); "Reconnaissance de l'autre mene-t-elle à Dieu: Dialogue avec Maurice Nédoncelle," [with Charles Lefevre], *Mélanges de Science Religieuse* 35:4 (1978), pp. 153-167; "Sensation, valuer esthétique et transcendance," *Diotima Athinai* 6 (1978), pp. 90-93.

And finally Nédoncelle also wrote a few theological essays including: "Chronique de théologie fondamentale," *Revue des sciences religieuses* 28 (1954), pp. 140-154; "Le sens de la résurrection," *Bible et terre sainte* 6 (1962); "Fidelité et celibat consacre," in Coppens, Joseph, ed., *Sacredoce et célibat* (Gembloux: J. Duculot, 1971), pp. 673-691; "La revelation en tant qu'experience," *Revue des Sciences Religieuses* 45 (1971), pp. 240-243; "Devoirs des intellectuels envers leur foi," in Soulages, Gérard, ed., *Fidelité et ouverture* (Paris: Mame, 1972), pp. 38-42.

For a partial bibliography of Nédoncelle see his *Explorations personnalistes* (Paris: Aubier, 1970), pp. 283-297 [lists his works up until 1970], *Intersubjectivité et ontologie* (Louvain: Nauwelaerts, 1974), pp. 381-383 [works from

1970-1974], and *Sensation séparatrice et dynamisme temporel des consciences* (Paris: Bloud et Gay, 1977), pp. 165-166 [works from 1974-1976].

78 Consequently for Nédoncelle the classic definition of the person given by Boethius (and adopted by the Scholastics) is incomplete. Boethius defines the person as an individual substance of a rational nature, but this ignores the openness and communicability of the person.

79 It is true that our initial congenial encounter with another person can quickly degenerate into indifference, pettiness, or antagonism. And if this occurs the course of reciprocity is at least temporarily halted (RECC, Part One, I, 8, 12, pp. 16, 20; Part Two, I, 96, 101, pp. 129-130, 135-136; Part Two, III, 142-143, 146-148, 152, pp. 178-185, 187-188; Part Two, IV, 159, 161, 170-171, pp. 193-196, 203-205; PLP, I, 3, pp. 76-77, 79; II, 4, p. 95; II, 5, p. 107; Conclusion, XIII, p. 220; HPN, I, 4, pp. 9-10; IO, I, pp. 9-11 [18-21]).

Yet Nédoncelle responds that, as we have seen, the initial meeting with another at least is full of a true interest in and regard for the other; it is a liberating and loving perception. Thus the first movement in which minds approach each other is generous, no matter how quickly this grace may later be denied (PLP, Conclusion, p. 217).

Second, a mutual joyful love is possible to attain, even if only partially, temporarily, and episodically (PLP, I, 3, p. 77-79). As Nédoncelle notes: "No matter how troubling the tears, no matter how copiously and long they flow, they are born of a paradoxical hope whose sweetness is inexplorable yet invincible. To absorb so many sorrows we must go beyond them and the exile is bitter only if there is a paradise. The truth is that the invisible soul of mutual promotion can never be completely identified with the painful task in which it is incarnate and which is always constricted, multiple and refractory in places" (PLP, I, 2, pp. 50-51 [63-64]).

80 This love can take different forms in a beautiful quote from Nédoncelle: "Here is a couple tenderly embraced who walk in ecstasy; this, certainly, is a loving behavior, and one must also suppose, a loving state of soul. But here is a mother who cradles her child and this, too, stems from love. And there is a school boy leading his little brother by the hand, ready to defend him against the brutality of larger kids, this, too, is love. The clasp of hands that I exchange with my friend, the coin that I insert in the blind beggar's bowl, the bitter generosity of hidden self-sacrifice ... what a multitude of forms! Powers which protect and sensitivities which make one cower, the frank exchange of a common gift, the tears that beg pardon or which grant it, the visit to the sick, the wrath of Hermione and the blade [of Abraham] poised over Isaac— nothing is common to all these things save the love which evokes them" (PLP, Introduction, p. 6 [12]). Love then can be reflected in a glance, gesture, gift, or sacrifice of sensible or spiritual goods. It is a pledge of future work ever incomplete (PLP, I, 2, pp. 37-38, 43-44).

81   I must not then love others for any of their qualities (even their good-ness or beauty; or even solely for the sake of God), says Nédoncelle, for in that case I fail to love my beloved for him or herself (RECC, Part One, I, 4-5, pp. 11-13; I, 31, p. 44; III, 78, p. 108; PLP, I, 1, pp. 8-9, 12). For to treat the other as a means in any way is to treat the other as a non-self [non-moi] (RECC, Part One, I, 31, p. 44).

82   Nédoncelle has his doubts about the validity and effectiveness of the traditional proofs for God's existence (though he does allow some merit to the ontological argument). He argues that the cosmological argument which reasons to God as a first cause of the world's changing beings illegitimately extends the idea of cause from the visible causes we can see (interontic causes) to a cause of the whole world (a supraontic cause). And the teleological argu-ment from the order of the universe to God has to deal with the fact that the world can seem indifferent to the existence of human beings and even if it can be beneficial to humans, it does not seem to have achieved its full plan. At most then it can give us a hope in the existence of God. Furthermore, all of these traditional proofs have the danger of reducing God to a God of dialectic (a God of the philosophers, one situated beyond the last star as with Kant) rather than a personal God (RECC, Part One, III, 76-77, 81, 92, pp. 104, 106, 110-112, 121; Part Two, II, 139, 141, pp. 175-177; II, 158, pp. 192-192; PLP, Conclusion, XIII, p. 223; PE, I, 4, pp. 53-54, 60-61; CL, I, 6, pp. 139-142; II, 2, pp. 190-193, 207-208; IO, XVII, pp. 193-197 [211-215]; "PHT", p. 102; cf. however RECC, Part Two, II, 128, 140, pp. 162-175-176; Part Three, IV, 255, p. 299).

83   Nédoncelle here argues against Aquinas that beauty, not being, is the fundamental transcendental. For truth is the beauty of relations and good-ness is the beauty of behavior (RECC, Part Three, I, 178, 183-184, pp. 217, 220-221).

84   Nédoncelle agrees with Blondel (and against the Thomists) in holding that nature and supernature are best not thought of as two floors [nature as the ground floor present in all humans and grace as the higher floor which perfects the lower and is given to some humans only]; but as an osmosis or transmutation of degrees in which nature is gradually enriched by supernature [where grace is considered the inside, hidden vocation (source), and nature the outside, visible expression (derivation)]. For the supernatural is always present in nature and humans to some degree, and indeed over time nature is increas-ingly enriched by the supernatural. Thus each human possesses a minimum of the divine (a minimal supernatural apprehension) and a vocation to increase in this divine possession (ITCP, IX, pp. 139-143; Conclusion, pp. 151-152; IO, XVII, pp. 193-197 [211-215]; "PHT", pp. 103-104; "FTP," pp. 17-18).

Nédoncelle does distinguish between a natural love and a supernatural love, however. Love of another human being does begin with our natural sentiments and through them we can achieve a state of promotion of the other. Thus humans do have a natural generosity [contra Anders Nygren] (RECC, Part One, I, 16, p. 24; Part One, II, 47, p. 57; PLP, I, 1, pp. 16-17). Yet the natural sentiments cannot surmount our infirmities and overcome our tendency to isolation. For this we need divine grace to elevate our nature (RECC, Part One, I, 7, 12, 16, pp. 15-16, 20, 25; Conclusion, 269, pp. 324-325; PLP, I, 1, pp. 16-17). We also need divine grace to perfect our love and make us capable of loving another person in his or her singularity (and not archetype) and for loving our enemies [i.e. overcoming hate] (RECC, Part One, I, 12, p. 20; Part Two, IV, 167-168, pp. 201-202; Part Three, 4, 268, p. 318).

85   As philosophy, through a form of the moral argument, can establish the existence of God and the immortality of the soul, as well as several other truths, it is rightly held to be autonomous from theology. At least in the sense that it appeals to its own rational methods of intelligibility in discovering various items of knowledge (RECC, Part One, III, 69-70, pp. 94-95; PLP, Conclusion, p. 223; ITCP, VII, pp. 119-120, 124; IX, p. 139-146 and n. 2 on p. 147, p. 148; Conclusion, pp. 150-152; IO, XVII, pp. 190-192 [208-211]; "PHT," pp. 95, 97). In fact, claims Nédoncelle, it is better to conceive of philosophy as the sister of theology than as its handmaiden (for in the latter case it is subordinate to theology rather than its equal).

Theology in its turn at a minimum should recognizes the need to adopt a language of philosophy (to incorporate such notions as essence, substance, or cause) and a logic (to establish the existence of God and an immortal soul), that is to say it must recognize the need for an underlying philosophy. It is even the case that theology can be renewed by philosophy, and in this manner come to understand revelation better and discover things it didn't suspect. Thus, for instance, philosophical reflection on death allows us to better grasp the death of Christ, on motherhood to better grasp Mariology, on human solidarity to more perfectly understand the Incarnation, on intention and love to more profoundly grasp the sacraments, on anthropology to better appreciate the supernatural, and on fatherhood to learn more about the Trinity. Hence theologians should try to learn from and understand philosophy and not just dictate to it (theology is thus both autonomous and heteronomous as it were) (ITCP, IX, pp. 139-143; Conclusion, pp. 151-152; IO, XVI, pp. 186-188 [201-205]; XVII, pp. 190-197 [208-215]; "PHT," pp. 97-100, 103).

Yet philosophy, like theology, is itself both autonomous and heteronomous (or better yet theonomous and obedient) as it is called to find its perfection through supernatural faith (PLP, I, 3, p. 71; III, 12, pp. 202-203; Conclusion, p. 227; ITCP, VI, pp. 112-113; IX, pp. 138, 143-146; n. 2 on p. 147; IX, p. 148; Conclusion, p. 150; IO, XVI, pp. 186-188 [201-205]; HPDP, II, 1, pp. 80-83).

In the first place Christian Revelation has value for philosophy in helping it to open up new routes for philosophical exploration (to in fact open up what was once considered non-philosophical), and so cooperate with the progress of philosophy (RECC, Part Three, 4, 268, p. 315; ITCP, VII, pp. 116-117). For instance, reflection on divine providence, the Incarnation and Person of Christ, Christ's ethical teachings, and the Trinity, can enrich metaphysics and ethics (ITCP, Preface, pp. 9-11; IX, pp. 139-146, 148; Conclusion, pp. 149-152).

Secondly, Revelation can help to draw limits to reason's competencies. Here Nédoncelle follows Maurice Blondel's (1861-1949) conception of Christian philosophy wherein reason (which pledges to leave nothing undone in the search for all truth) can acknowledge it is insufficient to know the whole of reality and so give a rational expectation of a Word coming to us from heaven (a summons of divine grace). For one can recognize a divine exigency in one's innermost being and yet that by nature we fall short of a complete union with God. Philosophy then can prepare one to engage in a faithful acceptance of God's revelation (ITCP, Preface, pp. 9-10; VI, pp. 112-113; VII, pp. 128-129, 131; IX, pp. 137, 140-141, 143-146, n. 2 on p. 147, p. 148; Conclusion, p. 150; IO, XVII, pp. 190-197 [208-215];"PHT, pp. 96-97, 102). Nédoncelle accordingly describes Christian philosophy as "a philosophy which, proclaiming the insufficiency of human nature to resolve the whole problem of the human, discerns and in some sense delimits a supernatural gift that would resolve the problem but which it itself cannot replace" (ITCP, Conclusion, p. 149 [115]).

Lastly, to Nédoncelle's mind, only revelation lets us encounter other persons and Christ as living and unique individuals (allowing for intimacy and prayer). While philosophy searches for the universal in the personal (and so substitutes a *tutti* [whole; many] for the *duo* [dyad]), theology searches for the personal in the universal (it is concerned with a Revealer and not just a Revelation, a Savior and not just salvation, a Father, Son, and Holy Spirit and not just a Trinity) (ITCP, VII, pp. 128-129, 131; Conclusion, pp. 150-151; IO, XVI, pp. 186-188 [201-205];"FTP," p. 24). This is because philosophy is committed to "the handling of ideas rather than to direct commerce with persons" (ITCP, VII, p. 131). Or as Nédoncelle puts it "It is not the autonomy of the thinker which prevents Christianity from entering into our thoughts, rather it is the existential intimacy of the call [*interpellation*]. A philosopher does not name persons. They are for the philosopher a bottomless abyss. It belongs to others to designate them to the philosopher. The task of the historian and the theologian is to know about Jesus in his earthly life, but the philosopher knows only the ideas of which Jesus is the center of radiance" (ITCP, VII, p. 129 [99-100]).

All of the above makes it clear why in the end Nédoncelle says that the most complete philosophy is Christian and the most complete Christianity makes use of philosophy (ITCP, VII, pp. 116-117). For, concludes Nédoncelle in a nice quote "The dignity of reason lies in its ability to establish contact between all the orders and to belong to all of these orders: its weakness lies in its inability to bring any of them to completion [*achever*]" (ITCP, Conclusion, p. 151).

86   We can single out from among around 75 Catholic Personalists: the Italian politician Fr. Luigi Sturzo (1871-1959); Peter Maurin (1877-1949) who
helped found the Catholic Worker Movement (1933-); Fr. Romano Guardini
(1885-1968); Fr. Theodor Steinbüchel (1888-1949); August Brunner, S.J.
(1894-1985) [also a Phenomenologist]; the death-bed convert Arnaud Dandieu (1897-1933), founder of L'Ordre Nouveau (1930-); Maurice Laudrain
(c. 1900-1985), founder of the journal *Terre Nouvelle* (1935-); Jean Lacroix
(1900-1986); the near convert Paul-Ludwig Landsberg (1901-1944) [who
died in a concentration camp]; Canon Jean Mouroux (1901-1973); the Spaniard Fr. Manuel Mindan Manero (1902-2006); Eugenio Frutos Cortes (1903-
1979); Pierre-Henri Simon (1903-1972); André Cruiziat (1904-1998),
founder of La Vie Nouvelle (1947-); the Jewish convert Alexandre Marc
(1904-2000), founder of L'Ordre Nouveau (1930-); Étienne Borne (1907-
1993); Jean-Pierre Maxence (1906-1956) [also a Thomist]; Jean de Fabregues
(1906-1983); Louis Janssens (1908-2001); the Belgian Jan Walgrave, O.P.
(1911-1986) [also an Integralist]; Otto Semmelroth, S.J. (1912-1979); Jean-
Marie Doménach (1922-1997), editor of *Esprit*; the Mexican Jose Ruben
Sanabria (1923-); Armando Rigobello (1924-); Claude Tresmontant (1925-
1997), of the Sorbonne; Cardinal Marian Jaworski (1926-); Ada Lamacchia
(1927-); John Cowburn, S.J. (1927-); Paul Thibaud (1933-), editor of *Esprit*;
Fr. Joaquin Ferrer Arellano (c. 1934-); Enrico Berti (1935-); Vittorio Possenti
(c. 1940-) [also a Thomist]; the Spaniard Carlos Díaz (1944-) [founder of
Institutio Emmanuel Mounier in Madrid]; Bernhard Langemeyer, O.F.M. (c.
1944-); Olivier Mongrin (1951-), editor of *Esprit*; Giancarlo Galeazzi (1942-
) [also a Neo-Thomist]; Guy Coq (c. 1955-), editor of Esprit; Marc-Olivier
Padis (c. 1955-), editor of Esprit; Kenneth L. Schmitz (c. 1955-); Tomas Trigo
(c. 1955-); Juan Martínez Porcell (1960-); Juan Manuel Burgos (1961-); Fr.
Thomas D. Williams (c. 1965-).

Personalism has been critiqued by John Cowburn, S.J., Robert Johann,
Charles de Koninck, Pedro Descoqs, and Louis Mercier; see also Baisnée,
Jules, "Two Catholic Critiques of Personalism," The Modern Schoolman 22
(1945), pp. 59-75.

87   Additionally World War II saw the imprisonment of the French
Catholic philosophers Jacques Chevalier (1882-1962) [pro-Vichy], Jean Guit-
ton (1901-1999) [pro-Vichy], Yves Congar, O.P. (1904-1995), Emmanuel
Mounier (1905-1950) [pro then anti-Vichy], and René Laurentin (1917-),
and the death (by imprisonment or execution) of the French Catholic thinkers
Yves de Montcheuil, S.J. (1900-1944) and the German-born Jewish convert
Paul-Ludwig Landsberg (1901-1944). Indeed over 200 French priests died
in World War II and around 500 were imprisoned.

88   For more on the life and thought of Lavelle see: DTC (1950), Tables
générales, p. 2909; CAP (1955), pp. 95-96; SHP (1955), p. 939; CRHP
(1957), pp. 485-487; CMCT (1960), pp. 43-64; CEP (1961), pp. 208-209,

310; PTCW (1964), pp. 555-568; PPF (1966), pp. 48-55; MHP (1967), p. 439; TPC (1967), pp. 269-272; RPF (1968), pp. 107-112; BHP (1969), vol. VI, pp. 258-259; TCP (1969), pp. 108-113; HWP (1971), vol. V, pp. 332-334; OB (1971), pp. 45-48; CHP (1974), vol. IX, pp. 307-310; CHAD (1975), vol. VII, pp. 89-92; PFPM (1977), pp. 139-141; CP (1990), vol. III, pp. 465-478; BBKL (1992), vol. IV, pp. 1267-1269; DP (1993), vol. II, pp. 1692-1694; BDTC (1996), pp. 439-440; DPR (1996), p. 296; LTK (1997), vol. VI, pp. 692-693; TCRT (1998), pp. 362-363; FPTC (2001), p. 84; NCE (2003), vol. VIII, p. 387; EMFT (2004), pp. 400-401; EP (2005), vol. X, pp. 214-216; EF (2006), pp. 6244-6247; TWFP (2006), pp. 151-152; Benrubi, Isaak, *Les sources et les courants de la philosophie contemporaine en France* (Paris: Alcan, 1933), vol. II, pp. 495-499; Bénisti, Edmond, *La main de l'écrivain* (Paris: Stock, 1939), p. 210; Truc, Gonzague, *De Jean-Paul Sartre à Louis Lavelle* (Paris: Tissot, 1946); Collins, James, "Louis Lavelle on Human Participation," *Philosophical Review* 56 (1947), pp. 156-183; Therive, André, *Moralistes de ce temps* (Paris: Amiot Dumont, 1948), pp. 93-150; Smith, Victor, "Lavelle and Le Senne: University Philosophy in France," *Thought* 23 (1948), pp. 245-280; Deledalle, Gérard, *L'existential: Philosophies et littératures de l'existence* (Paris: Lacoste, 1949), pp. 253-274; Copleston, Frederick, "The Human Person in Contemporary Philosophy," *Philosophy* 25 (1950), pp. 3-19; Foulquié, Paul, *Existentialism* (New York: Roy, 1950), pp. 115-123; "Louis Lavelle," *La Croix* (September 7, 1951); "Monsieur Louis Lavelle," *Bulletin Paroissial du Canton de Villeréal* (October, 1951); Sellars, Roy Wood, "The Spiritualism of Lavelle and Le Senne," *Philosophy and Phenomenological Research* 11 (1951), pp. 386-393; *Giornale di Metafisica* 7 (1952) [Special Issue on L Louis Lavelle]; Le Senne, René, "Louis Lavelle," *Giornale di metafisica* 4 (1952), pp. 405-421; *Recherches et Débats* 18 (1952) [Special Issue on Lavelle]; *Rivista di Metafisica* 4 (1952) [Special Issue on Lavelle]; Lacroix, Jean, "A Philosopher of Acceptance: Louis Lavelle," *Downside Review* 71 (1953), pp. 372-36; Davy, Georges, *Notice sur la vie et les travaux de Louis Lavelle* (Paris: Firmin-Didot et Cie, 1957); École, Jean, *La métaphysique de l'être dans la philosophie de Louis Lavelle* (Louvain: Nauwelaerts, 1957); Sargi, Bechara, *La participation à l'être dans la philosophie de Louis Lavelle* (Paris: Beauchesne, 1957); *Études Philosophiques* 13 (1958) [Special Isssue on Louis Lavelle]; Weze, A.M., "Personal Dimensions in the Spirituaism of Louis Lavelle," *Philosophy Today* 2 (1958), pp. 37-45; Piersol, Wesley, *La valeur dans la philosophie de Louis Lavelle* (Paris: Vitte, 1959); Levert, Paule, *L'être et le reel selon Louis Lavelle* (Paris: Aubier, 1960); Sciacca, Michele Federico, ed., *Les grands courants de la pensée mondiale contemporaine* (Paris: Fischbacher, 1964), vol. VI, pp. 831-859; Smith, Colin, *Contemporary French Philosophy* (New York: Barnes and Noble, 1964), pp. 47-74; Murphy, Wesley Piersol, "Louis Lavelle: An Approach," *Philosophy Today* 9 (1965), pp. 168-173; D'Ainval, Christiane, *Une doctrine de la présence spirituelle: La Philosophie de Louis Lavelle* (Paris: Nauwelaerts, 1967); Hardy, Gilbert, *La vocation de la liberté chez Louis Lavelle* (Louvain: Nauwelaerts, 1968); Hardy, Gilbert,

"Louis Lavelle on Freedom and Participation," *Philosophy Today* 13 (1969), pp. 19-25; Hardy, Gilbert, "Louis Lavelle on the Mystery of Freedom," *Philosophy Today* 13 (1969), pp. 243-246; Quito, Emerita, *La notion de la liberté participé dans la philosophie de Louis Lavelle* (Fribourg: Éditions Universitaires, 1969); Lechner, Robert, "Experience in the Thought of Louis Lavelle," *University of Dayton Review* 8 (1971), pp. 39-42; Reymond, Christiane, *Autrui dans la Dialectique de l'éternel présent de Louis Lavelle* (Paris: Presses Universitaires de France, 1972); Quito, Emerita, "The Paradox of Freedom in Louis Lavelle," *Unitas* 46 (1973), pp. 224-239; Chiari, Joseph, *Twentieth-Century French Thought* (London: Gordian Press, 1975), pp. 117-134; Jeantin, Paul, "Louis Lavelle," *Revue de l'Agenais* 105 (1979), pp. 235-247; Cauchy, Venant, ed., *Philosophy and Culture* (Montreal: Montmorency, 1983), pp. 303-314, 323-331; Hardy, Gilbert, "Value and Free Choice: Lavelle's Attempt at a Reconciliation," *Philosophy Today* 28 (1984), pp. 308-318; École, Jean, ed., *Louis Lavelle* (Agen: Société académique d'Agen, 1987) [including personal reminiscences]; Bretonneau, Gisèle, *L'exigence des valeurs chez Louis Lavelle* (Paris: SEDES, 1987); École, Jean, *Métaphysique de l'être, doctrine de la connaissance et philosophie de la religion chez Louis Lavelle* (Genova: L'Arcipelago, 1994); École, Jean, ed., *De Christian Wolff à Louis Lavelle* (Hildesheim: New York, 1995); *Actes du XXIVᵉ Congrès International de l'Association des Sociétés de Philosophie de Langue Française* (1996) [Special Issue on Lavelle]; École, Jean, *Louis Lavelle et le renouveau de la métaphysique de l'être au XXe siècle* (Hildesheim: Georg Olms, 1997); Halbwachs, Maurice, "Ma campagne au Collège de France," *Sciences Humaines* 1:1 (1999), pp. 189-229, especially pp. 209-210; Veillard-Baron, Jean-Louis, ed., *Philosophie de l'Esprit* (Hildesheim:Georg Olms, 1999); Ekogha, Thierry, *Liberté et création chez Nicolas Berdiaev et Louis Lavelle* (Lille: ANRT, 2000); Veillard-Baron, Jean-Louis, *La philosophie française* (Paris: Armand Colin, 2000); *Filosofia Oggi* 24:96 (2001) [Special Issue on Louis Lavelle]; École, Jean, *Les grandes notions de la métaphysique lavellienne et son vocabulaire* (Genova: L'arcipelago, 2003); École, Jean, *Louis Lavelle et l'histoire des idées* (Hildesheim: Geog Olms, 2004); *Revue des sciences philosophiques et théologiques* 89 (2004), pp. 219-332 [Special Issue on Lavelle]; Veillard-Baron, Jean-Louis, ed., *Autour de Louis Lavelle* (Paris: Harmattan, 2006); Robert, Sébastien, *La philosophie de Louis Lavelle* (Paris: Harmattan, 2007); Petit, Jean-François, *Histoire de la philosophie française au XXe siècle* (Paris: Desclée De Brouwer, 2009); Capelle, Philippe, ed., *Philosophie et Théologie* (Paris: Le Cerf, 2010), vol. IV.

89   The "Philosophy of the Spirit" series published works by such authors as Aimé Forest (1898-1893), Louis Lavelle (1883-1951), René Le Senne (1882-1954), Gabriel Marcel (1889-1973), Maurice Nédoncelle (1905-1976), and Jacques Paliard (1887-1953).

90   The former forms part of Lavelle's major and four-volume (1837 page) work The Dialectic of the Eternal Present [La Dialectique de l'éternal present]

consisting of *On Being* [*De l'être*] [OBG] (1928; 1932; 1947), *On Act* [*De l'acte*] [OA] (1937; 1946; 1992), *On Time and Eternity* [*Du temps et de l'éternité*] [OTE] (1945), and *On the Human Soul* [*De l'âme humaine*] [OHS] (1951); as well as *On Wisdom* [*De la sagesse*] (1951) [an unfinished manuscript that was to form the last part of his Dialectic of the Eternal Present]. Portions of these works have been translated by Robert Alan Jones, *The Act of Presence: Key Readings from the Philosophy of Louis Lavelle* (Bingil Bay: Robert Alan Jones, 2010). Pagination will be from the English translations unless in brackets indicating it is from the original French editions.

Lavelle wrote several other metaphysical works (indeed the sociologist Georges Davy (1883-1976), who was a student of Lavelle's, called him "Metaphysics Itself") including: *Total Presence* [*La presence totale*] [TP] (1934) [winner of the Prix Charles Levêque from the Academy of Moral and Political Sciences]; *Inaugural Lesson Given at the College de France on December 2, 1941* [*Leçon inaugurale faite au Collège de France le 2 décembre 1941*] [IL] (1942); *Introduction to Ontology* [*Introduction à l'ontologie*] [IO] (1947; 2008); *Reality and the Spirit* (1951) [unfinished manuscript]; *Manuel of the Dialectical Methodology* [*Manuel de méthodologie dialectique*] (1962); *On Existence* [*De l'existence*] (1984) [an unpublished manuscript of 1912 from Limoges].

Lavelle is also famous for his moral works including: *The Consciousness of Self* [*La conscience de soi*] [CS] (1933; 1951; 1993); the aforementioned *The Error of Narcissus* [*L'erreur de Narcisse*] [EN] (1939; 2003) [translated as *The Dilemma of Narcissus*, tr. William Gairdner (New York: Humanities Press, 1973; 1999)]; *Evil and Suffering* [*La mal et la souffrance*] [ES] (1940; 2000) [translated as *Evil and Suffering*, tr. Bernard Murchland (New York: Macmillan, 1963)]; *Speech and Writing* [*La parole et l'écriture*] [SW] (1942; 2005) [winner of the Prix Broquette-Génin of the French Academy]; *The Powers of the Self* [*Les puissances du moi*] [PS] (1948); *Four Saints* [*Quatre Saints; De la sainteté*] [FS] (1951; 1993) [translated as *The Meaning of Holiness* [*Four Saints*], tr. Dorothea O'Sullivan (Notre Dame: University of Notre Dame Press, 1963)]; *Conduct in Regard to the Other* [*Conduite à l'égard d'autrui*] [CRO] (1957); *Rules of Everyday Life* [*Règles de la vie quotidienne*] [REL] (2004). I make use of these translations throughout.

Finally he published a two-volume theoretical ethical work *Treatise of Values* [*Traité des valeurs*], 2 vols. [TV] (1951-1955; 1991). Lavelle also wrote several works on the history of philosophy based on his Chroniques philosophiques for the journal *Le Temps* (1930-1942) including: *French Philosophy between the Two Wars* [*La Philosophie française entre les deux Guerres*] [PBTW] (1942; 2009); *Morality and Religion* [*Morale et religion*] (1960).

Lavelle also wrote several articles including: "Solitude et communion," *Bulletin de l'Association Fénélon* (April, 1934), pp. 1-53; "Être et acte," *Les Études Philosophiques* 9 (December, 1935), pp. 104-108; "La liberté et la personne,"

Bulletin de l'Association Fénélon (April, 1935), pp. 1-41; "Être et acte," *Revue de Métaphysique et de Morale* 43 (April, 1936), pp. 187-210; "Acte réflexif et acte créateur," *Bulletin de la Société Française de Philosophie* 36 (July, 1936), pp. 141-180; "Observations sur le ma et la souffrance," *Bulletin de l'Association Fénélon* (June, 1937), pp. 1-66; "Principes généraux de toute philosophie de la participation," in *Travaux du IXe Congrès International de Philosophie* (Paris: Hermann, 1937), vol. IX, pp. 170-176; "Entretiens sur l'affectivité et la valeur," *Bulletin de l'Association Fénélon* (1938), pp. 1-61; "Remarques sur le thème: Légitimité et signification de la métaphysique," *Études Philosophiques* (April, 1938), pp. 39, 60-64; "De la vertu généra et particulièrement de la vertu de sincérité," *Bulletin de l'Association Fénélon* (1939), pp. 1-63; "La découverte du moi," *Annales de l'École des Hautes Études de Gand* 3 (1939), pp. 65-97; "Réflections philosophiques sur l'Encyclique," *Les Temps* (November 21, 1939); "De l'insertion du moi dans l'être par la distinction de l'acte et de la donnée," *Tijdschrift voor Philosophie* 3 (November, 1941), pp. 713-736; "La métaphysique ou la science de l'intimité spirituelle," *Revue Internationale de Philosophie* 3 (April, 1941), pp. 43-65 [translated as "Metaphysics or the Science of Spiritual Inwardness," ["SSI"], *Philosophy Today* 16 (1972), pp. 66-80]; "L'âme et ses puissances," and "La correspondence entre les different sens et les principales fonctions de la conscience," *Annuaire du Collège de France* 44 (1945), pp. 82-89; "L'existence et la valeur," and "La vue, sens de l'intelligence," *Annuaire du Collège de France* 42 (1945), pp. 81-86; "Formes et degrés de la participation," and "La participation dans la philosophie platonicienne," *Annuaire du Collège de France* 44 (1945), pp. 94-99; "Science et humanisme," *La Nef* 15 (1946), pp. 72-73; "Existence spirituelle et existence matérielle," *Actes du Congrès International de Philosophie* (November, 1946), vol. II, pp. 291-300; "Saint François de Sales ou l'union de la volonté et de l'amour," *Bulletin de l'Association Fénélon* (1946), pp. 1-21; "Anayse de l'être et dissociation de l'essence et de l'existence," *Revue de Métaphysique et de Morale* 52 (July, 1947), pp. 201-227; "Epitomae metaphysicae spirituais," *Giornale di Metafisica* 2 (September, 1947), pp. 37-408; "Être et connaître," and "De Descartes à Malebranche," *Annuaire du Collège de France* 44 (1947), pp. 104-113; "L'église ni la famille ne peuvent absorber l'état," *Giornale di Metafisica* 4 (1949), pp. 597-610; "La liberté comme terme premier," *Giornale di Metafisica* (December, 1949), pp. 597-610; "Les différentes espèces des valeurs," and "La philosohie de Plotin," *Annuaire du Collège de France* 50 (1950), pp. 136-145; "Métaphysique de la participation," in Barone, Francesco, ed., *La mia prospettiva filosofia* (Padova: Nuovo Ciclo, 1950), pp. 123-143; "La relation de l'esprit et du monde," *Actes du Congrès International de Philosophie* 2 (1950), pp. 825-829; "La sagesse comme science de la vie spirituelle," *Actes du Ve Congrès des Sociétés de Philosophie de Langue Française* (September, 1950), pp. 5-11; "Les trois moments de la métaphysique," in Farber, Marvin, *L'Activité Philosophique en France et aux Etats-Unis* (Paris: Presses Universitaires de France, 1950), vol. II, pp. 132-148 [translated as "The Three Stages of Metaphysics," in Farber, Marvin, ed., *Philosophic Thought in France* (Albany: State University of New York Press, 1968), vol. I, pp. 121-135]; "Une solitude ouverte sur tout l'univers," *Archivio di Filosofia* (1950), pp. 9-17; "Comparison du pessimism et de l'optimisme," *Bulletin de l'Association Fénélon* (1951), pp. 1-17; "L'esprit au service au monde ou le monde au service de l'esprit," *Citta di Vitta* 1 (1951), pp. 18-28 [translated as "Spirit in the Service of the World and the World in the Service of Spirit," *Cross Currents* 10 (1960), pp. 221-231]; "Le mal et l'individu," *Atti del Congresso Internazionale di Studi Umanistici* (Milan: Carlo Marzorati, 1951), pp. 265-275; "Donner et Recevoir," *Giornale di Metafisica* 3 (July, 1952), p. 402; "Réflexions sur l'idée de l'homme," *Recherches et Débats* 18 (1952), pp. 3-4; "Grandeur réelle et grandeur apparente," *Bulletin de l'Association Fénélon* (1954), pp. 1-20; "Sur la notion d'existence," *Études Philosophiques* 13 (1958), pp. 3-13; "In the Presence of Being," ["IPB"], in Caponigri, Aloysius Robert, ed., *Modern Catholic Thought* (New York: Harper & Brothers, 1960), pp. 43-64 [a translation of part of Lavelle's *On Being*, IX, pp. 248-284]; "How Being is Encountered," in Drennan, D.A., ed., *A Modern Introduction to Metaphysics* (New York: Free Press of Glencoe, 1963), pp. 240-250; "La destinée," *Études Philosophiques* 3 (1965), pp. 257-280; "Manuel de methodologie dialectique," and "Introduction to Ontology," ["IO"], *Philosophy Today* 9 (1965), pp. 171-189; "L'éternisation," [extract of chapter 3 of unpublished work *La réalité de l'esprit*], *Études Philosophiques* (July, 1983), pp. 257-269; "L'existence des deux mondes," *Revue Philosophique de Louvain* 81 (1983), pp. 5-36 [extract from chapter 2 of the unpublished work *Système de la participation icipation*]; "La intériorité en tant qu'elle déborde le moi," [extract of chapter 3 of unpublished work *Système de la participation*], *Revue Philosophique de la France et de l'Étranger* (January, 1983), pp. 25-47; "De quoi participle-t-on?," and "La participation religieuse," [chapters 8 and 10 of *Système de la participation*], *Filosofia Oggi* (July, 1985), pp. 1-20, 393-408; "La négation et l'absence," and "Le possible et le vouloir," [extracts from chapters 1 and 2 of the unpublished work *La réalité de l'esprit*], in École, Jean, ed., *Louis Lavelle* (Agen: Sociétè Acadèmique de Agen, 1987), pp. 489-553 [chapter one translated as "Negation and Absence," ["NA"], *International Studies in Philosophy* 25 (1993), pp. 37-53]; "La participation créatrice," and "La participation morale," [chapters 5 and 9 of *Système de la participation*], *Presenca filosofica* (January, 198), pp. 18-83. Lavelle also gave a radio interview in 1937. Some of these essays have been collected as *Of Spiritual Intimacy* [*De l'intimité spirituelle*] [OSI] (1955).

For a Bibliography of Lavelle see: École, Jean, *La métaphysique de l'être dans la philosophie de Louis Lavelle* (Louvain: Nauwelaerts, 1957), pp. 259-293; École, Jean, ed., *Louis Lavelle* (Agen: Société académique d'Agen, 1987), pp. 491-553. There is a Fonds Louis Lavalle, Collège de France. For a list of some of his posthumous works including *Bienheureuse solitude*, "Dieu," *De l'existence* (c. 1912), *Le langage ou le verbe de Dieu, La mort et le sacrifice, La réalité de l'esprit* (1950), *Système de la participation* (1950), *La religion métaphysique, De la sagesse* (1950), *Spiritualité et religion, Style et pensée*, see École, Jean, *Louis Lavelle et le renouveau de la métaphysique de l'être au XXe siècle* (Hildesheim: Georg Olms

Verlag, 1997), pp. 48-49. The Association Louis Lavelle has also published several unpublished philosophical fragments online and in their *Bulletin*.

91 Lavelle is clear, however, that God transcends the world and so is not a pantheist even if his language sometimes suggests such an interpretation. For as he puts it, participation does not have as its goal the extinction of the part in the whole but rather the formation of a spiritual society among the parts and the whole (OA, 1937, p. 165). So though being is instated in the I from the start, being surpasses our thinking (TP, I, pp. 9-11). For according to Lavelle, and following Blondel, there is an interval or gap separating our being from God. God is absolute act (the total presence of Being; realizing element) but humans are participated acts (light and shadow; realized element) (OA, I, 1, pp. 48-49, 53, 55; I, 7, pp. 74-75, 78; I, 8, pp. 96, 99; I, 9, p. 104; II, 18, p. 155; OTE, III, 7, pp. 181, 190).

92 Lavelle is justly famous for two other ideas of his. The first is that we find our destiny and God in all the moments of life, for all instants are opportunities for consent to being (TP, I, pp. 18-19; II, p. 30; OA, I, 9, p. 106; II, 12, p. 148; FS, Introduction, pp. 2-6; CS, V, 5, pp. [104-106]; EN, IV, 1, pp. 77-78). He argues:"We must not despise all those little events which, though fleeting, nevertheless fill the passing hours of each day, all those incidents of our daily life which leave no trace behind and awaken no echo. Our whole being is wholly involved in them; they are the only ones which have a full and lively meaning for us, and which, indeed, enable us at every moment to establish contact with the absolute. If every man could fix his attention upon them and devote himself entirely to them, there would be no further need of the important schemes by which we seek to change the face of the earth. It would be changed without our intervention" (EN, X, 5, p. 181). Or again"It is extremely dangerous to imagine that our vocation is something remote and extraordinary, for it is, in fact, always familiar and close at hand, hidden from our sight beneath the commonest circumstances in which life has placed us. Each of us must recognize his own in the tasks which come his way, not despising them, or seeking some mysterious destiny which he will never find" (EN, VII 5, 7, pp. 128-129).

The last is his optimism, indeed he often remarked that the most beautiful word in language was Yes [*Oui*]. Or in a famous quote:"Love is like a return to the very source of our existence. It is the perfection of our will, the point where our will reaches its fulfillment and is dissolved in the will of God. ... We need not be surprised to find that in its own development the will must endeavor to elicit love; that its sole task must be to increase the measure of its love; it must do nothing save for love, and all its labor and even death must proceed from love. But how can the will elicit love unless it first receives it in the form of grace? Love is only another name for grace itself to which the will needs only to consent. Will is the only road leading us from nature to grace. ... With love it must be all or nothing. Love knows neither prisoners nor slaves.

It is an infinity whose possession is always beyond us and which ought to fill us not with uneasiness but with admiration. As each new day dawns we ought to feel a thrill of joy at the thought of yet another day in which to love God" (FS, Conclusion, pp. 112-113; cf. TV, vol. I, II, 7, pp. [718-724]).

93   For more on the life and thought of Marcel see: RCSM (1938), pp. 55-61; CAP (1955), pp. 94-95; SHP (1955), p. 940; RPC (1956), pp. 176-180; CRHP (1957), pp. 482-484; HHP (1959), vol. II, pp. 631-632; CMCT (1960), pp. 109-123; PM (1960), vol. II, pp. 398-444; CEP (1961), pp. 180-184; PFA (1963), pp. 67-80; PTCW (1964), pp. 243-253, 421-444; TCT (1965), pp. 107-130; HYP (1966), pp. 488-490; PPF (1966), pp. 124-130; RP (1966), pp. 374-381, 807-808; MHP (1967), pp. 438-439; TPC (1967), pp. 395-399; RPF (1968), pp. 176-180; BHP (1969), vol. VII, p. 258; TCP (1969), pp. 135-140; HWP (1971), vol. V, pp. 276-285; CHP (1974), vol. IX, pp. 327-339; PFPM (1977), pp. 141-151; CHAD (1979), vol. VIII, pp. 403-407; LCN (1984), pp. 97-125; CTIC (1985), pp. 206-219; PHP (1988), pp. 362-363; TCRT (1988), pp. 360-362; CEWP (1989), p. 190; CP (1990), vol. III, pp. 411-437; WE (1991), pp. 209-213, 329-343; BBKL (1993), vol. V, pp. 761-769; DP (1993), vol. II, pp. 1910-1918; ATH (1994), p. 137; EMCT (1995), p. 359; TCFC (1995), pp. 224-225; BDTC (1996), pp. 506-507; TCFP (1996), pp. 46-57; EEP (1997), pp. 431-434; LTK (1997), vol. VI, pp. 1298-1299; CCP (1998), pp. 340-346; REP (1998), vol. VI, pp. 91-93; PCHP (1999), p. 718; RPFR (1999), pp. 30-33; MCT (2000), vol. II, pp. 138-140, 200; TEP (2000), pp. 146-150, 236-237; FPTC (2001), pp. 98-102; PAMP (2002), pp. 269-288; CAHP (2003), pp. 466-468, 792; NCE (2003), vol. IX, pp. 133-135; WPR (2003), pp. 319-322; EMFT (2004), pp. 453-456; ACP (2005), pp. 345-349; EP (2005), vol. V, pp. 699-703; OGP (2005), p. 554; EF (2006), vol. VII, pp. 6993-6997; TWFP (2006), pp. 163-165, 253-254; De Corte, Marcel, La philosophie de Gabriel Marcel (Paris: Téqui, 1938); Bénisti, Edmond, La main de l'écrivain (Paris: Stock, 1939), p. 113; Gilson, Étienne, ed., Existentialisme Chrétien: Gabriel Marcel (Paris: Plon, 1947); Troisfontaines, Roger, À la rencontre de Gabriel Marcel (Paris: La Sixaine, 1947); Chenu, Joseph, Le théâtre de Gabriel Marcel et sa signification métaphysique (Paris: Aubier, 1948); Grene, Marjorie, Dreadful Freedom: A Critique of Existentialism (Chicago: University of Chicago Press, 1948), pp. 122-140; Ricoeur, Paul, Gabriel Marcel et Karl Jaspers (Paris: Éditions du Temps present, 1948); Mounier, Emmanuel, Existentialist Philosophies (New York: Briston, 1951); Bernard, Michel, La philosophie religieuse de Gabriel Marcel (Le Puy: Cahiers du nouvel humanisme, 1952); Blackham, Harold, Six Existentialist Thinkers (New York: Macmillan, 1952), pp. 66-85; Collins, James, The Existentialists (Chicago: Henry Regnery, 1952), pp. 128-167; Prini, Pietro, Gabriel marcel et la méthodologie de l'invérifiable (Paris: Desclée de Brouwer, 1953); Troisfontaines, Roger, De l'existence à l'être: La philosophie de Gabriel Marcel, 2 vols. (Namur: Nauwelaerts, 1953); Copleston, Frederick, Contemporary Philosophy (Westminster: Newman, 1956), pp. 106-113; Michalson, Carl,

Christianity and the Existentialists (New York: Charles Scribiner's Sons, 1956), pp. 76-80; Bagot, Jean-Pierre, *Connaissance et amour: Essai sur la philosophie de Gabriel Marcel* (Paris: Beauchesne, 1958); Davy, Marie-Madelaine, *Un philosophe itinerant: Gabriel Marcel* (Paris: Flammarion, 1959); Schalden-brand, Mary, *Phenomenologies of Freedom: An Essay on the Philosophies of Jean-Paul Sartre and Gabriel Marcel* (Washington: Catholic University of America Press, 1960); Ralston, Zachary, *Gabriel Marcel's Paradoxical Expression of Mystery* (Washington: Catholic University of America Press, 1961); Galla-gher, Kenneth, *The Philosophy of Gabriel Marcel* (New York: Fordham Univer-sity Press, 1962); Tilliette, Xavier, *Philosophes contemporains: Gabriel Marcel, Maurice Merleau-Ponty, Karl Jaspers* (Paris: Desclée de Brouwer, 1962); Seymour, Cain, *Gabriel Marcel* (New York: Hillary House, 1963); Ewijk, Thomas, *Gabriel Marcel* (Glen Rock: Paulist Press, 1965); Miceli, Vincent, *Ascent to Being: Gabriel Marcel's Philosophy of Communion* (New York: Desclee, 1965); Parain-Vial, Jean, ed., *Gabriel Marcel et les niveaux de l'expérience* (Paris: Seghers, 1966); Keen, Sam, *Gabriel Marcel* (Richmond: John Knox Press, 1967); O'Malley, John, *The Fellowship of Being: An Essay on the Concept of Person in the Philosophy of Gabriel Marcel* (The Hague: Martinus Nijhoff, 1967); Widmer, Charles, *Gabriel Marcel et le théisme existential* (Paris: Cerf, 1971); Clyde, Pax, *An Existential Approach to God: A Study of Gabriel Marcel* (The Nague: Martinus Nijhoff, 1972); Chiari, Joseph, *Twentieth-Century French Thought* (New York: Gordian Press, 1975); Plourde, Simonne, *Gabriel Marcel, philosophe et témoin de l'espérance* (Montreal: University of Quebec Press, 1975); Boutang, Pierre, *Gabriel Marcel* (Paris: J.M. Place, 1977); Wall, Barbara, *Love and Death in the Philosophy of Gabriel Marcel* (Washington: University Press of America, 1977); McDown, Joe, *Availability: Gabriel Marcel and the Phenomenology of Human Openness* (Missoula: Scholars Press, 1978); Burr, John, ed., *Handbook of World Philosophy* (Westport: Greenwood Press, 1980), pp. 33-97; Gillman, Neil, *Gabriel Marcel on Religious Knowledge* (Wash-ington: University Press of America, 1980); Nseka, Ngimbi, *Tragique et inter-subjectivité dans la philosophie de Gabriel Marcel* (Kinshasa: Inkisi, 1981); *Bulletin de la Société Française de Philosophie* (January 28, 1984), pp. 32-63 [Special Issue on Marcel]; Ledure, Yves, *Lectures chrétiennes de Nietzsche: Maurras, Papini, Scheler, de Lubac, Marcel, Mounier* (Paris: Cerf, 1984); Schlipp, Paul, ed., *The Philosophy of Gabriel Marcel* (La Salle: Open Court, 1984); Davignon, René, *Le mal chez Gabriel Marcel* (Paris: Cerf, 1985); Plourde, Simone, *Vocabulaire philosophique de Gabriel Marcel* (Paris: Cerf, 1985); Applebaum, David, *Contact and Attention: The Anatomy of Gabriel Marcel's Metaphysical Method* (Lanham: University Press of America, 1987); Busch, Thomas, *Gabriel Marcel on Existence, Being, and Immortality* (Wash-ington: Catholic University of America Press, 1987); Hanley, Katharine, Rose, *Dramatic Approaches to Creative Fidelity: A Study in the Theater and Philosophy of Gabriel Marcel* (Lanham: University Press of America, 1987); Peccorini Letona, Francisco, *Selfhood as Thinking Thought in the Work of Gabriel Marcel*

(Lewiston: Edward Mellen Press, 1987); Traub, Donald, *Toward a Fraternal Society: A Study of Gabriel Marcel's Approach to Being, Technology, and Intersubjectivity* (New York: Peter Lang, 1988); Cooney, William, ed., *Contributions of Gabriel Marcel to Philosophy* (Lewiston: Edward Mellen Press, 1989); Parain-Vial, Jeanne, *Gabriel Marcel: Un veilleur et un eveilleur* (Lausanne: L'Âge d'homme, 1989); Konickal, Joseph, *Being and My Being: Gabriel Marcel's Metaphysics of Incarnation* (New York: Peter Lang, 1992); Moran, Denis, *Gabriel Marcel : Existentialist Philosopher, Dramatist, Educator* (Lanham: University Press of America, 1992); Randall, Albert, *The Mystery of Hope in the Philosophy of Gabriel Marcel, 1888-1973* (Lewiston: Edward Mellen Press, 1992); Kearney, Richard, ed., *Twentieth-Century Continental Philosophy* (London: Routledge, 1994), pp. 131-174; *Bulletin de la Société Américaine de Philosophie de Langue Française* 7 (1995) [Special Issue on Marcel]; Cain, Seymour, *Gabriel Marcel's Theory of Religious Experience* (New York: Peter Lang, 1995); Kipoy, Pombo, *L'esperance et l'immortalité: Étude sur l'ontologie intersubjective chez Gabriel Marcel* (Rome: Urbiana University Press, 1999); Fouilloux, Étienne, ed., *Un intellectuel en son siècle: Gabriel Marcel* (Paris: Présence de Gabriel Marcel, 2001); Bouëssée, Jol, *Du côté de chez Gabriel Marcel* (Lausanne: Age d'homme, 2003); Anderson, Thomas, *A Commentary on Gabriel Marcel's The Mystery of Being* (Milwaukee: Marquette University Press, 2006); Tilliette, Xavier, *L'église des philosophes: De Nicolas de Cuse à Gabriel Marcel* (Paris: Cerf, 2006); Treanor, Brian, *Aspects of Alterity: Levinas, Marcel, and the Contemporary Debate* (New York: Fordham University Press, 2006); Sweetman, Brendan, *The Vision of Gabriel Marcel* (New York: Rodopi, 2008).

94   This work has been translated by G.S. Fraser and René Hague as *The Mystery of Being* [MOB] (Chicago: Henry Regnery, 1960), 2 vols. I use this translation and others below throughout.

Marcel's other philosophical and literary critical writings include: *Journal Métaphysique, 1913-1923* (1927; 1935) [translated as *Metaphysical Journal* [MJ], tr. Barbara Wall (Chicago: Henry Regnery, 1952); *Being and Having* [*Être et avoir*] [BH] (1935) [translated as *Being and Having*, tr. Katharine Farrer (Westminster: Dacre Press, 1949)]; *From Refusal to Invocation* [*Du refus à l'invocation*; also titled *Essai de philosophie concrète*] (1940; 1967) [translated as *Creative Fidelity* [CF], tr. Robert Rosthal, New York: Farrar, Strauss, 1964)]; *Homo Viator: Prolegomena to a Metaphysics of Hope* [HV] (1944; 1963) [a collection of lectures] [translated by Emma Craufurd as *Homo Viator* (Chicago: Henry Regnery, 1951)]; *On the Ontological Mystery* [*Position et approches concrètes du mystère ontologique*] (1949; 1995) [translated by Manya Harari as *The Philosophy of Existence* [PE] (London: Harvill Press, 1949), pp. 9-46, and republished as *The Philosophy of Existentialism* (New York: Citadel Press, 1961); *Recherche de la famille* (1949); *Humans against Humanity* [*Les hommes contra l'humain*] (1951) [translated as *Man against Mass Society* [MMS], tr.

G.S. Fraser (Chicago: Henry Regnery, 1952)]; *The Decline of Wisdom* [*Le déclin de la sagesse*] (1954) [translated as *The Decline of Wisdom* (New York: Philosophical Library, 1955)]; *The Problematic Human* [*L'homme problématique*] (1955) [translated by Brian Thompson as *Problematic Man* [PH] [New York: Herder and Herder, 1967)]; *The Influence of Psychic Phenomena on My Philosophy* (1956) [Frederich W.H. Myers lecture of 1955]; *Un changement d'espérance à la rencontre du réarmement moral* (1958) [translated as *Fresh Hope for the World*, tr. Helen Harding (London: Longmans, 1960)]; *Presence and Immortality* [*Présence et immortalité*] [PI] (1959) [translated by Michael Machado as *Presence and Immortality* (Pittsburg: Duquesne University Press, 1967)]; *Fragments Philosophiques 1909-1914* [PF] (1961) [translated by Lionel Blain as *Philosophical Fragments, 1909-1914* (Notre Dame: University of Notre Dame Press, 1965)]; *The Existential Background of Human Dignity* [*La dignité humaine et ses assises existentielles*] [EBHD] (1963) [William James Lectures at Harvard University in 1961-1962]; *The Sacred in a Technological Age* (1963) [speech given in 1963 at Gonzaga University]; *Auf der Suche nach Wahrheit und Gerechtigkeit* (1964) [Speeches given at Freiburg University 1959-1965; translated as *Searchings* [SCH] (new York:Paul Press, 1967)]; *Der Philosoph und der Friede* (1964) [German Addresses]; *Man before the Death of God* (1966) [lecture given at the College of St. Catherine in St. Paul Minnesota in 1965]; *Toward a Tragic Wisdom* [*Pour une sagesse tragique*] [TWB] (1968) [translated as *Tragic Wisdom and Beyond*, tr. Stephen Jolin and Peter McCormick (Evanston: Northwestern Univerrsity Press, 1973)]; *En chemin, vers quel éveil?* (1971) [Marcel's autobiography; translated as *Awakenings*, tr. Peter Rogers, Milwaukee: Marquette University Press, 2002)]; *L'existence et la liberté humaine chez Jean-Paul Sartre* (1981); *Tu ne mourras pas* (2005) [a collection of articles; translated as *Thou Shall Not Die* (South Bend: St. Augustine's Press, 2008)].

Collections of Marcel's writings include those by Parain-Vial, Jeanne, *Gabriel Marcel et les niveux de l'experience* (Paris: P. Seghers, 1966); Busch, Thomas, ed., *The Participant Perspective: A Grabriel Marcel Reader* (Lanham: University Press of America, 1987); Sweetman, Brendan, *Gabriel Marcel Reader* (South Bank: St. Augustine's Press, 2010).

Marcel's philosophical articles include: "Existence et objectivité," *Revue de métaphysique et de morale* 32 (1925), pp. 175-195; "Médiation de Gabriel Marcel en réponse à une enquête sur Dieu," *Philosophie* (January-March, 1925), pp. 607-610; "À propos de l'Esprit," *Bulletin de l'union pour la verité* (May, 1926); "Fragments de Journal Métaphysique," *Europe* (January 15, 1926); "Fragments du Journal Métaphysique," *La ligne de coeur* (June, 1926); "Séance sur la querelle de l'athéisme," *Bulletin de la Société Française de Philosophie* (1928); "Carence de la spiritualité," *Nouvelle Revue Française* (March, 1929), pp. 375-379 [translated as "Death of Spirituality," tr. Angelo Bertocci, in O'Brien, Justin, ed., *An Image of the Twentieth-Century from the Pages of the*

Nouvelle Revue Française (New York: Farrar, Straus, and Cudahy, 1958)];"Dieu et la culture morale," *Bulletin de l'Union des libres penseurs et des libres croyants* (February, 1929); "Remarques sur l'irréligion contemporaine," *La Nouvelle Revue des Jeunes* (November 15, 1931); "Sur l'idée du philosophe," *Bulletin de l'union pour la verité* (December, 1932); "Esquisse d'une phénomenologie de l'avoir," *Recherches Philosophiques* (1933); "Position et approches concrètes du mystère ontologique," in *Le monde cassé* (Paris: Desclée de Brouwer, 1933) [translated as "Concrete Approaches to Investigating the Ontological Mystery," in *The Broken World* (Milwaukee: Marquette University Press, 1998)]; "Remarques sur les notions d'acte et de personne," *Recherches Philosophiques* (1934);"Réflexions sur la foi," *La Vie Nouvelle* (October 20, 1934);"De l'espérance," *Études* (April 20, 1935);"Note sur la fidélité," *La Vie Intellectuelle* (March 15, 1935), pp. 287-301;"Aperçus phénoménologiques sur l'être en situation," *Recherches Philosophiques* (1936); "De l'opinion à la foi," *La Vie Intellectuelle* (November 15, 1937); "Subjectivité et transcendance," *Bulletin de la Société Française de Philosophie* 37 (1937), pp. 172-182; "Le transcendant comme métaproblématique," *Travaux du IXe Congrès International de Philosophie* (Paris: Congrès Descartes, 1937); "Ebauche d'une philosophie concrète," *Recherches de Science Religeuses* (April, 1938); "L'Être incarné," in Bachelard, Gaston, ed., *Études Philosophiques* (Gand: L'École des Hautes Études, 1939); "La fidélité créatrice," *Revue Internationale de Philosophie* (October 15, 1939): "Méditation sur l'idée de preuve de l'existence de Dieu," *Le Semeur* (February, 1939);"Notes pour une philosophie du risque," *La Vie Réelle* (1939);"Réponse à une enquête sur l'enseignement de la religion naturelle," *Esprit* 9 (1941), pp. 236-238; "Moi et autrui," *Cité Nouvelle* (April 10, 1942); "Journal Métaphysique," *Confluences* (January, 1943); Le mystère familial," *Revue des Jeunes* (January-February, 1943); "Le vœu créateur comme essence de la paternité," *Chronique Sociale de France* (March-April, 1944); "Spectroscopie de la trahison," *Temps Présent* (September 1, 1944); "Hierarchie des fidélités," *Temps Présent* (September 15, 1944);"Autour de Heideger," *Dieu Vivant* 13 (August, 1945);"Devoir du philosophe," *Temps Présent* (August 24, 1945);"Il n'est pas mort pour nous: Phrase d'Albert Camus," *Temps Présent* (January 19, 1945); "Le phénomène Sartre," *Temps Présent* (November 9, 1945);"Le refus du salut et l'exaltation de l'homme absurde," *La Table Ronde* (March, 1945); "Responsabilités," *Eaux Vives* (September, 1945); "La science inhumaine," *Terre des Hommes* (December 8, 1945);"Existence et liberté," *Ombre et Lumière* (May, 1946); "L'existence et la liberté humaine chez J.-P. Sartre," in George, André, ed., *Les grands appels de l'homme contemporain* (Paris: Temps Présent, 1946), pp. 113-170;"Philosophie de l'épuration," *La Nouvelle Relève* (1946);"Le sens du profond," *Fontaine* (April, 1946);"Science et humanisme," *La Nef* (February, 1946); "Le témoignage comme localisation de l'existentiel," *Bulletin de la Société de Philosophie de Bordeaux* (March, 1946) [translated as "Testimony and Existentialism," in *The Philosophy of Existence*, tr. Manya Harari (London: Harvill Press, 1949), pp. 91-103];"Un existentialisme tonque," *Diogène* (April,

1946 "Regard en arrière," in Gilson, Étienne, ed., *Existentialisme chrétien* (Paris: Plon, 1947), pp. 291-319 [translated as " Essay in Autobiography," in Harari, Manya, ed., *The Philosophy of Existence* (New York: The Philosophical Library, 1949), pp. 104-110]; "L'audace en métaphysique," in *Revue de Métaphysique et de Morale* 52 (1947), pp. 233-243; "Désaccord avec Mounier," *Carrefour* (October 22, 1947); "Don et liberté," *Giornale di metafisica* (November, 1947); "Existentialisme et pensée chrétienne," *Témoignages* 13 (May, 1947), pp. 157-169; "Réfutation de J.-P. Sartre," *Ici-France* (September 18, 1947); "Note pour une métaphysique de l'acte de charité," *Jeunesse de l'Église* (May, 1948); "Pessimisme et conscience eschatologique," *Dieu Vivant* 16 (1948); "Pour une définition de l'homme de bonne volonté," *Les Cahiers des Hommes de Bonne Volonté* 1 (April, 1948); "Problème et mystère," *Revue de Paris* (July 7, 1948); "L'aventure technocratique," *La France Catholique* (April 8, 1949); "L'esprit d'abstraction comme facteur de guerre," *Cahiers du Monde Nouveau* (December, 1949); "Existentialisme et humanisme," *Archivio di Filosofia* 18 (1949), pp. 17-20; "L'homme et les techniques," *La France Catholique* (April 1, 1949); "Ontologie et axiologie," in Castelli, Enrico, ed., *Esistenzialismo cristiano* (Padua: Editoria Liviana, 1949), pp. 16-33; "The Malady of the Age: A Fanaticized Conscience," *Dublin Review* 1 (1950), pp. 1951; "Y a-t-il une nature humaine?," *Recherches et Débats* (1950); "Sartre, Anouilh et le problème de Dieu," *La Nouvelle Revue Canadienne* 1 (September-October, 1951), pp. 30-38; "Structure de l'espérance," *Dieu Vivant* 19 (1951); "L'homme moderne est-il libre?," in *L'Église et la liberté* (Paris: P. Horay, 1952)]; "Méditation sur la musique dans ma pensée," *Revue Musicale* (November, 1952); "Le primat de l'existentiel," *Actas del Primer Congreso Nacional de Filosofía* (Argentina: Universidad Nacional de Cuyo, 1949), vol. II, pp. 408-415; "Theism and Personal Relationships," *Cross Currents* 1:1 (1950), pp. 35-42; "Remarques sur la dépersonnalisation de la médicine," *La France Catholique* (January 18, 1952); "Notes pour une philosophie de l'amour," *Revue de Métaphysique et de Morale* 59 (1954), pp. 374-379; "Réponse à une enquête sur l'idée de Dieu," *Age Nouveau* 90 (1955), pp. 3-103; "L'athéisme philosophique et la dialectique de la conscience religieuse," in Mauris, Édouard, ed., *L'Athéisme contemporaine* (Geneva: Éditions Labor et Fides, 1956), pp. 67-92; "L'influence des phénomènes psychiques sur ma philosophie," *Revue Françaises de Recherches Métapsychiques* 1:3 (July, 1956); "Témoin de l'absolu," in Davy, Marie, ed., *Simone Weil* (Paris: Éditions Universitaires, 1956); "Behaviorisme et dualisme," *Bulletin de la Société Française de Philosophie* (January-March, 1957); "Universal against the Masses," in Burnett, Whit, ed., *This Is My Philosophy* (New York: Harper, 1957); "Vers une ontologie concrète," in Febvre, Lucien, ed., *Encyclopédie Française* (Paris: Société Nouvelle de L'Encyclopédie Française, 1957), pp. 2-6; "Aperçus phénoménologique sur la fidélité," in Beirnaert, Louis, ed., *Qu'est-ce que vouloir?* (Paris: Cerf, 1958), pp. 39-49; "Le crépuscule du sens commun," in *La Dimension Florestan* (Paris: Plon, 1958); "Dieu et la causalité," in Le Blond, Jean-Marie, ed., *De la connaissance de Dieu* (Paris: Desclée de

Brouwer, 1958), pp. 27-33 [translated as "God and Causality," in Leibrecht, Walter, ed., *Religion and Culture* (New York: Harper, 1959), pp. 211-235]; "Fragments du Journal métaphysique," in Castelli, Enrico, ed., *La Diriaristica Filosofica* (Padua: CEDAM, 1959); "Esquisse d'une problématique de la tolérance religieuse," *Choisi* (November, 1959); "Mystère et existence," in *Le Mystère* (Paris: Pierre Horay, 1959), pp. 197-202; "What Can One Expect of Philosophy?," *Irish Studies* 48 (Summer, 1959), pp. 151-162; "Authentic Humanness and Its Existential and Primordial Assumptions," in Schwartz, Balduin, ed., *The Human Person and the World of Values* (New York: Fordham University Press, 1960), pp. 82-96; "Contemporary Atheism and the Religious Mind," *Philosophy Today* 4 (Winter, 1960), pp. 252-262; "My Life," in Caponigri, Aloysius, ed., *Modern Catholic Thinkers* (New York: Harper, 1960), pp. 109-123; "Vérité et liberté," in Jolivet, Régis, ed., *La Philosophie et ses problèmes* (Lyons: Vitte, 1960), pp. 245-260 [translated as "Truth and Freedom," *Philosophy Today* 9 (Winter, 1965), pp. 227-237]; "Un septuagénaire cherche à voir clair," *Réalités* (January, 1960); "Participation," and "My Death and Myself," *Review of Existential Psychology and Psychiatry* 2 (1962), pp. 94-116; "Philosophical Atheism," *International Philosophical Quarterly* 2 (1962), pp. 501-514; "The Sacred in the Technological Age," *Theology Today* 19 (April, 1962), pp. 27-38; "On the Concept of Love and Peace: An Exchange of Letters between Daisetz T. Suzuki and Dr. Gabriel Marcel," *France-Asie* (January-April, 1963); "The Philosopher Meets the Scientist," *Philosophy Today* 8 (Fall, 1964), pp. 173-175; "Some Reflections on Existentialism," *Philosophy Today* 8 (Winter, 1964), pp. 248-257; "Dieu n'est pas une idole," *Janus* (February-March, 1965); "Philosophie négative, théologie, athéisme," *Wissenschaft und Weltbilde* (March, 1966); "Solipsism Surmounted," in Rouner, Leroy, ed., *Philosophy, Religion, and the Coming World Civilization* (The Hague: Martinus Nijhoff, 1966), pp. 23-31; "Le Viol de l'intimité et le dépérissement des valeurs" in *Le fondement des droits de l'homme* (Florence: La Nuova Italia, 1966); "Desire and Hope," in Lawrence, Nathaniel, et al., eds., *Readings in Existential Phenomenology* (Englewood Cliffs: Prentice-Hall, 1967), pp. 277-285; "I and Thou," in Schlipp, Paul Arthur, ed., *The Philosophy of Martin Buber* (LaSalle: Open Court, 1967); "Intersubjectivity," in Matson, Floyd, et al., eds., *The Human Dialogue* (New York: Free Press, 1967); "Remarques pour une problématique de la foi," *La Table Ronde* (December, 1967-January, 1968); "La foi aujourd'hui," *Cahiers de La Table Ronde* (1968); "La dominante existentielle dans mon oeuvre," in Klibansky, Raymond, ed., *Contemporary Philosophy* (Florence: La Nuova Italia, 1969), vol. III, pp. 171-176; "Mon temps et moi," in Hersch, Jeanne, et al., eds., *Entretiens sur le temps* (Paris: Mouton, 1967), pp. 11-19; "Mon testament philosophique," *Revue de Métaphysique et de Morale* 74 (July-September, 1969), pp. 25-262; "Le mystère Marivaux," *Les Nouvelles Littéraires* (October 30, 1969); "Le préternaturel chez Padre Pio et sa portée pour le philosophe," *Ecclésia* (September, 1969); "Un homme vieillissant livré aux femmes," *Les Cahiers Littéraires de l'O.R.T.F.* (January 19-February 1, 1969);

"L'éclipse des valeurs fondamentales," *France Catholique* (November 13, 1970); "Esquisse d'une méditation sur l'essence et le destin de l'homme," *Mainichi* (May, 1970); "Hommage à Gabriel Marcel," *Revue de Métaphysique et de Morale* (June, 1970 "Mauvaise conscience ou mal-être," *Nouvelle Table Ronde* (May, 1970); "Remarques sur l'avenir de la médecin," *Tribuna Medica* (January 5, 1970); "À la recherche de l'humain dans l'homme," *L'Homme Nouveau* (May 16, 1971); "Allocution pour le colloque précédant l'Assemblée des silencieux de l'Église," *Carrefour* (November 17, 1971); "Le courage et l'esprit," in Casanova, Jean-Claude, ed., *Science et conscience de la société* (Paris: Calmann-Lévy, 1971), vol. II, pp. 525-541; "Du fond des catacombes," *Le Figaro* (April 14, 1971); "Réflexions sur le couple," *L'A.B.C.* (February 14, 1971); "Une expérience qui fut une clé," in Ebon, Martin, ed., *Communication avec les morts* (Paris: Fayard, 1971); "Vaincre la peur," *La France Catholique* (October 15, 1971); "L'âme de la culture," *Les Nouvelles Littéraires* (July 17, 1972); "L'homme et sa mort," in Rémond, René, ed., *Maîtraiser la vie* (Paris: Desclée de Brouwer, 1972), pp. 155-186; "Note sur l'attestation créatrice dans mon oeuvre," in Castelli, Enrico, ed., *La testimonianza* (Padua: CEDAM, 1972), pp. 531-534; "Commentaires des réponses données par Gabriel Marcel," *Revue de Métaphysique et de Morale* 79 (July-September, 1974); "Notres sur le mal," *Revue de Métaphysique et de Morale* 79 (July-September, 1974), pp. 402-408; "Vers un humanisme théocentrique," and "Vingt et une lettres inédites de Gabriel Marcel et Charles du Bos," in Leleu, Michèle, ed., *Cahiers Charles du Bos* (May, 1974); "La liberté en 1971," *Études Philosophiques* 30 (January-March, 1975), pp. 7-17; "De la recherche philosophique," in Belay, Marcel, ed., *Entretiens autour de Gabriel Marcel* (Paris: Diffusion Payot, 1976); "An Autobiographical Essay," in *The Philosophy of Gabriel Marcel*, Schlipp, Philip, ed., (La Salle: Open Court, 1984), pp. 1-68; "Science and Wisdom," in *Bulletin de la société américaine de philosophie de langue française* 7 (1995); "The Structure of Hope," *Communio* 23 (1996), pp. 604-611. Marcel also wrote a negative review of Maritain's work in the *Reveu des jeunes* which never saw the light of day after he agreed to squelch its publication upon Maritain's request. Some of the above essays have been translated and collected as Cooney, William, ed., *Contributions of Gabriel Marcel to Philosophy: A Collection of Essays* (Lewiston: Edward Mellen Press, 1989).

Marcel was equally famous for the many plays he wrote including: *Un homme de Dieu* (1925; 1950); *Trois pièces: La regard neuf, Le mort de demain, La chapelle ardente* (1931; 1950) [translated in *Three Plays* below]; *Le monde cassé* (1933) [translated as *The Broken World and the Rebellious Heart* (West Hartford: The McAuley Institute of Religious Studies, 1974) and as *The Broken World* (Milwaukee: Marquette University Press, 1998)]; *Rome n'est plus dans Rome* (1951); *Croissez et multipliez* (1955) [initially censored by the Archbishop of Paris and the Vatican]. See the translation *Three Plays: A Man of God, Ariadne, and the Funeral Pyre* (New York: Hill and Wang, 1958).

Marcel also wrote reviews of philosophical works and critiques of drama and music for French journals.

For a Bibliography of the writings of Marcel see: Lapointe, François, "Bibliography on Gabriel Marcel," *Modern Schoolman* 49 (1971), pp. 23-49; Lapointe, François, and Claire Lapointe, eds. *Gabriel Marcel and His Critics: An International Bibliography, 1928-1976* (New York: Garland Publishing, 1977); Schlipp, Paul, ed., *The Philosophy of Gabriel Marcel* (La Salle: Open Court, 1984), pp. 585-610.

Some of Marcel's unpublished works reside at the Gabriel Marcel Archives at the Harry Ransom Center at the University of Texas and at the Fonds Gabriel Marcel at the Bibliotheque Nationale in Paris.

95   So for Marcel truth goes beyond an adequation of thing and intellect, and a universally effective smelting procedure, a visual recording apparatus, a poll of the majority. Rather truth is actively being open to receive knowledge, to welcome knowledge, to allow access to reality's revelation of itself, the "sting of reality" (MOB, vol. I, Introduction, pp. 12-14; II, pp. 23-24; III, pp. 65-69; IV, pp. 70-72, 76, 79-87; V, p. 102; VI, pp. 144-150; VII, pp. 156-159, 167; VIII, pp. 185-186).

96   Thus according to Marcel the human is a mysterious union of body and soul, a soul incarnate, a body-subject (a sympathetic mediation of soul and body) (MOB, vol. II, II, p. 28; VIII, p. 142; CF, I, p. 26). For I have my own presence to myself, and I experience my conscious self as bound to a body which is mine and is not an object or instrument. So I can say 'I am my body,' (but I wouldn't say 'I am my bicycle or spade or watch'). For I possess it and it belongs to me and is uniquely experienced by me, though I am not identical with it and I and my body cannot be reduced to an object or instrument (for my body exists for an I) (MOB, vol. I, IV, p. 82; V, pp. 113-124; VI, p. 127; PE, I, p. 19; BH, I, pp. 9-12, 87-88, 108; II, pp. 156, 158, 162-164; CF, I, pp. 17-20, 22-23; VIII, p. 169; EBHD, II, pp. 45-47; PI, VIII, pp. 233-235; MJ, pp. 333-334).

97   Marcel notes here that critis will say that a Christian sacrifice which is inspired by the hope of recompense thereby ceases to be a sacrifice (BH, I, n. 1 on pp. 88-90). To which he replies: "But how false and how shallow is the psychology which represents the sacrifice of a believer as the result of a calculation! Such sacrifice is carried on the stream as it were, of hope and love" (BH, I, n. 1 on p. 89).

98   Marcel does not completely reject the classical proofs for God. Indeed he argues that they are not sophistical and that distinguished philosophers have continually produced and attempted to revamp these proofs. Moreover, they do express something essential about the cosmos even if incompletely. Yet on the other hand, Marcel argues that they have limitations (BH, I, pp. 29-30). First, he notes that they have not seemed convincing to everyone (and it is overly

simplistic to say atheists have a fundamental ill-will to God or have refused to follow a road that leads where they don't want to go; rather the proofs may seem incompatible with a fundamental data of experience such as suffering, or it may seem that they blunt one's *elan* as a free creature of inexhaustible potential). Yet the main problem with the proofs is that they are ineffectual when they are most necessary (i.e. in convincing an unbeliever) (MOB, vol. II, X, pp. 195-198). Indeed a person who has experienced the presence of God has no need of proofs and one may even consider demonstration a slur on what God is, an Absolute Presence, a Thou, as proofs tend to give us the God of the philosophers that believers don't care about (MOB, vol. II, I, pp. 4-5; II, 8, pp. 154-157; VIII, pp. 147-148; X, pp. 197-198; BH, I, n. 1 on p. 136; II, p. 170; III, pp. 197-198; CF, I, pp. 36-37; IX, pp. 175-183; X, pp. 188-189; PF, I, pp. 35-41; BH, I, pp. 98, 118-121).

99   According to Marcel an ethics based on biology alone either claims to translate biological truths into general terms in which case the field of such truths that biology could justify is enormous (i.e. adultery), or it considers life as a spiritual force or current or value and loses its experimental status (BH, III, p. 194-196). As if science could enlighten us about values and as it progresses reveal true values, as if it could one day assert the primacy of a selfish demand over a non-selfish one. Yet science cannot tell us what is right or wrong. For instance it can only tell us that certain conditions will lead to overpopulation but not that we should care about human life (MOB, vol. II, VI, pp. 110-111).

So too an atheist cannot justify heroic ardor over erotic ardor, or choice of French Resistance over Anti-Bolshevik Legion, unless he or she brings in new scales of consideration, such as social utility, that go beyond the biological (BH, IV, pp. 209-210; PE, II, pp. 87-88). Indeed if sacrifice if not based on transcendence, revealed by the love encountered in our depths, we can give no answer to a person who says it is ludicrous to sacrifice one's life to promote the future development of a world one will never see (MOB, vol. II, IX, pp. 167-169, 176; X, p. 191).

100   For more on the thought of Zubiri see: PM (1960), vol. II, p. 618; PTCW (1964), pp. 634-638; MHP (1967), pp. 463-466; CP (1990), vol. III, pp. 646-661; DP (1993), vol. II, pp. 2997-2998; BDTC (1996), pp. 874-875; LTK (2001), vol. X, p. 1493; OHYP (2001), p. 212; PWW (2002), pp. 402-408; CAHP (2003), pp. 475-476; EP (2005), vol. IX, pp. 888-889; EF (2006), vol. VII, pp. 12489-12491; BBKL (2010), vol. XXXI, pp. 1555-1597; Wilhelmsen, Frederick, *The Metaphysics of Love* (New York: Sheed and Ward, 1962), pp. 68-80; Kline, George, ed., *European Philosophy Today* (Chicago: Fisch Quadrangle Books, 1965), pp. 15-29; Caponigri, Aloysius, "The Philosophy of Xavier Zubiri," *Realitas* 4 (1979), pp. 567-589; Fowler, Thomas, "Xavier Zubiri: Science, Nature, Reality," *Faith and Reason* 6:1 (1980), pp. 7-25; Aisa, Isabel, "The Human Openness in Xavier Zubiri," *Analecta Husserliana* 29 (1990), pp. 275-284; Oliver Molero, Manuel, "The Philosophy of Zubiri as

a Phenomenological Philosophy," *Analecta Husserliana* 36 (1991), pp. 361-370; Sánchez Venegas, Juana, "Zubiri's Critique of Idealism," *Filosofia Oggi* 56 (1991), pp. 559-562; Latourelle, René, ed., *Dictionary of Fundamental Theology* (New York: Crossroads, 1994), pp. 1165-1169; Fowler, Thomas, "The Great Paradigm Shift: Xavier Zubiri and the Scientific Revolution, 1890-1990," *Faith and Reason* 20:2 (1994), pp. 163-198; Fowler, Thomas, "Introduction to the Philosophy of Xavier Zubiri," "The Formality of Reality: Xavier Zubiri's Critique of Hume's Analysis of Causality," and "Xavier Zubiri's Critique of Classical Philosophy," *Xavier Zubiri Review* 1 (1998), pp. 5-16, 57-73; Fowler, Thomas, "Causality and Power in the Philosophy of Xavier Zubiri," *Xavier Zubiri Review* 2 (1999), pp. 83-102; Rovaletti, Maria Lucrecia, "Man, Experience of God: The Problem of God in Xavier Zubiri" *Xavier Zubiri Review* 2 (1999), pp. 65-78; Fowler, Thomas, "Zubiri in the Third Millenium," *Xavier Zubiri Review* 2 (1999), pp. 3-4; Harman, Graham, *Tool-Being: Heidegger and the Metaphysics of Objects* (Chicago: Open Court, 2002), pp. 243-268; Burke, Kevin, *The Ground Beneath the Cross: The Theology of Ignacio Ellacuria* (Washington: Georgetown University Press, 2003), pp. 26-29; Lee, Michael, "Liberation Theology's Transcendent Moment: The Work of Xavier Zubiri and Ignacio Ellacuría as Non-Contrastive Discourse," *Journal of Religion* 83 (2003), pp. 226-243; Weber Moore, Celeste-Marie, "Human Essence: Existential Concerns and Zubiri's Theory of Open Essence," *Xavier Zubiri Review* 5 (2003), pp. 87-105; Costoya, Manuel, "Beyond Nomological, Hermeneutic, and Dialectical Knowledge: Zubiri's Radicalization of Scholastic Realism and the Hidden Ground of the Human-Social Sciences," *Xavier Zubiri Review* 6 (2004), pp. 61-71; Stone, Brad, "On the Very Problem of God in Zubiri and Unamuno," *Xavier Zubiri Review* 6 (2004), pp. 73-88; Burke, Kevin, *Love that Produces Hope: The Thought of Ignacio Ellacuría* (Collegeville: Liturgical Press, 2006), pp. 73-128; Cope, Theo, "Some Thoughts on Metaphor in Cognitive Psychology and Zubiri's Sentient Intelligence," *Xavier Zubiri Review* 9 (2007), pp. 133-154; Fowler, Thomas, "Reductionalism, Naturalism, and Nominalism: The Unholy Trinity and Its Explanation in Zubiri's Philosophy," *Xavier Zubiri Review* 9 (2007), pp. 69-87; Thoresen, Alberto, "Peace Studies and the Philosophy of Xavier Zubiri," *Xavier Zubiri Review* 9 (2007), pp. 99-109; Aqino, Maria, *Love that Produces Hope: The Thought of Ignacio Ellacuria* (Collegeville: Liturgical Press, 2008), pp. 86-90; Bourke, Vernon, *History of Ethics* (New York: Axios Press, 2008), vol. II, pp. 216-217.

101   This book has been translated by Thomas Fowler as *Nature, History, God* [NHG] (Washington: University Press of America, 1982)] and I make use of it and other translations throughout.

Other books of Zubiri include his: *On Essence* [*Sobre la esencia: Estudios filosóficos*] [OE] (1962) [translated by Aloysius Caponigri as *On Essence* (Washington: Catholic University of America Press, 1983)]; *Five Lessons of Philosophy* [*Cinco lecciones de Filosofia*] (1963); *El hombre, realidad personal*

(1963); *El origen del hombre* (1964); *Notas sobre la inteligencia humana* (1966-1967); *El hombre y su cuerpo* (1974); *Scritti religiosi* (1976); *Respectividad de lo real* (1979); *Inteligencia sentiente*, 3 vols. (1980-1983) [translated by Thomas Fowler as *Sentient Intelligence* [SI] (Washington: Xavier Zubiri Foundation of North America, 1999)]; *Reflexiones teológicas sobre la eucaristía* (1981); *¿Qué es investigar?* (1982); *Siete ensayos de Antropología filosófica* (1982); *Human and God* [*El Hombre y Dios*] [HG] (1984) [lectures; translated by Joaquin Redondo as *Man and God* (Wasington: Xavier Zubiri Foundation of North America, 1997), a translation I use througout]; *On the Human* [*Sobre el hombre*] (1986); *Estructura dinámica de la realidad* (1989) [translated as *The Dynamic Structure of Reality* [DSR] (Champagne: University of Illinois Press, 2003)]; *On Sentiment and Volition* [*Sobre el sentimiento y la volición*] (1992); *El problema filosófico de la historia de las religions* (1993) [translated by Joaquin Redondo as *The Philosophical Problem of the History of Religions* (Washington: Xavier Zubiri Foundation of North America, 1999)]; *The Fundamental Problems of Western Metaphysics* [*Los problemas fundamentales de la metafísica occidental*] (1994); *The Theological Problem of the Human: Christianity* [*El problema teologal del hombre: Cristianismo*] (1997) [translated as *The Theological Problem of Man: Christianity* (2001)]; *On the Problem of Philosophy* [*Sobre el problema de la filosofía*] (1996); *The Human and the Truth* [*El hombre y la verdad*] (1999); *Primeros escritos, 1921-1926* (1999); *Sobre la realidad* (2001) [work of 1966]; *El hombre: Lo real y lo irreal* (2005); *Escritos menores, 1953-1983* (2007).

Some of these works have been collected in Pintor Ramos, Antonio, ed., *Xavier Zubiri, 1893-1983* (Madrid: Ediciones del Orto, 1996).

Zubiri also wrote a few essays such as: "La crisis de la conciencia moderna," *La Ciudad de Dios* 141 (1925), pp. 202-221; "Sobre el problema de la filosofia," *Revista de Occidente* 115 (1933), pp. 51-80 and 118 (1933), pp. 83-117; "La idea de naturaleza: La nueva fisica," *Cruz y Raya* 10 (1934), pp. 8-94; "¿Qué es saber?," (1935); "Filosofía y Metafísica," *Cruz y Raya* 10 (1935), pp. 7-60; "En torno al problema de Dios," *Revista de Occidente* 149 (1936), pp. 129-159; "Note sur la philosophie de la religion," *Bulletin de l'Institut Catholique de Paris* 28 (1937), pp. 333-341; "Ciencia y realidad," *Escorial* 10 (1941), pp. 177-210; "Nuestra situación intelectual" (1942); "El problema del hombre," *Indice de Artes y Letras* 120 (1959), pp. 3-4; "El hombre, realidad personal," *Revista de Occidente* 1 (1963), pp. 5-29; "El origien del hombre," *Revista de Occidente* 2 (1964), pp. 146-173 [translated as "The Origin of Man," ["OM"] in Caponigri, Aloysius, ed., *Contemporary Spanish Philosophy* (Notre Dame: University of Notre Dame Press, 1967), pp. 42-75]; "Notas sobre la inteligencia humana," *Asclepio* 18 (1967), pp. 341-353; "El hombre y su cuerpo," *Asclepio* 25 (1973), pp. 9-19; "La dimensión histórica del ser humano," *Realitas* 1 (1974), pp. 11-69 [translated as "The Historical Dimension of the Human Being" ["HDH"], *Realitas* 1 (1974), pp. 11-69]; "El espacio," *Realitas* 1 (1974), pp. 479-514; "El problema teologal del hombre," in Vargas-Machuca, Antonio, ed., *Teologia y mundo contemporaneo* (Madrid: Cristiandad, 1975), pp. 55-64; "Respectividad de lo real," *Realitas* 3 (1979), pp. 13-43; "Un Prólogo inédito a la traducción norteamericano de Naturaleza, Historia, Dios," *Ya* (December 16, 1980), p. 33; "Palabras de agradecimiento con ocasión del primer Centenario de su fundación de la Universidad de Duesto," and "Reflexiones teológicas sobre la Eucaristia," *Estudios Eclesiasticos* 56 (1981), pp. 39-59 [the latter has been translated online at the Xavier Zubiri Foundation of North America website as "Theological Reflections on the Eucharist" ["TFE"]]; "¿Qué es investigar?," *Ya* (October 19, 1982), p. 43 [reprinted in *The Xavier Zubiri Review* 7 (2005), pp. 5-7]; "Palabras de agradecimiento," *Giornale di Metafisica* 9 (1987), pp. 261-264; "La fuentes espirituales de la angustia y de la esperanza," *Revista Latinoamericana de Teología* 8 (1991), pp. 91-97; "Sobre el problema de la filosofia," *Convivium* 5 (1993), pp. 81-98; "Sobre el Problema de la filosofia II," *Convivium* 7 (1995), pp. 118-136; "El ser sobrenatural : Dios y la deificación en la teología paulina," in Díaz Muñz, Guillerma, *Teología del ministerio en Zubiri* (Barcelona: Herder, 2008), pp. 136-221.

For a bibliography of the works of Zubiri see Widemer, Hans, "Bibliographia zubiriana," *Realitas* 2 (1976), pp. 545-572; Lazcano, Rafael, ed., *Panorama bibliographico de Xavier Zubiri* (Madrid: Revista Augustin, 1993); Lazcano, Rafael, ed., *Repertorio bibliográfico de Xavier Zubiri* (Washington: Xavier Zubiri Foundation of North America, 2006); and the online bibliography of the Fundación Xavier Zubiri. See also Ellacuría, Ignacio, *Sobre la esencia de Xavier Zubiri: Indices* (Madrid: Sociedad de Estudios y Publicaciones, 1965).

102   Now the method of investigating this reality is comprised of three moments. First one investigates a system of reference (a limited field of reality; a concrete situation); second one sketches a system of possibilities of what the real could be in its essence and ground (circumscribing its limits and discovering its in-depth nature, and determing why its traits pertain to it and its source); third one enters into experience to approve or reprove the sketch.

Importantly there are four modes of experiential verifications of reality (which are almost always open-ended and ongoing processes that become more and more viable as we work out consequences, concordances, and convergences (sufficiency) and as we grasp new predictions and new properties (exceedings) that can be subsequently verified): 1) Probation [*probación*]—experiments to uncover physical realities (forcing or manipulating the real to show itself); 2) Comprobation (verification)—the proving of mathematical realities [tracing the necessities involved in postulates and axioms and apprehending mathematical realities]; 3) Compenetration—the interpersonal experience of human life, history, and God (being present interiorly at a vision of the real); 4) Conformation (appropriation)—the self-appropriation of my own being a person (personeity) and as enacting or failing to enact moral realities (personality) (NHG, I, 1-2, pp. 11, 16-18, 25, 38-41; SI, III, 6, pp. 316-334, 336-346, 348-354).

103   Hence Zubiri is somewhat critical of argumentation for God. The classical proofs are not as solid of a foundation for belief as is the experience of relegation; they often involve unargued for presuppositions; and they give us more an entifying sketch of God than the personal God who is ultimate, possibilitating, and impelling (NHG, III, 1, 4, pp. 301, 327-329, 340; HG, III, pp. 93-98, 104, 114-115; VII, p. 266; Conclusion, p. 271).

104   Indeed God is less a resource humans need to fix their problems, than the ground of plenitude of life in all its being. So we turn to God not to escape from this world but to be able to be a relatively absolute I. We turn to God not out of indigence but in plenitude, not as a help for acting but as a ground for being, as Author, Actor, Agent (NHG, Introduction, p. vii; HG, III, p. 121). Zuburi writes: "The experience of God, consequently, *a parte Dei* [on the part of God] is God giving Himself as absolute to human experience; *a parte hominis* [on the part of the human] it is to incorporate the experience of the absolute into the constitution of my person. A human being does not encounter God primarily in the dialectic of necessities and indigencies. A human being encounters God precisely in the plenitude of its being and its life. Anything else is to have a sad concept of God. Of course—all of us are victims of inelegancies—we appeal to God when it thunders. Indeed, no one is exempt. But this is not the primary form in which the human proceeds towards God, and are now actually in God. Humans do not proceed by the way of indigence but of plenitude, the plenitude of their being, in the plenitude of their life and their death ...in making themselves persons. In the personal being, in the relatively absolute being of the person, is where each person finds God, giving Himself to humans in their experiences. This donation of God is precisely the reality of the person. And this human experience of the absolute is experience of this donation of God" (HG, VI, p. 251 [344-345]).

105   Besides the human being constitutively turning to God and making a personal surrender to God in theologal or theological faith (*teologal*) there is theologic faith (*teológico*) of positive and historical religions (HG, Introduction, p. 20; II, p. 85; Conclusion, p. 278).

106   Among the more than 250 Catholic Existentialists we can name: Francesco Bonatelli (1830-1911) [Italian Christian Spiritualism]; the near convert Henri Bergson (1859-1941), at the College de France [Intuitionist]; Miguel de Unamuno (1864-1936); Maurice Pradines (1874-1958) [Philosophy of the Spirit]; Armando Carlini (1878-1959) [Italian Christian Spiritualism]; the convert Theodor Haecker (1879-1945); Jacques Chevalier (1882-1962) [Intuitionist; Spiritualist; French Minister of Education in 1941]; the Spaniard Eugenio d'Ors (1882-1954); René Le Senne (1882-1954), at the Sorbonne [Philosophy of the Spirit; Academy of the Moral and Political Sciences]; the Mexican politician José Vasconcelos Calderon (1882-1959) [Intuitionist]; Leonardo Coimbra (1883-1936); Antonio Aliotta (1884-1964); Peter Wust (1884-1940); Francesco Olgiati (1886-1962) [Italian Christian Spiritual-

ism]; Jacques Paliard (1887-1953) [Philosophy of the Spirit]; Max Picard
(1888-1965); the convert Edward Ingram Watkin (1888-1982) [Intuition-
ist]; Alois Dempf (1891-1982); Régis Jolivet (1891-1966) [also a Thomist];
Renato Lazzarini (1891-1975) [Italian Christian Spiritualism]; Luigi Ste-
fanini (1891-1956) [Italian Christian Spiritualism; censored by the Vatican
in 1929]; André Marc, S.J. (1892-1961) [also a Transcendental Thomist];
Étienne Souriau (1892-1979), at the Sorbonne; Augusto Guzzo (1894-1986)
[Italian Christian Spiritualism]; Umberto Antonio Padovani (1894-1967)
[Italian Christian Spiritualism; also a Thomist]; Gabriel Madinier (1895-
1958); Jules Chaix-Ruy (c. 1896-1975) [Philosophy of the Spirit]; Dom
Mark Pontifex, O.S.B. (1896-1991) [Intuitionist]; Aimé Forest (1898-1983)
[Philosophy of the Spirit; also a Thomist]; Henri Gouhier (1898-1994) [also
an Thomist; member of the French Academy]; Jean Grenier (1898-1971); Jean
Nogué (1898-1940) [Philosophy of the Spirit]; Fritz-Joachim von Rintelen
(1898-1979) [dismissed by Nazis in 1941]; Pierre Mesnard (1900-1969)
[member of the Academy of Moral and Political Sciences]; Enrico Castelli
(1900-1977); the Belgian Fr. Albert Dondeyne (1901-1985); Jean Guitton
(1901-1999), of the Sorbonne [Philosophy of the Spirit; member of the
Academy of the Moral and Political Sciences and the French Academy]; Eric
Voegelin (1901-1985), Felice Battaglia (1902-1977) [Italian Christian Spiri-
tualism]; Gustav Siewerth (1903-1963) [also a Thomist]; Gustave Thibon
(1903-2001) [winner of the Grand Prize of Philosophy in 2000]; the convert
Hans-Eduard Hengstenberg (1904-1998); the Spaniard Maria Zambrano
(1904-1991) [also a Phenomenologist]; Max Müller (1906-1994); Jean Pu-
celle (1906-1981) [Philosophy of the Spirit]; Roger Verneaux (c. 1906-1987);
Bernhard Welte (1906-1983) [also a Thomist]; Alfred Delp, S.J. (1907-1945)
[killed by Nazis]; the convert Dom Illtyd Trethowan, O.S.B. (1907-1993)
[Intuitionist]; the physician Pedro Laín Entralgo (1908-2001) [Zubirian];
the convert from atheism Fr. Ignace Lepp (1908-1966); Michele Federico
Sciacca (1908-1975) [Italian Christian Spiritualism; founder of the *Giornale
di Metafisica* (1946)]; the near convert Simone Weil (1909-1943); the Dutch
Bernard Delfgaauw (1912-); Hermann Krings (1913-) [Chairman of the
German Board of Education in 1994]; Isabelle Mourral (1913-) [Philoso-
phy of the Spirit; Inspector General of Education in France]; Julián Marías
(1914-2005) [Zubirian]; Adolfo Munoz Alonso (1915-); Aloysius Robert
Caponigri (1915-) [Zubirian]; Vincent P. Miceli, S.J. (1915-1991), Pietro
Prini (1915-2008) [Italian Christian Spiritualism]; Mario Stefani (c. 1915-)
[Italian Christian Spiritualism]; the Peruvian Rodrigo Alberto Wagner de
Reyna (1915-2006); Romeo Crippa (1916-) [Italian Christian Spiritulaism];
the Belgian Roger Troisfontaines, S.J. (1916-); James Daniel Collins (1917-
1985); Fr. Cahil Brendan Daly (1917-) [Intuitionism]; Eugen Biser (1918-)
[Hermeneutics]; Alberto Caracciolo (1918-) [Italian Christian Spiritualism];
Luigi Pareyson (1918-1991) [Italian Christian Spiritualism]; Sergio Cotta
(1920-2007); Louis Millet (1921-) [Philosophy of the Spirit]; the Belgian

Fr. Antoon Vergote (1921-); Maria-Teresa Antonelli (1922-) [Italian Christian Spiritualism]; the Italian politician Vittorio Mathieu (1923-), Opus Dei [Italian Christian Spiritualism]; Andrea Mario Moschetti (c. 1925-) [Italian Christian Spiritualism]; Claude Geffré, O.P. (1926-) [Hermeneutics]; the Spaniard Leonardo Polo (1926-), Opus Dei; Richard Schaeffler (1926-); Ada Lamacchia (1927-) [Italian Christian Spiritualism]; Alfonso Lopez Quintas (1928-), Opus Dei [Founder of the Escuela de Pensamiento y Creatividad in Madrid]; the Belgian-American Jacques Taminiaux (1928-); Heinrich Beck (1929-); the Belgian Albert Chapelle, S.J. (1929- 2003); Pierre Magnard (1929-), of the Sorbonne; Michele Schiavone (1929-) [Italian Christian Spiritualism]; Adriano Bausola (1930-); Ignacio Ellacuría, S.J. (1930-1989) [murdered; Zubirian]; Bernhard Casper (1931-); Maurice Corvez (c. 1931-); Virgilio Melchiorre (1931-); the Pole Jozef Tischner (1931-2000); Ferdinand Ulrich (1931-); Leslie Dewart (c. 1935-); Ulrich Hommes (c. 1935-) [the son of Jakob Hommes]; Kenneth T. Gallagher (c. 1940-), at Fordham University; the Pole Tadeusz Jaroszewski (c. 1940-); Pier Paolo Ottonello (1941-) [Italian Christian Spiritualism]; Reiner Schürmann, O.P. (1941-1993) [who left the Dominicans and died of Aids]; Jean Greisch (1942-) [Hermeneutics]; Jean-Louis Vieillard-Baron (1944-) [Philosophy of the Spirit]; Sergio Givone (1944-) [Italian Christian Spiritualism]; Rémi Brague (1947-) [Hermeneutics]; the Mexican Mauricio Beuchot Puente (1950-) [Hermeneutics]; Henri Hude (1954-) [Intuitionist]; Marco Olivetti (c. 1955-) [Hermeneutics]; Renato Pagotto (c. 1955-) [Italian Christian Spiritualism]; Jorge Vicente Arregui (1958-2005), Opus Dei [Hermeneutics]; Jean-Marc Rouviere (1958-); Brendan Sweetman (1962-).

107   For more on the thought of Anscombe see: HYP (1966), pp. 513-515; CEWP (1989), pp. 16-17; DP (1993), vol. I, p. 107; BDTC (1996), pp. 25-26; REP (1998), vol. I, pp. 280-283; NCE (2003), vol. I, pp. 492-493; ACP (2005), pp. 406-414; DTCB (2005), vol. I, pp. 25-33; EP (2005), vol. I, pp. 212-214; OGP (2005), p. 38; EF (2006), vol. I, pp. 491-492; BBKL (2010), vol. XXXI, pp. 15-26; Meiland, Jack, The Nature of Intention (London: Methuen, 1970), pp. 36-51; Diamond, Cora, ed., Intention and Intentionality (Ithaca: Cornell University Press, 1979); Hudson, William, A Century of Moral Philosophy (New York: St. Martin's Press, 1980), pp. 154-157; Theron, Stephen, Morals as Founded on Natural Law (Frankfurt: Peter Lang, 1987), pp. 121-128; Kersey, Ethel, ed., Women Philosophers (New York: Greenwood Press, 1989), pp. 34-36; Davidson, Donald, Essays on Actions and Events (Oxford: Oxford University Press, 1990), pp. 3-20; Kelsay, John, ed., Cross, Crescent, and Sword: The Justification and Limitation of War in Western and Islamic Tradition (New York: Greenwood Press, 1990), pp. 3-33; Monk, Ray, Ludwig Wittgenstein: The Duty of Genius (New York: Penguin Books, 1991), pp. 497-498, 538, 544, 551-567, 572-580; Singer, Peter, ed., A Companion to Ethics (Oxford: Blackwell, 1993), pp. 478-480; Phillips, Dewi, Religion and Morality (New York: St. Martin's Press, 1996), pp. 250-298; Fricker, Miranda,

ed., *The Cambridge Companion to Feminism* (Cambridge: Cambridge University Press, 2000), pp. 127-145; LaFollette, Hugh, ed., *The Blackwell Guide to Ethical Theory* (Cambridge: Blackwell, 2000), pp. 325-347; Richter, Duncan, *Ethics after Anscombe: Post Modern Moral Philosophy* (Dordrecht: Kluwer, 2000); Teichmann, Roger, ed., *Logic, Cause, and Action* (Cambridge: Cambridge University Press, 2000); Baldwin, Thomas, *Contemporary Philosophy: Philosophy in English since 1945* (Oxford: Oxford University Press, 2001), pp. 193-196, 237-239, 258; Becker, Lawrence, et al., eds., *Encyclopedia of Ethics* (London: Routledge, 2001), pp. 74-77; Boxer, S., "G.E.M. Anscombe, British Philosopher, Dies at 81," *The New York Times* (January 13, 2001); Cahal, Daly, "Warrior for the Truth," *Tablet* 255 (April 14, 2001), p. 528; Dolan, John, "G.E.M. Anxcombe: Living the Truth," *First Things* 113 (May 2001), pp. 11-14; Haldane, John, "G.E.M. Anscombe, 1919-2001: In Memoriam," *Review of Metaphysics* 53 (2001), pp. 1019-1021; Kerr, Fergus, "Anscombe, G.E.M.," New *Blackfriars* 82 (2001), pp. 54-55; Martinich, Aloysius, et al., eds., *A Companion to Analytic Philosophy* (Oxford: Blackwell, 2001), pp. 315-325; "Professor G.E.M. Anscombe," *The Daily Telegraph* (January 6, 2001); "Professor G.E.M. Anscombe," *The Times* (January 8, 2001); Warnock, Mary, "Obituary of Elizabeth Anscombe," *St. Hugh's College Chronicle* 74 (2001), pp. 10-13; Fosl, Peter, et al., eds., *British Phlosophers, 1800-2000* (Columbia: Gale, 2002), pp. 3-11; O'Grady, Jane, "Elizabeth Anscombe," *The Guardian* (January 11, 2001); *Biographical Memoirs of Fellows* (Oxford: Oxford University Press, 2002), vol. I, pp. 31-50; Wilson, A.N., *C.S. Lewis: A Biography* (New York: W.W. Norton and Company, 2002), pp. 110, 210-236; Reppert, Victor, *C.S. Lewis's Dangerous Idea: In Defense of the Argument from Reason* (Downers Grove, Illinois, 2003), pp. 11-24, 44-71; Hyman, John, et al., eds., *Agency and Action* (Cambridge: Cambridge University Press, 2004), pp. 43-68; O'Hear, Anthony, ed., *Modern Moral Philosophy* (Cambridge: Cambridge University Press, 2004), pp. 75-83, 121-123, 137-139, 141-158, 237-242, 265-281, 287-292, 301-316; Rutler, George, "Memoir of Elizabeth Anscombe," *Crisis* 22:8 (2004), p. 62; Jones, David Albert, "Portrait of a Catholic Philosopher," *Pastoral Review* 2:3 (2006), pp. 51-55; Solomon, David, *Elizabeth Anscombe's Modern Moral Philosophy: Fifty Years Later* (Philadelphia: Routledge, 2008); Teichmann, Roger, *The Philosophy of Elizabeth Anscombe* (Oxford: Oxford University Press, 2008).

108   There have been numerous amusing stories about Anscombe (see the various obituaries noted above). For instance one day she and Wittgenstein were both deep in philosophical thought and so didn't see that a train had pulled in near the platform on which they were standing. When the train started to pull off Anscombe ran and jumped on board leaving Wittgenstein behind. A fellow traveler approached Wittgensein and told him not to worry as another train was bound for London in an hour, to which Wittgenstein replied, 'But she came to see me off!' And Anscombe apparently once taunted A.J. Ayer by saying 'if you didn't talk so quickly, people wouldn't think you

were so clever' to which he replied 'if you didn't talk so slowly, people wouldn't think you were so profound.' She also once made good on a threat to put her child on the train to Bicester if he misbehaved; she gave up smoking cigarettes after she promised God to stop smoking if he healed her son (though she later commenced smoking cigars and pipes after he son recovered since she reasoned her pledge to God did not include them); she took off her pants when she was told at a fancy restaurant in Boston that ladies could not wear trousers; and she would refuse to answer to Mrs. Geach ('there is no one here by that name') as opposed to Mrs. Anscombe.

Incidentally Anscombe is buried in the same cemetery as her friend Wittgenstein, for whom she arranged a meeting with a Catholic priest at the end of his life and a Catholic burial, even if Wittgenstein did not seem to have fully converted to Catholicism (Anscombe was even known to have adopted some of Wittgenstein's mannerisms, such as placing her anguished head with a furrowed brow in her hands when deep in thought, maintaining long silences, and speaking in an Austrian accent).

109   See Warnock, Mary, *Women Philosophers* (London: Orion, 1996), p. 203, Cameron, J.M., in *The New Republic* (May 19, 1982), p. 34, and the front cover of Anscombe's *Intention* (2000 edition).

110   Anscombe additionally wrote several books including *The War and the Moral Law* (1939) [with Norman Daniel]; *Mr. Truman's Degree* (1956); *Nuclear Weapons and Christian Conscience* (1961) [*Nuclear Weapons: A Catholic Response* (1962); reprinted in Woodward, P.A., ed., *The Doctrine of Double Effect* (Notre Dame: University of Notre Dame Press, 2001), pp. 247-260, and Haber, Joram Graf, ed., *Absolutism and Its Consequentialist Critics* (Lanham: Rowman & Littlefield, 1994, pp. 29-40]; *Causality and Determination* (1971) [lecture of 1971 at the University of Cambridge; reprinted in Ekstrom, Laura, ed., *Agency and Responsibility* (Boulder: Westview Press, 2001), pp. 57-73]; *On Transubstantiation* (1974); *Contraception and Chastity* (1975); *Time, Beginning, and Causation* (1975) [Henriette Hertz Trust Lecture of 1974]; *Has Mankind One Soul: An Angel Distributed through Many Bodies* (1985) [Cassasa Lecture at Loyola Marymount University of 1985]. Anscombe also edited and translated many works of her mentor Wittgenstein.

Anscombe is perhaps best known, however, for her many papers including: "A Reply to Mr. C.S. Lewis's Argument that Naturalism is Self-Refuting," *Socratic Digest* 4:2 (1948), pp. 7-16; "Intention," *Proceedings of the Aristotelian Society* 57 (1957), pp. 321-332; "Does Oxford Moral Philosophy Corrupt the Youth?," *The Listener* LVII: 1455 (February 14, 1957), pp. 266-271 [BBC Talk in 1957; Anscombe also wrote several letters to the editor in response to critics in *The Listener* of that year]; "Modern Moral Philosophy," *Philosophy* 33:124 (1958), pp. 1-19; "On Brute Facts," *Analysis* 18:3 (1958), pp. 69-72; "On Sensations of Position," *Analysis* 22:3 (1962), pp. 55-58; "Authority in Morals," in Todd,

John, ed., *Problems of Authority* (Baltimore: Helicon Press, 1962), pp. 179-188 [Paper given at Bec Abbey in 1961]; "The Two Kinds of Error in Action," *Journal of Philosophy* 60 (1963), pp. 393-400; "The Intentionality of Sensation. A Grammatical Feature," in Butler, R. J., ed., *Analytical Philosophy* (Oxford: Blackwell, 1965), pp. 158-180; "Contraception and Natural Law," ["CNL"] *New Blackfriars* 46 (1965), pp. 517-521; "A Note on Mr. Bennett," in *Analysis* 26:6 (1966), p. 208; "On the Grammar of Enjoy," *Journal of Philosophy* 64 (1967), pp. 607-614; "Who is Wronged?: Philippa Foot and Double Effect," *The Oxford Review* 5 (1967), pp. 16-17; "You can have Sex without Children: Christianity and the New Offer," in Shook, Laurence, ed., *Renewal of Religious Structures* (New York: Herder & Herder, 1968); "Contraception and Chastity," ["CCH"], *The Human World* 7 (1972), pp. 9-30 [with replies in *The Human World* of that same year]; "Memory, Experience, and Causation," in Lewis, Hywel, ed., *Contemporary British Philosophy* (London: Allen & Unwin, 1976), vol. IV, pp. 15-29; "Times, Beginnings, and Causes," *Proceedings of the British Academy* 60 (1974), pp. 253-270; "Whatever has a Beginning of Existence must have a Cause: Hume's Argument Exposed," *Analysis* 34:5 (1974), pp. 145-151; "The First Person," in Guttenplan, Samuel, ed., *Mind and Language: Wolfson College Lectures 1974* (Oxford: Clarendon Press, 1975), pp. 45-65; "On the Hatred of God," *Theology* 79 (1976), pp. 131-132; "On Frustration of the Majority by Fulfilment of the Majority's Will," *Analysis* 36:4 (1976), pp. 161-168; "Soft Determinism," in Ryle, Gilbert, ed., *Contemporary Aspects of Philosophy* (London: Oriel Press, 1976), pp. 148-160; "Will and Emotion," *Grazer Philosophische Studien* 5 (1978]), pp. 139-148; "On Humanae Vitae," in Santamaria, J.N., et al., eds., *Human Love and Human Life* (Melbourne: Polding Press, 1979), pp. 121-127 [1978 paper delivered at *Humanae Vitae* conference at the University of Melbourne]; "Prolegomenon to a Pursuit of the Definition of Murder: The Illegal and the Unlawful," *Dialectics and Humanism* 6:4 (1979), pp. 73-77; "Under a Description," *Noûs* 13 (1979), pp. 219-233; "What Is It to Believe Someone," in Delaney, Cornelius, ed., *Rationality and Religious Belief* (Notre Dame: Notre Dame University Press, 1979), pp. 141-151; "Commentary 2 on Harris' Ethical Problems in the Management of some Severely Handicapped Children," *Journal of Medical Ethics* 9 (1981), pp. 122-123; "Action, Intention, and Double Effect," ["AIDE"] *Proceedings of the American Catholic Philosophical Association* 56 (1982), pp. 12-25 [Aquinas Medal Address of 1982]; "Murder and the Morality of Euthanasia," ["MME"] in *Euthanasia and Clinical Practice: Trends, Principles and Alternatives* (London: The Linacre Centre for Health Care Ethics, 1982), pp. 24-36; "Morality," in Marneau, C, ed., *Pro Ecclesia et Pontifice* (Vatican City: Libreria Editrice Vaticana, 1982), pp. 16-18 [Talk in Vatican City of 1982]; "On the Notion of Immaterial Substance," in O'Hara, Mary, ed., *Substances and Things: Aristotle's Doctrine of Physical Substance in Recent Essays* (Washington: University of America Press, 1982), pp. 252-262; "Why Anselm's Proof in the *Proslogion* is not an Ontological Argument?," *The Thoreau Quarterly* 17 (1985), pp. 32-40;

"The Causation of Action," in Ginet, Carl, ed., *Knowledge and Mind* (New York: Oxford University Press, 1983), pp. 174-190; "Paganism, Superstition and Philosophy," ["PSP"] *The Thoreau Quarterly* 17 (1985), pp. 20-31 [The Gildersleve Lecture at Barnard College in 1984]; "Truth: Anselm or Thomas?," *New Blackfriars* 66 (1985), pp. 82-98; "Were you a Zygote?," in Griffiths, A.Phillip, ed., *Philosophy and Practice* (Cambridge: Cambridge University Press, 1985), pp. 111-117 [Lecture given at the Royal Institute of Philosophy in 1984]; "Knowledge and Reverence for Human Life," Hittinger, Russell, ed., *Linking the Human Life Issues* (Washington: Regnery-Gateway, 1986), pp. 170-178 [Lecture at Marquette University in 1981]; "Twenty Opinions Common Among Modern Anglo-American Philosophers," *Persona, verità e morale* (Rome: Città Nuova Editrice, 1987), pp. 49-50; "A Comment on Coughlan's Using People," *Bioethics* 4:1 (1990), p. 60; "Why Have Children?," *Proceedings of the American Catholic Philosophical Association* 63 (1990), pp. 48-53; "Embryos and Final Causes," in Fellon, J., et al., eds., *Finalité et Intentionalité: Doctrine Thomiste et Perspectives Modernes* (Paris : J. Vrin, 1992), pp. 293-303; "Practical Truth," *Ruch filozoficzny* 49:1 (1992), pp. 30-33; "On Wisdom," *Acta Philosophica* 2 (1993), pp. 127-133; "Russelm or Anselm?," *Philosophical Quarterly* 43 (1993), pp. 500-504; "Is Matter the Whole Story: The Existence of the Soul," in Varghese, Roy, ed., *Great Thinkers on Great Questions* (Rockport: Oneworld, 1998), pp. 52-56; "Making True," in Teichmann, Roger, ed., *Logic, Cause, and Action* (Cambridge: Cambridge University Press, 2000), pp. 1-8; "How Can a Man be Free?: Spinoza's Thought and that of Some Others," *Aletheia* 7 (2002), pp. 21-30; "My Interests in Philosophy," in Rorty, Amelie, *The Many Faces of Philosophy* (Oxford: Oxford University Press, 2003), pp. 498-502 [Intellectual Autobiography].

Many of these articles have been collected in *Ethics, Religion, and Politics* [ERP] (Minneapolis: University of Minnesota Press, 1981); *From Parmenides to Wittgenstein* (Minneapolis: University of Minnesota Press, 1981); *Metaphysics and Philosophy of Mind* [MPM] (Minneapolis: University of Minnesota Press, 1981); *Human Life, Action, and Ethics* [HLAE] (Exeter: Imprint Academic, 2005) [including unpublished papers]; *Faith in a Hard Ground: Essays on Religion, Philosophy, and Ethics* [FHG] (Exeter: Imprint Academic, 2008) [including unpublished papers and speeches]; *From Plato to Wittgenstein* (2011).

See the Bibliographies of Anscombe in Diamond, Cora, ed., *Intention and Intentionality* (Ithaca: Cornell University Press, 1979), pp. xvii-xix; Teichmann, Roger, *The Philosophy of Elizabeth Anscombe* (Oxford: Oxford University Press, 2008), pp. 231-239.

111   Anscombe notes that voluntary actions can also be known without observation (i.e. with one's eyes closed), such as knowing what one has written or the position of one's limbs (INT, 8, pp. 13-14; 45-46, pp. 82-83).

112   Anscombe follows Wittgenstein, however, in arguing that we need not and should not appeal to private inner mental states when discussing intentions. For contrary to common sense, an intention is not defined by a special interior act, one only authoritatively known and settled by the agent (INT, 4, p. 9; 28, pp. 49-50). In the first place, taking the example given earlier, an image of poisoning the Nazis could occur in this man but also in someone who did not poison them (for one can intend something without fulfilling it, or change one's mind). Hence a mental image is not part of an intention. Secondly, a person can be mistaken about his or her own intention or moral responsibility. For instance, if the person who was pumping water tried to claim that his intention was only to earn a living as a servant and not to poison the people, this would be incorrect. For the person is taking extra steps than normal (putting poison in the water or failing to remove it) and so must take responsibility for the action under its ultimate intention (INT, 24-25, pp. 41-42, 44-45; 27-30, pp. 47-49, 52-53). Lastly, we can describe the intentions of animals, such as a cat that is stalking its prey, even though these animals can utter no thoughts and may lack inner intentions (INT, 2, p. 5; 47, p. 86; MPM, XIX, pp. 210). Hence an intention is never just a thought, something inside one's mind, an interior mental act (which do not secure intentions or bring it about, but are merely accompaniments to it, albeit ones by which the agent can utter 'This is my intention'). Nor do we need to inquire into the contents of an agent's mind to grasp an intention. All we need to do is physically observe what takes place (an agent's outer acts) and infer the reason why it does so from this (INT, 4, p. 9). This is again because an intention is a behavior for which we can give reasons in response to the question 'why?' (INT, 2-3, pp. 5-7; 21, p. 34; 46-47, pp. 84-85). Anscombe is also famous for her controversial view that the word 'I' has no referent (see MPM, II, pp. 21-36).

113   Anscombe also rejects the view that the recent indeterminism in physics (i.e. quantum mechanics) can be helpful in defending the freedom of the will. For Anscombe argues that this is mere "hap" and as such could not lead to ethical behavior. For freedom involves the power of acting according to an idea or reason and not merely a non-predetermination; freedom then is not a mere physical haphazardness but an intentionalness and voluntariness (MPM, XIII, pp. 145-146).

114   According to Anscombe the natural law is a moral law promulgated by God to human reason that tells humans how to act to properly fulfill their nature. It is thus the content of ethics insofar as it is independent of revelation (ERP, VI, pp. 60-61; VIII, pp. 72-73; "CCH," pp. 12-17; "CNL" pp. 517-519; "PSP," p. 105). As Anscombe writes: "For the natural law is the law of man's own nature, showing how he must choose to act in matters where his will is free, if his nature is to be properly fulfilled. It is the proper use of his functions; their misuse or perversion is sin ... And in what it consists he can discover by reason, checked and guaranteed by the divine revelation of Scripture" (ERP,

VIII, pp. 72-73). Or again "Catholic thinkers ... believe the general precepts of morality are laws promulgated by God our Creator in the enlightened human understanding when it is thinking in general terms about what are good and what are bad actions. That is to say, the discoveries of reflection and reasoning when we think straight about these things are God's legislation to us (whether we realize this or not)" ("CCH," pp. 16-17).

Interestingly Anscombe argues (contra Étienne Gilson, Jacques Maritain, and Michael Dummett) that Scripture can reveal no moral truths unknowable to our natural reason; so the content of the moral law is not a matter of revelation. For God can only reveal as wrong and command as right what we can potentially grasp as wrong or right through reasons and facts, i.e. what is connatural to a virtuous person. So for Anscombe there are no moral truths that are *per se* [in themselves] revealed to us by God and so knowable only by revelation (ERP, V, pp. 48-49; "CNL, pp. 517-519). This is not to say, however, that there can't be moral beliefs known to us through revelation *per accidens* [accidentally]. For revelation may reveal a moral truth which we could naturally know but which we have not yet thought out for ourselves. In fact, Anscombe admits that Scripture can reveal some truths going beyond reason that relate to the moral life and so can better help us determine what ought to be done and inform us about the proper motives, spirit, and purpose of the moral life—such as those of original sin, the conditional promises of God, and asceticism (which indeed would otherwise be thought morbid or founded on a false view of life) (ERP, V, pp. 49-50).

Furthermore, according to Anscombe, the moral precepts of Christianity are identical to those of the Old Testament and its God – excepting the stricter laws regarding marriage (i.e. divorce; cf. Mt 5:31-32) by way of addition, and the total extermination of the tribes of Canaan (Deut 7:1-5), said to have been commanded by God, by way of subtraction. For example, the Old Testament reveals a law of love and even tells us that we must love our enemies (ERP, V, p. 50; cf. Lev 19:18; Ex 23:4-5; Prov 25:21). And even the so-called primitive law of an eye for an eye was a just punishment for a wrongful perjury done to another person in Old Testament (and was not taught as a principle of revenge which is a corruption of the Old Testament) (ERP, VI, pp. 56-57; n. 2 on p. 54; cf. Ex 21:22).

One could take issue with Anscombe's argument here, however, and respond that even if some of Jesus's precepts were found in the Old Testament, they were not found in as pure or extended a form. And Anscombe fails to consider several areas in which the ethics of Jesus (or his followers) seems to go beyond that of the Old Testament, namely: elimination of dietary laws (Mk 7:1-23); the view that happiness will not necessarily be found on earth but in heaven (see Mt 5:10; although see the book of Job and the Psalms); the importance of not just following the law but having the proper intention in doing so, including not loving others out of hope of earthly gain (Mt 5:8, 21-28, 43-48 and 6:1-6 and 25:31-46; cf. Deut 6:6 Jer 31:31-34; Lv 11:13); rejection of the need for circumcision (Acts 15:1-29; Deut 10:16; Jer 4:4); the call to love the neighbor not just as oneself but as God has loved us (Jn 13:34 and 15:12; 1 Jn 4:7-8); elimination of animal sacrifice; the combining and centering of ethics on the twofold love commandment, i.e. love of God and neighbor (Mk 12:31 and 22:30; Gal 5:14; cf. Lev 19:18 and Deut 6:4-5); the extreme willingness to lay down one's life for others (Mk 10:45; Mt 16:25, 26:35; Jn 10:11-16, 12:25; Jn 14:15-15:17; Acts 21:13-14); the extension of love of neighbor to love of stranger and foreigner, which goes beyond non-mistreatment (Mt 25:35-36; Lk 10:29-37; cf. Ex 22:21) and indeed to love of enemies which does, contra Anscombe, seem to go beyond the Old Testament view (see Lk 10:25-37; Mt 5:43-48); and the enactment of the positive golden rule versus the negative silver rule, i.e. 'do unto others what you want done to you' and not just 'do not do unto others what you don't want done to yourself' (Mt 7:12; cf. Tobit 5:15).

115   Indeed Anscombe emphatically adds "But if someone really thinks, in advance, that it is open to question whether such an action as procuring the judicial execution of an innocent should be quite excluded from consideration— I do not want to argue with him; he shows a corrupt mind" (ERP, IV, p. 42).

116   Anscombe also engaged in a polemic with the utilitarians Philippa Foot and Jonathan Bennett, and the Catholic proportionalist Richard McCormick, who rejected the doctrine of double effect and argued that there is no ultimate difference between direct and indirect killing. They did so by appealing to the example of a pot-holer (i.e. an explorer) who is stuck in the entrance of a cave which is unfortunately occupied by other people and also filling with water that will soon drown everybody (including the pot-holer who is positioned face-inward). Now Foot and McCormick ask us to suppose that there are two ways to rescue the people in the cave (both at the unfortunate expense of the pot-holer). In one case the pot-holer can be blown up with dynamite. In the other case a rock can be dislodged to create an opening but the rock will roll over the pot-holer and crush his head. And they claim that both actions are worthy and obligatory actions from a moral point of view (for there is an absolute necessity to save lives) and so that it is not philosophically warranted to say that the former action is wrong as one intentionally kills the pot-holer (i.e. direct killing) but the other is allowable as here one only has the intention to escape and not kill the pot-holer (i.e. indirect killing).

In response Anscombe argues that the example is not a true representation of the doctrine of double effect (or what she calls the principle of side-effects), and so does not represent a distinction between direct and indirect killing. For in the second situation, freeing the rock is immediately connected with the pot-holer's death (i.e. it is certain or nearly certain here that moving the rock will result in the pot-holer's death). So it is dubious to say that in this case one doesn't intend the death of the pot-holer (even if it is true that it is not a part of one's aim that the pot-holer's head should be crushed). For the immediate

circumstances and consequences of an action dictate under what description
an intention lies (and so what is part of the intrinsic nature of the act). For
we cannot choose any intentional description of an action we want and say
for instance that my intention here is merely that 'I am moving what blocks
the egress' or 'I am removing a rock which is in the way' [as if one could say
in bombing the cities of Hiroshima and Nagasaka that one only intended to
'bomb the city' and it was an unfortunate accident that people happened to be
living there at the time, or as if a servant can merely intend to be 'doing his job'
or 'avoiding punishment' in holding a ladder for his sinister master and no part
of his intent is helping the master commit a rape or robbery—a view, in fact,
rejected by the Catholic Church in 1665 and 1679 (see DH 2037-2038, 2114,
2130-2132, 2151); or lastly as if one could say that one is merely intending to
'move one's knife through such and such a region of space' even if that space
is occupied by a human neck or a rope supporting a climber]. Thus a proper
intentional description of an action must include the immediate effects of the
action. And since here crushing the pot-holer is a pretty certain immediate
effect of moving the rock, it is an intrinsically wrong act and forbidden. That
is to say, the intrinsic certainty or great likelihood of the death of the pot-holer
in moving the rock would exclude its morality. Likewise, a surgeon would be
murdering a patient who had volunteered as an organ donor if the surgeon
knew that the death of the patient was a near certainty as a result of the surgery.
So too an arsonist can be said to murder if the fire set by the arsonist (say to
get insurance money) destroys a home and kills people, even if this is not what
the arsonist sought to do. Hence Anscombe implies that the doctrine of double
effect would only allow the moving of a boulder to rescue a trapped and drown-
ing party if the boulder only had a possibility (or a less than high probability)
of resulting in someone else's death (and not a certainty or great likelihood of
doing so) ("AIDE," pp. 20-24; ERP, VI, pp. 58-59; HLAE, XXI, pp. 275-277;
"MME," pp. 38-39, 48-50; cf. Philippa Foot, "The Problem of Abortion and
the Doctrine of Double Effect," *Oxford Review* 5 (1967), pp. 5-15; Richard
McCormick, *Ambiguity in Moral Choice* (Milwaukee: Marquette University
Press, 1977), pp. 36-40; Judith Jarvis Thomson, "Killing, Letting Die, and the
Trolley Problem," *The Monist* 59 (1976), pp. 204-217 and "The Trolley Prob-
lem," *Yale Law Review* 94 (1985), pp. 1395-1415; Fischer, John Martin, and
Mark Ravizza, S.J., *Ethics: Problems and Principles* (Orlando: Harcourt, 1992).

117   For more on the thought of Taylor see: BDTC (1996), pp. 774-
776; REP (1998), vol. IX, pp. 276-279; ACP (2005), pp. 472-477; DTCB
(2005), vol. II, pp. 1027-1033; MAP (2005), vol. IV, pp. 2386-2391; OGP
(2005), pp. 909-910; EF (2006), vol. XI, pp. 11306-11307; *Philosophy and
Phenomenological Research* 54:1 (1994) [Special Issue on Charles Taylor];
Tully, James, ed., *Philosophy in an Age of Pluralism: The Philosophy of Charles
Taylor in Question* (Cambridge University Press, 1994); Dussel, Enrique,
*The Underside of Modernity: Apel, Ricoeur, Rorty, Taylor and the Philosophy
of Liberation* (Atlantic Highlands: Humanities Press, 1996), pp. 129-159;

Kerr, Fergus, *Immortal Longings: Versions of Transcending Humanity* (Notre Dame, Indiana: University of Notre Dame Press, 1997), pp. 136-158; Smith, Nicholas, *Strong Hermeneutics* (London: Routledge, 1997); Laforest, Guy, ed., *Charles Taylor et l'interpretation de l'identité moderne* (Paris: Cerf, 1998); *Eidos* 15:1 (1998) [Special Issue on Taylor]; Gutting, Gary, *Pragmatic Libralism and the Critique of Modernity* (Cambridge: Cambridge University Press, 1999), pp. 113-162; Johnston, Paul, *The Contradictions of Modern Moral Philosophy: Ethics after Wittgenstein* (London: Routledge, 1999), pp. 100-111; White, Stephen, *Sustaining Affirmation: The Strengths of Weak Ontology in Political Theory* (Princeton, NJ: Princeton University Press, 2000), pp. 42-75; Abbey, Ruth, *Charles Taylor* (Princeton University Press, 2001); Pelaby, Janie, *Charles Taylor, penseur de la pluralité* (Sainte Foy: Les Presses de l'Université de Laval, 2001); *Acta Philosophica Fennica* 71 (2002) [Special Issue on Charles Taylor]; Gagnon, Bernard, *La philosophie morale et politique de Charles Taylor* (Sainte-Foy: Presses de l'Université Laval, 2002); Redhead, Mark, *Charles Taylor: Thinking and Living Deep Diversity* (Lanham: Rowman and Littlefield, 2002); Smith, Nicholas, *Charles Taylor: Meaning, Morals and Modernity* (Cambridge: Cambridge University Press, 2002); Baker, Deane-Peter, ed., *Explorations in Contemporary Continental Philosophy of Religion* (New York: Rodopi, 2003), pp. 143-154; Baker, Deane-Peter, *Tayloring Reformed Epistemology* (London: SCM Press, 2003); Abbey, Ruth, ed., *Charles Taylor* (Cambridge: Cambridge University Press, 2004); Spence, Keith, *Charles Taylor: Modernity, Freedom, and Community* (Cardiff: University of Wales Press, 2004); *Philosophiques* 33:2 (2006) [Special Issue on Taylor]; Terlinden, Luc, *Le conflit des intériorités: Charles Taylor et l'intériorisation des sources morales* (Rome: Editiones Academiae Alfonsianae, 2006); Fraser, Ian, *Dailectics of the Self: Transcending Charles Taylor* (Exeter: Imprint Academic, 2007); Templeton, John, ed., *Professor Charles Taylor: 2007 Templeton Prize Laureate* (Phoenix: Templeton Foundation, 2007); Braman, Brian, *Meaning and Authenticity: Bernard Lonergan and Charles Taylor on the Drama of Authentic Human Existence* (Toronto: University of Toronto Press, 2008), pp. 24-46, 73-97; Laitinen, Arto, *Strong Evaluations without Moral Sources: On Charles Taylor's Philosophical Anthropology and Ethics* (Berlin: Walter de Gruyter, 2008); Sibley, Robert, *Northern Spirits: John Watson, George Grant, and Charles Taylor* (Montreal: McGill-Queen's University Press, 2008), pp. 177-270; O'Shea, Andrew, *Selfhood and Sacrifice: René Girard and Charles Taylor on the Crisis of Modernity* (London: Continuum, 2010); Meynell, Robert, *Canadian Idealism and the Philosophy of Freedom: C.B. Macpherson, George Grant, and Charles Taylor* (Montreal: McGill-Queen's University Press, 2011).

118   Taylor is also known for his historical works on Hegel and his works on ethics, politics, and the philosophy of mind including: *The Explanation of Behavior* (1967); *Language and Human Nature* [Alan B. Plaunt Memorial Lecture] (1978); *Theories of Meaning* (1983) [Dawes Hicks Lecture of 1982; McLuhan Lecture of 1983]; *The Ethics of Authenticity* (1991) [also issued as

The Malaises of Modernity (1991)]; *Multiculturalism and the Politics of Recognition* (1992; 1994); *A Catholic Modernity?* [ACM] (1999); *Modern Social Imaginaries* [MSI] (2004); *A Secular Age* [SA] (2008) [Gifford Lectures of 1998-1999]; *Laïcité et liberté de conscience* (2010) [with Jocelyn MacLure]; *Dilemmas and Connections* (2010) [Collected Essays];*Retrieving Realism* (2011) [with Herbert Dryfus].

Taylor has also written numerous essays on communitarianism and other topics including: "The Poverty of the Poverty of Historicism," *Universities and Left Review* 4 (1958), pp. 77-78; "Clericalism," *Downside Review* 78 (1960), pp. 167-180; "L'État et la laïcité," *Cité Libre* 14 (1963), pp. 3-6; "Mind-Body Identity, a Side Issue?," *Philosophical Review* 76 (1967), pp. 201-213; "Relations Between Cause and Action," in *Proceedings of the Seventh Inter-American Congress of Philosophy* (Québec: Les Presses de l'Université Laval, 1967), vol. I, pp. 243-255; "Two Issues About Materialism," *Philosophical Quarterly* 19 (1969), pp. 73-79; "Explaining Action," *Inquiry* 13 (1970), pp. 54-89; "The Explanation of Purposive Behavior," in Borger, Roger, et al., eds., *The Behavioural Sciences* (Cambridge: Cambridge University Press, 1970), pp. 49-79, 89-95; "How Is Mechanism Conceivable?," in Grene, Marjorie, ed., *Interpretations of Life and Mind: Essays Around the Problem of Reduction* (London: Routledge and Kegan Paul, 1971), pp. 38-64; "Interpretation and the Sciences of Man," *Review of Metaphysics* 25 (1971), pp. 3-51; "Conditions for a Mechanistic Theory for Behavior," in Eccles, John, et al., eds., *Brain and Human Behavior* (Berlin and New York: Springer-Verlag, 1972), pp. 449-470 "What Is Human Agency?," in Mischel, Theodore, ed., *The Self: Psychological and Philosophical Issues* (Oxford: Blackwell, 1977), pp. 103-135; "The Validity of Transcendental Arguments," *Proceedings of the Aristotelian Society* 79 (1978), pp. 151-165; "Action as Expression," in Diamond, Cora, et al., eds., *Intention and Intentionality* (Ithaca: Cornell University Press, 1979), pp. 73-89; "What's Wrong With Negative Liberty," in Ryan, Alan, ed., *The Idea of Freedom* (Oxford: Oxford University Press, 1979), pp. 175-193; "From an Analytic Perspective," in Kortian, Garbis, ed., *Metacritique: The Philosophical Argument of Jürgen Habermas* (Cambridge: Cambridge University Press, 1980), pp. 1-21; "Understanding in Human Science," *Review of Metaphysics* 34 (1980), pp. 25-38; "Consciousness," in Secord, Paul, ed., *Explaining Human Behaviour: Consciousness, Human Action and Social Structure* (Beverly Hills: Sage, 1982), pp. 35-51; "The Diversity of Goods," in Sen, Amartya, et al., eds., *Utilitarianism and Beyond* (Cambridge: Cambridge University Press, 1982), pp. 129-144; "Rationality," ["RAT"], in Hollis, Martin, ed., *Rationality and Relativism* (Oxford: Blackwell, 1982), pp. 87-105; "Foucault on Freedom and Truth," ["FFT"], *Political Theory* 12 (1984), pp. 152-183; "Politics and Ethics: An Interview," in Rabinow, Paul, ed., *The Foucault Reader* (New York: Pantheon, 1984), pp. 373-380 [with Michel Foucault]; "Connolly, Foucault and Truth," *Political Theory* 13 (1985), pp. 377-385; "The Person," in Carrithers, Michael, ed., *The Category of the Person: Anthropology, Philosophy, History* (New York: Cambridge University

Press, 1985), pp. 257-281; "The Motivation Behind a Procedural Ethics," in Beiner, Ronald, ed., *Kant and Political Philosophy* (Cambridge: Harvard University Press, 1993), pp. 337-360; "The Nature and Scope of Distributive Justice," in Lukash, Frank, ed., *Justice and Equality Here and Now* (Ithaca Cornell University Press, 1986), pp. 34-67; "Overcoming Epistemology," in Baynes, Kenneth, et al., eds., *After Philosophy: End or Transformation?* (Cambridge: MIT Press, 1987), pp. 464-488; "The Moral Topography of the Self," in Sass, Louis, et al., eds., *Hermeneutics and Psychological Theory* (New Brunswick: Rutgers University Press, 1988), pp. 298-320; "Symposium: Religion and Politics," *Compass* 6 (1988), pp. 5-23; "Explanation and Practical Reason," *Wider Working Paper* WP72 (Helsinki: World Institute for Development Economics Research of the United Nations University, 1989), pp. 1-23; "Taylor and Foucault on Power and Freedom: A Reply," *Political Studies* 37 (1989), pp. 277-281; "Irreducibly Social Goods," in Brenna, Geoffrey, ed., *Rationality, Individualism and Public Policy* (Canberra: Australian National University, 1990), pp. 45-63; "Religion in a Free Society," in Hunter, James, ed., *Articles of Faith, Articles of Peace* (Washington: The Brookings Institution, 1990), pp. 93-113; "Heidegger, Language, and Ecology," in Dreyfus, Hubert, ed., *Heidegger: A Critical Reader* (Oxford: Blackwell, 1992), pp. 247-269; "The Deep Challenge of Dualism," in Gagnon, Alain, ed., *Quebec: State and Society in Crisis* (Toronto: Nelson, 1993), pp. 82-95; "It is Strange and Wonderful that We Exist," *Compass* 11 (1993), pp. 21-22; "Charles Taylor Replies," in Tully, James, ed,. *Philosophy in an Age of Pluralism: The Philosophy of Charles Taylor in Question* (Cambridge: Cambridge University Press, 1994), pp. 213-257; "The Modern Identity," in Daly, Markate, ed., *Communitarianism: A New Public Ethics* (Belmont: Wadsworth, 1994), pp. 55-71; "Reply to Commentators," ["RC"], *Philosophy and Phenomenological Research* 54 (1994), pp. 203-213; "A Most Peculiar Institution," in Harrison, Ross, ed., *World, Mind and Ethics* (Cambridge: Cambridge University Press, 1995), pp. 132-155; "Iris Murdoch and Moral Philosophy," in Antonaccio, Maria, ed., *Iris Murdoch and the Search for Human Goodness* (Chicago: University of Chicago Press, 1996), pp. 3-28; "Spirituality of Life—and Its Shadow," *Compass* 14 (1996), pp. 10-13; "A World Consensus on Human Rights?," *Dissent* 43 (1996), pp. 15-21; "Living with Difference," in Allen, Anita, ed., *Debating Democracy's Discontent* (Oxford: Oxford University Press, 1998), pp. 212-226; "Modes of Secularism," in Bhargava, Rajeev, ed., *Secularism and Its Critics* (Delhi: Oxford University Press, 1998), pp. 31-53; "Qu'est-ce qu'une philosophique morale réaliste?," in Laforest, Guy, ed., *Charles Taylor et l'interpretation de l'identité moderne* (Sainte Foy: Les Presses de l'Université Laval, 1998), pp. 365-368 [Interview]; "Analytical Thomism," *New Blackfriars* 80 (1999), pp. 206-210; "Conditions of an Unforced Consensus on Human Rights," in Bauer, Joanne, ed., *The East Asian Challenge for Human Rights* (Cambridge: Cambridge University Press, 1999), pp. 124-144; "In Defence of Positive Freedom," in Rosen, Michael, ed., *Political Thought* (Oxford: Oxford University Press, 1999), pp. 128-129; "The

Immanent Counter-Enlightenment," in Beiner, Ronald, ed., *Canadian Political Philosophy* (Oxford: Oxford University Press, 2000), pp. 386-400; "McDowell on Value and Knowledge," *Philosophical Quarterly* 50 (2000), pp. 242-249; "Modernity and Difference," in Gilroy, Paul, et al., eds., *Without Guarantees* (London and New York: Verso, 2000), pp. 364-374; "A Place for Transcendence," in Schwartz, Regina, ed., *Transcendence: Philosophy, Literature, and Theology Approach the Beyond* (London: Routledge, 2004), pp. 1-12; "Religion Today," *Transit* 19 (2000), pp. 11-20; "What's Wrong with Foundationalism?," in Wrathall, Mark, ed., *Heidegger, Coping, and Cognitive Science* (Boston: MIT Press, 2000), vol. II, pp. 115-134; "The Articulated Life," *Reason in Practice* 1:3 (2001), pp. 3-9 [Interview]; "Plurality of Goods," in Dworkin, Ronald, ed., *The Legacy of Isaiah Berlin* (New York Review of Books, 2001), pp. 113-120; "Modern Social Imaginaries," *Public Culture* 14:1 (2002), pp. 91-124; "On Identity, Alienation and the Consequences of September 11th," *Acta Philosophica Fennica* 71 (2002), pp. 165-195 [Interview]; "Risking Belief: Why William James Still Matters," *Commonweal* 129 (March 8, 2002), pp. 14-17; "Charles Taylor on Secularization," *Ethical Perspectives* 10 (2003), pp. 78-86 [Interview]; "Closed World Structures," in Wrathall, Mark, ed., *Religion After Metaphysics* (Cambridge: Cambridge Unviersity Press, 2003), pp. 47-68; "Ethics and Ontology," *The Journal of Philosophy* 100 (2003), pp. 305-320; "Foundationalism and the Inner-Outer Distinction," in Smith, Nicholas, ed., *Reading McDowell: On Mind and World* (London: Routledge, 2003), pp. 106-120; "The Immanent Counter-Enlightenment: Christianity and Morality," *South African Journal of Philosophy* 24:3 (2005), pp. 224-239; "Redefinir la famille," *MokaSofa* (March 21, 2003); "Sacred Killing: The Roots of Violence," *Voices across the Boundaries* 1 (2003), pp. 11-16; "The Twice-Born," in *Cross Currents* 53:3 (2003), pp. 339-352; "Language and Human Nature," in Ostry, Bernard, et al., eds., *Visions of Canada* (Montreal: McGill-Queen's University Press, 2004), pp. 389-418; "Notes on the Sources of Violence: Perennial and Modern" in Heft, James, ed., *Beyond Violence: Religious Sources of Social Transformation in Judaism, Christianity and Islam* (New York: Fordham University Press, 2004), pp. 15-42; "A Place for Transcendence," in Schwartz, Regine, ed., *Transcendence* (New York: Routledge, 2004), pp. 1-10; "What is Pragmatism?," in Benhabib, Seyla, ed., *Pragmatism, Critique, Judgement* (Cambridge: MIT Press, 2004), pp.73-92; "A Philosopher's Postscript: Engaging the Citadel of Secular Reason," ["PP"] in Griffiths, Paul, ed., *Reason and the Reasons of Faith* (New York: T & T Clark, 2005), pp. 339-353; "The Weak Ontology Thesis," *The Hedgehog Review* 7:2 (2005), pp. 35-42; "An Issue about Language," in Jourdan, Christine, et al., eds., *Language, Culture, and Society* (Cambridge: Cambridge University Press, 2006), pp. 16-46; "Benedict XVI," *Public Culture* 18:1 (2006), pp. 11-14; "Religion and European Integration" in Michalski, Krzysztof, ed., *Religion in the New Europe: Conditions of European Solidarity* (Budapest; Central European University Press, 2006), pp. 1-22; "Religion and Modern Identity Struggles," in Gold, Nilufer, ed., *Islam in Public: Turkey, Iran* and Europe (Istanbul: Istanbul Bilgi University Press, 2006), pp. 481-524; "Religious Mobilizations," Public Culture 18 (2006), pp. 281-300; "Sex and Christianity: How Has the Moral Landscape Changed?," Commonweal 134 (September 28, 2006), p. 12; "The Future of the Religious Past," in De Vries, Hent, ed., Religion: Beyond a Concept (New York: Fordham University Press, 2007), pp. 178-244; "Modern Moral Rationalism," ["MMR"], in Zabala, Santiago, ed., Weakening Philosophy (Montreal: McGill-Queen's Press, 2007), pp. 57-76; "On Social Imaginaries," in Gratton, Peter, et al., eds., Traversing the Imaginary: Richard Kearney and the Postmodern Challenge (Evanston: Northwestern University Press, 2007), pp. 29-47; "The Sting of Death: Why We Yearn for Eternity," Commonweal 134 (October 12, 2007), pp. 13-16; "What is Secularity?," in Vanhoozer, Kevin, ed., Transcending Boundaries in Philosophy and Theology (Aldershot: Ashgate, 2007), pp. 57-76; "Charles Taylor Interviewed," Prospect Magazine (February, 2008) [Debate with A.C. Grayling and others]; "Challenging Issues about the Secular Age," Modern Theology 23 (2010), pp. 404-416; "The Perils of Moralism" in De Vries, Hent, Religion: The Concept (New York: Fordham University Press, 2011).

These papers have been collected as: Human Agency and Language [HAL] (1985); Philosophy and the Human Sciences (1985); Philosophical Arguments [PHA] (1995).

For a bibliography of Taylor's writings see: Tully, James, ed., Philosophy in an Age of Pluralism: The Philosophy of Charles Taylor in Question (Cambridge University Press, 1994), pp. 258-264; Abbey, Ruth, Charles Taylor (Princeton University Press, 2001), pp. 229-245; Smith, Nicholas, Charles Taylor: Meaning, Morals and Modernity (Cambridge: Cambridge University Press, 2002), pp. 262-274.

119   Strong evaluation thus seeks the higher goods, those that are more important than others, those which make life worth living, and provide a standpoint from which things can be weighed. Examples of these higher goods would be such things as self-expression, family life, a fulfilling job, decency, and sensitivity. Taylor also introduces the notion of hypergoods which are the highest of these higher goods, those of overriding importance, such as universal justice, world peace, love of God, and religion (SOS, III, pp. 62-64).

120   Atheists of course have argued that religious-based moralities have led to authoritarianism, social oppression, the domination of women and minorities, the exclusion or murder of heretics, the mortification of sensual desire and the rejection of ordinary human living (such as with Nietzsche, Foucault, and New Atheists such as Ferry, Dawkins, Dennett, Harris, Hitchens, and Zizek) (SOS, I, pp. 5, 15-19; SA, XIV, p. 515; XV, pp. 561-562; XVI, p. 596; "PP," pp. 351-352). In response Taylor admits that religion can be manipulated in order to mobilize people, as with Milosevic, the Bharatiya Janata Party, the Kataeb Party, and the Ustase regime. And religion can even be used for violence as

with Aztecan sacrifice, the Spanish Inquisition, and Al-Quaeda. Yet, as Taylor notes, deism and atheism have their own potentiality for violence as with the French Revolution, Stalin, Hitler, and Pol Pot (SA, XV, pp. 548-549; XVIII, p. 688; XX, p. 769). Moreover, just because some hypergoods, including religion, have been interwoven with relations of dominance and violence, this does not show that all its tenets are false or all religious morality bad. For positive ideals can be misapplied and lead to harm, and potentially destructive ideals can be directed to genuine goods. Indeed honest non-believers have seen the good contributed by religion to society, such as being a great force in the anti-slavery movements in England and the United States (SOS, III, pp. 70-71; IV, p. 100; XXV, pp. 518-519; SA, VIII, pp. 305-306; X, p. 370; XV, p. 546; ACM, I, p. 19-22, 26-28, 36; n. 1 on p. 37; VI, pp. 109-110). So arguments that religion encourages violence represent a triumph of selective attention over reality (SA, n. 19 on pp. 833-834). What is needed then is not the elimination of our highest spiritual aspirations (i.e. religion) but making sure our religious behavior is in line with our modern aspirations for benevolence and happiness (SOS, XXV, pp. 519-521).

121   Taylor is an unashamed advocate of the modern identity with its key features of: the importance of human well-being and flourishing; a notion of inwardness stressing freedom, autonomy, self-control, and self-expression (indeed pluralism or the right to express and develop one's own opinion and define one's own life); the affirmation of ordinary life, the life of work and family; and the emphasis on universal justice, rights, equality, and benevolence (SOS, I, pp. 4, 11-15, 22-25; III, p. 98; XXV, pp. 503, 511-512; VRT, III, pp. 89, 101; SA, IV, p. 179). Indeed Taylor controversially holds that some of the goods and advantages of the modern identity depended upon a break with Christendom, albeit not a break with Christian belief per se, but a break with the view that the structures, institutions, culture, and ideology of society are supposed to reflect the Christian condition (A Christian Modernity?, I, pp. 17, 37). Indeed he asserts that modern culture, properly understood, has carried certain facets of Christian life further than they ever were taken or could have been taken within a traditional Christian state, such as the affirmation of universal human rights to life and benevolence, affirmation of freedom, self-realization, and the ordinary life, and new forms of inwardness (so in Taylor's mind organizations such as Amnesty International and Doctors without Frontiers could only occur after a breach with the culture of Christendom). Paradoxically then the enlightenment critiques of traditional religion (such as those by Voltaire) allow us to live the Gospel in a new and purer way, one unencumbered by arms and spiritual stultification, freed from the bloody forcing of conscience, and freed from hypocrisy, confusion of faith and power, and the "crushing weight of being the right answer." For the voice of God is heard most clearly when the loudspeakers of armed authority are silent (ACM, I, p. 15-19, 26, 29-30, 35; VI, p. 107-108; SA, X, p. 371; XVII, p. 637; VRT, III, p. 114). So the contemporary Christian must enter into the "Ricci project" of

reconciliation and try to find what in modern culture represents a valid truth and advance and what is incompatible with the Christian faith.

122   According to Taylor, the proofs of God, while not without merit, no longer appear unproblematic. For these demonstrations tend to be most accepted in cultures deeply convinced of the existence of God, but have not achieved a universal acceptance (due to various factors including inadequate catechesis and volitional depravity) ("PP" pp. 339-340, 351-352; SA, XV, p. 551). Indeed Taylor argues that religious faith can be increased more by reflecting on the meaning of life and the sense of the love of God and God as a divine helper, than by the externals of cosmic design which seem bizarre, dry, and irrelevant, and make God into a fussy parent and puppet-master anxiously molding every detail of creation to our well-being and comfort (SA, VI, p. 226; VII, p. 294-295; IX, p. 329-330, 342; X, p. 375; XI, pp. 388-389; XII, p. 428; "PP," pp. 339-343).

123   Of course with the rise of Enlightenment Deism and Liberal Theology (which tended to reject miracles and sacraments and the need for grace to be benevolent, holding only reason or self-interest or feelings of kindness were necessary), and Atheism—religion was explained away as an error theory (wherein people, afraid of uncertainty or the unknown, or misery, or weak in the head, invented the deities) (SA, Introduction, pp. 12-13; VI, pp. 221-269; XII, p. 434; XIV, p. 518). Parallel to this, irreligion was presented as arising through what Taylor calls a "subtraction story" as humans sought to liberate themselves from earlier confining horizons, illusions, or limited knowledge (SA, Introduction, p. 22). For instance, in one subtraction story science increasingly gave a naturalistic explanation of the world, and so science, due to the findings of Darwin and other thinkers, eventually refuted the Bible and theism and crowded out religious belief (SA, Introduction, p. 4; I, p. 26; XVI, p. 600). And in other substractory stories, the world was disenchanted as final causes and spiritual forces (spirits, miracles, magic, relics, sacred spaces) were eliminated from reality (with Francis Bacon), or as the self became buffered and a resident in a cosmos where meanings are only in the head (with Freud and other naturalists), for things only have meanings as they awaken a response in creatures with feelings, desires, aversions, thoughts (SA, I, pp. 27, 31, 36-38; II, pp. 98, 131, 135, 143; VII, p. 271; VIII, p. 316; IX, pp. 324, 329-330; XII, p. 428; XV, p. 539; Conclusion, pp. 773-775).

Yet there are several problems with such subtraction accounts according to Taylor. First, there are no cast-iron intellectual arguments for atheism (indeed it is based on rather inconclusive ones). So the slide to deism and atheism was not just due to science and a rational examination of belief (as the theories of Gibbon, Trevor-Roper, Hume, and Weber would have it). Indeed science only conflicts with a very literal account of the Scriptures such as fossils exceeding the 5000-6000 years of the Mosaic story, and only with certain conceptions of the divine and His providence (SA, IX, p. 328; XV, p. 566). This is why most accounts of the conflict between science and religion draw heavily on an oversimplification between faith and science, that science is based on rigid logic and faith on belief without any evidence. Yet this fails to grasp that science is not completely free of faith elements. In fact, to hold that there are no assumptions in a scientist's work that aren't already based on evidence is surely a reflection of a blind faith, one that can't even feel the occasional tremor of doubt. Few religious believers are so untroubled (which is why honest atheists such as Félix LeDantec or Richard Lewontin will admit that "science" has a prior commitment to materialism and hence tolerates unsubstantiated just-so stories. So it is not so much that the methods of science compel a material explanation as that a prior allegiance to materialism induces some people to create an apparatus of investigation and a set of concepts that do not allow the divine a foot in the door (SA, XV, p. 568; n. 27-28, p. 835) [unfortunately those in the grip of an immanent worldview are under the influence of a clouding and cramping picture wherein they often cannot see important aspects of reality suggesting the spiritual and often have disinterest or even contempt for religion] (SA, XV, p. 551). Moreover, we can check the supposed claims of science to disprove religion against our religious life, against our sense of how God impinges on our existence, and our best account of values and beauty (SA, XV, pp. 567-568) So religion is not irrational.

Second a large motivation for secularism was a deep-seated moral distaste for a religion that sees God as an arbitrary tyrant who sends most people to hell (SA, VII, pp. 270-280; VIII, p. 306). In fact to the extent that one's own faith remains childish, and one has immature images of God, the easier it is for a person to become convinced that science has discredited religion, or that science will one day come up with conclusive proofs of naturalism or God's inexistence (i.e. the promissory view that science will eventually reduce everything to physics or neuroscience). And to the extent that one is engaged in an adult life of prayer, meditation, spiritual discipline, and religious contemplation, which involves letting go of childish images of God, secular views will find little traction (SA, VII, p. 289; IX, pp. 363-366; XV, pp. 548, 563; XVI, p. 603; n. 17 on p. 833). Thus argues Taylor "conversions from religion under the influence of science turn not on the alleged scientific proofs of materialism or the impossibility of God (which turn out on examination not to go through anyway), but rather on other factors which in this case consist in attachment to in-essential doctrines which can be refuted" (SA, IX, p. 367-368).

Third, such accounts often are not historical as for instance the new mechanistic science of the seventeenth century wasn't always seen as threatening to God and indeed was based at times on Christian motives.

Fourth, exclusive humanism is not just a subtraction story but positively asserts an immanent source of the moral life. That is to say it is not like a withering away of religious and metaphysical beliefs, on its own, made room for a purely human motivation. Rather there was need of a positive notion that motivation to beneficence and justice can lie in ourselves, in our own human resources (that we possess a natural instinct to benevolence or the pleasures of virtue as with Diderot and Montesqieu and Hume, or a disengaged instrumental reason with Hutcheson and Kant) (SA, VI, pp. 244-269; VII, p. 288, 294). So it is a unique and positive achievement to consider the world as purely immanent, to hold that all order, meaning, and morality come from humans (SA, X, p. 376).

Fifth there can be an avid embrace of reductionism as with Renan, Douglas Hofstadter, Dawkins, and Richard Lewontin, who find the ultimate religion in explaining away God and the soul, a deep awe in the fact that feeling and thought emerge out of an immense purposeless machine, in how the ultimate reality is a myriad of ephemeral swirling vortices of nearly incomprehensible mathematical activity, in how humans are nothing but a fleeting life-form on a dying star (SA, VIII, pp. 305-306; IX, pp. 367-368; XV, pp. 547, 561-562, 569-570, 583-586) [often contrasted with a crude religion which tries to explain things in terms of spirits, relics, miracles, demons, and other mythical explanations]. In fact, secularism is most often based on an unchallenged framework, something we have trouble thinking ourselves out of even as an imagined exercise, it is a picture, a spin, a master narrative, a background to our thinking wherein we can imagine no alternative, a picture that holds us captive to use the words of Wittgenstein (SA, XV, p. 549-550, 555-557, 573).

Sixth and most importantly, Taylor argues that the turn to secularism, rather than being based on science, argumentation (which as we have seen are weak reasons for it), is rather made on the basis of ethical considerations (SA, IX, p. 362):"What happened here was not that a moral outlook bowed to brute facts. Rather we might say that one moral outlook gave way to another" (SA, XV, p. 563). For proponents of secularism regularly paint religion as an outdated and primitive form of understanding, and atheism as what is rational and at the forefront of human progress. Typically this takes the form of the secularist arguing that there is something more mature and courageous in facing unvarnished reality with a scientific stance, as opposed to a person of faith who childishly craves for comfort in the face of a meaningless world. So the religious believer is pictured as someone who is afraid to face the fact that we are alone in an indifferent universe and without cosmic support, who is unready to eschew all easy comfort and consolation and acknowledge unpalatable truths, unlike the secularist who takes a stance of manliness against childish fears and sentimentality (SA, VII, p. 289; IX, pp. 363-368; XV, pp. 548, 563; XVI, p. 603; n. 17 on p. 833). Such a view is repeated over and over again by deists and atheists such as Spinoza, Goethe, Nietzsche, John Stuart Mill, Darwin, Freud, Weber, Gauchet, Stephen J. Gould, Hardy, Camus, Sartre, Isaiah Berlin, and Dawkins (SA, VIII, p. 318; XV, pp. 562-563, 574-575, 582) [what all of these people miss, however, is that it is legitimate that we are called to be like little children, to be humble, and have fidelity in a transformation of our heart ("PP," pp. 351-352)].

So secularism is woven into a story of disengaged scientific enquiry, a reliance on one's own reason against authority, courageous adulthood and renunciation of the childish comforts of meaning and beatitude (i.e. that we live in God's embracing love, that there is a warm fuzzy meaning to it all), and indeed it is crucial to this outlook that it grasp itself as science and reason driven, since to accept that it is based on moral considerations would be to admit that there is something that needs defense and yet has received none (SA, XI, pp. 387-388; XV, pp. 561-562, 565-566, 569, 579, 591; XVI, p. 596; "PP," pp. 351-352). Taylor writes "experience was carved into shape by a powerful theory which posited the primacy of the individual, the neutral, the intra-mental as the locus of certainty. What was driving this theory? Certain values, virtues, excellences: those of the independent, disengaged subject, reflexively controlling his own thought-processes, self-responsibility in Husserl's famous phrase. There is an ethics here, of independence, self-control, self-responsibility, of a disengagement which brings control: a stance which requires courage, the refusal of the easy comforts of conformity to authority, of the consolations of an enchanted world, of the surrender to the promptings of the senses. The entire picture, shot through with values, which is meant to emerge out of the careful, objective, presuppositionless scrutiny, is now presented as having been there from the beginning, driving the whole process of 'discovery'" (SA, XV, pp. 559-560).

124   Other French analytic philosophers include Jacques Bouveresse, Jules Vuillemin (his teacher), Gilles-Gaston Granger, Jean Nicod, Jacques Herbrand, and Jean Cavaillès.

125   For more on the life and thought of Francis Jacques see: DP (1993), vol. I, pp. 1473-1474; EF (2006), vol. VI, p. 5907; Griffiths, A. Phillips, *Contemporary French Philosophy* (Cambridge: University of Cambridge Press, 1987), p. 7; Gochet, Paul, ed., *Cinquante ans de philosophie de langue française* (Paris: Vrin, 1988), pp. 225-239; Schmidt, C.T., "The Systematics of Dialogism," *Journal of the American Society for Information Science* 48 (1997), pp. 1073-1081; Bloechl, Jeffrey, ed., *Face of the Other and the Trace of God* (New York: Fordham University Press, 2000), pp. 62-89; Fiddes, Paul, *Participating in God* (London: Darton, Longman, Todd, 2000), pp. 54-60; Searle, John, "Ethics and Speech Acts: Reply to Francis Jacques," *Revue Inernationale de Philosophie* 2 (2001), pp. 290-292; Armengaud, Françoise, ed., *Du dialogue au texte: Autour de Francis Jacques* (Paris: Éditions Kimé, 2003); Barrotta, Pierluigi, et al., *Controversies and Subjectivity* (Amsterdam: John Benjamins, 2005), pp. 173-178; Capelle, Philippe, *Finitude et mystère* (Paris: Cerf, 2005), pp. 30-32; Pembroke, Neil, *Renewing Pastoral Practice* (Burlington: Ashgate, 2006), pp. 57-69; Gron, Arne, *Subjectivity and Transcendence* (Tübingen: Mohr Siebeck, 2007), pp. 106-112; Goyard-Fabre, Simone, *Philosopher autrement ou de l'interrogation radicale* (Paris: Éditions Kimé, 2010).

126   The former work has been translated as *Dialogue and Personal Relation* [DS], tr. Andrew Rothwell (New Haven: Yale University Press, 1991). I use this translation throughout.

Other works of Francis Jacques include: *Dialogics: Logical Studies on Dialogue* [*Dialogiques: Recherches logiques sur le dialogue*] [DIA] (1979); *The Logical Space of Interlocution* [*L'espace logique de l'interlocution*] [LSI] (1985) [winner of the prix Louis Liard of the Academie des Sciences Morales et Politiques; Dialogics II]; *On Significance* [*De la signifiance*] (1987); *The Visible Other* [*L'autre visible*] (1998) [with Jean-Louis Leutrat]; *The Order of the Text* [*L'ordere du texte*] (2000); *Questioning and Categorizing in Fundamental Theology* [*Interroger et catégoriser en théologie fondamentale*] (2000) [Theological Thesis]; *On Textuality* [*De la textualité: Pour une textologie générale et comparée*] (2002); *Belief, Knowledge, and Faith* [*La Croyance, le savoir et la foi: Une refondation érotétique de la métaphysique*] [BKF] (2005); *The Tree of the Text* [*L'arbre du texte*] (2007).

Jacques has also written such articles as: "Faut-il une philosophie au christianisme? Le sens d'une question, le non-sens d'une problématique," *Recherches et débats* 49 (1967); "A Terminological Note about Reference," in Ryle, Gilbert, ed., *Contemporary Aspects of Philosophy* (Stocksfield: Oriel Press, 1976), pp. 103-110; "Croyance commune, croyance communiquée," *Dialectica* 33 (1979), pp. 263-281; "Sur la logique de l'argumentation," *Revue internationale de philosophie* 8 (1979), pp. 47-69; "L'espace logique de l'interlocution," *Bulletin de la Société de Philosophie* 4 (April 26, 1980), p. 144; "L'explication dans les sciences humaines: Entre le déterminisme du comportement et la détermination de l'action," in Richelle, Marc, ed., *L'éxplication en psychologie* (Paris: Presses Universitaires de France, 1980), pp. 77-110; "Les conditions dialogiques de la compréhension ou le paradoxe de Narcissme," in Parret, Herman, ed., *Meaning and Understanding* (Berlin: De Gruyter, 1981), pp. 353-388; "L'interrogation, force illocutaire et interaction verbale," *Langue française* 52 (1981), pp. 70-79; "L'analyse des énoncés théologiques," in Lauret, Bernard, et al., eds., *Initiation à la pratique de la théologie* (Paris: Cerf, 1982); "La dimension dialogique en philosophie du langage," in Sojcher, J., ed., *Philosophie et langage* (Bruxelles: Editions de l'Université de Bruxelles, 1982), pp. 78-89; "La parole tronquée: Pour une pragmatique du phénomène excommunicatoire," in Lyotard, Jean-François, ed., *Langage et Excommunication* (Cabay: Louvain-la-neuve, 1982); "Communicabilité et référence," in *La vérité* (Paris: Beauchesne, 1983); "La mise en communauté de l'énonciation," *Languages* 18 (1983), pp. 47-72; "Les vertus dialogales: Interprétation et dialogue," in De Lubac, Henri, ed., *Mélanges Henri de Lubac* (Paris: Aubier, 1983); "Communicabilité et dialectique," *Archives de philosophie du droit* 29 (1984), pp. 7-25; "Dialogue exige, communicabilité et référence," *Archives de Philosophie du Droit* 29 (1984); "Du dialogisme à la forme dialoguée," in Dascal, Marcelo, ed., *Dialogue: An Interdisciplinary Approach* (Philadelphia: John Benjamin, 1985), pp. 27-56; "De l'intersubjectivité à l'interlocution: Un changement de pardigne?," *Archivo di Filosofia* 14 (1986), pp. 195-218; "Questions, problèmes, problématiques: Pour une approche interrogative de la connaissance," *Études de Lettres* (Lausanne: Presse Université de Lausanne, 1986); "Dialogisme et argumentation: Le dialogue argumentatif," *Verbum* 12:2 (1989), pp. 221-237; "Référence et différence: La situation originaire de la signification," *Encyclopédie philosophique* (Paris: Presses Universitaires de France, 1989), vol. I, pp. 492-512; "La construction pragmatique," in *Science et sens* (Lyon: Etudes Epistémologiques de Lyon, 1990), pp. 41-48; "Peut-on définir un a priori communicationnel?," in *Du Dialogue* (Paris: Vrin 1992); "Expérience et textualité en philosophie de la religion," *Revue des Sciences Philosophiques et Théologiques* 77 (1993); "Interprétation et textualités," in Greisch, Jean, ed., *Comprendre et interpréter* (Paris Beauchesne, 1993); "Des jeux de langage aux jeux textuels: Le cas du rite," *Concilium* 259 (1994), pp. 13-37 [translated as "From Language Games to Textual Games: The Case of the Religious Rite," in Chauvet, Louis, ed., *Liturgy and the Body* (London: SCM Press, 1995), pp. 1-21]; "Interrogativité et textualité: Une contribution à la théorie du texte," in Ellrodt, Robert, ed., *Mélanges offerts à Robert Ellrodt* (Paris: Presses de la Sorbonne Nouvelle, 1994); "Qu'est-ce qu'une catégorie religieuse?," in Capelle, Philippe, ed., *Le Statut contemporain de la philosophie première* (Paris: Beauchesne, 1996), pp. 73-120; "Entre théologie et philosophie: problèmes catégoriaux," *Revue des sciences philosophiques et théologiques* 4 (1997), pp. 439-479; "Définir la catégorisation religieuse," *Recherches sur la philosophie et la langue* 19 (1998), pp. 109-145; "Apologétique et théologie fondamentale: Après M.Blondel," in Capelle, Philippe, ed., *Apologétique et Philosophie* (Paris: Cerf, 1999), pp. 259-293; "L'impossible interrogation?: Entretien à trois voix," in Capelle, Phillip, ed., *Subjectivité et transcendence* (Paris: Cerf, 1999), pp. 129-167; "Philosophie religieuse ou philosophie de la religion: Blondel, Lavelle, Marcel," in Vieillard-Baron, Jean-Louis, ed., *Philosophie de l'Esprit* (Hildesheim: Georg Olms Verlag, 1999), pp. 2-20; "Dialogue, dialogisme, interlocution," *Actes du VIIIème Congrès internationale Bakhtine* (Calgary: North-Wester University Press, 1999); "Interroger: Interrogation philosophique et interrogation religieuse," *Transversalités* 73 (2000), pp. 5-72, 75-107, 109-121 [including debates with Jean Ladrière and Pierre Beauchamp]; "Avec: Éloge de la réciprocité interpersonnelle," in *Colloque Enrico Castelli* (Padua: Cedam 2001); "De la fracture à la conversion: L'interrogation de foi," *Réflexions chrétiennes* 25 (2001); "Qu'est-ce qu'un texte religieux?," *Raisons politiques* 4 (2001), pp. 40-56; "Apologétique de l'être et/ou apologétique du sens," *Réflexions chrétiennes* 26 (2002); "Pour un paradigme érotétique en théologie fondamentale: De l'appropriation catégoriale," in Doré, Joseph, ed., *La responsabilité des théologiens* (Paris: Desclée de Brouwer, 2002), pp.737-753; "Le statut de la pensée apophatique: Dire, dédire, redire," in Olivetti, Marco, ed., *Théologie négative* (Padova: CEDAM, 2002), pp. 13-56; "De la juste place: Un philosophie néo-critique de la religion est-elle possible?," in Casatillo, Monique, ed., *Criticisme et religion* (Paris: L'Harmattan, 2004), pp. 89-126; "L'option néo-critique en philosophie de la religion," *Revue*

Réflexions chrétiennes 3 (2004), pp. 30-45; "Sagesse, sens et salut: Comment évaluer le thème sapientiel dans Fides et ratio," in Capelle, Philippe, et al., eds., *Raison philosophique et christianisme à l'aube du troisième millénaire* (Paris: Cerf, 2004), pp. 53-97; "Après la mort de Dieu: Pour une théologie en interrogation?," in Van den Kerchove, Anna, ed., *Variations sur Dieu: Langages, silences, pratiques* (Bruxelles: Presses Universitaires Saint-Louis, 2005), pp. 119-146; "Réductions et réductionnisme," *Réflexions chrétiennes* 29 (2005 "Loi naturelle et impératif catégorique," *Réflexions chrétiennes* 30 (2006); "Transformer la philosophie de la religion," ["Transforming the Philosophy of Religion"] ["TPR"], *Revue d'histoire et de philosophie religieuse* 86 (2006), pp. 41-65; "Lui: statut du tiers personnel et structure d'altérité," *Archivio di Filosofia* 75 (2007), pp. 101-122; "Thomas d'Aquin et Emmanuel Kant: Loi naturelle et impératif catégorique. Et après?," *Doctor Communis* 10 (2007), pp. 93-128.

127   Jacques however disagrees with the postmodern views of Heidegger (somewhat) and Marion that God is a God without being (BKF, VI, pp. 330-332; Conclusion, pp. 378-379). For with Dominique Dubarle he argues that the God known to humans is not a univocal God of ontotheology [*ontotheologie*], but an analogous God of theological ontology [*theologale ontology*] (BKF, I, pp. 2, 8-10, 15, 18; II, pp. 72-73; V, pp. 232-236; VI, pp. 332-343, 348; Conclusion, pp. 366, 369-378; "TPR," pp. 45. 54, 63). Still we must proceed carefully here and recognize it is best not to think of the situation as one of being coming to God—wherein we have God Being [*Dieu-être*]—but one of God coming to being—wherein we have Being God [*l'être-Dieu*]. In this way we make it clear that God's being is the being by which all is (being determined by itself; *l'être par lui-même*), being in the causal sense of making be, not the common being of the world (being determined by being; *l'être par l'étant*). Again God's being is not that of an object [*l'etant*] but of a personal and pure being [*l'être; esse*], one who provides gifts, grace, and salvation, and is sacrificial love and judge. Divine being then names not a substance but an inexhaustibleness [*l'inepuisable*] (BKF, VI, pp. 344-350; Conclusion, pp. 374-375). Indeed contra Marion it is only because God is being that we can also say that God is love and goodness (BKF, VI, pp. 351-353, 356-357; Conclusion, p. 376; "TPR," pp. 57-58)

128   Jacques also argues that a metaphysics of a substantive ego results in loving the neighbor as oneself and so egoistically as well as on the basis of their qualities and so replaceably. Yet if we understand the person as relational then we can see that we love not a substance for its qualities, merits, charms, or possessions, but a person for him or herself, for his or her irreplaceable ipseity (selfness), without expectation of reciprocation (DS, II, pp. 73-90).

129   Based on this notion of dialogical relation, Jacques reconstitutes thought as a method of interrogation [*dialogisme*], or what he calls an erotetics [*érotétique*], following Littré. For all thought involves entering into interrogation with another about a world to be jointly said [and as what we seek to grasp

often involves interrogating a text, thinking is often textualizing] (LSI, III, p. 131-154; IV, pp. 181-196, 212-220; DS, Preface, pp. xvii-xviii; BKF, IV, pp. 256-257). Jacques, as can be suspected, also advocates an erotetic theology, i.e. an interrogative theology (BKF, I, pp. 25-31, 33; LSI, VII, pp. 288-290). In this way Jacques hopes to reconstruct both metaphysics, which has fallen on hard times in light of French postmodernism, and theism, which has fallen on hard times in light of atheism (BKF, I, p. 2, 8-10, 15, 18; Conclusion, p. 366; "TPR," pp. 45. 54, 63). For what is real is not what is sensible but what is questionable, whatever that may be (BKF, V, pp. 305-307). As a result, truth is more the *adaequatio cogitationis et vitae* [the adequation of thought and life] of Augustine, Pascal, and Blondel than it is the *adaequatio rei et intellectus* [the adequation of thing and thought] of Aquinas (BKF, II, pp. 86-91; IV, pp. 256-257).

Now Jacques argues that faith and reason are in harmony (BKF, II, pp. 111-113; IV, pp. 192-194) and involve a combination of faith seeking understanding (*fides quaerens intellectum*) and understanding seeking faith (*intellectus quaerens* or *collocans fidem*) (BKF, II, pp. 113-114; VI, p. 341).

On the one hand, faith is reasonable and Christians can legitimately make use of philosophy (an order of truths for intelligence) as did Clement of Alexandria who cited Paul about 200 times but Plato more than 600 times (BKF, II, pp. 104, 107-109). For as Jacques puts it, "Religion thinks in an original register of interrogation and experience" ("TPR," p. 58; cf. BKF, I, p. 7; IV, p. 191). That is to say, the rationality of faith can be based on an interrogation of an experiential encounter with being and the Absolute wherein we discover in the end that there is something greater than the self in the self—for we experience ourselves as existing not through ourselves, nor even through God as totally other, but through the divine relationship that unites with and precedes us—as well as an interrogation of Scriptural and other texts and their significance and presuppositions (content) (BKF, I, p. 59; II, p. 83; III, p. 178; V, p. 232; VI, pp. 360-361; DS, V, pp. 236-240). Ultimately such a religious philosophy is based on what Jacques labels a structure of Question/Response (Q/R) wherein we accept premises conditionally (BKF, II, pp. 126-131; III, pp. 165-166, 177; V, pp. 270, 275). Through this structure of Question/Response we can attain such metaphysical categories as those of causality, change, essence/existence (following Gilson), identity, necessity, permanence, possibility, property, relation, space, time, the transcendentals (being, true, good, one), and the Absolute (BKF, V, pp. 260-262, 264, 269-270, 284, 287-293, 297-300).

On the other hand, one cannot live by reason alone and without faith. First, because there are times in life where if one doubts one fails (or falls), such as when doing something risky like jumping over a pit. Second, as Newman noted, because there are things we believe on account of the testimony of others such as that Australia exists even thought we have never been there, or that planets are from errant stars, etc. In fact a great deal of our knowledge is based on one's belief in and the testimony of orators, the powerful, experts, influential people, the elderly, traditions, and the wisdom of the nations. Third, as Marcel recognized, because one believes without scientific proof that one can keep one's promises, achieve one's destiny, and have confidence in one's ability to display honor, cooperation, love, and friendship.

Indeed ultimately one has need of and can receive a religious faith proper [la croyance-foi] (BKF, I, pp. 20-22, 42, 54; III, pp. 180-183). Such a faith, according to Jacques, has three levels: credere Deum, credere Deo, and credere in Deum. Credere Deum [believing God] is a belief that God exists and has a divine nature of truth, goodness, light, and life. As such it overlaps with philosophy. Credere Deo [believing by God] is a belief in the Word of God, in the authority of divine revelation (particularly in the Scriptures), through which mysteries of the faith exceeding reason are revealed. Lastly credere in Deum [believing in God], following Rousselot, is an absolute confidence in another, a voluntary adhesion to and a credit extended to another, based on a friendship and its promises (DS, II, pp. 45-48, 70-72; BKF, I, pp. 51-57; II, pp. 70-72, 85; IV, pp. 189-190, 216-228). Finally, such a faith is, following Rousselot, a seeing of things with the eyes of God, albeit without vitiating human experiential knowledge (BKF, IV, p. 215). So faith, rather than being a unilateral theology of divine initiative or an anthropological theology of human auto-transcendence, is more a Wittgensteinien language game wherein responding to a prevenient grace or call one comes to believe that a divine love is stronger than death and one consents to its Word in a dialogue of salvation (BKF, I, pp. 62-68, 73; II, pp. 86-88, 91).

In fact according to Jacques faith is ultimately based on the structure of an Appellation/Response (A/R) [Call/Response], a call or autocommunication of God in His Word to which we relate and respond, and one wherein presuppositions (mysteries of the faith) are given to us by revelation and held unconditionally (BKF, I, pp. 63-64; IV, pp. 226-227, 229, 232, 248-249; "TPR," pp. 61-63). Through the structure of this Appellation/Response we can acquire such categories as those of bodily resurrection, conversion, creation, Holy Spirit, Incarnation, justification, original sin, purification, sacrament, sacrifice, salvation, suffering, Trinity, and vocation (BKF, II, p. 89, 95-96, 103; III, pp. 160-166, 170-172, 176-177, 179-180; n. 1 on p. 171; IV, pp. 227-244; VI, pp. 338-340, 359; "TPR," pp. 50-55).

Now according to Jacques there have been historically five specific notions regarding the relation of philosophy to theology (ancillary, concordant, asymptotic, parallel, and erotetic [which he favors]).

First is the medieval notion of philosophy as ancillary to theology, as a handmaiden [ancillaire]. Here philosophy exists to serve theology and has an obedience to faith, a subalternation, and so is not completely autonomous. Such a view is found in Origen, Maximus the Confessor, Peter Damian, Anselm, Aquinas, and Gilson (BKF, II, p. 102, 115-122).

Second comes the concordant relation of philosophy to theology. Here philosophy is autonomous and has its own proper rationality and domain (often because God guarantees various eternal, metaphysical, and mathematical truths). Hence by itself and independent of theology, philosophy can and should treat such subjects as human nature, bodily resurrection, creation, and God's existence and nature. Such a view is found in Albert the Great, Descartes, Malebranche, as well as in Mercier and the Louvain and Fribourg Thomists (BKF, II, pp. 123-126).

Third is the asymptotic relationship of philosophy to theology. Here philosophy is open to faith as its limit, reason recognizing it must in the end disavow itself and embrace the faith which it needs. This view is found in Augustine, Pascal, Hegel, Blondel, Marcel, Claude Bruaire, Hans Urs von Balthasar, and John Paul II (BKF, II, pp. 126-131; III, p. 165; IV, p. 187).

Fourth is the parallel relation of philosophy to theology seen in Eusebius of Cesarea, Aquinas again, Gilson again, and Chenu, according to Jacques. On this view philosophy and theology are parallel in their modes of argumentation but have different domains. On account of this philosophy can take over and incorporate the truths of theology into itself. Here then we have Gilson's famous notion of Christian Philosophy wherein philosophy borrows from revelation such categories as creation from nothing, God as pure act (*ipsum esse subsistens* [self-subsistent being]) and personal (*ego sum qui sum* [I am who am]), the human as a spiritual and dignified being, and sin, which Aristotle and Plato did not know. In a way then here philosophy profits more from theology than vice versa (BKF, II, pp. 71-73, 115-122, 132-134; III, pp. 154-156, 167-168; IV, pp. 241-245; V, p. 298; n. 61 on p. 350).

Finally we have the erotetic relation of philosophy to theology (*interrogo ut intelligam* [I interrogate in order to understand]) favored by Jacques himself and also found in Clement of Alexandria, Augustine, Origen, Kierkegaard, Blondel, Berdiaev, Lavelle, and Marcel. Here philosophy and theology differ both in their domains (as with the parallel relation) and in their modes of interrogation.

In terms of their domains philosophy interrogates what agrees with our proper nature as humans, as well as the metaphysical nature of reality (questions of meaning), whereas theology interrogates what agrees with our relation to God (the Gospels and its mysteries of the faith) (BKF, II, pp. 136-138; III, pp. 154-156, 177-178; IV, p. 210). And much like with Gilson's notion of Christian philosophy, here philosophy and theology can aid each other, all the while keeping their categories distinct for Jacques. For faith does not oppose the autonomy of philosophy and its domain of questioning, indeed it rather welcomes an autonomous philosophy and turns to it for elucidation (as for instance making use of the notion of the hypostases of Plato, Plotinus, and Proclus to better understand the Trinity). Hence faith is a knowledge arising from the interrogation of matters of faith in accordance with the status of the thinkable. And reason, even though it is autonomous and has its own norms, must not be closed-off from and blind to potential contributions coming to it from theology. Rather it should incorporate into its tissue the presuppositions given to it by revelation, as it has done with the notions of creation, the person, the Trinity, as well as like notions mentioned above – for the reason that depriving itself of Biblical sources would in fact be unreasonable. So as Jacques puts it, a philosophy founded on natural reason comes to find the blessings of faith, and a theology commencing with the stability of faith advances to find the serenity of reason (BKF, II, pp. 134-136; IV, pp. 253-254; VI, pp. 359-360; DS, V, p. 232). Or said differently, an ideal "religious philosophy" occurs when a tendency of philosophers to theologize meets a tendency of theologians to philosophize, in other words, where there is found a philosophizing in the faith [philosophant dans la foi]—in the presence of the Logos (BKF, II, pp. 138-142; III, pp. 143-149, 153, 156-160, 164-168, 172-175, 178-179; IV, pp. 196, 241-242).

In terms of their modes of interrogation, philosophy and theology are two distinct yet parallel ways of questioning. For philosophy, as we have seen, is a profane interrogation based on the mode of a Question/Response (Q/R) wherein we find the sense of humans and utilize the categories of logic and metaphysics. But theology is based on the matrix of an Appellation/Response (A/R) wherein we find the Sense of the human (a concern for salvation and a hope in and promise of the world to come) and with humility and homage utilize the categories of revelation (BKF, IV, p. 207-210, 213; VI, p. 348; Conclusion, pp. 369-375).

130   If one had to single out the key Catholic Analytic Philosophers among a total of about 125, one would have to include: Fr. Juan David Garcia Bacca (1901-1992) [Vienna Circle]; the convert Peter Geach (1916-) [husband of Elizabeth Anscombe; Pro Ecclesia et Pontifice in 1999; Aquinas Medal in 2000]; Sebastian Moore, O.S.B. (1917-); Walter E. Stokes, S.J. (c. 1920-1969) [Process Thought]; the convert Yorick Smythies (c. 1920-1982) [a student of Wittgenstein]; Leslie Dewart (1922-) [who opposes the use of Greek categories in Christian theology]; Cornelius Ernst, O.P. (1924-1977); the Australian Max Charlesworth (1925-); the convert Sir Michael Dummett (1925-), of the University of Oxford [Rolf Schock Philosophy Prize in 1995; Aquinas Medal in 2003]; the Spaniard Manuel Garrido Jimenez (1925-) [Opus Dei; the convert Nicholas Rescher (1928-) [Pragmatist; Alexander von Humboldt Prize in 1984; Cardinal Mercier Prize 2005; Aquinas Medal in 2007; AAS]; Vincent G. Potter, S.J. (1929-1994) [Pragmatist]; the convert Alasdair MacIntyre (1929-) [though something of a critic of pure analytic philosophy; Analytical Thomist; Aquinas Medal in 2010]; Fergus Gordon

Kerr, O.P. (1931-) [Analytical Thomist]; James F. Ross (1931-2010) [Analytical Thomist]; the Norwegian Dagfinn Föllesdal (1932-); Donald L. Gelpi, S.J. (1934-) [Pragmatist]; William Edward Walmesley St. George Charlton (1935-); Philip L. Quinn (1940-2004); Patrick Sherry (c. 1940-); Jorge J.E. Gracia (1942-) [Suárezian]; the Irishman Patrick Quinn (1944-); Raymond Gaita (1946-); George Peter Schner, S.J. (1946-2000); the Austrian Edmund Runggaldier, S.J. (1946-); Linda Trinkhaus Zagzebski (1946-) [Analytical Thomist]; Fr. Modesto Santos Camacho (c. 1947-); Gareth Edward Moore, O.P. (1948-2002); Janet Martin Soskice (1951-), at the University of Cambridge; Paul Moser (1957-); Luke Gormally (1962-) [Analytical Thomist; Son-in-Law of Elizabeth Anscombe]; John Greco (c. 1963-); the Australian David Oderberg (1963-); Roger Teichmann (1963-); Mario Micheletti (1966-) [Analytical Thomist]; Alexander Pruss (1973-). As one can see one important contemporary strand of Analytic Philosophy is that of Analytical Thomism.

Mention should also be made of some of the more than 250 Catholic Philosophers of Logic and/or Science: the physicist André-Marie Ampere (1775-1836); Fr. Bernhard Bolzano (1781-1848) [some of whose works were placed on the Index of Forbidden Books]; the mathematician Fr. François-Napoléon-Marie Moigno (1804-1884); the French biologist and reconvert Claude Bernard (1813-1878); Fr. Léger-Marie Pioger (c. 1821-1905); the convert biologist St. George Jackson Mivart (1827-1900) [who was later excommunicated]; Fr. L. A. Sorignet (c. 1820-1870); Dalmace Leroy, O.P. (1828-1905); the Belgian physicist Ignace Carbonnelle, S.J. (1829-1889); Auguste-Théodore Paul de Broglie (1834- 1895); José Mendive, S.J. (1836-1906); the physicist Fr. Raffaelo Caverni (1837-1900); Fr. Franz Brentano (1838-1917) [who later left the Church]; the Belgian mathematician Paul Mansion (1844-1919); Émile Boutroux (1845-1921), of the Sorbonne [member of the French Academy]; Fr. Martin Stanislaus Brennan (1845-1927); Manuel Polo y Peyrolón (1846-1918); John Gmeiner (1847-1913); the Suplician Albert Farges (1848-1926); the physicist John Augustine Zahm, Congregation of the Holy Cross (1851-1921); the neuroscientist Santiago Ramón y Cajal (1852-1934) [winner of the Nobel Prize]; the convert biologist Sir Bertram Windle (1858-1959) [member of the Royal Society]; the biologist Erich Wasmann, S.J. (1859-1931); Juan Gonzáles de Arintero, O.P. (1860-1928); the physicist Fr. Pierre Duhem (1861-1916); Antonin Eymieu, S.J. (1861-1933); the psychologist Jules de la Vaissiere, S.J. (1863-1941); the biologist Hermann Muckermann, S.J. (1866-1962); Kasimir Twardowski (1866-1938) [who eventually distanced himself from Catholicism]; Hubert Gruender, S.J. (1870-1940); the biologist Alexis Carrel (1873-1944) [atheist Nobel Prize winner who converted to Catholicism after visiting Lourdes]; the convert physicist Edmund Taylor Whittaker, F.R.S. (1873-1956); the physicist Johannes Stark (1874-1957) [Nobel Prize winner]; the physicist Joseph Wilbois (c. 1874-1950); the Hungarian Akos Pauler (1876-1933);

Agostino Gemelli, O.F.M. (1878-1959); the Pole Jan Łukasiewicz (1878-1956); the biologist Fr. Pierre Teilhard de Chardin, S.J. (1881-1955); the physicist Friedrich Dessauer (1881-1963); the Austrian Rudolph Allers (1883-1963); Pierre Lecomte du Noüy (1883-1947); Fr. Augustin Jakubisiak (1884-1945); the Irish physicist Alfred O'Rahilly, S.J. (1884-1969); Aloys Wenzl (1887-1974); the Pole Tadeusz Czezowski (1889-1981); the convert chemist Michael Polyani, F.R.S. (1891-1976), at the University of Oxford; Roland Dalbiez (1893-1976); Pawel Siwek, S.J. (1893-1986); the physicist Fr. Georges Lemaître (1894-1960) [who proposed Big Bang origin of cosmos]; the convert chemist Frank Sherwood Taylor (1897-1956); the mathematician Marcel Légaut (1900-1990); William Humbert Kane, O.P. (1901-1970); the Pole Alfred Tarski (1901-1983); the convert mathematician George Frederick James Temple, O.S.B. (1901-1992) [Royal Society]; the Pole Józef Innocentius Maria Bocheński, O.P. (1902-1995); Jean Cavailles (1903-1944) [who died in World War II]; the Australian neuroscientist John Eccles (1903-1997) [winner of the Nobel Prize]; Fr. Jan Salamucha (1903-1944) [who died in World War II]; Bishop Otto Spülbeck (1904-1970); Jean Daujat (1906-1998); the Pole Stanislaw Jaskowski (1906-1965); Charles de Koninck (1906-1965); Fr. Augustin Sesmat (c. 1906-1960); Dominique Dubarle, O.P. (1907-1987); the Dutch Norbert A. Luyten, O.P. (1909-1986); the Pole Fr. Stanislaw Mazierski (1915-); Vincent Edward Smith (1915-1972); Raymond Nogar, O.P. (1916-1967); William Wallace, O.P. (1918-); Patrick K. Bastable (1919-); the Belgian Jean Ladrière (1921-2007); the Spaniard Fr. Vincente Munoz Delgado (1922-1995); the Pole Andrzej Grzegorczyk (1922-); Vittorio Mathieu (1923-); Fr. Stanley Jaki, O.S.B. (1924-2009) [winner of the Templeton Prize in 1987]; Fr. Ernan McMullin (1924-); the physicist Walter Thirring (1927-), at CERN; Alexandre Ganoczy (1928-); the physicist Patrick Heelan, S.J. (c. 1928-); Edward M. MacKinnon, S.J. (1928-); the Italian biologist Fr. Fiorenzo Facchini (1929-); Karl Schmitz-Moormann (c. 1929-1996); the chemist John Polanyi (1929-) [Nobel Prize winner]; the physicist Antonino Zichichi (1929-), at CERN; the Pole Stanislaw Kaminski (c. 1930-); Cardinal Paul Poupard (1930-); the physicist Wolfgang Smith (1930-); Robert A. Brungs, S.J. (1931-2006) [founder of ITEST]; the physician Maurice Caillet (1933-) [an atheist who converted to Catholicism after visiting Lourdes]; George Coyne, S.J. (1933-); Evandro Agazzi (1934-); the biologist Francisco Ayala (1934-) [winner of Templeton Prize]; Enrico Berti (1935-) [also a Personalist]; the physicist Nicola Cabibbo (1935-2010); the physicist Fr. Michael Heller (1936-) [winner of the Templeton Prize in 2008]; Jean-Marie Moretti, S.J. (c. 1937-); Daniel N. Robinson (1937-); Fr. Mariano Artigas, Opus Dei (1938-2006) [winner of the Templeton Prize in 1995]; Jean-Michel Maldamé, O.P. (1939-); Dario Antiseri (1940-); Alfonso Perez de Laborda (1940-); the neuroscientist Eugene D'Aquili (1940-1998); the convert Frederick Suppe (1940-); the Canadian convert Bas van Fraassen (1941-); the Belgian physicist Jacques Demaret (1943-1999); William

Stoeger, S.J. (1943-); John F. Haught (c. 1945-) [Process Thought]; Hans-Dieter Mutschler (1946-); Christoph Theobald, S.J. (1946-); the biologist Gerard Verschuuren (1946-); the Polish Bishop Jozef Zycinski (1948-); Ulrich Lüke (1951-); the physicist Stephen M. Barr (1953-); the physicist Fr. Thierry Magnin (c. 1955-); the physicist Anthony Rizzi (c. 1950-); the biochemist Michael Behe (1952-) [Intelligent Design Movement]; Guy Consolmagno, S.J. (1952-); Fr. Gianfranco Basti (1954-); Francois Euve, S.J. (1954-); Orlando Franceschelli (c. 1955-); the mathematician Jacques Vaulthier (c. 1955-), of the Sorbonne; Fr. Giuseppe Tanzella Nitti (c. 1957-); Fr. Rafael Pascual (1959-); the Belgian physicist Dominique Lambert (1960-); Jacques Arnould, O.P. (1961-), at CNES; Dinesh D'Souza (1961-); Lorella Congiunti (c. 1962-); Jerry Korsmeyer (c. 1962-); the biologist Georg Souvignier (1963-); Michele Malatesta (c. 1965-); the neuroscientist Fr. Tadeusz Pacholczyk (1965-); Albert Bagood, O.P. (c. 1968-).

131   See here the works of Dominique Janicaud (1937-2002), *Le tournant théologique de la phénoménologie française* (Combas, L'Éclat, 1991) and *La phénoménologie éclatée* (Paris: L'Eclat, 1998). These works have been translated as *Phenomenology and the Theological Turn* (New York: Fordham University Press, 2000) and *Phenomenology Wide Open* (New York: Fordham University Press, 2009).

132   Namely in such secularists as Jean-François Lyotard (1924-1998); Michel Foucault (1926-1984); Jacques Derrida (1930-2004); Alain Badiou (1937-); François Laruelle (1937-); Luce Irigaray (1939-); the former Catholic Jean-Luc Nancy (1940-); Julia Kristeva (1941-); and Quentin Meillassoux (1967-).

133   For more on the thought of Marion see: DP (1993), v. II, pp. 1931-1932; BDTC (1996), p. 513; PCHP (1999), p. 717; RPFR (1999), pp. 153-164; MCT (2000), pp. 505-506; TEP (2000), pp. 238-239; FPTC (2001), pp. 376-377; OYHP (2001), p. 263; PAMP (2002), pp. 528-530; TT (2002), pp. 63-66, 205; WPR (2003), pp. 446-452; ACP (2005), pp. 532-542; GF (2005). pp. 186-206; EF (2006), v. VII, pp. 7018-7020; TWFP (2006), pp. 165, 255; Verneaux, Roger, *Étude critique du livre Dieu sans l'être* (Paris: Téqui, 1986); Charrak, André, ed., *Revue de Métaphysique et de Morale* 96 (1991) [Special Issue on Marion]; *New Blackfriars* 76 (1995) [Special Issue on Marion]; Ciapalo, Roman Theodore, ed., *Postmodernism and Christian Philosophy* (Washington: Catholic University of America Press, 1996); Sichère, Bernard, *Cinquante ans de philosophie française* (Paris: Ministère des Affaires Etrangères, 1998), vol. 4, pp. 27-31; Caputo, John, and Michael Scanlon, *God, the Gift, and Postmodernism* (Bloomington: Indiana University Press, 1999), pp. 185-222; Carlson, Thomas, *Indiscretion: Finitude and the Naming of God* (Chicago: University of Chicago Press, 1999), pp. 190-237; De Vries, Hent, *Philosophy and the Turn to Religion* (Baltimore: John Hopkins University Press, 1999), pp. 53-85, 124-129; Horner, Robyn, *Rethinking God as Gift: Marion,*

RECENT CATHOLIC PHILOSOPHY ❦ THE TWENTIETH CENTURY

Derrida, and the Limits of Phenomenology (New York: Fordham University Press, 2001); Benson, Bruce, ed., Graven Ideologies: Nietzsche, Derrida & Marion on Modern Idolatry (Downer's Grove: InterVarsity Press, 2002), pp. 169-223; Greisch, Jean, Le buisson ardant et les lumières de la raison: L'invention de la philosophie de la religion (Paris: Cerf, 2002), v. II, pp. 291-333; Janicaud, Dominique, Phenomenology and the Theological Turn: The French Debate (New York: Fordham University Press, 2002), pp. 31-32, 50-66; Philosophie 78 (2003), pp. 1-96 [Special Issue on Marion]; Faulconer, James, ed., Transcendence in Philosophy and Religion (Bloomington, Indiana: Indiana University Press, 2003), pp. 120-144; Maxwell, Patrick, et al., eds., Explorations in Contemporary Continental Philosophy of Religion (New York: Rodopi, 2003), pp. 9-22; Vanhoozer, Kevin, The Cambridge Companion to Postmodern Theology (Cambridge: Cambridge University Press, 2003), pp. 58-75; Benson, Bruce, and Norman Wirzba, eds., The Phenomenology of Prayer (New York: Fordham University Press, 2005), pp. 134-141, 168-184, 276-281; Ford, David, ed., The Modern Theologians (London: Blackwell, 2005), pp. 330-338; Horner, Robyn, Jean-Luc Marion: A Theo-logical Introduction (Burlington: Ashgate, 2005); Leask, Ian, and Eoin Cassidy, Givenness and God: Questions of Jean-Luc Marion (New York: Fordham University Press, 2005); Wainwright, William, ed., The Oxford Handbook of Philosophy of Religion (Oxford: Oxford University Press, 2005), pp. 472-493; Boundras, Constantin, Columbia Companion to Twentieth-Century Philosophy (New York: Columbia University Press, 2007), pp. 609-612; Cunningham, Connor, ed., Transcendence and Phenomenology (London: SCM Press, 2007), pp. 50-110; Gschwandtner, Christina, Reading Jean-Luc Marion: Exceeding Experiences (Bloomington: Indiana University Press, 2007); Hart, Kevin, Counter-Experiences: Reading Jean-Luc Marion (Notre Dame: University of Notre Dame Press, 2007); Reali, Nicola, ed., L'amore tra filosofia e teologia: in dialogo con Jean-Luc Marion (Vatican City: Lateran University Press, 2007); Miller, Adam, Badiou, Marion, and St. Paul: Immanent Grace (London: Continuum, 2008); MacKinlay, Shane, Interpreting Excess: Jean-Luc Marion, Saturated Phenomena, and Hermeneutics (New York: Fordham University Press, 2009); McCaffrey, Enda, The Return of Religion in France: From Democratisation to Postmetaphysics (Basingstoke: Palgrave Mc-Millan, 2009), pp. 132-145; Benson, Bruce, ed., Words of Life: New Theological Turns in French Phenomenology (New York: Fordham University Press, 2010).

134   These works have been translated as God without Being [GWB], tr. Thomas Carlson (Chicago: University of Chicago Press, 1991) and Being Given: Toward a Phenomenology of Givenness [BG], tr. Jeffrey Kosky (Stanford: Stanford University Press, 2002). I use these translations here.

Other postmodern works of Marion are With or Without God? The Future of Christian Values [Avec ou sans Dieu? L'avenir des valeurs chrétiennes] (1970) [with Alain de Benoist]; The Idol and Distance [L'Idole et la distance] [ID] (1977) [winner of the Prix Charles Lambert de l'Académie des sciences morales *et politiques* (1977); translated as *The Idol and Distance*, tr. Thomas Carlson (Fordham University Press, 2001)]; *La difficulté de Dieu* (1981; 1990) [*Au risque de croire*, v. III; with Jacques Lacourt]; *Prolegomena to Charity* [*Prolégomènes à la charité*] [MPC] (1986) [translated as *Prolegomena to Charity*, tr. Stephen Lewis (New York: Fordham University Press, 2002)]; *The Crossing of the Visible* [*La croisée du visible*] [CV] (1991) [translated as *The Crossing of the Visible*, tr. James Smith (Stanford: Stanford University Press, 2004)]; *Reduction and Givenness: Investigations of Husserl, Heidegger, and Phenomenology* [*Réduction et donation: Recherches sur Huserl, Heidegger et la phénoménologie*] [RG] (1989; 2004) [Part I of his Trilogy; translated as *Reduction and Givenness*, tr. Thomas Carlson (Evanston: Northwestern University Press, 1997)]; *In Excess: Studies of Saturated Phenomena* [*De surcroît: Études sur les phénomènes saturés*] [IE] (2001) [Part III of his Trilogy; translated as *In Excess: Studies of Saturated Phenomena* (New York: Fordham University Press, 2002)]; *Le phénomène érotique* [MEP] (2003) [translated as *The Erotic Phenomenon*, tr. Stephen Lewis (Chicago: University of Chicago Press, 2007)]; *Au lieu de soi: l'approche de Saint Augustin* (2008) [forthcoming translation from Stanford University Press]; *Certitudes négatives* (Paris: Grasset, 2010); *Le croire pour le voir: réflexions diverses sur la rationalité de la révélation et l'irrationalité de quelques croyants* (2010) [Collection of Articles]. Marion is also famous for his influential studies on Descartes. Marion was also the editor of the French journal *Communio* (1975-1985), *Bulletin Cartésien* (1970-), and of the collection *Épiméthée* (1981-).

Marion's key articles are his: "Note sur l'athéisme conceptual," *Résurrection* 38 (1971), pp. 119-120; "Présence et distance: Remarques sur l'implication réciproque de la contemplation eucharistique et de la présence," *Résurrection* 43-44 (1974), pp. 31-58; "Le verbe et le texte," *Résurrection* 46 (1975), pp. 63-80; "Le présent et le don," *Communio* 2:6 (1977), pp. 50-70; "La rigueur de la louange," in Bruaire, Claude, ed., *Confession de la foi chretienne* (Paris: Fayard, 1977), pp. 261-276; "De connaître à aimer: L'ébouissement," *Communio* 3 (1978), pp. 17-28; "Fragments sur l'idole et l'icone," *Revue de Metaphysique et de Morale* 84 (1979), pp. 433-445; "La double idolâtrie," in Kearney, Richard, et al., eds., *Heidegger et la question de Dieu* (Paris: Grasset, 1980), pp. 46-74, 304-309; "Sur l'onto-théologie de Descartes," *Bulletin de la Societe Francaise de Philosophie* 76 (1982), pp. 117-158 [translated as "Descartes and Onto-theology," in Blond, Phillip, ed., *Post-Secular Philosophy* (London: Routledge, 1998), pp. 67-106]; "La vanité de l'être et le nom de Dieu," in Marion, Jean-Luc, and Pierre Gisel, eds., *Analogie et dialectique* (Geneva: Labor et Fides, 1982), pp. 17-49; "Le don glorieux d'une présence," *Communio* 8 (1983), pp. 35-51; "L'étant et le phénomène," in Marion, Jean-Luc, et al., eds., *Phénoménologie et métaphysique* (Paris: P.U.F, 1984), pp. 159-209; "Splendeur de la contemplation eucharistique," in Marion, Jean-Luc, et al., eds., *La politique de la mystique* (Limoges: Criterion, 1984), pp. 17-28; "L'avenir du catholicisme," *Communio* 5-6 (1985), pp. 38-47; "La croisée du visible et de l'invisible," in Marion, Jean-

Luc, and Alain Bonfand, eds., *Trois essais sur la perspective* (Paris: Editions de la Différence, 1985), pp. 9-56; "De la mort de dieu aux noms divins: L'itineraire théologique de la métaphysique," *Laval Théologique et Philosophique* 41 (1985), pp. 25-42; "La fin de la fin de la metaphysique," *Laval Theologique et Philosophique* 42 (1986), pp. 22-33 [translated as "The End of the End of Metaphysics," tr. Bettina Bergo, *Epoche* 2 (1994), pp. 1-22]; "L'aveugle à Siloé," *Communio* 12:6 (1987), pp. 17-34 [translated as "The Blind Man of Siloe," tr. Janine Langan, *Image* 29 (2001), pp. 59-69]; "À Dieu, rien d'impossible," *Revue de Métaphysique et de morale* 5 (1989), pp. 43-58; "L'argument relève-t-il de l'ontologie," *Archivio de Filosofia* 1-2 (1990), pp. 43-69 [translated as "Is the Ontological Argument Ontological? The Argument According to Anselm and Its Metaphysical Interpretation According to Kant," *Journal of the History of Philosophy* 2 (1992), pp. 201-218 and in Bulhof, Ilse, and Laurens ten Kate, eds., *Flight of the Gods: Philosophical Perspectives on Negative Theology* (New York: Fordham University Press, 2001), pp. 78-99]; "Le sujet en dernier appel," *Revue de Métaphysique et de Morale* (1991), pp. 77-95 [translated as "The Final Appeal of the Subject," tr. Simon Critchley, in Critchley, Simon, and Peter Dews, eds., *Deconstructive Subjectivities* (Albany: SUNY Press, 1996), pp. 85-104 and in Caputo, John, ed., *The Religious* (London: Blackwell, 2002), pp. 131-144]; "Apologie de l'argument," *Communio* 17 (1992), pp. 12-33; "Christian Philosophy and Charity," tr. Mark Sebanc, *Communio* 19 (1992), pp. 465-473; "Le Phénomène saturé," in Courtine, Jean-François, ed., *Phénoméno-logie et théologie* (Paris: Criterion, 1992), pp. 79-128 [translated as "The Satu-rated Phenomenon," ["SP"], tr. Thomas Carlson, in Langdorf, Leonore, and John Caputo, ed., *Philosophy Today* 21 (1996), pp. 103-124, and in Janicaud, Dominique, ed., *Phenomenology and the Theological Turn* (New York: Fordham University Press, 2002), pp. 176-216]; "Le Possible et la Révélation," in van Tongeren, Peter, et al., eds,. *Eros and Eris: Contributions to a Hermeneutical Phenomenology* (Dordrecht: Kluwer, 1992), pp. 13-34; "Pour une philosophie de la charité," *France Catholique* 2355 (15 May 1992), pp. 15-21; "Métaphy-sique et phénoménologie: Une relève pour la théologie," *Bulletin de Littérature ecclésiastique* 94:2 (1993), pp. 189-206 [translated as "Metaphysics and Phe-nomenology: A Summary for Theologians," in Ward, Graham, ed., *Postmodern God: A Theological Reader* (Oxford: Blackwell, 1997), pp. 279-296]; "Note sur l'indifférence ontologique," in Greisch, Jean, and Jacques Rolland, eds., *Em-manuel Lévinas* (Paris: Cerf, 1993), pp. 47-62 [translated as "A Note Concern-ing the Ontological Indifference," tr. Jeffery Kosky, *Graduate Faculty Philosophy Journal* 20/21 (1998), pp. 25-40]; "Philosophie chrétienne et herméneutique de la charité," *Communio* 18:2 (1993), pp. 89-96; "Esquisse d'un concept phé-noménologique du don," *Archivo di Filosofia* 62 (1994), pp. 75-94 [translated as "Sketch of a Philosophical Concept of Gift," ["PCG"] in Westphal, Merold, ed., *Postmodern Philosophy and Christian Thought* (Bloomington: Indiana University Press, 1999), pp. 122-143]; "Metaphysics and Phenomenology: A Relief for Theology," tr. Thomas Carlson, *Critical Inquiry* 4 (1994), pp. 572-

591; "Saint Thomas d'Aquin et l'onto-théo-logie," *Revue Thomiste* 95 (1995), pp. 31-66 [translated as "Thomas Aquinas and Onto-Theology," ["TAOT"], in Kessler, Michael, and Christian Sheppard, eds., *Mystics: Presence and Aporia* (Chicago: University of Chicago Press, 2003), pp. 38-74]; "L'autre philosophie première et la question de la donation," *Philosophie* 17 (1996), pp. 29-50 [translated as "The Other First Philosophy and the Question of Givenness," tr. Jeffrey Kosky, *Critical Inquiry* 25:4 (1999), pp. 785-800]; "La fin de la métaphysique?," *Page* 38 (1996); "Nothing and Nothing Else," in Lilly, Reginald, ed., *The Ancients and the Moderns* (Bloomington: Indiana University Press, 1996), pp. 183-195; "Liturgy and Kenosis," in Ward, Graham, ed., *Postmodern God: A Theological Reader* (Oxford: Blackwell, 1997), pp. 249-264; "The Idea of God," in Daniel, Garber, et al., eds., *The Cambridge History of Seventeenth-Century Philosophy* (Cambridge: Cambridge University Press, 1998), v. I, pp. 365-304; "A Note concerning the Ontological Difference," *The Graduate Faculty of Philosophy Journal* 20:2 (1998), pp. 25-40; "Au nom: Comment ne parler de théologie négative," *Laval théologique et philosophique* 55 (1999), pp. 339-363 [translated as "In the Name: How to Avoid Speaking of Negative Theology," ["IN"], tr. Jeffery Kosky," in Caputo, John, and Michael Scanlon, eds., *Of God, the Gift, and Postmodernism* (Bloomington: Indiana University Press, 1999), pp. 20-53]; "Christian Philosophy: Hermeneutic or Heuristic?," ["MCHH"] in Ambrosio, Francis, ed., *The Question of Christian Philosophy Today* (New York: Fordham University Press, 1999), pp. 247-264; "L'évènement, le phènomène et le rèvèlè," *Transversalités* 70 (1999), pp. 4-25; "The Face: An Endless Hermeneutics," *Harvard Divinity Bulletin* 28:2-3 (1999), pp. 9-10; "On the Gift: A Discussion Between Jacques Derrida and Jean-Luc Marion," ["OG"] in Caputo, John, and Michael Scanlon, eds., *Of God, the Gift, and Postmodernism* (Bloomington: Indiana University Press, 1999), pp. 54-78; "The Other: First Philosophy and the Question of Givenness," tr. Jeffery Kosky, *Critical Inquiry* 25 (1999), pp. 785-800; "Le paradoxe de la personne," *Études* 391:4 (1999), pp. 349-360; "Le visage, herméneutique sans fin," *Conférence* 9 (1999) [translated as "The Face of the Other: An Endless Hermeneutics," *Harvard Divinity Bulletin* 28:3 (1999)]; "D'autrui à l'individu," in Marion, Jean-Luc, et al., *Positivité et transcendance* (Paris: P.U.F., 2000), pp. 287-308 [translated as "From the Other to the Individual," tr. Robyn Horner, in Schwartz, Regina, ed., *Transcendence: Philosophy, Literature and Theology approach the Beyond* (London: Routledge, 2004), pp. 43-60]; "La conscience du don," in Dumont, Jean-Noël, ed., *Le don: Théologie, philosophie, psychologie, sociologie* (Lyon: AVM, 2001); "Ils le reconnurent et lui-même leur devint invisible," in Duchesne, Jean, et al., eds., *Demain l'Eglise* (Paris: Flammarion, 2001), pp. 134-143 [translated as "They Recognized Him and He Became Invisible to Them," ["TRH"], tr. Stephen Lewis, *Modern Theology* 18:2 (2002), pp. 145-152]; "La phénoménalité du sacrament: Être et donation," *Communio* 26 (2001), pp. 59-75; "Ce qui ne se dit pas: Remarques sur l'apophase dans le discours amoureux," in Olivetti, Marco, *Théologie négative* (Rome: CEDAM,

2002), pp. 65-81 [translated as "The Unspoken: Apophasis and the Discourse of Love," tr. Arianne Conty, *Proceedings of the American Catholic Philosophical Association* 76 (2002), pp. 39-56]; "Notes sur le phénomène et son événement," *Iris: Annales de philosophie* 23 (2002) [revised as "Le phénomène et l'évènement," in Esposito, Constantino, et al., eds., *L'existenzia/L'existence/Die Existenz/Existence* (Bari: Turnhout, 2004); and translated as "Phenomenon and Event," *Graduate Faculty Philosophy Journal* 26:1 (2005), pp. 147-159]; "La raison formelle de l'infini," in Michon, Cyrille, ed., *Christianisme: Héritages et destins* (Paris: Le livre de poche, 2002), pp. 109-131 [translated as "The Formal Reason for the Infinite," ["FRI"] in Ward, Graham, ed., *Blackwell Companion to Postmodern Theology* (London: Blackwell, 2004), pp. 399-412]; "The End of Metaphysics as a Possibility," tr. Daryl Lee, in Wrathall, Mark, *Religion after Metaphysics* (Cambridge: Cambridge University Press, 2003), pp. 166-189; "The Event, the Phenomenon, and the Revealed," ["EPR"], in Faulconer, James, ed., *Transcendence in Philosophy and Religion* (Bloomington: Indiana University Press, 2003), pp. 87-105; "Le phénomène érotique," *Études* 399 (2003), pp. 483-494; "Ce que donne cela donne," in Capelle, Philippe, et al., eds., *Le souci du passage* (Paris: Cerf, 2004), pp. 291-306; Kearney, Richard, "A Dialogue with Jean-Luc Marion," *Philosophy Today* 48 (2004), pp. 12-26; "The Hermeneutics of Revelation," [A Debate with Richard Kearney], in Kearney, Richard, ed., *Debates in Continental Philosophy* (New York: Fordham University Press, 2004), pp. 15-32 [reprinted in Manoussakis, John Panteleimon, ed., *After God: Richard Kearney and the Religious Turn in Continental Philosophy* (New York: Fordham University Press, 2006), pp. 318-339]; "L'impossible pour l'homme—Dieu," *Conférence* 18 (2004), pp. 329-349 [translated as "The Impossible for Man—God," ["IMG"] in Caputo, John, and Michael Scanlon, eds., *Transcendence and Beyond* (Bloomington: Indiana University Press, 2007), pp. 17-43]; "On Love and Phenomenological Reduction," tr. Anne Davenport, *New Arcadia Review* 2 (2004), pp. 1-14; "La raison du don," *Bijdragen* 65:1 (2004), pp. 5-37 [translated as "The Reason of the Gift," ["RG"], in Leask, Michael, et al., eds., *Questions of Jean-Luc Marion* (New York: Fordham University Press, 2005), pp. 101-135]; "La banalité de la saturation," in Bousquet, François, and Philippe Capelle, eds., *Dieu et la raison: L'intelligence de la foi parmi les rationalités contemporaines* (Paris, Bayard, 2005), pp. 159-191 [translated as "The Banality of Saturation," ["BS"], tr. Jeffrey Kosky, in Hart, Kevin, ed., *Counter-Experiences: Reading Jean-Luc Marion* (Notre Dame: Notre Dame University Press, 2007), pp. 383-418]; "La fin de la métaphysique comme possibilité," in Zarka, Yves-Charles, et al., eds., *Y-a-t-il une histoire de la métaphysique?* (Paris, P.U.F., 2005), pp. 343-367 [translated as "The End of Metaphysics as a Possibility," in Wrathall, Mark, ed., *Religion after Metaphysics* (Cambridge: Cambridge University Press, 2003), pp. 166-189; "La foi et la raison," in Lustiger, Jean-Marie, ed., *Dialogue entre la foi chrétienne et la pensée contemporaine* (Paris: Parole et Silence, 2005), pp. 11-30) [translated as "Faith and Reason," in *The Visible and the Revealed*, VIII, pp. 145-154]; "Giving More," [with Richard Kearney], in Leask, Ian, and Eoin Cassidy, *Givenness and God: Questions of Jean-Luc Marion* (New York: Fordham University Press, 2005), pp. 243-257; "God and the Gift: A Continental Perspective," in Shortt, Rupert, ed., *God's Advocates: Christian Thinkers in Conversation* (Grand Rapids: Eerdmans, 2005), pp. 141-152; "Mihi magna quaestio factus sum: Le privilège d'inconnaissance," *Conférence* 20 (2005) [translated as "Mihi Magna Quaestio Factus Sum: The Privilege of Unknowing," tr. Stephen Lewis, *Journal of Religion* 85:1 (2005), pp. 1-24]; "L'irréductible," *Critique* 62 (2006), pp. 79-91; "La reconnaissance du don," *Communio* 33 (2008), pp. 169-182; "The Present and the Gift," ["PG"], in DeRoo, Neal, et al., eds., *Phenomenology and Eschatology* (Lewiston: Ashgate, 2009), pp. 193-214; "Lacoste ou la correction de l'analytique existentiale," *Transversalités* 110 (2009), pp. 171-175; "The Phenomenality of the Sacrament: Being and Givenness," ["PS"] in Benson, Bruce, et al., eds., *Words of Life: New Theological Turns in French Phenomenology* (New York: Fordham University Press, 2010), pp. 89-102.

Several of these articles have been collected in *Le visible et le révélé* [VR] (2005) [translated as *The Visible and the Revealed*, tr. Christina Gschwandtner (New York: Fordham University Press, 2008)].

See the bibliography of Jean-Luc Marion in Horner, Robyn, *Jean-Luc Marion: A Theo-Logical Introduction* (Surrey: Ashgate, 2005), pp. 151-190; and Hart, Kevin, *Counter-Experiences: Reading Jean-Luc Marion* (2007), pp. 419-469.

135   Marion argues, however, that he does not ultimately reject the Thomistic notion of God as *esse* [being] properly understood. For he claims that Aquinas understands the being of God as analogical (non-univocal) with that of humans. Indeed for Aquinas God's *esse* [being] immeasurably surpasses and is hardly analogous with that of creatures, for in God alone essence merges with *esse* [being]. Hence the divine essence cannot be related to the common essence of creatures and remains unknown to humans (and no name can be applied in the same way to creatures and God). As Marion explains "if *esse* [being] characterizes God in Thomism, *esse* [being] itself must be understood divinely, thus having no common measure with what Being can signify in metaphysics" (GWB, English Preface, p. xxiv; III, p. 72). Nor is God for Aquinas, says Marion, the ground of being or self-caused. God is free from any causality or ground ("TAOT," pp. 51-55, 66-68). Hence according to Marion Aquinas doesn't chain God to Being or metaphysics. Still, Marion criticizes Aquinas for conceiving God's proper name as *esse* [being] over love (GWB, English Preface, p. xxii; BG, III, pp. 155-156; "TAOT," pp. 44-45, 47-49, 60-64) [Marion's interpretation of Aquinas here is somewhat disputable].

136   Marion argues that Exodus 3:14 is best translated not as "I am who am" but "I am who I am" (GWB, III, pp. 73-74). Hence the highest name of God as revealed to Moses attests the impertinence of every essential name or description of God—I am who I am; I am the one that I want to be—and

opens the field to an endless litany of names (GWB, II, p. 45; BG, V, p. 297; n. 91 on p. 367; RG, IV, pp. 141-143; cf. Ex 3:14; Mt 26:65; Jn 8; Jn 18:6-7).

137   This does not mean for Marion that God does not exist. Rather it means God is beyond existence, greater than it: "God is, exists, and that is the least of things. At issue here is not the possibility of God's attaining Being, but, quite the opposite, the possibility of Being's attaining to God" (GWB, English Preface, pp. xix-xx; cf. GWB, Introduction, p. 2).

138   In this way Marion responds to Derrida who argued that a gift (a gratuitous offering where one expects nothing in return) is impossible as it is always implicated in a system of exchange, which makes the gift regulated by causality (the giver gives as an efficient cause) and given in pursuit of a final cause (the egoistic one of self-goodness or self-glory or self-approval). For any sort of repayment or return (such as by greeting, invitation, favor, money, or even awareness of having given) amounts to an economy, a countergift, a reimbursement, and reduces the gift to calculation and utility (i.e. to a commodity). Even the mere recognition of the gift of a giver bestows a burden to repay and makes the gift pure commerce. So to be a gift the giver (as well as the givee) must lack awareness of a gift (the presence of the gift undoes the present) which is impossible (BG, II, pp. 75-78, 81, 85-86; RG, IV, p. 174; "PCG," pp. 123-130; "ROG," pp. 103-104).

Now Marion accepts the analysis of Derrida on the gift (what he calls the natural attitude on giving) but argues such conditions do not make the gift impossible. For Marion argues that one can phenomenologically reduce the transcendence of the gift in a triple reduction and show how a gift involves no givee, giver, or given, and hence is free of the economy of exchange (BG, II, p. 84).

The givee is bracketed when one gives to an other who cannot pay one back for the gift, and may not even want the gift in the first place, or one gives to someone who is unknown. This may occur when one gives money to a humanitarian organization (such as the United Way). Here the giver does not know the exact amount that will be given out to the needy, its exact use, its result, or to whom it will be given. Nor is there an expectation of return as one recognizes that a gift is given in anonymity, ignorance, geographical and cultural separation, and that one may die before the end of the campaign (BG, II, pp. 86-87, 90). So too one may give to one's enemy. Here the givee is incapable of reciprocity and indeed repays only by striking back and harming. As Marion writes: "Only the enemy makes the gift possible; he makes the gift evident by rightly denying it reciprocity—in contrast to the friend, who involuntarily lowers the gift to the level of a loan with interest. The enemy thus becomes the ally of the gift, and the friend the adversary of the gift" (BG, II, p. 89 [129]; cf. BG, II, pp. 88-89; "ROG," pp. 110-111). Likewise I can give to an ingrate who refuses the charge of incurring a debt, of having been offered a gift (BG, II, pp. 88-92; "OG," pp. 62-64; "PCG," pp. 137-140). Thus anonymity, hostility, and ingratitude bracket and reduce the transcendence of the givee. We can also bracket the givee through the fact that Christ is present in all humans and so when we give to the poor we give to Christ as well (see Mt 25:31-46). Thus Christ is an absent face (eschatological delay), one in whom the gift can come into play, when he opens the universal place of his own face in every human face (BG, II, pp. 91-93). Finally one can bracket the givee (give without expecting a return) in devotion to a community, the gift of self for nation (death for the fatherland), the gift to humanity out of fraternity, and the gift to one's children. Here what is given of oneself (time, energy, life, love) will never be returned, and indeed the givee accepts that the gift will not be returned to the giver but will be transferred to future givees yet to come (here there is an obligatory delay) (BG, II, pp. 76, 80, 93-94; MEP, XVIII, pp. 84-89; XXXIX, p. 205; "ROG," pp. 116-122).

The giver is bracketed when someone unknown to us gives to us. This can happen for instance in the case of an inheritance where the giver remains unknown to his future offspring. In this case the giver is empirically absent (as the giver has died) and so I cannot repay the gift. Indeed the giver intended that I not repay it. Something similar can happen in the case of an anonymous donor such as with an endowment (BG, II, pp. 95-96). Additionally givers may give unbeknownst to themselves or without full knowledge of what they do or the effect it produces on a givee. This can occur with the athlete, artist, or lover who give pleasure of which they are unaware (BG, II, pp. 97-98; n. 38 on pp. 346-347; "ROG," pp. 113-114).

Finally we can bracket the gift. For while the presence of a gift would disqualify it as gift, a gift does not have to enter into the domain of presence, to be or to subsist, in order to give itself. Thus the present can be given without presence (BG, II, pp. 79-81). This happens as givenness abandons itself and produces an other besides itself, the given, in whom it disappears (it is a "letting appear without reserve and in person." It thus never appears as such in the gift. It never occurs as a being, substance, or subject, but saturates without measure (BG, I, pp. 35-36, 60-62, 74 [107]). So too the gift can manifest itself of itself and by itself without depending on an efficient cause (giver) or final cause (givee), hence without origin, genealogy, dependence, or cause (and hence without interest or motive). The gift here has no other justification than its givenness, its own arising without cause, its appearing at its own initiative. The gift gives itself in deciding to give itself, beyond the principle of sufficient reason (BG, II, pp. 62, 64-65, 68, 72-74, 83, 108, 111, 115, 117; "PCG," p. 142). So when one makes a promise, reconciles with someone, or begins a friendship or love (by giving one's power, time, life, confidence, word, or body to another), it is not the gift of an object or its transfer but its own happening, without object or transfer (BG, II, pp. 102-104, 108, 111; "ROG," pp. 125-134).

Hence when a gift occurs, we can say that the gift decides itself as a gift through the twofold consent of the givee and giver, who are less actors of the gift than acted on by givenness. Thus the giver and givee give under impetus of the gift itself. The giver gives him or herself over to the gift as it first gives itself and so accepts an obligation to give. The giver is then swept up by the allure of the gift and lets it give itself through him or her. Similarly the givee receives the gift and a debt of gratitude to another as the recipient agrees to be put in debt by the gift through the allure of the gift itself. This is the gifting of the gift wherein the horizon of economy is replaced with a horizon of donation wherein the gift gives itself through humans. In human giving therefore there is a saturating givenness, a hypergivenness of the inconceivable non-present saturating phenomenon (friendship, loyalty) (BG, II, pp. 108, 111-112; MEP, XXI, p. 103; "PCG," pp. 131-135).

139   Not unexpectedly, Marion reconfigures Catholic apologetics in light of his postmodernism. He thus finds wanting what he sees as the goal of a rational apologetics, that is, the goal of convincing someone of the truth of the Catholic faith by necessary reasons (wherein adherence arises as a simple consequence of the evidence) (MPC, III, pp. 56-57). In the first place the Church itself, he argues, has recognized that a rigorous proof of the truth of Christianity is impossible. For it rejected the semi-rationalism of Hermes and like thinkers (MPC, III, p. 52; n. 1 on p. 52). In the second place, a purely rational apologetics would have no room for a will to freely embrace faith and love (MPC, III, pp. 57-58). For an apologetics conducted solely on the basis of argumentation would merely fill in the abyss where the voluntary decision for or against faith and love must intervene—where the will or heart passes across evidence (the play of reasons) to love (MPC, III, pp. 58, 61). In the third place faith takes the form of a voluntary poverty, self-denial, and humility, not the arrogance of reasoning out all things (MPC, III, p. 52). Finally, by renouncing all rational confirmation of faith, and abandoning an argumentative apologetical machine, we can better respect the identity of the non-Christian and atheist, as well as facilitate our warm welcome into the cultural surroundings (MPC, III, p. 54).

Hence in a new apologetics, or what Marion is even willing to label a non-apologetics, rather than developing an argumentative apologetical machine in hopes of converting others to Christ by force, necessary reason, or popular slogans (all of which betoken a will of domination), we must instead try to engender a humble availability toward God in the hearts of others, an open-ness to a gesture of revealing Love (MPC, III, pp. 54-55, 60). Apologetics then demands not an appeal to reasons (which at most constrain our possible beliefs), but a confiding exchange of opinions, a silent communication of lived experiences, a sharing of hopes and struggles, all done in order to allow a conviction that Jesus is Lord to arise in the heart of hearts (GWB, VII, pp. 185, 189, 192-194; MPC, III, pp. 52, 56-58). For faith is an act where the will decides for or against the love of Love in a manner quite free of argumentation

(GWB, II, p. 52; MPC, III, pp. 62, 69). The rules that validate the confession of faith therefore are not those of syllogisms but of charity, namely, a logic of love (GWB, VII, pp. 192-196; VR, VIII, pp. 145-154). For ultimately only love can bear to gaze upon Love's excess (MPC, III, pp. 61-62, 66-68) and it does so by transgressing itself in "risking love, love—bare [à nu], raw [à cru]" (GWB, Introduction, p. 3 [11]).

As a result, one can give no answer to someone who says they don't have faith. One can only ask them to believe despite the belief that they do not believe, to believe in Love and that Love loves them in spite of their belief that they don't have faith, i.e. to abandon themselves to the gift of God (GWB, Introduction, p. 3; MPC, III, pp. 63-65; "MCP," p. 261). At times then, as Marion sees it, "Alone with itself, the will must will to believe, even when it does not possess the means for believing, or rather, when it does not believe it possesses the means for this" (MPC, III, p. 64).

140   For more on the thought of Lacoste see: RPFR (1999), pp. 197-202; GF (2005), pp. 207-225; Bloechl, Jeffrey, "Dialectical Approaches to Retrieving God after Heidegger: Premises and Consequences, Lacoste and Marion," *Pacifica* 13:3 (2000), pp. 288-298; Verhack, Ignace, "Response to Jean-Yves Lacoste," in Boeve, Lieven, and Lambert Leijssen, eds., *Sacramental Presence in a Postmodern Context* (Leuven: Peeters, 2001), pp. 232-235; Greisch, Jean, *La buissojn ardent et les lumières de la raison* (Paris: Cerf, 2002), vol. II, pp. 266-291; Janicaud, Dominique, *Phenomenology and the Theological Turn: The French Debate* (New York: Fordham University Press, 2002), n. 23 on p. 100; Schrijvers, Joeri, "Jean-Yves Lacoste: A Phenomeology of Liturgy," *Heythrop Journal* 46:3 (2005), pp. 314-333; Hart, Kevin, and Barbara Wall, eds., *The Experience of God: A Postmodern Response* (New York: Fordham University Press, 2005), pp. 104-112; Schrijvers, Joeri, "Ontotheological Turnings?: Marion, Lacoste, and Levinas on the Decentering of Modern Subjectivity," *Modern Theology* 22:2 (2006), pp. 221-253; Costantino, Giovanni, *Paradosso e gloria: Analisi e confronto con il pensiero di Jean-Yves Lacoste* (Assisi: Cittadella, 2008); Simmons, J. Aaron, "God in Recent French Phenomenology," *Philosophy Compass* 3:5 (2008), pp. 910-932.

141   This work has been translated as *Experience and the Absolute: Disputed Questions on the Humanity of Man* [EA], tr. Mark Raftery-Skehan (New York: Fordham University Press, 2004) [and the last section, sec. 63-73, has also been translated by David Thompson in Ward, Graham, ed., *Postmodern God: A Theological Reader* (Oxford: Blackwell, 1997), pp. 249-294]. I make use of these translations here.

Lacoste has also written works such as: *Notes on Time: Essay on the Rationality of Memory and Hope* [*Notes sur le temps: Essai sur la raison de la mémoire et de l'espérance*] [LNT] (1990); *Narnia, monde théologique?: Théologie anonyme et christologie pseudonyme* (2005).

And he is the editor of the famous *Dictionnaire critique de la théologie* (1998; 2007) [translated as *Encyclopedia of Christian Theology*, 3 vols. (London: Routledge, 2005); and abridged as *Histoire de la théologie* (Paris: Seuil, 2009)] to which he contributed several articles, of which the most important are "Atheism," "Credibility," "Faith" [with Nicolas Lossky], "Fundamental Choice," "God," "Knowledge of God," ["KG"], "Philosophy," "Rationalism," "Reason," and "Revelation."

Lacoste has additionally written many articles and book reviews on philosophy, the most important of which are: "Ontologie et mystère chrétien," *Nouvelle Revue Théologique* 102 (1980), pp. 707-715; "Expérience, evénement, connaissance de Dieu," ["Experience, Event, Knowledge of God"] ["EEKG"], *Nouvelle Revue Théoligique* 106 (1984), pp. 834-861; "Sacrements, ethique, Eucharistie" ["Sacraments, Ethics, Eucharist"] ["SEE"], *Revue Thomiste* 84 (1984), pp. 212-242; "Visages: Paradoxe et gloire," *Revue Thomiste* 85 (1985), pp. 561-606; "Du phénomène à la figure: Pour réintroduire à la gloire et la croix," *Revue Thomiste* 86 (1986), pp. 606-616; "Bâtir, habiter, prier" ["Building, Dwelling, Praying,"], *Revue Thomiste* 87 (1987), pp. 357-390, 547-578; "Penser à Dieu en l'aimant: Philosophie et theologie de Jean-Luc Marion," ["Thinking about God by Loving Him"] ["TGLH"], *Archives de Philosophie* 50 (1987), pp. 245-270; "La théologie et l'Esprit," *Nouvelle Revue Théologique* 109 (1987), pp. 660-671; "Anges et hobbits: le sense des mondes possibles," *Freiburger Zeitschrift für Philosophie und Theologie* 36:3 (1989), pp. 341-373; "De la phénomenologie de l'Esprit à la montée du Carmel" ["From Phenomenology of Spirit to the Mount of Carmel"] ["CARM"], *Revue Thomiste* 89 (1989), pp. 5-39, 569-598; "Théologie anonyme et christologie pseudonyme: C.S. Lewis, les chroniques de narina," *Nouvelle Revue Théologique* 112 (1990), pp. 381-393; "Urgence kérygmatique et délais herméneutiques," *Revue philosophique de Louvain* 92 (1994), pp. 259-280 [translated as "More Haste, Less Speed in Theology," ["MHLS"], *International Journal of Systematic Theology* 9:3 (2007), pp. 263-282]; "Le désir et l'inexigible," *Les Études philosophique* 2 (1995), pp. 232-238; "Le monde et l'absence d'oeuvre," *Revue des sciences philosophiques et théologiques* 80 (1997), pp. 377-413 [translated as "The Work and Complement of Appearing," ["WCA"], in Bloechl, Jeffrey, ed., *Religious Experience and the End of Metaphysics* (Bloomington: Indiana University Press, 2003), pp. 68-93]; "De la technique à la liturgie," *Telos* 113 (1998), pp. 19-40; ""Philosophie, théologie et vérité: Remarques frontalières," *Recherches de science religieuses* 89 (2001), pp. 487-510; "Présence et affection," ["Presence and Affection"] ["PAFF"], in Boeve, Lieven, and Lambert Leijssen, eds., *Sacramental Presence in a Postmodern Context* (Leuven: Peeters, 2001), pp. 212-231; "Presence and Parousia" ["LPP"], in Ward, Graham, ed., *The Blackwell Companion to Postmodern Theology* (London: Blackwell, 2001), pp. 394-398; "La connaissance silencieuse: Des évidences antéprédicatives à une critique de l'apophase," ["Silent Knowledge"] ["SK"], *Laval Théologique et Philosophique* 58:1 (2002), pp. 137-153; "Dieu: John N. Findlay et les raisons nécessaires" in Bourgeois-Gironde, Sacha, et al., eds., *Analyse et théologie* (Paris: Vrin, 2002), pp. 241-248; "Liturgy and Coaffection," ["LCA"], in Hart, Kevin, and Barbara Wall, eds., *The Experience of God: A Postmodern Response* (New York: Fordham University Press, 2005), pp. 93-103; "Témoignage mystique et expérience philosophique," in Capelle, Philippe, ed., *Expérience philosophique et expérience mystique* (Paris: Cerf, 2005), pp. 301-321; "L'apparaître et l'irréductible," *Revue philosophique de Louvain* 104:3 (2006), pp. 498-528 [translated as "The Appearing and the Irreducible," ["AI"], in Benson, Bruce, *Words of Life: New Theological Turns in French Phenomenology* (New York: Fordham University Press, 2010), pp. 42-67]; "Dieu connaissable comme aimable: Par delà foi et raison," ["God Knowable as Lovable"], ["GKL"], *Recherches de science religieuses* 95:2 (2007), pp. 177-197; "La frontière absente: Philosophie et/ou théologie dans les Miettes philosophiques," in Gaziaux, Eric, ed., *Philosophie et théologie* (Louvain: Louvain University Press, 2007), pp. 195-211; "La phénoménalité de l'anticipation," *Conférence* 24 (2007), pp. 511-542 [translated as "The Phenomenality of Anticipation," ["PA"], in DeRoo, Neal, et al., eds., *Phenomenology and Eschatology* (Lewiston: Ashgate, 2009), pp. 15-34]; "Voler amare: Note sull'amore e sulla fedeltà," in Reali, Nicola, ed., *L'amore tra filosofia e teologia: in dialogo con Jean-Luc Marion* (Vatican City: Lateran University Press, 2007), pp. 47-64; "Perception, Transcendence, and the Experience of God," ["PTEG"], in Cunningham, Connor, ed., *Transcendence and Phenomenology* (London: SCM Press, 2008), pp. 1-20; "La chose et le sacré," in Ciocan, Cristian, ed., *Philosophical Concepts and Religious Metaphors* (Bucharest: Zeta Books, 2009), pp. 29-62; "Continental Philosophy," in Chad Meister, ed., *The Routledge Companion to the Philosophy of Religion* (London: Routledge, 2010); "Theology and the Task of Thinking," in Pierre Gilbert, ed., *Theologies and Truth* (Louvain: Peeters, 2010), pp. 217-230.

These articles have been collected in: *The World and the Absence of Work* [*Le Monde et l'absence d'oeuvre*] [WAW] (2000); *Presence and Parousia* [*Présence et parousie*] [PP] (2006); *The Phenomenality of God* [*La phénoménalité de Dieu: Neuf études*] [LPG] (2008).

142   In the French language both *savoir* and *connaître* refer to forms of knowledge. Savior is knowledge of a fact, such as a mathematical theorem, or how to ride a bike. *Connaître*, on the other hand, refers to a knowledge born of familiarity with something, such as one's knowledge of a favorite city, a personal friend, or a song or book one loves. Lacoste, thus claims that only in the Parousia, or second coming of Christ, will we have an intimate knowledge [*connaissance*] of God, or at least to a full extent.

143   Lacoste is decidedly ambivalent on the importance of the feelings. Lacoste grants that the divine largesse can appear to us in our feelings, in an experience of peace and joy, if it so desires. That is to say it is always a possibility that we may feel the divine presence, feel a worldly inchoation or foretaste of the divine beatitude, especially in the liturgy (EA, Introduction, p. 2; III,

p. 51; IV, pp. 59, 73-74; V, pp. 85, 94-96; VIII, p. 146-148, 150; "PTEG," pp. 14, 16-17, 19; "SK," p. 146; "WCA," pp. 91-92; "LCA," pp. 101-103; "PAFF," pp. 229-230; "MHLS," p. 275; LNT, II, pp. 89-91, 101; III, p. 201).

Yet he cautions that no particular kind of religious experience can be considered paradigmatic, such as the Schleiermachian feeling of absolute dependence on an Almighty. For while God may be present, God transcends every side of Himself presented to me ("PTEG," pp. 19-20). Moreover, a God who appears to the feelings is also always subject to appearing in the modes of world and earth, and so to being shrouded in ambiguity and veiled. Indeed it is only by a careful discernment of spirits that we can ensure that our experience is genuinely one of God and not bound up with our own exaltation or idolatrous (more often than not such feelings of the divine are falsified rather than verified and so great hermeneutic caution must be taken here) (EA, III, pp. 48-49; IV, p. 63; V, p. 96; VI, p 101; VIIII, pp. 142-145; IX, p. 188; n. 6 and 8 on p. 206; "PTEG," pp. 14, 16-17). Finally, any legitimate feeling of God is bound up with a still greater inexperience (and so is primarily a knowledge [savoir] of God); only the Parousia could provide us with apodictic proof of God, with connaissance [familiarity] of Him. Accordingly no present experience of the Absolute is one wherein we can unambiguously utter the name of God (excepting perhaps mystical experiences which are a glimmer of the Parousia in the chiaroscuro of history). So we cannot fully silence the inexperience to which those who enter into liturgy must consent; liturgy is a place of prayer indifferent to feeling where normally nothing happens that manifests the grace of God. In other words, in the liturgy, God comes incognito (EA, III, p. 50).

Hence on the whole Lacoste is quite critical of a religion of Romanticism and proposes that liturgy is not to be equated with a school of sentiment (EA, Introduction, p. 2). For Hegel was right and Schleiermacher wrong: our present relation to God must take place in knowledge [savoir] not the feelings [les sentiments] (EA, VII, p. 134; n. 17 on p. 198; "PAFF," p. 214).

144   Lacoste remains skeptical of the so-called proofs for God. In order to see the world as a work of divine glory and let the heavens sing of God (i.e. accept the teleological argument), we must first name God beforehand in liturgy, or rather God must first name us before we name God. For such a feeling of the divine glory of creation is a projection of a meaning onto a phenomenon and not actually given with it (EA, VI, pp. 103, 105, 108). So too our feeling of our being as a gift (i.e. the basis of the cosmological argument) must be confirmed in liturgy (EA, VI, p. 106; VIII, p, 158-160; n. 8 on p. 206).

Lacoste admits that we can speak of a rational approach to God (as Vatican Council I did), but tends to reconfigure this as a way of knowing God by loving Him. For, as Lacoste sees it, knowledge and affection are bound up with each other, and we cannot know something if we do not love it. Moreover, Lacoste argues that the assent to God, even if based on natural knowledge, is ultimately voluntary. So while faith is not without reason, rare is the reason with which freedom does not collaborate. For God does not appear to us as the Alps do, as an object imposing itself on us, nor as a logical or mathematical proof, but as someone whom we can affirm and acquiesce in. Thus with God *ratio* [reason] and *caritas* [charity] are ever linked, God speaks to us through love (LNT, IX, pp. 229-230; XIII, p. 338; LPG, V, p. 132; "TGLH," p. 270; "Credibility," vol. I, pp. 387-390; "Reason," vol. II, pp. 1349-1351; "GKL," pp. 182-184, 187-191, 193-197). Lacoste writes: "... a divine manifestation occurring in history [i.e. the Incarnation] does not call for more assent (even if the logic of this assent is different) than a [divine] manifestation given always, everywhere, and to all. The God of the philosophers and learned paradoxically requires to be believed, and even to be loved. The rational affirmation of His existence includes an act of faith and an act of love" ("GKL," p. 196).

Lacoste also allows that humans have a basic restlessness for a divine surplus, even if they do not always know what they truly desire. For there is a fundamental awareness that the world and earth leave us unsatisfied (though we cannot infer from this an Absolute with which we would maintain an immemorial relation) (EA, III, pp. 41-42; V, pp. 85-90; VI, p. 105; IX, p. 190; WAW, II, pp. 49-54; III, pp. 92-101; LNT, II, pp. 96-100; "Reason," p. 1307). Thus our restlessness is the one palimpsest which can dissipate the chiaroscuro of the divine (by our boredom with world and earth and dreams of a beyond). In a way then the only experience we have of God is of wanting to know Him. Yet this restlessness must be informed by knowledge to become conceptual and ensure non-idolatry (EA, I, p. 20; V, p. 85; VI, pp. 101, 104-105; IX, p. 192; n. 20 on pp. 198-199; "EEKG," p. 854-858; "CARM," p. 15). Thus Lacoste writes that restlessness is a "mark of the humanity of the human which removes the human from every satisfaction to which world and earth hold the measure, and grants to the human the eschatological satisfaction, that by definition, the Absolute alone promises" (EA, n. 20 on p. 198 [n. 1 on p. 25]). So liturgy, "By subverting our earth and world, confirms that earth and world are indeed the native structures according to which our relation to place unfolds. And by affirming that our being is to be understood in the final instance as an (eschatological) vocation, in terms of an exposition to the Absolute and not in those of the opening onto the world, it very much ratifies the historical order in which this vocation 'is' perhaps, but it does not gain a hold over the native conditions of experience, except under the form of a restlessness (theology would speak here of a natural desire for the beatific vision) that does not yield all its meaning to a hermeneutics of facticity. One thus understands how we have come to form the suspicious affirmation according to which the divertissement would lie at the beginning (at the beginning, which does not mean at the origin)" (EA, V, p. 87 [106]).

145   For more on Desmond see: Martine, Brian, "William Desmond, the Artwork, and a Metaxological Understanding of Otherness," CLIO 20:4

(1991), pp. 333-351; Coolidge, Francis, "On the Nature of the Absolute: A Response to Desmond," *Southwest Philosophy Review* 13:1 (1997), pp. 67-74; O'Regan, Cyril, "Metaphysics and the Metaxological Space of the Tradition," *Tijdschrift voor Filosofie* 59:3 (1997), pp. 531-549; Rinaldi, Giacomo, "Metaphysics as a Cultural Presence: Dialectical and Metaxological Thought in the Philosophy of William Desmond," in Desmond, William, et al., eds., *Being and Dialectic: Metaphysics and Culture* (Albany: State University of New York Press, 2000), pp. 155-178; O'Regan, Cyril, "The Poetics of Ethos: William Desmond's Poetic Refiguration of Plato," *Ethical Perspectives* 8:4 (2001), pp. 272-306; *Ethical Perspectives* 8 (2001), pp. 221-331 [Special Issue on Desmond]; Hadley, Douglas, "To Be is To Be Determinate: Determination and Excess (and Neoplatonism) in William Desmond's Criticism and Construction of Metaphysics," *International Philosophical Quarterly* 42:3 (2002), pp. 329-348; Stambovsky, Phillip, *Philosophical Conceptualization and Literary Art: Inference, Ereignis, and Conceptual Attunement to the Work of Poetic Genius* (Madison: Fairleigh Dickinson University Press, 2004), pp. 81-133; Kohler-Ryan, Renee, "De Profundis Clavi Ad Te Domine: The Existential Significance of Depth for Berkeley, Merleau-Ponty, and Desmond," *Irish Philosophical Society Yearbook* (2005), pp. 237-253; Schulting, Dennis, "Hegel, Reason, and the Overdeterminacy of God," *Bulletin of the Hegel Society of Great Britain* (2005), pp. 51-52, 83-96; Zuba, Sonja, "Contemporary Retrieval of Platonic Themes: Murdoch and Desmond," *Irish Philosophical Society Yearbook* (2005), pp. 254-278; Coolidge, Francis, "On Divine Madness, Its Relations to the Good, and the Erotic Aspect of the Agapeic Good," *Tijdschrift voor Filosofie* 65:1 (2003), pp. 93-119; Kelly, Thomas, ed., *Between System and Poetics: William Desmond and Philosophy after Dialectic* (Burlington: Ashgate, 2007).

146   This work is the third book in his trilogy comprising also the earlier works *Being and the Between* [BB] (1995) [awarded the 1994 J.N. Findlay Award of the Metaphysical Society of America and the 1995 Prix Cardinal Mercier] and *Ethics and the Between* [EB] (2001).

Desmond has also written on Hegel and other works including: *Desire, Dialectic and Otherness* [DDO] (1987); *Philosophy and Its Others: Ways of Being and Mind* [PO] (1990); *Perplexity and Ultimacy: Metaphysical Thoughts from the Middle* [PU] (1995); *Is There a Sabbath for Thought?: Between Religion and Philosophy* [IST] (2005) [a collection of articles]; Philosopher

Additionally Desmond has penned many articles (and book reviews) the key ones being: "God, Kearney and Contemporary European Philosophy," *The Irish Theological Quarterly* 54: 3 (1988), pp. 237-242; "Being Between," *CLIO* 20:4 (1991), pp. 305-331; "Evil and Dialectic," in Kolb, David, ed., *New Perspective in Hegel's Philosophy of Religion* (Albany: SUNY Press, 1992), pp. 159-182; "Thinking on the Double: the Equivocities of Dialectic," *The Owl of Minerva* 25:2 (1994), pp. 221-234; "Being, Determination, and Dialectic: On the Sources of Metaphysical Thinking," ["BDD"], *The Review of Metaphysics*

48 (1995), pp. 731-769; "Between Finitude and Infinity: Hegelian Reason and the Pascalian Heart," in Ardis, Collins, ed., *Hegel on the Modern World* (Albany: SUNY Press, 1995), pp. 1-28; "The Mathesis of Nature, the Poeisis of Naturing," *Journal of Dharma* 20:4 (1995), pp. 321-333; "Perplexity and Ultimacy: Metaphysical Thoughts from the Middle," in Heim, Michael, and Nenos Georgopoulos, eds., *Being Human in the Ultimate* (Amsterdam: Rodopi, 1995), pp. 101-133; "Serviceable, Disposability, and the Blandness of the Good," *Ethical Perspectives* 5:2 (1998), pp. 136-143; "God, Ethos, Ways," ["GEW"], *International Journal of the Philosophy of Religion* 45 (1999), pp. 13-30 [also published in Sweet, William, ed., *God and Argument* (Ottawa: University of Ottawa Press, 1999), pp. 65-83]; "Hyperbolic Thoughts: On Creation and Nothing," in Sia, Santiago, and Andre Cloots, eds., *Framing a Vision of the World: Essays in Philosophy, Science and Religion* (Louvain: Louvain University Press, 1999), pp. 23-43; "God beyond the Whole: Between Shestov and Solov'ëv," in Van den Bercken, Wil, et al., eds., *Vladimir Solov'ëv: Reconciler and Polemicist* (Louvain: Peeters, 2000), pp. 185-210; "Neither Deconstruction or Reconstruction: Metaphysics and the Intimate Strangeness of Being," ["NDR"], *International Philosophical Quarterly* 40:1 (2000), pp. 37-49; "On the Betrayals of Reverence," ["BR"], *Irish Theological Quarterly* 65:3 (2000), pp. 211-230; "Philosophy of Religion," in Rosen, Stanley, ed., *The Examined Life* (New York: Random House, 2000), pp. 105-123; "Exceeding the Measure: On Ethics and the Between," *Ethical Perspectives* 8:4 (2001), pp. 319-331; "Religious Imagination and the Counterfeit Doubles of God," ["CDG], *Louvain Studies* 27 (2002), pp. 280-305; "Sticky Evil: On Macbeth and the Karma of the Equivocal," in Middleton, Darren, ed., *God, Literature and Process Thought* (Aldershot: Ashgate Press, 2002), pp. 133-155; "Maybe, Maybe Not: Richard Kearney and God," ["MMN"], *Irish Theological Quarterly* 68 (2003), pp. 99-118 [revised version published in Monoussakis, John Panteleimon, *After God: Richard Kearney and the Religious Turn in Continental Philosophy* (New York: Fordham University Press, 2005), pp. 55-77]; "The Need of Finesse: The Information Society and the Sources of Ethical Formation," in Conway, Eamonn, ed., *Ethics and Values in a Digital Age* (Dublin: Report of the Information Society Commission of the Government of Ireland, 2004), pp. 24-39; "Religion and the Poverty of Philosophy," ["RPP"], in Desmond, William, et al., eds., *Philosophy and Religion in German Idealism* (Dordrecht: Kluwer Publishers, 2004), pp. 139-170; "Tyranny and the Recess of Friendship," *Recherches de théologie et philosophie medievales* 6 (2004), pp. 99-125 [also in Kelly, Thomas, and Philipp Rosemann, eds., *Amor Amicitiae: On the Love that is Friendship* (Louvain: Peeters, 2004), pp. 99-125]; "Consecrated Love: A Philosophical Reflection on Marriage," *INTAMS Review* 11 (2005), pp. 4-17; "Consecrated Thought: Between the Priest and the Philosopher," ["CT"], *Louvain Studies* 30 (2005), pp. 92-106; "Hegel's God, Transcendence and the Counterfeit Double," *The Owl of Minerva* 36:2 (2005), pp. 91-110; "Is there Metaphysics after Critique?" ["MAC"], *International Philosophical*

Quarterly 45:2 (2005), pp. 221-241; "Neither Servility nor Sovereignty: Between Metaphysics and Politics," in Davis, Creston, et al., *Theology and the Political: The New Debate* (Durham: Duke University Press, 2005), pp. 153-182; "Pluralism, Truthfulness and the Patience of Being," in Taylor, Carol, and Roberto Dell'Oro, eds., *Health and Human Flourishing: Religion, Medicine and Moral Anthropology* (Washington: Georgetown University Press, 2006), pp. 53-70; "What's in an Ending?" *The Leuven Philosophy Newsletter* 15 (2006-2007), pp. 6-10; "Between System and Poetics: On the Practices of Philosophy," ["BSP"], in Kelly, Thomas, ed., *Between System and Poetics: William Desmond and Philosophy after Dialectics* (Aldershot: Ashgate, 2007), pp. 15-36; "Metaphysics and the Confidence of Thought," in Chandler, Peter, and Conor Cunningham, eds., *Belief and Metaphysics* (St. Mary's Works: SCM, 2007), pp. 11-40; "Ways of Wondering: Beyond the Barbarism of Reflection," in Deckard Funk, ed., *Philosophy Begins in Wonder* (Eugene: Pickwick, 2010), pp. 310-348. Desmond also published many popular articles on philosophy in the *Cork Examiner* (1980-1987).

See the bibliography in Kelly, Thomas, ed., *Between System and Poetics: William Desmond and Philosophy after Dialectic* (Burlington: Ashgate, 2007), pp. 293-302.

147   So too we are between Jerusalem and Athens and must listen to both religion and philosophy. For we must think the revelation of God in the best human wisdom we have, without sublimating theology to philosophy and forming an idol of God. And philosophy must be porous to religious communication, to the passion of prayer, in an *intellectus quaerens fidem* [intellect seeking faith] (GB, Introduction, pp. 8-9; V, p. 93; VI, p. 143; XIV, p. 282; "CT," pp. 95-98, 103-106; "CDG," pp. 298-299; "RPP," pp. 146-149, 161-170; BB, IX, pp. 202, 204; IST, Preface, pp. xi; Introduction, pp. 1-2; II, p. 66; III, pp. 106, 109-113, 127-133; X, pp. 348-356).

148   Desmond thus, while not rejecting, limits the usefulness of argumentative "proofs" for God. In the first place, we must get at what is prior to these "proofs" to find their enabling metaphysical conditions in our primal ethos, our mindfulness of life's vitality, mystery, and our ultimate sources. In the second place, some of the proofs are too tied to a univocal and determinate view of being, such as Anselm's ontological argument and Paley's argument from mechanical design. They thus give us a scarecrow abstraction of the divine, with God becoming the *ens realissimum* [most real being] or the *ens summum* [highest being], versus the living God (GB, Introduction, pp. 3-5; IV, p. 76; V, pp. 93-95, 108; VI, pp. 131-132, 140, 144; XIV, p. 340; "GEW," pp. 13-30, 66, 81-82; IST, Introduction, pp. 9-17). In the third place nature is too ambiguous to display God with sufficient luminescence (GB, IV, p. 82).

149   Desmond claims that God's power even extends beyond the law of contradiction which is but the limitation of human logic (GB, XIV, n. 21 on p. 316).

150   Other Catholic Postmodernists (of about 75 total including Neo-Platonists) are: the Passionist Stanislas Breton (1912-2005); the former priest Pierre Hadot (1922-), of the College de France [Neo-Platonist; winner of the Grand Prize of Philosophy in 1999]; Michel Henry (1922-2002); Michel de Certeau, S.J. (1925-1986); Fr. Adolphe Gesché (1928-2003) [winner of the Grand Prize of Philosophy in 1998]; Ghislain Lafont, O.S.B. (1928-); Pierre Aubenque (1929-), of the Sorbonne [Neo-Platonist]; Bernhard Casper (1931-); Pierre-Jean Labarriere, S.J. (1931-); Claude Bruaire (1932-1986), of the Sorbonne [Hegelian]; Paul Valadier, S.J. (1933-); the reconvert Philippe Sollers (1936-) [husband of Julia Kristeva]; Gianni Vattimo (1936-); John Caputo (1940-); Bishop André Léonard (1940-) [Hegelian]; Robert Magliola (c. 1940-); Mario Preniola (1941-); Emilio Brito, S.J., (1942-); Eugenio Trias (1942-); Merold Westphal (c. 1942-); Jean-François Courtine (1944-); Yves Labbé (1944-); Christoph Theobald, S.J. (1946-) [also Romanticism]; Claudie Lavaud (c. 1947-); the convert Jean-Louis Chrétien (1952-) of the Sorbonne; Kevin Hart (1954-); Tina Beattie (1955-); Richard Kearney (c. 1955-) [who speaks of a 'God who May Be']; Fr. Michael Purcell (1956-); Laurence Paul Hemming (1962-) [Radical Orthodoxyt]; Gerard Loughlin (c. 1965-) [Radical Orthodoxy]; Claude Romano (1967-), of the Sorbonne; and Maxence Caron (1976-).

Catholic critics of postmodernism include: Benedict Ashley, O.P., Gregory Baum, David Burrell, C.S.C., Dominique Dubarle, who responded to Marion's book with his own *Dieu avec l'etre* (Paris: Beauchesne, 1986), Michel Duquesne, Lawrence Dewan, Jean Griesch, Jean Guitton, Thierry-Dominique Humbrecht, John F.X. Knasas, Joseph Koterski, S.J., Peter Augustine Lawler, Hugo Meynell, Jean-Hervé Nicolas, O.P., Marie-Dominique Philippe, Vittorio Possenti, Géry Prouvost, Jean-Dominique Robert, O.P., James Schall, S.J., Kenneth Schmitz, Brendan Sweetman, Roger Verneaux, René Virgoulay, and see the volume Ciapalo, Roman, ed., *Postmodernism and Christian Philosophy* (Washington: Catholic University of America Press, 1996).

151   There has arisen the idea of a *sensus fidelium* (*sensus fidei; consensus fidei*), or sense of the faithful which designates as without error the doctrinal beliefs held by the whole body of the faithful, when "from the Bishops down to the last of the lay faithful they show universal agreement in matters of faith and morals" (*Lumen Gentium*, 12, 25; see DH, 1367, CCC, 904; Congregation for the Doctrine of the Faith, *Donum Veritatis*, 35).

BIBLIOGRAPHY

Agazzi, Evandro, *Il pensiero cristiano nella filosofia italiana del Noveceno* (Lecce: Milella, 1980).

Allitt, Patrick, *Catholic Politics and Conservative Intellectuals in America, 1950-1985* (New York: Cornell University Press, 1995).

Ariès, Philippe, ed., *Cinquante ans de pensée catholique française* [CAP] (Paris: Artheme Fayard, 1955), pp. 85-104.

Appleby, R. Scott, et al., eds., *Creative Fidelity: American Catholic Intellectual Traditions* (New York: Orbis, 2004).

Aubert, Roger, *Problème de l'acte de foi* [PAF], 3rd ed. (Louvain: E. Warny, 1958).

Auvergne, Dominique, *Regards catholiques sur le monde* [RCSM] (Paris: Desclée de Brouwer, 1938).

Bacik, James, *Contemporary Theologians* [CT] (Chicago: The Thomas More Press, 1989).

Baldwin, Thomas, ed., *The Cambridge History of Philosophy, 1870-1945* [CAHP] (Cambridge: Cambridge University Press, 2003).

Bautz, Friedrich Wilhelm, ed., *Biographisch-bibliographisches Kirchenlexikon* [BBKL] (Hamm: Bautz, 1990-2010).

Benrubi, Isaak, *Contemporary Thought of France* [CTF], trans. Ernest Dicker (New York: Alfred A. Knopf, 1926).

Benson, Bruce, ed., *Words of Life: New Theological Turns in French Phenomenology* (New York: Fordham University Press, 2010).

Berger, David, ed., *Thomistenlexikon* (Bonn: Nova und Vetera, 2006).

Berkhof, Hendrikus, *Two-Hundred Years of Theology* [TYT] (Grand Rapids: Eerdmans, 1989).

Berti, Enrico, "L'influenza della tradizione religiosa sulla filosofia Italiana del novecento," *Studia Patavina* 42 (1995), pp. 651- 668.

Bettoni, Efrem, ed., *La situation actuelle de la philosophie parmi les catholiques dans divers pays* (Utrecht: Spectrum, 1948).

Bird, Thomas, ed., *Modern Theologians: Christians and Jews* [MTCJ] (Notre Dame: University of Notre Dame Press, 1967).

Blandi, Giovanni, *Discussioni sul neo-tomismo* (Rome: Pontifical Lateran University Press, 1990).

Bobbio, Norberto, *Ideological Profile of Twentieth-Century Italy* (Princeton: Princeton University Press, 1995).

Bocheński, Józef, *Contemporary European Philosophy* [CEP], trans. Donald Nicholl and Karl Aschenbrenner (Berkeley: University of California Press, 1961).

Bogliolo, Luigi, *Il problema della filosofia cristiana* (Brescia: Morcelliana, 1959).

Boisset, Jean, ed., *Le problème de la philosophie chrétienne* (Paris: Presses Universitaires de France, 1949).

Bonifazi, Duili, *Filosofia e Cristianesimo: Discussioni recenti* (Rome: Pontifical University Lateranense, 1968).

Borchert, Donald, ed., *The Encyclopedia of Philosophy* [EP], 10 vols. (New York: Macmillan, 2005).

Bréhier, Émile, *History of Philosophy* [BHP], vols. 5-7, tr. Wade Baskin (Chicago: University of Chicago Press, 1967-1969).

Brezik, Victor, ed., *One Hundred Years of Thomism* [OHYT] (Houston: Center for Thomistic Studies, 1981).

Brillant, Maurice, and Maurice Nédoncelle, eds., *Apologétique* (Paris: Bloud et Gay, 1937).

Brosman, Catherine, and Tom Conley, eds., *Dictionary of Twentieth-Century French Culture 1900-1975* [TCFC] (Detroit: Gale, 1995).

Brown, Stuart, Diané Collinson, and Robert Wilkinson, eds., *Biographical Dictionary of Twentieth-Century Philosophers* [BDTC] (London: Routledge, 1996).

Brown, Stuart, ed., *Dictionary of Twentieth-Century British Philosophers* [DTCB], 2 vols. (Bristol: Theommes Press, 2005).

Burr, John, ed., *Handbook of World Philosophy: Contemporary Developments since 1945* (Westport: Greenwood, 1981).

Capelle, Philippe, ed., *Philosophie et Théologie* (Paris: Le Cerf, 2010), vol. IV.

―――. et al., eds., *Raison philosophique et christianisme à l'aube du 3ème millénaire* (Paris: Cerf, 2004).

Caponigri, Aloysius Robert, *Contemporary Spanish Philosophy* (Notre Dame: Notre Dame University Press, 1967).

―――. *A History of Western Philosophy* [HWP], vols. 3-5 (Notre Dame: University of Notre Dame Press, 1963-1971).

Carey, Patrick, *Modern Catholic Thinkers* [CMCT], 2 vols. (New York: Harper and Brothers, 1960).

Cernera, Anthony, and Oliver Morgan, eds., *Examining the Catholic Intellectual Tradition* (Fairfield: Sacred Heart University Press, 2000).

Cessario, Romanus, *A Short History of Thomism* [SHT] (Washington: Catholic University of America, 2005).

Chevalier, Jacques, *Histoire de la pensée*, 3 vols. (Paris: Flammarion, 1955).

Cohen, Paul, et al., eds., *Piety and Politics: Catholic Revival and the Generation of 1905-1914* (New York: Garland, 1987).

Colin, Pierre, ed., *Intellectuels chrétiens et esprit des années 1920* [ICEA] (Paris: Cerf, 1997).

Collins, James, *Modern European Philosophy* (Milwaukee: Bruce, 1954).

Connor, Charles, *Classic Catholic Converts* (San Francisco: Ignatius Press, 2001).

Copleston, Frederick, *Contemporary Philosophy* (London: Burns and Oats, 1956).

————. *A History of Philosophy* [CHP], vols. 3-9 (New York: Image Books, 1953-1977).

Coreth, Emerich, Walter Neidl, and George Pfligersdorffer, eds., *Christliche Philosophie im katholischen Denken des 19. und 20. Jahrhunderts* [CP], vols. 1-3 (Graz: Styria, 1987-1990).

Coulter, Michael, et al., eds., *Encyclopedia of Catholic Social Thought, Social Science, and Social Policy* (Lanham: Scarecrow Press, 2007).

Cox, James, *Key Figures in the Phenomenology of Religion: Formative Influences and Subsequent Debates* (London: Continuum, 2006).

Craig, Edward, ed., *Routledge Encyclopedia of Philosophy* [REP] (London: Routledge, 1998).

Critchley, Simon, and William Schroeder, eds., *A Companion to Continental Philosophy* [CCP] (Oxford: Blackwell, 1998).

D'Ales, Adhemer, ed., *Dictionnaire Apologetique de la Foi Catholique* [DAF], 4th ed., vols. 1-5 (Paris: Beauchesne, 1924-1931).

Daniélou, Jean, et al., eds., *Philosophies chrétiennes* (Paris: Arthème Fayard, 1955).

De la Torre, Teodoro, *Popular History of Philosophy* [PHP] (Houston: Lumen Christi Press, 1988).

De Laubier, Patrick, ed., *La philosophie d'inspiration chrétienne en France* (Paris: Desclée et Brouwer, 1988).

De Llera Estaban, Louis, "La filosofia catolica en la Espana de Franco, 1939-1975," *Hispania Sacra* 43 (1991), pp. 436-473.

Deledalle, Gérard, and Denis Huisman, eds., *Les Philosophes français d'au-jourd'hui par eux-même* [PFA] (Paris: C.D.U, 1963).

Delfgaauw, Bernard, *Twentieth-Century Philosophy* [TCP], tr. N.D. Smith (Albany: Magi Books, 1969).

De Lubac, Henri, "Retrieving the Tradition: On Christian Philosophy," *Communio* 19:3 (1992), pp. 478-506.

Denzinger, Heinrich, and Peter Hünermann, *Enchiridion Symbolorum definitionum et declarationum de rebus fidei et morum* [DH], 38th ed. (Freiburg: Herder, 1999).

Denzinger, Heinrich, *The Sources of Catholic Dogma* [Denz], 13th ed., tr. Roy Deferrari (Fitzwilliam: Loreteo Publications, 2002).

De Ruggiero, Guido, *Filosofi del novecento* (Bari: Laterza, 1966).

De Wulf, Maurice, *Scholasticism Old and New*, tr. Peter Coffey (London: Longmans, Green, and Company, 1907).

Dimnet, Ernest, *La pensée catholique dans l'Angleterre contemporaine* (Paris: Victor Lecoffre, 1906).

Doolan, Aegidius, *The Revival of Thomism* (Dublin: Clonmore and Reynolds, 1951).

Donegani, Jean-Marie, *La pensée catholique* (Paris: Presses de Science Po, 2001).

Drummond, John, and Embree, Lester, eds., *Phenomenological Approaches to Moral Philosophy* [PAMP] (Dordrecht: Kluwer, 2002).

Dulles, Avery, *A History of Apologetics* [HA] (Philadelphia: Westminster Press, 1971).

———. *The Assurance of Things Hoped For: A Theology of Christian Faith* [ATH] (Oxford: Oxford University Press, 1994).

Duméry, Henry, "Catholic Philosophy in France," in *Philosophic Thought in France and the United States*, ed. Martin Farber (Buffalo: University of Buffalo Publications, 1950), pp. 219-248.

———. *Regards sur la philosophie contemporaine* [RPC] (Tournai: Casterman, 1956).

Duquin, Lorene, *A Century of Catholic Converts* [CCC] (Huntington: Our Sunday Visitor Press, 2003).

Du Vauroux, Paul, *Du subjectivisme allemande à philosophie catholique* (Paris: Bloud et Gay, 1916).

Embree, Lester, ed., *The Encyclopedia of Phenomenology* [EEP] (Dordrecht: Kluwer, 1997).

Edwards, Paul, ed., *The Encyclopedia of Philosophy* [EP:1], 10 vols. (New York: Macmillan, 1967).

Egan, Philip, *Philosophy and Catholic Theology* (Collegeville: Liturgical Press, 2009).

Fernescole, Pierre, *Témoins de la pensée catholique en France su la IIIe république* (Paris: Beauchesne, 1940).

Fitzpatrick, P.J., "Neoscholasticism," in *The Cambridge History of Later Medieval Philosophy*, ed. Norman Kretzmann, et al. (Cambridge: Cambridge University Press, 1982), pp. 838-852.

Florian, Michel, *La pensée catholique en Amérique du Nord* (Paris: Desclée de Brouwer, 2010).

Floucat, Yves, *Pour une philosophie chrétienne* (Paris: Téqui, 1975).

Forment, Eudaldo, *Historia de la filosofía tomista en la España contemporanea* (Madrid: Ediciones Encuentro, 1998).

Fornero, Giovanni, and Salvatore Tassinari, *Le filosofie del novecento* (Milan: B. Mondadori, 2006).

Forte, Bruno, *Dio nel Novecento. Tra filosofia e teologia* (Brescia: Morcelliana, 1998).

Fouilloux, Étienne, *Une Eglise en quête de liberté: La pensée catholique française entre modernisme et Vatican II, 1914-1962* (Paris: Desclée de Brouwer, 1998).

Friedman, Maurice, ed., *Worlds of Existentialism* [WE] (Atlantic Highlands: Humanities Press, 1991).

Gambra, Rafael, *La filosofía catolica en el siglo XX* (Madrid: Speiro, 1970).

Gélinas, Jean-Paul, *La restauration du Thomisme soun Léon XIII et la philosophie nouvelle* (Washington: Catholic University of America Press, 1959).

Gény, Paul, *Brevis conspectus historiae philosophiae* (Rome: Universitatis Gregorianae, 1921).

Giammanco, Rosanna, *Catholic-Communist Dialogue in Italy: 1944 to the Present* (New York: Praeger, 1989).

Gilson, Étienne, et al., eds., *Recent Philosophy: Hegel to the Present* [RP] (New York: Random House, 1966).

Golinas, J., *La Restauration du Thomisme sous Léon XIII et les philosophies nouvelles: Etudes de la pensée de Maurice Blondel et du Père Laberthonnière* (Washington: Catholic University of America Press, 1959).

Grabmann, Martin, *Die Geschichte der katholischen Theologie seit dem Ausgang der Väterzeit* (Freiburg: Herder, 1933).

Grevillot, Jean Marie, *Les grands courants de la pensée contemporaine: Existentialisme, marxisme, personnalisme chrétien* (**Paris:** Édition du Vitrail, 1947).

Grieco, Eileen, *Love and Knowledge in Modern Thomism* (Frankfurt: Peter Lang, 2000).

Gugelot, Frédéric, *La conversion des intellectuels au catholicisme en France, 1885-1935* (Paris: CNRS, 1998);

Guillet, Jacques, *La théologie catholique en France de 1914 à 1960* (Paris: Médiasèvres, 1988).

Guitton, Jean, *Regards sur la pensée française* [RPF] (Paris: Beauchesne, 1968).

Gutting, Gary, *French Philosophy in the Twentieth-Century* [FPTC] (Cambridge: Cambridge University Press, 2001).

Haldane, John, *Modern Writings on Thomism* (Bristol: Theommes Continuum, 2003).

———. "Thomism and the Future of Catholic Philosophy," *New Blackfriars* 80 (1999), pp. 158-216.

Hankey, Wayne, "Neoplatonism and Contemporary French Philosophy," *Dionysius* 23 (2005), pp. 161-190.

Hastings, Adrian, *A History of English Christianity, 1920-1990* (London: SCM Press, 1991).

Hastings, James, ed., *Encyclopedia of Religion and Ethics* [ERE], 13 vols. (New York: Charles Scribner's Sons, 1908-1927).

Hellman, John, *Emmanuel Mounier and the New Catholic Left, 1930-1950* (University of
Toronto Press, 1981).

———. "The Opening to the Left in French Catholicism: The Role of the Personalists," *The Journal of the History of Ideas* 34:3 (1973), pp. 381-390.

Héraud, Marie, *Croyances d'incroyants en France, aujourd'hui* (Paris: Le Centurion, 1977).

Herr, William, *Catholic Thinkers in the Clear: Giants of Catholic Thought from Augustine to Rahner* [CTIC] (Chicago: The Thomas More Press, 1985).

Hirschberger, Johannes, *The History of Philosophy* [HHP], 2 vols., tr. Anthony Fuerst (Milwaukee: Bruce, 1958-1959).

Hocedez, Edgar, *Histoire de la Théologie au XIXe siècle* [HT], v. 1-3 (Brussels: Édition universelle, 1947-1952).

Honderich, Ted, ed., *The Oxford Guide to Philosophy* [OGP] (Oxford: Oxford University Press, 2005).

Hudson, Deal, and Dennis Moran, eds., *The Future of Thomism* [FT] (Notre Dame: University of Notre Dame Press, 1992).

Hughes, H. Stuart, *The Obstructed Path: French Social Thought in the Years of Desperation, 1930-1960* (New Brunswick: Transaction Publishers, 2001).

Huisman, Denis, *Dictionnaire des philosophes* [DP], 2 vols. (Paris: Presses universitaires de France, 1993).

———. ed., *Tableau de la philosophie contemporaine* [TPC] (Paris: Fischbacher, 1967).

Inglis, John, *Spheres of Philosophical Inquiry and the Historiography of Medieval Philosophy* [SPI] (Leiden: Brill, 1998).

Jacquemet, Gabriel, ed., *Catholicisme: hier, aujourd'hui, demain* [CHAD], 15 vols. (Paris: Letouzey et Ane, 1948-2000).

Janicaud, Dominique, ed., *Phenomenology and the Theological Turn: The French Debate* (New York: Fordham University Press, 2001).

———. *Philosophy Wide Open: After the French Debate* (New York: Fordham University Press, 2005).

John, Helen James, *The Thomist Spectrum* [TS] (New York: Fordham University Press, 1966).

Jolivet, Régis, *La Philosophie chrétienne et la pensée contemporaine* (Paris: Pierre Téqui, 1932).

Jones, Lindsay, ed., *Encyclopedia of Religion* [ER] (Farmington Hills: Thomson Gale, 2004).

Jones, W. Tudor, *Contemporary Thought of Germany* (New York: A.A. Knopf, 1931).

Jonkers, Peter, and Rudd Welten, eds., *God in France: Eight Contemporary French Thinkers on God* [GF] (Leuven: Peeters, 2005).

Jordan, Mark, "The Terms of the Debate over Christian Philosophy," *Communio* 12 (1985), pp. 293-311.

Judt, Tony, *Past Imperfect: French Intellectuals, 1944-1956* (Berkeley: University of California Press, 1992).

Kalinowski, Georges, and Stefan Swiezawski, *Philosophy during the Second Vatican Council* (Frankfurt: Peter Lang, 2006).

Kasper, Walter, ed., *Lexikon für Theologie und Kirche* [LTK], 11 vols. (Freiburg: Herder, 1993-2001).

Kerr, Fergus, *After Aquinas: Versions of Thomism* (Oxford: Blackwell, 2002).

———. *Theology after Wittgenstein* (Oxford: Blackwell, 1986).

———. *Twentieth-Century Catholic Theologians* [TCCT] (Oxford: Blackwell, 2007).

Knasas, John, *Being and Some Twentieth-Century Thomists* [BTCT] (New York: Fordham University Press, 2003).

Kolesnyk, Alexander, "Aspekte der Entwicklung der katholischen Philosophie seit 1945," *Deutsche Zeitschrift fur Philosophie* 27 (1979), pp. 1501-1510.

Kolpig, Adolf, *Katholische Theologie gestern und heute* (Bremen: Schünemann, 1964).

Köster, Peter, *Der verbotene Philosoph: Studien zu den Anfängen der katholischen Nietzsche-Rezeption in Deutschland* (1890-1918) (Berlin: Walter de Gruyter, 1998).

Labbé, Yves, "La réception théologique de la philosophie de Lévinas," *Revue des sciences religieuses* 79:2 (2005), pp. 193-217.

Lacoste, Jean-Yves, *Encyclopedia of Christian Theology*, 3 vols. (London: Routledge, 2005).

Lacroix, Jean, *Panorama de la philosophie française contemporaine* [PPF] (Paris: Presses Universitaires de France, 1966).

Langer, Albrecht, *Katholizismus und philosophische Strömungen in Deutschland* (Paderborn: Schöningh, 1980).

Lavelle, Louis, *La Philosophie entre les deux Guerres* [PDG] (Paris: Aubier, 1942).

Ledure, Yves, *Lectures chrétiennnes de Nietzsche* [LCN] (Paris: Cerf, 1984).

Livi, Antonio, *Il cristianesimo nella filosofia* (L'Aquila: Japadrek 1969).

―――. et al., *Le ragioni del tomismo, dopo il centenario dell'enciclica Aeterni Patris* (Milan: Edizioni Ares, 1979).

Livingston, James, Francis Fiorenza, Sarah Coakley, and James Evans, eds., *Modern Christian Thought* [MCT], 2nd ed., 2 vols. (Upper Saddle River: Prentice Hall, 2000).

Long, Eugene Thomas, *Twentieth Century Western Philosophy of Religion* [WPR] (Dordrecht: Kluwer, 2003).

Longpré, Anselme, *La pensée catholique* (Montreal: Éditions du Devoir, 1936).

Lopez Calera, Nicolás María, *Neotomismo e filosofia del diritto in Italia* (Bologna, Zanichelli, 1965).

López Quintás, Alfonso, *Pensadores cristianos contemporáneos* (Madrid: Editorial Católica, 1968).

MacIntyre, Alasdair, *God, Philosophy, Universities: A Selective History of the Catholic Philosophical Tradition* (Lanham: Rowman & Littlefield, 2009).

Macquarrie, John, *Twentieth-Century Religious Thought* [TCRT] (London: SCM, 1988).

Madigan, Arthur, *Catholic Philosophers in the United States Today* (Notre Dame: Erasmus Institute, 2002).

Malusa, Luciano, *Neotomismo e intransigentismo cattolico* (Milan: IPL, 1986).

Manent, Pierre, *Intellectual History of Liberalism* (Princeton: Princeton University Press, 1996).

Magnin, Étienne, ed., *Un demi-siècle de pensée catholique* (Paris: Bloud et Gay, 1937).

Marías, Julián, *History of Philosophy* [MHP], tr. Stanley Appelbaum and Clarence Strowbridge (New York: Dover Publications, 1967).

Marthaler, Berard, ed., *New Catholic Encyclopedia* [NCE], 2nd ed., 15 vols. (Washington: Catholic University of America Press, 2003).

Mascall, Eric Lionel, *The Openness of Being: Natural Theology Today* [OB] (Philadelphia: The Westminster Press, 1971).

Mascia, Carmin, *A History of Philosophy* [CRHP] (Paterson: St. Anthony Guild Press, 1957).

Masnovo, Amato, *Il neotomismo in Italia* (Milan: Vita e Pensiero, 1923).

Matthews, Eric, *Twentieth-Century French Philosophy* [TCFP] (Oxford: Oxford University Press, 1996).

Mazhar, Noor Giovanni, *Catholic Attitudes to Evolution in Nineteenth-Century Italian Literature* (Venice: Instituto Veneto di Scienze, Lettere e Arti, 1995).

McBrien, Richard, ed., *The Harper Collins Encyclopedia of Catholicism* [HCEC] (San Francisco: Harper Collins, 1995).

McCaffrey, Enda, *The Return of Religion in France: From Democratisation to Postmetaphysics* (Basingstoke: Palgrave McMillan, 2009).

McClelland, John, *The French Right* (New York: Harper & Row, 1970).

McCool, Gerard, *From Unity to Pluralism: The Internal Evolution of Thomism* [FUP] (New York: Fordham University Press, 1989).

————. *The Neo-Thomists* [NT] (Milwaukee: Marquette University Press, 1994).

————. *Nineteenth-Century Scholasticism: The Search for a Unitary Method* [NCS] (Fordham University Press, 1989).

McEnhill, Peter, *Fifty Key Christian Thinkers* [FKCT] (London: Routledge, 2004).

McGrath, Alister, *The Blackwell Encyclopedia of Modern Christian Thought* [EMCT] (London: Blackwell, 1995).

McLean, George, *Philosophy in the Twentieth Century: Catholic and Christian. A Bibliography* (Ungar, 1967).

Mehl, Roger, *La condition du philosophe chrétien* (Paris: Delachaux & Niestlé, 1947).

Melchiorre, Virgilio, *Enciclopedia Filosofica* [EF] (Milan: Bompiani, 2006).

Miller, Leo, *A History of Philosophy* (New York: Joseph F. Wagner, 1927).

Molitor, Arnulf, *Die Scheinstringenz der neuscholastischen Tranzendentalphilosophie* (Vienna: Gesellschaften Österreichs, 1974).

Mondin, Battista, *La metafisica di San Tommaso d'Aquino e i suoi interpreti* (Bologna: Edizioni Studio Domenicano, 2002).

Moody, Joseph, ed., *Church and Society: Catholic Social and Political Thought and Movements: 1789-1950* (New York: Arts, 1953).

Moran, Dermot, *The Routledge Companion to Twentieth-Century Philosophy* (London: Routledge, 2008).

Morkovsky, Mary, "Catholic Philosophy in Latin America Today," *Proceedings of the American Catholic Philosophical Association* 53 (1979), pp. 36-44.

Meunier, E.-Martin, *Le pari personnaliste: Modernité et catholicisme au XXe siècle* (Montreal: Fides, 2007).

Muck, Otto, *The Transcendental Method* (New York: Herder, 1968).

Murphy, Francis, *Catholics and Communists in France, 1936-1939* (Gainesville: University Press of Florida, 1989).

Murray, Christopher, ed., *Encyclopedia of Modern French Thought* [EMFT] (New York: Fitzroy Dearborn, 2004).

Nédoncelle, Maurice, *Is There a Christian Philosophy?* [ITCP]," tr. Illtyd Trethowan (New York: Hawthorn Books, 1960).

Nichols, Aidan, *Catholic Thought since the Enlightenment: A Survey* [CTE] (Leominster: Gracewing, 1998).

Niederbacher, Bruno, "Hundert und Fünfzig Jahre Philosophie an der Theologischen Fakultät in Innsbruck," *Zeitschrift für katholische Theologie* 129 (2007), pp. 345-366.

O'Leary, Denis, *Roman Catholicism and Modern Science* (London: Continuum, 2006).

Olgiati, Francesco, and Armando Carlini, *Neo Scolastica, Idealismo e Spiritualismo* (Milan: Vita e Pensiero, 1933).

O'Meara, Thomas, *Church and Culture: German Catholic Theology, 1860-1914* (Notre Dame: University of Notre Dame Press, 1991).

Oppy, Graham, ed., *The History of Western Philosophy of Religion*, 5 vols. (Oxford: Oxford University Press, 2009).

Pagani, Paolo, *Sentieri riaperti: Riprendendo il cammino della neoscolastica Milanese* (Milan: Jaca, 1990).

Passmore, John, *A Hundred Years of Philosophy* [HYP], 2nd ed. (New York: Basic Books, 1966).

Paul, Harry, *The Edge of Contingency: French Catholic Reactions to Scientific Change from Darwin to Duhem* (Gainesville: University Press of Florida, 1979).

Penzo, Giorgio and Rosino Gibellini, ed., *Dio nella filosofia del Novecento* (Brescia: Queriniana, 1993).

Perrier, Joseph, *The Revival of Scholastic Philosophy in the Nineteenth Century* (New York: Columbia University Press, 1909).

Pietroforte, Stefania, *Le origini della neoscolastica italiana, 1909-1923* (Bologna: Il Mulino, 2005).

Pizzardo, Giuseppe, ed., *Enciclopedia cattolica* [IEC], 12 vols. (Vatican City: Libro Cattolico, 1948-1954).

Popkin, Richard, ed., *The Columbia History of Western Philosophy* [PCHP] (New York: Columbia University Press, 1999).

Poulat, Émile, *Catholicisme, Democratie et Socialisme* (Paris: Casterman, 1977).

Prini, Pietro, "Che ne è dalla filosofia cattolica italiano, oggi?," *Rivista di storia della filosofia* 50:3 1995), pp. 657-675.

———. *La filosofia cattolica italiana del Novecento* (Bari: Laterza, 1996).

Prouvost, Géry, "Les relations entre philosophie et theologie chez E. Gilson et les thomistes contemporains," *Revue Thomiste* 94:3 (1994), pp. 413-430.

———. *Thomas d'Aquin et les thomismes* (Paris: Cerf, 1996).

Rahner, Karl, *Theologische und philosophische Zeitfragen im katholischen deutschen Raum 1943* (Ostfildern: Schwabenverlag, 1994).

Reardon, Bernhard, "Science and Religious Modernism: The New Apologetic in France, 1890-1913," *Journal of Religion* 56 (1977), pp. 48-63.

Reese, William, *Dictionary of Philosophy and Religion* [DPR] (Amherst: Prometheus Books, 1996).

Rénard, Alexandre, *La querelle sur la possibilité de la philosophie chrétienne* (Paris: Éditions École et Collège, 1941).

Roensch, Frederick, *The Early Thomistic School* (London: Burns, Oates & Washbourne, 1934).

Rowland, Tracy, *Culture and the Thomist Tradition: After Vatican II* (London: Routledge, 2003).

Ryan, Arthur, *Perennial Philosophers* (Dublin: Clonmore & Reynolds, 1946).

Ryan, John, ed., Ibid., *Twentieth-Century Thinkers* [TCT] (Staten Island: Alba House, 1965).

Sadler, Gregory, "Saint Anselm's Fides Quaerens Intellectum as a Model for Christian Philosophy," *Saint Anselm Journal* 4:1 (2006), pp. 32-58.

Salvaterra, David, *American Catholicism and the Intellectua Life, 1880-1950* (New York: Garland, 1988).

Sanabria, José Rubén, *Historia de filosofia Cristiana en Mexico* (Mexico City: Universidad Iberoamericna, 1994).

Schaeffler, Richard, *Die Wechselbeziehungen zwischen Philosophie und katholischer Theologie* (Darmstadt: Wissenschaftliche Buchgesellschaft, 1980).

Schaub, Edward, *Philosophy Today: Essays on Recent Developments in the Field of Philosophy* [PTRD] (Chicago: Open Court, 1928).

Schmiesing, Kevin, *American Catholic Intellectuals and the Dilemma of Dual Identities, 1895-1955* (Lewiston: Edward Mellen Press, 2002).

Schoenl, William. *The Intellectual Crisis in English Catholicism. Liberal Catholics, Modernists, and the Vatican in the Late Nineteenth and Early Twentieth Centuries* (New York: Garland Publishing, 1982).

Schoof, Ted Mark, *A Survey of Catholic Theology, 1800-1970* [SCT], tr. N. D. Smith (Glenrock: Paulist Newman Press, 1970).

Schrift, Alan, *Twentieth-Century French Philosophy* [TWFP] (Oxford: Blackwell, 2006).

Schultenover, David, *The Reception of Pragmatism in France and the Rise of Roman Catholic Modernism* (Washington: Catholic University of America Press, 2009).

Sciacca, Michele Federico, *Les Grands courants de la pensée mondiale contemporaine*, 6 vols. (Paris: Fischbacher, 1958-1964).

———. *Philosophical Trends in the Contemporary World* [PTCW], tr. Aloysius Robert Caponigri (Notre Dame: University of Notre Dame Press, 1964).

Sertillanges, Antonin-Dalmace Gilbert, *Le Christianisme et les philosophes* [CPH], 2nd ed., 2 vols. (Paris: Aubier, 1941).

Shanley, Brian, ed., *One Hundred Years of Philosophy* [OHYP] (Washington: Catholic University of America Press, 2001).

―――. *The Thomist Tradition* [TT] (Dordrecht: Kluwer, 2002).

Shook, John, ed., *Dictionary of Modern American Philosophers* [MAP] (Bristol: Thoemmes Continuum, 2005).

Souilhé, Joseph, *La philosophie chrétienne de Descartes à nos jours*, 2 vols. [SPC] (Paris: Bloud and Gay, 1934).

Spiegelberg, Herbert, *The Phenomenological Movement* [PM], 2 vols. (The Hague: Martinus Nijhoff, 1960; 2002).

Storia del Tomismo (Vatican City: Libreria Editrice Vaticana, 1992).

Sutton, Michael, *Nationalism, Positivism, and Catholicism: The Politics of Charles Maurras and French Catholics, 1890-1914* (Cambridge: Cambridge University Press, 1993).

Swidler, Leo, et al., eds., *Catholic-Communist Collaboration in Italy* (Lanham: University Press of America, 1988).

Swindal, James, and Harry Gensler, *The Sheed and Ward Anthology of Catholic Philosophy* [ACP] (Lanham: Rowman & Littlefield, 2005).

Terrier, Jean-Marie-Henri, *Le Transformisme et la pensée catholique* (Paris: Cèdre, 1950).

Theau, Jean, *La Philosophie Française dans la Première Moitié du XXe Siècle* [PFPM] (Ottawa: Éditions de l'Université d'Ottawa, 1977).

Thonnard, Francois Joseph, *A Short History of Philosophy* [SHP], tr. Edward Maziarz (Paris: Desclée, 1955).

Tilliette, Xavier, *Le Christ des philosophes*, 3 vols. (Paris: Institut Catholique de Paris, 1981-1983).

Tymieniecka, Anna-Teresa, ed., *Phenomenology World-Wide* [PWW] (Dordrecht: Kluwer, 2002).

Urdanoz, Teófilo, *Historia de la Filosofía* [UHF], 8 vols. (Madrid: Biblioteca de Autores Cristianos, 1998).

Urmson, J.O., et al., eds., *The Concise Encyclopedia of Western Philosophy and Philosophers* [CEWP] (London: Unwin Hyman, 1989).

Vacant, Alfred, et al., eds., *Dictionnaire de théologie catholique* [DTC], 15 vols. (Paris: Letouzey et Ané, 1909-1950).

Valbuena, J., "Actualidad de la filosofia escolastico-tomista en Norteamerica," *Salamanticensis* 2 (1955), pp. 90-102.

Vancourt, Raymond, *Pensée moderne et philosophie chrétienne* (Paris: A. Fayard, 1957).

Vanhoozer, Kevin, ed., *Cambridge Companion to Postmodern Theology* (Cambridge: Cambridge University Press, 2007).

Van Riet, Georges, *Thomistic Epistemology* [TE], 2 vols. (St. Louis: Herder, 1963-1965).

Viano, C., "La filosofia a Torino," *Rivista di filosofia* 91:1 (2000), pp. 5-45.

Vidler, Alec, *A Century of Social Catholicism* (London: S.P.C.K., 1964).

————. *Twentieth-Century Defenders of the Faith* (London: S.C.M. Press, 1965).

Vieillard-Baron, Jean-Louis, *La philosophie française* (Paris: Armand Colin, 2000).

Weiss, John, *Conservatism in Europe, 1770-1945* [TRC] (New York: Hartcourt, 1977).

West, J., "The Thomistic Debate concerning the Existence and Nature of Christian Philosophy," *Modern Schoolman* 77 (1999), pp. 49-72.

Winquist, Charles, and Taylor, Victor, ed., *Encyclopedia of Postmodernism* [TEP] (London: Routledge, 2000).

Wolf, Kurt, *Religionsphilosophie in Frankreich* [RPFR] (Munich: Wilhelm Fink Verlag, 1999).

Wolff, Paul, *Christliche Philosophie im Deutschland, 1920-1945* (Regensburg: Joseph Habbel, 1949).

Zybura, John, ed., *Present Day Thinkers and the New Scholasticism* (St. Louis: Herder, 1926).

INDEX